Developmental Disabilities

Introduction to a Diverse Field

Anthony M. Graziano
State University of New York at Buffalo

Allyn and Bacon

Boston ■ London ■ Toronto ■ Sydney ■ Tokyo ■ Singapore

Executive Editor: *Rebecca Pascal*
Editorial Assistant: *Whitney Brown*
Marketing Manager: *Caroline Croley*
Editorial-Production Service: *Matrix Productions Inc.*
Composition and Prepress Buyer: *Linda Cox*
Manufacturing Buyer: *Joanne Sweeney*
Cover Administrator: *Linda Knowles*
Electronic Composition: *Omegatype Typography, Inc.*

Library of Congress Cataloging-in-Publication Data

Graziano, Anthony M. [date]
   Developmental disabilities : introduction to a diverse field / Anthony M. Graziano.
      p.   cm.
   Includes bibliographical references and index.
   ISBN 0-205-32206-9
   1. Developmentally disabled.   2. Developmental disabilites.   3. Developmental disabilities—Etiology.   I. Title.

   HV1570 .G73 2001
   362.1 '968—dc21

                                                                        2001016065

Printed in the United States of America

10   9   8   7   6   5   4   3   2   1   06   05   04   03   02   01

This work is dedicated to:

The memory of Robert Guthrie: Scientist, Humanitarian, and Advocate for all persons with disabilities.

Charles Behling: My good friend whose convincing persistence 10 years ago turned this reluctant colleague to the creation of a new undergraduate course in developmental disabilities.

All of my undergraduate students, whose enthusiastic response helped to keep this project going.

All persons with disabilities and their families.

Sheila: For her patience, love, skill, and wisdom, especially in all things maternal.

Amy, Lisa, Michael, and Mark: Just for being.

C O N T E N T S

12   Seizure Disorders   299

PREFACE

It is estimated that more than 53 million persons in the United States have some form of disability, including 14 million persons with developmental disabilities. Each year, just over 4 million babies are born in the United States. Of those, 80,000 to 120,000 are born with developmental disabilities, and more are discovered during infancy to have disabilities. Mental retardation, autism, cerebral palsy, epilepsy and other neuromotor disorders, vision and hearing impairments, traumatic brain injury, and learning disabilities are the major categories of developmental disabilities. Emotional/behavioral disorders of childhood (i.e., developmental psychopathology) constitute another large group of disabilities but, as will be discussed later, are not included in this text.

Causes and Risk Factors in Developmental Disabilities

There are multiple causes of and risk factors for developmental disabilities—genetic and chromosomal origins and environmental factors such as toxins, radiation, drugs, disease, injuries, and maternal illness. We know that the quality of our physical and social environments contributes to developmental disabilities. How significant are the risk factors of environmental pollution, poverty, inadequate prenatal care, maternal and paternal use of tobacco and alcohol, legal medications, and illicit drugs? How much public knowledge is there of these and other factors? Because these are human-made risk factors, they are controllable, and, at least in principle, many of the disabilities can be prevented. But in the "real world," prevention is a psychologically complex, politically contentious, and economically expensive endeavor, and our society has a very long way to go before it matures into a consistently effective "prevention mode." If we accept the idealized notion of striving toward optimum human development, then our society will have to focus on these issues with a great deal more commitment than we have thus far shown.

The Professions in the Field

Professionals in many disciplines (see the list in Box 1.1) provide services for persons with disabilities. In addition, research scientists and technicians search for scientific and technical information and for understanding of the causes, characteristics, treatment, and prevention of disabilities. We know a good deal about developmental disabilities, but our current knowledge is only a small portion of what we need to know, and both basic and applied research need to be continued and in many directions.

Why This Textbook?

This textbook has developed through 10 years of teaching an advanced undergraduate course, Developmental Disabilities. My major goal has been to teach students about a large set of phenomena that are important as a scientific field of study and as information of personal significance for students. Any teaching endeavor is a two-way process, and I have learned many things in the process, three of which stand out.

First, I quickly realized that even advanced college students—among the best-educated of our young adults—lack basic information and understanding of the causes and prevention of developmental disabilities. Given this lack of information by this highly educated group, what, then, can be said of the knowledge level of the general population? This suggests that large-scale public education about developmental disabilities may be an important contribution to the nation's health.

Second, given the social and personal importance of understanding this topic, it seemed reasonable to believe that there would have been many available college courses on this subject. But I soon learned that such courses are not commonly offered. This was puzzling, given the importance of the topic and the positive student response that I have found.

One of the many factors that make a college course possible is the availability of an up-to-date, comprehensive college textbook. There are many excellent books on developmental disabilities, and they are cited throughout this text. Most of them, however, are professional-level discussions of research and clinical procedures; many serve very well as references, handbooks, and so on and are of importance to graduate students, researchers, and to practicing professionals in many fields. However, and this is my third point, only a small handful (e.g., Batshaw & Perret, 1992; Drew, Logan, & Hardman, 1998; Wallace, Biehl, MacQueen, & Blackman, 1997) have been written as integrated textbooks that are appropriate for college students—the group I want to address. This realization impelled me to organize my class notes and write this textbook.

The Goals for This Textbook

There are several goals for this text. First, there is direct teaching and educating a particular group: college students at the junior and senior levels. The content is appropriate for all majors, although students majoring in psychology, premedicine, biology, education, nursing, rehabilitation, sociology and social work, and health-related fields in general will probably be most interested.

My direct-teaching goal is to enhance students' knowledge and understanding of the facts and concepts of developmental disabilities. I aim to teach about the research, treatment, teaching, and training of individuals, about prevention, and about the personal human dimensions. I hope this direct teaching endeavor will also provide students with personally significant information, will stimulate their further explorations of this field, and perhaps bring some to consider professional careers in this important and growing field.

Learning about developmental disabilities carries a good deal of personal significance for young adults because most will soon be planning for parenthood. This textbook is intended to inform and alert you about important issues in conception, pregnancy, birth, and child development that affect millions of persons in the United States. For college students, the study of developmental disabilities has additional significance because this field includes many professions and scientific challenges that can be considered for possible career directions. Although this is not a career-oriented textbook, the information may stimulate and direct some of you toward further study of developmental disabilities.

Teaching also has a broader dimension. It is my hope that the information in this text will be shared, thus making a contribution to the cause of general public education about developmental disabilities.

It is my goal, too, that this text will provide a sufficiently complete and organized presentation of information for other instructors to create courses in developmental disabilities. To this end, the text includes pedagogical aids such as a list of key terms, study questions, and suggested readings for each chapter, an extensive glossary, a reference list, and author and subject indexes.

An important goal that guided this project is that of making a start in integrating some of the many diverse factors that constitute this field. There exists a loose collection of services provided by several professional disciplines that do not always communicate well with each other. In addition, the research activity is carried out at both applied and basic levels, investigates a great diversity of questions, and is conducted by persons in many different scientific disciplines. Needed is an integrated model within which multidisciplinary information can be organized. An integrated presentation would improve communication and the sharing of ideas and progress among the various disciplines and would help to highlight needed directions of new research. This text is an attempt at some of that integration. It is presented as a work in progress rather than a finished product. It is my hope that subsequent editions will improve the text and its success in integrating the information.

Finally, I should note that solving the general problems of developmental disabilities will depend, ultimately, on social action. We need to have an educated citizenry that is knowledgeable about disabilities, their causes, treatment, and prevention. In this text, there has been a heavy emphasis on etiology because I believe an understanding of etiology is necessary if we are to have successful treatment, education, and prevention efforts.

The Need for an Informed Citizenry

Persons need not be trained professionals in the field to make significant contributions to the prevention of developmental disabilities and to services for persons with disabilities. Through participation in social and political action, volunteering one's services in local programs, public education campaigns, altering one's own behavior toward better health, and imparting knowledge to one's children, well-informed individuals can contribute significantly through their normal roles as parents and citizens. It is my aim that this text, by helping to educate young persons about developmental disabilities, will contribute to that informed citizenry.

Organization of This Textbook

Chapter 1 is an introduction to the field, setting out some major guiding ideas and facts, incidence and prevalence figures, definitions, and a brief discussion of historical events. This chapter also emphasizes the importance of viewing developmental disabilities in a *full life-span context.* Persons with disabilities are living longer than ever before, many matching the life spans of most people. We are now learning that as persons with disabilities mature, personal needs change and so, too, must our knowledge, understanding, and service approaches. For example, providing service for a 60-year-old person with intellectual disabilities requires not only an understanding of etiologies and child developmental processes, but also a focused understanding of the special issues of aging processes in general and their interactions with the special characteristics of the developmental disability. This emerging life-span approach requires a new professional expertise, which in turn requires new facets to the education and training of future professionals.

Chapters 2 through 8 deal primarily with issues of etiology of developmental disabilities and include brief reviews of normal human development. These are important, for if we do not understand normal development and etiology of disabilities, then how can we ever successfully understand, treat, or prevent these conditions? These chapters lean heavily—but not exclusively—on biological factors. It is my belief that professionals, even those who are not directly trained in the biologically or medically related areas, must be aware of the major biological aspects involved. I will not try to develop a biology or medical textbook; rather, I wish to present important background information to help in the understanding of the nature of these conditions. But biological factors do not stand alone. I will stress the importance of recognizing the interactions of biological, environmental, social, and psychological factors in the etiologies of developmental disabilities. I will present a multifactorial model in which etiological and other developmental factors have their origins in and effect on the person's biological, psychological, and social development. These chapters also contain discussions of many specific conditions, primarily birth defects.

Chapter 10 presents a tentative theoretical social role model (the active socialization hypothesis) focusing for purposes of discussion specifically on intellectual disabilities (mental retardation). This social role model is presented to help us to understand the powerful effects of lifelong social learning on creating and maintaining much of the lifestyles and characteristic functioning of persons with disabilities. Role theory concepts are used throughout the remainder of the text in discussing types of disabilities and the nature of society's response to persons with disabilities.

Chapter 9 and Chapters 11 through 14 discuss major categories of developmental disabilities. There is considerable artificiality in placing people into discrete groups. Persons with disabilities, *just like everyone else, are complex individuals and do not fit neatly into categories.* Some fall between the groups, and others have characteristics of more than one group, including groups of persons who have no disabilities. In all, there is a mix of disability, normalcy, and strength, so who is to say we must define the person by his or her disability alone? Still, despite those problems and oversimplifications, it is useful to discuss groups separately, such as persons with cerebral palsy or with autism or with learning disabilities. In these presentations—one chapter for each—I focus on the personal, familial, psychological, and social characteristics of the persons and the disabilities. Each chapter refers to etiological and demographic information from earlier chapters, describes each condition, and discusses its developmental course. Family factors, education, treatment/training, and recent research are discussed for each. These chapters are, of necessity, overviews rather than detailed discussions, as each topic can command a separate text of its own.

Chapters 15 and 16 focus on modern service approaches for persons with disabilities, prevention concepts, and issues of public policy and public education. Topics such as parenting issues and family impact are discussed as they apply to all groups of persons with disabilities rather than to each specific subset. The text closes with a major emphasis on prevention concepts and approaches. Prevention, I believe, is a critical issue that needs greater attention, activity, and vastly increased social support. I consider what constitutes society's responsibility for persons with developmental disabilities and ask: Where, in society, does such responsibility lie?

Acknowledgments

I want to thank, first, Charles Behling, my friend and colleague who started me on this project and encouraged me to keep it going.

Several colleagues provided valuable commentary and critique in their reviews of the manuscript: Phillip Davidson, University of Rochester; Marcie Desrochers, College of Charleston; Matthew Janicki, State University of New York at Albany; Carol Reed, NOVA Southeastern University; and German Torres, State University of New York at Buffalo.

I want to express my gratitude to my undergraduate assistants, Allison Stooks and Stacy Durnan, who labored on many library search tasks. Their help on this project has been invaluable.

Rebecca Pascal, Executive Editor for Psychology at Allyn and Bacon, and Whitney Brown, Editorial Assistant, have been supportive and helpful throughout this project. I also wish to thank Merrill Peterson and Donna Simons for their production coordination, and Frank Hubert for copyediting the manuscript.

Anthony M. Graziano
Psychology Department
SUNY at Buffalo
Buffalo, NY

ABOUT THE AUTHOR

Anthony M. Graziano graduated from Columbia College, Michigan State University, and Purdue University and in 1960–1961 was a postdoctoral fellow at the Devereaux Institute. Since 1960 he has worked in developmental disabilities and developmental psychopathology, conducting research and clinical work with children and their families, teaching, and writing. From 1961 to 1969 he developed one of the first behavior modification programs for children with autism and other disabilities. In that program, he was, arguably, the first to employ relaxation and systematic desensitization to help teach self-control to children with autism. Training parents as active co-teachers and therapists was another development of that program.

Since 1969 Dr. Graziano has been on the faculty of the Psychology Department at the State University of New York at Buffalo, where he is now Professor Emeritus. He served as Director of Clinical Training, Co-Director (with Murray Levine) of the Research Center for Children and Youth, and continued his graduate and undergraduate teaching, clinical work, and research. His research has focused on treatment and education of children with disabilities and psychopathology and their families, reduction of severe fears in children, parent training, children's self-control training, social and health policy, and corporal punishment in childrearing. On the latter, he has been a longtime advocate for eliminating corporal punishment. His other books include:

Behavior Therapy with Children, Volumes I and II, 1971 and 1975

Child without Tomorrow: A Behavioral Program for Children with Autism, 1974

Children and Behavior Therapy (with Kevin Mooney), 1984

The Handbook of Practical Psychology (with Richard Bugelski), 1980

Research Methods: A Process of Inquiry (with Michael Raulin), Editions 1–4, 1989, 1993, 1997, 2000. The fifth edition is in progress.

CHAPTER

1 Defining Developmental Disabilities

I. Overview of the Text

This text is an introductory overview of developmental disabilities. Its goal is to help you develop knowledge about and sensitivity for the millions of people who are included under the developmental disabilities labels. This is a highly complex field involving more than a dozen professions (see Box 1.1). Each diagnostic category of persons can be studied through objective examinations of numerous biological, psychological, and social systems and their many interactions. We urge you not to lose sight of the *person* among the details. Whatever labels might be applied, however caught up we might become in clinical data, and whatever emphasis might be placed on *dis*ability, each person is a unique individual, a

1

complicated human being with needs, strengths, and weaknesses. Each is worthy of respect and human rights, and no one should be defined, understood, or approached primarily on the basis of clinical details or disability labels.

We begin with three vignettes of unique persons. To understand the persons represented in these vignettes, we must examine the systems and subsystems, the events that unfold, interact, and result in persons with developmental disabilities. Those causal events are often in place even before conception. Other events occur during pregnancy, during and after birth, and in complex human development right up to adulthood. It is in this maze of objective clinical detail that the person is presented in fragmentary ways, and students may easily lose the picture of whole persons. Examining those parts, however, is necessary in the study of developmental disabilities. The following case vignettes have been crafted based on more than 40 years of experience in this field. The problems described are real but the cases are not specific persons.

II. Three Vignettes

Frankie is 11 years old and has had a lifetime of serious developmental problems. His language is limited and distorted, and he does not communicate or relate well with others. He grimaces, makes repeated, stiff movements with his head and hands, and often shouts loudly. Indifferent to other people, including his own family, Frankie maintains an often agitated aloofness. He has never played with toys, as do his siblings. Rather, he sits for long periods engaged in simple repetitive motions such as spinning a pot cover on the floor or arranging kitchen utensils in a row in a rigidly fixed order. Frankie becomes agitated if anyone disturbs that arrangement. He has been in a special school program for 7 years but has made few gains socially or academically. His parents have tried several treatment, training, and educational programs, all with minimal or no success, and have finally accepted his condition as being permanent. Frankie has serious disabilities, has a poor prognosis for improvement, and has been diagnosed with autism and intellectual disabilities.[1]

At 13 years of age, Karen lives with her parents and two older siblings. She attends a public school, where she is in a special education program and is *mainstreamed* in two regular classes. Despite having mild mental retardation, Karen had been successfully coping and developing well personally and socially. In her stable and loving family, Karen has always been affectionate, responsive, and a generally happy youngster. Recently, however, Karen has become more anxious, unhappy, frequently crying, and often agitated. She no longer keeps up with her work in school and has apparently lost her friends. Karen sees them, all younger than she, as growing away from her, and she is hurt and perplexed as they move toward adolescent social life that is too fast-paced and complicated for her.

Ray, 48 years old, is happily married, has two children, and is a successful attorney in the county district attorney's office. He was diagnosed with *epilepsy* at age 6. Ray has seizures during which he loses consciousness and falls, which sometimes causes injuries.

[1]As of this writing, the term *intellectual disabilities* is beginning to replace *mental retardation*. The terms will be used interchangeably in this text. When referring to the concept in historical context, the older term is used.

BOX **1.1**

Professional Disciplines Involved in Services to Persons with Developmental Disabilities

Communication/Language Disorders
   Audiologist
   Speech Pathologist
   Speech Therapist

Medical Services/Counseling
   Dentist, Dental Hygienist
   Genetic Counselor
   Nurse
   Physician, Family Medicine, Pediatrician

Nutrition and Health
   Dietitian
   Nutritionist

Training/Rehabilitation
   Occupational Therapist
   Physical Therapist
   Recreational Therapist

Behavioral/Social/Emotional Aspects
   Psychiatrist
   Psychologist
   Social Worker

Education
   Art/Music Teacher/Therapist
   Special Education Teacher

Notes:

1. This list does not include all of the professional disciplines.

2. Several of the professionals listed (e.g., nurses, psychologists) have a wide scope of training and actually function in several domains of service.

3. Brief descriptions of the training and professional functions of each are presented in excellent handbooks such as those by Kurtz et al. (1996) and Wallaby et al. (1997).

4. One of the major foundations for the entire interdisciplinary field of services for persons with developmental disabilities is research, both basic and applied. Although researchers do not appear in this list of providers, their importance in each area cannot be overstated.

Because of the frequency of seizures despite his medication, Ray has decided to forgo courtroom appearances. Instead, he works behind the scenes preparing briefs, researching the law, and interviewing clients and witnesses. He has published a number of papers in law journals and contributes several hours a week to a local free legal clinic. His work is of high quality and importance, and Ray is well respected and liked by his colleagues and friends.

It has required an extraordinary and sustained effort by Ray to become an attorney and to maintain his professional position. He is determined to continue his success.

Frankie, Karen, and Ray have in common *developmental disabilities*—serious, permanent, disabling conditions that begin early in life and significantly handicap them. They have impairments, disabilities, and handicaps.

III. Impairments, Disabilities, and Handicaps

What does it mean to have impairments, disabilities, and handicaps? Consider a man who is of average intelligence, has a steady job and, with his wife, provides well for their family. He is in good health, is stable, mature, and dependable. He speaks clearly and no one has difficulty understanding him. With some sounds, however, particularly at the beginning of words, he hesitates, causing noticeable pauses in his flow of speech. This is a lifelong but minor pattern. Others hardly perceive it anymore, it causes no anxiety for him, and does not interfere with his life.

This man has a minor speech impairment. To impair a function is to diminish it. An *impairment* is a lessening or weakening in some organ system, ability, or state of health. Impairments can occur in any modality such as vision, hearing, locomotion, fine motor coordination, speech, intelligence, memory, and so on. A person with a deformed foot and a limping walk has impairments. To have impairments is to function in a diminished manner, less than optimally for that person's age. With his hesitant speech, he is impaired; but is he disabled? The impairment is so minor that it does not significantly affect his speech production; thus, his speech and communication are not *disabled*. A system that is disabled is incapable of functioning; it is ineffective or "put out of commission." This person has an impairment, but not a disability.

Is he handicapped? The speech impairment is not so great as to constitute a disability and make normal life achievements unusually difficult; that is, it does not handicap him. The term *handicap* applies to the person's overall functioning as affected by the impairment and disability. Handicap refers to the effects of the impairment or disability on one's pursuits of normal life activities; it involves the social consequences or disadvantages that result from the person's disabilities. For a handicap to exist, the impairment must reach the level of disability, and the disability must be severe enough that the person's pursuit of *normal life activities* is made unusually difficult or impossible. Normal life activities include self-care, language, learning, and so on. If the man with the speech impairment found it so difficult to communicate with others that he had serious problems in social relationships, securing employment, and living independently, then he would be handicapped. This man has an impairment, but he is neither disabled nor handicapped by it. The three terms—impairment, disability, and handicap—are labels for points along a continuum of severity. A person may have an impairment; if the impairment is severe, it might constitute a disability; if the disability is severe, handicaps can ensue.

> *Internal Summary*   Impairment is a condition of reduced health or functioning, and it might be to a minor or severe degree. If the impairment is severe, it can constitute a disability, which is a severe impairment in which some ability, functioning, or state of health is significantly disrupted, made ineffective, or in

the most severe case, "put out of commission." If a disability is severe enough to interfere with normal life pursuits such as self-care, language development, and capacity to learn, it is considered a handicap.

As shown in Box 1.2, disabilities and handicaps do not necessarily prevent a person's success. But handicaps do constitute uncommon burdens that are too often not appreciated by those without handicaps.

Social policy in the United States has begun to recognize not only that persons with handicapping disabilities have special needs but that it is to our nation's advantage to provide them with assistance such as access to public buildings, education, and legal protection against bias. Each person who is helped to achieve an independent, productive life becomes another strong link in the human web that constitutes our society and contributes to our nation's collective strength and success.

The modality in which a disability occurs is an important factor in the seriousness of the handicapping condition. Physical disabilities such as paraplegia are handicapping, seriously disrupting the person's life by posing major obstacles to the pursuit of ordinary life activities. Handicaps are not easy to deal with but can be partly compensated for with the use of physical, mechanical, and/or electronic aids such as canes and walkers, Seeing

BOX 1.2

Great Achievers: Persons with Disabilities

Persons with serious disabilities can nevertheless excel. Beethoven became deaf, surely a major handicap for a composer, but continued to create some of the world's greatest music. Contemporary musicians such as Ray Charles, Itzhak Perlman, and Thomas Quasthoff have become world-class performers despite their disabilities. Charles, jazz pianist, saxophonist, and singer, has severe visual impairments; Perlman, a superb classical violinist, has severe locomotion handicaps; Quasthoff, a powerful bass-baritone, was physically deformed by thalidomide but has become a world-renowned singer and teacher, with one of the finest classical voices.

Thomas Edison, Albert Einstein, Woodrow Wilson, General George Patton, former New York Governor and U.S. Vice President Nelson A. Rockefeller, and many others achieved great success despite their severe reading disabilities (dyslexia). Einstein and Edison were even considered by their teachers to be "dunces" and "backward." They failed repeatedly in school and came close to being institutionalized as "retarded" (Jordan, 1996). (At this writing, *Time* magazine has named Einstein as the most important person of the twentieth century!)

Stephen Hawking, physicist, continues to contribute to science and to science teaching despite severe physical handicaps (White & Gribbin, 1992). Temple Grandin has autism. She has earned a doctorate and writes about growing up without being able to speak or to perceive and learn subtleties of social behavior and communication (Grandin, 1992a, 1995a, b). Franklin D. Roosevelt became one of the greatest U.S. presidents despite his paralyzed legs (due to childhood poliomyelitis). Contemporary actor Chris Burke was a member of the cast of a popular television series despite having Down syndrome.

Countless persons with disabilities have overcome their handicaps and created successful, rewarding, and often outstanding lives.

Eye dogs, motorized wheelchairs, and speech-assisting computers. As discussed later in this text, an important area of medical and psychological technology known as *assistive technology* has developed to help reduce the handicaps of persons with physical disabilities. However, a cognitive disability, such as severe intellectual disabilities, is so pervasive in its effects on the person's entire development that it remains a lifelong, profoundly handicapping condition.

Disabilities abound in any society. This text focuses on a particular subset of disabilities, those arising early in life: *developmental disabilities.*

IV. Etiology: Causal Factors and Pathology

The term developmental disabilities refers to *functional impairments*—difficulties in functions such as speaking, walking, thinking, and socializing. Functional impairments have their roots in more basic *pathologies* (disease, disorders, illness). These pathologies can be biological in nature such as genetic defects, disease, or traumatic injuries, or they can be psychological such as low intelligence or language impairments. Pathologies are brought about by a number of causal factors. Box 1.3 represents part of the etiological picture, showing two categories: I. Genetic/Hereditary Factors and II. Environmental Factors. The two factors interact with each other and with two additional factors: the *stage of development* of the organism at the time of the pathology and the nature of the *particular organ system* involved. These additional factors will be discussed later and a more complete definition of etiology will be presented.

The term *etiology* refers to the study of all of the causes of a disease or pathology. These include (a) a direct link in producing pathology such as when a virus, microbe, or toxin (i.e., a pathogen) has a direct causal relationship to the illness and also (b) an indirect relationship in which some factors increase the probability that pathology will develop. An example of the latter is the influence of socioeconomic status (SES) on a baby's health. Poverty itself does not directly cause premature births or low birth weight. Rather, poverty is associated with poor maternal nutrition, use of tobacco and other drugs, and less competent prenatal care, all of which increase the risks of low birth weight and premature births. Thus, pregnant women living in poverty are at greater risk for premature births and low-birth-weight babies than are women who live in higher SES conditions. Poverty, then, is not a direct cause of premature birth, but it is an important etiological factor that increases the risk of the disorder (i.e., it is a risk factor). The etiology of a disability includes direct causes and indirect risk factors. Etiological factors in fetal alcohol syndrome, for example, include not only the pathogen (ethanol) but also risk factors such as the mother's psychological condition, education, and employment status (Stratton, Howe, & Battaglia, 1996). The causal sequence in developmental disabilities is diagramed in Box 1.4.

Pathologies that lead to functional impairments and handicaps are the bases for disabilities. Pathologies originate in a variety of etiological factors that can be grouped under two main headings, genetic/hereditary factors and environmental factors, as was shown in Box 1.3. The first category includes genetic defects, chromosomal anomalies, and metabolic problems. The environmental factors include pathogens for infectious diseases and illness

---

BOX **1.3**

Etiological Factors in Developmental Disabilities

Genetic/Hereditary Factors	*Environmental Factors*
Genetic Defects	Physical Traumas
Chromosomal Anomalies	Pathogens for Infections (microbes, viruses, toxins)
Metabolic Problems	Hypoxia
	Toxic Substances
	Nutritional Deficiencies
	Psychosocial Factors

(microbes, viruses, and toxins); physical trauma or injuries that can occur before or after birth; *hypoxia* (disruption of oxygen supply); nutritional deficiencies; psychological trauma or maltreatment; and social factors such as economic conditions. Many events can result in disability. Childhood physical trauma, for example, can be caused by automobile crashes and household accidents, playground injuries, parental child abuse, self-inflicted injuries, and so on. There are thousands of potential pathogens from naturally occurring microbes and from chemical substances including human-made toxins. Once pathology occurs, the person might suffer impairments, disabilities, and handicaps. As shown in Box 1.4, a

---

BOX **1.4**

Sequence of Causal Events in Developmental Disabilities

Etiology → Pathology → Impairment → Disability → Handicap

Definitions of Terms Used in the Developmental Disabilities Model

Etiology: All of the factors existing in direct and/or indirect causal relationship to pathology. Some of the factors are listed in Box 1.3. (Note that two additional etiological factors—developmental level of the organism and the nature of the organ system—are also important.)

Pathology: A condition of negative structural and/or functional changes; it is the disease, disorder, injury, or illness.

Impairment: A condition of reduced health or functioning in which one or more physical and/or psychological systems have been reduced by pathology to a less efficient, less healthy, less integrated level of functioning.

Disability: A severe impairment in which some system, ability, function, or state of health is significantly disrupted by pathology, is made ineffective, disabled, or "put out of commission."

Handicap: The severe, disruptive effects of disability on the person's success in carrying out life's normal activities which include: self-care, language skills, learning, mobility, self-direction, independent living, and economic self-sufficiency.

---

handicap can, theoretically, be traced back through disabilities, impairments, pathologies, and etiology. In many actual cases, however, the etiological factors are not known.

Note in Box 1.4 that the sequence of events begins with causal agents (the etiological factors) such as a genetic defect or a pathogenic event, and the process continues sequentially through one or more phases. However, the process might not continue all the way to a handicap. It may end at any point in the sequence, spontaneously or through medical or psychological intervention. For example, a causal agent such as a microbe might be present as a potential pathogen in the environment of a child who then suffers an infection with its symptoms including fever, headache, and muscle aches. Thus, a pathogen has resulted in pathology, in this case an infection. But the process might end there as the child's body, aided by antibiotics, successfully overcomes the infection, leaving no impairments, disabilities, or handicaps. Conversely, a disease such as meningitis, if not treated immediately and effectively, can leave the child brain damaged and permanently disabled. Box 1.4 describes a linear sequence from causal factors through handicaps. A developmental disability is the complex result of events proceeding through that sequence. Etiology, the causal factors that initiate the sequence of events, includes genetic/hereditary and environmental factors.

Developmental disabilities, like other complex human conditions, are *multiply determined.* To understand the development of a disability, we must consider not only the original causal agents (hereditary and/or environmental) but also the particular organ system(s) affected by the causal agents and the stage of development of those organ systems at the time that the pathogenic events occur. For example, it is not advisable for a woman to drink alcohol at *any* time during pregnancy. If she drinks during the first trimester, the potential destructive effects on the developing child will generally be greater than if she drinks an equal amount late in the pregnancy (Institute of Medicine, 1996).

Further, the nature of the organ system involved is important. To use an obvious example, a punch on a child's arm might have bruising effects, but a punch of equal force to the child's head or abdomen can have more serious effects.

> ***Internal Summary.*** Whether particular events (pathogens, genetic defects, traumas, etc.) contribute to a developmental disability depends on several factors: the occurrence and nature of the pathogenic events, the nature of the particular organ system(s) involved, and the stage of development of that system at the time the events occur. As a general rule, the earlier a pathogen occurs in the development of an organ system, the greater is the probability for disruption of that organ system's development.

Human development is continuous over a life expectancy of 79.6 years for women and 72.3 years for men (Monthly Vital Statistics Report, 1996). Developmental activity is greatest earlier in life as the child progresses through conception, prenatal development, birth, infancy, childhood, and adolescence. It slows—but does not cease—in late adolescence and early adulthood. It is the first quarter of life, approximately 18 years, in which the etiological events, impairments, pathologies, and handicaps occur to define developmental disabilities.

A pathology that is the basis of a *developmental* disability has its major effects prior to adulthood. During these early years, development is most rapid, and the person at any one time can be quite a different biological/psychological system than at any other time. This is particularly true earlier in life when, in a month, a week, or even days, important developmental changes can occur. Because organ systems change significantly during development, the pathogen-by-system interaction will also vary across time. Hereditary and environmental factors can have very different effects depending on *when* they occur in the person's development. Thus, the etiologies of developmental disabilities involve the interaction of at least four major variables: (a) heredity, (b) environment, (c) the specific organ system(s) involved, and (d) the child's (or organ system's) level of development at the time pathogenic events occur. Pathology leading to developmental disability is the result of an (a) × (b) × (c) × (d) interaction, as follows:

Heredity × Environment × Organ System × Time of Development

The degree to which each of these four major factors contributes to the etiology of pathology will vary from one case to another, as the possible combinations of factors and their respective weighting are very large. The etiology of developmental disabilities, then, has a very complex makeup.

V. Defining Developmental Disabilities

Some Historical Considerations

This section briefly notes some history of societies' responses to human disabilities. Readers who wish a full discussion should consult the excellent work by Safford and Safford (1996), *A History of Childhood and Disability.*

At this writing we are witnessing the emergence of a general guiding view of disability that is startling in its contrast to social themes that prevailed through most of human history. What is emerging is a theme of advocacy, dignity, personal achievement, and equality. It is a theme that is constructed around an emerging central idea we have labeled *social role sensitivity,* which will be discussed in detail in Chapter Ten. This view maintains that persons with disabilities are moral equivalents of all citizens, possessing the rights to pursue the highest quality of life possible and being accepted and integrated into society as fellow citizens with all of the respect, freedoms, and safeguards provided for all citizens. To help such persons overcome the particular obstacles they face and to achieve autonomous, successful, and dignified lives, society must advocate for them and help encourage their self-advocacy. Every person who becomes a successfully contributing member of society, to whatever degree he or she is able, strengthens the entire interactive social web, and that is to everyone's gain. This is an emerging model, not yet fully developed or realized by everyone, but it is a strong movement. It is enlightened, fair, and humanitarian. It is also revolutionary. As it continues to develop, it will bring about markedly improved lives for millions of persons with disabilities and will help produce a stronger society.

The history of social responses to disabilities has largely been determined, until recently, by the history of childhood. One might write, "As go the fortunes of children, so go the fortunes of those with disabilities." In many ways, persons with disabilities have long been viewed as members of a special class of childhood. For example, attributions of child-like qualities have traditionally been made to adults with intellectual disabilities. At some points in history, such attributions may have been useful by engendering a more kindly and even slightly nurturing view of persons with disabilities. Now, however, such characterizations are degrading and are hindrances to progress. Fortunately, our views are changing in that regard.

Throughout most of human history, adults have maintained a dual view of childhood. In the abstract, children have been highly valued—after all, continuation of humanity depends on the survival of children. However, such an abstract value of children does not guarantee the recognition of children as individuals nor does it guarantee kindly nurturing of particular children (Aries, 1962). This is a historically long-lived paradox: Extolling the virtues and value of children in the abstract easily coexists with the debasement and abuse of children in particular instances (Safford & Safford, 1996). Coexistent in any historical era, we find practices of love and nurture as well as brutality and abuse. Treatment of children has improved as we move into the twenty-first century, but it has not been a straight-line progression to higher moral levels. Rather, it has been an uneven march, repeating errors, stumbling, and regressing. Nor has it been completed. In contemporary societies, there are still examples of the darker side of childhood (Safford & Safford, 1996).

Throughout history, many children—including those with disabilities—have been loved and well cared for by their parents (Shahar, 1990). But much of the picture of childhood is grim, indeed. Children died at high rates, succumbing to the diseases and malnutrition that afflicted even adults. Since mothers' deaths in childbirth were fairly common, there were many orphaned children left in the care of less-than-caring persons. Many children were abused and brutalized, abandoned and murdered, exploited for economic reasons as in child labor, taken as religious offerings, and used for adults' sexual and other pleasures (Safford & Safford, 1996). The lower a child's position on the socioeconomic ladder, the worse the child fared. Since only a minority of children were of the privileged classes, most children faced a succession of serious obstacles to survival.

With the Industrial Revolution (approximately 1800 to 1900), men of business saw the opportunity to exploit children—even as young as 4 years old (Todd & Curti, 1966)—as an easily available supply of very cheap labor. Children (as young as today's kindergartners) were sent, often chained and whipped, into mine shafts and factories, working 12- and 15-hour days at dangerous, often deadly, tasks (Felt, 1971). This period, during which children were forcibly fed into the industrial machine was, arguably, the worst of times for childhood. Gripping portrayals (e.g., see Dickens's 1839 novel, *Nickolas Nickleby*) helped bring to attention the plight of children. As a measure of the lives of these "factory children," consider The Factory Act of 1819 (England). It was enacted after years of agitation for humanitarian reform despite the powerful objections of business. This reform act prohibited the factory employment of children *8 years of age and younger* and limited the working hours of children under 16 years (i.e., from 9 to 15 years of age) to *no more than 12 hours a day, 6 days a week!* In the United States, child labor reforms were not enacted until 1933, when President Franklin Roosevelt signed the National Recovery Administration Act.

In twentieth-century Western countries, children arguably live better than ever before. But the majority of the world's children do not live in Western societies. Around the world, including developed countries, there are still, in the year 2001, enormous problems heaped on children such as abandonment, abuse, neglect, disease, starvation, prostitution, forced industrial labor, ethnic and sexual discrimination, and even infanticide (Powell, Aiken, & Smylie, 1982). In some countries, beating one's child is still considered a rightful duty of parenthood (Graziano, Kunce, Lindquist, & Munjal, 1991). In the United States, corporal punishment of children prevails (Graziano, 1992). It is largely a holdover of the religious support for corporal punishment that thrived in our English and American colonial history. (See Greven's 1977 work on the history of religion and corporal punishment, Samuel Butler's classic English novel of 1867, *The Way of All Flesh,* and Glenn's 1984 account of corporal punishment in antebellum America.) Lest you are tempted to think that brutal treatment of children lies in the past, consider that *today,* in the United States as reported by Greenhouse (2000), children continue to be legally exploited as farm laborers. In many states, 12 and 13 year olds, mostly migrant children, often work 10 to 12 hours a day, 6 days a week under extremely dangerous conditions of heavy pesticide spraying and unprotected machinery, and they are paid far less than minimum wages. As one measure of the danger, Greenhouse (2000) reported that only 6 to 7 percent of all jobs held by young people are in agriculture, but they account for more than 40 percent of all work-related fatalities of young people. In many states, it is legal for 14 year olds to work 70-hour weeks as farm laborers! As it has been throughout history, and it continues in the United States of A.D. 2001, it is the children of the poor who remain the most ill used by the business community. The exploitation of children as farm laborers in the United States is a continuing problem, and there appears to be little correction in sight.

What about persons with disabilities? As with children in general, the treatment of those with disabilities has been a conflicting coexistence of family and institutional care for some and neglect, rejection, and abuse for others. Safford and Safford (1996) identify three major themes of societies' treatment of children that emerge, submerge, and reappear throughout history and in various forms are still with us today: extermination, ridicule, and asylum. A fourth, education, is relatively recent, having emerged in the early nineteenth century. To these four themes, we will add a fifth that we call social role sensitivity. This, we will argue, is a current revolution in approach. The first three are strategies of exclusion from society; the latter two themes constitute significant shifts toward full social inclusion.

Most drastically, there was extermination practiced throughout history. Many unwanted children, including those with birth defects, were killed, largely by being abandoned. Lest one believe such exterminations ended centuries ago, recall that the Germans carried out Operation T-4 in the 1930s and 1940s to exterminate persons with disabilities (Herr & Weber, 1999b).

The advent of Christianity at about A.D. 300 apparently helped reduce infanticide in Western Europe but did not end the torment of people with disabilities. The theme shifted from extermination to ridicule. The well-to-do could purchase for their own amusement children and adults with physical disabilities. Jesters and "fools," particularly persons with physical disfigurement, became court fixtures for the nobility, and carnival sideshows developed for ordinary people to enjoy.

The ridicule and debasement had an even darker side in religious-based stigmatization. Children and adults with disabilities were considered "stained." From medieval times to the end of the nineteenth century, the "mark of the devil" was seen in facial anomalies, blindness, deformed limbs, and so on. (Shahar, 1990). Birth defects were regarded as punishment for errant parents or the whims of demons visited on innocent families. Many of the children were not welcomed or even acknowledged as the true progeny of their parents and were abandoned to die. Later, many were given up to the church to serve as laborers or acolytes (Boswell, 1988). Foundling homes and orphanages may have begun through this early practice of oblation, giving up stigmatized children to monasteries and convents (Safford & Safford, 1996).

Although many children were loved and nurtured in families, ridicule, amusement, disdain, and stigmatization constituted much of society's public response to human disability into the late nineteenth and early twentieth centuries. For example, in the early 1800s, a Sunday afternoon's outing for a family was a visit to Bedlam (London's Bethlehem Hospital) (Foucault, 1965). There and in other enlightened hospitals such as those in Philadelphia (Safford & Safford, 1996) were children and adults with amusing, shocking, and frightening disabilities and antics, all on public display for the cost of one penny. In the United States, carnival sideshows featuring dwarfs, midgets, giants, fat ladies, half-man, half-woman, girls with webbed necks, and so on were common into the middle of the twentieth century. (I recall such traveling sideshows coming into my hometown in downstate New York in the 1940s.) As discussed by Safford and Safford (1996), we still have jokes and stories that ridicule those with disabilities, and during the 1990s, "dwarf-tossing" was a briefly popular form of entertainment in some places. All of these common forms of insensitivity and maltreatment excluded those persons from normal social relationships. They were seen as aberrant individuals who could be safely mocked as persons not of "our kind."

Asylums for persons with disabilities and/or mental illness became a prominent theme in the nineteenth and twentieth centuries. Their development may be traced back to early Christian times (about A.D. 300–400) when children with disabilities were given to the church as an alternative to infanticide. Over many centuries, some monasteries and convents became places of sanctuary for persons with disabilities, and they eventually developed into asylums devoted to their care and housing. The concept of asylum means a place of refuge, safety, care, and protection. Moving from blatant ridicule to the asylum theme was a humanitarian step. However, it was also another exclusionary tactic, removing from free society those persons seen as deviant. Housing them in walled institutions helped reduce, but did not eliminate, some of the more common and brutish forms of everyday ridicule. A kindlier social response than extermination, the asylum approach developed its own problems. In time, they evolved into overcrowded and poorly staffed mental hospitals and institutions for those with disabilities. The asylums became warehouses for human beings who had little to do but sit and wait and obey orders in dulling surroundings.

This was a convenience to society: It kept those people off the streets and out of sight, gave them shelter and food, and relieved families of responsibility. However, the people placed in these asylums became highly dependent on the institutions for their everyday care and submissive to the dictates of their keepers. Teaching autonomy and self-respect was not part of the asylum theme. After years in such institutions, people would find it difficult or impossible to adjust successfully to the outside world if they were ever released. In any event, the outside world was not ready to accept them.

The Greek term *iatrogenic* refers to a process in which a disorder is inadvertently induced by a physician while trying to treat an original disorder. Humanitarian reformers throughout history recognized that the manner in which we treat people has significant effects on how those people function; that is, our treatments may have iatrogenic effects. About A.D. 300, the Roman physician Soranus released mental patients from jails and dungeons. He argued that if we chained up "the insane" in darkness and isolation and treated them harshly, then they would surely become even more deeply insane. The treatment itself, he argued, causes much of the person's bizarre behavior. Some 1500 years later, the Italian physician Chiarugi rediscovered iatrogenic effects and created many important reforms in the treatment of mental patients. But it was not until the nineteenth-century humanitarian reform movement was in full effect that a more general social acceptance of the iatrogenic notion took hold. Pinel in France and Tuke, Rush, Dorothea Dix, and many others in the United States all advocated improvements in the physical care of persons in institutions. At that time in the Western world, there was a wide sweep of demands for reform: Democratic political reform, antislavery movements, child labor reform, improved treatment of women and prisoners, and education for children were all major issues in that great humanitarian reform movement.

As a result, the asylums were improved, and physical care improved. In time, however, the institutions grew into crowded warehouses once again. The people were no longer chained up, physically brutalized, or ridiculed, but they were subjected to the dulling iatrogenic effects of years of a dulling, dependent existence. A child with intellectual disabilities, for example, consigned to such an institution, had little chance of learning to become an alert, autonomous, self-respecting person. The asylums—now called institutions, training schools, hospitals, and so forth—continued to grow into large, overcrowded human warehouses well into the 1970s and 1980s. It was then that the concept of iatrogenics was yet again rediscovered and applied to the practice of lifelong institutionalization of persons with developmental disabilities. Through a series of legal, legislative, professional, and social actions, a modern humanitarian reform movement, *deinstitutionalization,* emerged in the late twentieth century. This movement continues today and is one of the major themes of the current revolution in thinking about and treatment of persons with disabilities.

The central concept in the idea of iatrogenic effects is that people's functioning is powerfully and permanently affected by the ways in which they are regarded and treated by others and, specifically, by the very practices that are applied as treatment. The current term, *developmental iatrogeny,* recognizes that our treatment approaches may have negative effects on a child's development (Northam, 1997) and care must be taken to avoid or at least minimize them. For example, the relative isolation and specific focus of special classes may improve academic learning for a child with intellectual disabilities but might also prevent many hours of critical development through normalizing social experiences. Likewise, the use of some drugs to control hyperactive behavior may also impede a child's alertness and learning in school. In the year 2001, the iatrogeny concept appears to be a statement of the obvious, and it is difficult to realize that a history of more than 1700 years unfolded before our current acceptance of this idea took hold. (We will return to this idea in the Chapter 5 discussion of Down syndrome and in the Chapter 10 discussion of social roles.)

The fourth historical theme in social responses to disabilities discussed by Safford and Safford (1996) is *education.* Training children to serve the interests of the state, church, commerce, or others has long been a human tradition. However, to be *educated* was long the prerogative of privileged classes; to educate children of all classes (universal education) and to do so based on a growing understanding of the psychological nature and needs of children are primarily twentieth-century developments. To educate those with disabilities is truly revolutionary.

In the American colonies, a beginning at public education was made in Massachusetts in 1647. It aimed to provide some basic literacy and to promote citizens' skills in self-government (Safford & Safford, 1996). Relatively few children were educated and only for a short time, but it was a beginning. By about 1820, the government-supported grammar schools had become virtually schools for the poor, while the more affluent attended public academies, which were open to all who could afford them. A long history ensued in which reformers brought about public education of children of immigrants and the poor, of former slaves, and they advocated full, equal education for girls and women. By the early twentieth century, public education was also provided to some children with physical and mental disabilities.

Universal public education is certainly one of the finest achievements of the twentieth century. Today, in most developed countries, all children, including those with disabilities, are entitled to an education, and society presumably provides the resources for each child to achieve his or her fullest potential. However, as in all social developments, the actual implementation of these excellent goals has been uneven. Compulsory education laws were enacted by all states in the United States by 1918, but over the years, exclusion policies barred many children from attending school, usually on the assumption that certain children could not profit from the usual classes. Children with intellectual, hearing, and visual disabilities and those with cerebral palsy, emotional problems, and many others were by law excluded. By the mid-1970s, good progress had been made in fostering the concept that all children can benefit from education and in bringing most formerly excluded children into public education. Even then, there remained millions of school-age children who were not enrolled in schools (Washington Research Project, 1974): Children of the poor and the homeless and some ethnic minorities are prevented from full benefit by circumstance and by the operation of lingering prejudices. In addition, many developing countries still do not provide universal education for children. But the concept of universal education, the policies, and much of the needed infrastructure are in place in much of the world.

We are currently in the midst of a true revolution or paradigm shift in our views of and interactions with persons with disabilities. Many long historical developments coalesced in the last decades of the twentieth century to form this new view, and it continues to grow. Contributing to these shifts is the twentieth-century realization of developmental reality: Children are not miniature adults, but are qualitatively different, and they proceed through a developmental sequence. As children mature, their needs, knowledge, skills, and abilities also change. Education and training thus need to be aimed at appropriate levels of maturation.

Full inclusion in society of persons with disabilities and the encouragement and help for each to develop as much autonomy and personal success as possible are now major goals. Accompanying this is an insistence on personal regard and respect for persons with disabilities. A *person-first* consideration has been adopted in which we recognize the *person* as distinct from the *disability* (e.g., "a person with autism" rather than "an autistic person"). This helps avoid defining the person in terms of the disability.

Underlying these changes is a growing advocacy for the rights of persons with disabilities, and we cannot overestimate the positive impact on governmental policy and services that such advocacy groups (e.g., parent associations) have had. We finally seem to be accepting the notion that persons with disabilities have the same basic rights as everyone else and that society has the responsibility of ensuring those rights for all persons (see Box 1.5).

B O X **1.5**

Basic Rights of Persons with Developmental Disabilities

The rights of persons with developmental disabilities are not different in concept from those of anyone else. An orderly, fair, and humane society needs to safeguard the rights of everyone, and particular care needs to be taken for those persons who may be most vulnerable. The ideals listed here converge on the concept that each person *must not be deprived by society of the opportunities* to create and enact his or her own individualized set of successful, meaningful, and personally satisfying social roles. Specifically, each person with disabilities, *like everyone else,* has the right to:

adequate health care and other services from conception throughout life;

a safe, secure, and loving human and physical environment for children and youth, with caring and responsible parents or other caregivers;

play, grow, and develop relationships with peers;

develop an individual personality and a positive regard for and sense of oneself;

learn and be educated in the least restrictive environment and to the fullest extent the child or adult is capable and/or desires;

develop personal autonomy and live as independently as possible, in settings of one's own choice, as normally as possible;

develop emotional relationships such as in friendships and romantic love;

be regarded and treated with respect and dignity, to be regarded as a "person" and not as a "disabled individual";

prepare for, develop, and practice a meaningful, satisfying occupation;

economic security and an adequate standard of living;

work, retire, and age in comfort and dignity.

Overall, society needs to guarantee the rights of each person to live and to die in dignity.

Presidential and Legislative Action in the United States

Human anomalies have been recognized throughout history, but the field of developmental disabilities is relatively new. It has been defined largely by federal legislation that was stimulated by President Kennedy in the early 1960s. The legislation recognized that disorders previously dealt with separately (conditions such as mental retardation, epilepsy, cerebral palsy, and learning disabilities) have enough in common that they could be defined as a group of related problems and could be better understood and treated. It brought together existing treatment and research under a new, unified focus, defining the field of developmental disabilities. President Kennedy's initial focus was on intellectual disabilities, a concern of the president because his sister was diagnosed with mental retardation. In 1961, President Kennedy appointed The President's Panel on Mental Retardation. Professionals in psychology, medicine, law, social sciences, and education carried out its mandate to study mental retardation and to produce a plan for reducing its incidence. Using existing information in the clinical, educational, medical, and research literature, the panel integrated most of what was then known about mental retardation. One year later, the panel presented its recommendations to the president in its report, *National Plan to Combat Mental Retardation* (1962) (for more complete discussions of the panel's work, see Hormuth, 1963; Mayo, 1963; Thompson & O'Quinn, 1979).

The panel noted that at that time there were 5.4 million children with retardation in the United States, and the cost of their care approached $600 million annually. Some retardation, they noted, is of known causes and may be preventable by application of existing knowledge. Most retardation, however, was of unknown origin, and more research was needed. The panel's discussions and recommendations identified important ideas that stimulated legislative and professional action.

For example, a high proportion of the mild levels of retardation seemed to be associated with poor socioeconomic conditions, and a successful program to reduce mental retardation would have to include solutions for those issues of poverty and their associated health-care problems. They had identified poverty as a risk factor in mental retardation. Their recommendations emphasized the need for a new major focus on *prevention* of retardation. This would include emphases on parent training and parent–child early enrichment programs. They emphasized the concept that care of persons with mental retardation requires the carefully selected blending of efforts of medical, educational, psychological, and social services disciplines, and they urged that such services need to be provided throughout the person's life to minimize disability. They recommended creation of community-based services such as diagnostic clinics, preschool programs, education of parents, educational, recreational, and vocational programs, group homes, legal aid services, and so on. Finally, they emphasized the need for increased and continued research to inform service providers about progress in basic and applied research in the field. To this end, the panel recommended close ties between universities with their research and training missions and agencies with their direct service missions. It was a forward-looking document that is still valid today.

Following that report, President Kennedy presented a message to Congress that was to have significant effects on stimulating national health policy. He called for a comprehensive approach to mental retardation and mental health that would include prevention, community services, research, and training. As a result, federal legislation was enacted in 1963 (Public Law 88-156 and Public Law 88-164) that placed new emphasis on research, training, and treatment in mental retardation and mental health.

Subsequently, the original law was amended to account for new information. There was a realization that many people had multiple problems requiring multiple solutions. Among the most important amendments were:

1. The exclusive focus on mental retardation had ignored millions of persons who were not labeled retarded but who were under a variety of different diagnostic labels, such as cerebral palsy.
2. Many persons with mental retardation had other problems that were not included under the old law, but which required attention.
3. Service needs for many people with various diagnoses were similar or identical.

The law enacted in 1970, Public Law 9s1-517, brought together persons with different diagnostic labels but with common service needs. This was the Developmental Disabilities Service and Facilities Construction Amendments of 1970. In this new version of the law, the focus on mental retardation was replaced by the expanded concept of developmental disabilities, thus increasing the number of people and types of disabilities included under the new law. Its intent was to facilitate actions by the states to meet the needs of those with developmental disabilities.

By 1978, the Developmental Disabilities Act (Public Law 95-602) had been amended further. The concept of developmental disabilities continued to be refined: It was broadened to include not only mental retardation but also cerebral palsy, epilepsy, autism, and some learning disabilities; it turned its focus to the shared *functional* problems of those disorders; it incorporated developmental data into the definition.

The Developmental Disabilities Act of 1984 (Public Law 98-527), subsequent amendments in 1987, and related legislation (i.e., the Federal Americans with Disabilities Act, 1990) have provided the basic definition that is in use today (Box 1.6). This is not a precise definition of specific clinical conditions, nor does it denote what disorders are included. Rather, it is an umbrella term that is useful for organizing information and for helping to direct governmental planning and funding programs for citizens with disabilities.

Definitional Concepts

Early Onset. To be considered a developmental disability, an impairment must have originated early in life, during the person's most significant developmental growth (from conception to about age 20). The rate of development slows significantly (but continues throughout life) as that period nears its end. Most developmental disabilities are attributed to events in early childhood. Disabling injuries also occur after age 20. A 40-year-old who suffers severe head injury in an automobile collision and has severe lifelong impairment has a disability but not a *developmental* disability.

It is during the early years, including prenatal development, that the person's physical, cognitive, and psychological growth are most rapid. People continue to change and learn throughout life, long past the twentieth birthday, but the early years constitute the

BOX **1.6**

A Working Definition of Developmental Disability

A developmental disability is a severe and chronic condition that:

1. is attributed to mental or physical impairment or their combination;
2. occurs before age 21;
3. is likely to continue indefinitely (i.e., is permanent);
4. results in substantial functional limitations in at least three of the following major areas of life activities:
   a. self-care
   b. receptive and expressive language
   c. learning
   d. mobility
   e. self-direction
   f. capacity for independent living
   g. economic self-sufficiency
5. requires professional services that are:
   a. of lifelong duration
   b. planned and coordinated on an individual basis
   c. drawn from many disciplines

The working definition has developed over many years and will continue to be refined as new understanding is attained through research and practice.

From Developmental Disabilities Act

---

most active growth period. The important point here is that when a severe disability occurs during this most active growth period, it affects not only the person at the time of the disability, but will interfere with the person's subsequent development and may curtail or prevent the acquisition of important knowledge and skills. The growth of a child with a developmental disability markedly deviates from normal growth and development. Thus, developmental disabilities are defined not only by impairments but also by the impairments' negative effects on subsequent development.

Impairments early in life have longer developmental paths in which to interfere than do impairments occurring much later. An obvious example is the child born with impaired cognitive abilities. That child's significantly low intelligence will have marked detrimental effects on all of his or her subsequent learning and socialization. As a general rule, the earlier in life the disability occurs, the greater are the negative developmental effects.

Functional Severity. To be diagnosed as a developmental disability, the impairment must be disabling and severe enough to cause significant limitations in the area of impairment (e.g., speech, sight, intelligence, etc.). Blindness, deafness, significant difficulties in motor control, and significantly subaverage intelligence are all impairments severe enough to be considered disabilities.

Notice, too, the emphasis in this definition on the long-term functional aspects of the person rather than on structural aspects or on clinical categories. There are many possible hereditary and environmental causes of a developmental disability, but regardless of the origins, emphasis is placed on how the person functions in life and on what successes and difficulties the person has in mastering the sequences of life tasks. Earlier definitions emphasized diagnostic categories such as mental retardation and cerebral palsy. But since about 1980, the emphasis has shifted to the common functional issues involved regardless of specific diagnoses. Given this functional emphasis, many conditions can be included under the developmental disabilities label.

The concept of functional severity is also reflected in the concept of handicap—a developmental disability is, by definition, a handicapping condition. It is severe enough to make the pursuit of common life activities uncommonly difficult or impossible. While some persons might have disabilities that are at less severe levels and therefore not handicapping, our focus is on the more severe end of the continuum, which involves those that are handicapping. How is "handicap" or "significant disruption and limitation" defined? The generally accepted criteria involve the concept that most people master several basic areas of functioning or life activity. Among these are the following seven areas (they were noted earlier): self-care, receptive and expressive language, learning, mobility, self-direction, capacity for independent living, and economic self-sufficiency. A developmental disability is defined when impairments cause limitations in at least three of those life activity areas. Thus, a person with early onset, severe, and permanent dysfunction in, for example, language development, learning capacity, and self-care would meet this definition of developmental disabilities. There is a clear judgmental factor here (some would call it "arbitrary") in setting diagnostic criteria at limitations in at least three functional areas.

Permanence.   The disability must not only be severe but also permanent. This concept must be qualified, and the statement should read "permanent in nearly all cases." For example, some children with epilepsy seem to "grow out it" by adolescence. Some researchers have noted cases of apparent mild intellectual disabilities in which the persons gradually develop sufficient skills so they are no longer functionally limited in any significant way (Haskins, 1986; Rowitz, 1991). In nearly all cases, however, a child with cerebral palsy or with intellectual disabilities, autism, brain injury, or any of the developmental disabilities will maintain that condition throughout his or her lifetime. Temporary disabilities, no matter how severe they may be, do not belong in the category of developmental disabilities. For example, persons injured in accidents might be seriously disabled with broken bones for months. During their convalescence, they will need to rely on others to care for them. But as they heal and regain control over their bodies and lives, the disabilities diminish and, ideally, disappear. They may have been severely disabled by injuries, but those temporary conditions do not constitute developmental disabilities.

Because the disabilities are permanent, they affect the person's development, treatment, education, training, and occupations throughout his or her lifetime. Developmental disabilities and handicaps do not end with childhood, and a full life-span perspective is necessary in research, treatment, and education.

VI. Conditions Included in Developmental Disabilities

Major Diagnostic Categories

Adults have a limited array of serious disabilities and chronic illness such as strokes, heart conditions, and cancer, and those occur at high frequencies (Ireys & Katz, 1997). Children, however, are prone to more than 200 chronic conditions (Hobbs, Perrin, & Ireys, 1985). Among that large group are disorders comprising the subset developmental disabilities, which include the conditions that best meet our criteria of early onset, functional severity, and permanence.

A number of textbooks have presented organized outlines of types of developmental disabilities (e.g., Batshaw & Perret, 1992; Craft & Wolraich, 1997; Kurtz, Dowrick, Levy, & Batshaw, 1996; Widerstrom, Mowder, & Sandall, 1991; and many others). Because of the lack of a clearly inclusive definition, each text is somewhat different. In this text, the organization is based on the commonalties of earlier work and our own judgments. No particular organization at this time is perfect or complete. The resulting organization of conditions presented in Box 1.7 is not an exhaustive list of all the possible conditions, but it does include those most commonly encountered by professionals. Box 1.7 shows seven groups of children's disabilities, with some specific disorders identified in each group. For example, included under the heading Cognitive Disabilities are learning disabilities, mental retardation, and communication disorders. Each of these includes several more specific disorders, totaling more than 200.

Notice that the inclusion in Box 1.7 of attention deficit-hyperactivity disorder and Behavioral/Emotional Disorders is tentative. Although a valid case can be made that these are properly included in the listing of developmental disabilities, it is our view that they are best considered (at least for now) within the professional domain of *developmental psychopathology*. This text will not deal with these disorders in any detail.

Likewise, other than having basic definitions presented, a number of conditions will be discussed only briefly. These include chronic illness such as AIDS, rheumatic disease, congestive heart disease, and diabetes; sensory disorders such as auditory and visual impairments; many physical disabilities such as amputations and facial anomalies; and communication disorders. Sensory and communication disorders, for example, are often associated with and secondary to other conditions, and separate discussions of each may be too repetitive. This is not to suggest they are less important than other conditions. Rather, some limits must be imposed on the scope of any useful textbook.

What remains, then, is our focus on cerebral palsy, muscular dystrophy, seizure disorders (e.g., epilepsy), neural tube defects (e.g., spina bifida, anencephaly), autism, intellectual disabilities, learning disabilities, traumatic brain injury, and disabilities associated with toxic effects of environmental substances (e.g., alcohol and other drugs, radiation, industrial toxins, etc.).

BOX **1.7**

Conditions Included under the Heading *Developmental Disabilities*

Physical Disabilities
    Cerebral Palsy
    Muscular Dystrophy
    Congenital Amputations

Chronic Illness
    AIDS
    Rheumatic Disease
    Epilepsy
    Congenital Heart Defects
    Diabetes

Birth Defects
    Craniofacial Anomalies
    Neural Tube Disorder
        Spina Bifida
        Anencephaly
        Myelomeningocele

Sensory Disorders
    Auditory Impairments
    Visual Impairments

Cognitive Disabilities
    Learning Disabilities
    Mental Retardation
    Communication Disorders

Behavioral/Emotional Disorders
    Attention Deficit Hyperactivity Disorder
    Autistic Spectrum Disorders
    Emotional/Behavioral Disorders (see Box 1.8)

Environmentally Induced Impairments
    Drug and Alcohol Syndromes and Effects
    Physical Trauma (Traumatic Brain Injury; Spinal Cord Injury)
    Passive Environmental Toxins (e.g., lead, mercury)

Based on Batshaw & Perret, 1992; Craft & Wolraich, 1997; Jackson & Vessey, 2000; Kurtz et al., 1996; Widerstrom et al., 1991

It is important to emphasize that developmental disabilities are not defined by particular diagnostic categories such as autism or epilepsy. These categories are useful in diagnoses and treatment, but the concept of developmental disabilities is more inclusive, encompassing any condition of severe, permanent disability that occurred in the formative years and interferes with at least three areas of normal life functioning.

As the types of pathogens, diseases, and numbers of persons grow and as finer distinctions are made among types of disabilities, so too will the need for more and newer services. For example, our increasingly toxic world is creating major challenges for researchers, clinicians, teachers, and policymakers. It is critically important to maintain, improve, and expand our services to those with developmental disabilities and to create new services. In the long term, however, the most important demands will be for researchers to determine how to *prevent* the occurrence of developmental disabilities, as was called for by President Kennedy's commission in 1962. It is the responsibility of our local, state, and federal policymakers to translate the science into effective social actions aimed at prevention, and it is the responsibility of professionals in many disciplines to implement those prevention measures. In another generation or two, this field will be much larger and possibly look very different than it does today.

The Problems Held in Common

However varied the disorders may be, the persons affected share similar problems of coping with the myriad developmental issues common to all of us, but they must do so while handicapped by some form of severe disability. If we think of life as a complex journey along a path littered with physical and psychological demands, obstacles, successes, failures, relationships, and emotions, then it is clear that those with developmental disabilities are hobbled in this journey by handicaps that are not of their own making. These persons are forced into grossly unequal and never-ending life contests with all others, causing them to fall ever farther behind others who proceed more smoothly through life.

VII. Developmental Delay, Developmental Psychopathology, and Dual Diagnoses

The terms developmental delay, developmental psychopathology, and developmental disabilities refer to impairments in child development, but they each focus on different aspects of development. Each of these overlapping concepts refers to "normal development gone awry," an aptly descriptive term used by Wenar (1990).

Developmental Delay

Normal child development proceeds as a continuing sequence of growth in which children encounter and master various tasks at predictable ages. For example, most children can sit alone at about 7 months, creep at 10 months, walk unassisted at about 15 months, use their first words between 10 and 15 months, and utter simple two-word sentences by 20–25 months. There is an average age for the appearance of each of these and many other skills, and there is also a great deal of normal individual variation around these average ages.

Many children, however, experience developmental delays—when a normal ability fails to appear at the expected age—in which some aspects of development fall significantly below the age norms. The term *developmental delay* is a nonspecific descriptive term used with children under about age 5. Most parents are alert to their children's progress in relation to what is expected of normal children, comparing their younger children with their older children and with children of relatives, friends, and neighbors. Parents seek normative developmental information from child care manuals and from pediatricians, psychologists, and other child health professionals. Table 1.1 shows approximate age norms for normal child development in locomotion and language.

Delays are usually seen earliest in motor functioning (e.g., coordination, sitting, standing, walking, etc.). Later, delays in language and social functioning may occur. There may be known reasons for the delays, such as illness, psychological trauma, birth injuries, genetic factors, and so on. In other cases, there may be no obvious causes of the delays. Children showing developmental delays should be examined to determine if they have a permanent developmental disability or if the delay is minor and/or temporary. All children with developmental disabilities are developmentally delayed, but a delay does not necessarily mean the child has a developmental disability. Parents often do not know if their

TABLE 1.1 Approximate Age Norms in the Development of Locomotion and Language

Locomotion

Lifts head	Neonatal
Holds head steady	1 month–5½ months
Crawling movements	Neonatal–3 months
Sits with support	1–5 months
Grasps small cube	2–7 months
Rolls over	4–7 months
Reaches for object, one hand	4–8 months
Grasps, fine control	7–10 months
Sits alone	5–9 months
Pulls self to standing	5–12 monhts
Stands up alone	6–12 months
Early stepping movements	5–11 months
Walks, with help	7–12 months
Walks alone	9–17 months
Walks upstairs with help	12–23 months

Vocal and Language

Crying	At birth
Cooing	1–3 months
Babbling	4–8 months
Echoes babbling	Approximately 9 months
First words	Approximately 12 months
Hololphrastic speech	12–18 months
Two-word combinations	Approximately 18 months
Multiword sentences, simple conversations	24–30 months

Based on the summaries by Rosenblith, J. F., & Simms-Knight, J. E. (1985). *In the beginning.* Monterey, CA: Brooks/Cole; and by Mussen, P. H., Conger, J. J., & Huston, A. C. (1990). *Child development and personality* (7th ed.). New York: HarperCollins.

children's delays are temporary or permanent until the duration of the delay is determined through diagnostic examinations or the passage of time.

A developmental delay might affect only one functional area and perhaps not to a severe degree. For example, a child might show a motor delay in locomotion but have no delays in other areas. A delay might be a temporary slowness that is overcome eventually, leaving no serious or permanent problem. However, it might be an indication of permanent developmental disability and should be evaluated when the delay becomes known.

Typically, developmental disabilities are first noticed by parents as developmental delays in the child's first 2 or 3 years and are diagnosed as developmental disabilities usually by the time the child enters school, at about age 5. With good prenatal and postnatal care, not only will the risks for impairment and disabilities be reduced but also the impairments that do occur will be diagnosed earlier, thus increasing the chances for effective remedial action to ameliorate future disabilities and handicaps. But when such care is lacking, as in many low socioeconomic status families, then the delay/disability might not be diagnosed until much later, in some cases not until school age. Corrective measures taken only then are generally not as effective as those taken earlier.

Largely spurred by pressure from advocates, particularly parent groups, Congress enacted PL99-457 in 1985–1986 (W. Brown, Thurman, & Pearl, 1993). That legislation provided funds to encourage states to develop early intervention programs for infants, toddlers, and children from birth through 5 years of age who have disabilities. That law required participating states to determine the nature of developmental delays in children with disabilities in each of five developmental domains: physical, cognitive, communicative, social/emotional, and adaptive. It is assumed that developmental delays can occur on a continuum of severity in each domain: mild, moderate, severe, and profound. States were also required to develop fourteen specific components such as specifying:

    methods of determining delay (e.g., tests, clinical/school observation)
    a definition of developmental delay
    multidisciplinary evaluation procedures for each eligible child
    an individualized family service plan (IFSP)
    child-find procedures
    public awareness procedures
    data-compiling procedures
    and seven other program components

Under provisions of that law, states could also create systems to determine the at-risk status of children—that is, of children who do not have disabilities but who, by virtue of medical history and/or environmental/family conditions, have a high probability of developing substantial delays if early intervention is not forthcoming (W. Brown et al., 1993). Two main categories of at-risk components are biological and environmental factors. The former includes events such as low birth weight, acute illness or accident, infant respiratory disease, and so on. The environmental factors include parental mental illness, teenage mother (younger than 20 years), homeless family, drug-dependent parent, and poverty or near poverty.

While all states now have systems for identifying developmental delay, there is considerable variability among states and even among municipalities within states.

Developmental Psychopathology

It can be argued that the field of developmental psychopathology is a special subset of developmental disabilities because it shares a focus on early-onset impairments that cause substantial functional limitations. However, the two fields have significantly different emphases. In *developmental psychopathology*, the emphasis is on emotional and behavioral (i.e., psychological) impairment of functioning. It is a relatively new area of research and practice. Its major journal, *Development and Psychopathology*, was first issued in 1989, and major textbooks that aim to define the field have appeared (e.g., Gelfand, Jensen, & Drew 1988; Kauffman, 1989; Lewis & Miller, 1990; Wenar, 1990; Wicks-Nelson & Israel, 1991). It is a "clinical psychology" of childhood, focusing on issues of psychological malfunctioning such as childhood anxiety, aggression, traumatic stress reactions, fears and phobias, depression, borderline and schizophrenic disorders, eating disorders, sexual disorders, and so on. It is assumed that these disorders are not necessarily permanent and can be treated through psychological means such as psychotherapy and training.

It is the psychological/behavioral domain that is emphasized in developmental psychopathology, but it overlaps with developmental disabilities. For example, children with developmental disabilities, such as intellectual disabilities or cerebral palsy, may also have emotional/behavioral problems. They experience anxieties, fears, depressions and may exhibit aggressive behavior, self-injurious behavior or hyperactivity, and so on. The incidence of such dual conditions is high, and persons with intellectual disabilities have twice the rate of severe emotional/behavioral problems as do persons of normal intelligence (Menolascino, 1990). Many of the psychological therapies that are useful for children with psychopathology are also appropriate for those who are primarily developmentally disabled but who also have psychological problems. The term *dual diagnosis* refers to these children. Another example is childhood autism, a severely handicapping disorder that occurs early in life and is permanent, thus fitting the definition of developmental disability. But characteristic of autism is severe functional disruption in virtually all aspects of life, and that functional aspect makes it a disorder of considerable interest to developmental psychopathologists. In fact, early, now discarded models of autism, such as the psychoanalytically based model of Bettelheim (1967), attributed the disorder to emotional distortions in the child's developmental experience. Disabilities such as autism, learning disabilities, and attention deficit disorders are now studied in both professional areas.

The field of developmental psychopathology is the study of psychological problems of children and youth. A major assumption is that most of the disorders are, at least theoretically, reversible through treatment. Box 1.8 lists the major disorders usually included under the heading developmental psychopathology.

As noted earlier, while some of the conditions clearly fall into one or the other group, other conditions such as autism overlap both. The two domains are not categorically separate. It might be better to think of them on a continuum of developmental disorders. These range from disorders whose origins are most clearly associated with genetic and biological factors and which are permanent disorders to those whose origins are most clearly related

BOX **1.8**

Conditions Usually Included under the Heading
Developmental Psychopathology

Developmental Psychopathology

A. Undercontrolled Disorders
  1. Attention Deficit Disorders
  2. Conduct Disorders and Aggressive Behavior

B. Overcontrolled Disorders
  1. Anxiety Disorders
  2. Posttraumatic Stress Disorders
  3. Fears and Phobias

C. Depression

D. Pervasive Disorders
  1. Autistic Spectrum Disorders
  2. Borderline Disorders
  3. Childhood Schizophrenia

E. Highly Specific Disorders
  1. Eating Disorders
  2. Sleep Disturbances
  3. Enuresis and Encopresis
  4. Tourette's Syndrome and Tics
  5. Stuttering
  6. Sexual Disorders

(based on Miller & Lewis, 1990)

to experience and learning (are functional disorders) and which might not be permanent conditions. The biological/functional distinction is a difference of degree. That is, both biological and learning factors apply across the entire continuum with different degrees of emphasis. The professional disciplines within developmental disabilities tend to cover the disorders in which biological factors appear to make the major contributions and that tend to be permanent. The disciplines within developmental psychopathology focus primarily on disorders of a more functional nature (i.e., disorders in which learning and other psychological factors appear to make the major contributions) and which might not be permanent. But keep in mind that across much of this hypothetical continuum the two areas are overlapping (see Box 1.9).

Dual Diagnoses

According to Parsons, May, and Menolascino (1984), an estimated 20 to 35 percent of non-institutionalized persons with intellectual disabilities also have some significant psychiatric

BOX **1.9**

Theoretical Continuum of Developmental Disabilities and Developmental Psychopathology

Developmental Disabilities   Developmental Psychopathology

Biological $\longleftarrow$ $\longrightarrow$ Psychological

Relative Emphasis in Etiological Factors

---

disorder (i.e., psychopathology). This rate is higher in persons with intellectual disabilities compared with the 15 to 19 percent of mental illness in the general population (Menolascino & Stark, 1984). The term *dual diagnosis* has traditionally referred to persons for whom intellectual disabilities and mental illness coexist. Usually, as we have found in our own work, the psychiatric diagnosis is not made until later in the person's life, long after the original intellectual disabilities had been determined, perhaps because the psychiatric conditions develop later or could not be easily diagnosed in childhood.

The diagnostic evaluation of mental retardation is carried out by a multidisciplinary team of professionals. In the evaluations, a multidimensional classification system as outlined in Box 1.10 is used. As shown, psychological/emotional status is considered within Dimension II. If mental illness is found as well as mental retardation, then the person is given the dual diagnosis.

Diagnoses are made to identify specific problems that can then be addressed with appropriate professional services including rehabilitation, education, language and speech training/therapy, social skills training, physical therapy, medication and other medical

---

BOX **1.10**

Multidimensional System for Diagnosis and Classification of Persons with Mental Retardation

Dimension I.   Intellectual Functioning and Adaptive Skills

Dimension II.   Psychological/Emotional Considerations

Dimension III.   Physical/Health/Etiology Considerations

Dimension IV.   Environmental Considerations

From: *Mental Retardation: Definition, Classification, and Systems of Support*, 9th Edition. Washington, D.C.: American Association on Mental Retardation, page 23. Reproduced by permission.

treatment, psychological counseling, family training/support, and so on. A dual diagnosis has considerable impact on the service plans for the person; both domains—intellectual disability and psychopathology—need to be considered carefully in planning a particular mix of services for that person. For example, if the person is diagnosed as "mental retardation with major depression," then treatment decisions must be made not only about the education and training usually provided for persons with mental retardation but also about the use of medication and behavior therapy to help control the depression. With the dual diagnoses, we can see how the two realms of developmental disabilities and developmental psychopathology come together. (Multidimensional diagnoses of mental retardation will be discussed more completely in Chapter 9.)

VIII. Developmental Disabilities in a Life-Span Context

This text emphasizes etiology and the developmental years, or approximately the first quarter of a normal life span. But we must also consider several significant facts about longevity that have emerged over the past century and their current and future implications. In 1900, 44 percent of the population of the United States was under 18 years of age, while only 4 percent was age 65 and older. By 2050, when most readers of this text will most likely be retiring from their occupations and looking forward to many years of deserved leisure, those figures are predicted to be, respectively, 23 percent and 26 percent (U.S. Senate Special Committee on Aging, 1991). Factors such as improved health care, education, safety, nutrition, and stable economic growth that may largely account for this marked demographic shift to an older society have affected everyone, including persons with developmental disabilities. As discussed by Herr and Weber (1999a), longer and healthier lives have become normal for most persons with developmental disabilities. In addition, our expectations for the functioning of persons with developmental disabilities have grown significantly over the past half century. No longer is institutionalization the primary goal. Today our goal is to foster the greatest degrees of autonomy, personal growth, achievement, and life quality for each person in spite of disabilities. We aim to foster their inclusion in mainstream life rather than their exclusion and assignment to high-control institutions. We value and support their *self-determination,* rather than their total dependence on social agents to make critical life decisions. For each person, we strive to replace the traditional provider-centered planning with *person-centered* planning in which the client becomes an important part of the planning procedures. The client's own views, goals, and preferences become major factors in determining what types of services to offer. We expect to help persons develop in parallel experience with everyone else and to take their places alongside others in the occupational world. Policy decisions have been made and new laws have been enacted to ensure that society recognizes and meets its newly defined obligations to these persons. We expect this social investment in resources will be amply repaid as each person becomes, to the levels of his or her ability, a contributing, strong link in our social fabric rather than a dependent, noncontributing resident of some institution.

These shifts in demographics and in our social expectations create new demands on society in general and on the professions in particular. One major set of demands—so important that it is helping to redefine the field—is to create, maintain, evaluate, and improve our professional services and other social resources across all disciplines to help individuals meet these new expectations to live fuller lives in dignity, personal fulfillment, and success. Thus, we now evaluate persons not only in terms of what disabilities they might "have" but also in terms of what strengths they each possess, what personal needs will emerge throughout their full life spans, and what resources such as support services they may need to help them realize their maximum achievements. This requires a focus on and continued support and services for each person's *full life span* because, as we continue to mature, we face newly unfolding issues, develop new needs, and require new solutions.

The life issues facing persons with developmental disabilities are essentially the same as those faced by everyone else (Herr & Weber, 1999a, b). These include having age-appropriate learning experiences (e.g., play, school, social interaction) and physical and emotional care when needed. As individuals grow into adulthood, they need to maintain an adequate living standard, learn occupational skills, and work. Throughout life, all people try to develop positive and meaningful roles, positive personal identities, and to form relationships and deal with friendship, love, sex, and loss. People seek respect, want to live in dignity, experience happiness, and grow into healthy and comfortable old age.

However, in these pursuits, persons with developmental disabilities are much more vulnerable than are most others to the disruptions and damage caused by physical and social obstacles. If they are to achieve goals similar to those pursued by most of us, then society needs at least to be more sensitive to their vulnerabilities and ensure that such obstacles are reduced or eliminated. To these ends, our responses to persons with developmental disabilities have changed since the 1950s. A view is emerging that recognizes not only the potentials for development of persons with developmental disabilities but also their human and legal *rights* to pursue quality lives and society's obligations to safeguard those rights (see the earlier discussion on rights). This dual recognition of potentials and rights is a major foundation for current views and social and professional responses to developmental disabilities. Today, services for persons with developmental disabilities are ideally driven by those dual concerns, and in our judgement, the professions are developing the expertise and other resources needed to apply this person-centered model.

Unfortunately, not everyone with developmental disabilities has had the same opportunities to benefit from this new model. First, most older adults with developmental disabilities came through their formative years 60, 70, or more years ago, before the general acceptance of the new person-first concepts. As noted by Heller (1999), it was only in the 1990s that we began to pay particular attention to older persons with developmental disabilities. As a result, many may now be more dependent and less capable of autonomous living than are younger persons. Thus, there are special demands made upon the developmental disabilities field to deal with the specific issues of this particular group of older, still-dependent persons. To what degree can these persons be brought into the new person-centered experience? Special programs for older persons with developmental disabilities are being developed, and these issues are being faced with considerable success (Janicki, 1994).

The newer service model has been adopted largely in the developed world—North America, England, and Western Europe. There are an estimated 500 million children and adults with disabilities worldwide (Annan, 1997). The majority of these people live in developing nations and are still treated under the old paradigm (Herr & Weber, 1999a, b) in which they are vulnerable to severe neglect and discrimination and are relegated to the poorest levels of society. Given the economic and political state of so much of the world, it seems unlikely that resources will be devoted soon to this large group of people. At present, it seems to be up to the developed nations to lead the world and to continue creating new concepts and services to form the models that will one day be used throughout the world. (Current service models for persons with developmental disabilities will be discussed more fully in Chapter Fourteen.)

IX. Social Attitudes about Persons with Disabilities

An important point must be made before proceeding with our study of developmental disabilities: *Every person is a unique individual.* That point is often lost in the details of diagnoses, group characteristics, and our own attitudinal biases and expectations of what "disabled" people, as a class, are like. In many cases, the disability and its effects on how the person looks and functions are so overwhelming that other people see *only* a disabled person, and the disability becomes the paramount defining feature of that person. Once that occurs, a response tendency is created in which (a) individual, personal characteristics of the person with disabilities are ignored and (b) all of the person's functioning is explained by others as being due to the disability.

What are the implications of such response tendencies? First, by ignoring other characteristics of the person with disabilities, one never becomes fully acquainted with that person. For example, one sees a young man with cerebral palsy, with spastic movements and speech articulation problems. Despite his severe disabilities, he might be an alert, aware, person with observations and ideas that would astonish you if you were ever to give him the opportunity to express them. It is true that about half of those with cerebral palsy have intellectual disability, but an equal proportion do not. Other people, seeing the physical limitations, can easily infer that the person is intellectually limited, has no worthwhile ideas, and is thus not able to engage in any meaningful verbal interaction or even has any capacity for friendship.

The nondisabled person in this situation would lose an opportunity to know a unique person, and the child, man, or woman with the disability is denied an opportunity for another human interaction. Whatever the developmental disability might be, there is a tendency for others to ignore most of the person's nondisabled characteristics, thus denying to both of them what could be an opportunity for a rich and interesting human interaction.

Second, by attributing all the person's functioning to the disability, the human complexity of the person is reduced to a single dimension—the disability. That disability is then used to explain all of the person's actions and problems. This view can result in the unfortunate loss of opportunities for friendships, personal development, and even for services.

For example, consider an 18-year-old boy with moderate intellectual disability. He is in a special school program appropriate for his cognitive level. This youth has recently displayed a number of problems—he becomes moody and unresponsive, easily upset, occasionally disruptive, and moderately difficult to control. Although he has not yet caused any serious problems, his teachers fear that a more serious outburst might occur.

It is easy to attribute all of this youngster's difficulties to the general condition of retardation. "Well", one might note, "I understand why he has so many problems in school and so little emotional control. After all, he *is* retarded!"

Given that attribution, one ignores other explanations for his behavior. Perhaps he is worried about the illness of a parent, and that concern is having an effect on his school behavior; perhaps he has developed deep concerns and doubts about himself and his abilities and is feeling frightened, anxious, even becoming depressed. He may have developed social or academic fears, perhaps to phobic levels. In short, he may be experiencing any of a number of psychological stresses that are common among other, nonretarded, adolescents. In the other cases, the youths are apt to be seen as normal youngsters who are under temporary psychological stress. An array of help can be offered such as counseling for their feelings of inadequacy and personal uncertainties, cognitive/behavioral self-control training to reduce anger and outbursts, systematic desensitization for the fears and phobias, remedial academic work, and so on.

But for this youth, those options might seldom be offered once the attribution is made that the behavior stems directly from the retardation that, after all, is a condition we cannot readily change. What is lost is the recognition that the youth with retardation has feelings, fears, concerns, and uncertainties like everyone else. In reality, those human dimensions are not lost because of the retardation. Indeed, some have argued that persons with disabilities have an even greater risk than others for developing psychological problems, and therefore, psychological treatment is needed even more urgently by them (Cullen, 1992; Van Hasselt, Lutzker, & Hersen, 1990). Therapeutic and remedial efforts commonly provided to other youngsters can be helpful for those with retardation, but they are not ordinarily made available to them.

This tendency to let the condition, retardation, define the person and serve as an explanation for all of the person's functioning has been called *diagnostic overshadowing* (Levitan & Reiss, 1983; Reiss, Levitan, & Szyszko, 1982); that is, the diagnosis of mental retardation overshadows all else about the person. Thus, real psychological disorders may be ignored, and potentially effective treatments might not be offered to the person who carries the retardation label; real skills and human uniqueness can easily be overlooked. Diagnostic overshadowing is a limitation in the thinking and perceptions not of the person with intellectual disability, but of the persons responsible for the programs serving those with intellectual disabilities. Reiss et al. (1982) found that even psychologists give lower ratings to a person's psychopathology when the person is labeled retarded. This tendency is apparently so strong that it is not moderated by experience with persons with retardation (Reiss & Szyszko, 1983) or by the theoretical orientation of the psychologist (Alford & Locke, 1984).

This attributional tendency is rooted in our biases, attitudes, perceptions, and fears concerning those with severe disabilities. Persons have been handicapped not only by their disabilities but also by social discrimination against them. Negative social attitudes against persons with disabilities and the effects of such attitudes have been discussed by many (e.g., Aloia & MacMillan, 1983; Jackman, 1983; Reiss et al., 1982; Siller, Chipman, Ferguson, & Vann, 1967). Asch (1984), reviewing some of the work on reactions to disability, noted that people without disabilities avoid social contact with those who are disabled and, when in contact with them, react in uneasy, distorted, and formal ways. Historically, persons with disabilities have been viewed by others as helpless, dependent, and incompetent (Jackman, 1983). There is little doubt that the ways in which others react to persons with disabilities has powerful effects on the disabled person's life. (Social factors in developmental disabilities will be discussed more completely in Chapters Nine and Ten.)

A real-life example of such distortion is the case of a 35-year-old woman with Down syndrome (a chromosomal anomaly and form of mental retardation) who was rejected for a desperately needed heart and lung transplant. The surgeons decided that, because of her intellectual disability, she was not intelligent enough to follow-through with the demanding postoperative regimen that is required for success (taking antirejection drugs, maintaining a proper diet, engaging in regular prescribed exercise, avoiding strenuous activity, and maintaining regular postoperative contact with the physicians). They did not know the person as an individual, but only as a member of a class (i.e., a mentally retarded person), and they based their decisions about this particular individual on what they believed about a class of people. What they did not know is that she is a high school graduate, is an advocate for persons with Down syndrome and other forms of mental retardation, has lived independently for several years, and attended President George Bush's signing of the Americans with Disabilities Act in 1990 (Cole, 1996). Early in 1996, when that information was provided to the surgeons by her advocates, the decision was reversed and the surgery was carried out. As of this writing, the patient has successfully recuperated.

Let us return to the opening statement of this section: *Every person is a unique individual.* If we consider the vast number of possible genetic factors that combine to form each individual, plus the infinite combinations of events that shape each person's social and personal development, then it seems clear that no two people are the same—each person is unique. This is no less true of persons with disabilities. Their disabilities may be overwhelming, but it is a disservice to fail to see the unique person behind the disability. This disservice keeps the person invisible.

X. Prevalence and Incidence of Developmental Disabilities

Prevalence refers to the number of persons in a population at a given time who exhibit a particular characteristic (e.g., Down syndrome) and is usually reported as the number of current cases per unit of population (e.g., 25/1000). *Incidence* refers to the number of new cases occurring in a specified period of time, usually 1 year, and/or in a unit of population, typically 1000. Prevalence and incidence are important for planning medical and other services, in studying factors of etiology, and in helping to predict future service needs. The relationship between incidence and prevalence is complicated, and we need not pursue it here. It is important, however, to note that prevalence and incidence estimates of disabilities are widely variable and are difficult to calculate. There are still no complete national recording or reporting standards. There is a lack of complete agreement on what types of disabilities to include. There are persisting differences among practitioners and researchers in their definitions of specific disabilities. It is often difficult to agree on what severity of impairment is necessary to define a true disability. The methods used in making estimates vary among different studies. One point seems clear: The total number of persons with disabilities (prevalence) will continue to increase as our population increases (see Table 1.2), thus making more demands on the availability of services. It also seems likely that incidence will increase, although ideally, at a slow pace. These increases, we believe, will be due in part to improved medical care which has reduced the mortality rate of children with developmental disabilities, thus adding to the total number. Further, new populations of children with disabilities will continue to emerge. For example, children with AIDS due to the mother's HIV infection were unheard of less than a generation ago, and newborns with fetal alcohol syndrome or drug addiction were quite rare. Because their numbers are still relatively small—for example, it is estimated there are now about 2000 children in the United States with AIDS (Craft & Wolraich, 1997)—they have not greatly affected prevalence.[2] But other emerging populations with newly discovered disabilities will continue to be identified in the future, and although not high in numbers, these emerging populations will add their own demands on already-stretched service-provider systems and will require new research on the causes and treatments for those conditions.

As these pressures operate to increase disabilities, there are also moderating influences. These include the generally improving health of the population, improved and more available services which help to stabilize disabilities of individuals and thus prevent their worsening, and primary prevention efforts, such as increased prenatal screening, smoking- and alcohol-control programs, and so on. These moderating influences depend on public policy and social actions and are thus heavily influenced by political values, budgets, special interests, and the public's will. It seems to have been our experience in the United States that every significant public step to strengthen disability-prevention efforts has been caught up, blocked, slowed, and weakened by special interests operating through political and legal systems. The nearly half-century-old antitobacco public health campaigns in the United States and attempts to reduce environmental lead and to control air pollution are examples (similar antismoking campaigns have hardly even begun in the rest of the world).

Prevalence estimates for all disabilities and chronic illnesses of children and youth range from 2 to 32 percent of persons under 18 years of age (Ireys & Katz, 1997). As those reviewers explain, the large differences in estimates are due to the range of severity of the particular disorders that are included. Conditions such as mental retardation, autism, and cerebral palsy impose severe restrictions on the child's functioning. Other conditions, such as ear infections and respiratory allergies, which are the most commonly reported chronic illness (Newacheck & Taylor, 1992), although serious and distressing, impose milder restrictions on overall functioning. They are far less handicapping or are not handicapping at all. The higher estimates of disabilities are for the less handicapping and thus more prevalent conditions such as common chronic illness; the lower estimates focus on the more severe, less prevalent conditions, such as those included in developmental disabilities.

This text is concerned with the more severe, more restricting levels that meet the developmental disabilities criteria of functional impairment, severity, and permanence. Prevalence estimates for developmental disabilities, drawn from a number of recent sources, range from about 3 to 5 percent of children and youth.

---

[2]This picture is very different in sub-Sahara Africa where AIDS is a major epidemic that has significantly reduced the very life expectancy of some populations (Kahn, 2000).

Despite the difficulties in making estimates, a tentative picture of the incidence and prevalence of disabilities has emerged. The Centers for Disease Control and Prevention analyzed health data from the Survey of Income and Program Participation (SIPP) for 1991–1992. The sample included 97,133 persons in 34,100 households (McNeil, 1993). They reported that 19.4 percent of the sample had some disability and that nearly 7.9 percent of those disabilities occurred in people 17 years of age or younger. Applying those percentages to the U.S. population (280,000,000 in 2000) yields national prevalence estimates for all ages and for persons younger than 18 years. Table 1.2 shows those percentages applied across several years of estimated U.S. population. As shown, the year 2000 estimates are over 53 million persons of all ages in the United States with disabilities, including over 4 million children (i.e., under 18 years). There is a steady increase in prevalence across the years as the population grows, and the increase in all disabilities from 1991 to 2000 is over 4 million persons!

Of the 53 million persons with disabilities, how many have developmental disabilities—the group in which we are most interested? A common estimate is 5 percent of the total population, yielding for the United States in the year 2000 an estimated 13.75 million persons of all ages with developmental disabilities (see Table 1.2).

Table 1.3 lists in the order of their frequency of occurrence the major developmental disabilities and the incidence for each. As can be seen, the highest incidence of disabilities per 10,000 live births is mental retardation, followed by fetal alcohol syndrome, epilepsy, anencephaly, and congenital heart defects. Other disabilities are shown in descending order of incidence. Notice that autism, one of the conditions that will be discussed in detail later, is relatively infrequent. The most frequent of the disabilities usually diagnosed by school age or later are learning disabilities, speech and language disorders, and traumatic brain disorder. Taken together, the most frequently occurring are, in descending order,

TABLE 1.2   Estimated Prevalence of All Disabilities and of Developmental Disabilities in 1991, 1994, and 2000

	1991	1994	2000
U.S. Population	252,800,000	260,341,000	280,000,000
All Disabilities, All Ages	49,043,000	50,506,000	53,350,000
All Disabilities under 18 Years of Age	3,874,000	3,990,000	4,214,650
All Developmental Disabilities, All Ages	12,640,000	13,017,050	14,000,000

Notes:

All disabilities for all ages = 19.4% of the total population (based on McNeil, 1993).

All disabilities of persons under 18 years of age = 7.9% of all disabilities (based on McNeil, 1993).

All developmental disabilities, all ages, = 5% of total population (based on Batshaw & Perrett, 1993; Craft & Wolraich, 1997; Kurtz et al., 1996).

Population estimates are based on United States Department of Commerce (1995). *The statistical abstracts of the United States.* Washington, DC: U.S. Government Printing Office.

speech and language disorders, learning disabilities, traumatic brain injury, and mental retardation.

The estimate of 14 million persons with developmental disabilities in the year 2000 is tentative, but it provides some idea of the magnitude of serious, handicapping, lifelong disabilities that begin in childhood or youth. These are the people we are addressing. It is a large group, and the demands for service and research are great. One of the important needs in this field is improved early diagnoses and development of standard recordkeeping throughout the country if we are to have more accurate data to guide our prevention, service, and research endeavors.

Impairments and disabilities can occur at any time of life—before birth, in childhood, or in adulthood. There is a large variety of causes and types of disabilities, of handicapping conditions, of ages and persons involved. This book will not deal with this entire domain of

TABLE 1.3   Estimated Incidence of Developmental Disabilities in the United States

I. Of every 10,000 Live Births

Mental Retardation	250–300
Fetal Alcohol Syndrome	100
Epilepsy	50–100
Anencephaly	50–100
Congenital Heart Defects	40–100
Hearing Disorders	30–60
Diabetes	20
Cerebral Palsy	5–20
Neural Tube Disorders (other than ancephaly)	10
Autism	4–15
Congenital Amputations	2–8
Visual Defects	2–3
Muscular Dystrophy	0.3

II. By School Age per 10,000 Children

Learning Disabilities	700–800
Speech and Language Disorders	300–1000

III. By Late Adolescence per 10,000 Youth

Traumatic Brain Injury	330

Notes:

1. These figures are estimates and therefore tentative.

2. The list is not exhaustive in its inclusion of developmental disabilities.

3. New cases annually of developmental disabilities are estimated at 2 to 3 percent of the 4,000,000 live births—an annual incidence of 80,000 to 120,000 new cases from among the birth cohorts.

4. Incidence rates have been derived from data supplied by the New York State Department of Health, Division of Community Health and Epidemiology, and from reviews by Batshaw & Perret (1993), Craft & Wolraich (1997), Kurtz et al., (1996), and Jackson and Vessey (2000).

the population of persons with disabilities but, instead, will focus on the smaller subgroup, developmental disabilities.

XI. The Person and the Professions

The term *developmental disabilities* refers to three related sets of concepts. First, it refers to the condition of a person, that is, to the person's development of pathologies, impairments, disabilities, and handicaps beginning in his or her first 20 years of life. Second, it refers to the universe of professional disciplines that focus on the human conditions that are subsumed under the label developmental disabilities. Third, it refers to a body of scientific and clinical knowledge about those conditions. Recall that this is an umbrella label, and it includes a large variety of conditions. They in turn present a multitude of causes, developmental results, corrective treatment, care, training, education, and so on. There are so many different factors or dimensions that operate under this umbrella label that addressing them requires varied professional expertise and, therefore, a multiplicity of professional disciplines. This multiplicity creates compelling challenges for persons in professional roles of clinicians, researchers, therapists, social workers, teachers, trainers, and all other care providers. Those professional roles represent many applied fields and research disciplines (see Box 1.1). This book's focus, however, is on the person and his or her condition of disability rather than on the professions. Ideally, ideas about career possibilities will be stimulated, but that is not the major intent of this work.

XII. Chapter Summary

Chapter 1 has defined developmental disabilities, distinguished this class of disorder from developmental delay and developmental psychopathology, and introduced important concepts for understanding the development of the conditions: etiology, pathology, impairment, disability, and handicap. Early onset, functional severity, and permanence were discussed as necessary conditions for the diagnosis of developmental disabilities, and we have introduced the concept of dual diagnoses.

It was stressed that developmental disabilities are multiply determined by the interactions of pathogenic events, the particular systems affected, and the level of development at the time of the pathogenic events.

A brief discussion of the history of this field was presented, the importance of prevention in the future development of the field was noted, and a discussion of social attitudes toward those with disabilities was presented. In that discussion, the problem of diagnostic overshadowing was examined, and students are urged to keep in mind that *every person is a unique individual* and should be viewed and treated as such. The chapter also pointed out that whatever diagnostic differences prevail among persons with developmental disabilities, they all share similar problems of coping with the myriad developmental issues common to all of us, but they must do so while handicapped by some form of severe disability. A major point is that our society is now undergoing a humanitarian and scientific revolution in our response to persons with developmental disabilities.

KEY TERMS

Know these important terms. Check the chapter and the Glossary for their meanings. They are listed in their approximate order of appearance in the chapter.

Iatrogenic effects	Prevention	Childhood
Person-first philosophy	Impairment	Youth and adolescence
Autism	Disability	Adulthood
Intellectual disabilities	Etiology	Multiply determined
Mental retardation	Pathology	Early onset
Cerebral palsy	Handicap	Functional severity
Epilepsy	Functionally impaired	Permanence (of disability)
Grand mal seizures	Pathogen	Developmental delay
Lead poisoning	Risk factor	Developmental psychopathology
Chelation therapy	Spinal meningitis	Dual diagnosis
Paraplegia	Prenatal	Diagnostic overshadowing
Developmental disability	Perinatal	Down syndrome
Assistive technology	Neonatal	Prevalence
Hypoxia	Postnatal	Incidence
Mainstreamed	Infancy	

SUGGESTED READING

Aries, P. (1962). *Centuries of childhood: A social history of family life.* New York: Knopf.

Boswell, J. (1988). *The kindness of strangers. The abandonment of children in Western Europe from antiquity to the Renaissance.* New York: Pantheon Books. An excellent account of this practice over centuries.

Butler, S. (1867). *The way of all flesh.* Modern Library edition (1950). New York: Random House. A masterful account of the paternalistic middle-class family, its rigidity, and its "righteous" abuse of children by parents in the Victorian age.

Dickens, C. (1978). *Nicholas Nickleby.* New York: Penguin English Library. A classic novel that arguably had major impact on stirring humanitarian reforms in child labor practices. (Original work published 1839)

Glenn, M. C. (1984). *Campaigns against corporal punishment: Prisoners, sailors, women, and children in antebellum America.* Albany: State University of New York Press.

Grandin, T. (1995). *Thinking in pictures: And other reports from my life with autism.* New York: Doubleday. This book (and others by the same author) provides a personal account by an individual with autism.

Greven, P. (1977). *The Protestant temperament: Patterns of child rearing, religious experience, and the self in early America.* New York: Knopf. This excellent book is essential in understanding the contemporary use of corporal punishment in the United States.

Herr, S. S., & Weber, G. (Eds.). (1999). *Aging, rights, and quality of life: Prospects for older people with developmental disabilities.* Baltimore, MD: Paul H. Brookes. Twenty chapters discuss issues and developments pertaining to the changing conditions of persons with developmental disabilities who are aging, and the social, professional, and policy responses. It is an excellent and highly informative book.

Jordan, D. R. (1996). *Overcoming dyslexia in children, adolescents, and adults.* Austin, TX: Pro-ed. This is an excellent discussion of dyslexia, its history, characteristics, and treatment, written by a teacher. The book includes an interesting chapter that presents vignettes of famous persons who overcame their severe dyslexia.

Safford, P. L., & Safford, E. J. (1996). *A history of childhood and disability.* New York: Teachers College Press.

Shahar, S. (1990). *Childhood in the middle ages.* London & New York: Routledge. A detailed account of childhood at that time.

STUDY QUESTIONS

1-1. What is "mainstreaming"? What is its purpose?

1-2. Define and distinguish etiology, impairment, disability, handicap.

1-3. Explain this statement: Etiology, impairment, disability, and handicap can be thought of as points along a continuum.

1-4. Explain, as if to someone who knows little about it, the distinctions between *developmental* disabilities and other disabilities.

1-5. Explain this statement: Developmental disabilities are multiply determined. Think through the implications of that idea for treatment, prevention, and social policy.

1-6. According to this chapter, what have been the major historical changes in our culture's treatment of children? Of persons with disabilities?

1-7. Think of the potential health problems of child exploitation on U.S. farms today and answer the following:

How might such treatment affect developmental disabilities?

Aside from disabilities, how might this affect children?

If you could "correct" this situation, what steps would you take?

1-8. How would you explain the concept of iatrogenics to someone who has never before heard of it?

1-9. Distinguish among these concepts: developmental delay, developmental disabilities, developmental psychopathology.

1-10. Think through the implications of "person-first" philosophy. What might be the important implications of this?

CHAPTER

2 Normal Prenatal Development

I. Human Development Is a Continuous Process

The etiology of developmental disabilities is complex, with at least four major etiological factors and their interactions (genetic/hereditary; environmental; the organ system involved; the level of development of the organ system). Those factors interact and can develop through the sequence:

Etiology → Pathology → Impairment → Disability → Handicap

Developmental issues are central in the interactions among these four factors. To understand developmental disabilities, it is necessary to know normal sequences of development. That is the task of this and the next chapter.

When we think of child development, we tend to picture a newborn growing into a cute infant, then into a pudgy toddler, taking those first hesitant steps and not a few bumps. The baby gains physical, personal, and social experience, does a prodigious amount of learning, develops an astonishing array of skills, and grows into childhood, adolescence, and adulthood.

Human development is continuous. It begins long before the child's birth and does not rest until the final dissolution of death. From conception through approximately 38 weeks of prenatal development, significant events occur and influence the physical, mental, and social characteristics of the growing baby. Even prior to conception, genetic and environmental factors are in place that will help determine much about the child's physical characteristics, personality, and even survival.

The baby who emerges at birth has been formed largely through the unfolding of genetic factors contributed by both parents. The normal course of prenatal development involves many events—including some that are disruptive and damaging—that can occur prior to conception, during pregnancy, and during the birth process.

The neonatal period is the baby's first 28 days after birth. The baby enters a complex physical and social world. The growing child perceives the world and develops concepts about self, objects, events, and other people. He or she progressively learns to master an enormous variety of skills and to cope with innumerable issues, including increasingly complex social interactions. All of this occurs within the actively pervasive context of unceasing cognitive and bodily change. In these complex, continuous developmental processes, the child ideally is supported and guided by many people, the most important being the parents. In time, relatives, neighbors, teachers, and peers will exert increasing influence. Symbolic events—abstract representations of actions and ideas such as are presented on television, in newspapers, and as discussed with peers—will also become important to the growing youth.

Human development is an unbroken stream, but it is not always smooth. Events often conflict and can be mutually inhibiting. There are failures, injuries, interruptions, regressions, and disappointments, but also growth spurts, achievements, and satisfactions. With all of its surges, lapses, and twists, developmental activity is continuous. In our discussions, we will draw arbitrary lines across that continuous sequence of development, making distinctions among prenatal, perinatal, and postnatal time periods. These distinctions are made for convenience and are not meant to suggest any breaks in the continuous developmental process.

II. Determinants of the Neonate's Health

The neonate's basic characteristics and health are determined by the interactions of genetic factors that are fixed at conception and environmental factors, including those which affect conception, intrauterine conditions during gestation, and the birth process. In the complex unfolding of genetic processes, events occur that normally result in a healthy baby. However, genetic and chromosomal factors may cause innate pathologies and impairments.

Likewise, environmental factors can affect development during pregnancy and at or after birth. These include:

congenital infections such as rubella and herpes simplex virus
postnatal infections such as bacterial meningitis
physical trauma at birth or later
teratogenic substances during pregnancy such as alcohol, lead, and nicotine
maternal nutrition during pregnancy
postnatal environmental toxins such as lead and tobacco
psychosocial factors such as socioeconomic status of the parent(s)

Psychosocial factors are important but are too often overlooked. They contribute to the intrauterine conditions, making them more or less healthy and supportive of good prenatal development. Socioeconomic status (SES) is a contributing factor for developmental problems. Generally, the lower the SES, the less adequate is the mother's prenatal care, and that can have negative effects on the pregnancy. Likewise, personal stress on the mother can contribute to problems in pregnancy, as can the mother's physical and psychological health, traumatic injuries to the mother and/or fetus in abusive relationships, and the effects of environmental toxins that cross the placenta and harm the fetus.

Factors that promote healthy prenatal development of the child include:

healthy genetic and metabolic processes and structures
a pregnancy that is safe, without physical trauma
good maternal physical health during pregnancy
a clean environment without infectious diseases or chemical toxins
good prenatal care of the mother
good nutrition and a generally supportive psychosocial environment

In short, conducive to healthy prenatal development is a stable, physically and psychologically healthy prenatal environment for the mother, with good personal support and help from family and friends. Unfortunately, such ideal conditions are not available to millions of pregnant women in the United States and many millions more throughout the rest of the world.

It is a perilous journey from conception through birth, childhood, youth, and adulthood. Of all the conceptions that occur, fewer than 50 percent survive to the successful birth of a healthy child. Half of all conceptions are miscarried or spontaneously aborted because of **genetic defects** or disorders during pregnancy (Plomin, DeFries, & McClearn, 1990). It has been estimated that 90 percent of conceptions with chromosomal abnormality and 50 percent of malformed fetuses are spontaneously aborted (Stein, 1984). Natural abortions are useful events that benefit the species. Elective abortions end another proportion of pregnancies. Others are carried to term but are stillborn. Of the live births, 10 percent have some form of impairment but only 2 to 3 percent are developmentally disabled (Moore & Persaud, 1993). There are just over 4 million births per year in the United States (Bureau of the Census, 1993), and they are the survivors of more than 8 million conceptions. The drop in survival is sharp just after conception, and then it slows through the remainder of pregnancy, infancy, and childhood. However, it is important to remember that the majority of live births—some 90 percent—are healthy babies without disabilities.

Human gestation requires about 280 days, or just over 9 months. Normal, full-term pregnancy ranges from 38 to 42 weeks, depending primarily on the mother's condition. In pregnancy, a microscopic fertilized egg cell, bearing the genetic blueprints of both parents, develops into a full-term fetus, ready for birth. Most neonates weigh 6 to 8.5 pounds and are about 21 inches long with a large variation in size. The size and weight of the newborn are determined primarily by the characteristics and the physical condition of the mother and not by the size of the father. Most babies are born without complications after an average of 14 hours of labor for a first pregnancy and about 8 hours for subsequent pregnancies, and they are quite healthy little people.[1]

In the United States, there are more than 52.9 million persons with some form of disability and 13.5 million persons with developmental disabilities (see Table 1.2), including both sexes and all socioeconomic levels and ages. A large proportion, perhaps most, of the etiological factors in developmental disabilities appears to occur at conception or during prenatal development. To help understand those factors, we will review the course of normal prenatal development.

III. Prenatal Development

Genetics: A Brief Review

Chromosomes and Genes.   Most of the trillions of cells in the human body are **somatic cells** (body cells), and the others are **germ cells** (sex cells). Each cell consists of a cell membrane surrounding the **protoplasm,** the living portion of the cell. The cell **nucleus** is enclosed by a nuclear membrane and contains a number of structures including the chromosomes. The protoplasm within the nucleus is called **nucleoplasm,** and that within the cell but outside of the nucleus is called **cytoplasm.** The cytoplasm contains granules or bodies with various functions, including the ribosomes, the sites at which protein is synthesized. Figure 2.1 shows a schematic of a human cell.

Long thought to be 100,000 in number (B. Brown, 1999) human genes are now estimated to number 30,000 to 50,000 (Claverie, 2001; Venter, 2001; Wade, 2001). Genes are carried on the chromosomes and are the chemical determinants of inherited characteristics. Stored in the genes, ready to be activated at the proper times, is the genetic code that will direct the development and functioning of each cell. Genes control the development of the zygote, embryo, and fetus and determine the characteristics that are inherited by the offspring from the parents. The nucleus contains all of the genes and genetic information (i.e., the blueprint) for that person's development. That inherited genetic information, the person's **genotype,** is determined at conception.

In humans, the nucleus of each somatic cell has twenty-three pairs of chromosomes, the carriers of genes. Each chromosome is a long, coiled, tightly packed strand of repeating molecules. The structure of genes is deoxyribonucleic acid, or DNA, the basic genetic material of organisms. In the 1940s, Oswald Avery discovered that DNA is crucial in genetic

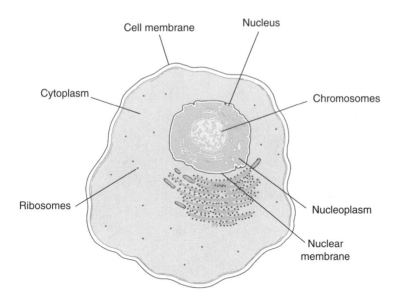

FIGURE 2.1 A Schematic Drawing of a Human Cell

transmission. As described later by Watson and Crick (1953) in their Nobel prize-winning research, the DNA molecule is a long, twisted ladder with two sides consisting of molecular chains of phosphate and sugar. These chains twist around each other, forming a double helix (*helix* is from Latin, meaning a "spiral form"). The two molecular strands are joined by four nitrogen-based molecules (nucleotides)—adenine (A), thymine (T), guanine (G), and cytosine (C), as diagramed in Figure 2.2. These four repeated molecules are the basic building blocks of DNA. They are held together in specific pairs by hydrogen bonds; that is, adenine bonds only with thymine (A-T), and guanine bonds only with cytosine (G-C). These A-T/G-C pairs are known as **base pairs.** When DNA reproduces itself, it does so by separating at the hydrogen bonds, rather like a zipper opening down the middle of the long DNA molecule. The two sides pull apart, each with its long alternating strand of sugar and phosphate molecules and half of the A-T/G-C molecules (see Figure 2.2). Each half of the original DNA molecule is then reproduced, and each new portion is attached to one of the original two, thus forming two new DNA molecules. Each of the two molecules then consists of one strand from the original molecule and one newly synthesized strand.

The general function of genes is to determine the characteristics that are inherited by the offspring and to control the organism's development. The genes accomplish this by transmitting biochemical information that results in the synthesis of specific proteins that are needed at various points in development. The genetic action is triggered by hormones secreted by the endocrine glands. When activated at the appropriate time, a gene duplicates itself, and in that chemical process, the DNA produces *ribonucleic acid,* or RNA (called messenger RNA). Its function is to carry a particular genetic message from the nucleus to ribosomes in the cytoplasm, which then synthesize (manufacture) the protein being called for. The cell is a protein factory in which activity is triggered by hormones and controlled

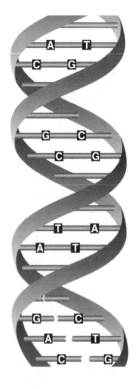

FIGURE 2.2   A Schematic Drawing of a DNA Molecule. *The two strands have begun to separate in the process of replication.*

by the DNA blueprint. The ribosomes synthesize perhaps a million different proteins from a basic pool of twenty forms of amino acids. The activation of each gene or, usually, a combination of genes, sets that process in motion.

It can be said that if the genes are the blueprints of heredity, then proteins are the building blocks for the body. Specific proteins are needed in the formation of new tissue and organs during development of the embryo. If the needed proteins are not synthesized at the right time or if they are manufactured in insufficient amounts or in a distorted manner, then the tissues and/or organs might not develop properly and developmental disabilities or death can result. As will be discussed in later chapters, many factors—genetic, chromosomal, and environmental (including stress and other psychological factors)—can cause disruptions of that process and result in disabilities.

High-magnification photomicrographs of stained chromosomes (usually obtained from scrapings of the inside of the mouth) reveal their relative sizes, shapes, and patterns of gene banding. The pictures of the chromosomes are then arranged into chromosome pairs according to shape and size. The result is a **karyotype,** a picture of all twenty-three chromosome pairs in a cell. Figure 2.3 shows a karyotype of a male and a karyotype of a female with the chromosome pairs arranged in order of size. The two chromosomes in each pair are about the same size, are of similar shape, and have similar patterns of gene banding. Twenty-two of the pairs have such similarities and are said to be **homologous** (i.e., having the same or similar structure). These twenty-two homologus pairs are called **autosomes.**

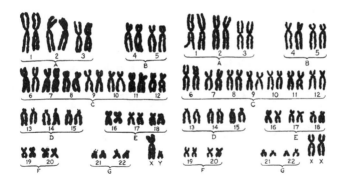

FIGURE 2.3   Human male and female karyotypes

From: Shaffer, D. R. (1996). Developmental psychology: Childhood and adolescence. (4th ed.) Pacific Grove, CA: Brooks/Cole Publishing Company.

As can be seen in the karyotypes , the twenty-third pair, the sex chromosomes, shows such similarity in the case of females (XX) but not in males (XY).

Through gene mapping, geneticists have identified chromosomes that carry the gene(s) that control some human characteristics. For example, the gene that determines sex in humans is on the Y chromosome of pair 23; chromosome 9 contains the gene that determines blood type (Scarr & Kidd, 1983). Gene mapping has also determined the loci of genes responsible for a number of human disorders, some of which are listed in Table 2.1.

TABLE 2.1   Genes That Control Some Human Disorders

Disorder	Located on Chromosome
Glaucoma (Juvenile onset)	1
Venous thrombosis (severe blood clotting)	1
Huntington's disease	4
Cri du chat	5
Cystic fibrosis	7
Basal cell carcinoma (a skin cancer)	9
Sickle cell anemia	11
Thalassemia (a type of anemia)	11
Phenylketonuria (PKU)	12
Tay Sachs	15
Tuberous sclerosis	9 & 16
Neurofibromatosis	17 & 22
Duchenne's muscular dystrophy	X
Diabetes mellitus	X
Hemophilia	X
Fragile-X	X

Based on Scriver, C. R., Beaudet, A. L., Sly, W. S., & Valle, D. (1995). *The metabolic and molecular bases of inherited disease (Vol. 1).* New York: McGraw-Hill.

The loci for genes controlling many characteristics have now been mapped, providing information that has led to an increasing ability to determine many genetic defects and diseases prior to birth. (The international Human Genome Project involves geneticists around the world mapping and sequencing the genome in order to describe and to understand all genetically determined human characteristics; see Box 2.1).

BOX **2.1**

The Human Genome Project

The international Human Genome Project was started in 1990 and is overseen by the National Institutes of Health and the U.S. Department of Energy. Its first director was James Watson who, with Francis Crick, in 1953 first described the structure of the DNA molecule. That work was an important breakthrough for which they received the Nobel Prize in 1962. The Human Genome Project has the ambitious goals of *mapping and sequencing* the entire human genome and those of several other organisms that are important in genetics research (e.g., *E. coli,* yeast, *Drosophila,* and the mouse). Researchers around the world are cooperating in this endeavor. The target date for completion was set at 2005 and has since been moved up to mid-2001.

Mapping the genome involves finding the location of each gene on each chromosome. Since we have an estimated 30,000 genes, this is a sizable task. Essentially, the goal is to create a detailed physical map of the genome. With this map, individual genes can be located, isolated, and studied. This would help lead to full understanding of the structure and functions of each gene and to the characteristics and processes that each gene controls. The implications for the treatment and prevention of gene-related disorders are enormous. Presumably, we would be able to identify specific genes that are responsible for given disorders, allowing detection of the potential disorders even before they appear in the person. Further, it may then be possible to take corrective action to "repair" the genes and thus prevent or ameliorate the disorders. Such applications on a large scale are far in the future, but the basic research that is necessary for such applications is well on its way to completion.

Sequencing the genome is an even more ambitious task. As was discussed earlier in this chapter, the two halves of the DNA double helix are held together by A-T, T-A, G-C, or C-G base pairs, called **nucleotides.** Each "rung" of the DNA "ladder" (see Figure 2.2) is composed of the base pairs. Each gene is a portion of the DNA strand and is made up of many such base pairs, ranging from several hundred to a million base pairs per gene, and averaging about 1000 nucleotides in each gene. The particular sequence of these nucleotides in the gene is critically important because it is this sequence that constitutes the *genetic code* that is carried by that particular gene, and the gene's functioning is directed by that particular sequence.

This project involves mapping the approximately 30,000 genes in the human genome and specifying the genetic codes of the approximately 3 billion base pairs. Late in 1999, chromosome 22 (the next-to-smallest chromosome) was the first to be completely mapped and sequenced.

It may be that each person will someday have a full "genetic ID," perhaps carried on a computer disk. The implications for understanding human behavior and health, for medical and psychological treatment, and even for law enforcement are profound. The ethical issues involving individual rights of privacy, misuse of genetic "surgery," and human engineering can only be imagined. To use an old metaphor (and no pun intended), "the genie may already be out of the bottle," and the twenty-first century promises to be a most dramatic time.

There is order in the arrangement of genes on chromosomes. Each chromosome is a string of genes, and each gene that determines a characteristic or function has a specific position, or **locus,** on the chromosome; that is, for all individuals of a species, a particular gene has the same locus on the same chromosome.

Cell Multiplication: Mitosis and Meiosis. In humans, somatic cells contain twenty-three pairs of chromosomes for a total of forty-six. These somatic cells reproduce through the process of **mitosis** in which the nucleus of a cell duplicates itself and the cell splits, forming two identical cells each with twenty-three pairs of chromosomes, as shown in Figure 2.4. These cells, containing their full compliment of forty-six chromosomes, are in the **diploid** ("double") state, referring to all forty-six chromosomes. In mitosis, the DNA molecules are duplicated and the cells divide in half, thus providing copies of the original chromosomes with all of their genes and biochemical information.

Virtually all cells in the body, except for the gametes, reproduce through mitosis. Germ cells, or gametes, are also originally in the diploid state with forty-six chromosomes, but before they mature and operate as reproductive cells, they undergo changes that occur in the reproductive organs, the **gonads** (female ovaries and male testes). Reproduction of the germ cells is achieved through **meiosis** in which the original diploid cell (see Figure 2.4) with forty-six chromosomes begins to duplicate itself much as in mitosis. However, each new cell then splits into two cells in the **haploid** (half) state, each of which has half the number of chromosomes, one from each pair in the original diploid cell. (All of the genetic information contained in a haploid cell constitutes the genome of that individual.) Meiosis, then, is a reductive process. These new cells, now called germ cells, or **gametes,** are the sperm in males and ova in females, and each contains twenty-three chromosomes, one from each original pair. As diagramed in Figure 2.4, meiosis in males (called spermatogenesis) results in four haploid spermatozoa from the original diploid cell. However, meiosis in females (oogenesis) results in only one viable haploid ovum from the original diploid cell because in oogenesis the secondary cells at each step disintegrate. When one sperm and one ovum unite in conception, each contributes its twenty-three chromosomes and the fertilized ovum (zygote) will then be in the diploid state with the full number of twenty-three chromosome pairs (forty-six chromosomes), half of each pair from the father and half from the mother. As will be discussed later, errors can occur during the replication processes resulting in pathological development of the embryo and/or fetus.

> *Internal Summary: Mitosis and Meiosis.* In mitosis of somatic cells, chromosomes are replicated and the original diploid cell splits into two, resulting in two diploid cells that are identical to the original.
>
> In meiosis of germ cells (spermatogenesis and oogenesis), the original cell duplicates as in mitosis, producing two diploid cells that are identical to the original. Each of these diploid cells then undergoes a reductive process in which each cell splits into two haploid cells, resulting (in the case of spermatogenesis) in four haploid sperm cells. In oogenesis, the process results in only one viable ovum because the others disintegrate.
>
> The steps in mitosis and meiosis are more complex than indicated in the diagram. For more detail, a good source is Russell, P. J. (1994). *Fundamentals of genetics.* New York: HarperCollins.

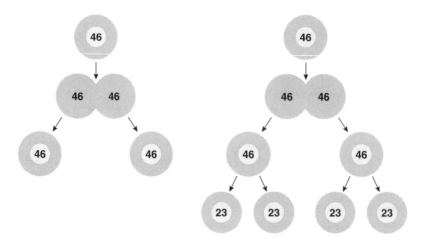

FIGURE 2.4   Mitosis and Meiosis.   *In mitosis and meiosis, chromosomes replicate and cells split to form new cells. In mitosis, each cell produces two new cells in the diploid (forty-six chromosomes) state, each cell identical to the original. In meiosis, a reductive process, the final step produces cells in the haploid (twenty-three chromosomes) state.*

Genetically Determined Characteristics.   Because children inherit half of their genetic makeup from each parent, they tend to be more like their own parents than like other people. However, genetic inheritance also operates to establish genetic diversity and individuality. Children tend to be similar to their parents and siblings, but they will also be very different in many respects (with the exception of identical twins who are formed from a single fertilized ovum). Most of a person's genes are identical to those of all other unrelated humans (Plomin et al., 1990). We share the many characteristics that make us human—a similar body form, skeletal organization, upright bipedal locomotion, speech and language, and so on. The diversity occurs because in the production of gametes each person can produce 2^{23} or about 8 million genetically different ova or sperm. The possible combinations of 8 million genetically different sperm and eight million genetically different ova mean that each male and female pair can create more than 60 trillion offspring that are genetically different! Thus, despite some familial similarities and with the exception of identical twins, *each human being is a genetically unique person.* The chances are small of finding two persons with the same genetic makeup. Recall the section in Chapter One in which we asserted that every person is a unique individual. That uniqueness begins right at conception.

Genetic inheritance is most obvious in many physical features such as blood type, eye, skin, and hair color, gender, and facial features. Behavioral tendencies may also have a genetic basis. Temperament, for example, is a set of stable biases in a person's behavior, the general tendency to behave in certain broad ways. It includes general activity level, overall tendency to be distressed, fretful, or happy, the general tendency to withdraw from novel situations or to engage them, and so on. These general temperamental tendencies are partly learned and therefore are influenced by prenatal and postnatal environmental factors, but they also have a major genetic component. Other behavioral characteristics or personality traits such as aggression, shyness, moodiness, and fearfulness may also have genetic components (Tellegen et al., 1988).

Cognitive characteristics, too, are thought to have genetic components. Although there is still controversy over the degree to which intelligence is inherited and the degree to which it is developed through experience, there is general agreement that there is an interaction of the two factors.

The twenty-third pair of chromosomes, the sex chromosomes, determines the gender of the child. Each ovum carries an X chromosome, and each sperm carries either an X or Y chromosome. If the sperm that unites with the ovum carries an X chromosome, then the child will be XX, or female; if the sperm carries a Y, then a male (XY) will result. Contrary to tradition, especially in royal families, the father and not the mother is "responsible" for the gender of the child. The other twenty-two pairs of chromosomes are shared by both males and females and are called **autosomes.**

At conception, the male and female gametes each contribute their twenty-three chromosomes to the ovum which, now fertilized, develops through zygote, embryo, and fetus. Recall from the earlier discussion that throughout these processes the genes, through messenger RNA, direct protein synthesis to form tissues and organs at the appropriate times and, generally, to direct embryonic and fetal development. At conception, all of the genetic factors are in place—whatever characteristics are to be genetically inherited are already determined. Likewise, hereditary pathologies (some of which might not appear until years later in development) are already set in place. Development proceeds through the unfolding of whatever factors have already been genetically determined and their interaction with environmental factors. If all goes well, in about 38 to 42 weeks, a normal, healthy baby will be born.

Development from Conception to Birth

Conception. Approximately every 28 days, a single ovum (the female gamete with its twenty-three chromosomes) is released by one of the two ovaries in a mature female, with the two ovaries usually alternating monthly. A sexually mature woman has her full number of ova and does not continue to produce new cells, unlike males who continue to produce sperm throughout most of their lives. The matured or "ripened" ovum moves along the Fallopian tube toward the uterus. Enzymes in the Fallopian tube cause a loosening of the covering around the ovum, leaving it accessible for penetration by a sperm cell. (The ovum, about 90,000 times heavier than a sperm, is the largest cell in the human body, and the sperm is the smallest.) The ovum continues moving into the uterus, and if not fertilized within about 24 hours in the Fallopian tube, it will disintegrate and soon be expelled in menstruation.

The ovum is viable for only about 24 hours, so it appears that there is a very narrow time each month in which conception can occur. However, sperm, traveling from the vagina into the Fallopian tubes, are viable for about 85 hours, or about 3 to 4 days. This means that the sperm that have reached the Fallopian tubes can fertilize an ovum released within a 3- or 4-day period, thereby increasing the number of days per month in which sexual intercourse can result in conception (the fertile period). Indeed, under some conditions, sperm can be caught in the folds of the cervix (the uterine "neck") where they remain viable for as long as 8 days.

While only one ovum is typically released each month, approximately 250 million sperm cells are introduced into the vagina with each ejaculation during sexual intercourse. Most of the sperm cells die before reaching the Fallopian tubes, but thousands succeed in moving through the cervix and uterus and hundreds enter the Fallopian tubes where, if an ovum is present, it may be penetrated by a single sperm. The sperm moves into the ovum and to the nucleus where, in about an hour after penetration, its twenty-three chromosomes are added to the twenty-three already there. Conception will have taken place, and the new diploid cell, now called a zygote, has its full complement of twenty-three pairs (i.e., forty-six chromosomes).

Conception normally takes place only in the Fallopian tubes during the few days an ovum is present. The zygote, fertilized in the Fallopian tube, moves into the uterus where the long period of gestation takes place (see Figure 2.5).

From the time of conception, normal, full-term human gestation ranges in duration from 38 to 42 weeks, or about 265 to 294 days. Common usage divides that time into three equal intervals, called trimesters, of approximately 3 months each. However, researchers typically use another type of division that has three parts of unequal duration. These periods are defined not in terms of time but rather in terms of events occurring within the developing child: the germinal stage, the embryonic stage, and the fetal stage. Figure 2.6 shows both of these measures and the relationship between them. Note that the first trimester includes the germinal stage, the embryonic stage, and the beginning of the fetal stage. The

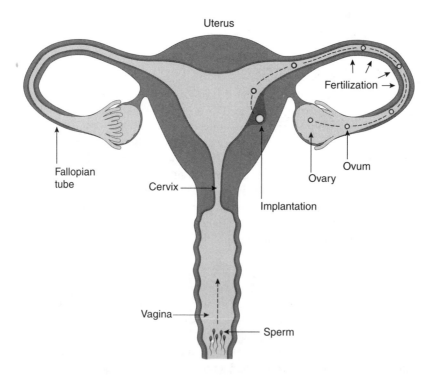

FIGURE 2.5   Path of Movement of Ovum from Ovary to Uterus

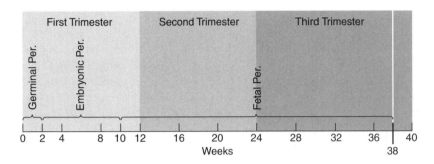

FIGURE 2.6   A Comparison of Two Measures of Time during Human Gestation

second and third trimesters refer to the fetal stage only. As represented in Figure 2.6, the first trimester is one of rapid development in cell multiplication, cell differentiation, and in establishing the basic conditions for the success of the long fetal stage that is to follow. This is a **critical period** because so much development is occurring that the child is particularly vulnerable at this time. In the first several weeks, many women are not even aware that they are pregnant, and they might engage in behaviors that are high-risk, such as smoking and using alcohol or other drugs.

The Germinal Period.   This is approximately 7 to 14 days beginning with conception and ending at the time of implantation, when the fertilized ovum becomes anchored to the endometrium, the uterine wall. Although this is a short period of time, it is critical, and a very high rate of basic activity and development occurs.

Following conception, the zygote continues moving toward the uterus, and in about 24 to 36 hours, cell division through mitosis begins and occurs rapidly. By the end of this 1- to 2-week period, the original single cell will have multiplied to about 150 cells (Tanner, 1978). Not only do the number of cells rapidly increase, but in this short time period of about 4 days following conception, **cell differentiation** begins. The zygote begins to resemble a tiny, hollow ball with an outer surface of cells and an inner mass of cells, and it is now called a **blastocyst.** From the outer cells of the blastocyst (ectodermal layer), structures necessary to support the developing organism in the uterus—the placenta, amniotic sac, amniotic fluid, and so on—are developed. The inner cells (endodermal) will develop into the embryo.

This germinal stage ends in about 7 to 14 days when the blastocyst becomes implanted in the endometrium, which provides the nutrients necessary for continued development. In this first "journey," the ovum migrates from the ovary to a Fallopian tube and continues to the uterus where it finally comes to rest in the endometrium.

The germinal stage of only 7 to 14 days includes conception, rapid cell division, cell differentiation, and implantation. It is a critical period because so much rapid development occurs that is basic to the health and even survival of the new organism.

Beginning with conception, the organism develops in what seems a disproportionate, although systematic, manner as some organs and parts of the body develop earlier than others. This general tendency is called **cephalocaudal** and **proximo-distal** development.

Cephalocaudal development means that development occurs in a head-to-tail, "top-down," fashion. For example, the head of the 8-week-old fetus is fully one-half the length of the entire body, compared to about one-fourth for the newborn and one-eighth for an adult (these comparisons are shown in Figure 2.7). The upper portions grow first and the lower portions catch up later. Generally, the head grows fastest, and then the arms, trunk, and later, the legs. The development of motor skills also follows this principle. The baby can lift the head, hold it steady, and grasp objects before he or she can sit alone, stand, take steps, or walk.

Proximo-distal development refers to the tendency for physical and motor skill development to proceed from the center of the body outward to the extremities. Prenatally, the trunk develops before the arms or fingers. Motor skills also proceed in this direction.

The Embryonic Period.   The next approximately 6 weeks, beginning with implantation, are the embryonic period (gestation weeks 3 through 8). This period involves completion of the supporting systems (placenta, amnion, umbilical cord, etc.) and the continuing differentiation of various embryonic systems (organs, limbs, nervous system, vascular systems, etc.). Early in this embryonic stage, three layers of cells have become differentiated (ectoderm or outer layer, mesoderm or middle layer, and endoderm or inner layer). These are the cell structures from which will develop: skin, central nervous system, and sense organs from the ectoderm; muscles, circulatory system, and blood from the mesoderm; internal organs, digestive system, and respiratory system from the endoderm. At the end of the 6-week embryonic period (8 weeks after conception), cell differentiation is completed, and every organ system will exist at least in rudimentary form. These 6 weeks are particularly important because this is when the major differentiation and beginning development of organs and systems such as the central nervous system (brain and spinal cord), respiratory, and circulatory systems occur. During this critical period, a great deal of basic developmental activity is taking place, and the organism is especially vulnerable to injury due to disruptions caused by disease, microbes, toxins, and trauma.

As was noted earlier, a major development during the embryonic period is that of supporting systems—the amnion, amniotic fluid, placenta, and umbilical cord. The embryo

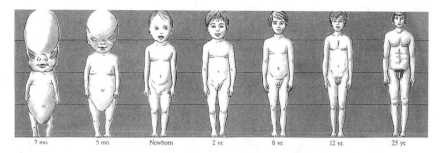

| 2 mo. | 5 mo. | Newborn | 2 yr. | 6 yr. | 12 yr. | 25 yr. |

FIGURE 2.7   Relative Body Proportions in Human Fetal–Adult Development

Source: Santrock, J. W. (1990). *Children.* Dubuque, IO: William C. Brown. Adapted from Patten, H. (1933). *Human embryology.* McGraw-Hill, N. Y., N. Y. Reprinted by permission.

(and later, the fetus) floats in amniotic fluid enclosed within the amnion (amniotic sac) (see Figure 2.8). This hydraulic arrangement protects the embryo and fetus from possible injury due to normal movements of the mother and the occasional more powerful physical movements or even trauma as might occur if the mother falls or is in an automobile crash.

The bloodstreams of the mother and the embryo are *not* directly linked. Rather, a filtering system composed of the placenta and the umbilical cord allows nutrients to pass from the mother to the embryo and digestive wastes and carbon dioxide to pass from the embryo to the mother, from whose body those wastes will be expelled. The placenta, a flat group of cells, lies against the uterine wall, and it is there that the filtering and transfer processes occur. Many substances that are potentially harmful for the embryo are composed of molecules that are too large to pass through this placental barrier and are therefore filtered out. Not long ago, it was believed that the placenta was a highly efficient barrier, filtering out potentially harmful material and providing a good deal of protection for the developing child. As we have since learned, however, as efficient as it is in transferring nutrients and wastes between mother and child, it does allow many hazardous substances to reach the embryo or fetus. Many of these substances, including commonly used pregnancy drugs and medications, some disease organisms, and others such as lead and nicotine, are composed of molecules that can pass through the placental barrier and enter the bloodstream of the fetus. They may create serious disease and malfunction in the developing child. Pathogenic substances that cross the placenta into the embryo or fetus are called **teratogens.** They are important in the etiology of many developmental disabilities. Teratogens and teratogenic effects will be discussed in more detail in Chapter 6.

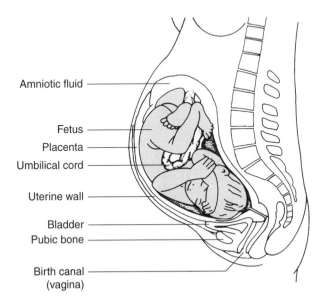

FIGURE 2.8   A Full-Term Fetus

Source: Turner, J. S., & Helms, D. B. (1991). *Lifespan Development.* Fort Worth, TX: Holt, Rinehart and Winston. Reproduced by permission.

Of the systems that become differentiated during this embryonic period, one of particular concern for our study is the brain and nervous system. Early in the embryonic period, at about the 15th day after conception, embryonic ectodermal cells begin to form the neural tube which is critical in the development of nerves, spinal cord, and brain. By the 4th week, rapid development is occurring around the neural tube. Its ends are open, and as development continues, they begin to close. First the head (cephalic) end closes and then shortly after the tail (caudal) end closes. The brain and spinal cord become differentiated, and by about the 5th week, the nervous system actually begins to function. As will be discussed later, failure of the neural tube to close properly will result in serious impairments—**anencephaly** if the cephalic end fails to close and **spina bifida** if the caudal end fails to close. Both conditions are associated with neural impairments and mental retardation.

Reflexive movements can be elicited in the embryo and faint brain waves can be recorded. Although movement begins in the embryonic period, it is not detected by the mother because the embryo is still so small. (The first fetal movements will not be detected by the mother until about the 16th to 18th gestational week.)

The next several weeks of the embryo involve rapid development of the brain and nervous system. This brain development is so great that the head grows to half of the embryo's total length. Bear in mind that *the embryonic period is critical for the development of the brain and spinal cord, and disruptions during this time can affect the child's intellect, as well as other functions.* This earlier development of the brain compared with the lower extremities is an example of cephalocaudal development that was introduced earlier.

By the completion of the embryonic stage (about 8 gestational weeks), supportive systems are developed and functioning, and all organs are in place, having been developed in rudimentary form. The embryo is then ready for the next period, that of the fetus. What remains is the long and complex task for those organ systems, now in primitive form, to be finalized; the fetus will grow, gain size, weight, and strength; movement will increase, and eventually, the birth process will begin.

The Fetal Period.   The duration of the fetal period is approximately 30 to 34 weeks, from about the end of the 8th week to birth at about 38 weeks. This is the longest of the three periods, and it begins when organ differentiation has been completed and bone starts to replace the cartilage of the embryonic skeleton. This period involves the refinement of all of the various systems that had been developed in primitive form during the first 8 weeks. During the embryonic period (gestation weeks approximately 3 through 8), the developing skeleton is composed of cartilage. At about the 8th week (the end of the embryonic period and beginning of the fetal period), cartilage starts to form into bone (Moore, 1977). The fetal period, then, starts with the formation of true bone, continues for about 30 to 34 weeks, and ends with the birth process.

At the start of the fetal period, the fetus is about 1 inch long, weighs about one-thirtieth of an ounce, and already has clearly humanoid features although the proportions are far from what they will be at birth and later. But even at the start of the fetal period (about the end of the 8th week of gestation), eyes, arms and legs, fingers and toes, and buds for tongue and teeth are evident.

In addition to the refinement of organs, increase in size and weight, and marked change in body proportions, the fetal period is also characterized by significant growth in functional capacity. Connections among organs grow, making the fetus a more coherent entity. For example, in the limbs, which were apparent as buds in the embryonic stage, joints and fingers develop, and networks of veins and connecting muscles form to make motion possible, bringing the limbs to a more complete functional level. There is a fetal heartbeat, digestive juices are produced by the stomach, the kidneys can filter uric acid from the bloodstream, and the nervous system begins to function.

By about 12 weeks, genitals can be discerned and the child's sex can be observed. The fetus kicks, and it can now curl its fingers and toes, which are fully formed. At about 16 weeks, the mother can feel the fetus moving, and this is a very significant and exciting event for the parents. Fetal movement (called **quickening**) increases until shortly before birth, when it slows, probably because of the increasingly crowded quarters for the fetus. Breathing and crying are possible by about the 6th month. Around that time, as the fetal period is moving toward its final phases, there is rapid development of the fissures and convolutions on the cerebral hemispheres—the portions of the brain that are most responsible for complex thinking. It should be noted that during the fetal period the central nervous system develops rapidly, but its development will not be completed until the child is several years old.

Although reflexive lung movement and some breathing can be noted at about 6 months, the fetus is not yet a viable organism. It could probably not survive outside of the uterus if premature birth were to occur at that time.[2] At 6 months, the fetus' neural and respiratory functions are not yet mature enough for survival. At that age, the fetus does not yet produce sufficient **surfactin,** a material that enables lungs to transmit oxygen from the air to the fetal bloodstream. Respiratory failure poses one of the greatest threats to premature infants. By about 7 months, the refinement of organs and systems, including respiration, the growth of supporting connections (blood vessels, nerves, muscles), and the increase in weight and size make the fetus a viable organism. The fetus is then developed and functioning well enough so that its chances of survival outside of the uterus are greatly increased if birth were to occur at that time.

The final few months are marked by major gains in weight and length. From about the 7th month through birth, the fetus gains about 6 pounds and grows in length by about half. Over approximately the final 2 months, the average weight gain is about a half pound each week. The development of subcutaneous fat accounts for much of that weight gain. This fat deposit helps to insulate the fetus and to protect it from the lower and more variable temperature outside the uterus after birth.

As the fetal growth and refinement continue, the fetus becomes less vulnerable to pathogenic agents, and its chances of survival increase. As was pointed out earlier, such threats to the developing child are generally greatest early in pregnancy.

Throughout most of the fetal period, the organs and systems already in place at the end of the embryonic period are perfected and finalized, the fetus grows larger, and its bodily proportions change markedly, continuing to change after birth and into adulthood. In about the final 2 months of gestation, no new structures or systems develop, and the fetus remains engaged almost entirely in the process of growth. By the final week of gestation, with little room to move now that it is attaining full size, it is ready for one of the most massive changes in its development—the total change from the uterine environment to the outside world.

Perinatal Development. The term *perinatal* refers to the time and events at and around birth, extending from about the 28th week of gestation to the end of the first postnatal month (Krasnegor, 1987), for a total of about 16 weeks (about 12 prenatal and 4 postnatal weeks). This period is of particular interest to researchers because the proximity of the biology of the final prenatal weeks and the behavioral developments of the early postnatal weeks provide a ground for studying basic biological/behavioral interactions. This relatively new field of study is creating a psychobiology literature that, as noted by Krasnegor (1987), should improve our knowledge of the basic mechanisms of learning, cognition, and social and emotional development.

During the perinatal period, no new organs or systems appear, but the fetus is growing rapidly, adding inches and pounds. From the 28th week onward, the fetus is in a viable state (i.e., there is a good probability of survival if birth were to occur from the 28th through 38th week). The longer it remains in the uterus until full term, the greater are its chances of healthy birth and future development. However, a much longer than normal pregnancy is generally not encouraged. The problem is that as the child remains longer in the womb, he or she continues to grow larger, and the increase in size can cause problems during birth for both child and mother.

As the fetus grows and fills the uterus, its movements slow in the final month, presumably from lack of room for movement. As the time for birth approaches, the fetus rotates into the head-down position. When the birth process has been completed, the fetus will have been transformed into a neonate, and its physical and social environment will have been drastically altered. This is arguably the biggest, most sudden, and momentous change in a person's lifetime. We had noted earlier that human development is continuous, and so it is. Even in the transition from the womb to the outside world, there are active and continuous processes spanning that change. However, moving in a few hours from womb to world is clearly a major and abrupt change.

The perinatal period is the interface between floating in the womb and living in the drastically different outside world. It is a prenatal time of preparation for that change and a postnatal period of swift but crucial adjustment. The demands for successful adjustment fall on the parents as well as on the baby.

Most of the serious developmental disabilities are already in place by the time of birth. They are due to poor maternal health during or even preceding pregnancy; events that involve genetic and chromosomal factors in place at the point of conception; embryo and fetal damage occurring at any time in prenatal development; perinatal and birth events that cause damage to the neonate. In addition, postnatal events, such as poisoning by environmental toxins (e.g., lead) and childhood injuries and disease, are responsible for additional numbers of developmental disabilities.

Prenatal Screening and Genetic Counseling

Social and legislative action needs to aim at improving maternal health, nutrition, and prenatal care. Worldwide inoculations can reduce the occurrence of maternal diseases such as rubella. Improved care of infants and children, safer products and more public awareness and training about accident prevention, and public education about environmental toxins can make substantial contributions. More available genetic counseling can be helpful to prospective parents by providing them with information about the probabilities of birth defects were they to conceive. Many of the genetic and chromosomal conditions that lead to birth defects can be detected early in pregnancy, allowing potential parents to make decisions about continuing the pregnancy and, in some conditions, actually correcting the defects. Prenatal testing and diagnoses of the health status of the pregnant woman, such as blood and urine tests, are routinely carried out. In addition, several types of procedures that more directly test the status of the fetus have been developed and, while not used routinely, are applied in a growing number of cases when medically indicated. These procedures, briefly described here, are amniocentesis, chorionic villus sampling, fetoscopy, ultrasonagraphy, and alpha-fetoprotein assay.

Amniocentesis. This is a complicated, costly, and invasive procedure with risk to the fetus and mother. It is usually employed in cases where high-risk of birth defects is suspected, as when the mother is over 35 years of age or when both parents are known to be carriers of a genetic disease or closely related to persons afflicted with the disease. Amniocentesis involves taking a sample of amniotic fluid. This cannot be done safely until midpregnancy—about 16 weeks postconception—when a sufficient amount of amniotic fluid to allow safe sampling has been developed. About half an ounce of amniotic fluid, with skin cells that have been sloughed off by the developing fetus, is drawn out through a syringe. The thin, 3-inch needle is carefully inserted through the mother's abdomen and must be guided by a thorough ultrasonographic examination (W. A. Miller, 1990), which outlines the fetus and placenta to avoid injuring them. The cells are drawn out and are cultured for 2 to 4 weeks, and then they are analyzed. A karyotype is made to check for chromosome anomalies, and biochemical tests are performed to detect enzyme deficiencies, protein defects, and gene alterations. Amniocentesis is the most commonly used prenatal screening procedure to detect chromosome anomalies (R. D. Wilson, 1991). The amniotic fluid can also be analyzed for the presence of fetal spinal fluid which, if found, indicates neural tube problems, specifically spina bifida. Rh incompatibility of fetal and maternal blood and fetal sex can also be determined through amniocentesis. At the midpoint of pregnancy, some seventy defects can be identified through amniocentesis. These include anencephaly, Down syndrome, muscular dystrophy, Rh incompatibility, sickle cell anemia, spina bifida, Tay-Sachs disease, and X-linked disorders such as hemophilia. As discussed in Chapter 5, virtually all cases of anencephaly and spina bifida can now be detected prenatally and the parents advised of the conditions. (Even more optimistically, as will be discussed in a later chapter, the incidence of these neural tube defects is now being drastically reduced through the preventive use of folic acid in the diets of women prior to and during pregnancy.)

Although generally a safe procedure, there is some risk of miscarriage and fetal injury estimated to be about 1 case in 600 (Cherry, 1987). Another limitation is the lateness in pregnancy of this procedure. It is not until the 16th week that the amnionic sac has grown large enough to contain sufficient fluid for safe sampling, and another 2 or 3 weeks are usually required for laboratory test results. If chromosomal anomalies are detected, the pregnancy will have progressed to the 19th week or later by the time the parents are advised of it, and that is very late in a pregnancy for an induced abortion.

Chorionic Villus Sampling (CVS).   This is another invasive technique for prenatal screening. A membrane layer composed of embryonic tissue (the chorion) surrounds the fetus and placenta. A biopsy or tissue sample is taken from the chorion by inserting a needle through the abdomen or biopsy forceps or a catheter through the vagina with the aid of ultrasound guides. The same analyses can be made as in amniocentesis (M. W. Thompson, McInnes, & Willard, 1991). The advantages of this procedure are that it can be carried out as early as the 8th to 12th week of pregnancy and, because a sufficient number of cells are taken from the chorion, there is no need for additional time for a laboratory culture. Thus, the findings can be given to the parents many weeks earlier than with amniocentesis.

The disadvantages are that it is a relatively new technique, and although the risks are low in either procedure, the rate of spontaneous abortion is greater in chorionic sampling: 1 to 3 cases in 100 (1 to 3 percent compared with about 1 case in 600, or 0.166 percent, for amniocentesis) (Cherry, 1987).

Fetoscopy.   Fetoscopy is an invasive procedure that is ordinarily not used until the 16th week of pregnancy. A small incision is made in the abdomen, and a thin tube is inserted into the uterus. Through that tube an optical device is inserted that allows visual scanning of the fetus. Congenital anomalies such as limb defects, cleft lip, and severe neural tube defects can be observed (Carlson, 1994). Fetoscopy is not used as frequently as other prenatal scanning procedures because it is an invasive procedure with higher risks to the fetus of about 5 percent (Behrman, 1992) and to premature delivery of about 10 percent. Furthermore, the images are not as clear as those in ultrasonagraphy (W. A. Miller, 1990). For these reasons, fetoscopy is being replaced, largely by ultrasonagraphy.

Ultrasonagraphy.   A noninvasive procedure that can be used in any stage of pregnancy, ultrasonagraphy uses high-frequency sound waves to create a picture of the uterus and embryo or fetus. A hand-held sound-emitting device is moved over the abdomen, the pulses bounce off the contours of the fetus, and are translated into pictures (sonograms) on a display screen. Unlike x-rays, it will reveal soft tissues as well as bone. Fetal organs such as kidneys, bladder, heart, and liver can be scanned for abnormalities. The sonograms can reveal the placement of the embryo or fetus, its size, and whether there are multiple fetuses. Because the fetal skull can be accurately measured in the sonogram, good estimates of fetal age are possible, and microcephaly and macrocephaly can be detected. Male genitalia can usually be discerned, making sex identification possible. Most neural tube defects such as anencephaly and severe spina bifida are also readily apparent in the sonograms (W. A. Miller, 1990). Ultrasonography is now used in about half of all pregnancies in the United States and is generally considered a very safe procedure.

Alpha-fetoprotein Assay (AFP).   Severe spina bifida is a neural tube defect in which there is a failure of closure of the vertebral arch, exposing a portion of the spinal chord (see Chapter 3). In such cases, a substance, alpha-fetoprotein (AFP), escapes from the spinal cord tissues into the amniotic fluid. The resulting concentration of AFP in spina bifida is markedly high not only in the amniotic fluid but also in the mother's blood. Therefore, blood serum testing of the mother can reveal the presence of high AFP, indicating the possibility of spina bifida. In about the 16th week of pregnancy, maternal blood testing can be carried out to test for AFP. This procedure has a high rate of false positives. Thus, when high AFP blood levels are found, an AFP assay is usually followed up with other tests such as amniocentesis.

It has been estimated (Moore & Persaud, 1993) that 99 percent of severe spina bifida can be detected prenatally with a combination of AFP testing and ultrasonographic scanning. The latter can show pictures of obvious protruding spinal tissues in the fetal spinal cord. A low level of AFP indicates the presence of trisomies such as Down syndrome and other chromosomal defects.

Genetic Counseling.   This is a fairly new professional field that offers to help prospective parents learn the probabilities of conceiving a child who will have disabilities or genetic-based diseases. It is generally a good idea for any prospective parents to know about their family genetic histories and disorders that seem to "run" in their families. But there are particular groups who are at higher risk, and genetic counseling is especially important for them (see Box 2.2).

Genetic counseling is an educational process in which detailed family and medical histories and physical examinations are carried out to identify heritable diseases and disabilities. The counseling is carried out both as preconception screening and as postconception, prenatal evaluation. For example, karyotypes and blood tests can be carried out to determine some chromosomal anomalies such as trisomies and conditions such as PKU. If risks are identified, they are categorized for etiology—genetic, chromosomal, environmental, or multiple causes. Based on the information, the counselor communicates to the prospective parents the probabilities of their having a child with heritable genetic defects. A major goal is to provide information to help the couple decide whether to conceive or, if pregnancy has already begun, whether to abort or continue it. In some cases, where anomalies are detected in pregnancy but abortion is not acceptable to the parents, the information can help them prepare for and adjust to the probability of having a child with disabilities. This may reduce the duration of parental disappointment and the feelings of anger and despair that ordinarily occur when a child is born with severe disabilities (W. A. Miller, 1990).

B O X **2.2**

Persons at High Risk for Having Children with Developmental Disabilities

Women over age 34 and men over age 40
Persons with relatives who have genetic disabilities
Parents who have already conceived a child with genetic problems
Persons who have been infertile
Women who have had three or more spontaneous abortions or miscarriages
Known carriers of a genetic disorder
Members of high-risk ethnic and age groups (e.g., adolescent mothers)
Individuals with high exposure to drugs, radiation, and toxins (as in the workplace)

IV. The Birth Process

As noted earlier, more than 50 percent of conceptions are naturally terminated, most in the first trimester (germinal and embryonic stages). Of those surviving, the average neonate at birth is 18 to 21 inches long and between 6 and 8.5 pounds. Boys are a little heavier and longer than girls. About 75 to 80 percent of all births are normal, a healthy baby emerges, and the mothers generally fare well.

About 10 to 14 days before delivery, the mother feels a signal called **lightening,** telling her the birth is imminent. This is a feeling of reduced pressure on some of the mother's organs caused by the fetus' head settling lower, into the pelvic inlet. The birth process begins with the first pangs of labor—the contractions of the uterus that make the cervix (the neck or opening of the uterus leading into the vaginal canal) open and flatten. The process ends with the birth of the baby and, shortly after, expulsion of the placenta, or "afterbirth." The birth process takes some 14 hours for first-time mothers and about 6 hours less for mothers who have given birth before. Some mothers experience "false labor" as early as 2 weeks before delivery, feeling contractions of the uterus. Unlike the later contractions in true labor, those in false labor do not have any real effect on the cervical opening. False labor, however, may have a function—it might help prepare the uterus for the true labor to come.

Dilation/Effacement Phase

There are three phases in the birth process. The first, the **dilation phase,** lasts about 12.5 hours for first-time mothers, from the first true labor contraction to full cervical dilation. At first, the contractions are fairly mild and brief, lasting about 30 seconds. As labor continues, the contractions become stronger and last longer. The uterine contractions bring about changes in the cervix (effacement and dilation). **Effacement** is the shortening of the cervical canal from its normal 2 centimeters to 0 (i.e., to where there is no canal at all). **Dilation** is the enlarging of the cervical opening to about 10 centimeters in diameter.

Expulsion Phase

The second stage of the birth process, **expulsion,** begins with the full dilation of the cervix and lasts about 1 hour and 20 minutes. The amnionic membranes rupture usually during the early part of this stage (less frequently during the first stage or earlier), and the amniotic fluid is expelled. Abdominal and uterine muscles contract and push the baby head-first through the uterus and into the birth canal. This movement is slow so as not to injure the head. The head emerges first, and slowly, the shoulders emerge, first one and then the other. With another contraction, the rest of the baby appears, usually face-down.

Placental Phase

The third or **placental phase** lasts 10 to 20 minutes and begins right after the baby has fully emerged. The remainder of the amniotic fluid is expelled, the placenta separates from the uterine wall, and the placenta and the remainder of the umbilical cord are expelled.

V. The Mother, the Neonate,
Postnatal Monitoring, and Care

Postpartum Depression

More than half of all mothers experience postpartum depression over a period of about a week after delivery. Overwhelming sadness, sudden crying, and fears about responsibility for the new baby are all part of this reaction, which is most probably due to the rapid, roller-coaster hormonal adjustments that occur after giving birth. Such feelings are not constant, but seem to reach peaks on the 3rd, 5th, and 7th days postpartum (Rubin, 1984). After about a week, the depression ends, presumably as the mother's hormonal adjustments near completion.

Neonatal Care

The postpartum perinatal period is one of adjustment to the postnatal world, and the delivery room staff is kept busy assisting the neonate in that adjustment. Immediately following birth, the baby is vulnerable, particularly to respiratory malfunctions. To prevent anoxia, it is important that the neonate begins breathing without delay. Toward that end, the baby is held head-down immediately following delivery to allow fluids to drain out and prevent their entering the respiratory system; the nose, mouth, and face are cleaned of mucus and fluids using gauze and/or a suction bulb. As mucus is removed from the airways, the baby begins to gasp and cry, thus signaling that respiration has begun. A gentle rubbing of the baby's back will induce crying and respiration. It is not necessary, and may even be dangerous, to slap the baby on the buttocks to stimulate breathing.

The neonate's weight, temperature, head-to-toe length, and head and chest circumferences are recorded. For identification purposes, the baby's footprints are taken, as is the mother's fingerprint. Silver nitrate eye drops are administered to prevent eye infection (a legal requirement in all states in case gonorrhea is present); vitamin K-1 is injected to help prevent excessive bleeding. Later, just before discharge from the hospital, about 75 percent of the boys will be circumcised—a controversial practice in the United States.

In many birth settings, once breathing, the baby is placed on the mother's chest, "skin-to-skin contact," for their first real postnatal social contact. Only the mother (and the father, if present) could say with any heartfelt sincerity that the baby is "beautiful." The little creature is one of strange proportions with an oversized head and often wrinkled body. The face is puffy and the eyes seem to bulge; the baby is toothless, crying, and squirming; there are still flecks of blood on the body, and a portion of the umbilical cord is still attached. But, yes, with all of that, he or she is, still, beautiful.

Neonatal Screening

The immediate postnatal period is critical, and decisions must be made quickly as to whether the baby requires special procedures. Early identification of problems is important in helping prevent subsequent disabilities (Meier, 1975). A number of screening procedures have been developed, standardized to some degree, and are in fairly extensive use, as reviewed by Francis, Self, and Horowitz (1987).

Obstetric optimality measures (e.g., Prechtl, 1977) attempt to determine the degree of positive or healthy status surrounding birth. From forty-two to seventy-four items (depending on the form used) are scored for information such as maternal and paternal smoking, family history of congenital anomalies, delayed birth, vaginal bleeding in pregnancy, length of pregnancy, birthweight, and so on. The total score is used as a screening for the probable health of the neonate.

Complication scales (e.g., Littman & Parmelee, 1978) attempt to measure the problems that may have occurred during pregnancy, birth, and immediately after birth. Items include gestational age, maternal age, presence or absence of prenatal care, drugs used during pregnancy, respiratory distress after birth, and so on.

The most widely used screening procedure is the **Apgar Scale** for newborns (Apgar, 1953; Apgar & James, 1962), which is now used routinely in most hospital births. At 1 minute after birth and again at 5 minutes, the infant is evaluated with the Apgar Scale. The baby is observed carefully and is rated 0, 1, or 2 on each of five critical life signs (shown in Table 2.2). (Notice that APGAR is also an acronym, composed of the first letter of each of the observed dimensions: Appearance, Pulse, Grimace, Activity, and Respiration.) The score on the baby's life signs is the total of all five ratings. Thus, scores can range from 0 to 10. Low scores at 1 minute tend to improve by the 5-minute rating, but if they do not, the procedure is repeated at 10 minutes. A total score of 3 or lower on the life signs indicates the baby is at significant risk and requires immediate intensive medical care including resuscitation (Reeder & Martin, 1987). A score of 4 to 6 indicates only "fair" condition. These infants show signs of cyanosis (blue tinge to the skin due to poorly oxygenated blood) and need to have airways cleaned out and the need for oxygen to be administered without delay to prevent neurological damage. At the 5-minute postbirth evaluation, about 85 to 90 percent of all babies score at 9 or 10 (National Center for Health Statistics, 1984). The Apgar Scale has contributed to the health of children, as many neonatal fatalities and developmental disabilities have been prevented by the large-scale use of this very simple procedure.

The Apgar Scale is used immediately following birth to determine if the baby is at high risk and if measures such as resuscitation are needed. It is a quick screening in a situ-

TABLE 2.2   The Apgar Scale

Score	A Appearance (Color)	P Pulse (Heart Rate)	G Grimace (Reflex)	A Activity (Muscle Tone)	R Respiration (Breathing Effort)
0	Blue skin color	Absent	No response	Flaccid, limp	Absent
1	Pink body, blue extremeties	Less than 100	Some grimace	Weak, inactive	Irregular, slow
2	Whole body pink	Rapid, over 100	Coughing, sneezing, crying	Strong, active	Good, baby is crying

Source: Apgar, V. (1953). A proposal for a new method of evaluation in the newborn infant. *Current Research in Anesthesia and Analgesia, 32,* 260.

ation that demands rapid decisions. A more extensive assessment of the newborn's neurological status is the Neonatal Behavioral Assessment Scale (NBAS) developed by Brazelton (1973, 1989; Brazelton, Nugent, & Lester, 1987). This evaluation is usually made on the infant's 3rd day, is repeated a few days later, and for various purposes, may be repeated several more times after the baby has been taken home. The infant's behavior is observed in twenty-six categories that include reflex reactions to various stimuli, general muscle tone, motor activity, and responses to the examiner such as the infant's "cuddliness." Each category may include several observed behaviors. To assess cuddliness, for example, nine behaviors are described and scored by the examiner, ranging from the infant's active resistance to being held through molding his or her body to the examiner, relaxing, grasping, and clinging to the examiner. Scores on the twenty-six items are combined into four groups: physiological, motoric, state, and interaction. Based on those scores, the neurological status of the infants is classified as "worrisome," "normal," or "superior."

Beyond assessing the infant's neurological status, the NBAS has been used as a guide for training parents of infants with only moderate scores on the social reaction items (Brazelton, 1989). Based on the NBAS, parents can be trained in how to interact with and socially stimulate and teach their infants. Research indicates that such training can improve the social interaction of infants (Widmayer & Field, 1980).

VI. Genotype and Phenotype

Genotype is the totality of a person's inherited genetic information. It is the genetic blueprint that is determined at conception. The genotype helps to determine much about each individual, contributing to the person's physical as well as psychological characteristics (emotional, behavioral, and cognitive). In complex interactions with other factors, the genetic information is expressed in the person's entire being.

Each person has a set of measurable characteristics, both physical and psychological. Some of these are easily observable, such as height, weight, facial features, hair color, and typical behavior patterns. Other characteristics, such as intelligence, disposition, maturity, and emotional stability, are more subtle but can be readily inferred from the person's overt behavior. The totality of observed and/or inferred physical, psychological, and behavioral characteristics is a person's **phenotype.** Tall, short, thin, fat, male, female, pleasant, or not all make up our phenotypes. Children with Down syndrome, for example, are phenotypically recognizable because, despite significant individual differences, they share particular physical and psychological characteristics. Each of us has our own particular size, shape, intelligence, behavior, and so on. We share phenotypical characteristics with others, particularly those in our own biological family, and we also display other more individual characteristics.

Unlike genotypes, which are biologically determined and fixed at conception, phenotypes result from interactions within and between genetics and environment. Phenotypes change throughout life, and their dynamic nature is due to their sensitivity to environmental factors. That is, experiences in our environments can significantly alter the way we act, think, and even the way we look. A person is phenotypically different at age 20 than he or she was at age 4, although genotypically he or she is the same person.

A person's phenotype is neither a simple, direct expression of one's genotype nor a direct expression of one's environment. Rather, it results from interactions of the countless variables that are included in those two categories. For example, as will be discussed in Chapter 4, phenylketonuria (PKU) is a disorder based on the presence of a recessive gene that disrupts metabolism and results in progressive cognitive deterioration. As the genetic information is played out in early infant development, the child's phenotype is progressively altered, and mental retardation becomes a likely characteristic. In this case, it is the interaction of genetics, metabolism, and diet that causes the irreversible disorder. However, it was discovered that manipulating one of these interactive factors, diet, could affect metabolism and prevent the cognitive deterioration. Thus, the person could maintain normal intelligence throughout his or her life. In this way, the usual outcome of the genetic factors is modified by environmental factors (i.e., diet).

As another example, one may be genetically predisposed to high intelligence and hence to high intellectual achievements. But that person might be born into an environment that fails to nurture intellectual accomplishment or that even interferes with cognitive growth (e.g., a toxic environment). As a result, that person may function far below his or her intellectual potential. In that case, the eventual expression of the genotype will have been modified by the person's experiences. On the other hand, a person who is genetically below average intellectually may grow up in an environment that attends closely to his or her special needs to learn and to develop socially. This person might ultimately display well-organized, independent, personally satisfying, and successful functioning, despite low genetic intellectual potential.

The interactions involved in producing one's characteristic phenotype include interactions among genes, interactions among environmental events, and interactions between genes and the environmental events. Several genes may interact (**polygenic determinism**) to produce a phenotypic tendency. But exactly how that genetic propensity is actually expressed phenotypically will also depend on the environment in which the person grows. Many factors determine the phenotype (**multifactorial transmission** of characteristics). These ideas will be referred to again in Chapter 4 in the introduction to birth defects and developmental disabilities.

Several theoretical models have been proposed to describe the nature of the gene–environment interaction. Perhaps the most basic is that of Gottesman (1974) who proposed that the genotype sets upper and lower limits for various characteristics—such as intelligence, size, physical strength, temperament, and artistic, musical, and athletic ability—producing a range (the **reaction range**) within which the person can, potentially, develop and function. Thus, depending on the nature of the environment—the degrees to which it is restricted or enriched—the person will develop and function higher or lower within that range but not beyond the genetic limits. There is considerable overlap in the potential reaction ranges so that persons of dissimilar genotype might function similarly, or those with similar genotypes might function quite differently, depending on the natures of their particular environments.

Other models (Bronfenbrenner & Ceci, 1994; Plomin, 1990, 1994; Scarr, 1993) differ in the emphases each places on the relative degrees of contributions made by genetics and environment. Whatever the differences between these theoretical models, all assume that phenotype results from interactions of genetics and environment and that each of these two complex factors is critical to our becoming who we are.

A final point needs to be made in this section. Environmental and genetic factors interact, modify each other, and affect the expressed phenotype. However, there are limits to how much of an effect each can have on the other and on the characteristics of the eventual phenotype. In the PKU example, if the diet control is never initiated, then the genetic factors will prevail, the cognitive deterioration will occur, and mental retardation will be a likely result no matter what other environmental conditions are present. In that case, the environment cannot alter what has been genetically programmed. Likewise, a severe brain injury to a normal adult can cause severe and permanently reduced intellectual functioning. That person's genetic program for normal or even superior intelligence will not overcome the massive head trauma and its resulting cognitive decrements.

VII. Chapter Summary

This chapter has reviewed basic concepts in human genetics and the normal, uncomplicated conception, development, and birth of a human baby. Prenatal and perinatal periods were discussed and divided into conception, germinal period, embryonic period, fetal period, perinatal, and neonatal periods. The perinatal sequence covers development from the 28th week of gestation through the first postnatal month.

The concepts of critical periods and teratogens were introduced and will be discussed further in Chapter 6. Just over 4 million babies are born in the United States each year, and more than 90 percent of those births are full-term, uncomplicated, and the infants are ushered into life as intact, well-developed, healthy neonates. The transition from womb to world is a major one, and critical care is needed, including careful assessment of the newborn's condition through observational scales such as the Apgar Scale and Neonatal Behavioral Assessment Scale. However, some 10 percent are born with impairments that are of varying types and degrees of seriousness, with only about 2 to 3 percent meeting the criteria for developmental disabilities.

The reaction range concept was discussed. This range of potential development and function is thought to be determined genetically, but the actual accomplishments within that range are the results of complex interactions of our genetic endowments and the quality of our particular environments.

KEY TERMS

Know these terms. Check them in the chapter and the Glossary for their meanings.
They are listed here in the approximate order of their appearance in the chapter.

Chromosomes	Ribosomes	Homologous
Genes	Genotype	Autosomes
Germ cells	Phenotype	Mitosis
Protoplasm	Ribonucleic acid	Meiosis
Nucleus	Deoxyribonucleic acid	Diploid
Nucleoplasm	Base pairs	Haploid
Cytoplasm	Karyotype	Gonads

Gamete	Gene mapping	Neural tube
Spermatogenesis	Locus	Amnion
Oogenesis	Genome	Teratogens
Autosomes	Ovum	Anencephaly
Temperament	Surfactin	Spina bifida
Conception	Amniocentesis	Surfactin
Critical periods	Chorionic villus sampling	Lightening
Germinal period	Fetoscopy	Perinatal
Cell differentiation	Ultrasonagraphy	Dilation phase
Blastocyst	Alpha-fetoprotein assay	Effacement
Cephalocaudal development	Zygote	Expulsion
Proximo-distal development	Fetus	Placental phase
Embryonic period	Fallopian tube	Postpartum depression
Quickening	Uterus	Apgar scale
Perinatal development	Cervix	Brazelton NBAS
Fetal period	Ectoderm	Psychosocial factors
Miscarriage	Mesoderm	Polygenic determinism
Gestation	Endoderm	Multifactorial transmission
Abortion	Endometrium	Genetic counseling
Somatic cells	Embryo	Genetic defects
DNA	Amniotic fluid	Reaction range
Double helix	Placenta	
RNA	Umbilical cord	

SUGGESTED READING

There are a number of excellent undergraduate textbooks in child development that provide a great deal of information on normal development.

Moore, P. K., & Persaud, T. V. N. (1993). *The developing human: Clinically oriented embryology* (5th ed.). Philadelphia, PA: Saunders. This graduate level text provides excellent information on embryology and birth defects.

Russell, P. J. (1994). *Fundamentals of genetics.* New York: HarperCollins. This undergraduate textbook provides a wide and deep view of genetics for any student who wants to go into much more detail than is provided here.

STUDY QUESTIONS

2-1. What four major factors interact in the etiology of developmental disabilities?

2-2. If you were responsible for arranging a community program of prenatal care to maximize healthy pregnancy and birth, what factors would you include in your program?

2-3. Naturally occurring miscarriages and abortions affect some 50 percent of conceptions. These are regarded as generally "positive" occurrences. How can these be positive?

2-4. What is the Human Genome Project? Think this through: What are the implications of this research for developmental disabilities?

2-5. What are teratogens? Some believe the threat of teratogens is increasing rapidly in our modern world. Can you explain this?

2-6. What are the early neonatal characteristics looked for to assess the newborn's health?

For the following, assume that you are a graduate assistant for this course. Your task is to explain each concept to your undergraduate students. Carefully think through each one.

2-7. Describe the processes of mitosis and meiosis.

2-8. The first trimester in gestation is considered a "critical period." Explain this.

2-9. How can socioeconomic status be an etiological factor for developmental disabilities?

2-10. Explain the concept of reaction range to your students. Be sure to define and explain the concepts of genotype and phenotype.

NOTES

1. For more detailed presentations of genetics, see sources such as Russell, P. J. (1994). *Fundamentals of genetics.* New York: HarperCollins.

2. In modern intensive care nurseries (ICN), the age of viability has been decreased and some premature in-fants as young as 23 weeks now survive because of the improved procedures. The chances of serious disabilities, however, are very high in such early births.

CHAPTER

3 Normal Postnatal Development

To understand developmental disabilities, we need an understanding of normal development. The previous chapter discussed normal *pre*natal development, and this chapter briefly summarizes normal *post*natal development. There are so many dimensions of human development, so much concurrent activity within dimensions, and uncounted interactions among them that any attempt to divide and arrange the topics for discussion will have an unwanted artificiality. This chapter also, of necessity, presents only brief discussions of each topic.

Let us assume that conception, gestation, and birth have proceeded without mishap, that the neonate is a healthy 7-pound, 5-ounce, 21-inch-long baby, and that mother and father are also doing fine. The child and the family have begun the long, cooperative venture of growth and development. Their success will depend on many factors, including genetics, parental skill, the child's temperament, the family's socioeconomic status, and even chance occurrences.

Development progresses with multiple systems growing and operating simultaneously and in interaction. The growth timetable is largely genetically determined, but how well the child develops also depends on the parents' success in meeting the baby's needs such as nutrition, safety, physical, sensory, and intellectual stimulation, teaching and guidance, socialization, attachment, and so on. Clearly, as was discussed in Chapter 2, heredity-by-environment interaction operates to create the child's emerging phenotype.

I. Physical and Sensory Development

Infancy is a rapid growth period, second only to the prenatal rate. After an initial 10 percent weight reduction soon after birth due to water loss, the baby gains weight rapidly, nearly tripling weight in the first year. Much of that is fat, but after 8 to 10 months, it is largely due to the growth of muscle, bone, and organs. During the first 2 years, the child grows to an average of about 30 pounds and a length of 35 inches (Behrman, 1992). More remarkable are the changes in body proportions (see Figure 2.7).

The rapid growth rate in the first 2 years slows during childhood to about age 11 or 12 when an adolescent growth spurt begins, reaching nearly 100 percent of adult growth by age 20. Body systems grow at different rates. Brain and head growth is rapid during the first 6 to 7 years, reaching virtually adult weight by about age 10 or 11. Sexual maturity, however, shows a very different growth curve, with little development during childhood and then a sharp increase from about age 13 to adulthood.

Sensation is the response to stimuli by sensory systems, and a baby's senses are in many ways well developed early in life. For example, both taste and smell are already well-developed in newborns. Indeed, an ability to discriminate among sweet, sour, bitter, and salt has been demonstrated by infants only 2 hours old (Rosenstein & Oster, 1988). Taste, smell, and touch are well developed in early infancy and functioning acutely by 1 year of age. As anyone who has observed infants and young children knows, touch is an extremely important sense for exploring the environment with fingers, lips, and tongue. Toddlers touch everything, and they learn to recognize sensations of hot and cold, hard, soft, rough, smooth, and so on. All of these sensations add to their store of knowledge, on which they will continue to build (Cataldo, 1984; Reisman, 1987), and these experiences are thus very important.

Hearing is evident in newborns. They react to sudden, startling sounds and to soothing, rhythmic sounds. By 1 month, they can distinguish among similar speech sounds (Eimas, Sigueland, Jusczyk, & Vigorito, 1971) and by 8 months can make fine discriminations among many sounds (Olsho, 1982). Vision is less developed at birth, but it improves sharply as neural development proceeds. Brightness sensitivity and the ability to focus are evident by about 3 months; primary colors (red, yellow, blue) can be perceived by about 4 months (Adams, 1989); clearly seeing small objects is developed by 9 months, and children can track remote objects by 1 year (J. S. Turner & Helms, 1991). Depth perception is developed by the time children are crawling and is an important ability for ongoing development in locomotion as well as vision.

Again, we see the importance of the environment in providing sensory stimulation and experience. These are critical not only in developing the senses further but also in actually stimulating the growth of neural networks in the brain (Parmelee & Sigman, 1983). As noted earlier, at or shortly after birth, sensory structures are present and functioning to a considerable degree. Sensory experiences are necessary to "fine-tune" the sensory responses, making mature sensory responses possible. The importance of sensory development cannot be overstated because it is through our senses that we know the world around us. The developing child uses continually occurring new information in sharpening his or her attention skills and must continually organize and make sense of sensory stimuli (i.e., perception). Sensation and attention are necessary precursors to **perception** and understanding, and they function hand-in-glove with other developmental processes.

Internal structures continue to develop. For example, skeletal development (ossification) begins about 8 weeks prenatal as cartilage starts its transformation into bone. Ossification continues into late adolescence and young adulthood when wrist and ankle bones are completed, providing a gradually strengthened bone structure that is necessary to support the body's growth in size, weight, and mobility.

In the first 2 years, gross and fine motor control, vision, and hearing all sharpen. Creeping, crawling, toddling, walking, and reaching for and grasping objects emerge. Before 1 year of age, the child can hold an object, turn it around, finger it, poke, probe, and visually examine it. By 2 years, these skills have further integrated and the child is able to coordinate movements, to manipulate, examine, and explore the environment at an amazing rate of activity, and to take great delight in those explorations. The 2-year-old is already a complicated person, a fast-changing, rapid learner, impelled to explore everything around.

From age 2 to about 6 (the preschool years or the play years), the child grows taller, a bit slimmer, and better coordinated. These are called the **play years** for good reason: Children now engage in constant play. In so doing, they explore and discover, and they practice basic motor, perceptual, social, and emotional skills. They delight in running, jumping, rolling around, and in general, discovering and exercising their growing physical abilities. Their bodies are still somewhat babyish—large head, chubby trunk, short arms and legs—and their coordination is not yet smooth and certain. The activity level is very high and their play, which is their major "occupation" in those years, may become intense and at times out of control and even dangerous. Physical injuries increase during these years as children become more mobile but have not yet developed smooth coordination or cautious worldly sense.

Several times, we have emphasized the importance in child development of environmental stimulation and support. Among other important things, the environment provides uncountable opportunities for the practice or rehearsal of emerging abilities. It is in children's play that we see this in its most intense, varied, and persevering form. Using whatever props are available, children can link their imaginations with their growing motor, language, and social abilities to create intense play situations in which they practice emerging skills across virtually all areas of development. The most obvious results of play are enhancing motor coordination, sensory sharpening, and muscular strength. But social skills are also developed in play, and cognitive growth is stimulated. Children practice their imaginative and creative abilities and toy with important make-believe ideas that help provide bases for later more abstract and hypothetical thinking (see Section III on cognitive development). Play can also help children to define and understand themselves. By enacting in play their feelings and ideas about themselves, they can examine, refine, and modify those self-defining elements. Play is critical for children. Good parents will be sure to provide the opportunities, support, and some good guidance in their children's play.

Play does not stop with childhood. Adolescents devote a good deal of time to play and, if we are honest in our observations, so do adults. Play serves different purposes as we grow older, but it remains an important part of development throughout most of our lives. Just observe adults at football games, cocktail parties, fancy dinners, or even at work and you will see play of all kinds. Most of us engage in what might be called a "play spurt" when we become parents, now playing with our children presumably because they like and need it. Fathers play more than mothers do with their children, and this may be an important contribution to the child's healthy development (Pruett, 1987).

By school age, a range of coordinated physical activities has been mastered. Watch children in a playground where 6-year-olds are running with good coordination, climbing and swinging like monkeys, throwing balls, although not yet with Little League proficiency, and making a lot of noise, enthusiastically displaying their coordinated and sustained body control.

Middle childhood (the schoolyears) is from about ages 6 through 12. There is a more gradual physical growth from the still chubby 6-year-old to the slimmer, longer, more muscular body of the preadolescent, as well as a gradual refinement of motor skills and physical abilities.

A growth spurt begins with puberty. By about age 18, adult height of about 5 feet 8 inches for boys and about 5 feet 4 inches for girls is reached. This is a time of rapid and uneven growth in virtually all physical dimensions, including height and weight, increase in muscle and fat, growth in size of internal organs (e.g., lungs and heart), and changes in the reproductive systems. Accompanying such growth is a rapid increase in physical strength and endurance and a high interest and involvement in athletics. In puberty, sexual development increases toward maturity, with enlargement of the penis and testes, the vagina, ovaries, and uterus. For boys, the first ejaculation of semen occurs, and for girls, the first menstrual period. Secondary sexual characteristics become apparent—body hair, changes in overall body shape, development of breasts in girls, deepening voice for boys, and so on (Malina, 1990).

More than a dozen hormones help to control body growth (Tanner, 1978). Hormones released by the pituitary gland stimulate the increased production of testosterone and sperm in boys; others stimulate progesterone and estrogen production in the ovaries. These hormones also stimulate secondary sexual characteristics such as body hair and body shape. The approximately 6 years of adolescence are as turbulent internally as they often seem to be socially. With all of these rapid changes, it is no wonder that adolescents seem to have such a hard time trying to define themselves.

II. Brain Development

Underlying the child's development, particularly cognitive and language development, is brain growth and maturation. The baby's head is disproportionately large (see Figure 2.7) to accommodate the large brain. The brain at birth is about 350 grams or one-fourth of its eventual adult weight. It grows rapidly during the first 2 years, reaching 50 percent of its adult weight by the first 6 months and 75 percent by 2 years (the adult human brain weighs about 3 to 5 pounds). The rapid rate of brain growth slows over the next several years, and by about age 5, it is 90 percent of its adult weight and 95 percent by 10 years (Tanner, 1978). Thus, the first 8 to 10 years after birth constitute a lengthy critical period for brain development. Physical trauma and illness causing brain damage during this period—and particularly during the first 2 years—can have significant and permanent effects on intelligence and language as well as on sensory and motor development. An indication of how rapidly the brain grows in comparison with other body systems is that while the 5-year-old brain is 90 percent of its eventual adult weight, the overall body weight is about 30 percent of eventual adult weight (Lowrey, 1986).

The postnatal growth of the brain is not primarily in **neural proliferation** (creation of new neurons), which at birth is almost what it will be at adulthood (see Chapter 2). Rather, the growth is largely a process of **neural differentiation** (Tanner, 1978), which involves the rapid development of supporting and connecting neural networks. In this process, the size of the neurons and the length of dendrites and axons increase, and **myelination** and the formation of new connections with other neurons speed up. The rapid activity of neural differentiation continues throughout childhood and enhances brain functioning. Myelination, for example, a process of developing an insulating sheath around axons, is related to cognitive development. The myelin sheath helps to speed up transmission of neural impulses, which in turn helps the early school-age child to acquire new cognition-related skills such as the visual and motor skills necessary for reading. Much of the neural differentiation occurs in the cerebral cortex that is responsible for intellectual functioning and higher sensory and motor functions.

The **cerebral cortex** is the one-eighth-inch thick gray matter that constitutes the brain's outer layer. It has specialized areas of specific functions: motor, sensory, auditory, and visual as well as generalized functions. As the neural connections become more dense and interrelated, the child's abilities that are controlled by these areas are better developed, refined, and integrated.

Much of that neural development is heavily influenced by the child's experiences in the environment (Kalil, 1989). Environmental stimulation of the various specialized brain areas enhances neural differentiation and the growth of sensory, motor, and cognitive functioning. These developments occur through heredity–environment interactions (Suomi, 1982). That is, given a sound genetic basis, a child also needs a rich and stimulating environment filled with learning and exploring opportunities to maximize brain development and motor, sensory, and cognitive abilities.

III. Cognitive, Perceptual, and Language Development

Cognitive development proceeds rapidly in tandem with the brain's growth and the child's experience in the environment. **Cognition** includes attention and perception, language, and all intellectual activities such as learning, thinking, memory, and problem solving. The importance of a stimulating and supporting quality of the environment is evident in cognitive development.

Very early, even at 1 and 2 days after birth, infants are selectively responsive to human language (Condon & Sander, 1974), orienting the head in the direction of the mother's voice. Crying is the first vocalization and has many variations (whimpering, sharp cries, variations in volume and duration, etc.). Parents learn to distinguish among the cries, and the baby thus communicates its needs to the parents. By about 3 months, babies make sounds along with a mother who talks to the baby. Cooing sounds emerge around 3 months, and **babbling** (e.g., mamamama; babababababa) occurs at about 6 months and is produced until about 12 months when single words begin to appear. Babbling allows the baby to practice with its strengthening vocal apparatus. Because it is the first vocalization that resembles speech, parents are particularly responsive to babbling by paying attention, mimicking, answering, and stimulating more babbling, thus helping the child to practice and hear its own growing range of sound production.

Between about 12 and 18 months, the first true word emerges, often to designate a parent. These are largely imitations of the vocal sounds heard by the child, and they increase in number, slowly at first and then in a **vocabulary spurt** (Barrett, 1985). Primarily nouns and verbs, these words are used with consistent meaning, usually referring to familiar people, pets, toys, other objects, or food (Nelson, D. L. 1984). **Holophrases,** single words that express a complete thought, can pack a great deal of meaning. For example, "baba" (a favorite word of my oldest daughter) might mean variously, "I want my bottle," "That's my bottle," "Where is my bottle?" The first few holophrases expand rapidly to several dozen, and by about 18 months, two-word phrases and then simple telegraphic sentences appear, such as, "Amy baba," which meant, "I (Amy) want my bottle!" or a plaintive, "Kitty go," which informed us that the cat had left the room (undoubtedly to avoid Amy's pestering). Phrases then are increasingly accompanied by meaningful gestures, and simple gestures such as reaching for and pointing emerge around 7 months (Oller & Eiler, 1988). While such **productive language**—the language produced by the child—is growing, **receptive language**—the language the child is able to understand—progresses even more rapidly. Throughout our lifetimes, receptive language ability is usually greater than that for productive language.

Without continuing experiences in close interaction with a supportive caregiver who is usually—but not necessarily—the mother, language might not develop beyond basic levels. This development requires a "special kind of fit" between the alert, responsive behavior of the adult and the emerging explorations of the infant (Kaye, 1982; Kaye & Fogel, 1980). The social/interactive aspect of language development continues as the child meets and interacts with other people, including siblings and other relatives, friends and acquaintances of all ages, neighbors, teachers, and so on. All of those social interactions provide opportunities and supports for further language development.

The average 3-year-old has about a 900-word vocabulary and can be an active participant in conversations with other children and adults (Dunn & Shatz, 1989). Language continues to develop as the child interacts socially and learns from the opportunities provided by family members and others. By about school age, vocabulary has grown to some 8000 to 14,000 words (Carey, 1977). Likewise, complex sentences, correct tense, and the understanding and use of negatives and questions are all growing. By school age, the normal child is able to communicate complicated ideas by using complex and grammatically correct sentences.

Cognition and intelligence in infants and preschoolers are different from that of older schoolchildren, adolescents, and adults. Younger children have already developed an amazingly complex set of cognitive skills based primarily on what they experience—what they see, hear, feel, taste; what their parents provide, emphasize, and reinforce for them. It is a set of skills that is very close to the concrete reality that they perceive—the world of people, things, actions, sounds, and images—and not yet so much the world of ideas. But that is coming. Their growing language use helps children think in language terms. Gradually, they learn to go beyond the immediate, concrete realities of their lives, begin learning skills in abstraction (Andrich & Styles, 1994), and think not only about what is, was, or will be, but also what *might* be. Throughout later childhood, more abstract words and concepts are learned and can be more readily manipulated, largely because of language growth.

Children's growing skills with abstractions develop largely from their learning to read and their continuing experiences with written rather than with spoken language. Reading thus becomes extremely important because it provides practice and enhances abstraction abilities to understand concepts, to reason, to go beyond immediate concrete facts, to draw inferences about future events and their probabilities, and to experience a growing set of skills in problem solving. Many children do not engage in much reading because they have difficulty doing so, because reading is not a supported activity in their environments, or because they devote inordinate time to other activities such as watching television. They will probably have less of those cognitive, reasoning, and abstracting abilities to use in their adult lives. In normal child development, people master those cognitive skills sufficiently to operate successfully as adults. For success in higher education and in more intellectually focused professions, those skills in abstracting are, of course, particularly important.

Through middle childhood, from about age 7 to 10 or 11, several dimensions of cognitive growth can be described. One is the child's increasing ability to employ **selective attention.** This includes the skills to focus on some particular segment of complex stimuli and ignore the rest, which are distractions. These skills help the child become more methodical and focused in studying, thinking, reasoning, and problem solving (Flavell, Miller, & Miller, 1993). **Memory skills,** including rehearsal and organization, storage strategies, and speed of processing new information, as well as a continually expanding knowledge base, all continue to develop in middle childhood.

An important cognitive development of the school-age child is that of **metacognition** (Flavell et al., 1993; Lovett & Flavell, 1990). This is what Flavell has termed "the game of thinking," the growing knowledge that learning requires not only active work but also the use of consistent cognitive strategies about how to go about learning and problem solving. An intellectual task can be examined and strategies developed about how to approach the task, solve the problem, and monitor one's own progress and success. For example, the older school-age child can assess a task in terms of how difficult it is likely to be and thus generate a sense of how much effort and time will be required compared to other less difficult tasks. He or she can determine if it is sufficient in a given task to try and memorize the material or whether that particular task requires more effort at understanding concepts. Other strategies include note taking and making lists, perhaps necessary in some tasks but not in others. The preschooler has not yet developed these skills, which may be described as *learning how to think about thinking.*

In adolescence, the growth in cognitive skills in thinking, remembering, selective attention, metacognition, and learning that occurred throughout childhood continues. The adolescent becomes far more adept with metacognition and has significantly increased skills in monitoring, assessing, and regulating one's own thinking in increasingly systematic ways. The adolescent is more likely than younger children to be critical and skeptical of the ideas of others, and even of his or her own ideas, and less likely simply to accept someone else's ideas or pronouncements. Intellectual activity increases along with these skills, and adolescents become involved in an amazing array of learning, from poetry through science, art, and mathematics. It is somewhat like children in the play years who delight in discovering their growing physical abilities and dive into a seemingly nonstop whirl of high-energy motor activities that leaves adults breathless. High rates of physical activity are also part of adolescence as seen in their intense involvement in athletics. What is new is the adolescents' intense and far-ranging penchant for exercising his or her growing intellectual powers.

While those skills continue to grow, a new cognitive development emerges in adolescence: logical thinking, specifically, **hypothetical-deductive reasoning** and **theory building.** Thus, adolescents' thinking ability is not only the further development of earlier skills, but there is a new, qualitatively different dimension in thinking (Andrich & Styles, 1994). Younger children are more concrete in their thinking, maintaining their focus on what they perceive as immediate and concrete reality. School-age children are beginning to learn to consider "what if?" ideas that are patently untrue, perhaps fanciful, and that conflict with what they know about reality. Adolescents can go even further, moving greater distances from concrete ideas, tentatively accepting such statements for the purpose of discussion or thinking, and then intellectually "playing" with the abstract ideas and considering their logical implications. For example, adolescents can consider the proposition, "Suppose there is a land on this earth in which people are only two-dimensional—length and width. What would their lives be like?"

In like manner, the adolescent can consider for analysis any ideas that conflict not only with objective reality but also with currently held beliefs. They can thus easily question and rethink their parents' acceptance of religious beliefs, patriotism, materialism, the value of the work ethic, and so on, often arriving at very contrary views, to the dismay of their parents.

In addition to thinking hypothetically ("what if?"), adolescents can engage in deductive reasoning. The school-age child develops the ability to use **inductive thinking,** a process of thinking that proceeds from specific, more concrete ideas to general, more abstract ideas. On the other hand, **deductive thinking** begins with the abstraction or more general propositions and proceeds to the specific conclusion. For example, the younger school-age child might think concretely as follows:

"This man has a nice smile. He is giving candy to me, and he is saying nice things to me." (the concrete facts or observations)

"If he is doing all these nice things, he is a nice man." (the more general conclusion)

The adolescent, however, can consider the same behavior very differently, starting with a more general, theoretical, or abstract idea:

"People may actually be very different from what they appear to be." (the abstract, theoretical, or more general proposition)

"This man is being very nice to me."

"But he may really not be very nice at all and may even want to hurt me." (the deductive conclusion about a specific possible event)

(This particular example will be used again later in this text when we consider some of the social problems that persons with cognitive disabilities such as mental retardation can run into.) By combining inductive and deductive thinking skills, adolescents are able to develop complex logical ideas or theories that can then be used to understand and to learn about the world and to make predictions about future events. This level of intellectual ability (hypothetical-deductive thinking and theory building) develops in adolescence, but it is thought that not all adolescents reach this level. Apparently, experience in more formal education is necessary to develop this level of thought.

As will be discussed later in this text, the developing realms of metacognition and logical thought, and their attendant skills such as selective attention, are severely limited in many developmental disabilities (e.g., mental retardation) that involve serious cognitive impairments. The lack of development of these processes leads to the question of whether they can be taught to youth with developmental disabilities, and this question will be taken up in a later chapter.

The capacity for language development and for later logical thinking is genetically programmed, but success also depends to a considerable degree on the stimulation, support, and guidance of the child's environment. This begins with repeated, close, one-to-one interactions of the baby and parent. The adult stimulates, reinforces, leads, teaches, and so on in countless little exchanges each day, and each one is a miniature but powerful teaching situation. The support given the child throughout infancy and childhood in his or her intellectual development is critical. A good environment supports thinking, problem solving, and reading and limits distracters such as viewing television. As with so much in child development, adult characteristics are products of a long, dynamic heredity-by-environment interaction.

IV. Emotional Development

An important factor in child development, particularly in emotional development and expression, is **temperament.** The term *temperament* refers to tendencies that bias the infant toward certain levels and styles of reactivity. Early research (A. Thomas & Chess, 1977; A. Thomas, Chess, & Birch, 1963) found that infants as young as a few weeks are observably different on several dimensions of temperament. There is some disagreement as to how much temperament is determined genetically (Goldsmith, Buss, & Lemery, 1997). However, there is general agreement that temperamental differences between babies can be seen almost from birth and may even be predicted by prenatal factors such as heart rate and activity level (DiPietro, Hodgson, Costigan, & Johnson, 1996). Babies differ in their general level of activity, intensity of reaction, approach-withdrawal in new situations, sensitivity to stimuli, distractibility and "fussiness," emotionality, sociability, fearfulness, mood quality, attention span, and so on. A. Thomas and Chess (1977) categorized infants based on their temperament as "easy," "slow to warm up," or "difficult" babies. These temperamental qualities seem to affect parental responses to their children. Generally, more patient, attending care is given to the easy compared with the difficult babies. It is generally thought that temperament interacts with the child's environment, helping to determine much of the person's characteristic behavior and moods.

Bonding and **attachment** are additional processes in emotional development. From the first physical contact of the newborn and the parents, emotional bonds are presumably formed. In healthy situations, they are positive emotions of parental love and feelings of responsibility. The importance of early bonding in some mammals for later care of the offspring has been established by research (Klopfer, 1971; Rosenblatt, 1982). Whether bonding is of critical importance in human infant care has not yet been determined (Ewer, 1992). Indeed, some research has indicated that early bonding has no lasting effects for humans (Grossman, Thane, & Grossman, 1981). The current practice in hospitals of providing the mother and father with immediate physical contact with their new baby is probably a good idea that should be continued, but it will not guarantee permanent bonds or good parenting later. The development of emotional bonds continues over the lifetime of interaction of the child with parents, siblings, and others. The quality of those emotional bonds will depend on many factors that unfold as the child grows.

Distress and sadness are among the first emotions clearly recognizable in infants, and by about 4 to 7 months, babies are able to combine distress with expressions of anger (C. R. Sternberg & Compos, 1990). Positive emotions are also evident early. A social smile is a clear smile in response to another person, and this is evident beginning around 6 weeks. By about 4 months, smiles are well developed and the baby can even laugh (Malatesta, Culver, Tesman, & Shepard, 1989).

The 4-month-old is already associating emotional meaning with facial expressions (Caron, Caron, & MacLean, 1988) and by around 8 months is alert and responsive to a range of emotions presented in the facial expressions and vocalizations of others. Around 8 to 9 months, there is a spurt of emotional development, and children are more alert to the social aspects of emotional communication and increasingly expressive themselves (Zelazo, 1979). At this time in development, the child is able to look to the parent or others for emotional cues which become important aspects of social interaction. At about 8 to 14 months, children display distress when meeting strangers and clear anxiety over any separation from mother (R. A. Thompson & Limber, 1990).

Among the important emotional developments that arise out of infants' social interaction is the development of attachment—a powerful, enduring emotional tie between parent and child (Ainsworth, 1993). Unlike bonding, which occurs rapidly, attachment is thought to develop over time through repeated, close parent–child interaction. As the newborn's sensory and other abilities develop, parent–child interactions become more active, with increased alertness and responsiveness by both child and parents. The baby becomes increasingly responsive to language and to the sights, sounds, and smells of the parents, and these provide more sensory, physical, and emotional dimensions through which they can interact. Their interactions increase, including more face-to-face contact (focused talking, cooing, and singing to the baby, laughing, playing, etc.), a general increase in active touching, and simple enjoyment of each other. In those processes, attachment normally grows, and ideally, by the time children reach about 18 months of age, they and their parents have strong, positive feelings for each other. Attachment processes normally occur throughout childhood and are not limited to parents. For example, children can become strongly attached to teachers and others in high-quality day-care centers (Howes & Hamilton, 1992).

It is generally thought that the quality of infant care by the caregiver determines the quality of the attachment. If the care has been good, the child presumably develops a **secure attachment;** if not, a more negative **anxious-insecure attachment** may develop. Research has related the type of early attachment to adjustment in the preschool and early school-years (e.g., Main & George, 1985; Sroufe, Fox, & Pancake, 1983). The quality of early attachment is only one factor that contributes to later adjustment, but it is regarded as an important contributor.

Researchers have considered factors that are thought to prevent or disrupt the development of secure attachment. For example, the quality of infant care (R. A. Thompson, 1991), the quality of the marriage (Fantuzzo et al., 1991; Pianta, Egeland, & Erickson, 1989), parental loss, illness, or child maltreatment may have negative effects (Cichetti & Carlson, 1989). Little is known about the relationship of developmental disabilities and attachment. It is reasonable to infer that the quality of the parent–child relationship depends heavily on the child's alertness and responsiveness, which in turn depend in part on the child's sensory, motor, and cognitive development. If developmental disabilities have curtailed the child's development, then it must be asked if there are negative effects on attachment formation. Is attachment prevented, moderated, or delayed? Research on attachment-disabilities relationships may be difficult to conduct, but these are interesting and important questions.

The year-old child clearly recognizes, responds to, and expresses basic emotions such as fear, anxiety, sadness, surprise, and joy. As children mature and gain social awareness and cognitive skills, their emotional lives become more complex. Children learn to anticipate events and can begin to display emotions over things that are apparently about to happen, showing eager anticipation, fear, disappointment, and so on. Likewise, they develop self-awareness and a sharpened recognition of others. With these developments, children can—and do—begin to respond with feelings such as affection, jealousy, pride, embarrassment, and disappointment (Dunn & Munn, 1985). By school age, most children have experienced and coped with a large array of emotions.

As they grow into the schoolyears, children can experience a full array of emotions, although their emotional control is not yet fully developed. In these years, the child's peer group becomes important, and emotions are increasingly associated with other children and events outside of the home. Feelings about being accepted, having friends, sharing jokes and humor, social rejection, personal accomplishments, and so on become the emotional focal points for the schoolyears.

In adolescence, emotional experiences are heavily involved with sexual development, desires for independence, identity, and achievement. In these years, the adolescent struggles to integrate all of the different and sometimes conflicting dimensions of prior growth into a coherent, identifiable, whole person who functions successfully in a complex world and fills various social roles. The adolescent typically can enact the many emerging but still incomplete roles of son or daughter, male or female, student, boyfriend or girlfriend, employee, athlete, friend, child, adult, and so on. They try to resolve many role conflicts such as the roles of independent adult versus dependent child or youth. These and other conflicts and the unfinished nature of their role developments complicate the tasks of finding a single well-defined identity. The youth's success depends heavily on family, social support and resources, and the degree to which their prior development succeeded in providing the bases for their attempted personal integration.

V. Social Development

As briefly summarized in this chapter, human development occurs across many interactive dimensions, and even though we present them in separate sections, the reality is that development proceeds with an interactive unity within a total, overall context. Development is not piecemeal; everything that a child develops is in the context of everything else the child develops. All of the child's previous development forms a complex web of form and function that is a dynamic background for all of the child's subsequent development. Any break in the web, such as a severe developmental impairment, will have effects in other parts and functioning of this complex system. The key ideas here are that the different areas of development are dynamic (growing, changing), interactive, and interdependent.

These ideas are evident in the case of social development, or **socialization,** which is the lifelong process of learning a culture's mores, prescribed behavior, values, and so on. Children live in a social context, and as they develop in all the ways previously described, they are gaining in abilities that allow them to learn and interact socially with increasing complexity. Healthy, mature socialization depends on continuing development in all other areas.

The infant's day-by-day interactive experiences with a caregiver and the development of attachment provide bases for the child's social development. As we noted earlier, by about 8 months children can respond emotionally to the social expressions of others, such as the parent. This growing ability to respond to social cues is called **social referencing** (Feinman, 1985) and indicates the child is becoming increasingly attentive to social events involving parents and other trusted persons (Camras & Sachs, 1991). While social referencing increases, children are also becoming much more self-aware—that is developing a sense of self, of "me," and of "mine." By about 2 years, most children can identify themselves and distinguish themselves from others (Pipp, Fischer, & Jennings, 1987). Having a more developed self-awareness enables the preschooler to enjoy greater recognition of others (i.e., those who are "not me") and thus provides the child with bases for more complex social learning. **Self-awareness** is also necessary in learning **self-regulation,** which in turn is important in social interactions with the child's growing circle of peers. Through the play years, children continue to experience social situations, to sharpen their perceptions of themselves and others, to develop increasing self-regulation, and to practice and learn interactive social skills. In a word, they are being quite rapidly socialized.

In the schoolyears, children continue to develop their self-understanding and their self-regulation. They also gain rapidly in **social cognition** (i.e., understanding other people). The child's peer group becomes increasingly important now. Children at this age become more dependent on their peer groups and look to their peers for friendship, guidance, advice, and criteria for self-evaluation. Children learn the peer group's rules for how they should behave and even how they should look and what they should wear. During these years, they also become more sensitive to the rules of the general society. In addition to all else that is developing, the child is becoming increasingly social-oriented during these schoolyears of about 6 to 11.

Social development in adolescence is given a new urgency by the powerful physical changes and the heavy pressure of newly energized sexuality. The peer group now has an added dimension of sexual meaning, and it grows even more important. By the end of adolescence, the youth has normally developed a fairly stable identity that incorporates what they have been learning of morality, values, politics, religion, and so on. In his or her emerging identity, the adolescent tries to maintain group values but also has a major focus on establishing individuality—the youth as a unique person and a separate individual.

VI. Normal Developmental Tasks:
Social Norms, Expectancies, and Roles

Successive **developmental tasks** need to be mastered as a person grows (Havighurst 1972, 1980). The origins of these tasks include biological needs and physical maturation, family, peers, society and culture, and one's own emerging personality (personal needs, desires, abilities, etc.). To function successfully, adults must have mastered skills at appropriate times in development, such as locomotion and language, social interaction, moral values and behavior, vocational plans, personal responsibility, and so on. Success in meeting these demands, according to Havighurst, contributes to success with later demands and leads to satisfaction and personal happiness. Failure to do so means greater difficulty in meeting later tasks and in achieving personal satisfaction and social acceptance. We will not use Havighurst's model in any formal manner, but the idea that humans have bio/psycho/social demands to meet and developmental tasks to master is a good general guide. Box 3.1 outlines some of the major tasks that persons in our society are expected to have mastered by the time they reach adulthood.

To put Havighurst's model into a more social context, these demands can be seen as stemming from the **expectations** that society in general has of persons at different ages. We expect children of 2 years to walk and to communicate verbally. We expect children in the schoolyears to form friendships and self-regulation, to learn to read and write, and to develop other academic skills. We expect adolescents to seek independence from parents, to have close ties with peers, to have understanding of moral principles, to be well on the way to developing a unique identity, and to have some direction for future education and/or employment. We expect adults to be responsibly mature, self-directive, and self-supportive, to be moral and law-abiding, and so on. That is, society has a historical collective sense of what is normal and specifies and communicates those **norms.** When we use the term *expectations,* we mean *the communication of norms.* Most people perceive those expectations and become alert to the norms. There are large individual differences, but overall, most people learn and incorporate the norms to some reasonable, but never complete or precise, degree. In this model, one's personal success is seen as the degree to which one meets or exceeds that myriad of norms.

The obverse, of course, is that lack of personal success can be seen as the degree to which persons fail to meet or exceed social expectations. There are many reasons for failure, including physical and/or psychological impairments. Such impairments can effectively interfere with development in both direct and indirect ways and make it difficult or impossible for a person to meet some of the norms. Persons with developmental disabilities are prevented from meeting many of those norms. Indeed, their difficulties in doing so have been recognized and incorporated into the very definition of developmental disabilities, as was discussed in Chapter 1 (see Box 1.3). It should be apparent that this concept of society's age-appropriate norms or demands is one of the bases for the concept of handicap. That is,

B O X **3.1**

Major Tasks: Social Expectations for Normal Growth and Functioning

By late adolescence, each person in our culture is expected to have met norms in each of the following dimensions of development.

Physical and Sensory Development
> Normal size, weight; muscular, skeletal, internal organ development
> Adequate sensory development (vision, hearing)
> Good physical health (no chronic disease, disorder)
> No physical anomalies
> Good neurological development and integration

Motor Coordination and Body Control
> Coordinated locomotion, mobility
> Normal eye-hand coordination
> Normal limb, muscle control
> Able to engage in normal physical activities for age

Cognitive Development
> Thinking, reasoning, memory
> Ability to learn intellectually
> Has developed cognitive problem-solving skills; indications of formal logical operations (e.g., hypothesis formation, induction, and deduction)
> Normal academic achievement; reading and math skills; abstract thinking; reasoning, memory, recognition, comprehension
> Normal fund of information for age

Language and Speech Development
> Development of expressive and receptive language
> Age-appropriate vocal and written language comprehension and use
> Able to use standard grammar in speech and writing
> Able to communicate clearly through language

Emotional Development
> Able to experience the full range of human emotions (i.e., affection, sexual ardor, joy, surprise, disgust, sadness, fear, anger)
> Able to recognize those emotions in oneself and others
> Developed self-control over emotions and appropriate expression of feelings
> Has developed emotional attachments; filial, friendships, love
> Has achieved emotional independence from parents

Integration of Cognitive/Emotional Skills
> Able to plan ahead intellectually
> Able to delay rewards and work toward intermediate and long-term goals
> Emotional/cognitive interaction—balancing emotions and intellect
> Development of cognitive self-control
> Aesthetic appreciation and expression—imagination; creativity (art, writing, music)

(continued)

BOX **3.1** **Continued**

Social/Interpersonal Skills
Able to recognize and to function appropriately in social situations
Develops mature relationships (friendships, acquaintances)
Recognizes responsibilities to friends etc.
Able to cooperate with others in socially responsible behavior
Develops appropriate social roles (including gender roles)
Anticipates and prepares for adult roles (e.g., marriage, family, career)

Moral Development
Has developed a clear sense of right and wrong
Has concern for welfare of others
Is developing a guiding code of moral/ethical values
Abides by social rules—legal and ethical behavior
Has developed control over one's aggression
Respects group's and others' needs
Has developed altruism (helping others without expecting benefits to in return)

Personal/Self-Development
Autonomy, sense of self; self-esteem; self-expression
A sense of responsibility for self
Self-care skills
The ability to make future plans (personal, vocational, academic)
Has developed self-direction; aspirations; goals
A capacity for learning

it is the functional limitations in various areas of life activities (self-care, language, mobility, etc.), the very skills that are expected of most people, that define disabilities. This is another way of saying that to understand developmental disabilities, we must first understand normal development and appreciate the power of norms and their communication (i.e., social expectations). The communication of norms among persons, their importance in defining and guiding an individual's social behavior, is accomplished through various social structures and events, primarily social positions and social roles. These concepts will be discussed in detail in Chapters 8 and 9 in our presentation of a social role analysis of mental retardation.

Most persons achieve those norms well enough to maintain mature, responsible, and self-satisfying lives that include a balance of personal independence and intimate sharing with others. The presence of developmental disabilities, however, alters that picture. The general effect is disruption of normal developmental processes and functions, with the severity of disruption depending largely on the type and degree of disability. The disruptive effects occur directly and indirectly. Direct disruptions are natural results of the impairments. A child with cerebral palsy will have had brain damage that disrupts motor functioning. A child with severe fetal alcohol syndrome will show not only intellectual disabilities but also a characteristic facial appearance. The direct effects of neural tube developmental failure in an embryo include severe conditions such as anencephaly and spina bifida.

Indirect or secondary effects are no less important. A child with impairment is at risk for further developmental disruptions because the impairment, once in place, will interfere with other developmental processes. Indeed, this continuing interference is at the center of the concept of *developmental* disabilities. For example, the impairment may affect the child's appearance, development, and behavior; these in turn may affect the caregiver's response to the child. Consider a point that we have made several times: Although children are genetically programmed to grow in normal directions, a supportive environment is necessary to guide and sustain that growth. Basic care is needed: nourishment, protection, physical, social, and cognitive stimulation, guidance, and so on. A responsive, alert, healthy baby makes the task easier and more pleasant for the parent. Fortunately, most babies are sufficiently responsive to make good use of the many developmental supports provided. Some children, however, particularly those with congenital or very early occurring developmental disabilities, are not able to respond and interact as effectively as other children. They are at risk for losing many learning/developmental opportunities. A relatively unresponsive child or one who is slow to develop physically and socially may be less reinforcing for parents who may then, through a process of response extinction, gradually give less time and attention to the child, thus losing many teaching opportunities. Likewise, a child with a physical handicap or subaverage intellectual ability may be rejected by other children and suffer even more social deprivation and loss of social learning opportunities.

The child with developmental disabilities is thus subjected to a double imposition: first from the direct effects of the impairment and second from all of the physical, social, and psychological complications set in motion by the impairment. Both seriously interfere with normal development. Notice that so far in this text we have postulated a negative effect, essentially it is an **interference hypothesis;** that is, developmental disabilities result in a decrement in functioning through their interference with normal development. In a later chapter on social role development in disabilities, we will take these ideas a significant step further. In that discussion we will develop our **direct socialization hypothesis.** That is, we will maintain that the development of persons with developmental disabilities is not only interfered with in this negative, decremental manner, but that persons are also directly and actively socialized into a significantly limited level of functioning. The latter direct socialization occurs because the child is put on a socialization course that eventuates in a powerful **social role** of disability. That is, developmental disabilities consist of the impairments, their direct and indirect negative effects on functioning, and a defined, learned, powerful social role of disability. In essence, we have expanded the definition of developmental disability given in Chapter 1 to include the social role aspects. These ideas will be further developed in Chapters 8 and 9.

VII. Growth beyond the "Developmental" Years

This text has its major focus on the developmental years, approximately from conception through age 20. Of course, human development does not cease as we attain our legal majority around age 18 to 21. We continue to grow, develop, and change. Most of us think of our childhood and youth as developmental in nature, whereas our adult years are more apt to be thought of as a process of aging. However, aging can be seen as a lifelong continuous process that begins at conception. The person develops along age-graded dimensions of growth (or aging) from conception to death. Most people tend to think of the first third of life, to about age 20–25, as the years of development of their skills and physical, psychological, and social role systems. We think of persons gaining in size, strength, coordination, intellectual, social, and personal skills, and of becoming the essential person we define as our "self." It is typically viewed as the period of preparation, in so many ways, for the more independent functions of adult life.

The second third of life, the adult "middle years," to about age 50–55, is typically viewed as a time of consolidation and maintenance of developed characteristics. Here we use the skills developed earlier to create our own niche in the world and to generate our work or professions, our families, and our most intimate relationships with life partners. We enter new social positions and enact new roles. We establish our status in life, and ideally, we make our own greatest contributions to others and to society in general. By any measure, these adult years involve a great deal of development, growth and change, gaining new skills and sophistication, and becoming someone who is different in significant ways from the more immature adolescent of the preadult years.

The final period of life, about age 55 and older, is what we typically think of as "aging," although aging has actually been occurring throughout life. We idealize this as a period in which we become more reflective, devote more time to enjoying what we had developed throughout our earlier life, and recognize that we need to move aside for the younger people who are "coming up." Mostly, however, people still think of this as a period of decline in which the body is naturally subjected to growing weakness and illness. Of course, people become ill earlier in life due to unpredicted and unfortunate events. In this later period, however, decline is seen as natural events that are integral to development and an inevitable, natural dimension of aging. Research tells us that many of these processes are triggered by sequences of gene expression and modified by environmental factors. The resulting "aging phenotype" varies somewhat from one person to another, but occurs to all who survive the requisite number of years. This inexorable developmental sequence is the aging process that grips all people. We remain in its progressions, many years for some, too few for others, but people, like it or not, are committed to these natural processes.

We are also learning that whatever gene expression may help to control the process, there is considerable leeway for individual and social control. Nutrition, physical activity, good health behavior and care, love and other positive personal relationships, active intellectual interests, and so on can make significant differences in the overall quality of this period (World Health Organization, 2000). Decline may be inevitable, but theoretically at least, the quality of life during this time is to a significant degree under personal control. Recall the "reaction range" concept (Gottesman, 1974) discussed in Chapter 2 and applied to the phenotypic expression of the developing child's genotype. The concept applies equally well to human development throughout life.

For the child with developmental disabilities, however, aging is even more complex. Not only does this person progress along the natural aging dimension experienced by everyone, but he or she is also subject to the special developmental dimensions imposed by the person's primary disability and its many functional consequences. This idea constitutes the basis of a conceptual model proposed by Turk, Overeynder, and Janicki (1995). In this model, the aging of the person with disabilities is understood in terms of two independent factors and their interactions:

1. *Factor A:* the complex natural aging sequences experienced by all persons
2. *Factor B:* the specific complex sequences due to the nature of each disability
3. *Interactions* of the two factors (A × B interactions)

Each factor, A and B, is complex and composed of many single events and sequences. It can be seen that when both are operating simultaneously, as in a person with disabilities, the total of all the processes becomes even more complicated. Add to this all of the myriad possible potential effects created by the interactions of the various parts of the two factors. An interaction of factors is not simply the addition of one to another. Rather, an interaction effect is greater than the simple sum; it is a new condition that has been created (Graziano & Raulin, 2000). Thus, the total impact of the two independent factors plus the newly created conditions due to the interactions can be very complex indeed.

For example, a person with Down syndrome will be subject to all of the processes and changes that occur in normal aging. We can anticipate the normal depletions of energy, the decrement of cognitive and physical skills, and the encroaching potential for age-related diseases and illness. However, we need to ask if there are any additional aging events that are introduced and controlled by the condition itself. For example, Down syndrome, as we will discuss in a later chapter, is the result of a particular chromosomal anomaly. Does this special chromosomal condition trigger age-related changes that will occur independently of the other usual age changes or that will interact with normal aging and produce new factors? Some evidence indicates that persons with Down syndrome have a shorter life expectancy than most persons and that cognitive deterioration, much like that occurring in normal senescence and in Alzheimer's disease, may begin years earlier in Down syndrome than normally occurs. Is this early senescence (if it occurs) an interactive effect of the two major factors: Down syndrome and normal aging? Are these aging events specific occurrences of the additional aging factor, the disability itself? Turk et al. (1995) raise these questions regarding another disability, cerebral palsy, a condition in which brain damage very early in life affects the condition and use of muscles. Cerebral palsy can be present to a mild, moderate or severe degree. The afflicted person may thus have a relatively minor impairment (e.g., walking with a stiff gait) or severe impairments (e.g., being mentally retarded and unable to talk or unable to control the arms, legs, and trunk). Turk et al. (1995) point out the importance of determining if and how these impairments impact on the normal aging process. Do the two factors interact to create even new aging problems for the person? Might those lifelong motor impairments in some ways alter the physical and psychological reserves of the person, decreasing the adaptive responses to physiological stressors that occur with aging? If these interactive effects do occur, do they pose significant new threats to the person's independence? Are they new demands and stressors that will significantly affect the progress of the person's life from that point on? This model has implications not only for the conceptual understanding of and research into developmental disabilities but also for planning, management, treatment, education, and prevention programs for individuals and for large-scale applications.

Persons with disabilities are living longer lives (Janicki, 1999; Maaskant, 1993) largely due to better medical and social care (Seltzer & Seltzer, 1985). In addition, the rate of disabilities in the general population increases after about age 50 to 55 (Janicki & Jacobson, 1986), so the prevalence of older Americans with disabilities (developmental and all others) will continue to increase. The field of developmental disabilities needs to address these changes and learn more about the progressions of continued aging in later years for persons with those disabilities. Most of what is currently known about aging and disabilities has been learned from work with persons with mental retardation (e.g., Janicki, 1993, 1994b; Seltzer, 1992). But what of the persons with primary disabilities that are not cognitive in nature, such as cerebral palsy, who can be expected to live well into their adult years? The questions posed by Turk et al. (1995) need to be addressed in research:

How do the normal aging processes play out in persons with disabilities?

What additional processes occur due to the nature of each particular disability?

How do these differ among the different disabilities?

What specific events result from the interactions of normal aging and the specific disability-related aging processes?

Older persons with disabilities have the right to the best possible life within their disability limits, just as we assume for younger persons. An array of social, educational, and treatment programs is appropriate for this group. Assistive technology can and should be utilized to enrich their lives appropriate to their ages and conditions. Increased research is needed to understand these later year aging processes if we are going to provide adequately for this growing population of older Americans who have disabilities. (This topic will be revisited briefly in Chapter 15.)

VIII. Chapter Summary

This chapter has briefly outlined some of the dimensions of normal postnatal development, pointing out the complexity of this task of "growing up." The child's growth timetable is largely genetically determined, but how well the child develops depends also on the parents' success in meeting the growing youngster's needs, such as nutrition, safety, physical, sensory, and intellectual stimulation, attachment, and guidance. In the discussion, it was emphasized that a child's development occurs in interrelationships; it does not happen in isolated segments. Child development forms a complex web of form and function, a dynamic background for all of the child's subsequent development. At any time and in any particular systems, developmental interruption such as the occurrence of an impairment may have disruptive effects in other systems and times in that child's development. This notion of interrupted development is part of the definition of developmental disabilities (i.e., it forms the interference hypothesis).

The discussion of socialization suggested that social norms for behavior are communicated to individuals through the expectations of other persons. Those norms are incorporated by growing children in the process of their socialization and become basic components of the various social roles that each person develops throughout life. We suggested that in the case of developmental disabilities those expectations lead the person into self-limiting roles. That is, society adds to the disabilities by actively socializing the child into a disabled—and therefore, a self-limiting—role. This social role model of disabilities will be further discussed in Chapter 9.

Aging is a normal part of human development, and there may be special circumstances and aging processes for persons with disabilities. Much more research is needed on these aging processes to understand the life spans of persons with disabilities and to provide them with adequate services.

KEY TERMS

Know these terms. Check them in the chapter and the Glossary for their meanings.
They are listed here in the approximate order of their appearance in the chapter.

Sensation	Selective attention	Socialization
Perception	Memory skills	Social referencing
Play years	Metacognition	Self-awareness
Neural proliferation	Hypothetical-deductive	Self-regulation
Neural differentiation	reasoning	Social cognition
Myelination	Theory building	Developmental tasks
Cerebral cortex	Inductive thinking	Expectations
Cognition	Deductive thinking	Norms
Babbling	Temperament	Interference hypothesis
Vocabulary spurt	Bonding	Direct socialization hypothesis
Holophrases	Attachment	Social role
Productive language	Secure attachment	
Receptive language	Anxious-insecure attachment	

SUGGESTED READING

As was recommended in the previous chapter, a number of excellent child development undergraduate texts are available, and they provide a great deal of information on child and life-span development.

STUDY QUESTIONS

3-1. Of what significance for developmental disabilities is the fact that a child's brain continues to grow for many years after birth?

3-2. Assume that you are in charge of creating a child development program for children from birth to age 5 for your community. The overall goal is to foster physically and psychologically healthy children (i.e., fostering health and wellness). What would you include in your program?

3-3. What do you think might be the major negative effects on children if they are not allowed or are unable to play a great deal?

3-4. Define and describe neural proliferation, neural differentiation, and myelination.

3-5. Explain, as if to your students, the possible negative effects on a child if a consistent and responsive caregiver is not available up to about age 4.

3-6. Why is it important to encourage and support reading for children?

3-7. Explain the concept of metacognition. What is its importance in child development?

3-8. Explain, as if to your students, the characteristics of inductive and deductive thinking.

3-9. Consider a person with significant intellectual disability (i.e., mental retardation). At age 18, he or she will not have developed strength in deductive thinking skills. What are the implications of this relative weakness for this person's intellectual and social development?

CHAPTER

4 Endogenous Etiological Factors in Disabilities: Genetic Defects

Prenatal development is complex and continuous, proceeding in a regular and predictable manner from conception to birth. Directed by the genetic information set in place at conception, the developing zygote, embryo, and fetus draw on the mother's resources, synthesizing various proteins to develop and sustain tissues and organs. The earliest phases of pregnancy are the most critical for survival, and it is in the first few weeks that nearly half of the pregnancies are naturally terminated because something has gone wrong and the zygote or embryo is not viable (Plomin, DeFries, & McClearn, 1990). Few women even know they are pregnant in those first few weeks. By the time the pregnancy is known, nearly all of the terminations have occurred. More than 80 percent of known pregnancies continue in their predictable, healthy, undisturbed, and successful development toward birth (Moore & Persaud, 1993). That should be reassuring to the young adults reading this text with its emphasis on disabilities.

The processes of prenatal development are played out largely as the results of maturation—of innate, biological, and gene-directed events supported by a healthy uterine environment. Fortunately, the limits of what is a healthy environment are generous, natural processes are robust, and this marvelous natural system tolerates a good deal of variation and even assault.

But problems do arise in a small proportion of known pregnancies, and it is from this minority that most children with developmental disabilities emerge. Of the 4,084,000 live births in 1992 in the United States (U.S. Department of Commerce, 1995), more than

80 percent were born with no discernible abnormalities, and just about 17 percent (about 700,000) were born with some degree of birth defects. But most of these birth defects (about 14 percent) are minor and do not constitute developmental disabilities. Overall, 90 percent of births are healthy, some of which show minor noncritical defects. The remaining 10 percent do have defects that are more serious, but only about 2 to 3 percent of births are developmentally disabled (Moore & Persaud, 1993). However, that is still about 80,000 to 120,000 new cases per year from the birth cohorts.

Many etiological factors operate during the first 18 years and result in developmental disabilities. Illness and traumatic injuries at any time during the first 18 years can cause developmental disabilities. *However, most developmental disabilities have prenatal etiologies, and most of those occur early in pregnancy.* That fact reinforces how important it is to understand these early processes and to aim research efforts at the prevention of early pathologies that lead to developmental disabilities, a focus we will discuss later in this text.

To paraphrase Charles Wenar (1990), developmental disabilities are instances of normal development gone awry. That is, in the processes of normal development, something intervenes, upsets that development, and causes it to be skewed in a pathological direction. What are those disruptive factors? As noted in Chapter 1 (see Box 1.3), the two major categories of etiological events in developmental disabilities are (a) hereditary factors (genetic and chromosomal) and (b) environmental factors. These interact with (c) the particular organ system affected and (d) the level of development of that organ system (i.e., heredity × environment × organ system × level of development).

I. Birth Defects

Birth defects and the equivalent terms, **congenital anomalies** and **congenital malformations,** are general terms referring to the condition of neonates born with some discernible developmental pathology. The emphasis is on the *presence at birth* of the defects ("congenital" is from the Latin *congenitus,* meaning "born with"). Birth defects can occur as single or multiple anomalies and can be of minor to major degrees of seriousness. Obvious birth defects are observable structural (physical) anomalies. But birth defects may also involve the ways in which parts of the body operate (functional), the chemical basis of body functions (metabolic), the psychological functioning of the person (behavioral), or the playing out of genetic and chromosomal factors (hereditary). Structural defects are most apparent at birth, while some of the others are more difficult to discern and may not be detected until later in life. Thus, estimates of the incidence of all defects discernible at birth are approximate. As has been noted, birth defects occur in about 17 percent of live births, but 14 percent of birth defects are of such a minor nature as to be negligible. Only about 3 percent of births present major structural anomalies such as spina bifida, and as children grow, birth defects become apparent in more children (Table 4.1). Birth defects can involve pathologies in any organ systems, with distortions in the brain and heart being the most common, as shown in Table 6.1. As noted, severe birth defects meet the criteria for and constitute a significant proportion of developmental disabilities.

The etiological factors in those defects are hereditary (genetic/chromosomal) and environmental. This chapter focuses on defects with genetic etiologies. These factors are in-

TABLE 4.1   Percentage of Detected Birth Defects by Age

3% of newborn
6% of 2-year-olds
8% of 5-year-olds

Data for this table are From Moore, K. L., & Persaud, T. V. N. (1993).
The developing human: Clinically oriented embryology. Philadelphia:
Saunders.

herent, and their origins lie within the organism (the cell, the embryo, or fetus). They are **endogenous factors** that are passed on to the next generation through genetic inheritance. A large proportion of developmental disabilities is determined by such endogenous factors.

Events leading to prenatal pathologies and birth defects can occur spontaneously or be induced by environmental factors such as temperature, toxins, and radiation. In addition, the developing organism can be harmed by nonhereditary factors such as disease, drugs, and physical injuries. These are environmental **exogenous factors,** whose origins are external to the organism. They affect gross structure and function, but do not cause changes in genes or chromosomes. Such exogenous factors during gestation include maternal disease and malnutrition, oxygen deprivation, drugs and other chemical substances, and maternal stress. They will be discussed in some detail in Chapters 6 and 7.

II. Polygenic and Multifactorial Transmission

The remainder of this chapter discusses endogenous etiological factors in human disabilities, specifically **genetic defects** and **chromosomal anomalies.** It may appear that each gene has only one specific function or that genetic or chromosomal aberrations are inevitably and directly played out. It may seem that the genotype is directly expressed phenotypically and that a gene controls one particular characteristic. As pointed out in Chapter 2, the relationship between genotype and phenotype is a good deal more complicated than we have presented. Keep in mind that the impact of prenatal events on development is through the interaction of at least four factors: heredity, environment, organ system, and level of development. Most inherited human characteristics are not the results of a single etiological factor, such as a particular gene. Instead, these traits are determined through two major patterns of interaction: **polygenic determinism,** in which several genes interact at the level of protein synthesis and contribute to the trait's emergence, and **multifactorial transmission,** which occurs through the interaction of genetic material with environmental factors. Most human inherited characteristics are polygenic and multifactorial traits (Scarr & Kidd, 1983).

In polygenic inheritance, genetic interaction occurs in various patterns: additive, nonadditive, and chromosome-linked patterns. In the additive pattern, the resulting phenotype is due to the average influences of several genes. Height, for example, is probably due to the influences of genes from different family members who were tall, short, or medium in height. Because of the genetic blending, any child in that family might be taller or shorter than the parents.

Of more significance for developmental disabilities are the nonadditive patterns, one of which is the dominant–recessive gene interaction pattern. A dominant gene may completely mask a recessive gene and thus be expressed phenotypically. Some types of blindness, dwarfism, and asthma are dominant-gene-based disabilities (see Box 4.1). If a child inherits one such dominant gene, then the disorder will be evident phenotypically.

If both parents are carriers of a particular recessive gene, neither parent will phenotypically express that characteristic. However, that combination of two inherited recessive genes will be expressed phenotypically. Examples of disorders due to recessive-gene inheritance (discussed later in this chapter) are phenylketonuria, sickle cell anemia, and Tay-Sachs disease. Phenylketonuria is a recessive-gene-based inherited enzyme deficiency that progressively interferes with brain development and can result in mental retardation. If each parent is a carrier of this recessive gene, then any child has a one in four chance of inheriting both recessive genes and therefore of phenotypically expressing the disorder (see the discussion in Chapter 3).

Another nonadditive polygenic pattern is a gene-chromosome interaction, in which particular genes are associated with specific chromosomes. Hemophilia and some types of muscular dystrophy are caused by recessive genes on the X chromosome. Down syndrome (Chapter 5) occurs when there is an excess of genetic material due to an extra chromosome 21.

Human traits are also multifactorial—that is, determined not only by more than one gene, but also by the interaction of genetic and environmental factors. Alcoholism, for example, is known to be a multifactorial trait. There is a genetic predisposition to abuse alcohol, although the specific gene or genes have not yet been identified (McClearn, Plomin, Gora-Maslak, & Crabbe, 1991). However, the genotype might not be played out phenotypically unless the predisposed person is in an environment that supplies alcohol and or in some manner encourages alcohol use (McGue, 1993). A person's genotype might predispose him or her to obesity or to be tall or short, but whether and to what degree the person develops obesity, or how tall he or she become, will be heavily influenced by the nutritional environment. Likewise, high or low intelligence is partly determined by genotype, but the person's phenotypic intellectual development is also heavily influenced by the subsequent learning environment.

As noted, most human characteristics are polygenic and multifactorial, and this also holds true for the major developmental disabilities. Thus, while the focus of the following sections is on genetic and chromosomal factors, bear in mind that the conditions discussed and the resulting degree of impairment depend on a more complicated mix (i.e., they are polygenic and multifactorial).

III. Genetic and Chromosomal Mutations

Genetic material is normally transmitted through cell duplication—mother cell to daughter cell—and from one generation to another. However, DNA material can be mutated, or altered, and transmitted in that altered form. Mutations are sudden changes in DNA material at the gene and/or chromosomal level, and these changes are departures from what is considered the standard form of that material. These changes in DNA can be spontaneous (i.e., naturally occurring through errors in the process of cell replication) or induced (i.e., caused by the application of **mutagens** such as radiation, high temperature, chemicals, and physical trauma). There are several natural mechanisms for correcting such changes in genetic material, but the repair processes do not occur with perfect reliability. Those DNA changes that are not corrected—and are thus passed on to the offspring—are **mutations.**

Of the several types of mutations that can occur, two are of particular interest: gene mutations (genetic defects) and chromosomal mutations (chromosomal anomalies). Gene mutations affect the smallest unit of heredity, the **base pairs** in specific genes. A genetic mutation is a sudden DNA alteration in which changes in one or more base pairs occur, the errors are not corrected by natural mechanisms, and the alteration is inheritable (i.e., can be passed on to the offspring). Several types of base-pair changes can occur such as when a G-C sequence is replaced by an A-T sequence or one or more sequences are lost. There are four major types of gene disorders, and the type depends on whether the affected gene is on an autosome or sex chromosome and whether it is dominant or recessive. The types are autosomal dominant, autosomal recessive, X-linked dominant, and X-linked recessive.

In contrast with genetic defects, chromosomal anomalies affect the organization of one or more whole chromosomes or parts of chromosomes. In both genetic and chromosomal mutations, the alteration can be passed on to the next generation and, depending on other factors such as the dominance or recessive nature of the characteristic and the nature of the child's immediate environment, may be phenotypically expressed in the offspring.

Many of these mutated genetic defects and chromosomal anomalies constitute *pathologies,* which can lead to impairments, disabilities, and handicaps. Genetic and chromosomal mutations are major etiological factors for many birth defects and, thus, for developmental disabilities.

Recall that half of all conceptions are lost early in pregnancy. Most of these losses occur because genetic defects and chromosomal anomalies make the zygote incapable of normal development. Further, those mutations can occur in either the autosomes (the twenty-two pairs in which the two chromosomes in each pair have very similar structure) or in the sex chromosomes (the twenty-third pair where the chromosome pair might or might not be very similar, i.e., either XX or XY). Genetic defects and chromosomal anomalies in conception are common, affecting half of all conceptions. Almost all of these are naturally terminated early in pregnancy, but some do survive and some of the anomalies are passed on to the next generation. An estimated 4000 human disorders have been identified as being linked to specific genes (National Research Council, 1988).

Autosomal Dominant-Gene Defects

Dominant-gene-controlled disorders will be presented only briefly since they do not play a significant role in developmental disabilities. Some disorders can be passed on directly through genetic inheritance if the parents carry and transmit the genes responsible for those disorders. Such inheritance can occur through the transmission of autosomal recessive or dominant genes, and some 100,000 babies are born annually with dominant- or recessive-gene disorders. Of that total of affected births, most are not serious disorders, but about 20,000 babies do have seriously debilitating disorders (Kowles, 1985). According to McKusick (1988), there are more than 2500 known or suspected autosomal dominant-gene defects and an estimated 1500 recessive-gene defects. Scarr and Kidd (1983) estimate that more than 150 gene defects, most of which are recessive, are known to cause mental retardation and other developmental disabilities. The disorders may be detectable in utero, at birth, or may not be manifest until later in childhood or even in adulthood.

At each gene locus on the chromosomes, there are two or more forms of the gene, called alleles. A person typically has two alleles for each gene locus, one from each parent. If the two alleles are the same for that locus, the child is *homozygous;* if the alleles differ—that is, if they are two variants of the gene—the child is *heterozygous.*

When a person carries both a dominant and recessive gene for a characteristic, the dominant gene takes precedence, and those particular characteristics will be expressed phenotypically. If a gene for some disorder is recessive, then if the person also carries a healthy dominant gene on the other chromosome in that pair (i.e., is heterozygous), the healthy gene takes precedence, and the person will not manifest the disorder (it will not be expressed phenotypically). The person will be a carrier and can pass on the recessive gene to his or her offspring. If a disorder is controlled by a dominant gene, then the parent with that gene will manifest the disorder phenotypically. If the person carries one dominant gene for the disorder and one recessive (nondisorder) gene (heterozygous) and the other parent carries only recessive nondisorder genes (homozygous), each child will have a 50 percent chance of inheriting the gene *and* the disorder from whichever parent is affected. There are an estimated 2500 disorders thought to be due to the transmission of dominant genes (McKusick, 1988). However, while dominant-gene disorders are high in number, they are rarely passed on because zygotes with serious dominant-gene defects tend not to survive, and if they do, these persons express the associated pathologies phenotypically and tend not to have children. They may not survive into adulthood or, if they do, are often too debilitated to reproduce. Thus, there is a tendency for dominant-gene defects to disappear gradually from the overall gene pool because they tend not to be transmitted to the next generation. There are exceptions, however. Some dominant-gene-controlled disabilities, such as some types of asthma and sensory disorders like deafness and blindness, do not necessarily impede marriage and/or procreation and are passed on to offspring (see Box 4.1).

Autosomal Recessive-Gene Defects

Recessive-gene disorders are important contributors to developmental disabilities with an estimated 1500 disorders, most of which are not developmental disabilities, attributed to recessive genes (McKusick, 1988). If a person has one recessive gene that is responsible for a disorder, he or she is a carrier, and thus shows no outward signs of disease (i.e., it is not expressed in the phenotype). These disorders are sometimes referred to as "silent" disorders. This person has the normal chance of growing to healthy adulthood and successfully reproducing. If only one parent carries a recessive gene for some disorder (is heterozygous), then the child has one chance in two of inheriting the recessive gene and becoming a carrier but will not manifest the disorder. If both parents carry the recessive gene, the child has one chance in four of inheriting and manifesting the disorder, one chance in four of not being affected, and one chance in two of inheriting one recessive gene and becoming a carrier but not manifesting the disorder. (This is illustrated by the PKU example in Figure 4.1B.) It is estimated that each person carries four such recessive genes. But whether they will be passed on or will cause disability in the next generation depends on genetic chance—the probability that a particular allele will be part of the genetic makeup of the particular ovum and/or sperm that creates the zygote. Most of the serious disorders due to genetic defects are carried by recessive rather than dominant genes. (Box 4.1 lists some of the inherited characteristics related to dominant and recessive genes and some for which the patterns are not yet known). The near universal prohibition against marriage among close relatives is a good safeguard for reducing the probabilities that two parents will each contribute a recessive gene for a serious disorder.

A group of autosomal recessive-gene disorders that cause developmental disabilities have their effects through hormonal disorders, that is, by blocking the body's production of enzymes that are needed for normal functions such as protein metabolism. Because of

---

BOX **4.1**

Some Dominant- and Recessive-Gene-Controlled Disorders

A. Dominant-Gene Traits
   Alzheimer's disease
   Asthma: Some types
   Baldness: Male pattern
   Blindness: Some types
   Blood type: RH negative
   Breast cancer: Some types
   Colon/rectal cancer
   Deafness: Some types
   Dwarfism: Some types
   Finger anomalies: Some types
   Huntington's disease
   Neurofibromatosis: Tumors on neurons

B. Recessive-Gene Traits
   Albinism
   Alopecia: Loss of body hair
   Baldness: In females
   Blindness: Some types
   Blood type: RH positive
   Cretinism: Some types
   Cystic fibrosis
   Deafness: Some types
   Dwarfism: Some types
   Muscular dystrophy (X-linked)
   Phenylketonuria (PKU)
   Sickle cell anemia
   Tay-Sachs disease

Based on Beaudet, et al., (1995); Committee on Genetics, (1996); and Sriver, et al., (1995).

that failure, toxic substances can accumulate in the body and interfere with the proper development of neurological and other systems. These are referred to as "inborn errors of metabolism." Examples of disabilities due to such hormonal disorders controlled by recessive autosomal genes are phenylketonuria, Tay-Sachs disease, sickle cell anemia, cystic fibrosis, and some forms of cretinism (hypothyroid condition).

Phenylketonuria (PKU).   **Phenylketonuria** (PKU) is an autosomal recessive-gene metabolic disorder that, until recently, was a major factor in severe intellectual disabilities, and persons with PKU were institutionalized for life. The condition is now controllable, leading many to believe, erroneously, that PKU is no longer a significant problem. However, we will devote considerable space to it because its history of research, treatment, and prevention illustrates so well the success, complications, and unintended effects that can occur.

The incidence of PKU in white populations (worldwide) is 1 per 10,000. In black populations (in the United States), it is 1 per 50,000 (Yule, 2000; Hofman, 1991). Despite recent advances, its incidence has remained at those levels (Yule, 2000). PKU is the result of over 400 mutations in a specific gene band on chromosome 12 (Yule, 2000). (This large number may partly account for the great variety of clinical signs in these children.) Currently, about one in fifty people (whites) carry the recessive allele for PKU. If only one parent is a carrier, a child will have one chance in two of becoming a PKU carrier (see Figure 4.1A). If both parents carry the recessive gene, then the child still has one chance in two of becoming a carrier, one chance in four of being unaffected, but also has one chance in four of having the disease (see Figure 4.1B).

PKU is one of many metabolic disorders, "inborn errors of metabolism," that are associated with intellectual disabilities. More specifically, it is among the large subgroup of amino acid disorders. Normally, the liver produces an enzyme that is needed to digest phenylalanine, an essential amino acid and a constituent of natural protein found in many foods, including milk (proteins in food naturally contain 4 to 6 percent phenylalanine). Because of the mutated gene, phenylalanine is not metabolized, and the body cannot convert phenylalanine into tyrosine, an important amino acid. As a result, phenylalanine accumulates and becomes converted to phenylpyruvic acid that damages the developing brain and nervous system. It is thought to interfere with the formation of myelin sheaths of brain neurons, although the exact mechanisms or damage is not yet known. As the infant feeds on milk, the phenylpyruvic acid continues to accumulate, compounding its damaging effects.

(A) One parent carries the recessive gene (r).

(B) Each parent carries a dominant (D) and a recessive (r) gene.

FIGURE 4.1   PKU Transmission

A less serious result is due to the lack of tyrosine. Tyrosine is a necessary amino acid that is important in protein synthesis, for producing some hormones such as adrenaline and thyroxin, and for creating melanin, the skin pigment. Lacking the ability to produce tyrosine, persons with PKU must rely on the small amount that is available in food. One result is an insufficient production of melanin, causing many persons to have very light skin color.

PKU creates a tragic condition, as the newborn may be healthy and normal in all other respects. During gestation, the excess phenylalanine passes from the fetus, through the placenta, and is properly converted by the mother, and no damage occurs to the child. But once born and separated from the mother's body, the baby must depend on its own systems that are not adequate for metabolizing phenylalanine, and the phenylpyruvic acid begins to accumulate. The baby appears to be developing normally over the first few months. But silently and invisibly, the toxic buildup continues, and between about the 3rd and 6th month, the child shows signs of developmental delay in motor coordination (e.g., sitting up, rolling over), may become listless or markedly irritable, and may begin to have infantile seizures. It has been estimated that ten IQ points are lost during the baby's first month and another ten by the end of the second month (Fishler, Azen, Friedman, & Koch, 1987; I. Smith, Beasley, & Ades, 1990). The intellectual deterioration continues, resulting in mental retardation. The time of appearance of these problems varies, depending largely on the rate of buildup of the phenylpyruvic acid. Generally, by 4 to 6 months, the parents are aware that their apparently healthy baby is now in serious developmental difficulty. But by that time, permanent damage has already been done.

The damage begins quickly, in the first few postnatal weeks, continues for several years while the immature brain is still developing, and cannot be reversed. The critical period—when potential damage is greatest—begins within the 1st month after birth and continues, with diminishing effects, throughout childhood. A major result is deepening and irreversible brain damage and mental retardation.

In the 1930s, an odor characteristic of some children with intellectual disabilities was traced to a high concentration of phenylpyruvic acid in the urine. Subsequent research determined the buildup occurs because of the lack of the enzyme needed to convert phenylalanine. This disorder was documented by Norwegian researcher Asbjorn Folling in 1934 and named phenylketonuria, or PKU. Later researchers discovered that PKU is genetically transmitted through an autosomal recessive gene. Subsequently, it was determined that the accumulation of phenylpyruvic acid has damaging effects on the brain, and severe intellectual disability results.

In concept, the treatment is straightforward although it is much more difficult in application. When the high concentration of phenylpyruvic acid is detected, the infant can be put on a special diet (first described by Bickel & Hickmans, 1953) of foods that are low in phenylalanine, such as fruits and other milk-free foods. Special milk-free formula is used for infants, and a low protein diet (little cheese, milk, meat, etc.) is prescribed. When that diet is started early, by about 65 days (Dobson, Williamson, & Koch, 1977), and is adhered to and carefully monitored, further damage can be prevented, the retardation can be avoided, and near normal IQ can be achieved. If PKU is detected later in the child's life, the diet should still be applied because there are still benefits (Yule, 2000). Of course, it cannot reverse already present neural damage or mental retardation.

Some amount of phenylalanine is necessary for normal growth of bones and other tissue. Thus, infants on this restricted diet also need phenylalanine supplements, usually in measured amounts of complete natural proteins such as is found in cow's milk.

Because serious damage occurs so quickly, diagnosis soon after birth is necessary so the protective diet could begin immediately. Robert Guthrie, a medical researcher in Buffalo, New York, developed a microbiologic assay to determine phenylalanine levels in the blood of newborns (Guthrie, 1961; Guthrie & Susi, 1963). A few drops of blood are put on filter paper that contains bacteria that grow if phenylalanine is present in excessive amounts. Since 1991, routine PKU testing of infants in the 1st week after birth has been required in all states of the United States and all Canadian provinces (Bellenir, 1996). But because phenylpyruvic acid has often not accumulated in that short time, some states require follow-up testing. In Massachusetts, for example, at 6 postnatal weeks, mothers are given filter papers to be placed on the baby's diaper. The filter paper absorbs urine and is then mailed to a health center for PKU testing. When such testing is routine, virtually all cases of PKU can be detected and treatment begun without delay.

Guthrie's screening procedure has been adopted in many countries and is estimated to have helped prevent over 30,000 cases of mental retardation by allowing early diagnosis and treatment. By any measure, Robert Guthrie, who died in 1995, has made a major contribution to human health.

However, several points should be made about the treatment of PKU. First, successful treatment means that more people with this genetic disorder will become independent, normally functioning adults and will have their own children, thus passing on the recessive genes for PKU. The incidence of this condition, then, may actually increase.

Second, despite successful treatment and prevention of mental retardation, these children are still not completely unscathed. Compared with their parents and their nonaffected siblings, PKU children still have lower IQ (Yule, 2000), display more emotional lability, have greater learning problems (Kopp & Parmelee, 1979), and may display hyperactivity and lower responsiveness to social stimuli (Smith, Beasley, Wolff, & Ades, 1988). It is believed that most of these problems are due directly to the biological condition, but a contributing factor might be differential treatment by parents once they learn of their child's disorder.

Third, it is not a simple task for either parents or children to maintain the low phenylalanine diet. Anyone who has attempted a diet of any kind surely knows the difficulties of self-restriction in a powerfully beckoning world. The diet is very restrictive and difficult to maintain because it is expensive, bland, and uninteresting. There are many appealing but prohibited foods that are high in phenylalanine with which the child comes in contact outside the home or even at home where other family members are not restricted. These foods include milk and milk products such as cheese, ice cream, custards, milk-based sauces, creams, cakes, cookies, and confections. To a child, these restrictions can seem most unfair. Some parents do not understand or even actively reject the importance of maintaining controls. For example, there are cases in which the children were being breast-fed at the time the condition was discovered, but mothers were reluctant to stop nursing (McAbe & McAbe, 1986). Additionally, it may be difficult to convince parents and children of the seriousness of the eventual disorder because those negative consequences are in the future. After all, when a child eats forbidden milk products that everyone else is enjoying, he or she does not become immediately or obviously ill.

Attempts by parents to monitor and control their children's food intake may cause stress that can contribute to the child's emotional and learning difficulties. The problems in restricting the child's diet become even greater as he or she grows older and begins to visit homes of friends and to buy food outside of home. Some popular commercial foods and diet soft drinks contain artificial sweeteners that include phenylalanine. Some of these products responsibly carry warning labels: "Phenylketonurics: This product contains phenylalanine." It is difficult, too, for parents to maintain the diet because they have little guidance, advice, and other professional support to help them.

Fourth, although phenylalanine at abnormally high levels is damaging, a certain amount is necessary for normal development. Thus, the phenylalanine level needs to be carefully monitored and maintained between minimum and maximum levels to make sure it does not rise dangerously high or drop below the minimum needed for normal growth. Blood tests may be required frequently, perhaps twice monthly, and that can be daunting for a child. The necessary phenylalanine has typically been met by prescribed amounts of cow's milk, and care is needed not to give too much. Breast-feeding, originally a problem in PKU as noted, has been successfully used as the source of the needed phenylalanine (McAbe & McAbe, 1986). The treatment for PKU demands a good deal of commitment, understanding, and effort by parents and child to maintain the diet and the optimum blood levels.

Fifth, until recently, dietary treatment was typically suspended in middle childhood. However, children who continue the diet into adolescence have significantly fewer deficits than those who discontinued before age 10 (Potocnik & Widhalm, 1994), and continuation is now recommended *at least* into adolescence. Indeed, the diet should be maintained lifelong (Fishler, Azen, Friedman, & Koch, 1989). In adulthood, the diet may be "liberalized" but not discontinued. This extends by many years the demands of dieting, blood-level monitoring, and self-control. Some adolescents and young adults are now being urged to return to the diets that they had abandoned years before. Unfortunately, compliance with long-term dieting and abstinence of any kind is not very successful. Keeping children, adolescents, and young adults on the diet is a demanding and difficult task. The difficulties in diet maintenance are long-term psychological issues that must be dealt with by the families affected and by the professionals who provide services. Hospitals and clinics generally offer very little guidance in this regard. This is an area where psychological research into families' maintenance of the PKU diet is needed. Research should address the questions of how best to educate parents and children about PKU and how to train them in the self-control skills necessary to maintain the diet adequately.

A sixth issue involves serious problems that can occur when treated homozygotic PKU children become adults of childbearing age. They do not necessarily have intellectual disabilities and are probably living independently and successfully. They may have somewhat lower IQ than non-PKU siblings but still be well above the retardation range. They may be more emotionally labile, causing some minor problems in ordinary living. However, if a person has the condition (i.e., is homozygotic for PKU), no matter how successful the treatment, he or she carries two recessive genes for the disorder.

The effects are much different for males than for females. A homozygotic PKU male who fathers a child will pass on one recessive gene to each child. If the mother has two dominant normal genes (D,D), then each child will have a 100 percent chance of becoming a PKU carrier but will not manifest the disease (see Figure 4.2A). If the mother is a carrier, with one dominant and one recessive gene (D,r) (and the father is PKU homozygotic), then the children will have one chance in two of being a carrier and will also have one chance in two of manifesting the PKU condition (see Figure 4.2B). That is, all children will be either carriers of or will have PKU.

The most severe problems, however, occur when homozygotic PKU women—*even those who had been treated successfully for PKU since infancy and have continued the diet*—become pregnant. The same rates of genetic transmission as noted earlier for the father will occur, but in addition, the children of mothers with PKU (maternal PKU, or MPKU) have extremely high rates of significant intellectual disability (Lenke & Levy, 1980, 1982; Yule, 2000). This occurs *even if the father is not a carrier of the recessive gene and the child has inherited only the one defective gene from the mother.* Despite the fact that this child may be heterozygous, with a dominant, healthy allele, he or she will have a high probability of mental retardation. The major reason is that the mother's abnormal metabolism that is characteristic of PKU—the high levels of phenylalanine and phenylpyruvic acid—creates a toxic intrauterine environment that interferes with healthy fetal development. If the mother resumes her low phenylalanine diet before and during pregnancy, the negative effects will be reduced but not avoided. There is real concern that the very success of diagnosis and treatment that has prevented so much mental retardation might inadvertently result in an increase of retardation in the children of MPKU mothers (Yule, 2000). More research is needed to follow-up successive generations of MPKU children. It is important for routine PKU testing to be carried out with all pregnant women, especially those with intellectual disabilities.

Tay-Sachs Disease.   Tay-Sachs is a fatal autosomal recessive-gene disorder that is the result of a single gene mutation on chromosome 15. It is a degenerative disease, causing progressive destruction of the central nervous system and leading to the child's death by 4 to 6 years of age. Like PKU, it is due to a metabolic disorder transmitted through an autosomal recessive gene. In Tay-Sachs disease, a deficiency of the enzyme *hexosaminidase A* (Hex-A) results in the accumulation of toxic fatty substances in the brain and in other body tissues. It is a tragic occurrence; the child is apparently normal at birth but progressively

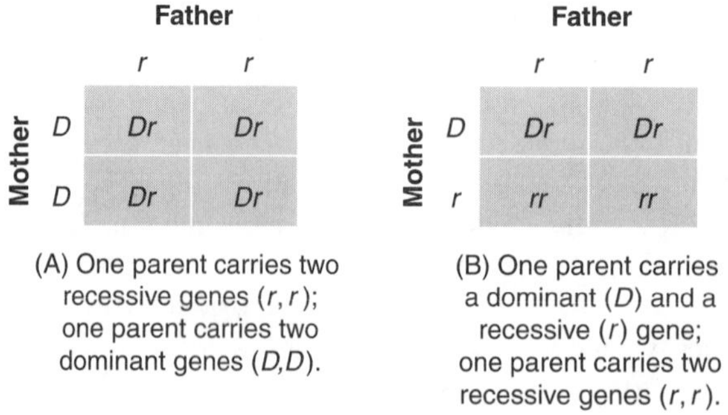

(A) One parent carries two recessive genes (r, r); one parent carries two dominant genes (D,D).

(B) One parent carries a dominant (D) and a recessive (r) gene; one parent carries two recessive genes (r, r).

FIGURE 4.2   PKU Transmission

deteriorates as the nervous system is destroyed. The deterioration is first noted at about 3 to 6 months; the child loses motor abilities, gradually becomes deaf and blind, and dies usually at about 5 years of age, perhaps as late as 6 to 8 years. Words cannot adequately communicate the psychological agony of the parents during and after their baby's brief life. And what of the child? Who can begin to understand the subjective life of the little child who suffers with this condition and comes to realize he or she will soon die?

Tay-Sachs is a rare disorder, occurring in about 1 in every 360,000 pregnancies. But it is much more common among Ashkenazic Jews (about 90 percent of all persons of Jewish descent in the United States) in whom about one in twenty-five persons is a carrier (Bellenir, 1996). Among persons of Jewish descent, the incidence is about 1 per 2500 pregnancies. Prior to the early 1800s, this disease did not exist. The original mutation causing Tay-Sachs occurred in Eastern Europe in the early 1800s among Jewish families and has since been genetically transmitted in this ethnic group. Because it is a recessive-gene defect, it will not tend to disappear from the gene pool.

Prenatal screening through amniocentesis or chorionic villus sampling can detect the levels of hexosaminidase A and thus indicate the possibility of Tay-Sachs disease. Given that information, the parents may want to terminate the pregnancy. Carriers of the recessive gene, both male and female, can be identified even before pregnancy with a blood test because, even if they are apparently normal, they have a lower level of the enzyme Hex-A. Thus, if both parents are carriers, they can be advised that their offspring will have one chance in four of having Tay-Sachs disease, one chance in two of being a carrier of the recessive gene, and one chance in four of being neither afflicted nor a carrier. With that information, parents can decide if they want to conceive, and if they do, they will be forewarned to have the amniocentesis or chorionic villus sampling carried out and to be prepared to make a decision about possibly aborting the fetus. Screening procedures have been effective, at least partly, because they can be readily limited to a relatively small number of prospective parents. As a result, very few babies are now born afflicted with Tay-Sachs disease.

Although carriers of the recessive gene can be identified among prospective parents and the presence of the disorder can be detected in pregnancy, there is no treatment if the person has the disorder (is homozygotic for Tay-Sachs). Unlike PKU, there is no diet or other treatment to reduce its destructive effects. The best help that these prospective parents can receive is through genetic counseling, and they are faced with the hard decision whether to have children or, if pregnancy has occurred, whether to terminate it.

An extremely rare form is *late onset Tay-Sachs disease,* which has only recently been recognized. There are no incidence or prevalence data, and little is known about the disease. Persons with this disorder are usually diagnosed in adolescence. They have very low levels of the enzyme Hex-A and have a variety of muscle control problems, weakness, and muscle cramps. Some with this disorder have been misdiagnosed with other muscular diseases. It is believed that life expectancy is not affected (Bellenir, 1996). As with Tay-Sachs disease, there is no known cure.

There are several other serious autosomal recessive-gene disorders described in the sections that follow.

Sickle Cell Anemia.   This disorder is the most common of several sickle cell diseases (Carroll, 2000), and it is carried by an allele on chromosome 11. It affects hemoglobin, and the red blood cells become distorted into a sickle or crescent shape instead of the normal disk shape (see Figure 4.3). Normal red blood cells are pliable disks, but these affected cells are more fragile and rigid. As a result, they tend to break, clog capillaries, and impede the flow of blood, thereby limiting the transport of blood and oxygen to organs. The resulting oxygen depletion can cause anemia, jaundice, severe abdominal and joint pain, rheumatism, heart and kidney failure, and low resistance to infections. Clinically, the person has recurrent "sickling episodes" (acute illness and often severe pain) that can be treated symptomatically at the time. For a child with sickle cell anemia, the overwhelming experience is pain. Clearly, frequent and/or severe sickling episodes can bring major interruptions to normal school, family, social, and occupational life.

It occurs in about 1 per 600 African American births and is prevalent in populations around the Mediterranean and West and central African areas in which a high occurrence of malaria is found. The children of two parents who are both carriers of the sickle cell anemia recessive gene will have a 25 percent chance of having the disease, a 50 percent chance of being a carrier, and a 25 percent chance of being completely free of the sickle cell gene. If only one parent carries the gene, each child will have a 50 percent chance of being a carrier and a 50 percent chance of being free of the gene. In the United States, it affects primarily African Americans, and it is estimated that about 10 percent of African Americans are carriers (Pierce, 1990).

It has been suggested that sickle cell anemia persists because its allele may provide survival value. As noted, it seems to occur most frequently in areas of high malarial infection. A recent report (*New York Times,* 2000) claimed that each day 3000 persons in Africa, mostly children, die from malaria. In some parts of Africa, 40 percent of the population are carriers (Diamond, 1989). Sickle cell carriers (those having only one affected gene) are less susceptible to malaria because their red blood cells do not support the malaria parasite very well. Therefore, compared with persons without the sickle cell gene, these sickle cell carriers have an advantage in malaria-prone areas of the world. Hence, there is survival value in being a carrier (Pierce, 1990) but not, of course, in having two recessive genes and thus manifesting the disease.

Diagnosis is usually made early, after the child's first 6 postnatal months. As described by Garrison and McQuiston (1988), the disease has a continuum of severity along which children tend to cluster in three ranges. About one-third of the cases are the most severe, suffering anemia and repeated bouts of swelling, infections, fever, and severe pain, requiring frequent hospitalizations. The other children have the same symptoms but at milder intensity and less frequent occurrence. It can be seen that the pain, discomfort, and repeated hospitalizations interfere with normal life pursuits, such as attending school, and can create psychological fears and other problems.

Although usually diagnosed after birth, sickle cell anemia can be detected by about the 10th week of pregnancy. As noted earlier, if both parents are carriers, then any child has a 50 percent chance of being a carrier and a 25 percent chance of having the disorder. A recently reported procedure, however, (Xu, et al., 1999) gives parents information much earlier in pregnancy and more options. Called *preimplantation genetic diagnosis,* this procedure uses ova and sperm from the parents, in vitro fertilization, and genetic examination of resulting embryos. If the embryo is affected with sickle cell, it is discarded; if not affected, the embryo is implanted with the goal of a full-term pregnancy. This procedure has

**FIGURE 4.3   Diagram of Normal Round Red Blood Cells
(left) and the Elongated Sickle Cell Shapes (right)**

been used with other genetic disorders, including Tay-Sachs disease and cystic fibrosis. There are ethical issues in examining embryos and deciding which ones will be allowed to survive and which ones will be discarded.

Newborn screening procedures can identify infants with sickle cell disease before acute episodes occur. While there is yet no treatment for the condition, the sickling episodes can be treated symptomatically, the pain and discomfort eased, and the possibility of fever and infections reduced. Research is exploring medical prevention of the episodes (Carroll, 2000), but general application of prevention is not yet available.

Cystic Fibrosis (CF).   Cystic fibrosis is a chronic disease caused by a recessive autosomal genetic defect located on chromosome 7 (Keren & Rommens, 1990). It is transmitted genetically in the manner of recessive genes (see the earlier discussions of recessive-gene transmission). A surprisingly large proportion of persons—one in every twenty to twenty-five Americans—is a carrier. CF incidence is 1 in 3200 live births in Caucasians, but considerably less in African American, Asian, Hispanic, and Native American populations (McMullen, 2000). It is the most commonly occurring life-threatening disorder of Caucasian children (McMullen, 2000). CF is a progressive disease in which many organ systems, particularly the lungs, can be involved (e.g., liver, pancreas, small intestine, and reproductive tract). There is a variety of symptoms and a wide range of severity, and this variability can cause problems for the early diagnosis of the disease. Three common clinical patterns are seen at the child's first diagnosis of CF: pancreatic dysfunction, sweat gland dysfunction, recurrent or chronic respiratory infections (chronic lung disease). The sweat gland dysfunction results in a high concentration of sodium and chloride in the child's sweat and gives rise to laboratory "sweat testing" for salt as an important diagnostic procedure. The most lethal aspect is the progressive filling of the lungs with mucus, causing severe respiratory distress, eventual lung infection, with relatively early death. CF has long been considered a *terminal disease* of childhood, with a life expectancy of fewer than 10 years. With modern treatment, however, the median longevity is now 30 years with some living into their 40s (CF Foundation, 1997), and it is now classified as a *chronic illness* (McMullen, 2000).

Therapy focuses on treatment of pancreatic dysfunction and lung disease. There is often daily physiotherapy to relieve lung congestion. This includes clap-percussion methods (i.e., carefully presented slaps on the back) and aerosol bronchodilators to open the airways, both of which help clear the lungs of mucus. Treatment typically includes antiviral and antibacterial medication to combat infection. Enzyme treatments and dietary control are often used. There is no cure for CF. However, by the 1980s, with vigorous treatment, survival rates improved so that 90 percent survived past the age of 10 years, 80 percent survived 20 years, and a few reached their 30s and 40s (Rudolph, 1987). As noted, by the mid-1990s, the *median* longevity was 30 years (i.e., there were as many survivors over 30 as there were under 30).

But even with improved survival rates, the quality of life is equivocal. First, treatment slows the progress, provides some relief for the person, but cannot cure the disease. A fairly young death is inevitable.

Second, CF is one of the most physically and psychologically devastating childhood diseases. The treatment is rigorous, frequent (often needed daily), often distressing, and the parents and child know that it is of value for only short-term relief. The child struggles with what for most people is the simplest act—breathing. He or she suffers growth delays, physical debilitation, and weakness. The child cannot engage in much of the normal play with peers and easily develops feelings of despair and fear of a rapidly darkening future. The family is faced daily with the reality of their dying child and his or her often intense suffering. Psychological distress can be intense, and counseling must inevitably devolve into making one's peace with the inescapable outcome and, eventually, processing the grief over the child's death. This is certainly one of the cruelest of childhood afflictions.

Some recent research suggests the possibility that cystic fibrosis might eventually be cured through gene therapy procedures with the fetus (Welsh & Smith, 1995). Larson, Morrow, Happel, Sharp, and Cohen, (1997) using laboratory rats, assumed that the gene responsible for cystic fibrosis is a mutation that prevents the synthesizing of protein that is necessary for healthy lung development. Shortly before birth of the pups with the affected gene, these researchers injected a genetically engineered "therapeutic virus" into the amniotic fluid. The action of this material lasted only a few days but was apparently sufficient to stimulate production of the needed proteins and to "cure" the condition. Whether the procedure holds up in subsequent research or will be effective with humans remains to be determined.

Ironically, the fact that the allele for this fatal disease is carried by a high proportion of persons suggests that, as in sickle cell disease, the heterozygous individual (carrying only one recessive cystic fibrosis allele) may have some kind of advantage. That is, the gene may have some survival value for the species, although it is not yet clear what that value might be.

Cretinism or Hypothyroidism.   This disorder is brought about by several different causal factors, all of which result in an underactive thyroid gland. Its most common forms appear to be carried by a recessive gene, although environmental factors may also be significant. It occurs in 1 to 1.5 per 1000 births (Fryers, 1984). Thyroxin, produced by the thyroid gland, helps control metabolism and general growth. Because thyroxin is deficient in this condition, growth and development are severely retarded virtually from the time of birth. The baby's body is short and stunted, with a relatively large head and a short, thick neck, low forehead, thick lips, protruding tongue, flabby body, and poor skin and muscle tone. The damage to the central nervous system is progressive, and severe mental retardation occurs quickly. In the past, cretinism has accounted for a significant portion of persons institutionalized for mental retardation.

Neonatal screening can detect the condition, and if treatment with thyroxin is started within 10 weeks of birth (Fryers, 1984) and continued lifelong, the most severe damage can be avoided and mental retardation averted. Although it is a treatable condition, there are not yet enough data to inform us of the long-term effects on development or, as in the case of PKU, on future pregnancies and offspring.

X-Linked Genetic Disorders

Genetic mutations occur not only in the autosomes but also in the sex chromosomes. Both hemophilia and Duchenne's muscular dystrophy are X-linked recessive-gene disorders. To avoid repetition of some of the material, these conditions will be discussed in Chapter 5.

IV. Chapter Summary

This chapter has focused on endogenous genetic factors that constitute prenatal etiologies of some of the more common congenital anomalies and developmental disabilities. These prenatal hereditary factors and congenital anomalies account for most of the many types of developmental disabilities. Mutations are uncorrected spontaneous or induced changes in DNA material that constitute variations from the usual or standard form or composition of genes or chromosomes. Many mutations are pathological and constitute hereditary defects that can be in the autosomes or the sex cells, can be dominant- or recessive-gene defects, and can involve specific genes (genetic defects) or whole chromosomes or parts of chromosomes (chromosomal anomalies). When mutations occur at the genetic level, they involve base-pair changes, such as when a G-C sequence is replaced by an A-T sequence or one or more sequences are lost. Genetic defects are associated with many known disabilities, several of which were discussed in this chapter. In the next chapter, chromosomal mutations will be discussed.

KEY TERMS

Know these important terms. Check in the chapter and Glossary for their meanings.
They are listed here in the approximate order of their appearance in the chapter.

Birth defects	Mutations	Sickle cell anemia
Congenital anomalies	Mutagens	Cystic fibrosis
Congenital malformations	Dominant gene	Clap-percussion methods
Endogenous factors	Recessive gene	Cretinism
Exogenous factors	Autosomes	Hypothyroidism
Genetic defects	Sex chromosomes	X-linked recessive-gene
Chromosomal anomalies	Phenylketonuria (PKU)	disorders
Polygenic determinism	Phenylalanine	Base pairs
Polygenic traits	Phenylpyruvic acid	
Multifactorial transmission	Tay-Sachs disease	

SUGGESTED READING

Guthrie, R. (1986). Lead exposure in children: The need for professional and public education. In H. Wisniewski & D. A. Snider (Eds.), *Mental retardation: Research, education, and technology transfer.* New York: New York Academy of Sciences. This is an excellent article by a leading researcher and advocate for prevention.

McMullen, A. H. (2000). Cystic fibrosis. In P. L. Jackson & J. A. Vessey (Eds.), *Primary care of the child with a chronic condition.* St. Louis, MO: Mosby.

STUDY QUESTIONS

4-1. Identify some important endogenous and exogenous etiological factors in birth defects.

4-2. Several concepts discussed so far in this text are important in the origins of a person's phenotype: genetic determination, gene–environment interaction, reaction range, polygenic and multifactorial transmission. Define each and put them together to describe how we believe phenotype is determined.

4-3. Polygenic patterns may be additive, nonadditive, or chromosome linked. What do these mean?

4-4. What are the probable inheritance results for offspring of the following dominant–recessive gene patterns?

One parent has two normal dominant genes; the other parent has one normal and one recessive mutated gene for those particular alleles.

Each parent has one normal and one recessive mutated gene for a particular locus.

One parent has two normal genes at a particular locus; the other parent has one normal recessive gene and one mutated dominant gene at that locus.

4-5. What are some of the common environmental mutagens?

4-6. Distinguish between genetic defects and chromosomal anomalies.

4-7. Explain this statement: Dominant-gene disorders do not constitute significant factors in developmental disabilities.

4-8. Describe the etiologies of each of the following conditions: PKU, sickle cell disease, Tay-Sachs disease.

Endogenous Etiological Factors in Disabilities: Chromosomal Anomalies

This chapter continues the discussion begun in Chapter 4 of endogenous etiological factors in developmental disabilities. These are primarily hereditary factors and include both gene mutations (*genetic defects*), which affect specific base pairs as discussed in Chapter 4, and chromosome mutations (**chromosomal anomalies**), which affect the organization of whole chromosomes or parts of chromosomes. Chromosomal anomalies are the major focus of the present chapter.

One set of disorders—**neural tube defects**—is included at the end of this chapter, although they are not due to chromosomal anomalies. The discussion is placed here because the etiologies stem from events early in pregnancy, and endogenous and exogenous factors—currently unknown—are thought to be involved.

I. Chromosomal Anomalies of the Autosomes

Chromosomal anomalies caused by mutations are defects not limited to specific genes. They involve changes in whole chromosomes, parts of chromosomes, or both. They also involve gains or losses of whole chromosomes in a chromosome pair. Chromosomal anomalies occur in the autosomes and in the sex chromosomes and cause severe problems because they involve missing or extra whole chromosomes or parts of chromosomes or disruptions in the patterns or organization of chromosomes. These mutations can constitute changes in the *structure* of chromosomes and/or in the *number* of chromosomes in what are normally chromosome pairs. Typically, most of these mutated cells do not survive.

Changes in Chromosome Structure

There are four types of mutations that involve changes in chromosome structure (i.e., changes in parts of single chromosomes): deletions, duplications, inversions, and translocations (see Box 5.1). **Deletions** and **duplications** involve changes in the amount of DNA material in a segment of a chromosome. **Inversions** involve changes in the arrangement of a DNA sequence on a chromosome. **Translocations** involve changes in the location of DNA sequences, moving either to other locations on the same chromosome or moving a DNA segment to another chromosome. These errors can occur in autosomes or sex chromosomes, in the egg cell or the sperm, and during meiosis, mitosis, or in early embryo development. If they are fertilized, most of the affected cells do not survive. However, some do survive through birth, and they result in impairments. Of those types of mutations, deletions are particularly associated with some severe developmental disabilities in humans.

Deletions. Deletions are mutations in which some portion of a chromosome is lost due to breaks in the chromosome, thought to be caused by radiation, heat, or toxic substances. The loss of genetic information may have serious effects depending on which chromosomes are affected, how much DNA material is lost, and whether the defect is homozygous or heterozygous. If the defect is heterozygous, the effects may be tempered if the other chromosome in the pair is intact, with its own copy of the missing allele. On the other hand, homozygotic deletions tend to be lethal, and the fetus is generally not carried to birth.

Two human birth defects that are believed to be caused by heterozygous deletions are **cri du chat,** or "cat's cry," syndrome (a deletion on the short arm of chromosome 5) and **Prader-Willi syndrome** (a deletion of a portion of the long arm of chromosome 15). The missing DNA material results in mental retardation and physical anomalies in both syndromes. It is believed that the severity of the conditions is related to how much genetic material has been deleted in each case.

Cri du Chat (Cat's Cry) Syndrome. Because their vocal cords are deformed by the mutation, cri du chat infants have a characteristic catlike mewing sound, hence the name given

BOX **5.1**

Types of Chromosomal Changes

Changes in Chromosome Structure

Deletion: A chromosome mutation involving loss of a DNA segment.

Duplication: A chromosome mutation involving doubling of a DNA segment.

Inversion: A chromosome mutation involving a 180° rotation of a DNA segment.

Translocations: A chromosome mutation involving a change in position of a DNA segment.

Changes in Chromosome Number (Aneuploidy)

Cause

Nondisjunction: A failure of chromosomes to separate during mitosis.

Resulting Condition (Types of Aneuploidy)

Nullisomy: The loss of one pair of homologous chromosomes, leaving the person with twenty-one instead of twenty-two homologous pairs.

Monosomy: The loss of a single whole chromosome from a pair, leaving what should be a pair with only one chromosome and therefore only one copy of each allele.

Trisomy: The addition of a single chromosome to a pair, resulting in a set of three chromosomes instead of the usual pair of chromosomes.

Tetrasomy: The addition of a chromosome pair, resulting in four copies of that type of chromosome instead of the usual two copies.

---

to this disorder. Thought to be due to a partial deletion on the short arm of chromosome 5, this disorder occurs in about 1 per 20,000 births. These babies are generally *microcephalic,* low birth weight, severely mentally retarded, suffer many physical deformities, and have associated congenital heart defects. They characteristically have malformed ears, epicanthic folds, divergent strabismus (poor eye-movement control), asymmetric faces, and short stature. Most die in early infancy, but some survive into adulthood, requiring many years of complete care. As medical care for these babies improves, their survival and the need for institutional care will increase. Amniocentesis and chromosome analyses can detect the presence of the syndrome.

Prader-Willi Syndrome (PWS). This birth defect was first described by Prader, Labhart, and Willi (1956). It is now receiving increasing attention because it is severe, it affects a relatively large number of persons, and Prader-Willi babies usually live into adulthood, thus requiring long-term, specialized care.

   The incidence of Prader-Willi syndrome is 1 per 10,000 to 1 per 25,000 (Alexander & Hanson, 1988; Bellenir, 1996) making it one of the more frequent birth defect syndromes. Males and females are affected equally, and it is not associated with any particular ethnic, social, or geographic groups. Although generally thought to be associated with one or more deletions on the long arm of chromosome 15, there is some discussion that PWS might be controlled by a recessive gene. In the first model, the mutation (i.e., deletion) is a chance event and has little probability of occurring again in the future children of those parents. However, the picture is quite different if PWS is controlled by a recessive gene and if both parents are carriers, which would be true if they have already conceived one Prader-Willi child. Their future children will have one chance in four of having the disorder, one chance in two of being a carrier, and one chance in four of being normal. In either model, the PWS individual can, theoretically, pass the chromosomal defect to future children. However, because of their characteristic poor sexual development, this is not probable.

The etiology is not yet clear, but the phenotypic development has been observed and described in more than 300 cases (Alexander & Hanson, 1988). There is now considerable information on infants and children, and data on longer life-span development into adulthood are now being gathered. The many clinical descriptions of cases leave no doubt that Prader-Willi is a severe lifelong disorder.

There are at least two distinct phases of this syndrome (Zellweger, 1884). The first phase is prenatal and up to about 2 years of age. The Prader-Willi fetus shows low fetal activity, growth retardation, and marked hypotonia (poor muscle tone). At birth, the baby is small, limp (due to hypotonia), and has underdeveloped sex organs (hypogonadism and hypogenitalism) and a weak sucking reflex.

Infancy and childhood are marked by growth retardation, developmental delays, short stature, small hands and feet, abnormal physical weakness, and a characteristic facial formation (almond-shaped eyes, triangular-shaped mouth, narrow face). The child is mildly to severely mentally retarded. Some eventually test within the normal IQ range, but nevertheless, for other reasons, they function at a retarded level. In addition, the Prader-Willi child is *emotionally labile* (unstable) and difficult to raise (Alexander & Hanson, 1988).

Because of the weak sucking reflex, feeding is a major problem for the neonate and parents. Poor nutrition and parental concern and frustration then compound the child's problems. For about the first 2 or 3 years, the parents' major struggles focus around getting their resistant child to eat sufficiently. The babies are often difficult to wake for feeding. When awake, they are unresponsive, listless, have poor head and neck control, and insufficient rooting and sucking reflexes. Because of their poor physical condition, low cognitive functioning, lack of normal weight gain, general growth retardation, and developmental delays, some have been erroneously diagnosed as **failure to thrive.**

At some point, from about age 2 to 5 years, the phenotype undergoes a radical change—presumably as it plays out the genetic blueprint—and the child begins to eat greater quantities of food. By this time, the musculature and coordination have developed somewhat, and feeding activity can be sustained. At first, the parents are relieved but soon recognize that now, in addition to the mental retardation and all of the other developmental problems, the child has developed a major eating disorder. This constitutes the second recognized phase of the disorder, and it remains a major lifelong problem.

By about age 5, Prader-Willi children become compulsive eaters, leading to severe, life-threatening obesity. They are insatiable and, unless closely controlled, cannot stop eating. These children have been described not just as overeaters, but as driven, voracious eaters who engage in virtually continual and often bizarre food foraging and eating. Behavior problems increase and include stubbornness and hyperactivity, aggression, self-injurious behavior, rages, and depression (Alexander & Hanson, 1988). The behavior problems may in part be genetically determined or perhaps are the results of a great deal of struggle with parents over the eating disorder. In some ways, the family life of this child is similar to that of the child with PKU (see Chapter 3), but the Prader-Willi situation may be even more tense and explosive. In both cases, a restricted diet may be imposed, and the child must struggle with the unequal treatment he or she receives compared with that of siblings. The parents' childrearing burdens become oppressively difficult.

As Prader-Willi children grow into adolescence, their divergence from normal youth becomes even more marked. Not only are they cognitively limited, and thus academically and socially impeded, but their grossly evident bizarre eating behavior, their size and body shape, physical weakness, and poor physical skills make normal social interactions and development virtually impossible. The Prader-Willi adolescent can become a social isolate and fail to develop appropriate social skills. To complicate this picture, the failure to develop normal secondary sex characteristics and the continued hypogonadism and hypogenitalism add significantly to the adolescent's feelings of inferiority and personal anxiety. Serious personality problems can develop (Hall & Smith, 1972). In adults, all of these problems continue.

There is no direct treatment for this condition, but increasing knowledge and sophistication among health-care providers have made better management possible. Early diagnosis, which includes genetic screening of the child to search for the chromosomal deletion, is crucial to help parents and pediatricians avoid many mistakes in diagnoses and treatment. Once the correct diagnosis is made, Prader-Willi management includes:

> Parent education and counseling aims to help parents understand the nature of the disorder and probable course of their child's development, access appropriate agencies and support groups, and avoid the common tendency for destructive self-blame.

> Detailed planning for dietary and nutritional management is critical and includes behavioral training for the family and child to learn how to control overeating behavior. This is important to avoid the early obesity which, if left uncontrolled, results in much more intractable eating control problems later.

> Special academic, social, and recreational programs are needed for skills development. In many cases, full day-care or even residential institutions are necessary.

> Psychological counseling and cognitive-behavioral therapy and training for the Prader-Willi child are used to teach self-control of eating behavior, tantrums, and aggressive outbursts. For the adolescent, counseling around issues of sexuality is important.

> Occupational training such as in sheltered workshops must focus on the special needs of Prader-Willi youth and adults. It would be destructive, for example, to place this person in an inappropriate job-training program in a cafeteria, with its easy access to food.

> Community-residential and possibly institutional-residential programs are needed for long-term living.

Problems in middle and old age have not yet been sufficiently investigated, but special needs will become apparent in those periods, too.

In recent years, a number of all-year residential programs and special summer camps specifically for Prader-Willi individuals have been developed in the United States. Every state has child advocacy and protection agencies, and many (perhaps most, by now) have information on Prader-Willi syndrome and its management. The Prader-Willi Syndrome Association provides information for parents and professionals. Greenswag and Alexander (1988) have written an excellent book on the management of the syndrome.

Although there is no direct treatment for PWS, the syndrome can be managed (as just discussed) and can be predicted through prenatal screening of the pregnant mother. If the deletion on chromosome 15 is detected in fetal cells, the parents can be counseled that the fetus, if brought to term, has a high probability of being PWS.

Duplications, Inversions, and Translocations.   Duplications are mutations that involve a chromosome segment being doubled. This can occur with small or large segments, and clearly, the normal amount of genetic information is significantly altered.

Inversions involve the removal (excision) of a chromosome segment that is then reintegrated into the chromosome but inverted 180 degrees. The result is a significant reordering of the genetic sequence on the chromosome.

Translocations are the transferring of some portion of one chromosome to a different chromosome. When that occurs, the number of chromosomes remains the same (i.e., twenty-three), but one chromosome will have some portion of its original structure replaced by a portion of the other chromosome, constituting an abnormal chromosome. The additional material might constitute, for example, a partial trisomy. If this were to involve chromosome 21 and the fertilized cell survived and developed, then a variation of Down syndrome will occur. It is estimated that 3 to 4 percent of cases of Down syndrome are due to translocation.

Changes in Chromosome Number (Aneuploidy)

The loss or addition of one or more whole chromosomes or chromosome pairs is called **aneuploidy,** and it occurs during mitosis or meiosis. There are four types of aneuploidy, one of which (trisomy) is particularly important for human developmental disabilities. The brief descriptions (see Box 5.1) are for only one occurrence of the condition, but they can involve more than one chromosome or more than one pair of chromosomes. For example, in a double monosomy, there has been a loss of one whole chromosome from each of two pairs.

Most aneuploid anomalies of the autosomes have such serious effects that the cell or zygote ordinarily does not survive. However, some trisomies do survive to birth, but most of those have a short postnatal survival. Trisomy 13 (Patau syndrome) occurs rarely, in only about 1 of 15,000 live births; trisomy 18 (Edwards syndrome) occurs more frequently but is still rare, about 1 per 7500 live births. In both conditions, the babies are severely mentally and physically disabled and die within 3 to 6 months.

Trisomy 21, however, survives at a much higher rate, occurring in about 1 in 700 live births, and it is the only one of the autosomal trisomic conditions in which people survive into adulthood. This condition, also known as **Down syndrome,** accounts for a large proportion of persons with mental retardation, and it will be discussed in some detail. But before describing the condition, let us consider how trisomies develop.

If an extra chromosome should occur in an otherwise normal pair so there are three instead of two chromosomes (a trisomy), the extra genes—an increase of about 50 percent over the normal number—may have an impact on the child's development. Similarly, in the case of a missing chromosome (monosomy), the reduction of genetic material in that pair of some 50 percent will also have a devastating effect. However, as noted earlier, autosomal monosomic zygotes are not viable and are naturally terminated very early in pregnancy.

Causes of Aneuploidy

Most trisomic and monosomic conditions arise as a result of errors that occur during meiosis. Recall that meiosis is the reductive cell division process that forms the gametes or sex cells, in which diploid cells split to produce the haploid ovum and sperm (i.e., the matured ovum or sperm carries only one chromosome of each pair). During meiosis, several errors can occur and cause chromosomal anomalies. These errors leading to trisomies include **nondisjunction, translocation,** and **mosaicism.**

Nondisjunction.   Nondisjunction is an error that occurs during meiosis in which the homologous chromosomes in a cell fail to separate and therefore remain as a pair of chromosomes. Let us suppose that this error involves chromosome 21 in the female cell. The female gamete that is produced will have two, rather than the usual one, chromosome 21. If in the process of fertilization this female gamete with two chromosomes at 21 unites with a normal sperm with one chromosome 21 (a true haploid cell), then the resulting zygote will have three instead of two chromosomes for chromosome 21 (i.e., a *trisomy 21*). This condition is designated as 47,XX,21+ or 47,XY,21+ to indicate the abnormal total number of chromosomes (forty-seven instead of the normal forty-six), whether the sex cell carrying the extra chromosome is the ovum (XX) or sperm (XY), and the number of the chromosome pair in which the third chromosome appears (in this case, 21). Most trisomies occur in meiosis of the ovum, but some also are produced in sperm meiosis. The extra genes of that third chromosome apparently account in some as yet unknown ways for the characteristics of Down syndrome. It should be noted that occurrence of a nondisjunction does not mean that particular mother has more chance of repeating it than any other mother of equal age—that is, when age is taken into account, having one Down syndrome baby does not increase the probability of having another. As we will see in the discussion of Down syndrome, age is a crucial factor, as older women have a greater chance of producing a Down syndrome child.

When such errors produce monosomy or result in missing parts of chromosomes, zygotes that might result are usually not viable and are expelled early in pregnancy. This is probably because the missing DNA material leaves the zygote with insufficient material to develop properly. Trisomies, with their extra genetic material, also fail at a high rate. It is estimated that 75 percent of trisomy 21 zygotes are naturally aborted (Polani, 1966), but some 25 percent do survive. (Trisomies have the highest rate of survival of all these anomalies.) Thus, even though trisomies fail at a high rate, there will be many that continue to birth, presumably because they are not missing information that is necessary for continued development. As a result, some trisomies survive through birth, but very few monosomies survive. One exception is Turner syndrome (discussed later), a monosomic condition in which the person does survive prenatal development.

Overall, relatively few zygotes with chromosomal anomalies survive to birth and ever reach reproductive age. Those that do survive are typically severely impaired. A major category of mental retardation, Down syndrome, is associated with a trisomy of the twenty-first chromosome pair (trisomy 21). Currently, there are forty-three known chromosomal disorders associated with mental retardation, including nine autosomal trisomic conditions (American Association on Mental Retardation, 1992).

Nondisjunction is involved in Down syndrome and in several X-linked disabilities as discussed later. Translocation and mosaicism are additional chromosomal errors, and they will be included in the following discussion of Down syndrome.

Down Syndrome (Trisomy 21)

Trisomy 21 is one of the most frequent genetic causes of intellectual disability, with an incidence of about 1 per 800 live births (Lashley, 1998). This rate varies sharply according to the age of the mother, ranging from 1 per 2000 for mothers in their early 20s to 42 per 1000 live births for mothers over 45 years of age (Hecht & Hook, 1996; see Table 5.1). Although the reason for this age difference is not clearly understood, one hypothesis is that the higher rate is related to the aging of the ova. Unlike males, who begin to produce sperm in adolescence and continue to do so throughout adulthood, women have all of their ova when they are born. That is, by birth, their total number of egg cells (several hundred thousand) will have already been produced. These ova then mature and complete the process of meiosis over a number of years beginning at puberty. Maturation of the ova occurs with puberty and later, but the cells are as old as the woman. A 40-year-old woman who conceives a child must do so with forty-year-old ova. This might contain the reason for the higher rate of trisomy 21 as women grow older. It may be that biochemical changes with age may affect the ova stored so long in the ovaries. The father's age is also related to Down syndrome, but there is not as high a correlation as with mother's age. Some research has indicated that as much as 24 percent of Down syndrome conceptions involved a sperm cell rather than an ovum that carried the extra genetic material (Fuhrmann & Vogel, 1983). Thus, the aging processes in both men and women may affect the germ cells, with a disproportionate effect for women.

Another hypothesis (Epstein, 1995; Jacobs & Hassold, 1995) suggests that older women are less likely to abort spontaneously when there is a non-normal zygote, such as a trisomy. They will carry to term at a higher rate than will younger women.

It is interesting that some recent data indicate that most Down syndrome babies in developing countries are being born to younger mothers despite their lower risk for Down syndrome. The reason, it is suggested, is that in developing countries improved prenatal screening and counseling of older women and the increased use of safe elective abortion have reduced the rates of Down syndrome births in the older groups.

Some research suggests that Down syndrome is also related to the father's exposure to environmental toxins found in many work settings such as farms with fertilizers and pesticides and paint shops and factories where solvents and heavy metals are found (Olshan, Baird, & Teschke, 1989). These findings are still only suggestive, and much more research is needed to determine the possible paternal contribution to Down syndrome etiology.

Prenatal screening for Down syndrome is carried out between about the 14th and 16th week of pregnancy (second trimester) using amniocentesis or chorionic villus sampling.

TABLE 5.1   Increased Rates of Down Syndrome as Maternal Age Increases

Maternal Age at Birth and Incidence of Down Syndrome

15–19	1/2400 births
20–24	1/1500
25–29	1/1125
30–34	1/715
35–39	1/220
40–44	1/63
45–49	1/18

Based on Fryers, T. (1984). *The epidemiology of severe intellectual impairment: The dynamics of prevalence.* London: Academic Press.

More recently, a blood serum test has been developed that is less invasive and can be carried out before the 14th week of pregnancy (Haddow, 1998).

Down syndrome occurs in several forms, all of which are related to some abnormality of chromosome 21. A specific chromosome band has been identified, which means that it is not necessary to replicate the entire chromosome for Down syndrome to occur (Nehring & Vessey, 2000). Most cases of Down syndrome (95 percent) have an extra chromosome 21 (i.e., trisomy 21). About 94 percent of these are due to nondisjunction (described earlier). About 75 percent of nondisjunction occurs during meiosis of the ovum and about 25 percent in the sperm (Fryers, 1984). Although a good deal is known about the processes of nondisjunction in the etiology of Down syndrome, little is yet known about the conditions that cause nondisjunction to occur in the first place. When research provides that information, the potential for prevention of Down syndrome by reducing the factors leading to nondisjunction will be considerably advanced.

Translocation and Mosaicism in Down Syndrome.   While the majority of Down syndrome cases (about 94 percent) result from nondisjunction, about 3 percent result from translocation and the remaining 3 to 4 percent involve mosaicism. In translocation, during meiosis some material from chromosome 21 breaks away and either becomes attached to some other chromosome or is incorrectly reattached to chromosome 21 (e.g., the severed top of the chromosome might become reattached at the bottom). In mosaicism, it is thought that an error occurs not during meiosis but during mitosis early in embryonic development (i.e., after conception has occurred). The result is that only some of the body cells exhibit trisomy, while another proportion does not. The degree of severity of Down syndrome involving mosaicism is related to the proportion of body cells with trisomy. Thus, an affected person might show only some of the usual signs of the disorder and have less severe retardation or even have normal intelligence.

Clinical Characteristics of Down Syndrome.   As noted by Nehring and Vessey (2000), the condition we now call Down syndrome was first described by Esquirol (1838) and in 1866 was named "Mongolian idiocy" by Langdon Down (Down, 1866) who propounded an ethnic-based model of mental retardation. That label was later discarded in favor of Down syndrome. Beginning with those early descriptions, persons with this syndrome were viewed as severely limited intellectually, incapable even of simple understanding and learning. They were seen as congenitally in poor health and as having a very short life span. It is no surprise, given those expectations, that immediate institutionalization was prescribed for these babies. As discussed later, those expectations and treatment have undergone revolutionary changes in recent years.

Virtually all children with Down syndrome have intellectual disabilities, with IQs ranging from about 25 to 50. Indeed, Down syndrome is still the most common cause of mental retardation in the moderate range (Hickson, Blackman, & Reis, 1995), and therefore, children with Down syndrome have limited academic potential. Some range as high as 70; a few, perhaps 4 percent, can learn to read.

There are fifty physical clinical features of Down syndrome that can be identified at birth (Nehring & Vessey, 2000), but not all are expressed equally or appear in every child. Among the most common physical characteristics are a short, stocky stature, an unusually rounded head, an enlarged tongue, a small nose, a "simian crease" (i.e., a characteristic skin crease straight across the palm instead of being curved), broad, short hands and fingers, visual impairments, and generally poor muscle tone.

Several other disorders are not immediately apparent, including congenital heart defects, hypothyroidism, an abnormally high risk for leukemia, and metabolic and immunological problems that result in high susceptibility to many infections. Earlier in the twentieth century, children with Down syndrome had a life expectancy of fewer than 10 years. However, this has improved markedly since the 1970s. Herr and Weber (1999a) reviewed life-expectancy estimates and reported that life expectancy for persons with Down syndrome was *9 years* before 1929 and rose to 60–64 years by 1996.

Before about 1930, with such short lives, there was little expectation that these children could develop personally and socially, and they were given little opportunity to do so. Their mental retardation combined with low expectations by others and their very truncated lives, which gave them little time to grow and develop, assured their inadequate development. Their obvious physical features made diagnosis possible at birth. With such negative and restricted expectations held by society, with poor prognoses for the children, and because the obvious physical features made diagnosis possible immediately at birth, parents were typically advised to institutionalize their children quickly—before they became "too attached" to them. Parents were warned that the demands of caring for such children who were literally doomed to short, unhealthy, and unhappy lives could have disruptive effects on the whole family. As a result, many children with Down syndrome were sent away to specialized residential settings and state schools where the expectations were no better. There they languished, were not stimulated and guided, had few supports for personal, social, or occupational development, were crowded into situations where airborne and contact diseases were easily communicated, and died, as expected, at very young ages. The history of treatment of persons with Down syndrome shows the operation of iatrogenic effects of treatment that were discussed in Chapter 1.

I recall a neighbor who gave birth to a Down syndrome child in the early 1950s. The unfortunate label then used locally was Mongolian idiot. Those parents successfully resisted intense pressures from their doctors, social agencies, school, church, and relatives and insisted on caring for their son at home with the family. Their adamant stand in the face of tradition and strong and continued pressure required great commitment and bravery. Their obdurate rejection of all advice was a neighborhood scandal at the time. The child was maintained at home under the care of his family, and he attended special schools and training programs. That family was considerably ahead of its time as it practiced, in a very real sense, normalization for their child. That man with Down syndrome is now almost 50 years old, lives in a group home in his familiar neighborhood, enjoys a social life with friends, often visits his brothers and sisters and their families, and has worked many years as a custodian's assistant in a local business. He handles much of his own wages, buys things he wants (going to the movies with a friend is a favorite of his), and has a savings account. What would his life now be like had his parents accepted the advice given them half a century ago?

The care of children and the lives of adults with Down syndrome today are vastly different compared with just two generations ago (i.e., the 1940s) largely due to effective advocacy. Our society's view of persons with Down syndrome, our expectations of their longevity, their potential for growth, our social acceptance, and our provision of a range of supporting systems constitute a true humanitarian revolution.

Our modern approaches are organized around the expectations of a long life, the belief in optimum development through normalization, and the willingness to guarantee human rights and privileges and to provide necessary *lifelong* social supports. The thrust is to provide the supports to enable parents to maintain their children in as normal a family and learning situation as is possible and to help them and the child work toward the greatest degree of autonomy and achievement possible for that person. A lifelong outlook also means helping the transition from the family to other living settings such as group homes, from dependence to as much autonomy as is possible, and from birth into middle and old age. It also means a society that is sensitive to and ready to assist in the changing demands on this person as he or she matures into the 50s and 60s.

Children with Down syndrome are diagnosed by amniocentesis or chorionic villus sampling before birth or, at latest, at birth. This enables immediate professional steps to be taken, including parental counseling and guidance that will continue as long as is necessary and medical steps (surgery, diet, medication) as determined in each specific case. These initial steps are taken to improve the child's immediate and long-term health and longevity and to start the family on a path toward the child's optimal development.

Normalization is stressed at home, in preschool programs, and in school. Social skills training and personal self-control can be focused on in special classes, applying systematic cognitive-behavioral approaches. While special classes and activities may be necessary to a greater or lesser degree depending on the child, mainstreaming as much as possible is sought to ensure normal social contacts and experience. Each youngster is taught academic skills to his or her abilities and is involved in as much normal social activity as possible.

For older adolescents and young adults with Down syndrome, the focus of their education and training remains within the normalization principle and emphasizes preparation for transition from home, to more autonomy, and to occupational success. Classes, workshops, and on-the-job training become important. Eventual job placement and maintenance of occupation are now major goals. At this time, the person (and the family) is helped in the transition away from home to a more autonomous setting. Supports are provided to help this person maintain employment, live in cooperation with others, develop and maintain friendships, and in general, to experience a "normal" and rewarding life. This is a far cry from the institutionalization ethic of not too long ago.

As persons with Down syndrome approach middle age (40s and 50s), many display signs of **dementia** that are similar to those in **Alzheimer's disease** (Kolata, 1985). Dementia is a severe impairment in thinking, problem solving, or memory (Davies, 1988). It characteristically involves progressively more pronounced forgetfulness, loss of concentration, rambling speech, and confusion. In later stages, the person with dementia may pose severe danger to himself or herself and to others by failing to turn off stove burners, leaving home and becoming lost, refusing to stop driving their cars, and so on. In Alzheimer's disease, there is a marked loss of memory for once familiar faces, names, and people, among other problems.

Postmortem examinations of brain tissue show a heavy development of anomalies— "plaques and tangles" in the cerebral cortex of Alzheimer's patients (Roth, Wischik, Evans, & Mountjoy, 1985). Further, the amount of those tissue anomalies is highly correlated with the patient's intellectual impairment. Could there be brain-tissue similarity between the Alzheimer patients and the older persons with Down syndrome who were showing signs of dementia? Malamud (1964) carried out postmortem brain examinations of institutionalized persons with mental retardation, and a striking observation was made: Of those who were not Down syndrome, about 14 percent showed tissue anomalies—plaques and tangles—that were similar to those found in Alzheimer patients. However, of the persons with Down syndrome, nearly 100 percent showed the degeneration consistent with Alzheimer's. Perhaps the two disorders share some chromosome 21 genotypic characteristic. More research is needed.

Children born today with Down syndrome are expected to be still-functioning adults in the year 2060! Indeed, there is the expectation that, with continued health advances, longevity will be even greater (see Table 5.2). Our support programs must therefore assume this long-term, full-life view and continue to improve and provide lifelong services. Perhaps by that time, genetic research will have resulted in applied methods to reduce or even to avoid completely the occurrence of Down syndrome. In the meantime, of course, there will still be children born with Down syndrome, and our agencies must be prepared to provide the needed supports.

TABLE 5.2   Estimates of Life Expectancy for Down Syndrome

Year	Down Syndrome	All M. R.	All Devel. Disabilities
1929	9 years	20 years	(no estimates)
1980			58 years
1986	47 years		
1996	60–64 years		70–74 years

Data for this table are from Herr, S., & Weber, G. (1999). Aging and developmental disabilities: Concepts and global perspectives. In S. Herr & G. Weber (Eds.). *Aging, rights, and quality of life: Prospects for older people with developmental disabilities.* Baltimore, MD: Paul H. Brookes.

II. X-Linked Genetic Defects
and Chromosomal Anomalies

Thus far, this and the previous chapter have discussed genetic defects and chromosomal anomalies of the autosomes, but genetic and chromosomal defects can also occur in the sex chromosomes. When they do, the major disturbances are in the person's sexual development and not necessarily in motor or cognitive functioning. Sex chromosome defects and anomalies make only a relatively small contribution to developmental disabilities, while a larger proportion is contributed by defects in the autosomes. That is, children with sex chromosome disorders are not as severely disabled as, for example, those with trisomy 21 or with PKU. Mental retardation that occurs in sex chromosome anomalies is usually at mild rather than severe levels. In general, humans can tolerate anomalies in the sex chromosomes more readily than they can in the autosomes. This may be in part because the two chromosomes of the autosomes are much larger and carry more genetic information than do the sex chromosomes. Thus, distortions such as nondisjunction and translocation of the autosomes may disrupt a larger portion of gene-controlled functioning.

There are some 160 known sex-linked chromosomal defects, most of which occur in males. This sex disparity might be due to compensating processes that reduce the negative effects of additional X chromosomes in females, but there are no compensating mechanisms for the Y chromosome (P. J. Russell, 1994). Some of the sex chromosome anomalies are described briefly in the two groups, genetic defects and chromosomal anomalies.

X-Linked Genetic Defects

Hemophilia.   Hemophilia is an X-linked recessive-gene disorder in which the allele for blood clotting normally carried on the X chromosome is lacking. As a result, the protein antihemophilic globulin (AHG), which is needed for normal blood clotting to occur, is not produced. Hemophilia occurs in 1 to 3 per 10,000 male births but is rare in females. The Y chromosome does not contain the allele for blood clotting, so if a boy inherits the recessive allele from his mother, there will be no compensating allele for blood clotting available. For a female to have the disease, she must have two affected genes, one from the father and one from the mother, and this occurrence is rare. Women who are heterozygous for this allele are carriers of hemophilia, and they can pass on the recessive gene to daughters and sons. Fathers with the disease cannot pass on the allele to their sons because they contribute the Y chromosome to their sons and the defect is on the X chromosome only. These fathers, however, can pass it on to their daughters who can then be carriers and then can pass it on to their sons or daughters. Thus, hemophilia cannot pass from father to son, but can pass from father to daughter, to grandsons and granddaughters, and from mother to sons or daughters.

In hemophilia, blood clotting does not occur normally, and severe, possibly fatal, bleeding can occur from injuries. Even minor cuts can be serious. The hemophiliac easily bruises and bleeds excessively if injured. Hemophilia can be diagnosed prenatally, and the parents can be appropriately counseled.

Muscular Dystrophy.   This constitutes a group of degenerative diseases affecting primarily boys and occurring in about 1 of 3500 male births. Duchenne's muscular dystrophy is one type for which some genetic information has been found. The recessive gene for Duchenne's muscular dystrophy is carried on the short arm of the X chromosome. Because boys have only one X chromosome, there is no correcting or compensating allele available, and the disease appears in the phenotype. For a girl to suffer Duchenne's, she would have to be homozygotic, with the recessive Duchenne gene carried on each of the two X chromosomes. Duchenne's muscular dystrophy is age-related and appears in children between the ages of 2 and 5 years. This is a progressive disease resulting in muscle atrophy and loss of locomotion by about age 10 to 12 years. Death usually occurs before adulthood. About a third of the boys afflicted with Duchenne's are mentally retarded. There is no cure for the disease, and the progressive weakening as the child grows older, with the knowledge of the unavoidable result—early death—makes it a particularly devastating disorder for the child and his family.

X-Linked Chromosomal Anomalies

Klinefelter's Syndrome.   Klinefelter's syndrome (47,XXY) has an incidence of 1 per 500 to 1000 live-born males. The condition is caused by nondisjunction in meiosis of the ovum resulting in a female gamete with two X chromosomes. If that gamete is fertilized by a sperm carrying a normal Y chromosome, then a trisomy of the sex chromosome results, XXY. Because of the XY combination, these persons are male, but the extra female chromosome results in reducing some male characteristics and in adding female characteristics. They have small male genitalia, often have enlarged breasts, and have the overall body contours and slim, long legs of a female. Problems that often accompany Klinefelter's include diabetes and scoliosis (an abnormal spine curvature). As youngsters, they tend to be more compliant than most boys and often have behavior problems. Their feminine physical aspects become more apparent at puberty, and it is then that most are diagnosed. Treatment with androgen, a male hormone, can help stimulate the development of secondary sex characteristics but cannot alter the essential condition. They are usually sterile and have low-normal intelligence, with about 20 percent having IQs of less than 80. Like trisomy 21, this trisomic condition occurs more frequently in births by older women. Prenatal amniocentesis and chorionic villus sampling can detect the presence of the syndrome.

Turner's Syndrome.   Turner's syndrome (45,XO), caused by nondisjunction of the male gamete in meiosis, is a monosomic condition of a female in which the second X chromosome is missing. It occurs in about 1 of 10,000 female births (P. J. Russell, 1994). The person usually has a short neck with excess skin folds at the back giving a "webbed" appearance, short fingers, and short stature. At puberty, secondary sex characteristics do not develop because of the lack of female hormones, and these women do not reproduce because they are sterile. Estrogen treatment can help to improve their appearance and stimulate secondary sex characteristics (Baer, 1977) but cannot alter their basic condition or reverse their sterility. Although they are not usually mentally retarded, those with Turner syndrome do have learning problems, are socially immature, and often have problems in social relationships (McCauley, Ito, & Kay, 1986). Interestingly, girls with Turner syndrome develop feminine personalities and interests despite their genetic characteristics and lack of female hormones (McCauley, Kay, Ito, & Treeler, 1987). Turner syndrome can be prenatally diagnosed with amniocentesis or chorionic villus sampling.

Triple X Syndrome. This disorder (47,XXX) occurs in about 1 of 1000 female births (P. J. Russell, 1994) which to all appearances are normal. At puberty, persons with triple X syndrome develop female secondary sex characteristics. They have somewhat lower than normal intelligence but are not typically mentally retarded. There have been cases of females with as many as five X chromosomes, with associated greater levels of retardation.

Super Male Syndrome. The super male syndrome (47,XYY) is seen in about 1 of 1000 male births (P. J. Russell, 1994). These males have an extra Y chromosome that results from nondisjunction of the Y chromosome during meiosis, and later fertilization of a normal ovum with one X chromosome creates the trisomic condition, 47,XYY. The 47,XYY male is tall, below average in intelligence, although not necessarily mentally retarded, and has personality problems. As children, these boys are often aggressive, defiant, and hard to manage. In adolescence, it is common to find sexual problems and antisocial behavior. In the 1980s, it was suggested that the 47,XYY condition might explain a significant portion of highly aggressive, violent criminal behavior in men, but subsequent research has not supported that hypothesis (Schiavi, Thelgaard, Owen, & White, 1984).

Fragile X Syndrome (fra X). This disorder (fra X) is thought to be second to Down syndrome in prevalence of chromosome anomalies that account for mental retardation (Spitz, 1994), and it occurs equally in all tested ethnic groups (Sherman, 1996). In the MR population, there are 25 percent more males than females, and it was hypothesized that X-linked genes may be responsible. The fragile X syndrome was identified as accounting for much of that difference (reviewed by W. T. Brown et al., 1986, and Goldson & Hagerman, 1992). Fragile X has a high prevalence with an overrepresentation of males (16 to 26 per 100,000), and the prevalence for females is about half that rate (De Vries, B. B. A., van den Ouweland, & Mohkamsing, 1997; Murray, Youings, & Dennis, 1996; G. Turner, Webb, & Wake, 1996). In fragile X, the X chromosome has a narrowed, pinched, weakened, or breaking point near its lower end. As reviewed by Hagerman (1996, 2000), a *fragile X mental retardation-1* (fmr-1) gene was discovered in 1991 and identified as responsible for the chromosomal condition. It is thought that this gene effectively silences ("turns off") related protein production. It is the lack of the protein that presumably causes the fragile X condition. Depending on the extent of the mutation, a range of problems from mild cognitive and emotional problems to severe mental retardation can result. Because fragile X was recently discovered and has a variability of phenotypes, most persons with fragile X have probably not been diagnosed (Hagerman, 2000).

When fragile X occurs in females (XX), the negative effects can be partly compensated for by the other X chromosome with its healthy alleles. However, this does not completely nullify the effects, as about a third of the females have intellectual impairment, but most of those are at moderate levels. The effects on intelligence are more severe for males because when fragile X occurs in males (XY), there is no compensating healthy X chromosome as there is in females. Nearly half of the males with fragile X syndrome have severe levels of intellectual disability, about 30 percent have mild to moderate levels of retardation (W. T. Brown et al., 1987), and only about 13 percent have IQs above 70 and are not considered retarded. Reasoning and abstract ability are affected, and because of their impulsiveness, they cannot focus long on learning tasks. In school, they manifest many learning problems, speech delays, and language deficiencies. Because academic demands increase with grades, their cognitive functioning and tested IQ may actually decrease (Goldson & Hagerman, 1992). Clinical observations suggest that the fragile X youngster is easily influenced by the immediate environment, including the behavior of peers. One result may be that foul language seems easily adopted by the youngster and often occurs in an explosive manner, as if prompted by some uncontrolled speech pressure. These observations need more verification. Although fragile X does not affect females as severely, it is still a significant contributor to mental retardation in females.

Behaviorally, there is a high occurrence of hyperactivity, attention problems, aggressive outbursts, emotional problems, and a spectrum of autisticlike functioning. Unlike autistic children, however, the fragile X child is interested in relating to others. Many researchers have found a link between fragile X and autism (e.g., Largo & Schinzel, 1985) and have suggested that fragile X may be the most common biomedical cause of autism (W. T. Brown et al., 1986; Hagerman, 1996). (Autism will be discussed in more detail in Chapter 10.)

Fragile X males are fairly normal in appearance and can usually pass casual inspection in most groups. However, there are three major physical indications, one or more of which may occur in fragile X males: a long and narrow face, prominent, large ears, and enlarged testicles (Hagerman, 2000). More subtle indications include a small distance between the eyes and a large-circumference head. The facial characteristics are often difficult to detect before puberty in males but become more pronounced later (Hagerman, 2000). Orthopedic problems, joint laxity, hypotonia, and middle-ear infections are common in fragile X children. Signs of neurological disorder are "soft" rather than pronounced, and seizures may be associated with the condition.

The fragile X condition can be detected through amniocentesis and chromosome testing. If it is found, the parents can be counseled, trained, and helped to provide a good developmental environment. The fragile X baby, with cognitive and physical limitations, muscular weakness, poor attention, and hyperactivity, may be quite difficult to raise, and parents may erroneously attribute the various problem behaviors to a negative "willfulness." Thus, parent training, counseling, and assistance can be very important. Indeed, the parents' active involvement in the efforts to help the child toward more control and better functioning may be critical. This condition cannot be reversed, but a good deal can be done to help the youngster function better. Physical therapy, speech therapy, and special high-structure academic programs are important. Behavior therapy to teach better self-control and cognitive-behavioral therapy for reducing impulsive behavior and improving organized thinking and problem solving may be effective. Parent behavioral training is also recommended. In schooling, it is advisable to seek as much mainstreaming as possible, but other special approaches, as just noted, are also needed. Genetic counseling is important because fragile X can be passed on generation after generation, and this information may be important to a family.

III. Neural Tube Defects (NTDs)

A discussion of neural tube defects (NTDs) might be misplaced in this chapter on chromosomal anomalies because the latter are not known to be major etiological factors in NTDs. Both endogenous and exogenous factors are thought to contribute to this class of severe physical and neurological disorders (i.e., there is a multifactorial etiology), but the specific etiological factors are yet not clearly known. Neural tube defects occur in about the 4th week of pregnancy, but the etiologies for these defects may have occurred long before then. The incidence of NTDs varies across time and place, occurring in about 1 to 3 per 1000 live births in the United States (Harmon, Hiett, Palmer, & Golichowski, 1995). The occurrence in embryos is much higher, but the defects are so severe that most do not survive to birth. Those who do survive are severely disabled with some combination of physical, neurological, cognitive, and motor impairments, and many die as infants.

Recall that the first 2 months of pregnancy are the period of *organogenesis,* when rapid development of the body organs occurs. By the beginning of the 3rd week, the zygote has differentiated into three layers of cells. These are the ectoderm, or outer layer (from which the outer skin, brain and spinal cord, and peripheral nervous system develop); the mesoderm, or middle layer (circulatory system [heart, blood], skeleton, muscles, etc.); and the endoderm, or inner layer (lungs, stomach, intestines).

As was noted, NTDs occur early in pregnancy, in the 3rd and 4th weeks, before most pregnant women even know they are pregnant. At the start of the 3rd week, from the cells of the ectodermal layer, the embryo begins development of what will become the central nervous system—the spinal cord and brain. Cells at one end of the 15-day-old embryo grow rapidly, their two small bulges defining the cephalic end of the embryo and constituting the beginnings of brain development. A groove, which is the beginning of the spinal cord, is open along nearly the whole length of the barely 5-mm-long embryo, from cephalic to caudal end. Within a few days (around the 18th day of pregnancy), the groove closes, first at the cephalic end and then shortly after at the caudal end. It folds over and closes, creating the neural tube within which the spinal cord and its protective vertebrae will develop. This enveloping structure will also enclose the heart, lungs, and other organs that are beginning to develop.

During this period, cells for the brain and spinal cord are developing rapidly, and a primitive heart begins to flutter. Arm and leg buds and the beginnings of the urogenital system appear, and blood vessels start to develop in the 4th week. These 3rd and 4th weeks, with their rapid developments, define a critical and sensitive period, particularly for central nervous system development. Any interruptions or problems at this time can have serious effects on development and ultimate function.

One major difficulty that can occur is the failure of the neural tube to close properly. The reasons for such failures are not known in each case, but it is suspected that exogenous factors such as chemicals (drugs), maternal illness, and serious malnutrition during the 3rd and 4th weeks may be responsible (Cockcroft, 1991; Holmes, 1992). For example, it is thought that high fever of the mother during the 18th to 30th day might constitute high enough body heat to kill developing cells, disrupting neural tube and early brain development and causing severe brain, spinal chord, and other deformities. Some of the disabilities resulting from neural tube defects are anencephaly, spina bifida, and hydrocephaly. Severe mental retardation is associated with all of these conditions, although it does not occur in all cases of spina bifida and hydrocephaly.

Anencephaly

Prior to the 1970s, anencephaly occurred in about 1 to 2 of 1000 live births in the United States. Worldwide, all neural tube defects occurred at about the same rate. As will be discussed, the U.S. rate declined from 1970 to 1990 to about 0.6 per 1000 live births (Yen et al., 1992).

Anencephaly can result if failure to close properly occurs at the cephalic end of the neural tube, thus interfering with development of the brain. It is a severe cerebral malformation in which a large portion of the brain, scalp, and cranium are absent—literally, "lack of a brain." The condition can be diagnosed early in pregnancy with chemical indicators (i.e., an elevated maternal blood serum alpha-fetoprotein, AFP, in routine prenatal screening examinations). Follow-up ultrasonography is used to confirm the tentative diagnosis. Both maternal serum AFP screening and ultrasound examinations became widely used in the 1970s. In some hospitals, virtually all cases of anencephaly since then have been diagnosed prenatally (Limb & Holmes, 1994). When anencephaly is diagnosed, the parents can be counseled regarding aborting the fetus. Even though about half of these children can survive birth, most of the cortex is missing. The children cannot perceive most stimuli, will never learn to think, remember, recognize people, play, laugh, develop language, learn social or academic skills—in short, they will lack virtually everything that makes us human. These babies cannot long survive naturally and will usually die within a few weeks after birth. But heroic efforts with special equipment and around-the-clock monitoring and care can keep some of these babies alive, perhaps for several years. There have been cases of parents who, knowing their fetus is anencephalic, still insist for personal/religious reasons on bringing their child to term rather than terminating the pregnancy. In such cases, a difficult personal and ethical question is obvious: In the best interests of the child, parents, and society, should this pregnancy be terminated?

Limb and Holmes (1994) reviewed the cases of anencephaly in a Boston hospital from 1970 to 1990. Until about 1970, half of these children were born alive after a full-term or near full-term pregnancy. By 1990, because of routine prenatal diagnoses at that hospital, 100 percent were electively aborted. The current incidence of anencephaly in that facility is zero. Cuckle (1995) reports that the incidence at birth of all neural tube defects in England and Wales from 1970 to 1990 declined by 95 percent due primarily to prenatal diagnoses and elective terminations.

Thus, the technology exists to eliminate anencephaly. However, as reported by Cragan et al. (1995), from 1985 to 1993, there was considerable geographical variation in how routinely prenatal screening and ultrasonography were used to diagnose anencephaly and spina bifida. As a result, elective pregnancy terminations for anencephaly ranged from 20 percent in Arkansas to 69 percent in Hawaii; terminations for spina bifida were less frequent, ranging from 3 percent in Arkansas to 29 percent in California. When these screening and diagnostic procedures become more uniformly used, all parents affected will have the option of elective termination. In those situations using prenatal diagnoses, it is rare for parents to decide to continue a pregnancy once the prenatal diagnosis has been made.

Spina Bifida

Spina bifida may result if the failure to close occurs at the caudal end of the neural tube. Because of the incomplete closure, there remains an opening in the neural tube, and the spinal cord may develop abnormally, even protruding through the child's back (see Figure 5.1). The neural tube defects involve not only the spinal cord itself but may also involve the surrounding or overlaying spinal cord tissues—the meninges, vertebral (neural) arch, muscles, and skin. Spina bifida occurs when the neural arch (the bony arch enclosing the spinal cord) is defective. Literally, spina bifida means a failure of the lateral halves of the vertebral arches to fuse. In severe cases, body functions that occur below this level of damage, such as locomotion, are impaired, and paralysis of the legs may occur. Associated damage might also have occurred in heart development and possibly to other internal organs; thus, the child may also have serious heart, bowel, and other problems.

Meningocele is the condition in which the spinal cord defect allows a portion of the meninges, covered by a layer of skin, to protrude, forming a cystic sac filled with cerebral spinal fluid. As shown in Figure 5.1B, this condition does not include protrusion of the spinal cord. Neurological problems typically occur.

Myelomeningocele, a more severe type of meningocele, includes protrusion of the spinal cord (see Figure 5.1C). In this condition, hydrocephaly is virtually always present, and the neurological problems are more severe because the spinal cord itself is involved in the pathology.

The developmental effects on the child are widely variable, from lethal conditions to minor anomalies that have no clinical significance (Moore & Persaud, 1993) depending on the severity of the damage and the speed with which treatment is applied. (It is thought that very mild spina bifida conditions exist in many adults who function perfectly well and are not even aware of the condition.) Severe mental retardation occurs in at least 10 percent of cases (Fryers, 1984). The neural damage is not reversible, but surgery just after birth can help to stabilize the child and slow, but not completely prevent, further damage (Abel, 1989). Until recently, children with the most severe levels did not survive into adulthood, but with improved care, the life span is increasing. The disability is lifelong.

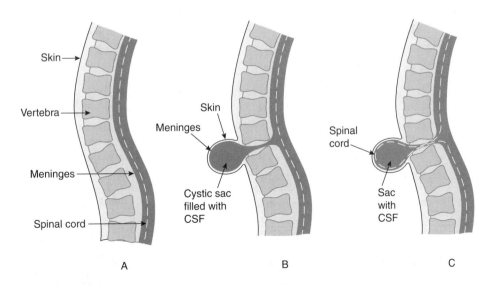

FIGURE 5.1   Diagram of a normal spine (A), meningocele (B), and myelomeningocele (C).
(B) and (C) illustrate the cystic sac filled with cerebrospinal fluid (CSF).

Hydrocephaly

Water or fluid around the brain (hydrocephaly) is also associated with neural tube defects. Normally, the brain is surrounded by cerebrospinal fluid, which naturally is able to drain out to keep its level in proper balance. However, due to developmental problems such as neural tube defects, the cerebrospinal fluid does not drain properly. This causes excess fluid to accumulate around the brain, creating pressure on the brain and skull, and resulting in an enlarged head (macrocephaly) and brain damage. Severe mental retardation results. The excess fluid can be drained off surgically, but the effectiveness will depend on how early the condition is diagnosed, how early the treatment is started, and the degree of severity of pathology. It is thought that early treatment, which is even possible in utero, can minimize the brain damage and the resulting mental retardation.

Microcephaly

The pressure of the growing brain on the malleable soft portions of the fetal skull and fibrous connective tissues results in the expansion of the calvaria (the cranial vault) in order to encompass the increasing brain size. Under some conditions, including genetic and chromosomal factors, environmental toxins, radiation, drug and alcohol abuse, and infectious conditions such as rubella and toxoplasmosis, the brain fails to develop. If the child is carried to term, most of the body, including the face, is of normal size. However, the brain, calvaria, and thus the exterior skull are abnormally small. This condition is known as microcephaly (small head). Because of the abnormally underdeveloped brain, these children are invariably severely mentally retarded.

These conditions can be detected in utero through prenatal screening and ultrasonagraphy, and the parents can be provided with counseling about elective abortion. Women who have a history of children with neural tube defects are at higher risk for subsequent neural tube defects, and screening early in the second trimester is usually recommended (Fryers, 1984).

Prevention of NTDs

It was noted that prenatal screening procedures such as AFP, ultrasound, and amniocentesis can identify a large proportion of NTDs. If these conditions are diagnosed in time, parents may want to terminate the pregnancy. More recently, research has found that the administration of **folic acid** (a water-soluble B vitamin) for a month prior to conception and for 3 months after can prevent a significant proportion of NTDs (a risk-reduction of 60 to 80 percent has repeatedly been shown; Farley & Dunleavy, 2000). In 1992, the Public Health Service recommended for all women of childbearing age a daily intake of 0.4 mg of folic acid. This can be obtained through vitamin supplements of synthetic folic acid (e.g., a multivitamin containing 0.4 mg of folic acid) or by maintaining a diet that includes foods with natural folic acid. These include green, leafy vegetables (e.g., spinach), beans (lentils, black beans), asparagus, citrus fruits and juices (e.g., orange and grapefruit juice), liver, and nuts (e.g., peanuts and peanut butter). The term *folic* is from the Latin *folium* (i.e., foliage such as green, leafy vegetables).

The dietary approach is a simple, effective, and low-cost prevention for severe disabilities. Unfortunately, it is not yet generally known by women of childbearing age, and some will needlessly give birth to children with severe NTDs. Since January 1, 1998, The

Food and Drug Administration has required folic acid enrichment of all fortified grain products (fortified bread, flour, corn meal, rice, and breakfast cereals). This is a good example of enlightened public action for primary prevention, and it might significantly reduce these severe birth defects. NTDs can be virtually eliminated, at least in developed countries. This can be brought about if sufficient folic acid is taken by women of childbearing age (which would significantly reduce the incidence of NTDs), if prenatal screening for NTDs becomes routinely used to diagnose those that do occur and if those pregnancies were then terminated. As is the case so often, enlightened public policy can bring about significant improvement in public health; whether such policies are developed and maintained depend on politics.

IV. Chapter Summary

This chapter has focused on endogenous chromosomal factors that constitute the prenatal origins of some of the more common developmental disabilities. Chromosomal anomalies are mutations that affect whole chromosomes or parts of chromosomes by altering the structure of single chromosomes or the number of chromosomes in a pair. A major cause of altered chromosome structure is a process called deletion in which some portion of a chromosome is lost. Other mutations (duplication, inversion, and translocation) can also occur. In all of these mutations, the effects can be significant because of the changes in genetic material (i.e., adding or deleting genetic information or in other ways altering it). Examples of developmental disabilities caused by deletions are cri du chat and Prader-Willi syndromes.

Nondisjunction is a major process in aneuploidy (changes in chromosome number) causing a gain or loss of chromosomes in what is usually a pair. Translocation and mosaicism are other processes. Trisomy 21 (Down syndrome) is an example of a major developmental disability caused by nondisjunction.

Genetic defects (i.e., base-pair alterations) and chromosomal anomalies occur in both the autosomes and the sex chromosomes. In sex chromosome mutations, the major disabilities involve sexual development, but in some types of disabilities, such as fragile X syndrome, other problems, such as mental retardation, also occur.

Neural tube defects (NTDs) are among the most severe birth defects, but they can be prevented with adequate diet. Further, amniocentesis can identify a fetus with NTD, and the parents can be counseled regarding termination of the pregnancy. Prenatal screening by amniocentesis and chorionic villus sampling can detect the presence of many of these disorders.

KEY TERMS

Know these important terms. Check the chapter and the Glossary for their meanings.
They are listed here in the approximate order of their appearance in the chapter.

Chromosomal anomalies	Inversions	Failure to thrive
Neural tube defects	Translocations	Aneuploidy
Deletions	Cri du chat syndrome	Nullisomy
Duplications	Prader-Willi syndrome	Monosomy

Trisomy	X-linked	Anencephaly
Tetrasomy	Hemophilia	Spina bifida
Nondisjunction	Muscular dystrophy	Meningocele
Translocation	Klinefelter's syndrome	Myelomeningocele
Mosaicism	Turner's syndrome	Hydrocephaly
Down syndrome	Triple X syndrome	Microcephaly
Alzheimer's disease	Super male syndrome	Folic acid
Dementia	Fragile X syndrome	

SUGGESTED READING

Jackson, P. L. & Vessey, J. A. (2000). *Primary care of the child with a chronic condition.* St. Louis, MO: Mosby. Presents more detailed coverage of the conditions discussed in this chapter.

Greenswag, L. R., & Alexander, R. C. (Eds.). (1988). *Management of Prader-Willi Syndrome.* New York:

Springer-Verlag. These chapters provide detailed clinical examples and discussions of Prader-Willi syndrome, its causes and management.

Russell, P. J. (1994). *Fundamentals of genetics.* New York: HarperCollins. Provides a full discussion of mechanisms of chromosomal anomalies.

STUDY QUESTIONS

5-1. Genetic defects and chromosomal anomalies are etiological factors in developmental disabilities. Do you understand what these are?

5-2. Explain, as if to a student, how neural tube defects occur, what forms they take and why, and what the associated phenotypic characteristics are.

5-3. Chromosomal deletions are involved in creating trisomies such as Down syndrome. What is the process of deletion and how can it result in *extra* chromosomes?

5-4. Describe the development of Prader-Willi syndrome. Why would there have been confusion of this with failure to thrive?

5-5. What is the current thinking on the reason(s) for the association of Down syndrome with maternal age?

5-6. Think this through: What are some major implications of the vastly increased life expectancy of persons with Down syndrome?

5-7. Explain what X-linked disorders are and why they might occur more frequently and more severely in males than in females.

5-8. If you were in charge of developing a program to prevent NTDs, what would you include?

6 Exogenous Etiological Factors in Disabilities: Prenatal Origins

I. Prenatal Environmental Factors in Birth Defects

While more than 80 percent of all live births in the United States are healthy, slightly less than 20 percent have some pathology. Most of those anomalies, about 14 percent of total births, are so mild as to be of no clinical significance. The remaining 6 percent have discernible disorders at birth, but only about half of these, 2 to 3 percent of total births, have serious structural defects (Moore & Persaud, 1998), most of which lead to developmental disabilities (see Table 6.1). Some defects become known only later, and the proportion of known malformations increases in early childhood (Table 6.2).

TABLE 6.1   Major Malformations at Birth

Incidence of Organ Malformation

Brain	10:1000
Heart	8:1000
Kidneys	4:1000
Limbs	2:1000
All Others	6:1000
Total	30:1000

Table reprinted from Moore, K. L., & Persaud, T. V. N. (1998). *The developing human: Clinically oriented embryology* (6th ed.). Philadelphia, PA: Saunders. Page 183. Reprinted with permission.

Chapters 4 and 5 discussed endogenous etiological factors in developmental disabilities that are of genetic/chromosomal origin. There are also **exogenous** factors of environmental origin that affect prenatal and postnatal development. Note in Box 6.1 that the etiologies of 50 to 60 percent of developmental disabilities are not yet known. That percentage should decrease as research continues. As we will discuss later, the unknown causes may be evenly divided between genetic and environmental factors. This chapter focuses on environmental factors and begins with a discussion of **teratogens.**

Controlled human experiments that directly assess the effects of suspected teratogens on child development are impossible to carry out. Ethical constraints prevent researchers from meeting the requirements of controlled experimental studies, such as administering measured doses of suspected teratogens to pregnant women in order to measure what damage occurs to the mother and/or child. Because true experiments of drug effects on pregnancy cannot ethically be carried out on humans, this experimentation is done with laboratory animals. Most human research, however, is **correlational** rather than **experimental,** assessing the extent to which substance exposure is associated with negative outcomes.[1] Correlation research requires large samples of participants and access to already existing data such as measurements of toxic substances in the environment. In the case of

TABLE 6.2   Rate of Structural Anomalies Diagnosed in Early Childhood

	Approximate Cumulative Percentage
Diagnosed at birth	3%
Diagnosed by 2nd year	6%
Diagnosed by 5th year	8%

Information for table from: Moore, K. L., & Persaud, T. V. N. (1998). *The developing human: Clinically oriented embryology.* (6th ed.). Philadelphia, PA: Saunders.

BOX **6.1**

Factors in Developmental Disabilities

Prenatal and Postnatal Factors

1. Genetic/Chromosomal (Endogenous Factors)
2. Environmental Factors (Prenatal, Exogenous)
   a. Teratogens
      Infectious Disease
      Drugs, Including Medications
      Environmental Hazards
   b. Other Maternal Conditions
      Maternal Malnutrition
      Stress/Emotions
      Maternal Age
   c. Oxygen Deprivation
   d. Physical Trauma
3. Environmental Factors (Birth and Postnatal, Exogenous)
      Childhood Illness
      Oxygen Deprivation
      Brain Infections
      Physical Trauma
4. Low Birth Weight and Premature Birth
5. Unknown Factors (these account for 50 to 60 percent of all developmental disabilities)

---

drugs, retrospective questionnaires are used, asking participants what substance, how much they had used, and when and for how long that use had occurred. Research on illicit drugs has additional problems in obtaining valid and reliable information from participants who may be reluctant to admit illegal behavior. Even if they are willing to provide information, they do not know the exact concentrations of the drugs used, the precise amounts taken, or the exact number of doses in any given time period. Further, there may be unmeasured interactive effects of multiple drug use and/or the presence of contributing factors such as nutrition or prenatal health care. Assessing the effects of teratogens on human pregnancies, especially at low dosage, is difficult because of the uncontrolled variability in virtually all of the factors that need to be measured. Despite those problems, researchers and policymakers must draw conclusions and set policies based on the available research information.

II. Teratogens

Teratogens are environmental factors that invade the uterine environment, affect cells and tissues, and disrupt the development of the embryo or fetus. Teratogens include chemicals, metals, x-rays and radiation, disease organisms, or viral infections. Other factors, such as maternal age, stress, malnutrition, and physical trauma, may also harm prenatal development. These are often discussed as additional teratogens, but this book treats them separately.

There are four main results or **endpoints of teratogens:** (a) death of the embryo or fetus (abortions and miscarriages), (b) malformation in births (birth defects), (c) fetal growth deficiency and/or premature births, and (d) postnatal functional problems (including cognitive deficits and behavioral and psychosocial problems). Some teratogens have specific effects on particular organ systems, and they produce a limited array of characteristic birth defects. Others, such as alcohol (i.e., ethanol), can lead to all four endpoints and thus have a broader spectrum of effects.

The severity of teratogenic effects in humans depends not only on (a) the nature (i.e., the type and concentration) of the teratogens but also on (b) the particular organ system that is affected and (c) its level of development at the time the teratogen is introduced. The embryo and fetus are subject to teratogenic effects throughout gestation. However, the time of greatest vulnerability for the most serious damage is during approximately the 2nd to the 16th week (the embryonic and early fetal periods) when organogenesis is occurring and organ systems are at their highest rates of development. As summarized by Moore and Persaud (1998),

> During the first two weeks of development, teratogenic agents usually kill the embryo or have no effect, rather than cause congenital anomalies. During the **organogenetic period,** teratogenic agents disrupt development and may cause major *congenital anomalies.* During the fetal period teratogens may produce morphological and functional abnormalities, particularly of the brain and eyes. (p. 196)

Teratology (from the Greek *terat,* meaning "monster") is the study of birth defects caused by teratogens. Teratogens have been recognized throughout human history, but controlled research is recent. In the 1960s, for example, thousands of babies were born with arm and leg deformities. By examining the mothers' pregnancy histories, it was discovered that thalidomide, a new sedative prescribed to control morning sickness in the first trimester, was the cause (thalidomide will be discussed in more detail later).

It had been thought that the developing child is superbly well protected in the uterus, where it is suspended in fluid and surrounded by maternal tissue. It was also believed that the placenta is a highly efficient organ that filters out virtually all toxic substances. But now we know that many pathogenic substances can reach and affect the embryo or fetus. These substances cross the placenta, perhaps because their molecules are small or they are in highly concentrated forms (Samuels & Samuels, 1986). In addition, radiation and physical shocks can affect the fetus directly, without going through the placenta.

Teratogens have always been present in the environment as naturally occurring substances and conditions such as lead and mercury, high heat, and radiation. Today, there is a justifiably increased concern about teratogenic threats because of the millions of tons of new chemical compounds that are being poured annually into the environment. The placenta may have no natural ability to control many of them. People are ingesting more medications and illicit drugs than ever before, and the environment is more replete with chemical compounds in our food, water, air, and in common products such as paint, cleaning substances, and cosmetics. The research task of determining which of these substances may be teratogenic is massive and perhaps ultimately impossible because new compounds are being created each year by a huge chemical and manufacturing industry.

Most discussions of teratogenic effects involve the three endpoints with a prenatal or perinatal focus (i.e., embryo or fetal death, growth retardation, and birth defects). These emphasize physical abnormalities. The fourth endpoint, functional aberrations, has a postnatal focus on the child's behavioral, intellectual, and emotional functioning. The study of the functional endpoints is a specialized area, **behavioral teratology,** which is the study of damage by teratogens to the brain and central nervous system and their effects on the child's functioning after birth and during the early years (Voorhees & Mollnow, 1987).

Numerous psychological problems of childhood are associated with teratogens. These conditions include intellectual disabilities, hyperactivity and attention problems, aggression, and social skill deficiencies. Teratogens and the resulting tissue damage may contribute to childhood psychological disorders that have traditionally been attributed to emotional or psychosocial etiologies. In what proportion of the cases of childhood psychopathology might teratogens operate and to what degree of influence are important issues yet to be determined by research. When children display psychological problems, one of the alternative etiological hypotheses—now rarely considered—is the influence of teratogens.

Principles of Teratogenics

Several principles of teratogenic effects are summarized here, based on the discussions by Voorhees and Mollnow (1987) and J. G. Wilson (1977).

1. *There are two main routes of access by teratogens to the uterine environment, and these routes depend on the nature of the teratogenic agent* (the principle of **target access**). First, teratogens such as radiation (one of the most invasive and potentially damaging teratogens), ultrasound, and some microwaves can move directly through maternal tissue and enter the uterine environment essentially unchanged. Other physical agents, including extremes of temperature and physical impact, can also affect the maternal body but are not transmitted directly to the conceptus. Instead, the mother's body has homeostatic responses that help to change the agent, such as reducing temperature and absorbing some or all of the force of physical blows, thus ameliorating the potential effects on the embryo or fetus.

Second, teratogens also occur in the form of chemical agents, and these reach the fetus by being carried across the placenta in maternal blood. The concentration of the chemicals that reach the fetus depends on many factors, including the maternal dose of the substance, the rate of absorption of the chemical into the maternal bloodstream, and the operation of maternal homeostatic responses that reduce the blood concentrations of the teratogens. Thus, chemicals entering the mother's body may or may not reach the fetus in sufficient concentrations to cause defects.

2. *Susceptibility to teratogens varies with genotype.* There are variations between species and among individuals within a species in the response of an embryo or fetus to a teratogen (the principle of **genetic determination**). For example, thalidomide was prescribed partly because in research on laboratory rats it had negative effects only at high dosages.

The human doses, however, were small, and therefore, thalidomide was thought to be safe. It was later realized that the human species, compared with rats, is far more susceptible to thalidomide at low dosages. Genotypic differences between individuals within species also contribute to susceptibility. Thus, a substance might have negative effects on some children but not on others, depending on genetically influenced vulnerability to the agent.

   3. *Susceptibility varies with the developmental stage at the time of exposure* (the principle of **critical periods**). The greatest teratogenic effects occur during more immature stages of the organism when the highest rates of developmental activity are occurring. Teratogenic effects in the first 2 weeks of pregnancy result mainly in prenatal death. Therefore, birth defects are not typically a result of teratogens that operate during this very earliest period of pregnancy. Most major abnormalities and birth defects due to teratogens occur during the 2nd through 16th gestational weeks involving the embryo and early fetal periods. During this time, major organ development occurs at rapid rates, and thus, much more (and more basic) developmental activity is interfered with.

   Organ systems develop at different times and rates. Thus, there are variations in when critical periods occur for particular organ systems. For example, as represented in Figure 6.1, teratogens can cause major anomalies in the central nervous system through about the 18th to 20th gestational week, but major limb anomalies are most probable in about the 4th to 6th weeks. Thus, thalidomide, when taken during this approximate time, can create severe limb anomalies, but taken earlier or later will have little or no effects on limb development.

   4. *There are several mechanisms through which teratogenic agents act on specific cells and cause deformities in organ systems.* Various environmental factors can stimulate cell and tissue changes and alter their development. Teratogens can cause changes such as genetic mutations and chromosomal anomalies (e.g., breaks and nondisjunctions). They can interfere with mitosis and cause enzyme inhibition and changes in nucleic acid.

   5. *There is a dose-effect relationship of teratogenic agents and resulting impairments.* Once a teratogen gains access to the fetus and its critical threshold is reached, its effects are related to the dosage. A small dose might have little effect, an intermediate amount might disrupt the development of specific organs, and a high dose might cause embryo death. Generally, the more the pregnant woman smokes or drinks alcohol or the higher the doses of drugs, of radiation, and so on, the more severe will be the effects.

   6. *The endpoints or final results of teratogens are death, growth retardation, malformations and birth defects, and functional disorders.* These endpoints depend on many factors such as the type of teratogenic agent, the developmental level of the organ system, the genotype of the individual, and so on. Each endpoint may be reached by a variety of teratogens, and because of interactions with other factors, the same teratogen will not always result in the same endpoints.

   7. *Some teratogenic effects might not appear until long after birth* (the principle of **delayed effects**). Many effects of teratogens are apparent at or immediately after birth, as in observable birth defects. However, the effects of some might not become apparent until much later. A classic example is the teratogen diethylstilbestrol (DES), a synthetic estrogen used to prevent miscarriages. It was used from the 1940s through the 1960s. An effective

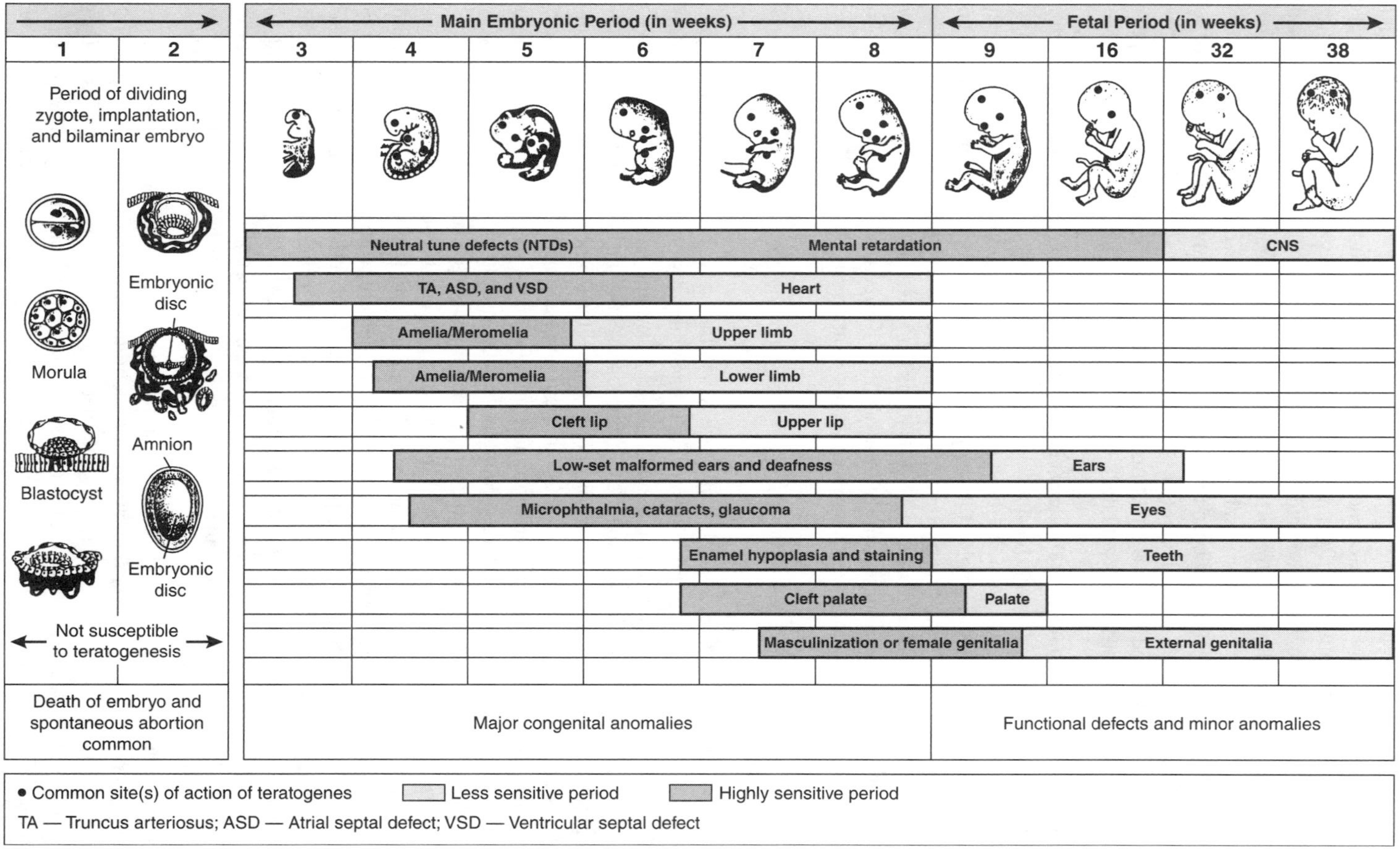

FIGURE 6.1 Critical Periods in Human Development

From: Moore, K. L., & Persaud, T. V. N. (1998). *The developing human: Clinically oriented embryology.* (6th ed.). Philadelphia, PA: Saunders. Reproduced by permission.

and safe medication, it protected the pregnancies of many women who had suffered earlier miscarriages. But when the children reached adolescence or adulthood, its teratogenic effects were recognized. Daughters of women who had been treated with DES showed higher than normal vaginal structural abnormalities, vaginal and cervical cancer, and increased risks of miscarriages and premature births during their own pregnancies. DES illustrates the possible delayed effects of some substances and suggests that the number of known teratogens may be underestimated because the effects of some might not be seen prior to or at birth. Other examples of delayed effects are juvenile paresis, caused by the mother's infection with syphilis, and a herpes infection (cytomegalovirus), both which might appear later in childhood (these are discussed later).

8. *The* functional endpoints *of teratogens are impaired cognitive, behavioral, and emotional (i.e., psychological) functions.* This is the principle of behavioral teratology (see the previous discussion). It is assumed that only those teratogenic agents that adversely affect the central nervous system are involved in the production of psychological anomalies. The focus is on the child after birth and during early psychosocial development.

Teratogens will be discussed under four headings: infectious disease and drugs in Chapter 6, and environmental hazards and maternal conditions in Chapter 7.

Infectious Disease

An infectious disease involves a number of processes in the body: invasion of microorganisms and their multiplication in body tissues, cellular injury resulting from toxins and/or from abnormal cell multiplication, and the normal defensive antigen-antibody responses to the invasion. The invading microorganisms causing disease may be bacteria, viruses, protozoa, or parasites. These organisms exist commonly in the environment, and anyone, including pregnant women, can come in contact with them and become infected. Infections can invade any body tissues, including the brain and spinal cord, of the mother or child, both prenatal and postnatal. If not effectively countered by the normal defenses of the body or by timely medical treatment, serious and even permanent damage can result.

The proportion of all developmental disabilities that can be attributed to infectious diseases is difficult to estimate. In one attempt, Iivanainen and Lahdevirta (1988) studied 1000 cases of mental retardation and concluded that 11 percent were clearly attributable to infectious disease alone and another 1.6 percent were due to infectious disease in combination with other etiological factors. Of those cases attributed to infectious disease (126 of 1000 cases), most of the infections occurred perinatally or postnatally (82 percent) and 18 percent occurred prenatally (i.e., as a result of teratogenic effects). They reported that the major prenatal infections were toxoplasmosis, rubella, influenza, and syphilis (these are discussed later).

They found that the cognitive deficits resulting from the various infectious diseases were very pronounced—just over 63 percent of the children were profoundly retarded (IQ less than 20) and 22 percent were severely retarded (IQ 20–35). Epilepsy was also diagnosed in 61 percent of these cases of mental retardation and cerebral palsy in 46 percent. The authors concluded that infectious diseases may account for a significant proportion of severe to profound mental retardation (about 12–13 percent) and other developmental disabilities. In theory at least, all of these are preventable—for example, vaccination programs to prevent rubella and influenza and timely treatment for syphilis and toxoplasmosis. *Any infectious disease in a pregnant woman can create problems for the mother and child.* Several infectious diseases of particular concern in pregnancy are summarized in the sections that follow.

Rubella. **Rubella** or congenital rubella syndrome (CRS), also called German measles and 3-day measles, is a viral infection that is usually of little consequence for children or nonpregnant adults. Rubella involves a mild, itching rash and a low-grade fever that may last for several days and leave no damage. However, it becomes a powerful teratogen when the mother is infected during the early weeks of pregnancy (Kopp, 1983), with a 20 percent risk of embryo/fetal infection (Gibbs & Sweet, 1989). There can be devastating effects on an embryo: cataracts, heart defects, deafness, growth retardation, and disrupted brain development. Mental retardation can occur, but severe intellectual deficits due to rubella are uncommon (Fryers, 1984). Congenital rubella syndrome is characterized by "cataract, cardiac defects, and deafness" (Moore & Persaud, 1998, p. 191). The teratogenic effects are strongest in about the first 8 weeks of pregnancy. Half of the children born to mothers who contract rubella in the first 4 weeks have birth defects. The percentage drops to 6 percent if contracted in the 3rd month, with virtually no defects after that (Moore, 1988). Recall from the discussion in Chapter 5 that high fever in about the 4th and 5th weeks of pregnancy can disrupt development of the neural tube, brain, and spinal cord.

The last major rubella outbreak in the United States was in 1964, before large-scale vaccination programs began. It caused the loss of over 20,000 pregnancies and 25,000 children with birth defects (Andiman & Horstmann, 1984). Rubella has since decreased to a handful of cases each year (about 1 per 10,000 births in the United States; Fryers, 1994) due to successful vaccination programs for schoolchildren (Freij, South, & Sever, 1988). Best given to children, the vaccine should not be given to women who are pregnant or within 3 months of becoming pregnant. Unfortunately, vaccination programs are lacking in most of the rest of the world, where rubella remains a major cause of preventable birth defects.

Cytomegalovirus (CMV). **Cytomegalovirus,** a herpes virus, is usually fatal to the embryo when the infection occurs during the first trimester. CMV is the most common human fetus viral infection, occurring in up to 23 per 1000 births (Fryers, 1984). Some 20 percent of the infected children will have congenital defects such as growth retardation, deafness, cerebral palsy, and mental retardation (Behrman, 1992). Like other herpes-caused diseases, there is a high probability of latency in symptoms, which might not appear for years. Outbreaks are not predictable, the disease cannot be treated, and no effective vaccine has been developed.

Varicella (Chicken Pox). A common communicable disease of childhood, **varicella** ordinarily leaves no lasting damage. But if the virus infects pregnant women, serious damage to the fetus can result. If the mother is infected during the first trimester, there is a 20 percent chance that congenital anomalies will occur, including mental retardation, muscle atrophy, skin scarring, and limb anomalies (Moore & Persaud, 1998).

Congenital Toxoplasmosis.   This blood and tissue infection is caused by a parasitic protozoan (*Toxoplasma gondii*). It is common throughout the world but is most prevalent in warmer climates. One characteristic of this protozoan is that it completes its life cycle only in cats. Infected cats can contaminate soil through their feces, and other animals, including human gardeners, coming into contact with that soil can then become infected. The parasite may be in animal tissues, on fur or feathers (from licking or preening), or in the stool in cat litter boxes. Under some conditions, the parasite can survive for a year in cat feces. Some 20 to 40 percent of adults in the United States have been exposed to the organism (Feldman, 1982). Human infection occurs by eating undercooked, infected meat (primarily pork and lamb) and eggs. It is also transmitted through close contact with domestic animals (e.g., cats, dogs, rabbits, birds), contact with infected soil, or contact with feces or the dust in litter boxes of infected cats.

There are mild symptoms of toxoplasmosis (minor rash and/or fever), and the infected person may not even be aware of the disease. Only about 3 percent of infected mothers pass on the disease to the fetus (MaCleod & Lee, 1988). In those cases, the parasite crosses the placenta and increases the risks of microcephaly, hydrocephaly, visual defects, and mental retardation (L. R. White & Sever, 1967). The best safeguard for pregnant women is to avoid animals and feces that might be infected and to avoid undercooked meat and eggs.

Influenza.   This group of highly contagious viral diseases is characterized by fever, severe aches and pains, progressive inflammation of the respiratory mucous membranes, and physical exhaustion often to the point of prostration. High death rates occurred in worldwide **influenza** epidemics early in 1919 and 1957. Now, with greater public health awareness, improved procedures to slow its spread through contagion, and the use of preventive vaccines, it is no longer so devastating a disease.

If contracted during pregnancy, however, particularly in the first trimester, influenza can be a serious teratogen and is associated with increased risk of early spontaneous abortion and low birth weight. Recall from Chapters 2 and 5 that neural tube development begins about the 2nd week of pregnancy and rapid development occurs through about the 5th week. During that time, high maternal fever may cause the death of developing cells in the embryonic central nervous system (CNS) and internal organs such as the heart. Although there is agreement on the effects of heat on neural tube defects, the effects of influenza specifically have not been well studied. However, it is not unreasonable to infer that the heat of the fever occurring in influenza may cause CNS damage and heart defects. One recent epidemiological study in England (Takei et al., 1995) found a positive correlation of the death rate of influenza and the rate of mental retardation from 1953 to 1980. Presumably, the viral infection causes an elevated temperature in the mother which interferes with neural tube development, causes CNS damage, and results in mental retardation. The hypothesized etiologic path of virus—elevated temperatures—neural tube defects—CNS damage—cognitive disability (i.e., MR) is plausible but as yet uncertain. Much more research evidence is needed to consider the idea to be anything more than a tentative hypothesis.

Epidemiologic studies of the influenza epidemics (e.g., Mednick, Machon, Huttenen, & Bonett, 1988; O'Callaghan, Sham, Takei, Glover, & Murray, 1991) suggest that maternal influenza during the second trimester is associated with greater risk for the offspring's development of schizophrenia in young adulthood. However, the notion of an influenza-schizophrenia link has been challenged (e.g., Crow & Done, 1992) as being the result of poorly controlled epidemiological studies. The inference that schizophrenia may be caused by a virus has intrigued researchers for nearly three-quarters of a century. It was first postulated by Menninger (1926), who later abandoned that hypothesis (Menninger, 1928).

Similar methods have been used to study the relationship between prenatal exposure in influenza epidemics and autism. Researchers have concluded that the two are not associated (Dasa, Takei, Sham, & Murray, 1995).

Sexually Transmitted Disease (STDs).   This group of diseases includes syphilis, herpes simplex, gonorrhea, chlamydia, and AIDS, totaling more than a dozen known STDs. The Institute of Medicine has labeled STDs the "hidden epidemic" (S. Sternberg, 1996), noting that the United States has the highest rate of infection of all industrialized nations, at an annual cost of $17 billion. STDs among adolescents are "skyrocketing" (Blake, 1990). However, despite the high rate of infection, *the United States has virtually no public health prevention or educational campaigns,* and American adults know very little about STDs.

STDs involve an infection of the maternal bloodstream and of the genitourinary tract where highly infectious lesions can exist. Thus, STDs can be transmitted to the child via the mother's blood through the placenta and/or through direct contact of the baby with infected birth canal tissues during birth. In many cases, AIDS has been transmitted to infants through breast-feeding (Koop, 1986).

Syphilis.   Syphilis causes increased risk for miscarriages, abortions, and stillbirths. Infected children have increased risks of seizures, hemiplegia, hydrocephalus, mental retardation, and infant death (Kurent & Sever, 1977). Blindness, deafness, abnormal teeth and bones, and damage to internal organs such as the liver may also occur (Moore & Persaud, 1998). Some infections show up later, in early childhood, as **juvenile paresis,** a gradual deterioration of motor and mental abilities and, eventually, a young death. The incidence of congenital (present at birth) syphilis is about 1 per 10,000 live births (Ricci, Fojaco, & O'Sullivan, 1989), but it has been increasing steadily for several decades (Moore & Persaud, 1998).

Syphilis is caused by a spirochete (*Treponema pallidum*). In the first 4 or 5 months of pregnancy, the fetus is relatively resistant to the spirochete. During that time, the mother can be treated with penicillin, and fetal infection can be prevented. However, after about 4 months, the fetus is susceptible to the infection. Thus, good prenatal care, early diagnosis, and timely treatment before the 16th week can prevent syphilitic infection of the fetus. Syphilis can be readily diagnosed with a **Wasserman Reaction** (WR) test on a maternal blood sample, and this is routinely carried out in most states during the first one or two prenatal care visits. If the mother is diagnosed and treated early in pregnancy, the child is unlikely to become infected. However, timely prenatal medical care is not available to many low SES women, and opportunities to diagnose, treat, and prevent the spread of the disease are too often lost.

Herpes Simplex Virus (HSV).   HSV is the most common sexually transmitted disease. Infected children have a high risk of death, blindness, deafness, brain damage, and mental retardation. An HSV infection early in pregnancy triples the rate of spontaneous abortions (Moore & Persaud, 1998). Although it can be transmitted through placental transfer, mother-to-child infection usually occurs during birth when the child comes into contact with herpes lesions in the birth canal. If the presence of the disease is known, Cesarean delivery is used to avoid the exposure. Herpes is not easily treated since it is caused by a virus, and unlike diseases caused by bacteria, antibiotic agents are not effective.

Gonorrhea.   Caused by a bacterial infection, gonorrhea is more common in men than in women, and it affects about 1 million persons a year. The infection usually lodges in the penis, vagina, throat, and anus and can spread to the eyes through contact, usually with the hands, with affected tissue. Gonorrhea can lead to blood infection, sterility, arthritis, and heart problems. Nearly all states require silver nitrate or penicillin eye treatment for all newborn children to prevent eye infections from the birth process.

Chlamydia.   Chlamydia is the most common bacterial STD. It is caused by a parasite (*Chlamydia trachomatis*) and affects more than 3 million persons each year. The infection occurs in the cervix, urethra, or rectum and can be successfully treated with antibiotics. However, symptoms do not usually appear until the disease is well developed. Women who contract chlamydia are at risk for serious infections of the reproductive organs, and pregnant women risk abortion, stillbirth, and fever. Serious eye infections and pneumonia can result in children who are infected during birth.

AIDS (Acquired Immune Deficiency Syndrome).   This is a recent, devastating worldwide health problem. AIDS is the endpoint of a disease process caused by the human immunodeficiency virus (HIV). The Centers for Disease Control estimate that up to 23,000 children in the United States are HIV infected, but its incidence and prevalence are underreported (Fahrner & Manio, 2000). A recent news report (France, 1999) notes that Native Americans (1.9 million persons) may be facing an epidemic because they are unwilling to acknowledge homosexuality and AIDS.

The global spread of AIDS, first recognized in the 1980s, may have originated through human contact with the blood of infected chimpanzees in west-central Africa about 1924 to 1946 (Christensen, 1999) through skinning and eating the animals. The virus, carried in the chimpanzees' blood, may have "jumped" to humans through scratches in the humans' hands as they butchered the chimps. Once established in humans, the virus then spread to other humans primarily through sexual contact. The chimpanzees are thought to have been the original reservoir of the **HIV-1** virus and a variant, HIV-2 (the human immune deficiency virus type 1 and type 2), that are responsible for AIDS. The HIV virus is transmitted among humans through exchange of bodily fluids such as blood and semen, usually during sexual contact and/or through sharing infected hypodermic needles. The time period between HIV infection and appearance of the AIDS symptoms varies from one person to another and may take many years. However, once AIDS symptoms are established in a person, the inevitable result is death. The virus attacks the immune system, leaving the person highly susceptible to many other infections. Death due to respiratory complications of pneumonia is common in AIDS patients. One-third of pregnant women with AIDS infect their children (Valleroy, 1990; Valleroy, Harris, & Way, 1990) through the placenta, through physical exposure of the baby to the infection during the birth process, or through breast-feeding by an HIV infected mother (European Collaborative Study, 1991). Research (e.g., Connor et al., 1994) has demonstrated a significant reduction in mother-to-child transmission of the virus by strengthening the mother's immune system with the drug AZT during pregnancy and strengthening the neonate's immune system immediately after birth. However, if the child does become infected with HIV and it develops into AIDS, the child sickens and dies frequently within 6 months, and almost all die within 3 years (Seabrook, 1987). Their lives are short and distressed.

Children are also exposed to HIV through contaminated food and sexual abuse. Adolescents contract HIV largely through sexual activity and contaminated needles in drug use. The mean time from HIV infection to the endpoint, AIDS, is about 11 years (Fahrner & Manio, 2000); thus, most young adults with AIDS were infected as adolescents.

The HIV virus not only causes AIDS in children but also can be a teratogen for other congenital disorders, including head and facial deformities, respiratory and other infections, and neurological damage with intellectual deterioration. This infection is one of the most severe threats to the health and lives of persons of all ages—children, adults, and adolescents.

It is clear that the virus is spread through human societies by virtue of human behavior: sexual contact with bodily fluid exchanges, shared needles in drug use, during birth, and infant nursing. Unfortunately, human behavior is difficult to change, particularly when so many of the people involved are the least accessible. In the United States, these include the young, poorly educated, homeless, drug abusers, and those in poverty (Dryfoos, 1994). Large proportions of the populations in developing countries are not educated about the causes of the spreading infections. A recent report (UNICEF, 2000) noted that large proportions of young people in developing countries—particularly females—have little knowledge about AIDS, its causes, effects, and prevention. Public education programs have been few, ill-designed, and not effective. Even if some persons are knowledgeable, their governments too often do not have the infrastructure needed to obtain and properly dispense medication that can help strengthen immune systems and delay, but not prevent, death. At this writing, the U.S. public has become aware through news reports that AIDS is a growing worldwide epidemic of huge proportions, particularly in many developing countries. High rates of infection are found in Asia, the Caribbean area, and sub-Saharan Africa. South Africa, for example, now has the largest single group of HIV-infected persons in the world—4.2 million—and more than one-third of pregnant women in some African countries are HIV infected (Altman, 2000). Throughout the African continent, an estimated 50 million people are infected with HIV (Kahn, 2000). There is no doubt that AIDS constitutes a growing and major threat to worldwide health.

Two additional points should be made about AIDS. The first, a hopeful thought, is that chimpanzees are carriers of the virus, but do not succumb to AIDS because something in their physical makeup protects them. If researchers can discover what the protective factors are, then a human protective agent might be developed from them. The genetic difference between chimpanzees and humans is very small, and it may be in that small area that this answer will be found.

The other point is more ominous. The virus is thought to have existed, possibly for thousands of years, in east-central Africa. Are there other equally virulent life forms there or in other parts of the world, now silently growing and capable of making the "jump" from animals to humans at some future time?

Drugs

Thalidomide.   Most drugs are taken deliberately, as either legitimate medication or for recreation. **Thalidomide** is a classic example of a legitimate medicinal drug that turned out to be a teratogen. It was prescribed in the 1950s and 1960s for pregnant women to control nausea in morning sickness. There were no known side effects, and it was thought to be safe and effective, which helps account for its widespread use. When taken in the first trimester—which is not only a critical period in embryo and fetal development but is also when morning sickness is greatest—thalidomide caused serious birth defects in 20 to 30 percent of the babies (Annas & Elias, 1999). The defects, known as thalidomide embryopathy, included deformed limbs, digestive and urogenital deformities, and congenital heart defects. As learned much later, it also had a depressive effect on intelligence, and many of the children had subnormal IQ scores. An estimated 8000 to 10,000 thalidomide babies, most of them in Germany where the drug had been used most heavily, were born with limb anomalies. Of that worldwide total, only seventeen were born of American parents (Annas & Elias, 1999), and most of them were Americans stationed abroad. This was largely because an alert researcher with the Food and Drug Administration (FDA), Dr. Frances Kelsey, rejected the drug for use in the United States based on early research reports.

Thalidomide still has legitimate medical uses and is considered safe, but not for women in the first trimester of pregnancy. Current research shows that thalidomide has an inhibiting effect on the production of some white blood cell factors, and this has implications for the treatment of AIDS, cancer, rheumatoid arthritis, tuberculosis, and macular degeneration (Adler, 1994). In mid-1998, the FDA concluded that thalidomide is effective in treating Hanson's disease (leprosy) and has approved its use for the 7000 leprosy patients in the United States (Annas & Elias, 1999).

Diethylstilbestrol (DES).   For about three decades, 1940s through the 1960s, a synthetic estrogen, **diethylstilbestrol** (DES), was an effective treatment to reduce miscarriages. Some 20 years later, it became apparent that the female children of those mothers suffered increased risks of vaginal cancer, miscarriages, premature births, and stillbirths. DES, it turned out, was a teratogen. Most of the problems were in young women, but it was later observed that male children had increased risks of urinary tract problems and infertility (Henle & Altman, 1978). Subsequent research has indicated that the effects on women were not as severe or widespread as originally thought. For example, although they had more difficulties with successful pregnancies, these women did succeed in giving birth about as often as women whose mothers had not used DES; only about 1 in 1000 daughters of mothers who used DES developed cancer (Moore & Persaud, 1998; Noller, 1990; Ulfelder, 1986).

A number of other medicinal drugs may have teratogenic effects, and their use during pregnancy must be carefully supervised. These include some antibiotics, phenobarbitol and other barbiturates, anticoagulants, anticonvulsants, tranquilizers, and hormones. Iodides, such as found in some over-the-counter cough suppressants, are normally harmless, but can be dangerous when used in pregnancy, as fetal iodide toxicity causes enlargement of the thyroid and problems such as cataracts in the developing child.

Alcohol.   **Ethanol,** the chemical term for alcohol, is the most-studied teratogen and one of the most severely destructive. The negative effects of alcohol use during pregnancy have been noted since antiquity, and in the last 30 years, significant research data have been gathered (e.g., Lemoine, Harousseau, Borteyru, & Menuet, 1968). Two important papers (Jones & Smith, 1975; Jones, Smith, Ulleland, & Streissguth, 1973) coined the term **fetal alcohol syndrome (FAS)** and described FAS children. In an important review of the research, M. Russell (1982) focused on the epidemiology of FAS. Since those early publications, more than 3000 papers and books have been published on this topic.

Maternal Alcohol Abuse.   This is the obvious cause of alcohol fetopathy. Defects can result from maternal drinking at any time during pregnancy, but the most severe effects are due to drinking in the early weeks, during organogenesis. Animal studies have established the teratogenicity of ethanol (as reviewed by Abel, 1990; Cicero, 1994; Coles, 1994; Little, Graham, & Samson, 1982), and studies with humans have further confirmed those findings (Coles, 1994). As reviewed by Michaelis and Michaelis (1994), when ethanol is applied to embryos **in vitro,** growth retardation results. In humans, alcohol is rapidly and nearly equally distributed in fetal and maternal tissues.

The mechanisms through which ethanol damages the embryo and fetus are not yet fully known, but several have been suggested (Pratt, 1984). In this model, different mechanisms or combinations of mechanisms operate at different points in the development of the embryo and fetus as follows:

> *At conception and first few weeks:* During this early stage of pregnancy, ethanol may be a cytotoxic and/or mutagenic agent, causing the death of the zygote or embryo and/or causing lethal chromosomal changes.
>
> *One month to about 10 weeks after conception:* Ethanol can continue as a cytotoxic agent, causing the death of cells developing at that time, principally in the central nervous system. The loss of cells and the disruption of normal brain and head development may lead to microcephaly, mental retardation, and to the characteristic facial anomalies in FAS.
>
> *From about 10 weeks and throughout pregnancy:* Ethanol may disrupt and/or delay cell development. If neural cell formation is disrupted, synapses might not form properly, resulting in neurological deficits. The characteristic cognitive deficits and neurological and behavioral problems may stem largely from this disruption.
>
> *Late pregnancy:* Ethanol interferes with neurotransmitter production. This may affect the hypothalamus, which in turn can lead to suppression of growth hormone. The characteristic growth retardation of FAS may be due to this deficiency in growth hormone.

A woman can be several weeks pregnant without knowing it. If she consumes alcohol at that time, her baby can be aborted or permanently disabled, all without her knowledge until much later. Women who drink alcohol might stop when they realize they are pregnant, but there is a lapse of time from conception to the recognition of the pregnancy, placing many children at serious risk. A dose-effect relationship also exists, with greater effects on the child associated with higher amounts of drinking by the mother.

One of the puzzles of FAS is that while ethanol is considered to be the most potent of all teratogenic drugs (Snodgrass, 1994), it does not affect all children of alcohol-using mothers. The probabilities of FAS in children of heavy-drinking mothers vary considerably—from 1 percent in some studies to 50 percent in others (Burd & Martsolf, 1989). Snodgrass (1994) estimates 10 percent of children exposed to heavy drinking in pregnancy will show major and specific effects (FAS), while less severe and nonspecific anomalies (**fetal alcohol effects, FAE**) will occur in somewhat more than 10 percent of the children. It appears, at least tentatively, that some 20 percent of the children of drinking mothers will show detrimental effects.

Researchers do not yet know the factors that result in some children suffering from FAS and FAE, whereas others, whose mothers drink just as much alcohol, are apparently not affected. The severity of effects are apparently due to combinations of events, including the amount of maternal drinking, the pattern of drinking (e.g., steady drinking, binge drinking), the time in embryo/fetal development when drinking occurs, maternal health, nutrition, genetic factors, and maternal and fetal metabolism. The exact combination of events leading to serious FAS is yet to be understood. The single most important predictor, of course, is maternal alcohol consumption.

Any consumption of alcohol just prior to and during pregnancy is dangerous. Some researchers believe that even one or two drinks during pregnancy can have irreversible effects (Light, 1988). Particularly damaging are drinking early in pregnancy, heavy drinking, or binge drinking (see Box 6.2). The latter is common among college women—consider the pervasiveness of the weekend beer blast or the reduced prices on "happy hour" and "ladies' night" that are so commonly used around college campuses to get young women into bars. Heavy drinking involves two or more alcoholic drinks daily. But in a weekend binge, a woman could consume six or more drinks in just a few hours. Even one night of binge drinking—particularly during the first few weeks of pregnancy, when the woman might not even be aware of the pregnancy—is a serious threat and can cause irreversible damage to the embryo or fetus (Short & Hess, 1995).

Alcohol easily crosses the placenta and is readily introduced to the child through maternal blood. In effect, when the mother drinks alcohol, the baby "drinks" alcohol, and the more the mother drinks, the more the baby drinks. Alcohol enters the fetal system in about the same concentration as in the mother's blood, but alcohol levels fall more slowly in the fetal system, and alcohol remains for several hours in the amniotic fluid (Griesbach & Polloway, 1990). Note, too, that the effects of several ounces of alcohol on a young woman weighing 120 pounds or so are observable; imagine the impact of that amount on a tiny embryo or fetus with its small tissue mass!

Alcohol may affect the embryo and fetus in several ways, and the most severe effects may occur through the depletion of fetal oxygen. A great deal of oxygen is used in alcohol metabolism. Therefore, the amount of oxygen available for fetal growth may be markedly reduced, thus slowing or disrupting development. It may also directly impede processes such as cell differentiation early in pregnancy, thus causing impairments in the embryo or fetus. Alcohol also reduces maternal respiration rate, further reducing fetal oxygen supply.

BOX **6.2**

Heavy Drinking and Binge Drinking Defined

Heavy Drinking: Two or more alcoholic drinks daily (two beers, 12 ounces each; or two glasses of wine, about 2 to 3 ounces; or two shots of distilled alcohol such as whiskey, gin, etc., about 0.5 ounce each)

Binge Drinking: Five or more drinks on one or more occasions

In a study by Day and Richardson (1994), 3 percent of *pregnant* women met the binge-drinking criteria, and 0.06 percent were heavy drinkers.

In another study (Serdulla et al., 1991), 25 percent of pregnant women reported having had an alcoholic drink.

FAS has a typical fetal and childhood pattern of growth retardation, a recognizable constellation of facial anomalies, and brain dysfunction, including mental retardation. The severity of these effects is related to the amount of alcohol consumed by the pregnant woman. It is at the high levels of consumption that FAS, with its obvious facial deformities, is most readily recognized and at which the child is most seriously disabled.

Fetal alcohol effects (FAE) also occur. FAS and FAE differ in degree along a continuum of effects (Burd & Martsolf, 1989). FAE includes the same characteristics of growth and mental retardation but to milder degrees. The differences are probably due to variations in the amount of maternal drinking, the time during pregnancy of the drinking, and varying susceptibility of mothers. FAE children can have behavioral, learning, and language problems, poor attention, and hyperactivity (Rosett & Weiner, 1984). Microcephaly and obvious facial deformities are generally not as severe in FAE as in FAS. The terms *alcohol-related birth defects (ARBD)* and *alcohol-related neurodevelopmental disorder (ARND)* are also used to distinguish full-blown FAS from the less severe effects.

Of the many substances that are abused, including heroin, cocaine, and marijuana, alcohol is the most severely damaging, producing in the fetus the most serious neurobehavioral effects (Stratton, Howe, & Battiglia, 1996). Alcohol is the leading known cause of mental retardation in the Western world (Abel & Sokol, 1987). Alcohol's effects, which begin during early fetal development, continue into adolescence and adulthood. FAS is a birth defect with significant *lifetime* disabilities (Abel, 1990).

Alcohol has effects at all four teratogenic endpoints, causing: (a) embryo and fetal death, (b) malformation and birth defects, (c) growth retardation, and (d) functional impairment. Alcohol, then, is particularly dangerous not only because of the seriousness of the damage but also because it has such a wide spectrum of serious effects across all endpoints.

There are no objective chemical or genetic tests that can detect FAS. The diagnosis is made clinically based on five sets of observations:

1. *Growth retardation,* both pre- and postnatal, in height, weight, and head circumference
2. *Central nervous system involvement* (cognitive deficits), subaverage intellectual functioning, and poor physical coordination

3. *Facial-cranial anomalies* in a fairly consistent pattern (in some cases, there may also be cardiac problems and limb involvement)
4. *Behavioral problems* such as hyperactivity and distractibility
5. *Documented maternal use of alcohol during pregnancy*

The characteristic features of FAS are summarized in Box 6.3.

The visible physical characteristics of children born with FAS include head and facial deformities such as microcephaly (smaller than normal head size), flattened profile, long midface, short, narrow, and unusually shaped eye openings, a long, thin, upper lip, and indistinct philtrum (see Figure 6.2). Children with FAS suffer growth retardation (retarded in height, weight, and head circumference). They are smaller, slimmer, and lighter than nonaffected children. Growth retardation usually begins prenatally. The children are typically below the tenth percentile in weight and height and below the third percentile in head circumference (Sokol & Clarren, 1989). The children grow in height at about 60 percent of the normal rate and at about 33 percent of the normal rate for weight gain (Aase, 1994). Joint and limb problems and congenital heart defects are often part of the FAS picture. Unlike children who are growth delayed due to prenatal maternal malnutrition, these FAS children are permanently affected—there is no correcting or reversing FAS once it occurs.

B O X **6.3**

The Major Identifying Characteristics of FAS

Central Nervous System: Mild to moderate mental retardation (might also include poor fine motor coordination, speech and language defects)

Growth Retardation: Extremely small size for age

Facial/Cranial Anomalies:
  small head
  jutting forehead
  short palpebral fissures
  epicanthic folds
  underdeveloped midface
  low-set eyes
  short, flat nose
  low-set ears
  indistinct philtrum (absence of vertical ridges between nose and mouth)
  thin upper lip (highly specific to FAS)

Behavioral Problems: hyperactivity, distractibility

Maternal Alcohol Use: history of maternal alcohol use during pregnancy

Information from: Short, R. H., & Hess, G. C. (1995). Fetal alcohol syndrome: Characteristics and remedial implications. *Developmental Disabilities Bulletin, 23*(1), 13–29.

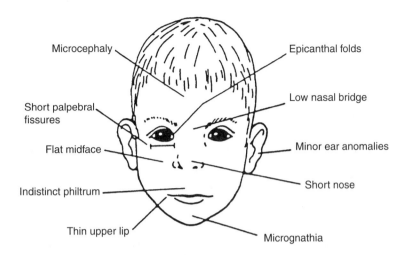

Microcephaly

Epicanthal folds

Low nasal bridge

Short palpebral fissures

Flat midface

Minor ear anomalies

Indistinct philtrum

Short nose

Thin upper lip

Micrognathia

FIGURE 6.2   Common Facial Characteristics in Fetal Alcohol Syndrome.
The characteristics on the left side are those most frequently seen in Fetal Alcohal Syndrome. Those on the right side are less specific.

From: Streissguth, A. P., Sampson, P. D., Barr, H. M., Clarren, S. K., & Martin, D. C. (1986). Studying alcohol teratogenesis from the perspective of the fetal alcohol syndrome: Methodological and statistical issues. In H. M. Wisniewski & D. A. Snider (Eds). *Mental retardation: Research, education, and technology transfer.* The New York Academy of Sciences, Vol. 477, 63–86. Reproduced with permission.

About 85 percent of FAS children are mildly to moderately mentally retarded (Abel & Sokol, 1987). Twenty years ago, FAS was considered the third major cause of mental retardation, following Down syndrome and *spina bifida,* and the major preventable cause of mental retardation. However, more recently, researchers believe that FAS is *the leading known cause* of mental retardation in the Western world, surpassing Down syndrome, cerebral palsy, and spina bifida (Phelps & Grabowski 1992; Streissguth et al., 1991), and FAS is the only one that is entirely preventable. Hagberg, Hagberg, Lewerth, and Lindberg (1981) examined the causes of mild mental retardation (IQ 50 to 70) in a sample of ninety-one Swedish children 8 to 12 years old. They found that 55 percent were of unknown cause, and 23 percent were due to prenatal causes. The largest single etiological factor in those prenatal cases, accounting for one-third of the cases, was alcohol fetopathy. These cases accounted for 8 percent of the total sample; in contrast, 5 percent of the total sample was traced to *all known genetic causes.* In this study, the importance of alcohol fetopathy in the etiology of mild mental retardation becomes obvious. These authors argue that more attention needs to be paid to drug abuse (including alcohol) in the etiology of mental retardation.

As summarized in reviews by Niccols (1994) and by Phelps and Grabowski (1992), newborns with FAS are difficult to care for. They are small, with a malformed appearance; they are irritable, difficult to soothe and to feed; and their sleep patterns are hard to establish. Motor and language development, toilet training, speech, and social development are delayed. It is difficult for many parents to form appropriate attachment to these children, with potentially negative effects on the children's emotional and social development. This may compound the problems these children already have.

Preschoolers with FAS are notably short and thin, with sudden, poorly coordinated movements. They are frequently diagnosed as having attention deficit hyperactivity disorder. Developmental delays are common and intellectual deficits are apparent even before they enter school. Although a small proportion may have average or even higher IQ, their mean IQ is 60 to 65, with a range of about 40 to 80 (Niccols, 1994). IQ varies inversely with the severity of the FAS (Streissguth & LaDue, 1985, 1987).

Because FAS has been studied for only about 30 years, there is still not a great deal of information on the course of the lives of persons with FAS as they grow into adolescence and adulthood. According to current data, FAS children continue to show the FAS characteristics that have been noted. They are smaller and lighter than non-FAS children and are characteristically very thin. The microcephaly and facial deformities continue, and the FAS phenotype remains clearly discernible throughout childhood.

Some data, however (see Streissguth & LaDue, 1987), indicate that the FAS phenotype for adolescents and adults may be different—that is, some visible changes seem to occur with age. With girls, menstruation occurs at the normal time, accompanied by an increase of body fat. They continue to be shorter than average, and thus, many of the adolescent girls with FAS may lose their earlier thin form and become much stockier in body shape. The facial anomalies continue to be evident, but the nose and mandible (lower jaw) continue to grow to larger than average proportions. According to Streissguth and LaDue (1987), FAS boys continue to be shorter and thinner than normal, and puberty is delayed. As with the girls, microcephaly and facial deformities persist, and the nose and mandibles continue to grow to abnormal size. These researchers noted that the most important and enduring characteristic of adult FAS patients is the effects on the central nervous system and the resulting intellectual deficits.

As these children grow into adolescence and adulthood, their poor social behavior becomes a major handicapping characteristic. They continue to function at low intellectual levels, have difficulty with decision making, seem restless and agitated (Driscoll, Streissguth, & Riley, 1990), and are poorly equipped for occupational or personal success.

Studies carried out in the United States and in Europe leave no doubt that FAS has lifelong consequences—hyperactivity, social delays, and cognitive difficulties continue into schoolyears, adolescence, and adulthood (Streissguth, 1994). For example, some of the first long-term studies (Streissguth, Randels, & Smith, 1991) found that adolescents and adults with FAS led "generally dysfunctional lives." In the latter study, although the mean chronological age of those studied was 17 years, their level of adaptive functioning as measured by the Vineland Adaptive Behavior Scales was only 7 years.

There may be additional general and pervasive results of alcohol fetopathy, but we are only beginning to recognize them. Persons with FAS continue to grow and to change, and their needs change with age. In addition to their cognitive deficits, adults with FAS may have serious psychological and behavioral problems that become more disruptive as they grow older. Streissguth (1994) reviewed research and clinical reports and concluded that it is no longer sufficient to conceptualize FAS as primarily a problem of childhood mental retardation to be handled through special education and training programs for children and youth. Rather, the psychological problems and dysfunctional living of these people *throughout their lives* need to be addressed in future research and clinical treatment.

While CNS damage may account for most of the characteristic functioning of FAS children and adults, there are also risk factors that may operate. For example, many FAS children are born into poverty to alcoholic and/or single mothers who cannot provide adequate parenting. Many of these children are removed from their homes and experience a succession of foster homes. The inconsistent and poor parenting, as well as other factors associated with poverty, may contribute to their characteristic adjustment problems.

The incidence and prevalence of FAS and FAE vary geographically, socially, and are difficult to estimate. Diagnoses cannot be made from a biological test, as with PKU or Down syndrome, and the physical anomalies may be very subtle at birth rather than being obvious such as in spina bifida. Abel and Sokol (1987) calculated an overall estimate of 1.9 FAS cases per 1000 live births worldwide. Stratton, Howe, and Battaglia (1996) list fourteen studies with prevalence ranges for FAS and FAE combined from 0.03 per 1000 (U.S. Asians) to 3.1 per 1000 (U.S., Boston) and two studies finding a prevalence of 4.2 per 1000 (southwest Native Americans) and 120 per 1000 (northwest Canadian Native Americans). With the exception of the Native American populations, the prevalence rates are on the order of about 1 to 3 per 1000 live births. However, among mothers who are alcoholic, FAS approaches 25 per 1000 live births, which is between eight and twenty-five times the general population rate. In addition, FAE is thought to occur at rates three to four times higher than those for FAS (Larsson, Bohlin, & Tunnell, 1985). It should also be pointed out that while there is considerable variation, FAS occurs in all ethnic and socioeconomic groups.

Alcohol is a serious teratogen, and public health campaigns to convince pregnant women to forego alcohol are well justified. But as reported by Dufour, Williams, Campbell, and Aitken (1994), American women of childbearing age have little knowledge of the facts of FAS. It is frustrating for health practitioners and researchers that this group of disorders, major contributors to developmental disabilities, is at least in theory *completely preventable*. If mothers did not drink when pregnant, nearly all of these disabilities would be prevented. Unfortunately, this problem is a complex mix of physical effects, psychological adjustment, and sociological factors that may be resistant to significant change. There is some evidence that drinking during pregnancy has decreased in recent years (Serdulla, Williamson, Kendrick, Anda, & Byers, 1991) from 32 percent in 1985 to 20 percent in 1988. In that study, 3 percent of the pregnant women fit the criteria for binge drinking and 0.6 percent for heavy drinking. Despite that decrease, 25 percent of the pregnant women in that study had consumed an alcoholic beverage in the past month. Further evidence suggests there has been a decrease in alcohol use by women since 1989 when the federal government mandated warning labels on alcoholic beverage containers (see Box 6.4). Hankin (1994) found a decrease in drinking rate reported by pregnant women shortly after the warning went into effect. However, the label seemed to have had an effect on drinkers who were least at risk (i.e., the lighter drinkers), whereas heavy drinking pregnant women seemed not to have been affected by the label. Rosenthal (1990) estimates that about 86 percent of women drink at least once during their pregnancy and 20 percent to 35 percent drink regularly, although not necessarily large amounts.

Risk drinking during pregnancy is associated with birth defects and other developmental disabilities. As has been discussed, the rate of risk drinking in the United States is

BOX 6.4

Warning Label Mandated by Public Law 100-690, November 1989

GOVERNMENT WARNING: (1) ACCORDING TO THE SURGEON GENERAL, WOMEN SHOULD NOT DRINK ALCOHOLIC BEVERAGES DURING PREGNANCY BECAUSE OF THE RISK OF BIRTH DEFECTS. (2) CONSUMPTION OF ALCOHOLIC BEVERAGES IMPAIRS YOUR ABILITY TO DRIVE A CAR OR OPERATE MACHINERY AND MAY CAUSE HEALTH PROBLEMS.

relatively low, but the damage to children of the 1 to 3 per 1000 cases of FAS is catastrophic for those individuals. Screening procedures to identify that small proportion of risk drinkers are of major importance for FAS prevention attempts. However, screening by asking pregnant women about how much they drink may not be very successful, as such direct approaches may trigger denial and mothers' reports that minimize their drinking (Sokol, Martier, & Ernhart, 1985). M. Russell (1994) and M. Russell et al. (1996) have developed more indirect screening procedures that are effective in the early identification of risk drinking. Psychological research on identifying risk drinkers, reducing drinking among childbearing age women, and eliminating it among pregnant women is of major importance.

FAS is a clear example of the growing realization that personal lifestyle has profound affects on physical well-being. The federal government initiated its *Healthy People 2000* agenda (U.S. Department of Health and Human Services, 1991) with its goals of reducing preventable death and disability and improving life quality by the year 2000. One of the more than 300 objectives was the reduction of FAS to an incidence of no more than 0.12 per 1000 live births. Unfortunately, that goal was not reached. Alcohol is clearly a teratogen, has severe negative effects on the developing organism, and is an important factor in the etiology of a large proportion of cases of mental retardation. However, in heavy drinking during pregnancy, there are a number of confounding factors: Heavy-drinking mothers are typically also cigarette smokers, single, older, have used other drugs, and tend to associate with men who are heavy drinkers. It is not yet known what mix of etiological factors is most responsible for FAS. But the advice is clear and available for every rational woman: Until we know with more precision which women are most at risk for FAS and FAE, and under what conditions, *it is wise for women to avoid all alcohol just prior to and during pregnancy.*

Paternal Alcohol Abuse and Effects on Offspring.   We have presented a standard picture, guided by the research, that alcohol fetopathy is the result of maternal drinking and that serious deficits are preventable if the mothers would only forego alcohol. Prevention efforts are still meager. They focus on the mother as the responsible agents, and that focus will probably remain in future programs. No one can deny the critical importance of maternal behavior in alcohol fetopathy.

However, little attention has been paid to the possible etiological contribution of the father's alcohol consumption. It is reasonable to expect that children of alcoholic fathers are at developmental risk from factors associated with alcoholism. These risk factors include lower socioeconomic status and fewer family resources, lower parental education, inadequate health knowledge, poor nutrition and medical care, and greater risks of physical abuse of both mother and child. Alcohol-abusing fathers may smoke cigarettes more than most and might subject their children to the dangers of secondhand smoke (see the section on tobacco). Childhood head injuries and brain damage in automobile crashes and other events more probably occur in the family of an alcohol-abusing father.

Might the father's drinking have more direct effects on child development? Cicero (1994) noted that human and animal research suggests paternal genetic contributions to some alcohol-related pathologies in offspring. For example, in humans, alcoholism appears to be genetically linked to the father, and male children of alcoholic fathers are at risk for hormonal and neurological anomalies, for behavioral problems such as hyperactivity, and for intellectual deficits. The research suggests that genetic factors related to the biological father's drinking might have direct effects on the children's intellectual and behavioral development.

In a series of studies, Cicero (1994) found that consumption of alcohol by male rats prior to their sexual maturity had significant negative effects not only on those animals but on their offspring. First, the moderate exposure to alcohol resulted in disruption of puberty and sexual maturity in those male rats. At sexual maturity, the rats' alcohol intake was discontinued, and the animals appeared to have recovered completely, showing only normal hormonal and reproductive signs. Nevertheless, later, when these animals sired litters, the offspring differed significantly from nonalcoholic-sired pups in three ways: the litters of the alcoholic sires were significantly smaller; the pups showed disrupted hormonal functions—i.e., lower testosterone levels and smaller seminal vesicles (the sperm-producing structures in the testes); the pups had difficulty with several spatial learning tasks, although other forms of learning seemed not to have been affected.

Cicero concluded that the exposure of male rats to alcohol prior to sexual maturity, despite being followed by a nonalcoholic period of apparently normal development, produced significant developmental disruptions in the offspring. Here, in controlled studies, a paternal contribution to alcohol-related disabilities in the offspring has been demonstrated. Although we cannot generalize these results to humans, we should be alerted by them, particularly in light of the apparent decreasing age of alcohol consumption by boys. Do these animal data suggest that the future children of early drinking boys may be at alcohol-related risk for both physical and cognitive disabilities? Here is another area in which much more animal and human research is needed.

Cicero speculates that if there are direct effects of paternal alcohol use on offspring, as shown by his research, several mechanisms may operate, singly or together:

alcohol might be a toxicant for sperm, causing genetic mutations in sperm cells

alcohol might affect the viability of sperm so that in alcohol-exposed sperm only certain sperm survive for eventual reproduction

alcohol might affect the chemical composition of semen, and that might alter the activity of the sperm that are ejaculated

Research evidence points to a paternal contribution to alcohol-related deficits in offspring. There does not appear to be a specific, clearly observed set of physical and cognitive characteristics such as in FAS. The deficits may be more subtle, less apparent, but still significant. They may include reproductive problems and cognitive deficits in specific types of intellectual tasks. The question must be asked, too, of the possible interactions of effects on children for whom both parents are alcoholic. For example, most alcoholic mothers also have alcoholic mates (Abel, 1992). Thus, when FAS occurs, the effects presumably due to maternal drinking may be directly or indirectly influenced by the father's drinking. Clearly, more attention—both in clinical evaluation and in research—is needed on the issue of paternal contribution to alcohol-related deficits in children. In clinical diagnoses, the father's drinking history as well as the mother's should be considered.

Tobacco.   Tobacco may be the most commonly used—and abused—drug in the world. There are more than 50 million cigarette smokers in the United States (Raloff, 1994). Tobacco use ranks as a major health problem in which annually half a million Americans and more than 3 million persons worldwide die from tobacco-related illness. That number is expected to more than triple to 10 million annual deaths within the next 20 years (Raloff, 1994). In the United States, tobacco accounts for nearly 20 percent of all deaths annually and more than 25 percent of deaths between the ages of 35 and 64 years, most from tobacco-related cancer and heart disease (Raloff, 1994). The yearly cost of tobacco in the United States in terms of health care and lost productivity has been estimated to be more than $100 billion (MacKenzie, Bartecchi, & Schrier, 1994).

Tobacco is used in various forms such as smoking, chewing, "pinching" it between gums and cheek, and inhaling it into the nostrils in the form of snuff. Since women do not typically use snuff, chew or pinch tobacco, or smoke pipes and cigars, the tobacco-use threat to prenatal development is primarily from cigarette smoking by pregnant women. Some 20 to 25 percent of American women smoke during pregnancy (Chomitz, Cheung, & Lieberman, 1995). The rate of smoking by pregnant women varies with several factors, one of which is education. Among pregnant women, only 5 percent of those with a college education smoke compared with 35 percent of those with less than a high school education (National Center for Health Statistics, 1989). While American men have had the good sense to reduce their smoking rates over the years, women have not. About 30 percent of American women—most of childbearing age—continue to smoke cigarettes. Indeed, women under 23 years of age constitute the fastest-growing group of smokers in the United States (Bartecchi, MacKenzie, & Schrier, 1995).

A 20-year period of decreased cigarette use in the United States has ended; tobacco consumption has leveled off, and there are signs of increased use, particularly among youngsters (MacKenzie et al., 1994). At the same time, tobacco use has increased markedly around the world, especially in Asia and Africa, and we can expect future high rates of tobacco-related deaths, illness, and economic and social costs in those areas. The United States is the world's leading exporter of cigarettes, exporting more than three times as many cigarettes as any other country (U.S. Department of Agriculture, 1992). This increase has been attributed to aggressive marketing by tobacco companies that have particularly targeted minorities, women, and children and spent more than $5 billion for marketing in 1992 (Bartecchi et al., 1995). Tobacco is second only to automobiles as the most heavily advertised products in the United States (MacKenzie et al., 1994).

The major active drug in tobacco is nicotine, but it is not clear how much nicotine directly affects prenatal development or how much the effects are due to related factors such as oxygen depletion and increased levels of carbon monoxide and cyanide compounds. There are more than 2000 compounds released in a burning cigarette (U.S. Public Health Service, 1979) and inhaled by the smoker, and their effects are not yet fully known. More than 450 of the compounds are known to be toxic (Jarvik, 1973), and the potential negative interactions of so many toxic substances cannot even be estimated at this time.

The teratogenic endpoints of tobacco use are primarily embryo and fetal deaths and growth retardation, with some indication of functional/cognitive effects on children, but the data on the latter are still meager. Smoking is a major cause of preterm deliveries (prematurity) and low birth weight, which in turn are major factors in infant mortality. Smoking during pregnancy retards fetal growth and reduces birth weight by 150 to 300 grams (5.3 to 11.4 ounces; Chomitz et al., 1995). Pregnant women who smoke are twice as likely as nonsmokers to have low-birth-weight babies.

The best-documented effects of smoking are on fetal deaths and prenatal growth retardation. The latter results in low birth weight (LBW). Cigarette smoking is "the single largest modifiable risk factor for low birth weight and infant mortality" in the United States (Shiono & Behrman, 1995, p. 11). Abel (1980) reported that maternal smoking during pregnancy is associated with increased spontaneous abortions, stillbirths, and infant deaths. Korones (1986) noted fetal growth retardation, lower birth weight, and decreased resistance to disease. Meyer and Tonascia (1977) studied over 50,000 births, comparing mothers who were heavy smokers (more than a pack daily), light smokers (less than one pack daily), and nonsmokers. The risk of fetal death increased by 20 percent for mothers who were light smokers and by 35 percent for heavy smokers. Note the dose-effect relationship: The more the mother smokes, the greater are the risks to the baby. Note, too, that even smoking *less than a pack daily* during pregnancy has negative effects.

There has been speculation but little data on the effects of paternal smoking on pregnancy. It has been suggested that the father's smoking might reduce his sperm count and/or activity, thus reducing the chances of conception. Perhaps, too, the man's secondhand smoke, surrounding a pregnant woman, might affect her health and, subsequently, the health of the developing child. Passive smoking (a nonsmoker inhaling the secondhand smoke of a smoker) accounts for an estimated 53,000 deaths annually. A nonsmoker who lives with a smoker has a 30 percent greater risk of heart disease and lung cancer (Bartecchi et al., 1995), and this poses a particular threat to children with their smaller body mass.

Research indicates that crib deaths (**sudden infant death syndrome, SIDS**) are significantly more likely to occur in homes where cigarette smoking occurs. SIDS occur within 6 months after birth, with peaks of occurrence, for unknown reasons, at 8 to 9 weeks and at 13 to 15 weeks. Babies who were in good health are found dead in their cribs with no apparent causes. There are several known risk factors for SIDS, including poverty, limited education, and maternal age (i.e., under 20 years). The baby's position while sleeping has been recognized as a risk factor: The risk is less when babies are put on their backs to sleep, and it is greater when they are placed on their stomachs (Beal & Finch, 1991). In England, a concerted "Back to Sleep" program has resulted in the general change from putting infants to sleep face-down to putting them on their backs or sides. A two-thirds drop in SIDS over a 5-year period has been attributed by some to this change Maugh (1996).

Estimates of the incidence of SIDS show considerable variation—4.6 per 1000 among Native North Americans and 2.1 per 1000 among Caucasians living in the same area (Bulterys, 1990). The SIDS rate in Sweden is 0.7 per 1000 (Haglund & Cnattingius, 1990), which accounted for more than a quarter of all the deaths of infants who had survived the 1st week after birth. That study of 190 SIDS cases over a 3-year period confirmed findings of earlier research that maternal smoking during pregnancy is a major risk factor for SIDS. Further, they found the strongest association to be with earlier compared with later SIDS (8 to 9 weeks vs. 13 to 15 weeks). The researchers concluded that maternal smoking may be the most important preventable factor in SIDS, and the amount of smoking may help explain why there are two peaks of occurrence. Bulterys (1990) also suggested that the high rate among Native Americans my be due to their high rate of maternal smoking.

SIDS is associated not only with maternal smoking during pregnancy, but with any smoking by any person in the infant's home. Thus, *passive smoking* effects due to the smoking of family members and even day-care providers, particularly when they smoke in the same room as the infant, may be a contributing factor (Klonoff-Cohen et al., 1995).

Smoking as a risk factor in SIDS is a relatively new finding, and researchers continue to study how tobacco has its deadly effects on infants. A group of researchers (Slotkin, Lappi, McCook, Lorber, & Seidler, 1995) provides evidence from animal studies that prenatal exposure to nicotine results in offspring who are deficient in their production of the stress hormones adrenaline and noradrenaline. As a consequence, if they are subjected to lowered oxygen, such as occurs when babies stop breathing during sleep (transient reduction of oxygen, or sleep apnea), the pups were not able to maintain normal heartbeat, and 30 percent died (100 percent of the control pups survived the oxygen reduction). The suggestion is that babies with pre- or postnatal exposure to tobacco may suffer in a similar manner and be at high risk (i.e, unable to maintain heart rate and/or restart breathing). The population studies just noted also support the notion of a dose-effect relationship of tobacco exposure and SIDS.

The clear advice to young parents, parents-to-be, child-care workers, or any persons in close contact with babies is: *Do not smoke while pregnant or when anywhere near children, especially infants. Don't take the risk!*

Effects of smoking on embryo and fetal deaths and growth retardation may occur through the reduction of oxygen in the blood of the mother and fetus. When the mother smokes, there is an increase of carbon monoxide in the blood, and that displaces oxygen in the red blood cells of both the mother and the embryo or fetus. Oxygen is necessary for fetal development, and oxygen restriction may have disruptive effects on that development.

In summary, maternal cigarette smoking during pregnancy is teratogenic for embryo and fetal deaths and for growth retardation, making tobacco use during pregnancy a major threat to the very lives of babies. It is, according to some investigators, the major preventable risk factor for infant mortality, including SIDS. There is not sufficient evidence that smoking causes severe CNS disruption or cognitive/intellectual deficits, and virtually no link with birth defects has been found. This probably reflects the fact that its major effects are to kill off the conceptus at an early point, leaving few to survive with deformities. Thus, tobacco is a serious teratogen, causing embryo and fetal deaths, growth retardation, and preterm deliveries. It contributes to infant mortality and has negative long-term effects but does not appear to contribute appreciably to specific developmental disabilities in surviving children. Paternal smoking may be a significant risk factor both pre- and postnatal.

Cocaine. It is estimated that in the United States between 7 and 15 percent of pregnant women use illicit drugs (Chomitz et al., 1995; N.P.H.S., 1996).[2] Annually, up to 375,000 babies are born to these drug-using mothers (National Association for Perinatal Addiction Research and Education, 1988), and nearly 1 million infants each year are exposed to illicit drugs (National Center for Addiction and Drug Abuse, 1996). Cocaine use by pregnant women is a growing problem, with more than 45,000 infants a year born to cocaine-abusing women (N.P.H.S., 1996). An estimated one in ten of the babies born in urban hospitals had prenatal exposure to cocaine (March of Dimes, 1993). The most commonly used illicit drugs by pregnant women are cocaine and marijuana, and they are often used concurrently with tobacco and alcohol (N.P.H.S., 1996).

Cocaine is a powerful, short-acting CNS stimulant with a half-life of an hour and a half. Within minutes of taking the drug and for 2 hours following, the risk of heart attack increases ten- to twentyfold (Carpenter, 1999). This occurs even with young people who are otherwise at low risk for coronaries. When used by pregnant women, cocaine crosses the placenta rapidly within about 3 minutes (Chasnoff, 1992). Cocaine is also ingested by nursing infants through the milk of the cocaine-using mother. Once in the fetal system, cocaine has the same effects as on adults, including tachycardia, vasoconstriction and reduced oxygen, and hypertension (Chasnoff, 1992; Keuhne & Reilly, 2000).

Maternal cocaine use is associated with fetal deaths, growth retardation, low birth weight, preterm births and stillbirths, birth defects, neurological defects, small head size, urinary tract and genital defects, seizures, and strokes (R. Taylor, 1989). Postnatal results include higher rates of infant crib deaths, developmental disabilities, and serious learning and behavioral problems (Keith et al., 1989; Kuehne & Reilly, 2000; Neerhof, MacGregor, Retsky, & Sullivan, 1989).

Postnatal care of cocaine-affected infants is difficult. Whether due to direct teratogenic effects or to associated pre- and postnatal factors, these babies are tense, irritable, have rapid, jerky movements, facial grimaces, and often have their eyes closed or averted from the mother. They are easily agitated and do not respond well to attempts at calming. Predictable feeding and sleep–wake cycles are hard to establish, and they show evidence of sensorimotor retardation (Chasnoff, 1992). Their high-pitched, grating cries are frequent, distressing, long-lasting, and highly noxious for adults. It is not easy to establish a warm, loving, caring bond with these children, and poor, neglectful parenting can easily develop, constituting still another risk factor for pathological development. A child who is born to a drug-addicted mother in poverty (which is most often the case for cocaine-affected babies) presents an onslaught of demands that would tax the best of mothers and children in the best of conditions. Under these poor conditions, the already stressed, economically deprived, poorly educated, probably isolated mother who has few good parenting skills in any event is often completely unable to care adequately for the child.

Although pregnancy and developmental problems are associated with prenatal cocaine use, it is also true that only a minority of all cocaine-exposed infants are significantly impaired (Hawley & Disney, 1992). There is no consistent pattern or syndrome in cocaine-affected babies, such as in FAS. Alcohol is a far more potent teratogen than cocaine

(Snodgrass, 1994), and the proportion of cocaine-exposed babies with severe disorder is less than the 10 percent of alcohol-exposed babies with FAS and the larger proportion with lesser effects (FAE). No "fetal cocaine syndrome" has been established, but it is clear that cocaine-exposed babies do have more abnormalities than babies of nondrug users.

It is not clear how many of the negative outcomes are due to cocaine or to other prenatal and postnatal risk factors related to cocaine use. Dow-Edwards, Chasnoff, and Griffith (1992) report that, compared with drug-free mothers, cocaine-abusing mothers had more pregnancy and birth complications of infectious disease (e.g., hepatitis and venereal diseases). They also abuse alcohol, tobacco, and other drugs, may be poor parents, and generally have lifestyles not conducive to good child development. The pre- and postnatal damage attributed to cocaine may thus be due to the direct or interactive effects of the other factors. Lester, Lagasse, and Brunner (1997) reviewed the research and concluded that such associated factors were not usually considered. Phelps, Wallace, and Bontrager (1997) and Phelps (2000) controlled for polydrug use and reported that cocaine per se had no independent impact on cognitive, social, language, and behavioral development. This is not to say that cocaine can be dismissed as a factor. We do not know, for example, if cocaine use is critical in creating the multihazard lifestyle associated with child defects.

When cocaine-abusing mothers are provided with medical care, nutrition, and social support, negative effects on the child are significantly less (Snodgrass, 1994). Cocaine, while a powerful drug for the user, may be a very weak human teratogen (Gonzalez & Campbell, 1994). Of all the major drugs, alcohol is by far the most potent human teratogen.

Heroin and Methadone.   These are possible teratogens because they are transmitted to the baby through the placenta and also through mother's milk. But their greatest danger may lie in their continued disruption of effective parenting.

As many as 60 to 90 percent of the newborns who are affected by cocaine, heroin, or methadone in utero can be addicted and can show withdrawal symptoms, including sweating, tremors, seizures, and diarrhea (Chasnoff, Hatcher, & Burns, 1980; Householder, Hatcher, Burns, & Chasnoff, 1982). Treatment using careful doses of drugs and gradual withdrawal can be effective in curing the baby's addiction. However, even with treatment, these symptoms can continue for as long as 6 months, and the child can become readdicted through the drug-using mother's milk.

There are short-term negative effects of heroin, as indicated by the number of heroin-exposed neonates with *neonatal abstinence syndrome* (i.e., drug-withdrawal symptoms). However, obvious long-term effects of prenatal exposure to heroin have not been determined (G. S. Wilson, 1992). The effects are more subtle. Minor neurobehavioral deficits in cognition and behavior appear to be associated with prenatal drug exposure, leaving these children at risk for academic failure. The major known effects on children seem to be due to the family/environment/socioeconomic risk factors that surround the growing child.

One of the research problems in assessing the long-term effects of maternal drug use in pregnancy is that moderate and heavy drug use is usually associated with many other risk factors for developmental problems. Drug users tend to be from lower socioeconomic groups, less educated, more socially and personally isolated, single mothers, prone to poor nutrition, to have poor health care, to use alcohol, tobacco, and other drugs, and to be subject to economic and personal stress. The continuing problems of children with prenatal drug exposure might thus be due in large part to these other postnatal factors rather than to the prenatal drug exposure itself. Some early research in the 1970s (reviewed by G. S. Wilson, 1992) reported data on children who had no prenatal drug exposure but had been raised in families in which one or both parents abused drugs, particularly heroin. A high proportion of these children had elevated rates of cognitive and behavioral problems compared with children raised in drug-free families. These data suggest the influence of family–environmental risk factors. Continued research is needed to separate the proportional contributions of the prenatal and postnatal factors.

The specific type and extent of fetal damage due to maternal cocaine use in pregnancy are not fully known, and more research is needed. The suspected effects on the child include mental retardation, attention and emotional control problems, growth retardation, and learning disabilities. With treated children who are not reexposed to the drugs, the effects diminish with age. Current data show that social and psychological pre- and postnatal risk factors are significant. Treatment and prevention programs, therefore, should focus on these social/psychological issues and not just on the drug use itself.

Marijuana.   As with so many health issues, social policy concerning marijuana has taken on ideological and political meaning, and much of our public controversy roils around the morality of its use. Against a background of political condemnation of marijuana use, some support its medical use, and in 1996, California and Arizona voters legalized its use for medical purposes, followed by six more states by late 1998. In its review of marijuana use in medical treatment, the National Academy of Science (1999) concluded that the drug is potentially useful for appetite stimulation and for control of pain, nausea, vomiting, and anxiety, all of which are severe problems secondary to chemotherapy and radiation therapy for cancer patients. However, its usual delivery system (i.e., smoking) is crude, inexact, and may create negative effects. Therefore, the academy recommended research on the development of effective, noninjurious delivery systems.

Marijuana, or cannabis, is prepared from the leaves of the plant *Cannabis sativa L* and is the most commonly used illicit drug. The substance that produces euphoric effects is delta-9-tetrehydrocannabinol (THC), and it is hallucinogenic. Its use is estimated to be between 5 and 34 percent of pregnant women, and prenatal use is maintained by most of those mothers postnatally (Astley & Little, 1990). Cannabinoids can be introduced to the fetus from the mother's blood through the placenta and to infants through mother's milk during breast-feeding (Dalterio & Fried, 1992). A drug-using mother who breast-feeds is particularly dangerous because THC transfers into mother's milk at *eight times* its level in maternal blood (Perez-Reyes & Wall, 1982). It is stored in mother's tissues, and although the concentration decreases considerably by the time it reaches the fetus, it can continue to be released over a long period of time to the fetus or to nursing infants. Cannabinoids also accumulate in amniotic fluid and fetal tissue and can later be released into the baby's bloodstream. It is thus reasonable to hypothesize that if it has negative effects, those effects might continue long after the mother's use has stopped, even postnatally as the substance is ingested through nursing and/or released from the baby's own tissues. Long-term storage and release of cannabinoids in humans have not yet been well studied.

The research does not reveal clearly established causal effects of marijuana, but it has been shown to be associated with some problems. Moore and Persaud (1998) noted that marijuana has not been shown to cause birth defects, but it is clearly associated with intrauterine growth retardation (IUGR) of the fetus. Astley and Little (1990) cited evidence for its association with labor and delivery problems, lower birth weight, higher frequency of preterm births, and in neonates, visual problems, tremors, and altered startle response.

Fried (1982) and Lester and Dreher (1989) reported that high-pitched cries in newborn infants, which may indicate neurophysiological damage, are associated with maternal marijuana use. The latter studied babies born in Jamaica, a society that generally accepts marijuana smoking, and reported that women who were heavy users of marijuana had a significantly higher rate of babies with such cries.

Voorhees and Mollnow (1987) reported that compared with controls, neonates of mothers who used marijuana in pregnancy had more pronounced startle responses and uncontrollable shaking and trembling. However, at 2 years of age, these babies appeared to have recovered and were not different from babies of nondrug-abusing mothers. These particular effects of marijuana thus appear to have been eliminated with age.

Other effects, however, are persistent. Fried (1986) compared children of nonusers with those of heavy users (smoking marijuana in excess of five times weekly or taking an equivalent amount in other forms). Potentially contributing factors such as income levels and the use of alcohol and cigarettes were controlled. In most respects, such as miscarriages, birth complications, birth defects, newborn activity levels, and alertness, there were no differences between the two groups of children. However, the heavy marijuana user group had shorter gestation periods, some minor facial anomalies around the eyes, including greater eye separation, and several days after birth showed less general responsiveness. Visual problems were also found, and they persisted into early childhood.

Astley and Little (1990) report that marijuana exposure through mother's milk during the 1st month postpartum is associated with a decrement in the motor development of 1-year-olds. However, (a) the seriousness and permanence of the effects are not clear and (b) because, as with other drugs, marijuana use is associated with so many variables (economics, education, health, tobacco, alcohol and other drug abuse, etc.), its direct effects on humans are not certain. Overall, there is little clear evidence of either major or minor physical anomalies associated with low levels of prenatal marijuana use. Dalterio and Fried (1992) suggest that the minority of studies that do report physical anomalies associated with prenatal marijuana use describe features of FAS that might be attributable to the high alcohol consumption associated with marijuana use.

In summary, marijuana can be stored in mother and child tissues and released at some later time. It can enter the fetal system in reduced concentrations by crossing the placenta and the neonate through breast-feeding. It is a known hallucinogen and causes euphoria in adults; thus, it has at least temporary CNS effects. At a minimum, it is a risk factor for some pregnancy and fetal problems. There appears to be a dose-effect relationship: Heavy use is associated with anomalies, although it is not clear how serious those effects are. There are no consistent findings of deleterious effects of low-level marijuana use.

However, the current lack of evidence of effects at low doses does not mean that marijuana is a "safe" drug. It is hallucinogenic, is transported to the fetus and to children of lactating mothers, is stored in maternal and child tissues, and at high-usage levels, is associated with fetal CNS impairment. The evidence for some negative effects of heavy use and the *possibility* of a dose-effect relationship should alert all women to caution. The best advice is clear: *Do not use marijuana prior to and during pregnancy and breast-feeding.*

Antiepiletic Medication. Epilepsy is a condition of repeated seizures and occurs to various degrees of seriousness, as will be discussed in Chapter 11. When a woman with epilepsy becomes pregnant, there is an increased risk of birth defects and of epilepsy in the child. The rate of birth defects in the general population is 2 to 3 percent. In women with epilepsy, it rises to 4 to 6 percent (Gumnit, 1997). However, it should be emphasized that 90 percent of pregnant women with epilepsy have normal children (Gumnit, 1997), which is the same as in the general population. It is not yet clear whether epilepsy results in birth defects, although it is accepted that severe epileptic conditions probably do have direct effects. However, seizure control medications, even those used during pregnancy, have teratogenic effects. Some drugs are implicated more than others, but no drug is completely safe during pregnancy (O'Donohoe, 1994). Neural tube defects, cleft lip and cleft palate, minor facial anomalies, and hirsutism (abnormal hairiness) are associated with antiepileptic drugs taken during pregnancy. Functional disorders such as mental retardation are associated with only some types of epilepsy but not with other types. Epilepsy will be discussed in Chapter 12. (Note: The summary for Chapter 6 is contained in the Chapter 7 summary.)

KEY TERMS

Know these important terms. Check the chapter and the Glossary for their meanings.
They are listed here in the approximate order of their appearance in the chapter.

Teratogens	Functional endpoints	Chlamydia
Endogenous	Behavioral teratogenics	AIDS
Exogenous	Dose-effect relationship	HIV-1
Experimental research	Paresis	In vitro
Correlational research	Rubella	Thalidomide
Endpoints of teratogenic	Cytomegalovirus	Diethylstilbestrol
Organogenetic period	Varicella	Ethanol
Birth defect	Congenital toxoplasmosis	Fetal alcohol syndrome (FAS)
Congenital anomalies	Influenza	Fetal alcohol effects (FAE)
Pathogenic substances	Sexually transmitted disease	Spina bifida
Teratology	(STD)	Risk drinking
Behavioral teratology	Syphilis	Sudden infant death syndrome
Target access	Juvenile paresis	(SIDS)
Genetic determination	Wasserman reaction	Passive smoking
Critical periods	Herpes simplex virus	Neonatal abstinence syndrome
Delayed effects	Gonorrhea	

SUGGESTED READING

Abel, E. L. (1990). *Fetal alcohol syndrome.* Oradell, NJ: Medical Economics Co.

Cicero, T. J. (1994). Effects of paternal exposure to alcohol on offspring development. *Alcohol, Health and Research World, 18*(1), 37–41.

Streissguth, A. P. (1994). A long-term perspective of AS. *Alcohol, Health, and Research World, 18*(1), 74–81.

For full discussions of experimental and correlation research, see appropriate chapters in any good undergraduate research methods textbook.

STUDY QUESTIONS

6-1. Do you understand the concepts of correlation and experimental research? If not, take a look at any good research methods textbook.

6-2. What are some of the major problems in doing good research on teratogens and human pregnancy?

6-3. Some teratogens, such as tobacco, have effects at all teratogenic endpoints. Explain this statement, as if to a student.

6-4. Behavioral teratology is concerned with functional endpoints. What does that mean?

6-5. The use of thalidomide in the 1950s is an example of teratogenic effects. At that time, many principles of teratogenics were not developed or well known. Think about the thalidomide problem, the research that was done before its use, and why some European countries allowed its use. What principle of teratogenics, had it been well known then, might have helped to avoid that problem?

6-6. Review so you fully understand it the concept of critical periods as it applies to teratogens.

6-7. Several factors in addition to the nature of the toxic agent determine the type and degree of teratogenic effects. Think this through: What are those factors?

6-8. Alcohol and tobacco are powerful teratogens, and yet so many women of childbearing age abuse them despite the readily available information. If you were to set up a community program to reduce conception, pregnancy, and birth problems due to the use of these substances, what kind of program would you create? What would your major goals be?

6-9. The effects of cocaine on embryo and fetal development provide an example of how a single factor (cocaine) may have many associated risk factors that contribute to the eventual disability. Think this through: What are some important cocaine-associated risk factors that might have effects on the developing child?

NOTES

1. Ethical constraints prevent researchers from meeting all of the requirements of controlled experimental studies, such as administering doses of drugs to pregnant women to see if expected damage does occur.

2. Schroeder (1992) based her conclusion regarding the negative effects of maternal marijuana use on studies carried out in the 1980s, including Fried (1982), Fried, Watkins, & Dillon (1987), Gibson, Baghurst, & Colley (1983), Greenland, Staisch, Brown, & Gross (1982), Hingson et al., (1982), and Lester & Dreher (1989).

7 Exogenous Etiological Factors in Disabilities: Prenatal Origins (Continued)

(**Author's note:** Chapter 7 continues the discussion begun in Chapter 6 of exogenous prenatal factors in developmental disabilities. This lengthy material has been presented in two chapters to avoid a single extremely long chapter.)

I. Environmental Hazards of a Passive Nature

The negative effects of illicit drugs and alcohol require an active involvement by the parents, engaging in behavior that brings the pathogenic substances into their bodies. Thus, there is a good deal of personal responsibility involved. However, there are many hazardous factors in the environment that may have teratogenic effects and that impinge on the mother, father, and child in a passive manner only because the people are in an unhealthy environment. Known hazardous events include radiation, lead and other heavy metals, and many chemicals. Some of the most important are discussed in the sections that follow.

Radiation

Radiation is a known teratogen; ionizing radiation, ultrasound, and certain microwaves pass directly through maternal tissues without undergoing any diminution or change. Their route to the embryo or fetus is direct. Of the three, only ionizing radiation appears to have selective effects on the embryo or fetus that result in birth defects. Pathogenic doses of ionizing radiation are difficult to calculate because the amount of radiation absorbed depends on many factors. These include the type of radiation (alpha or beta particles or gamma rays) and whether the radiation is introduced internally as in treatment or diagnostic procedures or is delivered from external sources such as x-rays. The effects vary with these factors, with the length of exposure, with the stage of gestation, and with particular biochemical affinities of some radiation for certain tissues. There are many radiation sources such as x-rays in dental and medical examinations, radioactive materials used in thyroid and cancer treatment, background radiation in some workplaces, and even radiation leaks from nuclear power plants. In animal studies, radiation has caused sterility in males and females, reduction in ova and sperm count, damage to sex cells, and genetic mutations (Brent, 1977).

According to Moore and Persaud (1998), there is no clear evidence that the low levels of radiation used in diagnostic medical procedures cause congenital anomalies in humans. Ultrasound techniques have replaced much of the use of x-rays, and the dangers to the fetus have thus been reduced. However, radiation continues to pose serious risks to women who are pregnant or who are planning to become pregnant in the near future.

Most dangerous in pregnancy is prolonged or very high levels of radiation, but few women of childbearing age encounter such prolonged or high levels. The effects of high levels of radiation include embryo and fetal death, genetic mutations, physical malformation and birth defects, and mental retardation. Radiation may have damaging effects at any time during pregnancy. It is particularly dangerous in the first 2 weeks, prior to implantation, when radiation can destroy the zygote. Malformations that constitute birth defects are very likely in the next 4 weeks, following implantation.

The dangers of radiation go beyond pregnancy, and its effects are cumulative. Repeated exposures to radiation even by children and adolescents can have mutagenic effects, thus possibly producing genetic and chromosomal anomalies later, when that person's gametes help to create a zygote. Keep in mind that the woman's ova can be susceptible to radiation for many years before she becomes pregnant, and mutagenic changes in sex chromosomes might occur. Men, however, continue to generate new sperm throughout most of their lives, and it is possible for sperm damaged at one time to be replaced by new undamaged cells.

Microwaves may have destructive effects on the mammalian embryo and fetus (Brent, 1977). It is thought that these effects may be thermal; that is, the damage may be due to elevated temperature in the tissues rather than direct effects of the microwaves. Normal use of microwave appliances appears not to pose any dangers to humans.

Lead

Lead, a toxic heavy metal, is particularly dangerous for children, both as a prenatal teratogen and as a postnatal environmental toxin (that will be discussed in Chapter 8). As a teratogen, its endpoint effects appear to be broadband, causing embryo and fetal deaths, malformations and birth defects, growth retardation, and functional disabilities such as mental retardation. The fetus is a passive recipient of lead through a mother who is in a toxic environment; contamination of the pregnant woman means contamination of the fetus. The placenta does not screen out lead (Angell & Lavery, 1982), and prenatal lead exposure increases the risks of fetal death and congenital malformations (Castellino & Alimandi, 1995; Castellino, Castellino, & Sannolo, 1995; Needleman, Rabinowitz, Leviton, Linn, & Schoenbaum, 1984). Most of the research has examined the effects of high levels of postnatal lead exposure. The data are convincing that growth retardation and, particularly, impaired brain development and cognitive deficits result from high levels of lead exposure. Recent studies are examining the effects of prenatal exposure at low and moderate levels of lead. They suggest that what used to be considered low and moderate levels of lead exposure may actually be toxic for children and dangerous in pregnancy.

Lead is not only a teratogen, affecting the embryo and fetus, but it continues to be a serious environmental toxin throughout childhood while the young brain is still developing, causing brain impairment and mental retardation. Preschoolers are most at risk, but serious dangers continue throughout the period of continuing brain development to about age 8. Even beyond that age, severe lead poisoning in youth and adults can cause illness and death, as has been documented throughout much of our history (Eisinger, 1996).

Humans are exposed to more than 5 million chemicals in the environment. Each year, manufacturing increases that number. Animal testing for teratogenicity has been carried out on only about 1600 of those 5 million chemicals (Shepard, 1986). Of those tested, half have been found to have teratogenic effects on laboratory animals. It is not known how many of these tested chemicals are human teratogens or what proportion of the remaining nearly 5 million might be human teratogens. The possible interactive effects of so many potential teratogens cannot even be estimated at this time.

Mercury and Other Hazards

Other known teratogens, such as paints and solvents, are found in many manufacturing settings, and workers are regularly exposed to them. Insecticides, herbicides, and animal feed additives are common factors in farms and rural feed mills, and traces are found in foods for humans. Cleaning materials such as soaps, detergents, and solvents, particularly where they are manufactured, pose risks to women of childbearing age. Health-care workers in hospitals and laboratories are exposed to x-rays, aerosol propellants, anesthetic gases, and chemicals used in cleaning and in laboratory procedures, any of which can be toxins with teratogenic effects. Most of these teratogens are found in workplaces, and some pose significant hazards for women. Many of these substances can be stored in the body for long periods and be released into the woman's system long after the exposure. Thus, even prenatal exposure may be significantly hazardous.

Mercury is a case in point. In 1953, fetal deaths and significant birth defects in Japan were seen to be associated with consumption of fish from Minimata Bay. The water was severely polluted by mercury from industry. Mercury became concentrated up the food chain and reached its peak when humans ate predatory fish such as tuna. The resulting CNS disorder came to be known as Minimata disease. For half a century, the teratogenic effects of mercury have been known. Recent newspaper reports (e.g., Revkin, 2000) noted that each year an estimated 60,0000 children are born in the United States with prenatal mercury exposure, most from maternal consumption of poisoned fish. The major sources of environmental mercury are coal-burning power plants, emitting over 40 tons of mercury each year, or about one-third of the total released into the environment (Revkin, 2000). Federal and state health agencies have repeatedly warned against consuming mercury-tainted fish, and this may have reduced the scale of the effects. However, federal efforts to reduce mercury emissions have been blocked by industrial interests for many years, and each year of delay has left still more children affected. In mid-2000, with the release of a National Academy of Science study, it appears that regulations will be drafted. How long this process will take and how effective the control measure will be are yet to be seen.

II. Maternal Conditions

Maternal Hormonal Disorders

Noninfectious maternal hormone conditions, maternal illness, or other pathological conditions of the mother can also cause fetal anomalies and birth defects. Phenylketonuria (PKU) is an example. As discussed in Chapter 3, pregnant women who are homozygous for PKU and who are not treated for that condition present an unhealthy prenatal environment for the developing child. Mental retardation of the child is an almost certain result.

Hyperthyroidism and Hypothyroidism.   Important hormonal conditions of the mother are hypothyroidism, in which the thyroid produces insufficient thyroxin (thyroid hormone), and hyperthyroidism, in which it produces too much. In both situations, the health of the mother and the development of the child are threatened. As discussed in Chapter 3, cretinism is a genetically determined condition in which an underactive thyroid gland fails to produce sufficient thyroxin. Cretinism is an extreme condition, and there are many persons with underactive thyroids who do not reach that extreme and in whom the condition is not genetically caused. Thyroxin helps to control the overall rate of growth and specifically brain development. Hypothyroidism in pregnant women causes an unhealthy reproductive environment but can be effectively treated with hormones to overcome the deficiency. If not treated, these mothers are prone to spontaneous abortions, preterm deliveries, and stillbirths. The children who survive birth are typically slower in motor and cognitive development and have a higher than normal incidence of mental retardation. Treatment of the mother prior to or early in pregnancy generally prevents these negative outcomes.

There is less information on the effects of hyperthyroidism on pregnancy. In adults, an overactive thyroid produces rapid heart rate, high blood pressure, and increased metabolic rate. Some earlier research (Burrow, 1965) shows high rates of fetal deaths and fetal goiter. One of the problems is that treatment is complicated because the drugs used to correct hyperthyroidism can cross the placenta and may cause damage to the developing child. We have no current data on the contribution of maternal hyperthyroidism to developmental disabilities.

Diabetes Mellitus.   This is a hormonal condition with multifactorial causes (a recessive gene in interaction with diet), in which the body fails to produce sufficient insulin. This results in poor sugar metabolism and a buildup of blood sugar (glucose). About 10 million Americans have diabetes mellitus. Most develop it in later adulthood, but about 1 in 500 children have diabetes mellitus (Berger & Thompson, 1995). Diabetes can be managed through diet and insulin but not cured. When it occurs very early in life, diabetes can be fatal if not vigorously treated. Its occurrence later in life is associated with greater risks from other diseases.

In diabetes, the person's insufficient insulin results in poor sugar metabolism and high blood glucose (sugar) level. *Gestational diabetes* is diagnosed in 1 to 5 percent of pregnant women (Bellenir, 1999). In those cases, the mother's high glucose level is transmitted to the fetus through the placenta. Insulin is needed to move glucose from the blood to muscle tissues where it functions as energy, and the fetal pancreas creates more insulin to deal with the elevated maternal glucose. Any extra glucose is converted to fat, and the fetus becomes larger than normal (macrosomia), which is a major risk to the fetus. Such large size can create serious problems during normal birth, and to avoid those problems, Caesarian procedures are used.

The effects on the fetus are most severe if gestational diabetes occurs early in pregnancy, during the most critical period of the first trimester, resulting in a doubling or tripling of birth defects (E. Miller et al., 1981). However, it does not usually occur until about the 24th gestational week, thus in most cases avoiding the most critical period. Even then, gestational diabetes is associated with increased risks of spontaneous abortion, miscarriage, and stillbirth (Weiss & Coustan, 1988). Babies born to mothers with diabetes have increased risks for congenital heart defects and vertebra and limb anomalies. One of the common problems is abnormally low blood sugar (hypoglycemia) in the neonate. This occurs because of the high insulin levels produced by the fetus in response to the mother's high blood glucose during gestation. After the birth, the mother's high glucose level is no longer a factor, but the baby's high insulin is still present, resulting in hypoglycemia.

Although serious for the baby, gestational diabetes ordinarily poses no serious threats to the mother's health, and the condition corrects itself after the end of pregnancy. Diabetes in the father is not associated with these risks, and thus, the effects on the infants appear to be due to environmental (uterine) and not to genetic factors. The exact mechanisms leading to birth defects are not yet known, and continued research is needed. It does appear, however, that vigorous treatment with diet, insulin, and close monitoring of the mother from the beginning and throughout pregnancy can prevent virtually all of the negative effects on the children (reviewed by Avery & Taeusch, 1984). Treatment of the neonate is necessary to deal with hypoglycemia and other chemical imbalances that may occur as a result of gestational diabetes.

Maternal Nutrition

Severe and chronic maternal malnutrition in pregnancy is associated with increased risk of spontaneous abortions, premature and low birth weight, stillbirth, susceptibility to illness such as pneumonia, high infant mortality, fetal neurological damage, and cognitive deficits in children, including mental retardation. Maternal malnutrition may have cross-generation effects, as the children who are born to malnourished mothers are at greater risk for problems in their own future pregnancies (Kopp & Kaler, 1989). In general, the effects of severe malnutrition on mother and child during pregnancy can have serious short-term and long-term effects.

Mild to moderate malnutrition is also thought to have seriously negative effects on cognitive development, but it is only beginning to be studied (Sigman, 1995). Some of the most important ideas drawn from research on the complex relationships between maternal nutrition and child health are discussed in the following paragraphs.

Poor nutrition for women affects their reproductive health even before they become pregnant. Poor diets are associated with delayed menstrual onset, menstrual irregularity, difficulty becoming pregnant, high rates of spontaneous abortions, and neonatal deaths. Severe malnutrition of girls in childhood is a risk factor for having premature or low-birth-weight babies. Good nutrition, not only during pregnancy but also throughout early development, is important in promoting healthy pregnancies and preventing birth defects.

There is a dose-effect relationship between the degree of maternal malnutrition and severity of child health problems. The most severe effects are found in situations where a population has been subjected to chronic and severe starvation such as in wartime and national revolutions. For example, at this writing, the United Nations is warning that 8 million people in Ethiopia will suffer hunger or starvation in 2000. More than 1 million died in the Ethiopian famine of 1984 (Crossette, 2000). Although climatic conditions such as sustained drought are sometimes implicated, political conflicts are usually at fault, and only political solutions can help those people. While we may think of chronic, severe malnutrition as a problem in poor nations, there are some parts of the United States where politics and poverty combine to create serious malnutrition.

Malnutrition is a health problem with many causes. In underdeveloped countries where malnutrition is a major problem, the causes may be political upheaval and armed conflicts; natural disasters such as floods, drought, and crop freezes; poverty and low purchasing power; poor education and consumers' lack of nutritional information; and general poor health conditions. In developed countries such as the United States, the more violent causes are not present, but we still have poor nutrition due to poverty and to poor consumer education across all socioeconomic groups. In addition, there may be another factor that is usually overlooked: Not only is there a lack of knowledge about nutrition, but there are sources of active misinformation and harmful guidance. Compare children's experience sitting through a single 15-minute nutrition lesson in school and their repeated exposure to highly polished and compelling television commercials urging them to consume high-fat, high-calorie, high-salt, high-sugar, and low-vitamin fast foods. Which message is going to stay with those children and affect their eating habits?

Maternal malnutrition can affect development throughout pregnancy, but most seriously during critical periods—specifically during the first trimester and during rapid growth periods of the central nervous system. In the first trimester (embryonic and early fetal periods), the heart, brain, and spinal cord may be particularly affected by maternal malnutrition. In addition, the infant brain develops rapidly in the last 12 weeks of pregnancy (the last trimester) and during the first 2 years after birth. Animal research (Winick, 1976) and postmortem studies of human infants (Winick & Rosso, 1969) show a relationship between malnutrition of the mother and of the infant and a decrease in number of infant brain cells. Winick (1981) estimates 20 percent fewer brain cells in a seriously malnourished fetus.

Other animal research (e.g., Galler, Tonkiss, Maldonado-Irizarry, 1994; Tonkiss, Galler, Formica, Shukitt-Hale, & Timm, 1990) has found that maternal protein malnutrition in rats affects fetal development, and the offspring show evidence of some learning impairments. Thus, maternal malnutrition, particularly in the first and third trimesters, and child malnutrition during the first 2 postnatal years are particularly risky.

Maternal malnutrition in pregnancy is thought to cause a decrease in the number of fetal brain cells and interference with the process of myelination, which occurs at a rapid rate in the early postnatal years. Myelin sheaths cover and insulate nerve cells and aid in the transmission of neural impulses. Infant malnutrition may impede the development of the myelin sheaths and thus interfere with the functioning of the neurons, resulting in cognitive deficits, including mental retardation (Davison & Dobbing, 1966).

The National Academy of Sciences concluded that for pregnant women in the United States, the energy intake (i.e., calories) and intake of certain vitamins and minerals were below recommended levels (Institute of Medicine, 1990). Some proteins, vitamins B-12, and vitamin C, however, exceeded the minimum levels. Although maternal nutrition in pregnancy is related to disabilities, it is not yet known if specific nutrients are responsible or how their lack affects fetal health (Chomitz, Cheung, & Lieberman, 1995).

Poor maternal nutrition alone, unless it is severe and chronic, might not contribute significantly to children's disabilities. It is thought that the developing child draws adequately from the mother's resources, even if the mother is somewhat malnourished. Further, if there are negative effects, they can be offset by improved child nutrition after birth. However, in some situations such as poverty, conditions might not improve after birth. A child might be born healthy to an undernourished mother, but if the child then continues to have insufficient nourishment because the family is poor, negative effects will probably occur. Thus, when maternal malnutrition occurs, it is a markedly more serious developmental problem for children born into poverty than it is for children born into more affluent homes (Lozoff, 1989).

Nutritional deficiency in mothers is usually measured as (a) insufficient number of calories, (b) inadequate protein intake, and (c) inadequate intake of vitamins and minerals. Insufficient calorie intake is probably the least damaging, while failure to obtain adequate proteins, vitamins, and minerals is the most harmful. The focus here is on micronutrients— that is, those substances such as iron, iodine, and vitamins that are needed by the body in only small amounts. They are not produced by the body and must be ingested in food or provided through dietary supplements. Their lack produces no dramatic, sudden problems and no immediately recognized cravings; thus, undernourished persons might continue for years not knowing of the progressive damage that may be occurring.

Dietary insufficiency is the main cause of maternal malnutrition, but it might also be caused by metabolic or other maternal problems (e.g., diabetes mellitus, thyroid malfunction, phenylketonuria, and anemia). Disorders such as these can disrupt a woman's ability to metabolize important nutrients even though she ingests a quality and amount that would be sufficient for other women. The demands on the mother of a multiple pregnancy such as triplets might reduce the nutrients available to each fetus. There may be problems in the structure and function of the placenta, leading to an insufficiency of blood flow to the fetus and thus to a decrement in the needed nutrients. But for the most part, insufficient dietary intake accounts for malnutrition.

The picture is complicated because malnutrition is associated with many risk factors, chiefly, economic status. People in poverty have more nutrition problems than do others, and this is a serious problem in pregnancy (Lozoff, 1989). But poor people also have fewer resources such as general medical care. They tend to be less healthy and less educated. They have a history of poor nutrition, inadequate prenatal and postnatal care, more teenage pregnancies, more pregnancies per person, more out-of-wedlock pregnancies, and less supportive personal and social environments. When several factors cooccur in a poor family, the risks for problem pregnancies and child impairments are greatly increased.

The women in the United States most at risk for poor nutrition and thus for negative effects on their children are poor, young, single mothers and those who are socially isolated. They have limited knowledge about nutrition (due to low education and/or cognitive limitations) and were themselves malnourished during childhood and youth. In addition, cigarette smoking and addictions to drugs or alcohol may reduce appetites, interfere with motivation and good judgment, and upset eating habits, thus increasing the risk of malnutrition (Dwyer, 1983).

There has been some dispute concerning the effectiveness of dietary supplementation programs. A small number of studies (reviewed by Sigman, 1995) present data from several countries in which pregnant women and infants were provided diets enriched with calories and/or protein. Among these studies, there is general agreement that dietary supplementation is associated with higher motor and cognitive abilities in children. The one long-term controlled study that has been published (Pollitt, Gorman, Engle, Martorell, & Rivera, 1993) not only indicates measured gains in cognitive, motor, and perceptual skills but also shows lasting effects. In that study, two Guatemalan villages were provided with daily high-calorie and high-protein supplements for 8 years. A follow-up several years later found the gains were still evident in adolescents who had been infants or children in the study, even as long as 12 years earlier.

Sigman (1995) concludes from her review that mild to moderate malnutrition has negative effects on children's cognitive development and that dietary supplementation for families in poverty can offset at least some of these effects. Whatever the causes, malnutrition is a serious problem for pregnancy and neonatal health, particularly for women with the at-risk characteristics noted earlier. Public health concern for proper diets in pregnancy and infancy is not misplaced.

Maternal Stress

Stress during pregnancy is a factor that, on the face of it, would seem to be important in prenatal development (Chalmers, 1984a, 1984b). Negative emotions, such as fear, anxiety, and depression, involve the mother's autonomic nervous system with resulting changes in respiration, heart rate and blood pressure, blood flow, muscle tension, and the release of chemicals into the blood, such as acetylcholine and epinephrine. The emotional responses due to severe and/or prolonged stress should create even more powerful effects. If high stress occurs during pregnancy, then blood flow to the placenta can be diverted, possibly teratogenic chemicals might be released into the bloodstream, and both of these factors could disrupt prenatal development. It has been hypothesized that anxiety during pregnancy might increase maternal metabolic rate, thus reducing fetal weight gain and contributing to preterm labor (Kramer, 1987). It has also been suggested that high stress might result in the mother engaging in tension-reducing behaviors such as smoking, drinking, or other drug use, all of which are teratogenic (McAnarney & Stevens-Simon, 1990). Across many different societies, it is traditionally believed that pregnancy and birth are best carried out under low-stress conditions (Samuels & Samuels, 1986).

The research literature on humans provides some evidence for negative effects of stress on the pregnancy, the fetus, and the neonate (Parker & Barrett, 1992), although not a great deal of research has been carried out. More complications during pregnancy and childbirth are found with women who have been under sustained stress (Katz, Jenkins, Haley, & Bowes, 1991). Stress, when present with other factors such as poverty, is a risk factor for low birth weight and preterm delivery (e.g., Newton & Hunt, 1984; Williamson, LeFevre, & Hector, 1989). Animal studies have shown that noise, shock, and crowding-induced stress are related to low birth weight (Istvan, 1986; Myers, 1975). Fenster et al. (1995) hypothesized that with more women working, work-related stress might have become an important factor in pregnancy. The research found a significant relationship between work stress and risk for spontaneous abortion only in older women who smoked cigarettes. Thus, stress appears to be a risk factor when associated with other factors (poverty, smoking), but stress alone has not yet been shown consistently to be a significant predictor of pregnancy problems in humans. However much those studies suggest a relationship between maternal stress and embryo/fetal development, the literature to date does not present a consistent picture (Chomitz et al., 1995; Collins, Dunkel-Schetter, Lobel, & Scrimshaw, 1993; Istvan, 1986; Norbeck & Tilden, 1983).

Perhaps the relationship for humans compared with that for laboratory animals is not clear because it is more complicated; that is, stress might be mediated by family resources and by psychological and other support available to the pregnant woman during the stressful situation (Smilkstein, Helsper-Lucas, Ashworth, Montano, & Pagel, 1984). When those resources are lacking, then high stress may be a risk factor for pregnancy and birth complications, including low birth weight (Norbeck & Tilden, 1983). Collins et al. (1993) reported that poor women who had good social support had better progress in labor, and their babies had higher Apgar scores at 5 minutes postbirth and higher birth weight. Both are important factors in infant health.

Maternal stress has not been found to be a direct causal factor in developmental disabilities, but it is a reasonable inference that it is a risk factor when combined with other variables. While the research is inconclusive, good judgment does call for low stress and high support from family and other resources for women during pregnancy and childbirth.

Maternal Age

Age at pregnancy is a risk factor for developmental disabilities, particularly in Down syndrome as we saw in Chapter 3. In general, young adolescent mothers and those over 35 have increased risks for pregnancy and birth problems and for developmental disabilities in children (see Box 2.3). Maternal age of about 25 to 35 years appears to be the optimal range for healthy pregnancies and births. Chromosomal abnormalities (e.g., Down syndrome) are more likely in older mothers, particularly those over 40. These chromosomal problems may be due to the aging of the ova, all of which have been produced by the time the woman reaches sexual maturity, unlike males who continue to produce new sperm throughout most of their lives.

Other problems such as growth retardation leading to low birth weight, more frequent illness during pregnancy, difficulties in labor and delivery, miscarriages, and stillbirths are also more likely with older mothers. But it is not clear whether they are due directly to age or whether they might be caused by factors related to aging. That is, women over 40 generally have more aging-related health problems, less stamina, longer recuperation time, less muscle tone, and so on, and these might contribute to the complications related to pregnancy and birth. However, if they are healthy, older mothers seem not to have any more pregnancy and birth problems than younger women (A. Stein, 1983). Pregnant women over the age of about 35 who maintain good health, nutrition, exercise, and prenatal medical care do as well as younger mothers. Except for the chromosomal anomalies, aging alone does not have to be a significant factor in pregnancy.

With procedures such as amniocentesis, older women can have the presence of chromosomal anomalies such as Down syndrome or sex chromosome anomalies diagnosed during approximately the 16th to 18th week of pregnancy (early in the second trimester) and then make informed decisions about aborting the fetus. Amniocentesis can detect some 100 genetically based diseases, and the procedure is an added safeguard for older women.

Age-related problems are more commonly found in young mothers, with increased risk for those under age 20 (McAnarney, 1987). Babies born to teenagers compared with those of young adult mothers (ages 25 to 35) have higher risks of premature birth and low birth weight, respiratory problems, neurological damage, and death in infancy (Osofsky, Osofsky, & Diamond, 1988). Problems due to chromosomal damage are rare in young mothers and are associated more with those over 35 years. Further, it is suspected that for very young mothers (under age 15), both the child's and the mother's growth appear to be slowed by the pregnancy (Hayes, 1987). This is not surprising because youngsters of 15 years are normally still in the process of considerable physical growth themselves. They are, in the words of a colleague, "children having babies."

There are about 500,000 births annually to teenage mothers (i.e., one in twenty teenagers), and 60 percent of those young mothers are unmarried (Children's Defense Fund, 1988). Clearly, the increased risks to so many newborns constitute a substantial public health problem.

There is an apparent contradiction here. Although this age group has higher childbearing risks, it is also considered by many to be the optimal biological age range for bearing healthy babies (Guttmacher & Kaiser, 1986). The answer may lie in the adequacy of medical care received by the expectant teenager, her lifestyle, and the personal and social supports available to her. As a rule, unmarried teenagers do not enjoy optimal conditions for pregnancy and birth. They are often alone, with no husband or companion to shoulder some of the hefty responsibility, and may be ostracized by their families, criticized, and psychologically maltreated. These youngsters typically have few social and economic resources, their knowledge of prenatal and postnatal care is meager, and their judgments for solving normal life problems are not mature. For example, the nutritional choices of adolescents in general are notoriously poor—imagine the quality of self-determined menus of an isolated, pregnant teenager! However, when adequate prenatal care is provided for these youngsters, the rates of pregnancy and birth difficulties decrease and are similar to those for other mothers (Lee & Corpuz, 1988). Thus, the health problems may not be related directly to the mother's young age but rather to the many accompanying social risk factors. In theory at least, all of those factors can be effectively dealt with by an enlightened society.

Rh Incompatibility

A potential pregnancy complication is a genetic–environment interaction that causes an incompatibility of the mother's and fetus' blood. That incompatibility is based on a protein substance (the Rh factor) that is in the child's blood but absent in the mother. The Rh factor, named for rhesus monkeys in which it was discovered, is a normal genetically inherited characteristic determined by multiple genes. Persons with this factor are classified as Rh positive and those without it are Rh negative. More than 90 percent of Western Europeans and North Americans fall into these two normal groups. The vast majority of these people are Rh+, and about 15 percent of Caucasians and 5 percent of blacks are Rh–. It should be stressed that the presence or absence of this factor is not in itself pathological.

The problems arise when an Rh– woman (lacking the protein) and an Rh+ man (with the protein) conceive an Rh+ child. If any of the child's Rh+ blood cells mix with those of the Rh– mother, the mother's system will begin producing antibodies to counteract the foreign protein substance (a condition called **erythroblastosis**). The first pregnancy is normally not a problem because the mother's and fetus' blood systems ordinarily do not mix during gestation. However, fetal blood cells will mix with the mother's during a miscarriage, abortion, Cesarean, or normal birth. The antibodies produced in the mother's blood will persist throughout her life, and subsequent Rh+ children born to that mother are at risk. The probability is that her children will be Rh+, since some 85 percent of people are. In future pregnancies, maternal antibodies can cross the placenta, enter the embryo and/or fetus' bloodstream, and attack and destroy fetal red blood cells. This may result in fetal death, miscarriage, or stillbirth. If the baby survives, anemia, jaundice, heart defects, brain damage, and mental retardation might result.

Diagnosis, prevention, and treatment have developed over several decades. Rh status of potential parents is easily tested, and they can be advised if the woman is Rh– and the man Rh+. Within 72 hours after a miscarriage, abortion, or the birth of the first child, the Rh– mother can be administered a vaccine (Rh immune globulin) that will prevent the formation of Rh+ antibodies (Apgar & Beck, 1974), and future pregnancies will be protected. Prior to the development of this effective prevention, some 10,000 babies each year in the United States were brain damaged or died as a result of Rh incompatibility (Rosenblith & Sims-Knight, 1985). Given proper maternity care, this should no longer be a source of developmental disabilities. The availability of prenatal care for all women, however, depends on public policy actions, which often move too slowly and uncertainly.

The Rh+ or Rh– condition is not, itself, a defect. Except for the particular combination of an Rh+ baby growing within an Rh– mother, the blood condition does not harm the individual. The incompatibility is a serious problem because the mother's Rh– system treats the baby's Rh+ blood as if it is a threatening foreign substance that must be destroyed. This is an example of a genetic X environment interaction in which a fetus with this normal genetic trait is in a hostile uterine environment.

III. Other Prenatal Factors

Other factors such as oxygen deprivation and physical trauma to the mother during pregnancy can cause developmental disabilities. As discussed earlier, some teratogens such as alcohol and nicotine can result in reduced oxygen for the developing embryo or fetus, and their effects on development are thus partly due to oxygen deprivation. Any severe interruption of the pregnant woman's breathing due to injury or illness can translate into reduced blood oxygen available to the developing child, and depending on the level of fetal development and the duration of the breathing interruption, disabilities can result.

Disabilities due to physical trauma during pregnancy are rare (Moore & Persaud, 1998) because the fetus, floating in the amniotic fluid and surrounded by the amnion and the mother's body, is well protected from physical force. The force from falls, for example, can often be safely absorbed by amniotic fluid. But many pregnant women suffer more traumatic force such as in automobile crashes or physical attacks by abusive men, and these can result in premature birth, loss of the fetus, or interruption of fetal oxygen supply.

If, for some reason, a significant reduction occurs in the amount of amniotic fluid, then the developing fetus is no longer well protected. It is believed that limb deformities may result.

However, developmental disabilities due to oxygen deprivation or to physical trauma most likely occur during and after birth. At those times, the child is no longer provided with oxygen by the maternal blood supply and is not protected physically by amniotic fluid and the mother's tissue mass.

IV. A Multi-Hit Model of Neurological Handicap

Snodgrass (1994) outlined a model of substance effects that describes the multiple nature of pathogenic assaults on the child. According to this model, the general failure to find clear, serious, teratogenic effects of illicit drugs such as cocaine, heroin, and marijuana does not mean they are safely used in pregnancy. Alcohol has its serious negative effects through several mechanisms and can operate during gestation and after birth. The effects of alcohol can arise first from a sudden, severe, concentrated "hit" on the developing child in utero (i.e., the teratogenic effects). This physical/chemical hit during sensitive periods accounts for the FAS syndrome, including the child's physical deformities and mental retardation. But alcohol abuse in a family continues to have multiple hits on the child. An alcohol-abusing family will most likely include less attentive, less competent parenting, and the child may thus be subject to poor nutrition, poor physical care, more illness and school interruption, less psychological support and guidance, and more abuse and neglect. All of these factors will affect the child's cognitive functioning, learning, personal/emotional development, and social competence.

Cocaine and other illicit drugs may not have the severe first hit, the teratogenic effects, but they can continue to have multiple physical, cognitive, and psychological hits on the child's development. Thus, even without teratogenic effects, the use of illicit drugs in pregnancy is a serious risk factor for child development.

V. Chapter Summary

Chapters 6 and 7 have discussed exogenous etiological factors with prenatal origins. A large class of factors, teratogens, includes environmental substances that can enter the pregnant woman's body, cross the placenta, and cause irreversible damage to the child at any stage of prenatal development. The degree of damage depends on the interaction of the nature and amount of the teratogenic substance, the child's genotype, the particular organ systems affected, and the stage of development at the time of the introduction of the teratogen. Maternal disease, drugs, heavy metals, chemicals, and radiation can have teratogenic effects. Other prenatal exogenous factors include fetal anoxia, physical trauma, and maternal condition such as age, malnutrition, and stress. Perinatal and postnatal exogenous factors also account for some portion of developmental disabilities and will be discussed in Chapter 8.

KEY TERMS

Know these important terms. Check the chapter and the Glossary for their meanings.
They are listed here in the approximate order of their appearance in the chapter.

Cocaine	Diabetes mellitus	Anencephaly
Alpha particles	Gestational diabetes	Hydrocephaly
Beta particles	Malnutrition	Microcephaly
Gamma rays	Undernutrition	Macrocephaly
Ionizing radiation	Risk factors	Spina bifida
Lead toxicity	Rh incompatibility	Multihit model
Hyperthyroidism	Erythroblastosis	
Hypothyroidism	Neural tube defects	

SUGGESTED READING

Two classic works are suggested for anyone interested in understanding and helping to solve the problems of environmental pollution. We suggest that these classics are essential in your reading.

Carson, R. (1962). *Silent spring.* Boston: Houghton Mifflin. This book is generally acknowledged to be the work that alerted the public to environmental issues.

Levine, A. G. (1982). *The Love Canal: Science, politics, and people.* Lexington, MA: D. C. Heath. The Love Canal disaster erupted in the 1970s and continues today to have powerful impacts on the well-being of many families. Levine's classic sociological study documents the psychological, social, and financial impacts on resident families of this industry and government-caused health crisis and many of the political factors dogging its solution.

STUDY QUESTIONS

If you have not worked through the study questions for Chapter 6, please do so now.

7.1. There can be passive or active teratogenic exposure. Active exposure refers to one's own behavior and lifestyle that increase exposure risks. Which teratogenic substances do you think are most apt to be involved in active exposure? Given your answer, what programs could society create to reduce those risks?

7.2. Explain, as if to a student, which teratogenic substances/events can pass directly through tissues to the fetus without diminution or change and which must cross through the placenta.

Would public policy have to be different for these?

7.3. Review for your own understanding the dangers of radiation. Consider radiation levels, the types of damage likely to occur with radiation, and what the short-term and long-term effects might be. How can radiation affect not just the current generation (the fetus/child) but also the *next* generation?

8 Exogenous Etiological Factors in Developmental Disabilities: Perinatal and Postnatal Environmental Origins

Trying to estimate the prevalence and incidence of developmental disabilities is complicated and at best provides only approximations. In Chapter 1, we estimated a total of 53 million persons in the United States with disabilities, of which 13.5 million (of all ages) have developmental disabilities. Thus far, we have focused on prenatal etiologies in developmental disabilities, but many impairments occur in the perinatal period and during infancy, childhood, and youth. To estimate the proportion of prenatal and postnatal occurrences, the rates derived by Hagberg, Hagberg, Lewerth, and Lindberg (1981) from their small sample of persons with mental retardation will serve as a guide. According to those estimates, 55 percent of the cases were of unknown etiology, 23 percent were of known prenatal origin, and 22 percent were of known postnatal origin. Applying these percentages to our estimate of 13.5 million persons with developmental disabilities in the United States yields about 7 million cases of unknown origin (55 percent), just over 3 million cases of known prenatal origin (23 percent), and just under 3 million persons (22 percent) of known postnatal origin. Therefore, factors occurring after birth and before age 21 account for about 45 percent of all cases of developmental disabilities of known etiologies. Assuming that about the same proportion (45 percent) of the currently "unknown" etiologies may be postnatal factors, we can see that the estimated proportion of cases due to all postnatal factors, 45 percent, is significant.

The major etiological factors during and after birth are oxygen deprivation (anoxia), physical trauma, environmental toxins, childhood illness, and malnutrition. To this list, we will add low birth weight (LBW) and preterm birth, although these do not fit neatly into our organization of material into prenatal and postnatal factors. LBW and preterm births are physical conditions diagnosed at or shortly before birth, but their etiologies are found much earlier among prenatal factors. Those five groups of etiological factors and LBW and preterm birth are discussed in the present chapter.

I. Etiologies and Disabilities

Oxygen Deprivation

Normal birth, from the start of labor through delivery of the baby and expulsion of the placenta, takes about 14 hours for first-time mothers and 8 hours for mothers who have given birth before. The actual birth of the child usually takes just over 1 hour. Most births, about 80 percent, are healthy, uncomplicated, and occur within these time spans.

However, there are potential problems such as **anoxia** (lack of oxygen) that may cause impairments and lead to brain damage and developmental disabilities. Anoxia can be caused by birth or postnatal factors that interrupt the oxygen supply to the child. Mild anoxia, due to only brief periods of oxygen interruption, does not appear to have serious or long-term negative effects. Prolonged anoxia of several minutes, however, can cause cell damage and even death. Damage may lead to cognitive, neurological, and motor disabilities such as mental retardation, epilepsy, cerebral palsy, learning disabilities, and poor coordination.

Anoxia is a potential problem, particularly during birth. The length of time required to complete the birth process is important. Delays in delivery as well as problematic presentations of the baby in the birth canal can cause anoxia. For example, when the baby is improperly positioned, as in breech presentation where the buttocks instead of the head are presented first, there is risk of umbilical cord constriction and therefore of interrupted blood flow and resulting anoxia. Manipulating the child's position in a breech presentation to aid its birth also carries some threat of physical injury to the baby. Breech presentations occur in about 3 percent of births (Creasy & Resnik, 1989), and they are now delivered by Cesarean section, thus avoiding many of the complications.

Abnormally rapid or precipitous birth, less than about 10 minutes, can cause anoxia and physical trauma to the baby. In **precipitous births,** umbilical blood flow might be cut off during contractions without sufficient time for the flow to begin again, causing anoxia.

The rapid squeezing of the child through the birth canal can also put severe pressure on the head, with the result that blood vessels in the brain may hemorrhage. The child's head will be deformed because of the pressure during birth on the still-malleable skull, but the deformity usually disappears over the next several weeks. However, there may have been numerous brain hemorrhages, too small to be detected. The baby is then at risk for as yet undetected brain damage and for subsequent neurological, cognitive, and motor problems that might not be apparent for months or perhaps years.

Another potential problem in delivery is the possibility of umbilical cord constriction of the baby's neck. This can happen during the late prenatal period or during birth, impeding blood flow and causing anoxia and subsequent tissue damage or even death.

If the child is low birth weight (LBW) and/or premature, he or she might not be sufficiently developed to survive without damage. Neural and lung development and the general strength that is needed to take over and maintain the task of breathing may be compromised, delaying the child's own breathing. Delays in initiating normal breathing can result in anoxia, cerebral hemorrhaging (Beckwitrh & Rodning, 1991), and brain damage.

Low Birth Weight and Preterm Birth

The average weight of the approximately 4 million live births annually in the United States is 7.5 pounds, or 3500 grams. About 7 percent (roughly 280,000) are full-term, low birth weight and about 11 percent (roughly 440,000) are preterm (see Table 8.1). The World Health Organization (1950) established the standard now generally used, defining LBW as less than 2500 grams. Traditionally, the term **low birth weight** included babies who are born at full term, but suffered some degree of growth retardation, and those who are small because they were **preterm births.** These are different conditions that need to be researched and understood separately. In a large proportion of cases, the low birth weight is due to preterm delivery as are nearly all of the **very low-birth-weight** (VLBW) and the **extremely low-birth-weight** (ELBW) babies with a weight of 3.75 pounds (1500 grams) or less. Preterm and LBW conditions are causally related to higher than normal risks for serious growth problems in infants and a high risk of infant death. Those risks increase sharply as the birth weight and/or gestation time decreases. The prevalence of LBW and preterm births is shown in Table 8.1.

TABLE 8.1   Birth Weights in the United States

Average Birth Weight	7.5 pounds; 3500 grams
Low Birth Weight (LBW)	< 5.5 pounds; 2500 grams
Very Low Birth Weight (VLBW)	< 3.75 pounds; 1500 grams
Extremely Low Birth Weight (ELBW)	< 2.2 pounds; 1000 grams
Preterm birth	< 37 full weeks gestation

Source of data: Paneth, N. S., (1995). The problem of low birth weight. *The Future of Children, 5*(1), 19–34.

In the United States, the infant mortality rate within the 1st year of life is about 1 percent of births (Paneth, 1995), or about 40,000 annually. Nearly 75 percent of these babies—30,000 each year—will die because they are born too early or too small (Shiono & Behrman, 1995). Thus, infant deaths are highly correlated with LBW and preterm delivery. They are also related to ethnic factors: Infant mortality among Caucasians is about 7 per 1000 (0.7 percent) but is nearly 18 per 1000 (nearly 1.8 percent) for African Americans (see Figure 8.1). Infant mortality decreased markedly in the United States during the twentieth century, but in spite of having one of the best medical systems in the world, the United States has a higher infant mortality rate than many other industrialized nations (see Figure 8.2). In 1993, the United States ranked 22nd in the world in infant mortality, with Japan, Singapore, England, Scandinavia, and nearly all of Western Europe having healthier rates. As noted, nearly 75 percent of the infant mortality is due to LBW and premature birth (Shiono & Behrman, 1995). The United States has one of the highest rates of prematurity and LBW, and that appears to account for its high rate of infant mortality. Recall from the discussion in Chapter 6 that tobacco use during pregnancy was seen as the major cause of LBW and premature birth in the United States and its relationship to SIDS. We suggest that the high rate of tobacco use in this country, particularly by women, may be a major cause of our high infant mortality.

LBW and preterm babies have achieved less than optimal prenatal development and, at birth, have weak respiratory and circulatory resources. These babies have postnatal difficulties in adjusting to the environment outside the womb where the baby's own systems must take over from those of the mother. A major problem during and just after birth is that of respiration and thus of getting enough oxygen to the brain and to other organs. At about 20 gestational weeks, the developing lungs begin to produce a substance, **pulmonary surfactant,** which forms a thin film over the walls of the primitive lung sacs. The substance facilitates lung development and, at birth, helps keep the air sacs open as the baby begins to breathe. At first, there is only a small amount, and in the final weeks of gestation, surfactant production increases markedly. When the baby takes its first breaths, the air opens up the alveoli (lung sacs or air pockets), and the surfactant coating prevents the sacs from closing. Preterm babies do not have enough surfactant, and thus have insufficient lung development, and the alveoli collapse after each breath. At birth, when the baby's own respiratory system must come into play, the preterm babies suffer from respiratory distress, and are at risk of oxygen insufficiency resulting in death and/or damage to the brain and other tissues. Until recently, respiratory distress syndrome or hyaline membrane disease resulted in some 7000 deaths annually of preterm babies (Olds, London, & Ladewig, 1988). Surfactant has now been synthesized and can be administered as a spray directly into the lungs. It is routinely administered to preterm babies to help keep the alveoli open, resulting in a significant reduction of deaths and chronic lung disease.

Little is known about the causes of LBW and preterm birth, but three factors are clearly predictors: cigarette smoking in pregnancy, low maternal weight gain during pregnancy, and low prepregnancy maternal weight (G. R. Alexander & Korenbrot, 1995). Cigarette smoking alone accounts for 20 percent of all LBW (Shiono & Behrman, 1995). Preterm births account for most LBW and are strongly related to infant death. If the rate of preterm births could be significantly reduced, then LBW, infant mortality, and a host of other problems would diminish.

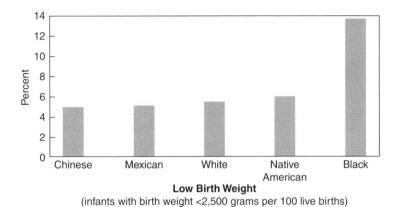

Low Birth Weight
(infants with birth weight <2,500 grams per 100 live births)

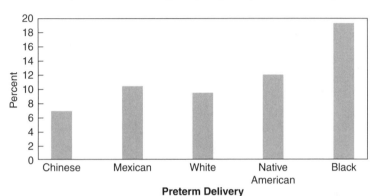

Preterm Delivery
(birth prior to 37 weeks gestational age per 100 live births)

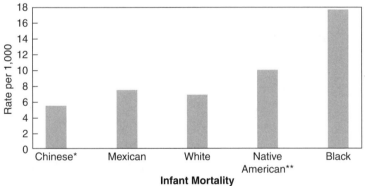

Infant Mortality
(infant deaths to age 1 per 1,000 live births)

* Infant mortality data for Chinese are from 1990.
** Infant mortality data for Native Americans are from 1992.

FIGURE 8.1   Ethnic Group Comparisons of Birth Outcomes in the United States, 1991

From: Paneth, N. S. (1995). The problem of low birth weight. *The Future of Children,* 5(1), 19–34. Reprinted with the permission of the David and Lucille Packard Foundation, Center for the Future of Children.

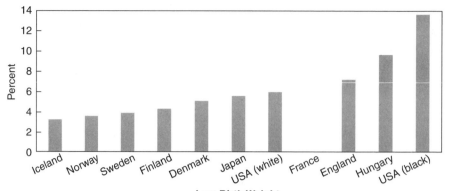

Low Birth Weight
(infants with birth weight <2,500 grams per 100 live births)

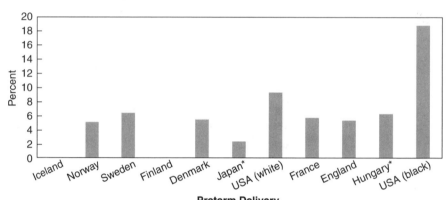

Preterm Delivery
(birth prior to 37 weeks gestational age per 100 live births)

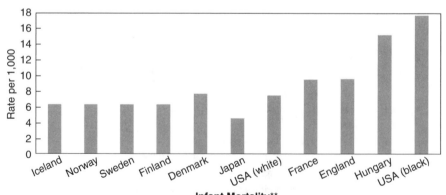

Infant Mortality**
(infant deaths to age 1 per 1,000 live births)

* Prior to 35 completed weeks.
** All infant mortality rates for 1991 except Finland and Hungary (1990).

FIGURE 8.2   International Comparisons of Birth Outcomes

From: Paneth, N. S. (1995). The problem of low birth weight. *The Future of Children,* 5(1), 19–34. Reprinted with the permission of the David and Lucille Packard Foundation, Center for the Future of Children.

Development during pregnancy is a series of complex events, as is the preparation for and carrying out of the birth process. Recent animal studies show that the duration of pregnancy is largely determined by processes in the fetus. As it develops toward birth, the fetus signals for preparation and for eventual initiation of labor and delivery. But what accounts for the premature signals that initiate labor and delivery too early? Continued research is needed into the genetic, hormonal, and other factors that control that signaling (Nathaniels, 1995). With more information and better understanding of the basic processes, it will be possible to prevent or reduce the rate of preterm labor and birth.

However, despite efforts at improving prenatal care, the rates of preterm and LBW infants in the United States have not diminished. They have remained fairly stable at about 11 percent for preterm and 7 percent for LBW. As seen in Figure 8.3, there has been a small but steady increase in preterm births. Apparently, prevention programs have either not been effective in reducing preterm and LBW births or, if successful in a technical sense, have not been applied consistently, across enough of society, to have affected the overall rate. Note in Figure 8.3 that while the rate of LBW and preterm babies has not declined, neonatal mortality (i.e., death within 28 days of birth) has decreased from about 20 per 1000 in 1949 to about 7 per 1000 in 1991. This large improvement is due to increasing success in the neonatal intensive care procedures that are keeping higher proportions of LBW and preterm

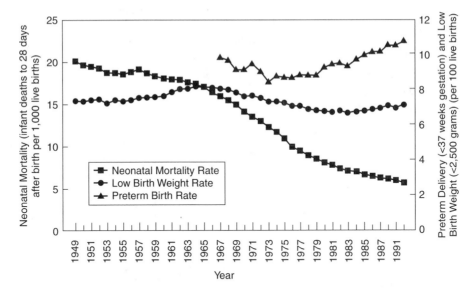

FIGURE 8.3 Low Birth Weight, Preterm Birth, and Neonatal Mortality Rates in the United States, 1950–1991

Sources: Lee, K., Paneth, N., Gartner, L., et al. Neonatal mortality: An analysis of the recent improvement in the United States. *American Journal of Public Health* (1980) 80: 15–21; National Center for Health Statistics. *Advance report of final mortality statistics.* Monthly Vital Statistics Report. Hyattsville, MD: Public Health Service, (1950 through 1991.); National Center for Health Statistics. *Advance report of final natality statistics.* Monthly Vital Statistics Report. Hyattsville, MD: Public Health Service, (1950 through 1991.)

From: Paneth, N. S. (1995). The problem of low birth weight. *The Future of Children, 5*(1), 19–34. Reprinted with the permission of the David and Lucille Packard Foundation, Center for the Future of Children.

babies alive. But despite success in saving these babies once they are born, we have not been able to reduce the rate at which they are born.

Infant mortality, LBW, and premature birth vary with ethnicity. The rate of LBW is 5.8 percent for whites and 13.6 percent for blacks (Paneth, 1995). Other ethnic minorities in the United States (e.g., Asian, Hispanic, Native American) have rates similar to American whites, and none approach the high rate shown by blacks. Similar ethnic variability is found with preterm deliveries. Blacks are at a far higher rate (see Figure 8.1). The contribution of socioeconomic factors has not been sufficiently studied independently of related factors such as ethnicity. It has been argued (Hughes & Simpson, 1995) that the higher rates for African Americans and the generally disappointing results of all prevention efforts through improved prenatal medical care may be due to socioeconomic factors that have thus far not been sufficiently addressed in either research or prevention programs.

As noted, LBW and premature birth are the principal causes of infant mortality, accounting for 75 percent of the deaths. In addition to being a risk factor for infant mortality, LBW is also associated with several short- and long-term outcomes. As expected of small and incompletely developed babies, these infants have a higher rate of poor health and functioning in all areas of development (Hack, Klein, & Taylor, 1995). These include greater susceptibility to injury during and after birth, cerebral palsy, blindness, deafness, chronic lung disease, learning disability, and attention deficit disorder.

Since the 1960s, the death rates and serious developmental disorders due to LBW have declined markedly, largely due to improvements in intensive care for LBW neonates. Within about 3 weeks of intensive neonatal care, the preterm baby's physical condition is stabilized, and feeding and weight gain improve. The baby is moved to a nursery and is eventually sent home. However, the parents' task of caring for this baby is difficult and demanding. The baby is small, weak, not well developed or responsive, and sleeps poorly and erratically. The baby's weak sucking reflex, frequent vomiting, and problems holding down needed medications are some of the difficulties facing the parents.

However, even with good neonatal intensive and home care, when compared with normal weight and full-term births, LBW babies still have substantially higher rates of serious problems. The postnatal development of most LBW babies is within normal parameters, although often at the lower limits. For example, the average IQ of LBW children is within the average range (low normal to normal levels). But this group also has significantly higher rates of subaverage intelligence (i.e., 80 and lower IQ) and mental retardation (70 and lower) (Hack et al., 1995). With the good neonatal intensive care now available, the vast majority of LBW children function within normal limits. However, the risks of various developmental problems are higher than they are for normal weight children, and a substantial minority suffer serious problems.

Those risks are greatest for the very LBW and extremely LBW babies. Although these children constitute only 15 percent of the total of LBW babies (Hack et al., 1995), they account for nearly all of the serious problems associated with LBW. Thus, babies at the higher levels of LBW (2500 grams or 5.5 pounds) who receive good neonatal care develop well within normal limits (see Table 8.2).

What are the risks associated with the 15 percent of LBW babies (1 percent of all births) that constitute very LBW and extremely LBW? First is the higher than normal risk of infant mortality, although it has decreased as a result of improved neonatal intensive care. This decrease in deaths is almost all due to the increased survival rate of the lowest

**TABLE 8.2   Prevalence of Low Birth Weight and Preterm Births
in the United States**

Total Births 1990	VLBW <1500 grams	%	LBW <2500 grams	%
4,158,212	52,915	1.3	289,418	7.0
By Gestation Age Total	Preterm	%	Term	
4,158,212	436,590	10.6	3,674,806	89.4

Source of data: National Centers for Health Statistics, Centers for Disease Control.
Prepared by March of Dimes.

weight babies—the group for whom the serious risks of developmental problems is highest. Second, because of the increased survival, there has been a modest increase in the number of babies with developmental problems, and specifically with cerebral palsy, one of the most common of the major abnormalities in LBW children (Bhushan, Paneth, & Kiely, 1993; Hack et al., 1995). Although the birth rate of cerebral palsy has remained fairly consistent since the 1970s, the improved survival of LBW babies has added to the absolute number of persons with cerebral palsy. Third, in addition to cerebral palsy, other neurosensory problems (e.g., hydrocephalus, microcephalus, blindness, deafness, and seizures) are clearly related to decreased birth weight (Hack et al., 1995) (see Table 8.3).

Two studies (Langerstrom, Bremme, Eneroth, & Janson, 1991, 1994) suggest that the effects of LBW and prematurity may vary with gender. They followed 494 LBW children born in Stockholm and evaluated them at ages 13 and 16, and the boys again at age 18 when they were examined for military duty. This long-term study found that LBW and preterm birth were not related to adjustment problems, psychiatric disorders, or to juvenile delinquency of both sexes at ages 13 and 16. Further, they found no differences on these measures between LBW and VLBW adolescents. When they compared the school grades at age 16 of the LBW, VLBW, and normal boys and girls, they found some interesting interactions. For the girls, the LBW condition was associated with significantly lower grades compared with normal birth weight girls; for the boys, however, it was the gestational age

**TABLE 8.3   Rates of Neurosensory Problems
as Related to Diminishing Birthrates**

Normal birth weight	< 5%
2499–1500 grams	6–8%
1500–1000 grams	14–17%
less than 1000 grams	20%

Source of information: Hack, M., Klein, N. K., & Taylor, H. G. (1995). Long-term developmental outcomes of low birth weight infants. *The Future of Children,* 5(1), 176–196. Page 183.

and not birth weight that was related to significantly lower grades. They concluded that the effects of LBW and preterm birth are gender related, with boys affected most by lower gestational age and girls by LBW.

Childhood Illness

As we saw earlier, numerous diseases contracted by pregnant women can have severe consequences for embryo and fetal development, resulting in developmental disabilities. Children are also subject to a variety of diseases and injuries during and following birth and these, too, can leave significant impairments. Childhood illness that involves major brain infections with high fevers (e.g., meningitis, encephalitis, etc.) and severe head trauma can cause brain damage and mental retardation. In a study reviewed in an earlier section, Iivanainen and Lahdevirta (1988) examined 111 cases of mental retardation in which infectious disease was the cause of the retardation. They concluded that twenty cases (18 percent) were due to prenatal infections and ninety-one (82 percent) were due to perinatal or postnatal diseases. The illnesses included encephalitis, meningitis, and gastrointestinal illness and dehydration. Generally, any illness that results in high fever, particularly over extended periods, poses potential risks for brain damage and disabilities.

Physical Trauma

Unintentional Injuries to Children.   Childhood injuries, particularly involving the head and spinal cord, can lead to serious disabilities. These injuries may be unintentional or intentionally caused. The term **unintentional injuries** refers to injuries that occur as a result of environmental factors or because supervising adults do not understand the developmental limitations and vulnerabilities of a child under given circumstances. Unintentional injuries are nearly always preventable, given proper supervision and care, and are therefore not "accidents."

Examples of unintentional injuries are those occurring in automobile, boat, bicycle, playground, and sports injuries. They can be toy related and can occur at home, on farms, in schools, on the job, and so on (O'Shea, 1990). Unintentional injuries involve millions of children each year with serious consequences for more than half a million children and permanent disabilities for 20,000 (see Table 8.4). **Intentional injuries** to children and youth include homicides and suicides, rape, assault, child abuse, and injuries resulting from any domestic violence.

The Centers for Disease Control no longer use the term *accident* because that implies that the event and the injuries were beyond anyone's control and therefore were not predictable or preventable. Too many people could too easily attribute to accident some sad events—particularly involving children—that may have been due to their own negligence and thereby absolve themselves of any responsibility. A recently reported case is that of a 10-month-old who died while allegedly having been left for 2 hours in a hot, closed automobile by his grandmother and another relative, each of whom thought the other had taken the baby out of the car. "It was just an accident! It was just an accident!" the baby's distraught grandfather was quoted as saying (*Buffalo News,* 1997).

TABLE 8.4   Unintentional Injuries to Children and Youth

Due to unintentional injuries each year in the United States:

3600 children die

20,000 children become permanently disabled

550,000 children are hospitalized

15,000,000 children are taken to hospital emergency rooms

Source of information: Legit, E. M., & Baker, L. S. (1995). Unintentional injuries. *The Future of Children, 5*(1), 214–222.

Unintended negative side effects of medications form a special class of potential unintended injury to children. Although there is not much hard evidence and virtually no research, it appears of potential importance and worthy of mention here. We are referring specifically to the rapidly growing practice of treating younger children with medications that have been developed for older children or adults. The use of stimulants, antidepressives, and other psychiatric drugs increased significantly in the first half of the 1990s (Goode, 2000; Zito et al., 2000) and has stimulated public concern. The most common is the use of methylphenidate (trade name Ritalin) to control preschoolers who are diagnosed with *attention deficit hyperactive disorder.* There are two major problems here. First is the increasing tendency to use the diagnosis for ever-younger children, thus possibly redefining some level of young children's behavior as a medical disorder. This might be erroneous and dangerous in its own right, serving only to mislabel children and misdirect professionals' views and actions. The other related problem is the possibility that the use of the drug might have disabling effects on the still-maturing brain of the young child. *We simply do not know if such damage occurs.* But prudence demands that we be very careful.

As shown in Table 8.4, each year in the United States, another 20,000 children become permanently disabled from unintended injuries. National data on the details of the disabilities—their type, treatment, rehabilitation, outcomes, and so on—are not available (Centers for Disease Control, 1991; Legit & Baker, 1995; National Committee for Injury Prevention and Control, 1989). Therefore, we do not know what proportion of the 20,000 disabled children meet the criteria for developmental disabilities, particularly the criterion of substantial functional limitations in at least three of the major areas of life activities (as discussed in Chapter 1). But it is clear that each year both unintentional and intentional injuries cause thousands of children to become developmentally disabled.

Intentional Injuries to Children: Child Abuse.   As difficult as it is to comprehend, many children are intentionally injured, permanently damaged, disabled, and even killed by their own parents and other caregivers. The endpoints of severe abuse include death or physical and emotional injury of the children. Each year in the United States, more than 2 million investigations of reported abuse involving more than 3 million children are carried out by child protection agencies (US:DHHS, 1998). More than 2000 children, most of whom are under 4 years of age, are killed and another 142,000 are injured in child abuse/neglect incidents (U.S. Advisory Board on Child Abuse and Neglect, 1995). Of those injured, an estimated 18,000 per year suffer "serious disabilities" (NCCAN, 1995). Causes of intentional death of children include beating, burning, drowning, hanging by the neck, scalding, starving, stabbing, suffocating, being thrown out of windows, entombed in cement, and many others (U.S. Advisory Board on Child Abuse and Neglect, 1995). The perpetrators are almost always parents, while a smaller number involves other caregivers such as boyfriends, baby-sitters, or relatives. It is inferred that a huge number of intentional injuries do not even come to the attention of social service agencies.

Reliable data are not available on what proportion of children who survive abuse become developmentally disabled. One estimate (Baledarian, 1991a), drawn from a review of the literature, puts the number at 18,000 children or more each year who suffer mental retardation and/or permanent sensorimotor disabilities. Diamond and Jaudes (1983) noted that many of those children are left with cerebral palsy. Given Baledarian's estimate of 18,000 cases due to abuse and our estimate in Chapter 1 of at least 120,000 new cases each year of all etiologies, then it can be seen that child abuse may be responsible for about 15 percent of new cases of developmental disabilities. This is a significant proportion and suggests that child abuse is a major factor in creating developmental disabilities, but to date, there has been very little interest in or investigation of this problem.

A related issue (covered later in this text) is the abuse of children who are already disabled. One would expect that children with disabilities are more vulnerable for abuse than are most children. Further, these children may have greater difficulty in reporting such incidents (Baledarian, 1991b), and therefore, very few facts are known. Because so many are isolated in institutions and have language barriers, social strategies for preventing the abuse of disabled people pose many difficult problems (Muccigrosso, 1991; Sobsey & Mansell, 1990). It is clear that much more attention needs to be paid by service agencies, and more research is needed on the extent of abuse of children with disabilities. We hope that, in time, researchers will investigate these issues that are so important in developmental disabilities.

Up to 5 percent of children admitted to pediatric hospitals suffer from a condition known as **failure to thrive** (Barlow & Durand, 1995). Usually afflicting infants, the condition is one of low weight, small size, and generally poor physical development. The babies appear as if they are starving, and indeed, limited nourishment is an important part of the picture. Many cases are due to medical conditions such as the early development of children with Prader-Willi syndrome, as discussed in Chapter 5. But many are due to psychosocial factors of poverty, ignorance, neglect, and even outright abuse. The family situation is pathogenic, but these children, usually diagnosed as "feeding disorders of infancy or childhood," can respond well if timely social service and medical action are taken. In many cases, however, the child dies or is left with lifelong disabilities.

A particularly dramatic and severe condition is **psychosocial dwarfism** (Money, 1992), or Kaspar-Hauser syndrome. The condition appears to be the result of severe physical and psychological abuse with its resulting stress over long time periods. The children are so thoroughly traumatized by the abuse that their physical, cognitive, and social development is drastically impaired. Stress is a normal experience, and all children must learn to cope with it. However, severe, prolonged stress has negative effects on endocrine function (Chrousos & Gold, 1992) and slows mental and physical growth (B. Brown & Rosenbaum, 1985). In a case described by Money, Annecillo, and Hutchison (1985), a boy who was apparently 8 years old in all physical, cognitive, and social respects was removed from his home after years of severe abuse. He had been kept by his stepmother for years locked in a dark closet and deprived of food and water for long periods. His three siblings were forced by this woman to beat him frequently with broom handles, and his arms and skull showed many fractures. After he was removed from the home, it was determined that he was actually 16 years old. He had been severely stunted not only physically, but in all intellectual, emotional, and social development as well. Although he recovered some physical growth, he will remain developmentally stunted (see Figure 8.4).

Traumatic Brain Injury and Diffuse Axional Injury.   Of particular concern for developmental disabilities is **traumatic brain injury** (TBI), the major cause of death or permanent disability in children and adolescents (Snow & Hooper, 1994).[1] TBI is caused by external force that results in an altered state of consciousness, brain damage, total or partial functional disability, and/or psychosocial and academic impairment. Its effects can be short or long term. Typically, TBI involves (a) a loss of consciousness, (b) some posttraumatic amnesia, and (c) neurological damage. It varies in severity with the power of the physical force, the type of injury, and the locus of the brain damage. The external force can be a

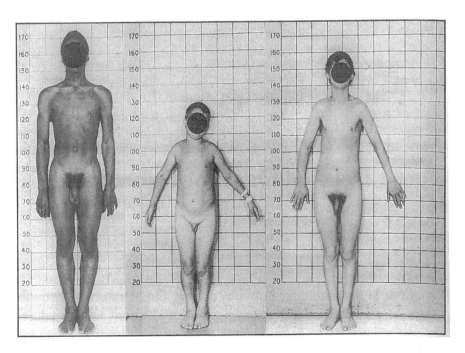

FIGURE 8.4   Kaspar-Hauser Syndrome. *Left: A 16-year-old with normal development. Center: A 16-year-old with psychosocial dwarfism. Right: The same boy at age 19.*

From: Money, J. (1992). *The Kaspar-Hauser syndrome of psychosocial dwarfism: deficient statural, intellectual, and social growth induced by child abuse.* Buffalo, NY: Prometheus Books. Reproduced by permission.

direct blow to the head or generalized, as in the violent acceleration–deceleration that can occur in automobile crashes, some playground injuries, and in **shaken baby** incidents. Note that the etiology is clearly exogenous. Not included is brain damage due to endogenous factors such as disease, strokes, and genetic/chromosomal factors.

TBI is not randomly distributed among the population of children and youth. In their excellent review, Snow and Hooper (1994) summarized the findings of several epidemiological surveys. They reported that TBI occurs at twice the rate in boys as in girls, increases sharply in the 15–24-year age range, particularly for males, and has an incidence rate of about 220–230 per 100,000 from birth to 14 years and 550 per 100,000 from 15 to 19 years. An estimated 150,000 children each year suffer TBI (Centers for Disease Control, 1991).

Not only do incidence rates change with age but so do the causes and the types of injuries. The largest group of head injuries in preschoolers occurs as unintentional injuries in the home and intentional injuries in child abuse. For school-age children, falls, pedestrian or bicycle collisions, and sports activities account for most of the mild TBI. The most severe brain injuries are, in general, due to automobile crashes and occur primarily to older adolescents and adults.

Brain tissue can be damaged by penetration and by nonpenetration injuries. In the former, estimated to be 2 to 5 percent of all brain injuries (Kampen & Grafman, 1986), brain tissues are pierced by bone fragments, missiles, or objects such as dashboard knobs in automobiles. In nonpenetration injuries (the remaining 95 to 98 percent), there is no piercing of the skull or brain, but the force of deceleration/acceleration causes concussions and the tearing and depression of tissues. **Diffuse axonal injury** (DAI) refers to the generalized damage that occurs in nonpenetration injuries. DAI includes the tearing, twisting, and breaking of axons and damage to connective cells in the brain (Snow & Hooper, 1994).

TBI ranges from relatively low severity, as in **concussions,** to severe damage, as in diffuse axonal injury. Concussions are common in emergency room admissions. They involve force to the head (as in a fall) causing momentary loss of consciousness from which the child recovers quickly and apparently completely, usually in minutes. In DAI cases, however, severe, violent motion, such as the buffeting of acceleration–deceleration that occurs in some automobile crashes, causes neural injury throughout the brain. Unconsciousness is immediate and, depending on the severity of the damage, recovery may take weeks, months, years, or may not occur at all. Children can remain in a coma for days, weeks, and even months. Motor, cognitive, sensory, emotional, language, and behavioral problems can occur and may persist, with their extent and severity depending primarily on the severity of the brain damage and the areas of the brain in which the damage occurred.

Primary injury is the immediate, direct result of the physical force. Secondary injury (e.g., cerebral hemorrhage, scarring, infection, seizures) can follow TBI immediately or develop some time later, further complicating the problems for the already injured child. In most cases, several types of injuries occur at the time of the injury or develop later. Each type of injury poses its own threats, adding to the severity of the condition (see Box 8.1).

The results of external physical force to a child's head are many and complex. Injury can be to any specific areas of the brain, causing different functional impairments. It may be diffuse, affecting many areas and functions. It may be mild to severe, leaving some persons quickly recovered, others never completely recovered, and still others killed by the injuries.

B O X **8.1**

Types of Injuries in TBI

The following medical conditions can occur at the time of the injury or may develop some time later. They may be direct (primary) or secondary results of the physical force to the child's head. Each poses its own threats, adding to the severity of the damage. In most cases, several of the following types of injuries will occur.

Scalp and skull injuries such as linear skull fractures (a thin crack in the skull that does not press on the brain) are common among childhood playground falls and ordinarily are not associated with neurological damage. However, in depressed skull fractures, the bone breaks pushes on brain tissue, and can cause significant brain damage.

Concussion occurs when there is a brief loss of consciousness or the child suffers amnesia for the occurrence of the injury. Concussions are relatively mild conditions from which the child recovers quickly and usually completely.

Contusions (bruises) involve breaking of small blood vessels and discoloration of the tissues affected. Contusions may appear over several days following the injury.

Diffuse axonal injuries (DAI) are at the most extreme ends of severity. These occur with severe, violent motion, such as in automobile crashes, causing immediate unconsciousness and the shearing, twisting, and breaking of neural axons. Severe functional disabilities can result.

Ischemia and *hypoxia:* Interrupted/obstructed blood flow to the brain (ischemia) and reduced oxygen content of blood (hypoxia). Additional brain tissue can be destroyed by the lack or reduction of blood and oxygen supply.

Brain swelling (cerebral edema): Swelling involves pressure on brain tissues, and compression can lead to tissue death or otherwise damage brain tissue.

Excess bleeding (hemorrhage): A hematoma or blood clot is a swelling of blood in a specific locus. When this occurs as a result of hemorrhage, the blood can collect at any point within the skull—that is, between the skull and the dura or brain covering (epidural hematoma) or between the dura and the brain (subdural hematoma). Pressure from the hematoma can cause additional neural damage.

Posttraumatic epilepsy: Posttraumatic seizures can occur within seconds of the injury (immediate) or may develop after a day or 2 (early seizures) or within about 2 years of the injury (late). In most cases, the seizure activity decreases, but the child may still be prone to occasional seizures for many years.

Note: This box on TBI draws heavily from the review by Snow and Hooper (1994). Acknowledgment and my indebtedness are given to these authors.

Impairments and disabilities are immediate, but some may occur later as injury-caused pathology continues to impair the person.

TBI can have negative effects in virtually all of a child's functioning, and the degree of impairment/disability depends largely on the severity of the initial damage, as does the rate and quality of recovery. Generally, the greatest degree of recovery is in the 1st year following TBI, and except in the cases of minor damage, even after several years, there often is still some evident disability. Language, memory, and intellectual performance are negatively affected by TBI. Attention deficits occur, and hyperactivity and decreased social adjustment are often noted. Motor deficits and visual-motor coordination problems occur.

The TBI child suffers a sudden, unexpected, and often violent and severe change of developmental progress. From being a normal, neurologically intact child, he or she can become, in a moment, a child with cognitive, motor, and social disabilities. In rehabilitation and therapy, the psychological issues need to be dealt with as well as the physical problems. Similarly, the psychological impact on the family can be severe, and those issues must also be handled in rehabilitation/therapy programs. For those children who survive, TBI treatment and rehabilitation can be arduous and long, even lifetime, in duration.

Lead and Other Environmental Toxins

Children are exposed to many environmental toxins (e.g., mercury, vinyl chloride, cadmium, formaldehyde, etc.). As discussed earlier, these are known environmental toxins and teratogens that are among the more than 5 million industrial chemicals in the environment, increasing in number every year. One of the best studied is lead, a toxic heavy metal. In Chapter 6, we discussed prenatal lead exposure. Lead is a teratogen, entering the mother, crossing the placenta, and poisoning the fetus. Lead is ubiquitous in the environment, and it continues to be a toxic threat even after the child is born. Postnatal lead exposure of children is the focus of this section.

Sources of Lead.   Before the 1970s, the major sources of lead poisoning in the general population were:

1. atmospheric lead, primarily from automotive exhausts of leaded gasoline and the mining, refining, and combustion of lead in industries
2. contamination of food by lead solder used to seal food cans
3. lead-based paint
4. lead in dust and soil
5. contamination of drinking water, largely by the lead-soldered plumbing that still exists in 90 percent of U.S. homes (Levin, 1986)
6. occupational contamination of workers in industries that use or smelt lead (Eisinger, 1996)
7. lead in fresh foods such as meat, vegetables, and fruit that have been lead contaminated by soil, water, and/or use of leaded pesticides

In addition to human-caused contamination, there is a natural background of lead released into the atmosphere, water, and soil through natural chemical and weathering processes (Sannolo, Carelli, DeLorenzo, & Castellino, 1995). Lead does not degrade, and whatever has been released into the environment since lead was first smelted more than 8000 years ago (Eisinger, 1996) has accumulated in the soil, water, and air. It has been estimated that some 300 million metric tons of lead have been produced throughout history, and most of that remains in the environment (National Research Council, 1993). It has also been estimated that present atmospheric lead levels are some 2000 times greater than those in pre-Roman periods (Environmental Protection Agency, 1986). The body burden of lead in humans has increased markedly during the industrial period. Comparisons have been made of lead levels in modern Americans with levels found in the remains of Native Americans who lived prior to European settlements in the Americas. The lead burden of modern North Americans is 300 to 500 times greater than it was in preindustrial society (Ericson, Smith, & Flegal, 1991).

Lead has a long history of use since pre-Roman times in metallurgy and industry and as vessels for cooking, storing, and serving food. It was used as an ingredient in food and wine preparation (lead has a sweet taste) particularly in European winemaking. In powdered and paste form, lead was used in cosmetics and even taken as medication, with generally disastrous results (Eisinger, 1996). Even today, lead is an ingredient in some nutritional supplements widely sold in the United States such as calcium tablets. It has been speculated that the heavy use of lead in everyday life over many centuries may have been an important factor in the decline of the Roman Empire (Eisinger, 1996).

As noted by Robert Guthrie (1986), in some countries such as India, Kuwait, and Pakistan, lead in ground black powder form is still used by women—even during pregnancy—as a facial cosmetic called **kohl** or **surma.** It is also applied around the umbilicus and eyes of newborn children and around the eyes of females from infancy and throughout their entire lives. The lead is absorbed through the skin, resulting in high rates of severe lead poisoning, brain damage, mental retardation, and death. Because it is a cosmetic used to enhance female attractiveness, the resulting disabilities are disproportionately borne by females in those cultures and secondarily by male babies through teratogenic effects due to the pregnant mother's use. Young girls are taught to apply it to themselves and continue to do so throughout their lives, unwittingly poisoning themselves and their eventual progeny. Guthrie points out that because there may be hundreds of thousands of persons from those countries living in the United States, it is therefore a problem that is beginning to affect our own population, and U.S. pediatricians need to be alert to it. But the use of this cosmetic is traditional, and convincing women to stop using it has been extremely difficult. Even governments have been slow to respond to Guthrie's recommendations. In the United States, there is current concern over the lead content of cosmetics such as hair coloring for men and women and some facial cosmetics such as eyebrow shadow.

Fairly recently, lead was used in the treatment of cancer, but it succeeded only in further poisoning the patients (Eisinger, 1996). Lead might still be used in some countries as a sweetener in food and beverage preparation. The leaded seals currently used on many wine bottles are sources of dietary lead. (At your next fancy candlelight dinner, when you open that nice bottle of wine, the careful removal of the leaded seal and wiping down the neck and lip of the bottle before pouring are recommended.)

From a public health standpoint, it is prudent to find nontoxic substitutes for lead and to end its mining and smelting. Environmental levels will never be decreased, but perhaps in time, the rate of increase might be significantly slowed. This of course requires values that place health above commerce and concerted political action around the world, so its prospects are not very good at all.

In the 1970s, the U.S. federal government imposed restrictions on lead use despite the hard opposition of industry. The new law mandated eliminating lead solder from food cans, removing lead from most paint, and reducing lead in gasoline by more than 95 percent (National Research Council, 1993). These moves have had significant public health effects in reducing the threat of lead toxicity, particularly for children who were highly vulnerable to the food contamination and airborne lead from gasoline. However, lead is still used in many imported food cans, and the continued use of lead industrially around the world ensures that its accumulation in the environment will continue to increase. For example, Mexico is one of the world's leading producers of lead and has such poor controls on leaded gasoline that some 32 metric tons of lead are released into the atmosphere each day by automobile exhaust in Mexico City alone (Sannolo et al., 1995).

The federal government's actions in the 1970s reduced airborne lead and lead in domestically produced canned foods, thus removing them as major sources of toxicity for children. The remaining major sources of lead exposure to children in the United States are shown in Table 8.5.

Children from about 2 to 6 years are particularly vulnerable to the lead in deteriorating paint in homes. The paint chips have a sweet taste (recall that lead was used for centuries as a food sweetener), and children tend to put things in their mouths. Some children, particularly if hungry, eat the sweet-tasting chips. Ingesting inedible material is a condition called **pica,** and children in poor families are particularly at risk. Their homes are apt to contain deteriorating lead paint, and the children may be hungrier than more affluent children. Brightly colored, sweet-tasting paint chips can be appealing to a hungry child.

It is ironic that removing lead paint from older homes, if not carried out properly, can actually increase the lead risk because the removal processes create lead-saturated dust that can be breathed in by children. When done carefully by trained technicians, the removal can be carried out effectively and without risk.

More than 90 percent of homes in the United States have lead-contaminated water from the lead used in water pipes. Even newer homes, which have copper instead of leaded pipes, have contaminated water because lead solder continued to be used to join the sections of copper pipe. While the lead threat to children from gasoline and from food cans has been significantly reduced, the threat from old paint and water contamination continues. Only focused political and social action can remedy that situation.

Federal legislation to date has had significant positive effects in protecting children, but much more needs to be accomplished. Programs to remove lead paint and lead plumbing from houses and schools and improved recycling of batteries and other lead items are

TABLE 8.5   Current Sources of Lead in Children

Prenatal	Maternal intake of lead
Birth–6 months	Milk and water
6 months–2 years	Leaded paint chips and dust
2 years–6 years	Leaded paint chips (pica); exposure to background lead through respiration and ingestion

Source of data: National Research Council (1993). *Measuring lead exposure in infants, children, and other sensitive populations.* Washington, DC: National Academy Press, p. 19.

needed. In addition, lead production and the use of leaded gasoline without concern for environmental impact, such as in Mexico, must be addressed by international actions. Unfortunately, economic values will continue to prevail, and action on health issues will probably remain far down the list for a very long time.

Clinical Effects of Lead Toxicity. What are the clinical effects of lead toxicity (**plumbism**) and the implications for developmental disabilities? Animal research has shown that *lead can interact with and disrupt virtually any existing biological system.* In high concentrations, it causes death, reproductive problems, teratogenic effects, and cancer (Masci & Bongarzone, 1995). Lead is toxic for all persons, but the most vulnerable are infants, children, and pregnant women (the latter as surrogates for the fetus). These groups comprise the **sensitive populations** for whom most of the recent lead-control regulations have been developed.

The severity of lead toxicity depends on many factors, chiefly the amount of lead in the body. The effects range from subtle, subclinical damage to severe lead intoxication and death. A generation ago, most of the concern was for the most obviously acute, life-threatening lead intoxication effects. As research has continued, however, it appears that even low-level exposure might result in serious and chronic damage. Scientific, policy, and health agencies (e.g., the National Research Council, Environmental Protection Agency, and Centers for Disease Control) have calculated the blood lead levels at which medical intervention is recommended. It has long been accepted that, for children and infants, a lead concentration of 150 ug/dL (micrograms per deciliter) of whole blood is a lethal level. The question is: At what concentration should medical treatment begin in order to avoid the lethal effects? In 1972, it was recommended that when blood lead levels reach 40 percent of the lethal level (i.e., about 60 ug/dL) treatment should be initiated. However, the recommendations changed as more research continued to show serious effects at much lower levels. In 1978, the recommended level for action was dropped to 20 percent (30 ug/dL); by 1985, it was dropped to 17 percent (about 25 ug/dL); and in 1991, it was lowered to 7 percent (about 10.5 ug/dL) (National Research Council, 1993, p. 17). Much of the recent research and public health measures have focused on subtle, chronic effects at lower exposure.

Medical treatment is now recommended at about 10.5 ug/dL in children, which suggests that levels below that are low or safe levels. But what does "low" mean? As noted earlier, the typical, supposedly nontoxic body-burden levels in modern North Americans are some 300 to 500 times greater than those for preindustrial Native Americans (Ericson et. at., 1991). Thus, we are now far above what might be considered the "natural" lead body burden for humans. The belief that there may be safe levels of toxins has been challenged by many researchers. Marlowe (1995), for example, argues that metals such as lead, cadmium, aluminum, mercury, and arsenic may be toxic at any levels, and the notion of safe levels may be a fiction.

There are four organ systems primarily affected by lead toxicity: the central nervous system (i.e., the brain, particularly for children), the peripheral nervous system (in adults), the kidneys, and the hematologic system (the blood-forming organs) for both adults and children. Lead poisoning can result in damage in all of these systems, with children being most sensitive. As noted, death occurs in children when blood lead levels reach about

150 ug/dL of whole blood. **Lead encephalopathy** in children (lead-caused brain disease) occurs at concentrations of about 100 to 150 ug/dL of whole blood. The clinical picture includes convulsions, paralysis, and mental retardation. Before the development of **chelation therapy** (discussed in the next section) to reduce blood lead levels, lead encephalopathy was fatal in 60 to 65 percent of cases (National Research Council, 1972), but mortality is now less than 2 percent. However, if children survive lead encephalopathy, the chances of permanent brain damage with mental retardation and severe behavior disorders are high (National Research Council, 1993). For adults, somewhat higher blood lead levels (above 120 to 150 ug/dL) are associated with encephalopathy. At high levels, such as those encountered by workers in high-lead industries, the clinical signs include dullness, irritability, headaches, hallucinations, convulsions, paralysis, and death.

In addition to the acute effects of high lead intoxication on these specific organ systems, there is growing research evidence that lower levels of chronic exposure also have negative effects on cognitive functioning and on growth in general. As reviewed by the National Research Council (1993), children exposed to lead prior to birth and/or postnatally have significant decrements in IQ and compared with nonexposed children are measurably smaller in size (length, weight, chest circumference) (Schwartz, Angle, & Pitcher, 1986). In his review of research, Marlowe (1995) cites studies that found increased body levels of various metals in children with mental retardation (lead and cadmium), learning disabilities (lead, cadmium, aluminum, mercury, zinc, and nickel), and behavior disorders (lead, copper, cadmium, and arsenic).

Chelation Therapy.   Chelation therapy reduces the lead level in blood. Chelation agents are organic compounds that bind to metals, including lead, and they are used in the treatment of metal poisoning. Bound with lead, the chelation compounds have their effects in two ways: They can be excreted, thus removing the lead from the body, and they can limit the absorption of the metal in the intestines. Chelation treatment must be repeated over time, and the chelation agents must therefore be well tolerated by the body. Some agents may have their own toxic effects, actually making the child ill, and care must be used in their application. A commonly used chelation agent is a calcium compound, calcium disodium edetate.

To be effective, the chelation agent should have a strong affinity for the metal to be removed. It must be able to compete successfully with naturally occurring chelation agents already present in the body, must bind the metal in a stable manner, and must be resistant to biological transformations that would make the chelation agent toxic were those transformations to occur. As noted earlier, other metals—cadmium, aluminum, mercury, and arsenic—are also toxic and have teratogenic effects. In a review of the literature, Marlowe (1995) concludes that there is a dose-effect relationship, with no "safe" levels. Further, he argues some research suggests that combinations of those metals at low levels may have significant deleterious effects on children's cognitive functioning, but these suggested **synergistic effects** have not yet been adequately studied. More research is needed on the effects on cognitive development of low-level exposure to toxic metals singly and in combinations. Because these metals are ubiquitous in our environment, and assuming they have effects even at low levels, then they pose threats to virtually all children in our society.

Lead poisoning is not limited to children. Adults can also suffer severe lead intoxication. Major sources of lead for adults are occupational environments in industries that use lead, canned foods, leaded gas, and lead-polluted air and soils. There are also many unusual sources of lead (Bologna & Castellino 1995), including wine, lead glaze on pottery, lead pellets such as in shotgun shells, cosmetics, and even illicit drugs. Some of these sources can also affect children.

Malnutrition and Undernutrition

Chapter 7 discussed the effects of maternal **malnutrition** and **undernutrition** during pregnancy. These do not appear to be major factors in developmental disability, at least not in the United States, but major nutritional problems occur in underdeveloped nations.

Severe malnutrition in infants causes a disorder called **marasmus.** In this disease, the child's growth literally stops, the child's body deteriorates, and death occurs. Another condition is **kwashiorkor,** in which the severe malnutrition results in skin sores, hair loss, and the accumulation of water and resulting swelling of the child's face, abdomen, arms, and legs. If the children survive severe malnutrition, they will suffer from cognitive deficits and physical disorders, thus contributing to increases in developmental disabilities. The severe endpoints of serious malnutrition, then, are disability and/or death. There are many thousands of children in the world today suffering from severe malnutrition and its aftermath. It is the major cause of child deaths in developing countries (Batshaw & Perret, 1997). The tormented lives and lingering deaths of these children are rarely due to "natural events" or "acts of God." Rather it is the actions, ignorance, greed, and callousness of competing factions—almost always people in conflict with each other—that cause such misery.

Undernutrition is a more common world problem, particularly in developed countries. There is ample evidence that undernutrition, such as is found in poor families, is associated with cognitive/intellectual deficits in children. Research in the 1960s showed that chronically undernourished children, such as many in poor homes, have lower academic achievement than do more adequately nourished children. Animal studies reported that overall brain size and number of brain cells were reduced due to chronic undernutrition. Thus, one might conclude from those early studies that chronic undernutrition in infancy causes intellectual deficits and might very well have a direct causal relationship to developmental disability, mental retardation in particular.

In response to such findings, it was concluded that a sensible approach would provide adequate nutrition to poor children, thus preventing the intellectual deficits. As Ricciutti (1991) has noted, the subsequent research in nutritional supplement programs for poor children has yielded mixed results, and it is not clear that a simple relationship exists between nutrition and mental deficit. Rather, the mechanisms accounting for the relationship may be more complex and indirect than was at first thought. Undernutrition might have direct negative effects on intelligence, but it seems more likely that the effects are mediated by other factors. For example, chronic undernutrition occurs in poor families. A host of poverty-associated variables in addition to undernutrition may contribute to it. The children may not have stimulating toys, books, videos, and so on. Their parents are generally less educated than middle-class parents and may not have the interest or skill to stimulate high intellectual growth. That is, these children might grow up in an intellectually stunting environment in addition to being chronically undernourished.

Another possibility is that chronic undernutrition might affect the child's general level of physical energy, thus failing to sustain not only physical growth but also the level of activity needed for continued intellectual growth (Schurch & Scrimshaw, 1990). This might reduce interest, curiosity, and motivation to explore and to learn and leave the children less responsive to what is available in their environments. Simply put, a constantly hungry child just might not have the energy for or much interest in active exploration of new things and therefore may not take advantage of the existing learning opportunities. Thus, undernutrition appears to be a crucial factor that interacts with many factors in the child's environment and has a depressive effect on intelligence and learning and, generally, may make problems likely to occur (Ricciutti, 1991). Simply providing the nutritional supplements, while undoubtedly useful in improving the child's health and therefore a desirable effort, might not be sufficient to overcome the entire complex of factors that lead to impaired cognitive ability. Nutritional adequacy is important but is only part of the issue, and children's learning and general home environments are equally important for cognitive development (Sigman, 1995). Nutritional supplement programs should be accompanied by social and educational programs to enrich the child's learning environments and to teach parents how to maintain enriched home settings.

While poverty is a risk factor for undernutrition, the problem seems most associated with specific factors within the family. For example, mothers who are depressed are often unresponsive to their children's needs and may not feed them properly (Drotan, Eckerle, Satola, Pallotta, & Wyattet, 1990). Parental drug and alcohol addiction and mental illness can also contribute. Ignorance of the nutritional needs of growing children is another risk factor, and it is associated with low education and poverty.

What are the developmental consequences of undernutrition? Undernourished children are generally smaller and lighter than normal. They have less disease resistance than do normally fed children, and they are often apathetic, fatigued, and lacking in interest and motivation. Their rates of learning and development may be slower as they will not benefit from the learning opportunities in their environments as will normal children. If left uncorrected, the children could suffer from attenuated intellectual and social development and might never achieve at their highest potential levels (Dobbing, 1987). Most will probably not be developmentally disabled, but they will most likely be delayed. In terms of our discussion in Chapter 1, they may be impaired in various functions but not necessarily disabled. As Ricciutti (1991) suggests, undernourishment is itself a risk factor, making deficits more likely if other risk factors, such as injury and disease, should also occur.

However, as discussed in Chapter 6, corrective steps can be taken and the children can regain a normal developmental growth curve. Despite undernourishment in infancy, improved diets and special physical, social, and intellectual stimulation and education can overcome developmental problems (Super, Herrera, & Mora, 1990). Thus, it appears that social programs to help poor, undernourished children by providing nutritious food, early stimulation, preschool education, and general learning-enriched environments may be a good investment for society, as well as personal aid for many individual children.

A related problem that has recently become of interest to researchers is **overnutrition**—children receiving too much food and becoming obese. There is no current evidence that obesity in infancy predicts obesity in adulthood (Epstein & Wing, 1987). However, obesity in childhood and adolescence does predict adult obesity. Two-thirds of obese adolescents will become obese adults (Epstein & Wing, 1987).

Obesity is associated with lower self-esteem and social problems in children, curtailed social and physical activity, and increased risks of high blood pressure and heart problems as adults (Epstein & Wing, 1987). To date, there has been no evidence that obesity in infants and children is a risk factor for developmental disabilities and no reason to expect it to be. However, there is concern that children with developmental disabilities are at increased risk for poor nutrition. Because they are particularly dependent on others for their care, these children may not receive adequate nutrition. They may not be able to make their needs known easily, and responses of caregivers may not be sufficiently timely or nutritionally adequate. Because of their physical handicaps, many children will not be able to make nutritional corrections on their own, seeking, obtaining, and self-administering proper food and/or nutritional supplements. Those with cognitive limitations may not be able to benefit by public education about nutritional care or take responsibility for rational, informed self-care. Similar questions also apply to adults with developmental disabilities.

These issues are of concern for research and for applied programs of care, training, and education of persons with developmental disabilities. Researchers should investigate the nutritional status of children and adults with developmental disabilities. Is their nutritional status as a group different from the norms or from some optimal theoretical condition? How does it change from childhood through adulthood and old age? Are there particular kinds of nutritional problems that are most prevalent and/or severe among people with developmental disabilities? Is there an interaction of nutritional problems and types of developmental disabilities? That is, are there nutritional differences between those with autism, retardation, and so on? Many important questions can be researched concerning the nutritional behavior and knowledge of persons with developmental disabilities.

In related fashion, professionals in educational, training, and care programs can address how best to provide proper nutrition for their clients, to educate and train the parents, and probably most important, how best to teach and train the clients for their own self-controlled, optimal self-care for proper nutrition.

II. Chapter Summary

The major etiological factors that operate during and after birth in developmental disabilities are oxygen deprivation (anoxia), physical injury including traumatic brain injury, environmental toxins, childhood illness, and malnutrition. In addition, preterm birth and full-term but low birth weight are conditions clearly associated with disabilities.

Anoxia is a potential problem particularly during birth, when many events (breech presentation, precipitous birth, head deformations, etc.) can interfere with oxygen and cause brain damage. In contrast, traumatic brain injury occurs largely to older adolescents and frequently in automobile crashes.

In addition to operating as teratogens during fetal development, environmental toxins, such as lead, can have severe effects on the postnatal child. One of the complications in lead toxicity is that the treatment (chelation therapy) may itself have negative effects on the child.

Low birth weight and preterm delivery both increase risks of developmental disabilities because these children are born smaller, weaker, less developed than normal, and thus have particular difficulties in adjusting to the postnatal demands of development.

Childhood illness such as severe infections and malnutrition also affect development. Malnutrition is a problem particularly in developing countries.

KEY TERMS

Know these important terms. Check the chapter and the Glossary for their meanings. They are listed here in the approximate order of their appearance in the chapter.

Anoxia	Intentional injuries	Plumbism
Precipitous birth	Failure to thrive	Sensitive populations
Low birth weight (LBW)	Psychosocial dwarfism	Pica
Very low birth weight (VLBW)	Breech presentation	Lead encephalopathy
Extremely low birth weight (ELBW)	Traumatic brain injury	Chelation therapy
	Shaken baby syndrome	Synergistic effects
Preterm birth	Meningitis	Malnutrition
SIDS	Diffuse axonal injury	Undernutrition
Pulmonary surfactant	Concussion	Overnutrition
Alveoli	Encephalitis	Marasmus
Infant mortality	Kohl	Kwashiorkor
Unintentional injuries	Surma	

SUGGESTED READING

Abel, E. L. (1990). *Fetal alcohol syndrome.* Oradell, NJ: Medical Economics Co.

Cicero, T. J. (1994). Effects of paternal exposure to alcohol on offspring development. *Alcohol, Health, and Research World, 18*(1), 37–41.

National Research Council. (1993). *Measuring lead exposure in infants, children, and other sensitive populations.* Washington, DC: National Academy Press.

Snow, J. H., & Hooper, S. R. (1994). *Pediatric traumatic brain injury.* London: Sage.

Streissguth, A. P. (1994). A long-term perspective of FAS. *Alcohol, Health, and Research World, 18*(1), 74–81.

STUDY QUESTIONS

8-1. Consider all of the reasons it has been so difficult to determine the incidence and prevalence of DD. What are the major factors in this problem? What can be done to arrive at reliable and valid figures?

8-2. Be sure that you understand the disabilities brought on by oxygen deprivation. What are the conditions under which this is likely to occur? How can we prevent/reduce this?

8-3. A number of developmental problems are associated with low birth weight. What are they?

8-4. How can a public health campaign reduce the problems associated with LBW?

8-5.   Here is a puzzler. The United States has, arguably, the finest health-care system in the world, and yet our infant mortality rate is still higher than in many other countries. What might the reasons be for this contrast?

8-6.   In this chapter, we took care to distinguish between intentional and unintentional injuries to children and youth. How do these differ? Why do you think we argue against the use of the label "accident"?

8-7.   What public health actions do you think will have the greatest effect on reducing TBI in children and youth? Outline a program that you think would be effective.

8-8.   Do you understand the dangers of environmental lead? What are those dangers?

8-9.   Let's bring this to a personal level. Look at your own life, the environment you and your family live in, and your lifestyles. In what ways are you vulnerable to toxic chemicals and to dangerous elements and other factors such as lead and mercury? What are the sources of these in your life? How can you protect yourself?

Mental Retardation (Intellectual Disabilities)

There are three major concepts that describe the 5 to 6 million persons in the United States, across all age groups, who are in the category "mental retardation" (MR, or persons with intellectual disabilities). The central concept is **limited cognitive abilities;** that is, mental retardation refers primarily, but not completely, to significant limitations in intelligence. The second major concept, deficits in adaptive behavior, refers to the person's functioning in pursuing common activities and goals of life. (For a diagnosis of MR to be made, significant deficits in both cognitive and adaptive behavior must be present.) A third important concept, one that applies to all of the developmental disabilities, is that deficits occur during the person's major developmental period (i.e., to about age 18 or 21). This chapter is organized around the first two major concepts: deficits in intelligence and adaptive behavior.

I. The Nature of Intelligence

Defining Intelligence

The literature on the nature and measurement of intelligence is vast, and a single chapter can touch upon only a few of the concepts. The volumes that have been written on the descriptions, definitions, and theories of intelligence (e.g., Detterman, 1994; Khalfa, 1994; Sternberg & Detterman, 1986; Zigler & Balla, 1982) illustrate the diversity. Intelligence has been conceptualized as a quality and/or quantity within individuals (e.g., a set of cognitive skills); the overt behavior of individuals; the successful interaction of persons and their external environments; success in meeting life's demands; and as one's capacity to learn. Major underlying factors in these definitions are biological, environmental, social, emotional, psychological, and/or their combinations.

Theorists conceptualize intelligence as being **global** and/or specific—that is, general in nature and/or as existing as specific components or independent abilities that operate together as a complex system (Detterman, 1986). Independent abilities include verbal and motor intelligence, metacognition, memory, comprehension, and so on. Most commonly, intelligence is thought to consist of some combinations of a general factor of intelligence plus combinations of specific abilities. Intelligence has been thought of as fixed at conception and therefore unchangeable. Conversely, it has been thought to be amenable to change through experience or even as created by environmental factors.

Finally, there are diverse ways of measuring intelligence, and they do not necessarily agree with each other. Among the problems of measurement are the issues of validity and reliability. **Validity** concerns whether a particular test really measures intelligence. Is it a fair test or has it been biased in some subtle ways to the disadvantage of particular groups and so on? **Reliability** concerns whether the test holds up and gives the same results for a person at different administrations of the test. That is, does an IQ test give substantially the same results over time and across different settings, such as school and work? The domain encompassed by the variously defined concept of intelligence is huge indeed. It is important to emphasize that concepts and measures of intelligence are variable, at best are incomplete approximations of reality, and many procedures and decisions are based on conventions rather than true understanding. However, as imperfect as they may be, these are the tools we possess and must use while continuing to improve them.

Our understanding of the general meaning of "intelligence" is based on Sternberg and Slater's (1982) definition of intelligence as thinking and behavior that are adaptive for individuals as they meet life's demands and pursue life's goals. In this definition, intelligence refers not only to the individual's quality of thinking but also to the quality of overt behavior. Traditionally, however, it has been the "thinking" (i.e., cognitive aspect) that has been emphasized in the study of MR and is sampled by most intelligence tests.

School-Based Criteria in Defining MR

The importance of certain kinds of intellectual skills is nowhere more evident than in our schools. Children who vary considerably in their abilities compete within the general arena of society and the specific arena of schools. As Parsons (1965) noted, the elementary school is, among other things, a critical mechanism for determining a person's future status in society. Those who are the brightest will, by and large, be the most successful students, will become the professionals, the governmental and business leaders, and the artists, writers, composers, teachers, and scientists who contribute to society far in excess of their numbers.

But what of the children who are significantly below the middle of the intellectual continuum and are excluded from or restricted in that academic arena? School is the **social agent** that is primarily responsible for identifying persons with MR (Haskins, 1986; Mercer, 1973). School personnel do so by judging the child in the academic context using school-based criteria. But academic demands and expectations do not necessarily represent those in the larger society. Haskins (1986) cites studies showing that for those with retardation school achievement does not correlate well with workplace success. He concludes that for persons with MR the adaptive skills appropriate in the academic setting are not necessarily the same as those required by the workplace and might not be the most appropriate for judging future social adjustment. Failure or poor performance in the classroom does not mean these persons will fail in social and occupational adjustment as they mature.

Defining retardation in terms of academic criteria has led to what Rowitz (1981, 1991) calls **6-hour retardation.** The term describes children who are labeled with mild retardation (IQ about 50 to 70) and who behave in ways that are consistent with teachers' expectations of children with retardation. However, outside of school, free from the persistent demands of focused intellectual tasks, most of these children function quite well and do not appear to be retarded. They interact successfully in peer groups, after-school jobs, with families, relatives, and friends, and might have no serious behavioral problems. That is, their "retardation" seems to be defined largely by the particular context (i.e., the school).

School-based criteria, which have defined most persons with MR, are not necessarily appropriate for assessing the person's postschool adjustment and success. This means that many—indeed, most—cases of MR are contextually defined rather than defined solely by the person's characteristics. Thus, when MR is contextually defined outside that context, the person is no longer mentally retarded. The retardation seems to "come and go" depending on the surrounding contexts. As will be discussed later, this is very different from persons for whom the MR results from clearly defined organic impairments such as neural tube defects and chromosomal anomalies. For these persons with organic etiologies, the MR functioning level is consistently apparent across all contexts.

Measuring Intelligence: IQ Tests

Intelligence is a complex set of cognitive skills and behaviors that develops as the child grows. In this sense, then, intelligence grows with one's continuing experience with life's increasingly complicated personal, social, educational, and occupational demands. All persons, including those with MR, become more sophisticated and "smarter" as we grow into adulthood and gain experience. But intelligence develops at different rates and levels of quality in different people. The variability of all human characteristics, including intelligence, is a "fact of life" (Graziano & Raulin, 2000)—simply, persons differ from one another on each characteristic. Intelligence is distributed along a range within the population, with most persons falling in the middle ranges and smaller numbers at the upper and lower ranges. Not only are there differences between people, but there are also variations within people. A person might be quite high in some area of intelligence such as verbal ability but comparatively low in some other area such as motor/performance ability.

Despite the varieties of intelligence tests and the still debated issues of validity, IQ tests continue to be used as the primary measure of intelligence in defining MR. Most modern intelligence tests assume that intelligence is not a unitary trait but rather is composed of mental abilities in different but related areas of cognitive functioning. Thus, memory, reasoning, numerical calculation, problem solving, general information, comprehension, and so on are all assumed to be components of one's general intelligence. Intelligence tests try to sample many areas by posing specific standardized questions that are constructed to probe specific areas (e.g., arithmetic problems, memory tasks, verbal reasoning) and by recording how many are answered correctly. From these answers, the psychologist derives the person's total score contributed to by all of the areas tested. In addition, an assessment can be made of the relative strengths of the different areas for each person tested. Two persons might have very similar total scores in spite of different patterns of strengths and weaknesses in specific areas. To arrive at a comparison of persons, each individual's score is compared with the scores of others of similar chronological age.

When we take measurements such as intelligence test scores of a large number of cases, the scores tend to distribute themselves along the shape of a **normal curve.** As seen in Figure 9.1, this is a symmetrical distribution in which the large majority of cases fall around the middle of the distribution. Half the cases fall above the middle (the mean or average score), half fall below the middle, and the extremes drop off sharply, with similar curves at the ends of the continuum. The vertical height of the curve represents the number of scores at each point (i.e., the number of persons tested), and their scores are represented across the base. As shown in Figure 9.1, intelligence test scores are distributed normally, ranging from the lowest scores on the left to the highest on the right. For convenience and comparability, many intelligence tests are constructed with 100 as the mean score and a standard deviation (SD) of 10 or 15. Figure 9.1 shows the normal curve distribution of IQ scores, with the mean and standard deviations, and the proportion of cases in each segment of the curve. As can be seen, 67 percent or about two-thirds of the tested population scores between 85 and 115 (–1 SD to +1 SD). Nearly all persons (95 percent) score between 70 and 130 (–2 SD and +2 SD). Only about 2.2 percent score less than 70 (> –2 SD) and another 2.2 percent score higher than 130 (> +2 SD). Any person's score, then, can be interpreted in standard deviation units and understood in relation to the other scores. For example, a score of 100 is exactly at the mean, 130 is 2 standard deviations above the mean, and 70 is 2 standard deviations below the mean. In the normal curve, the percentage of persons at various standard deviation units is known. For example, a person who scores 130 on this test is 2 standard deviations above the mean and is in the rare company of the

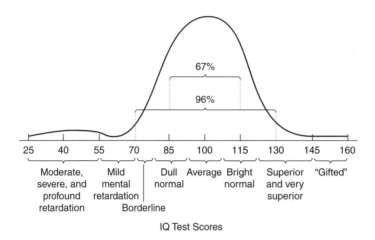

FIGURE 9.1   **Normal Curve of IQ Distributions Showing a Mean Score of 100 and SD of 15 and the Proportion of the Tested Population in Each Area of the Curve.** *Note the slight bulge of cases at the lower end.*

From: Bee, H. (1992). *The Developing Child* (sixth edition). New York: HarperCollins. Reproduced with permission.

highest 2.2 percent of the population of test takers. Likewise, a person scoring 70 on this test is 2 standard deviations below the mean and is in the company of the lowest 2.2 percent of persons. It has been a historical convention to categorize persons between 90 and 110 as "average," while a score of 70 or below is in the range of MR.

MR is defined by low intellectual functioning and by adaptive behavior deficits. In terms of the intellectual dimension, we can see that MR is indicated when the score is significantly subaverage, specifically 2 or more standard deviations below the mean. On most IQ tests, this is a score of 70 or less. Persons in this IQ range account for 2.2 percent of the population. In the U.S. population of 275 million persons, about 6.5 million persons, or 2.2 percent, are in this range as measured by standard IQ tests. However, because many persons in that IQ range do not have the adaptive behavior deficits, the actual number who are classified as mentally retarded is considerably less. Further, because of genetic defects, chromosomal anomalies, and brain damage due to injuries, there are more persons with very low IQ than there are at the upper extreme. Thus, in reality, there is a slight bulge in the curve at the lower end, so more than the theoretical 2.2 percent is actually included.

II. Intelligence and MR

Cognitive Development

Recall (or reread) the discussion in Chapter 3 on the development of cognitive skills. We described an integrated developmental process that includes the physical growth of the brain and the rapid and continuing development of connecting neural networks in which neural cells increase in size and myelination accelerates. These provide the continually growing neural structure for cognitive development—attention and perception, language, and all intellectual activities such as thinking, learning, memory, reasoning, and problem solving. These are the skills that we traditionally think of as comprising one's intelligence.

In young children, these skills are tied closely to concrete experiences. Children's growing perceptual skills, such as recognizing shapes, sounds, colors, and textures, are basic to their expanding knowledge about the world. As language develops, children begin to think in more abstract terms; they think about ideas as well as concrete things. Practice in reading is particularly important in developing skills in abstraction. The older preschooler can go beyond immediate concrete reality and draw inferences about what has not yet happened (the future) and speculate about what "might be" rather than only "what is." For the school-age child, a knowledge base grows rapidly, and memory skills accelerate, including learning how to organize, rehearse, store, and retrieve material (i.e., **metacognition,** learning how to think about thinking), as discussed in Chapter 3. Many, but not all, adolescents develop skills in **hypothetical deductive reasoning** and **theory building.** They can make **inductive** and **deductive inferences,** make predictions, and pose complex "what if?" questions. With these skills, they can comprehend and even create theoretical concepts and theories about nature and about their own functioning. These high-level skills constitute a qualitatively different dimension in thinking and intelligence (Andrich & Styles, 1994). Presumably, persons who are more developed in this range of cognitive skills are more capable of success in their life pursuits. In contrast, children with MR are seen to be deficient in some or all of those skills, and they are thus significantly subaverage in intelligence.

Children and adults with MR manifest significant delays in cognitive development, putting them far behind their average-intelligence age mates. Major intellectual characteristics of persons with MR are summarized in the sections that follow.

Attention

Short attention span (insufficient time spent on a task) and **stimulus overselectivity** (focusing on a small, often irrelevant portion of a total stimulus) are problems of attention in persons with MR. The person characteristically does not devote sufficient time to learning tasks, thereby failing to learn. In addition, by focusing on small, irrelevant aspects of a task, he or she fails to take in the whole task or other, possibly more important, cues, leading to poor learning. Attention span and overselectivity problems have to be addressed specifically in any training or teaching programs for persons with MR.

Generalization (Transfer of Learning)

The person with MR not only has difficulty in learning new tasks but also in the **transfer of learning** from one setting to another such as from the classroom to a job or from one social experience to another. It is important in normal learning to be able to carry out such generalizations. For the person with MR, however, learning seems to be situation specific, and the generalization across settings and time that is so easily carried out by most of us is not accomplished naturally. Thus, training and education programs for MR must include carefully developed and specific procedures for teaching new learning and also for establishing and maintaining the generalization of new learning across time and setting.

Incidental Learning

Most people in school, work, home, and other everyday situations are able to attend to many aspects of a complex situation. In learning settings, most people learn not only specific things to which we are directed but also many other things to which we pay only part or fleeting attention. Each situation is potentially rich for learning numerous things—some directly and some incidentally (**incidental learning**). Then, in other situations that contain factors similar to those incidentally learned factors, we can recognize them and respond successfully. For example, in a new job, perhaps we are being shown how to operate a particular computer program. While focusing primarily on the screen, the keyboard, and the supervisor's instructions, we are also incidentally attending to other aspects of the situation. We are simultaneously learning some things about our supervisor, the way the room is organized, or how many other people work in that room, what they look like, and so on. By the completion of the training session, we will have learned quite a variety of things, not just how to use a particular computer program.

Persons with MR, however, have difficulty with simultaneous attention to and perception of multiple aspects of a complex situation. Thus, training must include careful teaching to bring many of the important factors to the person's attention and ultimately within their scope of learning. This may entail simplifying the situation as much as possible and then seemingly endless, repetitious practice, each time making explicit another aspect of that situation, aspects to which most of us would naturally attend incidentally.

Concrete and Abstract Thinking

Persons with MR tend to think in concrete terms, focusing on the more obvious aspects of persons, things, and situations and on immediate rather than past or future events. There are difficulties in thinking in abstract terms, in making inferences about what might be, or in making predictions about the future and seeing accurately beyond immediate appearances. Long-range planning, goal setting, self-monitoring of progress toward personal goals, and postponing immediate satisfactions for the sake of much later rewards all require abilities in abstracting ideas and going far beyond immediate events. Such abstractions are difficult for persons with MR.

Metacognition

Learning new tasks, especially mental tasks, will be difficult, at least partly because of limitations in **metacognition** (i.e., "thinking about thinking"), knowing how to learn, and having skills in organizing, storing, and retrieving information. While one might be able to follow very carefully presented step-by-step directions with close supervision, it will be difficult for that person with MR, on his or her own, to approach a new task successfully. Limited metacognitive development leaves the person without skills in how to approach and analyze a new task, how to break it down into its parts, which parts to deal with in what order, and so on. Lacking these metacognitive skills, the person with MR faced with a new problem or task is apt to approach it in an unplanned, haphazard manner. Failing to find success quickly, he or she may soon become frustrated or lose interest and perhaps experience another personal failure. Metacognitive skills are extremely difficult to teach. (As we will discuss in Chapter 10, metacognitive skills deficits may also be critical in autistic disorders.)

Language

Expressive and receptive language are less developed in those with MR than in other persons, and academic tasks accomplished by normal age mates are difficult to achieve. Writing, reading newspapers and bus schedules, and managing checking or savings accounts will be far too difficult. Arithmetic ability, general intellectual problem solving, basic comprehension skills, and a general fund of knowledge will be significantly less than for persons of average or higher intellectual abilities. That does not mean that persons with MR are incapable of thinking, learning, solving problems, or functioning socially. They can and do, but at lower developmental levels of cognition and not with the facility, speed, and success of other people.

Social Communication

Subtle communications in many social situations are difficult for persons with MR. These persons can be easily influenced and taken advantage of because of their relative social naiveté and their inability to infer human motives that contradict outward appearances. Making such inferences requires a fund of knowledge about human behavior, some social maturity, and sophistication. There are many instances of young adults with mental retardation (e.g., with a mental age of 12 years or less) who are easily convinced by their normal-intelligence age mates to engage in dangerous or illegal actions and to be taken advantage of and victimized. In those situations, the submissiveness and compliant acquiescence of the victimized person are easily understood when we recognize the vast differences between the 11- or 12-year-old mentality of the targeted person and the adult mentality of the others. The younger mentality is simply no match for the older. Such exploitation in situations of disparate mental abilities in chronologically equal youth often takes the form of sexual abuse, such as the incident in which an adolescent girl with mental retardation was sexually abused by a group of adolescent boys (see Box 9.1).

Relative Rates of Cognitive Development

Consider a hypothetical case of a developmentally delayed 6-year-old with the mental development of a 4-year-old, and compare this child with an "average" child of 6 years. The average child has a chronological age of 6 years and a matching mental age of 6 years (an IQ of 100) and has developed the cognitive skills needed for early school success (see Chapter 3 and the preceding discussion). Another way of stating this is that early school demands are created for the ability levels of the average 6-year-old and not for the average 4-year-old. To use an oversimplified calculation just for illustration, consider that the delayed child—a

BOX **9.1**

Victimization and Sexual Abuse of a Girl with Mental Retardation

In his book *Our guys: The Glen Ridge rape and the secret life of the perfect suburb* (1997), Bernard Lefkowitz describes what happened to Leslie, a 17-year-old girl with mental retardation. A physically attractive girl, Leslie functioned on an intellectual level of about a 9- or 10-year-old. She loved sports and was infatuated with the swaggering adolescent boys who were the school's athletes. Leslie was not part of their various cliques and was never invited to their parties. She longed to become their friend, to be accepted by them, and to become part of their glamorous group.

Leslie was generally ignored by these high-status boys until one day in 1989 when she met a group of them in the park in baseball practice. She was excited when they invited her to a "party," her first invitation and indication of acceptance by them. They went to one of the boys' homes, into a basement recreation room where she was soon stripped of her clothes, forced to perform fellatio, and was raped by some of the boys who used a wooden drumstick.

She was not certain exactly what was going on, but she had some vague sense that they had been "bad boys" because what they did to her was painful. But she was reluctant to tell anyone what they had done because she did not want to get her "friends" in trouble and would not risk that they might not like her anymore.

Leslie, with her 17-year-old body and 10-year-old mentality, was no social match for the scheming of those adolescent boys.

6-year-old with a 4-year-old mental level—has developed only four-sixths, or .667, of the other child's mental development (an IQ of 67). This developmentally delayed child will not have the range of cognitive skills necessary for kindergarten and first grade. If put into those classrooms without compensating programming, this child will surely flounder. His or her cognitive resources are significantly less than those of the other child. The delayed child will continue to grow physically and intellectually, to experience, perceive, interpret, and understand the world, and to categorize and remember events and ideas (i.e., to learn a great deal). But that growth will be always significantly slower than in the average child—that is, the rate of intellectual development is much slower (Weir, 1982). At every point in their relative developments, the child with retardation will learn, incorporate, and master less because his or her intellectual resources are less. He or she will be continually disadvantaged in learning and understanding. All subsequent intellectual development will be adversely affected. As this continues, the delayed child will, of necessity, fall further behind the average child and will never "catch up." If the child had been 2 years delayed at age 6, he or she will be nearly 4 years delayed at age 12 and 5 years delayed by age 16. By 16 years, this youngster will have the approximate mental development of an 11-year-old. Had the child manifest a greater delay, then the mental disparity at each age level would be even greater.

However, the rate of intellectual development is not the only difference; in some ways not yet understood, the quality of what is developed is also affected. Consider that at each age level, every new experience is filtered through a set of intellectual resources that are only two-thirds of those available to the other child. The intellectual contexts for the two children are very different. For example, suppose that both are 14 years old, and they each encounter a new, complex social/learning situation. Both youngsters will learn, gain from the experience, and carry with them a new level of experience to use in future situations. However, what the delayed youth learns and takes away for future use is filtered through the mental level of a 9-year-old. Thus, the very quality of what is learned and generalized to other settings is different for the two youngsters. The intellectual deficits are not only in the rate of development (i.e., the delay) but also in the inevitable distortions due to incomplete understanding at each point in time and the subsequent problems as those distortions are incorporated into later development. We do not know how all of this plays out.

III. Heterogeneity among Persons with Mental Retardation

IQ Criteria for Mental Retardation

In conventional use (A.A.M.R., 1992), scores of 70 and lower (2 or more SD below the mean) define the intellectual range of MR. Statistically, 2 SD below the mean include 2.25 percent of the population. Two important points must be made about this range of scores. First, because of measurement errors and issues of reliability, no IQ score is precise but must be seen as representing a range of about 5 points above and below the score. An obtained score of 70, for example, is interpreted as falling in the range of 65 to 75. This 10-point range is the **zone of uncertainty** (Reschly, 1987).

Second, persons who score 70 or less and are therefore candidates for the MR diagnoses form a heterogeneous group. The functional differences between those at the higher portion of this group (70 to 75 IQ) and those at 30 IQ and below are considerable. In addition, two persons with the same IQ score can have different patterns of abilities and very different personalities. *Because persons in this category share the label "retardation" does not mean they are all the same!* The functional differences among these persons are labeled as shown in Figure 9.1 and Table 9.1.

The categorization and description of persons presented in Table 9.1 are no longer used in formal MR diagnoses. They are presented here to help describe the MR population and to underscore the functional heterogeneity within it. To understand the issues, we need to recognize the generally shared characteristics across all persons with MR and within each of the MR levels discussed here. Most important, however, despite the common aspects, we must not treat people as members of a class but must focus on each individual and help each to develop his or her best possible quality of life.

Mild Mental Retardation (MMR)

About 75 percent of all persons with MR are at this upper level of retardation (Grossman & Tarjan, 1987). Their intellectual functioning is about 50 to 70 IQ. Typically, children in this range are physically indistinguishable from their nonretarded peers, and for most, there are no known discernible organic etiologies (i.e., their retardation is due to "unknown causes"). However, they show developmental delays (i.e., are "slower" in achieving developmental milestones); their functioning, particularly cognitive, is notably different, and they have difficulties managing many social relations. Most are not diagnosed until they enter school and

TABLE 9.1   Percentage of All Persons with MR at Four IQ Levels

Level	IQ Range	Approximate Percentage
Mild Retardation	50–70	75–80 %
Moderate Retardation	35–49	10%
Severe Retardation	20–34	5–10%
Profound Retardation	Below 20	

Percentage estimates are based on Gajria, M., & Hughes, C. A. (1988). Introduction to mental retardation. In P. J. Schloss, C. A. Hughes, & M. A. Smith (Eds.), *Mental retardation.* Boston: Little, Brown, & Co.

are evaluated according to the school-based criteria that emphasize cognitive tasks. They are educable and can profit from primary education up to an equivalent of about sixth or perhaps seventh grade, developing some literacy and common social and communicative skills. Most children in the MMR range attend special classes in public schools. Some are mainstreamed into regular classrooms, which is an increasingly used and successful option for these children. Along with regular class placement, they are provided with modified academic material and resource rooms where special services are available such as individual tutoring in specific subjects.

When they become adults, many in this group will work regularly in low-skilled jobs and will attain some degree of independent living (Evans, 1983). Several years out of school, some may become so well integrated into the community as to be indistinguishable from nonretarded persons (Edgerton, 1988; MacMillan, Siperstein, & Gresham, 1996; Rowitz, 1991) and no longer considered to be "retarded" (Robinson & Robinson, 1976). They will have progressed beyond that label, maintain good social and occupational adjustment, although usually experiencing some maladjustment problems at some point (Edgerton, 1988; Rowitz, 1991), and lead largely independent lives, no longer appearing retarded. Thus, assuming no serious physical or emotional disabilities, many of the persons with MMR can carry out much of what constitutes successful, independent living. They will not achieve positions such as teachers, police officers, secretaries, businesspeople, or bus drivers. With natural environment supports (family, friends, employers) and professional programs, many will find useful occupations and will maintain successful and reasonably independent lives.

Most, however, will require some degree of lifelong services in settings such as group homes or will drift down into low socioeconomic levels. They will find adjustment acceptable to them and will probably not adopt working class values, behavior, and amenities. As Evans (1983) observed, many do not accept the legitimacy of the middle-class "success value," and therefore, by conventional standards, they will not be very "successful."

Cultural-Familial Retardation

Cultural-familial retardation is a term applied to a large subset of persons in the mild-moderate groups. These persons function at the higher levels of MR and have no known organic etiologies. What, then, accounts for their functioning?

Some researchers (e.g., McCarver & Craig, 1974; Mercer, 1970; Windle, 1962; Zigler & Balla, 1982) argue that the importance of intelligence in the performance of persons with MR has been overestimated. They maintain that about 20 percent of all MR cases are due to central nervous system (CNS) pathology. In contrast, the limited performance of most persons in the cultural-familial group (which accounts for some 70 to 80 percent of all MR) is best understood as the result of intellectual limitations due to genetic factors (the familial component) and to motivational and achievement factors (the cultural component). These persons, according to Zigler and Balla (1982) and Nichols (1981), are not categorically different from nonretarded persons and do not possess CNS "defects" that account for the retardation. Rather, they argue, most persons with MR are simply persons who are in the lower range of the normal distribution of intelligence. For these researchers, the difference is quantitative, not qualitative.

In this model, a combination of limited intellectual ability and deprived learning experiences leaves the person less capable than most of successful functioning. By definition, cultural-familial retardation is not attributed to any single cause, such as a genetic defect, but is due to multiple factors. These may include hereditary determinants of intellectual ability, biological risk factors associated with poverty, patterns of developmental neglect within a family context of poor childrearing skills, and limited resources that may lead to inadequate stimulation and guidance, resulting in a gradual decrement of functioning level. For example, children of MMR parents who are raised in a deprived social and economic environment will probably share their parents' genetically determined limits of intelligence and will suffer from social and learning deprivations affecting their performance. If the school performance of these children is poor, it may not be due to their cognitive level alone but also to personality and motivational factors arising from sociocultural deprivation.

Motivational and personality factors that affect performance include the person's expectations for failure, heightened sensitivity to social reinforcement, suspicion or wariness of others, overdependence, and as Weisz (1982) suggested, some degree of learned helplessness. Zigler and Balla (1982) proposed that the overdependence observed in persons with MR might derive from the child's heightened sensitivity to or need for social reinforcement. These children may learn to depend heavily on others for cues about how to behave in order for their actions to be approved by others. Zigler and Balla (1982) assert that one cannot emphasize enough the impact of such learned overdependence on the functioning of persons with retardation. They noted that for persons with retardation to become "self-sustaining" in society, the most important factor may be their success in shifting significantly from learned dependence to independence.

Personality and motivational factors are developed as consequences of the child's particular developmental history, such as growing up in socially deprived settings. It follows that if those developmental conditions could be improved, then the negative personality and motivational characteristics such as overdependence might be attenuated, and the person's cognitive and social performance might be enhanced. This position does not deny the subaverage cognitive abilities of persons in the cultural-familial group. There is little doubt that persons with MMR have fewer intellectual resources to draw upon than do those who are not retarded. Rather, Zigler and Balla (1982) emphasize that the performance of those persons is also strongly affected by the additional factors of personality and motivation.

This is an optimistic position. It assumes that while interventions designed to improve the limited sociocultural environments and personal motivational factors might not alter basic cognitive ability, they might nevertheless bring about significantly improved performance. Thus, the person's degree of independent living and vocational success or failure might be due to such motivational and personal factors.

Moderate Mental Retardation

Another approximately 10 percent of the MR population are in the IQ range of about 35 to 49. Children at this level and lower are generally diagnosed early in childhood, before school age. Physical anomalies are apparent, and syndromes such as Down syndrome account for a large proportion. Developmental delays across many functions (motor, coordination, locomotion, etc.) are characteristic. Their overall potential is clearly less than that for the mild group, but useful communication and social and vocational skills are well within their abilities. School achievement is possible up to about third- or fourth-grade levels in special education settings. These children can develop some basic skills in both arithmetic and reading by the time they are about 16 years of age.

Training in social skills, communication, personal self-help, and general skills in daily living is a major component of educational programs. These programs for children living at home have replaced the earlier near-automatic assignment to residential institutions. Vocational training is included for the older youth and young adults, making it possible for adults to maintain occupations in some lower-level jobs. With such programming and lifelong guidance and support, some degree of independent living is possible.

Severe and Profound Mental Retardation

About 10 percent of persons with MR are in these groups and range up to 35 IQ. They have the lowest levels of cognitive functioning and the highest incidence of organically based retardation. (Conversely, those at higher functioning levels [MMR] have the lowest incidence of organically based retardation.) In the lower-functioning group, there is a high proportion of severe birth defects and physical impairment, including low birth weight and high infant mortality. Those who survive infancy have genetic defects and chromosomal anomalies, brain damage, blindness, cerebral palsy, and impaired motor control and locomotion. Adaptive behavior, speech, language, and social skills are impaired significantly. There is a high incidence of behavior problems, usually involving poor personal control such as aggressive attacks on people, destruction of objects, severe tantrums, and self-injury. Feeding problems, including vomiting, pica, and hoarding food, are frequent.

Traditionally, institutionalization was the only placement, and it was assumed they could not learn from any attempts at training. However, we now know that individualized training can be successful in teaching a degree of self-control, basic communication, and even simple vocational skills. By creating individualized and specific training programs, we can help each to develop more socially adaptive and physically safer functioning. For those with severe mental and organic disabilities, this means living in a residential, hospital-like environment. For most, however, it means living at home with one's own family or, more commonly, in a small neighborhood residential facility where a "new family" atmosphere can be maintained. In any case, these persons remain highly dependent on others, and life-long support services are necessary.

Is Mild Mental Retardation a Valid Diagnostic Category?

Most persons diagnosed with MR are in the MMR range of about 50 to 70 IQ. Many researchers have argued for years that persons in this MMR range are significantly different from those who function at lower intellectual levels, and they should not be considered "mentally retarded" at all (e.g., Zigler & Hodapp, 1986). They maintain that persons diagnosed with MR comprise two major groups. Persons in the smaller group, named the "organic-etiology" group, account for about 25 percent of MR. This group has a high proportion of organic etiologies. Although most of these persons function around 30 IQ and lower, the group ranges upward with a few who function at higher IQ levels. Most persons in the larger group, the "nonorganic" or "familial" group, which accounts for about 75 percent of MR, function around 55 to 70 IQ and have a very low proportion of known organic etiologies.

As discussed by Macmillan, Siperstein, & Gresham (1996), there are significant differences between the two groups in intellectual functioning, personal adjustment, social skills, and overall adaptive behavior in their etiologies and responses to intervention. The lower-functioning group with its severe mental retardation has a high rate of organic etiologies, whereas the etiological factors for the familial group are characterized as primarily or wholly nonorganic. For the familial MR persons, parental IQ and socioeconomic status (SES) are risk factors, but no organic etiologies are clearly indicated; no genetic, chromosomal, or physiological impairments account adequately for the diagnosed familial retardation. The condition of the organic group is permanent, while that of the familial group can be improved.

The distinction between organic and nonorganic etiology defines the "two-group" model (Zigler & Hodapp, 1986). The organic MR group includes persons who range from a functional 0 IQ (as in cases of anencephaly) and peaks at about IQ 30, with a few persons ranging upward into the MMR group. This organic MR group includes those with retardation clearly linked with organic etiologies, such as genetic defects (e.g., PKU, Tay-Sachs disease, cretinism). As discussed in Chapter 4, these are transmitted through inheritance of dominant or recessive gene patterns. Heritable etiologies also include chromosomal anomalies resulting in mental retardation associated with specific syndromes such as cri du chat, Prader-Willi, and Down syndromes. Some of the chromosomal anomalies are known to be X-linked, such as Klinefelter's, Turner's, triple-X, and fragile X syndromes. MR due to conditions such as anencephaly, micro- and macrocephaly, and spina bifida is associated with neural tube defect (NTD) etiologies.

As discussed in Chapter 6, many teratogens are etiological factors in mental retardation. These include infectious disease such as rubella, herpes, toxoplasmosis, varicella, influenza, and sexually transmitted diseases (STDs) such as syphilis, gonorrhea, and AIDS. Chemical teratogens include alcohol, resulting in FAS and MR, heroin and other drugs, and heavy metals such as lead. Rh incompatibility, anoxia, and traumatic brain injury are additional organic etiologies. As indicated earlier, approximately 20 to 30 percent of all MR is attributable to known organic etiologies.

In contrast, the familial group has no known characteristic organic etiologies. Rather, the subaverage intellectual functioning seems related to parental intelligence and developmentally restrictive environments (Garber, 1988). The retardation in this group is largely defined contextually rather than organically—that is, the situation or context in which the person, with his or her subaverage intellectual abilities, and the environment, with its restrictions and its supports, interacts. An obvious example is the school context discussed earlier. Many children labeled MMR within the school context function quite adequately outside of school hours and after they age-out of school. That is, the impaired (i.e., MR) functioning occurs only in certain contexts. In very sharp contrast, the adaptive functioning impairments of persons in the organic group are evident across all contexts—they are not context dependent.

It is generally believed that some 75 to 80 percent of all persons with MR have no demonstrable organic etiologies and their MR is due to some combinations of risk factors, including poverty. Macmillan et al. (1996), however, believe that estimate will decrease as more cases are found to be organically related. For example, as discussed in Chapter 5, a growing number of cases have been found to be directly attributable to fragile X syndrome (e.g., Goldson & Hagerman, 1992; Spitz, 1994). Also, more cases than formerly believed are now known to be due to maternal substance abuse (Macmillan et al., 1996). But even with the shift of some proportion of cases from the familial to the organic group, the reality of the two groups, at present at least, is clear, and the impairments of most MMR persons are still contextually defined.

Given the etiological and functional distinctions between the organic and familial groups, it has been suggested that the term *mental retardation* be reserved for the organic MR group but discontinued for the familial group. For example, Reschly (1988) suggested the label *educationally handicapped,* while Macmillan et al. (1996) prefer a term such as *generalized learning disability.* These terms would apply to those persons who are in the MMR range and whose functional limitations are contextually defined. There are many important implications for the field if these suggestions are adopted. For example, the number of persons labeled MR would be drastically reduced because the majority would be redefined under a new label. The upper limit of the cognitive functioning for a label of MR would probably be dropped from the current 70 IQ to 50 and less. The study and identification of the etiologies of MR would probably be enhanced for the smaller group and perhaps prevention efforts would be stimulated to greater levels.

IV. Multidimensional Diagnosis and Service Planning for Mental Retardation

Until recently, the diagnosis of mental retardation was relatively simple but, unfortunately, problematic. An IQ of 70 or less on a standard test was sufficient for the diagnosis. But as we know, there are validity and reliability problems with exclusive reliance on strictly defined IQ scores. A score of 70, because of the reliability range of the test, might actually reflect an ability level of 75 or perhaps even higher. Categorizing that person as "retarded" could be damaging. Thus, it is important to have more than one test and more than one administration of a test to determine a reliable IQ figure.

Further, even when a reliable IQ estimate is obtained, there are factors other than IQ that influence one's personal and social competence and success. Two persons, both with reliable IQ scores of 65, for example, might nevertheless be very different from one another in terms of personal and social success and ability to continue managing a life of relative independence or, as most people have, a life of **interdependence.** That is, mental retardation should be defined not only by intellectual level but also by overt behavior. In particular, we need to attend to the person's emotional status and those social and personal skills that are necessary for developing successful interdependent living.

This kind of broad assessment of thought, adjustment, and behavior requires sensitivity to the person's supporting environment, including cultural diversity in language, behavior, and values. It requires recognition that adaptive functioning is truly socially interactive, interdependent, and not isolated. Therefore, we need to know the person's abilities and limitations, the nature of his or her immediate social and cultural environment, and the social resources needed by the person. An assessment is then made of which of the needed resources are already available in the natural environment and which will have to be provided by the agency. Inherent in this kind of assessment is an important shift from the old focus on personal limitations and disabilities to a focus on the person's abilities, strengths, and the supporting resources in the person's physical and social environments. The essence of this kind of broad assessment is the question: Whatever the obtained IQ score may be, how well can this person function in interaction with other people and with factors in the social and physical environment? At base, adaptive functioning involves person–environment interaction. It is a focus on how the whole person functions within the context of his or her environment (A.A.M.R., 1992), and that is what the newer diagnostic approaches try to assess.

This broader approach is basic to the A.A.M.R. (1992) definition of mental retardation and its application (summarized in Box 9.2). (The following discussion of multidimensional diagnosis is necessarily brief. A more complete discussion can be found in the publication, *Mental retardation: Definition, classification, and systems of supports.* Washington, DC: A.A.M.R., 1992.)

Given the AAMR definition and assumptions, the diagnostic process now involves a multidimensional approach—a study of four areas, or "dimensions," as follows (from A.A.M.R., 1992):

Dimension I. Intellectual Functioning, Adaptive Skills, and Age of Onset
Dimension II. Psychological/Emotional Considerations
Dimension III. Physical/Health/Etiology Considerations
Dimension IV. Environmental Considerations

For each person being evaluated, the diagnostic procedures are carried out in three successive steps, with each step focusing on one or more of the diagnostic dimensions listed. These steps are summarized in Box 9.3.

Step 1: Diagnosis of Mental Retardation

Dimension I: Intellectual Functioning, Adaptive Skills, and Age of Onset.   The first step in diagnosis focuses on Dimension I to determine if MR is present. This requires the diagnostician to determine that (a) the person's intellectual functioning is 70 to 75 or below,

---

BOX **9.2**

The A.A.M.R. Definition of Mental Retardation

Mental retardation refers to substantial limitations in present functioning. It is characterized by (1) significantly sub-average intellectual functioning, (2) existing concurrently with related limitations in two or more of the following applicable adaptive skill areas: communication, self-care, home living, social skills, community use, self-direction, health and safety, functional academics, leisure, and work; (3) mental retardation manifests before age 18.

The following assumptions are essential to the application of the definition.

1. Valid assessment considers cultural and linguistic diversity as well as differences in communication and behavioral factors;
2. The existence of limitations in adaptive skills occur within the context of a community environment typical of the individual's age peers and is indexed to the person's individualized needs for supports;
3. Specific adaptive limitations often co-exist with strengths in other adaptive skills or other personal capabilities; and
4. With appropriate supports over a sustained period, the life functioning of the person with mental retardation will generally improve.

From A.A.M.R. (1992). *Mental retardation: Definition, classification, and systems of support* (p. 5). Washington, DC: American Association on Mental Retardation. Reprinted with permission.

(b) there are significant disabilities in two or more adaptive skill areas, and (c) the age of onset is prior to 18.

A standardized intelligence test administered individually by a psychologist is required to measure intellectual functioning. Because we need a specific focus on the individual, including careful observations of how he or she proceeds through the testing, group intelligence tests are not to be used. The test selected must be appropriate for the individual, taking into consideration factors such as age, native language, and motor and sensory limitations (i.e., the person must not be put at a testing disadvantage because of language differences or physical/sensory handicaps).

The upper-limit criterion of 70 to 75 is 2 standard deviations below the mean of most standard IQ tests where the mean is 100 and the SD is 15. That is, this score is significantly below average. As noted earlier, we expect about 2 to 3 percent of the general population to fall at or below 70 IQ. Admittedly, this criterion for MR remains somewhat arbitrary, but in practice, it is still useful.

If IQ criteria are met, then the diagnostician must determine if the person also has significant limitations in two or more adaptive skill areas. This entails careful assessment of the person's behavior. **Adaptive behavior** refers to everyday behavior for meeting normal demands, and it therefore addresses the person's overall competence. It is clear that one's intellectual level affects one's everyday coping abilities, and thus the two functions—intelligence and adaptive behavior—have an important degree of overlap. The emphasis in this part of the assessment, however, is on the behavioral, coping aspects. The A.A.M.R. states it succinctly: "adaptive behavior refers to what people do to take care of themselves and to relate to others in daily living rather than [to] the abstract potential implied by intelligence" (1992, p. 38).

The person is carefully assessed in the ten areas of normal adaptive functioning that are specified in the A.A.M.R. definition shown in Box 9.2 (communication, self-care, home living, social skills, community use, self-direction, health and safety, functional academics, leisure, and work). Although a number of adaptive behavior assessment scales are available, they are not as complete, well-developed, or standardized as are the much older IQ tests. The diagnostician obtains adaptive skills information by using various scales, interviewing the person, family members, teachers, and so on, and making direct observations of the person during the assessment procedures and in the person's natural environment (home, school, etc.). Significant limitations in two or more of the adaptive living areas are necessary to meet the MR criteria.

In most cases, the diagnosis is made prior to age 18, thus meeting the third criterion, age of onset. For older persons being evaluated, the decision needs to be made whether the disability occurred prior to age 18. Medical records and history reported by family members usually provide that information, and it is ordinarily not difficult to obtain.

Step 2: Identifying Strengths, Weaknesses, and Service Needs

If the three definitional criteria are met in Step 1, then the diagnosis of MR is made. The evaluation procedure then moves to the next step, identifying strengths, weaknesses, and the needed support services. This step in the evaluation process focuses on Dimension II (psychological/emotional considerations), Dimension III (physical/health/etiology considerations), and Dimension IV (environmental considerations).

Dimension II: Psychological/Emotional Considerations.   Up to 35 percent of all persons with MR are also emotionally disturbed or mentally ill (Parsons, May, & Menolascino, 1984). These are persons with dual diagnoses for whom the primary diagnosis is MR and the secondary diagnosis is some form of mental illness, as defined by the *Diagnostic and statistical manual (DSM-IV)* (American Psychiatric Association, 1994). The presence of mental/emotional disorder in addition to MR has important implications for understanding and providing services to the person. Therefore, the diagnostic procedure must determine if mental disorder is present, define and describe it, and make recommendations for appropriate treatment. This mental health assessment uses information from direct observations of the person, clinical interviews, information from relatives, and formal psychodiagnostic testing. Psychologists and psychiatrists typically conduct this part of the evaluation. The psychodiagnostic criteria and nomenclature for each diagnosis are those put forth in the *DSM-IV* (American Psychiatric Association, 1994).

Dimension III: Physical/Health/Etiology Considerations.   The impact of physical health on adaptive functioning is as significant for persons with MR as it is for anyone else. Persons with MR might range in physical health from those with severe physical disorders such as cerebral palsy to those who are in exceptionally good health and can excel, for example, in competitive sports. It is important to assess physical health, and the diagnostician does so by taking a health history, obtaining birth and developmental information, making behavioral observations, and having a medical examination carried out. Examinations for sensory functions (vision, hearing, etc.) may also be ordered. The physical/medical information becomes important data in understanding the person's limitations in adaptive behavior and for planning services for the person.

In addition to assessing current physical health status, it is also important to obtain information on etiology. Here, knowledge of the material on etiology discussed in the first half of this text comes into play. As discussed in earlier chapters, developmental disabilities are multiply determined (i.e. more than one etiological factor has operated in causing the disability). The etiological factors in MR include combinations of (a) biomedical factors (e.g., genetic, nutritional, disease), (b) social factors (e.g., family, adequate parenting, etc.), (c) behavioral factors (e.g., maternal alcohol and drug use), and (d) educational factors (e.g., limited educational and developmental opportunities and supports).

Information to determine etiology is drawn from all of the sources used throughout the diagnostic process, particularly the medical and developmental information. The evaluator seeks information that will help to determine what the etiological factors were (or are) and when they occurred (i.e., prenatal, perinatal, or postnatal onset).

There are three major reasons for obtaining etiological information. First, the information helps to fill out our understanding of the nature of MR in general and of the particular person's disabilities. Even if there are no immediate practical uses for the information, we must believe that all valid and reliable information contributes to the total "universe" of knowledge upon which future discoveries will depend.

Second, etiological information can be of use in planning treatment or other services for the person being evaluated. For example, suppose it is found that the child's condition is due to the recessive gene for PKU, resulting in the typical PKU metabolic errors. With this etiological information, nutritional treatment for the child and training for the parents can be provided, with good chances of arresting or at least significantly slowing the child's cognitive deterioration. Likewise, if postnatal heavy metal toxicity (e.g., lead) is determined to be a major etiological factor, then chelation therapy can be started for the child and the home physical environment can be investigated for toxic sources. The contamination might then be corrected and/or the family moved to a noncontaminated home.

Third, and perhaps here is where it currently has its greatest potential importance, our knowledge of the etiologies of MR is essential for the development of MR prevention strategies. The etiologies of about half of all cases of mild MR and 30 percent of severe MR are not known (McLaren & Bryson, 1987), and much information can be gained from intensive study of individual cases. A major effort, of course, is needed to bring all of that information together. The issues of prevention will be discussed in Chapter 16.

Dimension IV: Environmental Considerations.   It is important to identify the person's physical and social environments and to determine how they impinge on the person to constrain or facilitate his or her adaptive functioning. The diagnosticians:

1. identify and evaluate the person's home, work, and/or school settings

2. consider how and to what extent these settings and intensities constrain or facilitate the person's functioning
3. determine the optimum environments for the person's best adaptive functioning according to his or her specific needs and mix of strengths, weaknesses, and other characteristics.

Step 3: Determining Needed Supports and Support Intensities

In this step, the information obtained in the prior steps is brought together to determine what kinds of supports are needed by the person and to what intensities these supports need to be developed. The concept of supports refers to any strategies and any resources the person can access to help him or her to achieve good adaptive functioning. Ideally, these support resources will be found in the person's own natural environment rather than in a restrictive institutional setting. Such resources can include the person's own skills, information, financial resources, family and friends, and technology such as assistive devices (wheelchair etc.). Natural environment supports include befriending a person with disabilities, helping with one's money management, providing in-home living assistance, health care, financial planning, and so on. Wherever natural support resources are not available, then support services, such as those provided by agencies, should be applied.

The supports needed will, of course, vary greatly from one person to another and even within each person's lifetime. For example, as people grow older, as they gain or lose skills, or as their family situations change, then their needs and associated supports will also change. Thus, the needed supports will vary in their type, duration, and intensities. The diagnostic steps that have been discussed above are summarized in Box 9.3 and the concept of support intensities is defined in Box 9.4.

V. Some Important Generalizations

This brief section highlights several important generalizations about persons with MR and the nature of our current work with them. Overall, persons with MR have common disabilities in thinking and learning and, by definition, operate at intellectual levels that are significantly below most other people. Intellectual deficits increase as the cognitive levels decrease. Despite that focus on deficits, professionals increasingly recognize the great variability among MR individuals and the success that can be achieved with education and training programs. As a result, we now focus much more on the strengths and support needs of individuals, and we work more assiduously to design and carry out individually focused programs. More than ever before, persons with MR are being maintained in their original families and in small familylike neighborhood group homes. More is being accomplished in education and training, and more persons are working in supervised work settings.

One of the most important underlying concepts in this development is the growing recognition that what we see as "retarded functioning" is largely affected and controlled by environmental factors and can be improved by altering the person's environment. For example, we now recognize that MR children can learn some academic material, and therefore,

BOX **9.3**

The Three-Step Diagnostic Process: Diagnosis, Classification, and Systems of Supports

Dimension I:
Intellectual
Functioning and
Adaptive Skills

Step I: Diagnosis of Mental Retardation
Determines Eligibility for Supports
Mental retardation is diagnosed if:

1. The individual's intellectual functioning is approximately 70 to 75 or below.
2. There are significant disabilities in two or more adaptive skill areas.
3. The age of onset is below 18.

Dimension II:
Psychological/
Emotional
Considerations
Dimension III: Physical/
Health/Etiology
Considerations
Dimension IV:
Environmental
Considerations

Step 2. Classification and Description
Identifies Strengths & Weaknesses and the Need for Supports

1. Describe the individual's strengths and weaknesses in reference to psychological/emotional considerations.
2. Describe the individual's overall physical health and indicate the condition's etiology.
3. Describe the individual's current environmental placement and the optimal environment that would facilitate his/her continued growth and development.

Step 3. Profile and Intensities of Needed Supports
Identifies Needed Supports
Identify the kind and intensities of supports needed for each of the four dimensions.

1. Dimension I: Intellectual Functioning and Adaptive Skills
2. Dimension II: Psychological/Emotional Considerations
3. Dimension III: Physical/Health/Etiology Considerations
4. Dimension IV: Environmental Considerations

From: American Association on Mental Retardation (1992), *Mental retardation: Definition, classification, and systems of supports.* (9th ed.) Washington, DC: A.A.M.R. Reproduced by permission.

we provide programs to help them do so (i.e., we are changing their school environments). Ideally, all of this has led and will continue to lead to the achievement of improved life quality for increasing proportions of people with MR.

Perhaps the most important point in this discussion concerns the majority of persons with MR, those in the mild and moderate groups. That is, some 70 to 90 percent have the capacity to learn some academic skills, to develop adaptive social skills, to achieve consistent self-controlled behavior, to function successfully in social relationships and in wage-

---

BOX **9.4**

Definition and Examples of Intensities of Supports

Intermittent

Supports on an "as needed basis." Characterized by episodic nature, person not always needing the support(s), or short-term supports needed during life-span transitions (e.g., job loss or an acute medical crisis). Intermittent supports may be high or low intensity when provided.

Limited

An intensity of supports characterized by consistency over time, time-limited but not of an intermittent nature, may require fewer staff members and less cost than more intense levels of support (e.g., time-limited employment training or transitional supports during the school to adult provided period).

Extensive

Supports characterized by regular involvement (e.g., daily) in at least some environments (such as work or home) and not time-limited (e.g., long-term support and long-term home living support).

Pervasive

Supports characterized by their constancy, high intensity, provided across environments, potential life-sustaining nature. Pervasive supports typically involve more staff members and intrusiveness than do extensive or time-limited supports.

From: American Association on Mental Retardation (1992). *Mental retardation: Definition, classification, and systems of supports* (9th ed.) Washington, DC: American Association on Mental Retardation. Reprinted with permission.

---

earning occupations, and to gain in knowledge, skills, and sophistication as they grow older and gain experience. For a variety of reasons, including severe physical disabilities afflicting some portion, not all will be successful. But with appropriate natural environment and professional program supports, most are able to achieve some degree of occupational and social adjustment and reasonably independent and successful lives. By working and earning a wage, the majority of persons with MR are thus able to make constructive contributions to society in their own manner, and that, after all, is what is asked of all people, MR or not.

VI. Social Factors in Mental Retardation

Mental Retardation and Socioeconomic Status

Most persons in the cultural-familial retardation group live at poverty levels. It is striking that cultural-familial retardation hardly ever occurs in middle-class and upper-class families (Haskins, 1986; Ramey & Finkelstein, 1981). Retardation that does occur at higher SES levels is almost always at the more severe levels and is associated with genetic and chromosomal factors and/or nervous system pathology. Cultural-familial retardation is clearly a problem of the poor. Years of research have demonstrated that retarded intellectual functioning is associated with lower socioeconomic status (Garber, 1988). Risk factors such as poor prenatal care, teratogens, low birth weight, poor nutrition in pregnancy and infancy, vulnerability to childhood toxic invasion (e.g., ingesting lead paint), and a higher probability of intentional and unintentional injuries are clearly associated with poverty. Low-income children are at high risk of exposure to many such harmful conditions. Also, when they do become ill, they are less likely to receive adequate treatment and are more likely to suffer long-term effects than are middle- and upper-SES children (Haskins, 1986). Poverty is not a direct cause in the etiology of retardation, but it constitutes a set of serious risk factors.

Clearly, low socioeconomic status is a factor associated with cultural-familial retardation. However, while virtually all persons with cultural-familial retardation are in the lower-SES groups, most poor people function well above the level of mild retardation (Garber, 1988), and a small minority of infants in low-SES families are at risk for retardation. Simply stated, although poverty is very much related to the problem, poor people in general are not mentally retarded.

Thus, it is not poverty per se but rather factors associated with poverty that raise the risk of retardation for some poor persons. Garber (1988) addressed the issue of why some children and not others are more affected by the poverty environment. Garber, like Hunt (1961), assumed that intelligence is modifiable within genetically determined limits. However, he took issue with the long-held cultural deprivation hypothesis (i.e., poverty is a condition of social deprivation that causes cultural-familial retardation). Garber reasoned that while poverty may be an important risk factor in MR, we need to discover the specific mechanisms that may operate for some families.

Garber proposed an interactive model in which the major factors were cultural-familial retardation and an inadequate early childhood microenvironment. He studied 3- to 6-month-old infants and their mothers who lived in poverty. The mothers' IQs tested at 75 or lower, with a mean of 67. According to Garber, the most important environmental factors in children's cognitive development are the continued, close, personal interactions between the child and the parent. It is the parent who mediates between the child and the external environment and who stimulates, teaches, guides, and supports the growing child. That detailed, daily parent–child interaction is the **microenvironment.** In general, children who experience a rich, healthy, microenvironment will fare much better socially and cognitively than those who do not have that rich environment, and it is no different for children born into poverty. Thus, it is not poverty alone that results in cognitive retardation but the inadequate microenvironment and its failure to mediate successfully between the child and the larger environment that may be the most critical factor. Cultural-familial retardation then, according to Garber, is the result of the interaction of parental IQ (a genetic factor), poverty, and an inadequate microenvironment (social/environmental factors). Children born into these families are at highest risk for cultural-familial retardation. Two families may be in very similar SES conditions but experience very different microenvironments. In one, the mother may have greater intellectual abilities, childrearing skills, and/or more support such as helpful relatives, a partner, or friends, all of whom can help mitigate the decremental effects of poverty. Garber's study suggests that early support and training of low-skilled mothers can reduce the risk of intellectual deterioration of their children.

The Social Surround

Edgerton (1988) proposed a model for secondary prevention of mild mental retardation. He assumed the interaction of genetic/physiological and social learning factors in the development of MMR. According to Edgerton, socialization of a child of low-IQ parents under limited family conditions (i.e., in Garber's terms, a limited microenvironment) creates a "lifetime of failure" experience in which the person is allowed only limited opportunities for normal socialization. The result may be a young adult who, in addition to limited cognitive skills, has developed a personal adjustment characterized by severe overdependence, poor self-concept, low personal expectations, and unwillingness to risk failure. According to Edgerton, most of those people improve their social adjustment and cognitive abilities over time and achieve some degree of independence. Simply, people become more socially sophisticated and generally "smarter" as they mature. However, despite such improvements, most persons with MR continue to require some level of special services and, perhaps most important, continue to view themselves as "retarded" and therefore seriously limited in virtually all of their abilities. Over more than 30 years of observation and research, Edgerton has developed a description of lifestyles that incorporate an **a-motivational syndrome.** That is, these persons have little belief in their own abilities or enthusiasm for vocational or other long-range planning. They have little or no commitment to self-improvement and little involvement in personal challenges. In short, a socialization of failure and disappointment has left them convinced of their own retardation, the hopelessness of expecting a better personal future, and the futility of trying.

Edgerton believes that with the appropriate supports (resources) persons with MMR would be able to function well even without highly specialized services and perhaps would no longer maintain the self-perception of being retarded. The intervention model proposed by Edgerton incorporates three major programmatic factors: (a) augmenting alternative cognitive skills, (b) formation of **symbiotic support groups**, and (c) providing more positive social roles.

Application of the first factor (augmenting alternative cognitive skills) entails cognitive skills training to improve the functioning of those with MR or who are at risk for MR. Although Edgerton focuses primarily on those already with retardation (i.e., a secondary prevention focus), primary prevention through early intervention such as Garber's (1988) program is compatible with this model. As will be discussed in Chapter 16, primary prevention aims to prevent the occurrence of the basic condition (i.e. mental retardation), and secondary prevention aims to reduce the duration of the condition once it has occurred. While there is a large social component to Edgerton's proposed cognitive training intervention, it is primarily aimed at augmenting intellectual processes that will presumably help the person achieve more successful adaptive behavior.

The other two intervention factors (formation of symbiotic support groups and providing more positive social roles) are clearly social factors. As an example of symbiotic support groups, Edgerton suggests communal living arrangements in which several adults with MMR live together, sharing incomes, housekeeping duties, and skills. With professional supports maximized at first and gradually faded, the residents should learn to become mutually dependent on each other (i.e., "symbiotic" in Edgerton's terms) and less dependent on agencies. Over time and with some success (and failure), an agency would presumably gain experience in creating such settings. It is reasonable to expect that success rates could improve as the agencies become more adept at selecting sites, helping individuals to choose compatible housemates, and to solve problems of daily living. Indeed, this model of semi-independent living units in the community has become common in the field.

The third factor, improving social roles, leads to our next topic—social role development in MR. The socialization of persons with MR, according to Edgerton, is so restricted and protected that persons do not have opportunities to experience more independent lives, and they therefore have little social success. Edgerton notes, "Even persons with normal intelligence can be socialized into social incompetence if they are denied the opportunity to live as ordinary people (and, although risky) we should allow persons with low I.Q. to try their hand at living more normal lives" (1988, p. 333).

Persons with MR are not well socialized into what are generally considered useful social roles, particularly vocational roles. Edgerton suggests that human service roles, such as aides in child care centers or in programs for the aged, are not only within the abilities of many persons with MMR but might be highly motivating for them because of the human service component. He observed that persons with MMR are not well motivated to develop vocations and that work does not hold the same value it does for most people. However, after years of dependence on others, many persons with MR express strong interest in helping others, and human services work might be effective reinforcing conditions.

Edgerton does not detail how to accomplish such role development, and he limits his discussion to occupational roles. His model assumes, as have a number of researchers, that a major deficit in the socialization of persons with mild MR lies in their social role development and that interventions aimed at role development might be of value.

The next chapter will explore the suggestions made by Dexter (1960, 1964), Edgerton (1988), Mercer (1970), Wolfensberger (1983, 1984, 1992), and many others of the importance of social role development in MR. We will explore social role concepts and will apply them to MR. Our underlying question will be: Can social role theory inform us about MR?

VII. Chapter Summary

The defining concepts of mental retardation are limited cognitive abilities, deficits in adaptive behavior, and advent prior to about age 21. All three criteria must be met in order to diagnose mental retardation. Intelligence is defined as thinking and behavior that are adaptive for meeting life's demands and pursuing life's goals. A child with mental retardation is cognitively delayed, and the rate of cognitive development remains lower than for normal children. Because development continues for all children, the child with MR will never "catch up" cognitively. In addition to the rate of development, the quality of cognition is also negatively affected for the child with MR. In general, this child has retarded cognitive abilities and will function primarily on a level of concrete thinking with a short-term focus.

IQ tests are the standard means for assessing intelligence. Traditionally, an IQ of 70–75 or less (2 standard deviations below the mean) indicates subaverage cognitive ability. Approximately 2.5 percent of the population is in this area, and it includes mild, moderate, severe, and profound retardation. A multidimensional definition of MR and diagnostic process is recommended by A.A.M.R. It includes: (a) diagnosing MR; (b) identifying the person's strengths, weaknesses, and needs for service; and (c) determining the type and degree of needed supports.

This chapter ended with a discussion of the importance of environmental and social factors in mental retardation. A particularly important set of factors, social role development, was introduced and will de developed in detail in the next two chapters.

KEY TERMS

Know these important terms. Check the chapter and the Glossary for their meanings. They are listed here in the approximate order of their appearance in the chapter.

Limited cognitive abilities	Normal curve	Mild mental retardation
Adaptive behavior (or skills)	Attention span	Cultural-familial retardation
Global intelligence	Stimulus overselectivity	Moderate mental retardation
Validity (of IQ tests)	Transfer of learning	Severe mental retardation
Reliability (of IQ tests)	Incidental learning	Profound mental retardation
Social agent	Concrete thinking	Interdependence
Hypothetical-deductive	Abstract thinking	Primary prevention
reasoning	Metacognition	Secondary prevention
Theory building	Zone of uncertainty	Tertiary prevention
Inductive inference	Social communication	Microenvironment
Deductive inference	Relative rates of cognitive	A-motivational syndrome
6-hour retardation	development	Symbiotic support groups

SUGGESTED READING

Detterman, D. K. (Ed.). (1994). *Current topics in human intelligence: Vol. 4. Theories of intelligence.* Norwood, NJ: Ablex.

Edgerton, R. B. (1967). *The cloak of competence: Stigma in the lives of the mentally retarded.* Berkeley: University of California Press.

Rowitz, L. (1991). Social and environmental factors and developmental handicaps in children. In J. L.

Watson & J. A. Mulick (Eds.), *Handbook of mental retardation* (2nd ed., pp. 158–165). New York: Pergamon Press.

Wolfensberger, W. (1992). *A brief introduction to social role valorization as a higher-order concept for structuring human services.* Syracuse, NY: Syracuse University Press.

STUDY QUESTIONS

9-1. Be sure that you understand the major concepts used in the diagnosis of mental retardation.

9-2. Reliability and validity are important characteristics of IQ tests. Explain these concepts and their importance.

9-3. Explain this statement: To some extent, MR is a school-based diagnosis.

9-4. A person with an IQ of 64 nevertheless has excellent social functioning. Is this person rightly diagnosed as MR? Discuss and explain.

9-5. What is the importance in MR of the concept "incidental larning"?

9-6. Will a child with significant intellectual deficit ever "catch up" to peers in intelligence? Discuss and explain.

9-7. What is the importance of multidimensional diagnosis in MR?

9-8. Explain, as if to a student, the concepts of "needed support" and "support intensities" and explain their application in practice.

I. Socialization

The Active Socialization Hypothesis

Developmental disabilities are complex conditions in which biological, psychological, and social factors interact in ways that are as yet only incompletely understood. As discussed in Chapter 3, risk factors operate in developmental disabilities (a) by interfering directly with normal development and function (the **interference hypothesis**), (b) by directly teaching impaired functioning (the **active socialization hypothesis**), or (3) by a combination of both. Most of our discussion of etiology has focused on biological factors operating through interference mechanisms and preventing normal development. However, we again remind the student that psychological and social factors are also critically involved in etiology.

This chapter examines the active socialization hypothesis in developmental disabilities; that is, *to what degree does society actively teach persons to function less than optimally?* As discussed earlier, social variables are critically important in the mix of risk factors for developmental disabilities. The most compelling cases are persons in the cultural-familial MR group. They show no discernible biological causality but function at significantly low intellectual and social levels. Causal factors include cognitive limitations, limited social and economic circumstances, poor motivation, and the lack of intellectual stimulation and guidance (Zigler & Balla, 1982). Even in cases where biological etiology is evident, social factors are presumed to intensify the already existing functional impairments.

The active socialization hypothesis goes further. It posits that in some significant ways social forces actively teach impaired and limited functioning to specific groups of persons, that persons with developmental disabilities are particularly at risk for these teaching effects, and without such active teaching, these persons could have learned to function at higher levels. It suggests that in some manner society is helping to create functional impairments (primary negative effects) and to exacerbate existing impairments (secondary negative effects).

Further, we hypothesize that the agents of society who carry out this active teaching are those who are closest to the individual—the parents, siblings, teachers, and acquaintances. We do not suggest deliberate intentions to harm or restrict anyone. Rather, we hypothesize that various social mechanisms have developed and become integral forces in culture and society, and those mechanisms operate to the detriment of individuals in a virtually automatic manner that is not easily recognized by the social agents. Without realizing it, these persons may be helping to create and maintain some of the deficits that impede the person with disabilities. No matter how much they may love, guide, support, teach, and encourage, they are also to some degree the unwitting agents in the active socialization process for functional disabilities.

What are those automatic social mechanisms through which the active socialization proceeds? That is the major question posed by this chapter. We try to identify these mechanisms and describe how they might function. It is suggested that they operate through the normal process of **social role development,** and we emphasize the importance of **social roles** in the creation and maintenance of developmental disabilities. We hypothesize that social role formation is an important normal part of socialization, that it has a powerful impact on human personality, and that the mechanisms operate automatically and "invisibly."

MR and Social Roles

Viewing mental retardation and other developmental disabilities in terms of social roles has been discussed since the 1960s. (e.g., Dexter, 1960, 1964; Edgerton, 1988; Mercer, 1970, 1973; Wolfensberger, 1983, 1984, 1992, and many others). However, the literature on social role theory has not been explored in a systematic manner specifically to guide theory, research, and application in mental retardation. Still to be identified are the specific social mechanisms by which social role development might contribute to the low functioning of persons with retardation. Our aim is to identify and describe those mechanisms. In essence, we wish to explore the question: Can social role theory inform us about mental retardation?

Defining the Population to Be Addressed

Social role development is important for everyone, including children with disabilities. The concepts apply particularly to persons with mild mental retardation (MMR) because of their generally high mobility, activity, and contact with other persons. They are subject to many of the same social forces that apply to others and have many opportunities for the operation of often subtle social role factors. (We assume that at lower intellectual levels of MR subtle social factors have less impact, while basic organic factors contribute relatively more to the functional limitations.) MMR is the largest single developmental disabilities group, accounting for some 75 percent of all MR. Thus, if the hypothesized social factors are significant in MMR development, then they must affect the majority of persons with MR. For these reasons, we will focus our discussion of social role development specifically on MMR, but with the understanding that the same mechanisms apply to all developmental disabilities with varying degrees of impact.

We propose a social role model for development of social competence of persons with MMR. This model posits a learned **mental retardation social role** (the MR role) into which persons labeled with "mental retardation" are socialized from an early age and forced into learning tracks that constitute lifelong careers in the MR role.

We hypothesize that the MR role is a **socially devalued role** that is characterized by imposed restrictions of learning opportunities and by repeated rehearsal and reinforcement of limited, submissive styles of behavior. We expect that through such socialization the adaptive behavior developed by the person will be congruent with society's views of the appropriate enactment of the MR role—that is, submissiveness toward others, a generally limited range of behavior, and general intellectual, social, and vocational incompetence.

We further hypothesize that the MR role is shaped and maintained by the expectations and behaviors of others and operates as a powerful, lifelong influence over persons with MMR, resulting in significant restriction of social and intellectual development. Much of the person's low achievement, social functioning, and submissive position relative to non-retarded persons, lack of tacit knowledge, low motivation, and poor self-concept are here seen as due, at least in part, to lifelong socialization into the MR role.

As discussed in Chapter 3, access to age-appropriate social resources is necessary for normal social development, and such access is available to most persons through the enactment of social roles. In this model, we hypothesize that for persons who are labeled MR, this **social role resource access** is systematically and continuously restricted, and these specific restrictive mechanisms are among the major factors that shape poor social and vocational competence. Thus, in this proposed model, **restricted role resource access** is identified as a major social mechanism in the development of the MR role. It follows, as will be discussed later, that expanding role resource access should be a major component in programs for persons with developmental disabilities, particularly for those with MMR.

A Double Handicap

In this model, persons with MR have a double handicap. First, their cognitive abilities are significantly below average, which slows their social and personal development. Second, they are channeled by society into a highly restrictive MR social role, thus further reducing their access to social resources, resulting in still further restrictions of development and skills. The overall result of this double handicap is significant lifelong restriction of **personal competence** and **adaptive intelligence** (see the Glossary for definitions).

In our proposed model, retardation is, to a significant degree, a reality constructed by society, and that reality operates powerfully and pervasively to limit the person's functioning. We propose that social mechanisms that define persons as MR and influence their functioning operate through a well-defined MR role with its primary effect of restricting access to normal social role resources. In the following sections, we define selected social role concepts and try to show how they operate in the socialization of the MR role. Box 10.1 provides a brief abstract of the assumptions and hypotheses that underlie the discussion.

II. Positions and Roles: Social Structure and Personal Function

Faced by a huge social role literature, our limited goal is to identify selected social role concepts and apply them to the socialization of persons with MR. There are many classic theoretical models of social roles, and we will draw on those of Biddle (1979), R. Brown (1965), and Stryker and Statham (1985). We begin with the distinction that **social position** is a structure created by society, and *social role* is the behavioral functioning of a person within that structure.

Social Positions

Social positions, created in large numbers by every society, are easily recognized categories of persons such as police officer, teacher, and parent. In Biddle's (1979, 1986) analysis, the two most important defining factors in social position are (a) the symbols or labels that identify the position (e.g., teacher, mother, police officer, mental patient) and (b) the characteristics that are thought to be shared by the position members. Those shared characteristics include the person's actual or imputed physical and psychological attributes, their characteristic behavior, and the behavior of others toward them (see Box 10.2).

BOX **10.1**

The Active Socialization Hypothesis in Developmental Disabilities: Summary of the Major Assumptions and Hypotheses

Major Assumptions

1. MR and other developmental disabilities are multiply determined.
2. Biological factors constitute one set of etiological variables and have their major effects on organ development, structure, and functioning, as well as on the person's overall functioning.
3. Social factors constitute another set of etiological factors and have their major effects on functional aspects (cognition, values, attitudes, self-perceptions, motivation, behavior, etc.).
4. Social role development is a critical part of normal human socialization.

Major Hypotheses

1. Society actively teaches impaired functioning to some persons and/or exacerbates already existing functional impairments.
2. This active teaching (socialization) occurs in both indirect and direct fashion.
3. The primary social agents for this active teaching are those persons who are closest to the individual (i.e., family, friends, teachers, employers, etc).
4. The social agents
   a. operate without harmful intent or design
   b. are not aware of the negative effects of some of their actions
5. The major social mechanisms through which social agents operate are those involved in the formation and operation of social roles.
6. The social agents' primary contact with and route of influence over the labeled person is through their complementary social role enactments.
7. Among those social roles
   a. there exists a mental retardation social role (MR social role)
   b. into which persons who are labeled "mentally retarded" are socialized from an early age and throughout their lives
8. The MR social role:
   a. is shaped and maintained by the expectations and behaviors of significant other persons (the social agents)
   b. has a powerful lifelong influence over persons with MR
   c. results in significant restriction of social and intellectual development
   d. is a markedly devalued role in society
9. One of the major social mechanisms in MR role development is restricted role resource access.
10. Much of the person's general low functioning, characteristic "retarded" behavior, submissive position relative to others, low motivation, poor self-concept, and relative lack of tacit knowledge and personal competence is due in part to socialization into the MR social role.
11. Once MR socialization has developed, it is difficult to exit the role or modify it significantly.

Implications for Service/Support Programs

1. Support programs need to focus on expanding role resource access.

(continued)

B O X **10.1**   **Continued**

2. Current programs actively and/or tacitly teach persons with MR to accept the reality of their impairments and disabilities, and it makes good psychological sense to do so. However, by doing that, the social agents are reinforcing the MR social role. The problem is that many of the MR role norms are self-defeating or limiting. This model suggests that training should distinguish the norms that have positive value from those with negative impact and differentially reinforce the positive norms.

Social Roles

Roles are organized groups of behaviors, beliefs, attitudes, and expectations that are engaged in (enacted) by persons. *A role is an enactment by a person of a position, and it is guided largely by what is expected by others concerning the role, as well as what is expected by the person in that role.* The role is a dynamic, socially interactive phenomenon. It is built on preexisting social structures, some of the most important of which are positions, norms, expectancies, status, and role resource access, as discussed in the sections that follow.

A social position is a structural social unit created by society. It also defines expected behaviors for that position. If no one "inhabits" the position, it remains an empty abstraction. When a person assumes (inhabits) a particular position, then individual personality and skills are brought to bear, and the result is a dynamic interaction of the person and the social position (i.e., a social role is created). In essence, a social position is a creation of society, an abstract category of persons and behaviors; a social role is a creation of a person,

---

B O X **10.2**

Some Bases for Defining Social Positions

Social positions are defined in terms of:

Occupation (using a general sense of that term): Examples are parent, mother, father, teacher, doctor, member of the clergy.

A Person's Attributes such as age, sex, and ethnicity: Examples are child, senior citizen, boy, girl, Hispanic.

The Characteristic Behavior of Persons: Examples are homosexual, heterosexual, "leader," etc.

The Behavior of Others toward a Person: Examples include the ways people behave toward positions of disability such as chronic illness and mental retardation. The example used by Thomas and Biddle (1966) of such a position is that of "scapegoat." Note that this is particularly important for our discussion (i.e., MR is a deviant social position that is largely defined not only by the behavior and characteristics of the person but also by the behavior of others toward that person).

a person's dynamic, behavioral enactment of a position. By enacting the role, a person puts "life" into the position.

III. Dimensions of Social Positions

Social positions have defining characteristics or dimensions, as discussed in this section.

Positional Norms, Expectancies, and Demands

Social positions do more than identify a category of persons; they also provide the rules of behavior (social norms) for the person in any given position. **Social norms** specify the *behavior* that is appropriate for a given position, the *person* who occupies the position, and the *setting* in which the behavior is to occur. For example, a teacher (the person) will instruct (the behavior) pupils in the classroom (the setting). Every social position has its predefined norms that specify appropriate behavior. For example, norms for the position of police officer include aiding and protecting citizens in distress; for elementary school teachers, norms include understanding children and enhancing their intellectual growth. For the position of parent, norms include physical and emotional care of children and responsibility for the children's well-being.

Many norms are **explicit norms**—that is, organized, spoken, and/or written such as certification for teacher, physician, and so on. Others are **implicit norms**—not written or codified but expected by others—and they are just as real and influential as explicit norms (R. Brown, 1965). However, they are often subtle, such as many of our norms for appropriate social behavior, and their subtle nature makes it difficult for persons with MR to recognize them and behave appropriately.

For common social positions, the implicit and explicit norms are well known by most persons. The norms specify behaviors that help define the position, and those behaviors are expected by society of the persons who occupy the position. Expectancies, or expectancy norms, include commonly accepted ideas about a given social position, the appropriate behavior for that position, and privately held beliefs, attitudes, and prejudices (E. J. Thomas & Biddle, 1966). Society has, for example, clear expectancies of how a grammar school teacher should and should not behave.

Expectancies must be communicated by society to the person in a position if they are to affect that person's behavior. Once communicated, social expectancies exert force on the person. That is, through the act of communication, largely subjective **expectancies** held by others are transformed to overt **demands** placed on a person in a given position to behave in certain ways. Norm communication occurs through a variety of social mechanisms. Norms can be communicated verbally and become demands through direct messages (e.g., "boys don't cry like that," "girls are not good in math and science"). Norms are also communicated through the person's active attempts to discern the unspoken intentions and expectancies of other people. These mental processes constitute attempts to develop a "theory of mind"—that is, understanding the mental life of other persons. (Theory of mind concepts will be discussed in Chapter 10 when we consider autism.) Norms are also communicated through direct modeling and imitation (i.e., observations of and interactions with real persons) and symbolic modeling and imitation (i.e., observations of people and situations in television, movies, magazines, etc.). Rewards and punishments of the role enactor's behavior ("you are being punished for talking back to your mother!") also help to communicate and reinforce norms. Expectancy norms are communicated to children in increasing variety as the children grow and have wider ranges of real and symbolic social experiences.

According to Biddle (1986), expectancies/demands are the major factors in the generation of social roles. Role theorists assume that although people are not aware of all factors that enter into the structure of social positions, most have learned considerable social awareness and are very knowing about a large range of expectancies for a large number of social positions. That is, people are believed to be thoughtful, socially aware human actors.

A role comes into existence when a person enacts the norms of a given social position. To use a theater metaphor, a position is like the script—it is the structure that preexists the actor. When the person brings that script to life by applying his or her own personality and skills to that enactment, then a role has been created. Thus, norms, taken together in a coherent grouping, define a position. A position that is enacted by a person becomes a role. A role is a behavioral phenomenon, a dynamic interaction of the person and the social position.

Position Entry, Maintenance, and Exit

How do persons enter social positions? Linton (1936) introduced a distinction between ascribed and achieved positions. Ascribed positions are entered through conditions not under our control or not due to our own efforts. For example, we are born into ascribed positions of gender, ethnicity, and socioeconomic status; we mature into age-graded ascribed positions of infancy, childhood, adolescence, adulthood, and old age. In contrast, achieved positions are entered largely through our own efforts. We study and pass examinations to become engineers or botanists; we campaign for public office; we seek compatible partners for marriage.

Each social position includes norms for **position entry, maintenance,** and **exit** (E. J. Thomas & Biddle, 1966). For example, to enter the position of teacher, a person must have a college degree and meet state certification criteria. To maintain the position, the teacher must responsibly prepare for and meet classes, develop courses, monitor student progress, and so on. Some behaviors are normatively proscribed. For example, the teacher must not be late for class, wear inappropriate clothing, tell smutty stories to children, or treat parents rudely, and so on. To exit the position, the teacher must meet criteria for promotion, retirement, dismissal. or resignation.

Position Status and Set

Each person assumes and maintains many positions throughout life, and multiple positions are held simultaneously. For example, an adult may hold simultaneous positions such as parent, spouse, son, uncle, student, teacher, and so on. Each position is implicitly ranked by society. The sanctions (i.e., rewards such as prestige, wealth, and authority and punishments such as incarceration, probation, etc.) applied to each position are indications of the value that society places on the position. In our society, positions such as chairperson of the local bank, university president, U.S. senator, and professional football player are accorded high positive status and extremely high rewards. Positions such as professor, teacher, town council member, nurse, parent, and pastor are accorded modest but still positive status, while immigrants and farm laborers are accorded far less. Near the bottom of the social status ratings are deviant positions such as mental retardation and mental illness and, lower still, criminals. There is an unfortunate elitist alignment here, but that is social reality.

When a person assumes a position, he or she also assumes the status of that position. Position status is important on a personal level because it helps determine how others will behave toward a person, particularly with regard to respectful behavior. Consider, for example, the difference in one's respectful behavior when meeting a U.S. senator compared with meeting the office cleaning person.

The multiple positions maintained by a person make up that person's **positional set.** A person's total social status is defined by his or her particular positional set.

Deviance Positions

Deviance will be discussed in more detail later. Here we point out that positions of deviance, such as mental retardation and mental illness, do not fit neatly into the ascribed/achieved distinction, but norms do exist for entry into deviance positions. The person is considered "deviant" when society recognizes he or she has exhibited behaviors that define the deviant position and then imposes a process of public labeling. Note that norms for deviant positions (e.g., psychotic functioning, subaverage intelligence, law breaking, etc.) are negatively valued. A person enters a deviant position not through ascribed or achievement processes, but through social recognition of their actual or imputed negatively valued behavior and social labeling processes (Becker, 1963; Lemert, 1967; Scheff, 1966).

IV. Dimensions of Social Roles

Imposition and Improvisation

A position can exist independently of any individual, but a role has no existence unless enacted by a person—it is a dynamic and individualized creation by a living person. In the terminology used by Powers (1980), role enactments are characterized by the norms imposed by the position (imposition) and by the behaviors created or improvised by the person (improvisation). Improvisation is the creative "ad-libbing" that occurs in social situations, whereas imposition suggests that a good deal of social behavior is predetermined by culture and society. Social behavior is the result of many forces that operate simultaneously and often in opposition such as the tendencies toward imposition and improvisation. In normal social development, people learn the skills to balance those opposing tendencies in role enactments (Stryker & Statham, 1985). As we will see, those learned skills and the ratio of improvisation and imposition in a person's role enactments are important elements in defining the MR role.

Role Complementarity

By their very nature, roles exist in a social matrix, a *web of interaction,* and they function with reference to other roles. Parent and child are **complementary roles** that operate together and serve to complete or complement each other. The role of parent is meaningful only in relationship to the role of child. The norms of the parenting role carry the expectations and specify the behaviors for the parent toward the child and have no meaning unless the child role exists. Every role implies at least one other role with which it functions in some complementary relationship. Aunt-nephew, pastor-parishioner, and friend-friend are complementary roles.

Complementary roles are in a special relationship to each other, serving important reciprocal functions in role definition, shaping, and maintenance. A college student, for example, is aware of the major norms for that position. Others, too, are aware of those norms, and they communicate expectancies for appropriate role enactments by the student. Those expectations are held by society in general but, most important, by the student's complementary role enactors (e.g., professors, administrators, other students, and parents). They have considerable social power in evaluating the student's performance and applying sanctions such as rewards and punishments for the student's role enactments.

Complementary roles together form a social unit, and they carry mutual expectancies and sanctions for the enactments of those particular roles. The influence of complementary roles on learned role behavior is of major importance. As will be discussed later, the nature of the complementary role enactments toward persons in MR roles is critical.

Role Multiplicity and Role Set Status

The web of social interaction for each person grows more complex as one matures and enacts a greater number and complexity of roles. Each person normally develops several roles (**role multiplicity**), many of which are age related and are altered or discarded as we mature. In a normal day, we cycle through several roles such as spouse, parent, employee, friend, or parishioner. These constitute our personal role set. The concept of status, discussed earlier with regard to social position, also applies to roles, and each person has an overall **role set status.** If all of a person's roles are enactments of low-status positions, the overall role set status will be low. A role set that includes sequential and often simultaneous enactments of high-status positions is a high-status role set. It seems reasonable to expect that a person's sense of satisfaction, accomplishment, and general self-worth may be strongly affected by his or her overall role set status.

Multiple roles can lead to complexities, conflicts, and strains but may also have positive effects. Each role enactment includes interactions—direct or symbolic—with persons in complementary roles. These include expectancies and demands, evaluation, rewards and punishments, and access to social resources. Thus, persons with multiple role repertoires (large role sets) will experience a great variety of social interaction, more social stimulation and rewards, more complementary role interactions, and greater access to social resources (Sieber, 1974). Their lives will presumably be richer, with greater personal satisfaction and more skills in meeting life's demands (Orden & Bradburn, 1969; Spreitzer, Snyder, & Larson, 1979). They might even be physically healthier and have greater perceived well-being (Menaghan, 1989; Verbrugge, 1983) than persons with restricted role repertoires.

Aging in America is a case in point. The aged have been stripped of virtually all their previous roles (Blau, 1973), and old age has become a *role vacuum* (Cavan, 1962). *One's quality of life may partly be a function of multiple role repertoires and role set status.*

Role Complexity

Social roles are enactments of learned behaviors, and roles can vary in their complexity. One dimension of complexity is the number of *role sectors* included in a role. For example, the role of father may include several sectors. The father might behave in a consistent manner with his young daughter but behave in a consistently different manner toward his older son. That is, the details of enactments vary with the identity of the complementary role enactor at any particular time. These variations within the same role are *role sectors*. Roles with more sectors are more varied and complex than are those with fewer sectors.

Two other dimensions of role complexity are the breadth and difficulty of role enactments. Roles that encompass a greater variety of norms, sectors, and characteristic behaviors are of greater breadth than roles limited to only a few. The difficulty of a role enactment involves the amount of skill and energy needed to perform the role. For example, the role of a surgeon is difficult, while those of a store clerk or mail carrier are less difficult (Biddle, 1979). Roles of greater complexity are generally accorded the highest social status and rewards. As we will discuss later, the MR role is significantly less complex than most other roles, and this may be one of the factors in that role's low status and few rewards.

Role Variation

A person enacts each social role many times, and the enactments vary because of differences in specific settings and the degree of imposition and improvisation during a social interaction. But if role enactments are largely determined by the preexisting structural factors in social positions, how do people ad-lib and create role variations? We have no research data on which to base an explanation but will suggest the hypothesis that the new elements in role enactments may be a function of the person's response to his or her own response-produced cues. A person's own behavior becomes part of the total stimulus setting, and the person observes, perceives, and responds to his or her own behavior. That is, the behavior we produce serves as cues for our subsequent behavior. In doing so, the person may be adding some improvisation to the role enactments. Thus, improvisation may be at least partly a function of an individual's idiosyncratic self-perceptions and responses to his or her own behavior. This would require a fair degree of social perceptiveness, self-awareness, and ability to view, monitor, and evaluate one's own behavior, goals, and motives. Most of us have developed the skills to alter our behavior and, thus, improvise. It follows that persons who are limited cognitively, in social and self-perception and self-evaluation (e.g., a person with MR), would be less capable of such improvisation, more dependent on impositional factors, and show less role variation.

Role Violation, Role Conflict, and Role Strain

If a person violates some norms by failing to carry out what is prescribed and/or by committing acts that are proscribed, the violations will usually be recognized by the role enactor and by persons in complementary roles. One of the functions of complementary roles is to evaluate others' role enactments and to provide appropriate feedback in the form of rewards, punishments, and guidance. These functions are most obvious in complementary roles such as parent-child, teacher-student, and employer-employee, but they are important components in any complementary role interaction.

When norm violations are minor (e.g., the teacher who wears tennis shoes to classes), the violation will be tolerated and may even add some "color" to the teacher's reputation. However, if the norm violation is major, such as a teacher arriving to class inebriated, the violation will not be tolerated, and the person may be removed from that position.

Role conflicts may occur when the norms within a role or those of complementary roles are in opposition to each other. Conflict may also occur when the demands of a role are unacceptable to the person in that position or when the role/position demands are so difficult or beyond the person's abilities as to be stressful for the person. Norm violations and role conflicts constitute pressures on the person and can cause a good deal of stress. This condition of personal stress is called **role strain.**

Role Resource Access

We now introduce the major concept of **role resource access** and emphasize that it is of particular importance in mental retardation. Each social position includes a number of potentially important social resources, and the role enactor in that position can have legitimate control over those resources. For example, a parent has control over resources that are needed by children such as protection, guidance, nurturing, and so on. In a work situation, position-related resources might include tools, personnel, workspace, and control over bonuses and pay raises. By virtue of entering a position, a person is accorded control over positional resources, and additional resource control can be achieved depending on the success of the person's role enactment. Thus, two people may have the same social position, but in their respective role enactments, one might have developed much more resource control than the other.

Of greatest importance for our discussion is *the sharing of positional resources with persons in complementary roles.* That is, a person's access to and control of positional resources allows some portion of those resources to become available to others through complementary role interactions. There is a sharing, an exchange of social resources. There may be more resources accruing to one than to the other, such as in a mentor-student interaction, because their relative control of resources may be disproportionate. In other relationships, such as friendship, the sharing may be more equal. But in any case, a person can increase access to social resources through complementary role enactments. An example is the graduate student who, by virtue of joining Professor Levine's lab, is provided with funding, lab equipment, training, ideas, interactions with other students, computer access, and so on. The social resources controlled by Professor Levine have become available to this student by virtue of the student's having entered a complementary position and role (e.g., mentor-student).

Each enacted role brings the person into contact with more complementary roles and therefore with more potential social resources. The greatest resource access is open to those persons with large role repertoires. This mechanism provides the person with resources for meeting needs, creating new experiences, learning new skills, developing more and more complex roles, and generally, furthering one's life quality. Conversely, if a person's roles are greatly restricted in number, complexity, variation, improvisation, and to complementary roles of low status, then that person's range and mix of complementary role interactions will likewise be restricted, resulting in limited social role resource access. This person will be at a distinct social disadvantage. We will argue that this is what happens to the person labeled "mental retarded" in our society.

The Personal/Organizational Value of Social Roles

Positions and roles serve important social purposes by providing organization and guidance for behavior. Much of our culture is transmitted to subsequent generations through the structures of social positions. We need not reinvent all of our behavior anew in each generation because much of it is already prescribed and passed on to us through preexisting social positions. Positions existing as coherent social units provide each of us with a great deal of information and useful guides for organizing, emitting, and evaluating our behavior.

The social value of positions and roles is not limited to individuals. Large-scale social change can be achieved through altering the norms in social positions, with no need to deal with the role enactments of every single individual. For example the role of father has undergone some significant changes by the addition of new parenting norms that were formerly prescribed primarily or exclusively for mothers. The general communication of new behavioral norms for the father role will presumably result in new role enactments by many individual fathers. In this regard, the behavior of high-status role models becomes very important for communicating the new norms (i.e., translating the role expectancies into role demands). Modeling changes in role enactments (e.g., showing well-known macho men tenderly, competently, and without embarrassment caring for their babies) may have significant impact on the role enactments of other individuals. The media, television in particular, may have such general effects. Think of examples of the impact on social norms of the symbolic modeling by television.

V. Social Role Development and Personal Identity

Social Role Development

We assume that role enactments are central to everyone's social existence. Role enactments depend on learned skills, involve considerable flexibility and creativity in behavior and in responsibility not only for one's own role enactments but also for monitoring, evaluating, and guiding those of others. Developing these social skills requires a long, complex socialization process that begins very early in life, includes learning norms, positions, and roles, and involves active participation by many persons.

Children live in a social environment, and their socialization begins from birth, growing through countless day-by-day parent–child interactions (as discussed in Chapter 3). A neonate's orienting toward a parent's voice is evident at 1 or 2 days, social referencing (the ability to respond to social cues) emerges before 1 year, and attachment with a caregiver will be well-developed by 18 months to 2 years. Language development and social communication progress rapidly. During the play years, children try out their versions of grown-up roles. They play at being teachers, doctors, parents, fashion models, soldiers, jet pilots, animals, athletes, criminals, monsters, and even at being children. As they grow, children are directed toward greater social interaction. They sharpen their perceptions of self and of others, develop emotional expression and self-regulation, and practice an ever-widening set of interactive social skills.

The child "plays with," experiences, and develops many role enactments, such as age-related roles of child and relational roles of brother or sister. Each role has its attendant complementary roles (e.g., child-parent, sibling-sibling), and the complementary role enactors communicate norms and help guide the child's role development through evaluating, rewarding, punishing behavior, and so on. Early role development, such as learning gender roles (social expectancies for appropriate boy and girl behavior), may serve as the prototypes for later role learning and perhaps provide good training for "learning how to learn" social roles. The sheer number of arranged and fortuitous learning situations, the innumerable repetitions of learning trials and exposure to models, and the reinforcements of appropriate gender behavior over so many years shape the child's gender role enactments. In addition to such specific teaching, children learn about roles, positions, and norms in more indirect ways through observation and imitation of the behavior of important live and symbolic portrayals.

By the time most children enter school, they have already experienced a great deal of socialization. They have become familiar with an astonishing array of social positions, the expectancy norms that define those positions, and appropriate enactment behavior. They have also developed skills in how to learn new roles (i.e., a **social role metacognition**).

In the schoolyears, self-understanding, self-regulation, and social cognition continue to grow. Dependence on peer groups develops, and the groups' norms and expectations become increasingly important, particularly by adolescence, when the youth's positional set has grown quite large. The adolescent enacts multiple roles, including those of gender, filial relationships (son, daughter, brother, sister), student, socioeconomic class, friendship, intimacy, and so on. For each role enactment, a variety of complementary roles is encountered, accompanied by access to the social resources associated with those complementary roles. Often in adolescence, conflicts occur between the norms of older familiar positions (e.g., parents, family, religion) and other newer and presumably more salient positions such as the adolescent's friends and all of their complementary roles and resources. The exact composition of the youth's positional set, how well he or she enacts the various roles, and which complementary roles become dominant in the set will vary from one person to another. Also, positional set status will have already been clearly identified in adolescence based on the perceived social value of each of the youth's enacted roles. The fact is that by adolescence the social reality of a person has already been developed to a high degree of complexity, and in adolescent society, there is a sharp awareness of roles, role evaluation, and role set status.

Role Interactions, Status, and Personal Identity

Much of the energy and concern of adolescence is aimed at developing and clarifying one's **personal identity** and **self-esteem,** which in part are derived from one's positional set and success in role enactments. "Who am I?" "How successful am I?" "How popular am I?" (a measure of role-set status). "Where am I going in life?" These are complex adolescent issues that involve the youth's social positions, role enactments, role set status, and complementary role enactments, particularly by one's peers. We cannot emphasize enough the importance of the quality of role development in creating one's personal identity and sense of worth or self-esteem.

By young adulthood, people are accomplished role enactors. Most have developed multiple role sets and can maneuver with skill and flexibility among their various roles, although often with a good deal of adolescent role conflict and strain. The role set of an older adolescent might include roles of son or daughter, brother or sister, student, employee, friend, or club member. For too many adolescents, the roles of parents, wife, or husband—roles they are poorly equipped to enact very well—may also be included. As people progress in life, they assume new positions, exit former positions, and modify their role enactments.

One's identity alters throughout life as new roles are developed and previous roles are modified or discarded. Dynamic interactions of the person and the social structure continue, and role activity remains a central part of social reality and self-identity for each person. However, as we grow into advanced age, the number and complexity of our positions and roles decline, and as noted earlier, old age can unfortunately devolve to a *social role vacuum,* with all of the attendant loss of position, status, and self-esteem.

VI. Can Social Role Theory Inform Us about Mental Retardation?

We have discussed basic social role concepts and the role mechanisms that operate in all normal development. Now we apply these ideas to the concept of mental retardation to see if they can enlighten our understanding of this condition (i.e., can social role theory inform us about mental retardation?).

Mental Retardation as a Deviant (and Devalued) Social Position

Because we hypothesize the existence of the MR role, we must also hypothesize a supporting **MR social position.** Recall that a social position is: (a) a category of persons who are identified (b) by labels or symbols and (c) by real or imputed characteristics of the position holders. Clearly, mental retardation meets the definitional requirements for a social position. First, it is a category of persons. The term *mental retardation* refers to more than 7 million persons in the United States and many more around the world. The term has a clearly understood referent, an identifiable category of persons.

Second, its labels and symbols identify the persons in the category. The labels "mentally retarded" and "mental retardation" clearly convey an identity of the person labeled. If we know nothing else about a person except that she or he is mentally retarded, we will recognize an identity. Our thinking about, evaluations, status assessments, and behavior toward that person will conform to our expectations about that particular social position.

Not only has this person been labeled and an identity specified, but the label carries with it powerful expectancies. When those expectations are negative and/or derisive, they may overwhelm any conflicting facts about that person and may have significant interfering effects on his or her development (Garber, 1988). Positional labels such as mental retardation can, as suggested by Garber (1988), communicate low expectations for these children and result in a child's exposure to repeated negative experiences that impede their social and academic development.

Third, a position is partly defined by selected human characteristics, and those are automatically imputed to the position members. Among the definitional requirements of this position are that persons be of significantly subaverage intelligence from an early age and have significant personal, social, or other deficits. When imputed to a person, they are made with the weight of evidence such as tested IQ, social skill evaluations, and professional observations and judgments. However, diagnostic errors are sometimes made. For example, Mercer (1973) long ago documented the erroneous labeling of low-income children as mentally retarded. However important this may be, faulty diagnoses are not the issue of discussion at the moment. The issue is the nature of the imputed characteristics of persons labeled mentally retarded.

When most people think of mental retardation, they are not apt to think in terms of significant subaverage intelligence. Rather, their descriptions would more likely be slow, dull, childlike, dependent, happy, naive, foolish, loud, unskilled, irresponsible, unkempt, limited, and so on. They might describe persons with mental retardation as being in need of care and supervision and as persons who cannot make important life decisions, assume responsibility, or live independent lives. Such descriptions, even when inaccurate, may become accepted by the person as his or her true characteristics.

Thus, mental retardation meets the definitional requirements of a common social position. It is (a) a category of persons and is defined by (b) its labels and symbols and (c) the characteristics, real or imputed, of the position members. Mental retardation has a social construction and, like any social position, is a foundation for role and complementary role enactments. This social position is definable and readily perceived. It is an available, common social category into which we traditionally place persons who bear the requisite characteristics.

Mental retardation is also a social position of deviance (i.e., a departure from norms). Deviance involves rule breaking and nonconforming behavior that carries a negative social evaluation which includes the idea that there is something wrong, objectionable, unacceptable, or undesirable about the person and/or behavior. Deviance is held in low status and is in one manner or another punished by society.

Deviance, however, is still more. For a person to acquire the identity of a deviant, the nonconforming behavior must be attributed not to happenstance or to the unavoidable press of external forces but to the essential character of the person. A person who lives a career of deviance, it is thought, is one whose very character leads him or her to pursue that nonconforming, negatively valued low status and often punished behavior. Any of us might commit some deviant act that is unintentional, fleeting, or forced on us by external events. But to have a **deviant identity** (Biddle, 1979) is a more substantial and often willful involvement in deviant functioning.

Deviant positions include criminality, mental disease, alcoholism, chronic illness (Biddle, 1979), and mental retardation. The person occupies a position of deviance and is readily identified by others as deviant. Personal characteristics that purportedly explain the deviance are attributed to the labeled persons in the same way that any positional characteristics are attributed to position holders.

Mental retardation is viewed by society as a deviant social position—the person is significantly different from normative standards in intelligence and social ability, and those differences are negatively valued by society. The label itself, despite continuing efforts by many in the field, remains a pejorative one, and the reasons for the inclusion of the person in that position are generally viewed as being ingrained within the very character of the person. Although overt punishment is no longer part of society's usual response to mental retardation, as it is for criminality, it has been argued (Garber, 1988) that the label may set up a pattern of discriminatory behavior on the part of others, putting that person in social and personal jeopardy. In essence, subtle social punishment does occur.

Position Entry for Mental Retardation

How does a person enter the social position of mental retardation? Role theorists assume that people are actively involved in creating and enacting their roles (Biddle, 1979). However, virtually all members of the MR social position entered the position when they were too young and/or unskilled to have been aware of that entry or to have had any directive influence over it. Of course, that is also true for many other positions, such as childhood, but there is a significant difference because we eventually exit such age-based positions by growing up. The child in the MR social position, however, will most likely never exit that position or have the normal opportunities to enter other nondeviant positions.

The process of entry into a deviant social position involves several events. First, the person is observed to display the characteristics (in this case, developmental delays) that help define the position. Later, a formal hearing is held, such as a hearing before the school's committee on education for the handicapped. The evidence is examined, and IQ testing, educational achievement, teachers' observations, and psychologists' reports are all considered. The parents and sometimes other parties, such as an attorney, may be present. As a result of the hearing, the child may be formally labeled "with mental retardation," "learning disability," and so forth, and recommendations are made for appropriate placement such as inclusion in regular classes with remedial students, resource-room assignments, special class placement, or removal from school and placement in a specialized institution. Because of the serious effects on the child and family, these decisions are not made casually. But however carefully the decision is made, the result is that a public label of deviance, with all of its negative connotations, devaluation, and imputed characteristics, has been placed on that child, and this process is clear testimony to the social dimension of mental retardation.

A series of public actions results in labeling the child as a person with mental retardation. The child is officially identified as a member of the social position of mental retardation, becomes regarded as a member of a deviant class who possesses the requisite MR characteristics, and will be treated accordingly, with the attendant status recognition and special program supports. We are not criticizing the need for the process or the positive intent of the labelers, but are trying to describe and understand the process and its effects.

MR Position Maintenance and Exit

Maintaining a social position depends primarily on the person's success in meeting the positional criteria for maintenance (i.e., enacting the role so as to meet the positional norms). Frequent or serious norm violations, either through errors of commission or omission, can result in the loss of that position. Thus, in positional maintenance, there is an important element of the person's awareness of the norm expectations, effort, and self-determination.

It does not seem reasonable to expect that a person in a deviant position will work hard to maintain that low-status position. Rather it seems reasonable to assume the person would desire to exit the position. Exceptions may include persons in deviant subcultures such as delinquent youth gangs whose needs are well met by that membership. For deviance such as chronic illness, physical handicaps, retardation, and other disabilities, it seems reasonable to assume (and this is only an assumption) that most persons would desire to exit rather than maintain that position.

What accounts for the maintenance of the MR position? Children are assigned to the MR position by the judgments and actions of others. They will remain in that position as long as they continue to be viewed by complementary role enactors as meeting the positional criteria. Unless there is a significant effort by the labelers to remove the MR diagnosis, the labeled children can exit the position only by challenging and overturning the norms (i.e., stop behaving in ways that validate the diagnosis and begin behaving in "nonretarded" ways).

But how is a person with mental retardation to accomplish that? It would require one's understanding of the constructs "position" and "role" and well-developed social, intellectual, and emotional skills to manipulate sophisticated social factors (e.g., managing impressions made upon complementary role enactors). In other words, the person would have to excel in the very cognitive and social skills in which they have already been found deficient!

With other social positions, effort is required to meet the norms to maintain the position membership. But with deviant positions, the norms are set negatively (lack of intelligence, lack of social skill, lack of good judgment, lack of self-control, etc.). Little effort is required to display a lack of those characteristics. Maintaining the MR position is thus relatively easy, requiring a tacit acceptance of the position expectations and refraining from challenging the norms. Behavioral inertia is on the side of position maintenance.

The MR position has evolved so as to maximize the probabilities of its maintenance and minimize the probabilities of exit. Thus, membership in the MR position is permanent, with its lifelong label and expectations. This is not only because in most instances the person possesses the defining normative characteristics of intellectual and social deficits but also because the construction and operation of the social position with its negative definitions helps to deepen and maintain those characteristics. The MR social position is a social construction that actively maintains and deepens MR functioning. Once labeled, the person is trapped in that position, and only by extraordinary and unlikely efforts can the person exit from that position and escape the negative expectations of others.

Positional Status and Personal Identity in Mental Retardation

As discussed earlier, positional status helps to determine how others will behave toward a person, particularly in terms of respectful behavior. Complementary role enactors behave in a generally respectful manner toward persons of high status, communicating their recognition of the other person's high status and positive characteristics attributed to them. It seems reasonable to infer that steady experiences of such respectful treatment will positively affect the person's self-evaluation. Conversely, steady experiences of being perceived as of low status would presumably contribute to a more negative self-evaluation and identity.

The general proposition that a person's identity and self-evaluation derive largely from the behavior of others toward that person is a central notion for many role and personality theorists (e.g., Blumer, 1980; Kuhn, 1964; Mead, 1934; R. H. Turner, 1956, 1978) and others as reviewed by Stryker and Statham (1985). In our long socialization, we observe others, we imitate their role enactments (i.e., role taking), and we evaluate and categorize those persons and their behavior. We not only observe and learn about other people but we also learn about ourselves by observing how others perceive us and behave toward us during complementary role interactions; that is, we learn how others see us. Through those complementary interactions, other people communicate their expectations and evaluations of us. In Mead's theoretical model, for example, the "self" is largely shaped by the responses of others toward us. As we evaluate and categorize other people, so, too, do we categorize and evaluate ourselves in comparison. The self in these models is one's own personal description, a set of ideas about oneself in relation to others.

The MR social position is not associated with wealth, prestige, or power; it does not cause others to behave respectfully; it does not command high positive social rewards. It is a negatively defined social position of deviance and low status.

The MR position member is nearly always placed in invidious comparisons with persons who occupy higher-status positions. Wherever persons with MR may go—in a bus, to a movie, to school or work, or just for a walk down the street—they are perceived to be of lower status than nearly everyone else. Note that this is a condition of *unrelieved* low status. Most persons, by virtue of their multiple roles, have varied status experiences. The relatively low status in one setting (e.g., work) may be much higher in another (e.g., at home, in social clubs, etc.). But not so for the person in the MR position who experiences a generalized, unrelieved, low-status positional set. That status does not improve with age because the MR position is readily maintained, exiting is difficult, and it is a lifelong position.

Membership in low-status positions, such as some ethnic minorities, may be sources of personal stress and related to maladjustment (Biddle, 1979; Lindzey & Byrne, 1968). We can infer that membership in the MR position, with its generalized, unrelieved, and permanent nature, may also be a source of stress and psychological maladjustment. Reflected to this person in many social contacts are perceptions of low status, of intellectual and social incompetence, and other negative inferences and attributions about their personal characteristics. All are expectancies commonly held in our society for the MR position, and all are communicated to the person through myriad complementary role enactments. It seems inevitable that the person's own identity and self-evaluation will develop a negative, self-demeaning aspect.

MR Status Validation

MR status validation is an important factor. As has been described, demands are made on the person in the MR position to behave as expected. When the person does so, others view that as validation of their original assessment of the person's position and status. This is a reciprocally reinforcing pattern; the person is reinforced for behaving appropriately in meeting the MR norms, and the complementary role enactors are reinforced for the correctness of their original evaluations, expectations, and demands.

> *Internal Summary 9.3.*   Mental retardation is a commonly recognized, low-status social position of deviance. The child who is labeled MR faces a lifetime of unrelieved low status, reinforcement for maintaining the MR norms, and repeated MR position and role validation. These processes occur through interactions with complementary role enactors. It is hypothesized that the negative impact includes diminished functioning, psychological stress and disorder, and the development of a negative self-evaluation.

VII. MR Social Role Enactments

Now let us consider MR role enactments of persons in the MR position. By placing the MR label on a child, society assigns that child to membership in the MR social position. The child's complementary role enactors recognize that membership. They then, through their expectancies and demands and their use of rewards and punishments, modeling, direct guidance, and teaching, consistently monitor and shape the behavior of the labeled child to conform to the norms of the MR position and role. This is done with benign intentions, is to a large extent necessary, and has many positive and enhancing effects on the growing child. However, there is an unintended negative side to it—the MR position is a socially devalued position of deviance, and the MR role is an enactment of appropriate norms that define that deviance. By so actively directing and supporting the child's repeated rehearsals and mastery of the norms defining the deviant position, social agents help *already existing deficits* become deepened and hardened into ever-more consistent and inflexible MR functioning; that is, they help to shape the person's deviance. These processes and social mechanisms constitute lifelong training for the child, youth, and adult and an active socialization into the MR role.

Complementary Roles for MR

Once labeled a member of the MR social position, the child begins to experience the active socialization process of MR role development. The most significant complementary role enactors are the child's parents or other primary caregivers and, later, siblings, teachers, and peers. These social agents pass along the culture and communicate to the child the social norms that define the MR position. They guide, teach, and reinforce the child's continuing rehearsal of the appropriate normative behavior for the MR role. They reflect to the child their views of his or her current and future abilities and limitations. They communicate their expectancies, which become normative demands, about how the child should function. What they allow and help the child to explore and achieve, what developments they encourage or discourage, what values they communicate, and how they evaluate the child are important factors in the child's experiential mix. From countless interactions with complementary role enactors, the child learns about others and about himself or herself in relation to others.

In the following paragraphs, we speculate on the child's experiences with complementary role enactors. We assume that complementary role enactments with children labeled MR (a) operate according to the same principles as those with other children but (b) are significantly different in their enactment details from those for other children and (c) take on an identifiable, characteristic form specifically geared to MR-labeled children. Thus, the social experiences of children with MR are significantly different from those of other children not only because of their developmental limitations but also because of the characteristic manner in which complementary enactors behave toward them.

Consider the number and variation of complementary roles available for the MR child's interactions. Most children will presumably encounter a large and expanding number of complementary role enactors as they mature and as their opportunities to interact with growing numbers of people increase. Ideally, most children will experience many variations in complementary role enactments and role status levels, and they will encounter social expectancies expressed in different ways according to individual complementary role enactments. Consistent with role theory, this multiplicity of persons and variations of complementary role enactments provide children with a richness of social stimulation, reinforcement, and social learning opportunities. Most important, in normal development, there are many and varied opportunities for role resource access, providing most children with many learning supports.

We hypothesize that, in contrast, the child with MR has a restricted number and variety of complementary role enactors. It follows that role resource access will be limited, and the child will be denied many learning opportunities and social supports.

MR Role Multiplicity, Complexity, and Variation

Most people occupy several social positions and enact numerous roles, but only a few roles are available to those with MR. Many of the role restrictions are reasonable, given the person's cognitive limits. However, many are due to the protective constraints applied by social agents. Most obviously, the large array of occupational roles available to most people is limited for persons with MR. They do not become secretaries, police officers, airline pilots, or other white-collar, professional, or clerical workers. The familial roles of spouse, parent, or grandparent are virtually denied to them. Membership roles in religions, clubs, and political parties are also limited. Some of those roles demand functioning that is beyond their abilities, but many do not. For example, membership in religious congregations is certainly feasible.

What are the roles into which persons with retardation are socialized? They include age and familial roles (e.g., child, sibling), pupil, client, group home residents, workers, and friends. But consider two factors about that brief list. First, the number of available roles is limited compared with those of most people. Second, except for the coequal friendship roles, all imply a *submissive-dependent character in role enactments* for the MR person. This point is particularly important. It suggests that the role enactments across the already limited MR array are further constrained by this generalized submissive-dependent component.

In their play, children rehearse a variety of adult roles (i.e., their versions of the adult roles which they observe in their normal interactions and through media such as television). They play at being cowhand, parent, teacher, police officer, nurse, firefighter, doctor, and so on. In each play enactment, children try out, rehearse, and learn about many adult roles and relationships among them. The question is raised whether children with mental retardation play at the same roles and at the same ages as other children. We suspect that children with mental retardation do attempt the same role playing as do other children, but when they are older, with some delay. We hypothesize that they will attempt to play much the same as their mental age peers. However, because of their greater chronological age and usually larger size, much of their play will be viewed by others as inappropriate and thus will not be supported by some complementary role enactors, both children and adults. Hence, the retarded child's later attempts at role-playing will be interrupted, inconsistently supported, sometimes punished, and therefore incomplete. Those children will miss many of the learning experiences available to other children. This interrupted social experience leaves those children less socially aware and skilled than they might have been had they been allowed the role-playing opportunities. We suggest that these and similar restrictions on allowable role-playing and rehearsal will continue to occur throughout the person's life, thus further limiting personal experience, learning opportunities, and adult role choices.

The social competence of persons with MR is limited by their subaverage cognitive levels and by specific role restrictions imposed by complementary role enactors. Which of the two types of restrictions, cognitive or social, is the more powerful in shaping the social behavior of persons with MR has not yet been answered. We assume that both are contributing factors, but we do not know the relative value of their contributions.

Imposition and Improvisation in Mental Retardation

Role variation in MR may be constrained by the degree of imposition/improvisation in the enactments. In normal socialization, persons learn to balance social tendencies toward imposition and improvisation so that each individual enacts prescribed role behavior, modifies current behavior, and even creates new role behavior (improvisation). Improvisation is another means of achieving role variation, and improvisational skills are normally taught through socialization. However, these skills probably demand a degree of independent behavior that is rare in the learning history of persons with MR. Rather, prescribed role enactments, largely controlled by society's expectations for submissive-dependent behavior of those persons, may be emphasized. Thus, we hypothesize that role variation for persons with MR will be further limited by the lack of role-improvising skills.

The degree of imposition/improvisation is particularly important for our application to mental retardation, as we assume that the character of a person's social role enactments is largely shaped by the degree to which preexisting social structures (the positional norms) are imposed on the enactment. Role enactments could, conceivably, range from totally structured by society (imposition) to totally created by the person (improvisation). We assume most roles have a mix of the two tendencies and most persons have a socialization history that includes training in role improvisational skills. Mental retardation, however, is a recognized position of deviance, and we hypothesize that it is tightly defined by the positional structure, leaving little opportunity for individually creative role improvisation. Thus, the role enactments of persons with mental retardation are characterized as heavily impositional in nature, and the persons in that position are viewed as not having been taught improvisational skills. In essence, the person in the paradigm is relatively weak and engages in his or her role enactments in a nearly fixed-role manner, displaying little variation or creative improvisation. If suddenly faced with a new situation, this person will be at a considerable loss to behave effectively, since he or she will have had little training and practice in role improvisation. This appears to be a major distinction between role enactments in MR and those within most other social positions in which the contributions of the enacting person are considerably stronger.

If MR role enactments are limited in type, and if they all include a submissive-dependent character, then we assume that role complexity is also limited, and each role enacted by the person includes only a limited number of sectors. The person with mental retardation is expected by most to behave consistently, in much the same manner (i.e., as a retarded, and thus limited, person) regardless of the identity of the complementary role enactor. We hypothesize that few demands will be made on the child and few supports provided to teach the child to discriminate among persons and to vary his or her role enactment accordingly. Thus, training in role variation for the child will be limited.

We believe the socialization of persons with MR is so restricted that their role enactments are few in number and severely limited in variety, complexity, and the creativity of improvisation. Remaining for these persons is a limited array of role enactments in which similar enactments are repeated in seemingly rigid fashion. Thus, a marked sameness or standardization of behavior is characteristic of persons with MR, given approximately equal levels of intelligence. That is, the person with mental retardation displays a characteristic set of behaviors. (Stereotypes held by others may in part be drawn from the reality of such commonly shared behavior exhibited by persons with MR.) Characteristic behaviors include:

> a limited array of social roles
> repetitiveness and lack of variety in behavior
> difficulty dealing with social situations in which novel aspects have been introduced
> dependence and submissiveness in most interactions with nonretarded persons
> poor social skills
> a general naiveté about social relationships
> a lack of creativity, initiative, and motivation to succeed in traditional paths

These behaviors are not necessarily due directly to limited intelligence. Rather, as has been discussed, two socialization factors may be primarily responsible for shaping such behavior. The first factor is lifelong training in the MR role in which sets of behaviors expected of the person with MR are learned. Through socialization, mentally retarded persons learn the acquisition of specific and characteristic "mentally retarded" behavior. Second, the characteristic sameness is also enhanced by the failure in MR role socialization to teach the person role variation and improvisational skills. Such skills, were they ready at hand, would allow the personal modifications of role enactments and thus help break the grip of the standardized or typical MR role enactments. The failure to allow the development of creative, improvisational skills is presented here as a factor that may be equal in its effects to those of the direct teaching of specific MR role-appropriate behavior.

This suggests that some changes in the typical MR socialization patterns might alter some of those "characteristic" MR behaviors. For example, in training and education programs, specific attention might be paid to training persons with mental retardation in improvisational skills to apply in their role enactments. An underlying assumption here is that they are capable of learning such skills if given the opportunity and support, although such learning will take longer than it does for nonretarded persons and will require special teaching settings and procedures. Hence, special education and training programs focused on this issue are needed. A potentially rich field of applied research exists here.

Role Violation, Conflict, and Strain in MR

We expect that persons in the MR position do not experience significant role strain due to problems of "living up" to their role expectations. This seems a reasonable expectation because the MR position is one of deviance, and norm conflicts are most likely to occur when the person attempts to override the limitations imposed by the expectancies of complementary role enactors. Examples might be when a young adult with MR begins to experiment with sex, wants to drive the family car, or to engage in other behavior that is normal for nonretarded peers but is proscribed for him or her. We assume this person is capable of recognizing that he or she is denied much of what is easily available for others. The person may develop a general observation that other people do and have desirable things that are not allowed to the person with MR. It seems reasonable to expect that perception of these differences may lead to a general feeling of dissatisfaction, sadness, longing, or even anger over the perceived inequities.

Thus, role strain may occur under these norm-override conditions—that is, when the person with mental retardation (a) actively attempts to override some imposed limitations and/or (b) recognizes inequities and develops a generalized feeling of dissatisfaction. However, we expect that the socialization of persons in the position of retardation will tend to minimize the more active norm-override efforts, and thus, role strain due to active norm violations or failures will be minimal. However, we hypothesize that role strain will occur, being manifest in generalized, usually low-intensity feelings of dissatisfaction (i.e., generalized low-level frustration).

In a similar manner, we expect that interrole conflicts, which other people experience because they enact many roles, will be minimal for those with mental retardation because of their limited role multiplicity and variability. They enact relatively few and minimally varying roles that, as discussed in earlier sections, share basic characteristics such as dependence and subordination. These few and fairly similar roles will have fewer chances of occasioning conflicts than do the wider array and varied enactments of most people. However, some interrole conflicts might nevertheless arise. For example, a parent might criticize a child with MR for some behavior the parent considers inappropriate for the child's gender or age and insist that the child correct it.

Of the types of role conflicts discussed earlier, intrarole conflicts may be the most likely to occur. Recall that intrarole conflicts occur when persons in complementary roles lack consensus about the norms. Parents might disagree on what is appropriate behavior for a child with retardation and what behaviors might be excused because of the retardation. The child could then be caught in an intrarole conflict, directed toward different behaviors by the parents. For example, a child with MR who has been well taught in submissive and dependent behavior might suddenly be exhorted by a parent to "stand up for your rights" when bullied by another child.

It seems reasonable to expect that for persons in the MR position, acute role conflict and strain are not a major problem. However, we have hypothesized that a generalized low level of role strain may be developed, leaving the person with general feelings of dissatisfaction. Whether this hypothesized low-level role strain phenomenon occurs and how debilitating might be the resulting stress are questions for which research is needed.

We must note here that persons with MR are subject to stress and anxieties from other than role-related sources, just as are all people. They can, and often do, develop fears and/or phobias, feel social anxieties, and become upset with social, academic, and/or occupational failures. The distress from such experiences is just as real and debilitating as it is for anyone else, and therapeutic procedures such as relaxation, desensitization, and modeling appear to be appropriate for application to persons with retardation.

The Dependent-Submissive Character in Mental Retardation

It was noted earlier that one of the mechanisms resulting in limited role enactment experiences for persons with MR is the generalized **dependent-submissive character** of the enactments expected of the person. Complementary role enactors appear to assume a dominant character over the submissive-dependent role enactments of the person with retardation. That is, adults, and even some children, who enact complementary roles are likely to assume their own superiority in all skills, knowledge, and feelings and to assert their dominance and authority over the person with MR. Teaching the child with mental retardation to adopt a dependent and subordinate position seems little different from the lessons taught to nonretarded children. But for children with MR, two additional factors enter that are not present for other children. First, the subordination of oneself is not only in relation to adults, as it is with most children, but may be in relation to all non-MR and thus seemingly more skillful persons, even if they are the youngster's chronological age peers. The experience for the child in terms of the subordinate status of childhood may thus be far different from that of other children. First, their subordination and dependence are generalized to a much wider array of other persons. Perhaps the only situations in which the person with MR is not clearly expected to be subordinate are interactions with other persons with MR (in which other factors may operate to determine relative dominance) and interactions with significantly younger non-MR persons.

Second, and perhaps most important, non-MR children are reminded frequently that their subordination and relative powerlessness is only a temporary condition of childhood that will alter as they grow older. The adults' expectancies are repeatedly communicated to non-MR children, who are told that in time they, too, will have jobs or professions and money of their own, that they will someday be parents "in charge" of their own families, and that they will eventually be independent of their parents. Such abstract notions about one's own not yet experienced future may at first be difficult or meaningless to the child. But the repetition in varied forms over many years will gradually clarify the ideas, and they become adopted as the child's own self-expectations. These expectations of the child's future are communicated by adults in a myriad of repeated ways, through what adults say and what they allow and encourage their children to do. For example, there is the common occurrence in many families of good-natured teasing about the young adolescent's first date, boyfriend or girlfriend. This is part of the ongoing age-graded acknowledgment by adults that the child is growing into the youth, and the youth now begins to exercise more freedom approximating the coveted powers of adults.

But where in the life of a child with MR are the repeated, varied, and easy assurances that the child is growing into greater individuality and self-determination and out of his or her accustomed position of near complete subordination? For what may be good reasons to many people, parents in particular, these children are not very well prepared for dating and courtship, marriage and parenthood. Nor do we communicate to them that a wide spectrum of personal futures—including military service, college or trade schools, and jobs and/or professions—are all available to them, only awaiting their eventual choice. Many of the options open to other children are obviously out of reach for children with MR, and in these respects, their future lots are as drawn blanks. But knowing of those limitations, have we created sufficient alternative self-directive opportunities for these children? It appears that we have not. Rather, driven by our own expectancies of the children's limitations, we offer them no sense that their subordinate positions of dependence may be only temporary. Instead, we teach them that such is their generalized and permanent lot, and in effect, we rob them of their futures.

It is not only their futures that are affected but undoubtedly also their present functioning. Without the repeated assurances that they are indeed shedding some of their dependence, the child's current functioning remains wedded to submissiveness and dependence. That child does not have the repeated opportunities to try quick and safe forays into greater independence and self-determination that are characteristic of other children.

The subordination and dependence of the child with MR, then, contrasted with that of other children, is a generalized dependence in relation to nearly every one else, and it is driven home as a permanent position of subordination and dependence.

Those two factors—the (a) generalized and (b) permanent nature of their subordinate childhood position—help to make the socialization experiences of the child with retardation different indeed from those of the nonretarded child, even though both are taught as children to be subordinate and dependent in relation to adults. For children with retardation, this socialization will eventuate in a generalized and permanent submissiveness, both in current functioning and in their expectations of their own personal futures. Submissiveness and dependence, as has been described by Edgerton (1967, 1988) and others, then become major de facto characteristics of persons who have been long socialized in the MR role.

Role Set Status in Mental Retardation

Earlier, we noted that the person with MR experiences a low *position* set status. Associated with that is a generalized low *role* set status. We assume that most persons experience a mix of status levels that defines their overall social status. But for persons with MR, role and position multiplicity is restricted. This means there will be fewer opportunities for role taking and role development and fewer opportunities to experience roles and positions that are associated with higher status. This person will not have the same opportunities to develop a mix of positions and roles and thus to experience higher- as well as lower-status positions. The restrictions on multiplicity will keep the person tied closely to only a few roles that will be predominantly associated with the deviant, low-status position of mental retardation. Thus, the overall role set status of the person with mental retardation is low, with little chance of changing its level. Such low, generalized, and unrelieved role and po-sition set status, we hypothesize, will have negative effects on the person's self-identity. Given the role restrictions on multiplicity, the person with MR faces a lifetime of low status and its associated demeaned self-identity.

Role Resource Access in Mental Retardation

This concept holds that each role enactment brings a person into contact with the resources (opportunities, knowledge, money, skills, status, etc.) that are controlled by complemen-tary role enactors. We hypothesized that greater role resource access is available to those persons who have large role repertoires, complex roles with many sectors, a high degree of role variation and improvisation, and a greater number, variety, and depth of interac-tions with those in complementary roles. Access is also greater for persons who interact with complementary role enactors who hold high status, skill, knowledge, and so on. Role resource access is an important social mechanism as it provides the person with resources for meeting needs, creating new experiences, learning new skills, gaining understanding of social diversity, developing more and/or more complex roles, and generally, in furthering one's own life quality. We maintain that in normal development access to such resources through experiences with complementary roles constitutes a framework of major social learning supports for children and youth as they mature and learn greater social and other skills and sophistication.

But what of the person with MR? Occupying the MR social position occasions a marked restriction in role multiplicity, variation, improvisation, and so on—that is, in the very social mechanisms, particularly role multiplicity, that enhance role resource access. In addition to having cognitive deficits and low status, the person with MR is further handi-capped by being denied the usual avenues to role resource access. Indeed, we propose that denial of this particular mechanism may be the major culmination of the restrictive social mechanisms that are imposed on the person with MR. That is, the effects of the various role restrictions may all bear on this single point of limited role resource access.

Consider the child who has been labeled MR, identified within the MR social posi-tion, and impelled along the career of MR role fulfillment. How are the restrictions on role resource access manifest? If the number of complementary role enactors for the child and the number of roles allowed to the child are restricted, then it seems apparent that the op-portunities to utilize complementary role resources will also have been restricted. The re-strictions will be manifest in at least three major ways. First, the number of complementary role enactors will be fewer than for non-MR children. This child will not have as many persons in different roles with whom to interact. This may not be so within a family as the child with MR will have the same number of relatives with whom to interact as will his or her siblings. The difference shows up primarily in the opportunities for complementary role interactions outside of the family. As the children grow older, the non-MR siblings increase their new contacts and interactions with peers and with the peers' complementary role enactors. For example, children will play in the homes of their friends and will meet and interact with the parents, siblings, and friends of the other family. They will sometimes stay overnight with a friend or go on outings with the other families. Each interaction with a new person offers expanded opportunities to utilize other resources, to learn new ideas and ways of doing things, and to be introduced to other roles that may not be available in one's own family. Their friend's family, for example, might include a live-in grandparent, or one of the adults might have a somewhat unusual social position such as a soldier or an artist. They may speak a different language, practice a different religion, or eat different foods. The friend may have different toys and activities. The differences may be new and enlightening for the visiting child and are all potential resources that are of value in that child's development. Through their friend's family, the child may be introduced to a variety of new ideas and allowed access to other new resources. This process continues as the children grow older and peer interactions assume greater importance and take up more time. They may become active in scouts, in church groups, in after-school clubs, athletic teams, and other activities. In adolescence, there will be a great surge of new role enactments and interactions, particularly around gender identity and sexual activities. The adolescent might work after school and on weekends and will learn new, appropriate occupational role enactments and interact with new complementary roles. All of these interactions bring the person into contact with an expanding array of complementary role enactors and thus with social resources. Their development of social knowledge and skills is heavily dependent on these mechanisms for social role resource access.

In contrast, the child with MR is limited in many of these opportunities to interact with such a variety of complementary roles. The restrictions grow as the children grow older; that is, the non-MR children gain greater social freedom and opportunities for complementary role interactions, while the child with MR is increasingly directed into what are considered to be MR role-appropriate activities. The child with retardation will not be allowed the same opportunities to develop freedom to interact with others, to visit other homes and stay overnight, and so on. Participation in special clubs, groups, and athletic teams is limited for this growing child, as are after-school and weekend jobs. And it will be the very rare adolescent with MR who goes on dates. The effect is that the child with retardation will not experience the normal, widening field of complementary role enactors, and thus will not have the same opportunities for access to those resources that are controlled by other persons. The limited range of complementary roles with which to interact is a serious obstacle to role resource access.

Second, the child will also be limited in the number of roles (multiplicity) he or she is allowed and/or encouraged to enact and in the variation and complexity of those roles. As noted, the nonretarded child matures into a variety of role enactments in school, in friendship and other social activities, in clubs and teams, at part-time jobs, and so on. But the child with MR is not encouraged to develop and to enact so many roles. This limitation is but another path to the same result stated earlier. This child, through restrictions on role enactments, will come into contact with fewer complementary roles, which in turn will allow only limited access to the resources controlled by those complementary role enactors. This child/youth, then, will have fewer opportunities to utilize the advantages (the role resources) offered to most others.

Third, the complementary role enactors with whom they do interact will selectively withhold certain resources. An obvious example is use of the family car, a resource often made available to non-MR adolescents. The selective withholding will be based on the complementary role enactors' expectancies regarding the retarded child or youth. The judgment is made that the retarded youngster is not capable of utilizing certain resources (e.g., a trip to the library to take out books, a weekend at a relative's home), and those resources may then be withheld. We suspect that in the daily lives of most children with MR many such resources that are ordinarily provided for others are withheld and, perhaps, without too much thought of the justification or consequences.

To summarize, we maintain that social role resource access is a critical and natural set of mechanisms in the development of children and youth. We hypothesize that, for the child with MR, role resource access is significantly limited by:

1. the restricted number of complementary roles with which the child interacts
2. the restricted number, variety, and complexity of roles the child is allowed to enact
3. the selective withholding by complementary role enactors of resources judged to be inappropriate for the child

We have also suggested that restricted access to social role resources is the major resultant of the various role-related restrictions imposed on the person with retardation. We hypothesize that if we could understand these resource access restrictive mechanisms and could systematically alter them, the person's development and general life quality would be enhanced. It is suggested that in the daily lives of many persons with retardation, a careful examination could identify the roles and resources not made available to them and could identify those that would be appropriate and useful if made available. The implication for research and training seem clear: Identify those factors that now limit role resource access, build in specific changes in daily programs, and evaluate the results.

VIII. Tacit Knowledge, Practical Intelligence, and the Zone of Proximal Development

None of the next three concepts, **tacit knowledge, practical intelligence,** and **zone of proximal development,** are social role concepts, but they are useful in our role analysis of mental retardation.

Tacit Knowledge and Practical Intelligence

The concept of tacit knowledge (R. J. Sternberg, 1982, 1985; Wagner & Sternberg, 1985) distinguishes the kinds of knowledge or intelligence that seem to be important in academic achievement and those needed for success in what Wagner and Sternberg (1985) label "real world pursuits" such as those in occupational roles. The concept seems to have grown out of the common observation that some persons, despite outstanding academic achievement, do not succeed in the social and/or occupational world, and conversely, some who are outstanding in their occupational/career pursuits had not been particularly successful in academic settings.

The distinction is between academic intelligence and practical intelligence. The former is of importance in the relatively structured, systematic, and overt teaching demands made in the school setting. Academic demands tend to be formulated for the student by other people, may be of little intrinsic interest to the student, and are largely divorced from the students' ordinary experience. Wagner and Sternberg (1985) add that academic tasks are also well defined, usually have only one correct answer, and allow only one correct solution. The typical measurement of academic intelligence is through the use of standard IQ testing.

Practical intelligence, on the other hand, applies to tasks carried out in natural settings (i.e., nonacademic settings) such as social and occupational roles. It is employed in the pursuit of our personal goals and is aimed at the solution of practical, personal, real-world problems that affect our own well-being and perhaps our survival. The problems are not necessarily posed by others nor are their details worked out in advance; they are of intrinsic interest to ourselves, are closely woven into our lives, and each problem undoubtedly has more than one solution. Practical intelligence incorporates our subjective emotions, motivations, and fears, as well as our more objective skills and our knowledge of facts about the world.

In R. J. Sternberg's (1985) model, one component of practical intelligence is tacit knowledge. This tacit knowledge is presumably gained by the person not through formal and systematic teaching, as in school, but in the everyday informal learning, which the person experiences in common situations and through his or her active involvement in the solution of the practical personal and occupational issues noted. With no formal "lessons" in tacit knowledge, the information is not easily verbalized or made systematic, although it could be if the person were to pay sufficient attention to that task. Tacit knowledge is viewed by Sternberg and others as constituting a major component of the practical intelligence that leads to success in real-world pursuits. This knowledge is practical rather than academic, informal rather than formal, and tacit rather than purposely taught (Wagner & Sternberg, 1985). The practical intelligence necessary to succeed in real-world pursuits is a mix of both academic intelligence and tacit knowledge. However, IQ tests, the usual measures of intelligence, assess only the academic intelligence aspect.

Now let us put the concept of tacit knowledge into the context of the MR role. In normal socialization, tacit knowledge is presumably developed through a myriad of informal lessons as the person proceeds through social, academic, and vocational experiences. The person confronts issues and problems, develops and tries out various solutions, at times seeks help, succeeds in some, fails in others, and in the process gains practical experience and knowledge about how to meet one's various needs and achieve personal goals. Hence, the person gains practical knowledge about the world and how to maneuver successfully in it and thus enhance one's own well-being.

These hypothesized processes of acquiring tacit knowledge and improving practical intelligence appear to require the person's being actively involved with other people across a variety of situations and grappling with numerous problems and tasks. A variety of interactions and tasks, it appears, would enhance the acquisition of such practical intelligence.

Referring to our earlier discussions, we can see that the mechanisms involved in role resource access may be major vehicles for providing people with the informal opportunities to develop tacit knowledge and contribute to practical intelligence. Through complementary role interactions, the person is allowed access to a variety of social resources. When there is an abundance and variety of both complementary roles and role resources, the person will have many opportunities to develop tacit knowledge and to enhance practical intelligence. When both are restricted, as in the MR social position and role, then the person will have limited opportunities for developing tacit knowledge and practical intelligence.

The Zone of Proximal Development

The concept zone of proximal development (Vygotsky, 1978) emphasizes two important points. First, according to Vygotsky, intelligence develops not only from the internal unfolding of maturational processes but primarily from the child's experiences in social interaction, particularly with parents. Thus, varied and continued social interaction is a major necessary factor in intellectual development.

Second, if social interaction is insufficient, the child may not develop intellectually to his or her latent potential. The difference between a person's actual functioning level and latent potential is the zone of proximal development. According to Vygotsky, this zone can be measured, and for some children (including those with mental retardation), specialized tutoring or training can move their intellectual functioning up to their potential.

The concepts of practical intelligence, tacit knowledge, and proximal development point to the critical importance of social interactions not only for the development of social behavior *but also for intellectual development.*

This bears obvious implications for any model of mental retardation. In normal socialization, an abundance of complementary role interactions and role resource access provides people with resources for meeting needs, creating new experiences, learning new skills, developing more and/or more complex roles, and generally, in enhancing oneself and furthering one's own life quality. Role resource access may be a major vehicle for providing the many informal opportunities to develop the tacit knowledge necessary for successful social interaction and personal achievements in a social world. A wealth of tacit knowledge is learned informally in normal socialization through the operation of abundant role resource access and is necessary for smooth and optimal social interactions. Intellectual development may depend largely on the nature, amount, and continuity of reciprocal-role interaction, particularly between child and parent. In many ways, the retarded social role results in restricted role resource access. Because of the positional and role restrictions discussed earlier, the tacit knowledge and practical intelligence base of persons with retardation will be meager and will lack many elements in common with those of nonretarded persons. Our everyday social interactions demand a great deal of tacit knowledge, including the idea that the interacting persons have a shared understanding of what is going on. If retarded and nonretarded persons do not share common tacit knowledge and cannot assume a shared understanding of each social situation, their interactions may end in confusion and failure.

We know that persons with MR are limited in those skills that Sternberg labels academic intelligence, and as a result, we have low expectations for their academic achievement. Indeed, academic achievement is one very clear area where the person with mental retardation does not do very well. But what of practical intelligence? Wagner and Sternberg (1985) show that academic and practical intelligence are not highly correlated. Thus, it may be that persons with retardation might be able to develop their practical intelligence far more than their academic intelligence and thus achieve some good measure of practical success. But a general observation made of persons with mild mental retardation is their naiveté of worldly things. To be naive, according to *Webster's Dictionary,* is to be "deficient in worldly wisdom or informed judgment," and that definition seems to apply to persons with mental retardation. It is easy to assume that their deficiency in worldly wisdom is highly related to their deficiencies in other intellectual skills, such as are appropriate for academic achievement. But as our analysis suggests, persons with mental retardation, already limited in academic intelligence, are under such role restrictions that they are not allowed the opportunities to develop practical intelligence that has much compensating value. Again, we find a double handicap. One is imposed presumably by genetic and familial factors, and the other is imposed by the restrictive mechanisms of the deviant position and role. The person with MR, then, does not have the skills to pursue success in either academic or real-world settings.

What this analysis suggests is that the practical intelligence of persons with MR might be enhanced through programs that remove current social barriers to role resource access. In addition, perhaps some of what is learned as tacit knowledge by most people can be identified, made more explicit, and directly taught within appropriately programmed social and occupational situations. Mildly retarded people can be taught, for example, what kinds of apparel and general personal bearing are expected and are valuable in enhancing work and social situations. The careful study of tacit knowledge in appropriate work situations appears to be a potentially useful investigation with many implications for the education and training of persons with retardation.

IX. Implications for Research and Service

The discussions in this chapter lead to some suggestions for research and training programs both for complementary role enactors and also for persons with mental retardation. For complementary role enactors, we suggest a more detailed consideration of how best to employ their role enactments. Increasing the number and variety of complementary roles as well as specific training for complementary role enactors in reducing their assumed dominance, altering their (hypothesized) tendency to withhold role resources, and supporting more varied and creative role enactments by the person with retardation are suggested.

For the person with retardation, we suggest that training programs include rehearsal in more and more varied role enactments, training in role improvisation, and training in how to best recognize and utilize the role resources that are made available. It was also suggested that programs include specific training to impart the practical knowledge that others gain in a tacit and informal fashion and treatment or training to counteract the (hypothesized) results of role strain—that is, the (hypothesized) generalized feelings of dissatisfaction and frustration.

The importance of primary caregivers as complementary role enactors and role-models in shaping the child's identity demands attention. We suggest that a focus on those complementary role enactors should constitute a major dimension of applied programming and of research in mental retardation. Research is needed to determine what expectancies are being communicated to the children; how those communications are typically carried out; what may be the effects of those communications on children's developing self-identities; what expectancies and procedures are of greatest enhancement value for children; and how they can best be applied. More applied research would focus on how to train and educate parents to understand and utilize their complementary roles for their children's enhancement. Parent training programs are commonly used. What is suggested here, however, is a specific focus on parent training and education in the importance and utilization of the complementary role mechanisms in the child's development in general and self-identity in particular.

We suggest that a major facet of all programs for young children with MR should be a carefully organized, specifically focused parent training program. The program would train parents to understand their complementary roles and their power in shaping the development of the child's identity. Methods for training parents in how to communicate consistent expectancies aimed at enhancement of the child's identity need to be developed and tested. Not all parents will benefit from or will even accept such enhancement roles, and some might not even have the abilities to do so, but most parents would learn something of value. (Perhaps parent training classes should be mandatory when children are accepted into programs.)

On what might such training focus? First, on a clear presentation of the processes involved in complementary role enactments and on the importance for the child of the parents' complementary role behavior. The parents should learn how they reflect the child's social reality to the child through their own behavior and how their expectations are crucial in the child's development. These expectations should be carefully examined by the parents and should be altered where necessary to direct them toward greater service for child enhancement. Parental management of how the other family members interact with the child should also be considered. The major aim here is to help parents to understand and reshape their complementary role enactments with their retarded children so as to maximize the positive enhancement value of their role enactments. It is, in effect, parents' role-modification training aimed at enhancing the child's functioning.

Thus, in addition to parents' detailed training of children (as discussed by Garber, 1988), parents need to be trained in the best utilization of their powerful relationship to the child—that is, in directing their complementary parent–child role enactments toward the child's identity enhancement.

Basic research is needed to investigate the nature and mechanisms of the parent–child complementary interactions; applied research is needed to determine the most effective ways of developing and enhancing complementary roles and of minimizing parental contributions to the child's negative self-identity. The types of training programs need to be researched, as well as the kinds of skills taught, the effects upon the parents, short-term and long-term effects on the children, and so on. Here is a rich area of potential research and application that needs to be followed up.

In passing, we should note that the influence of peers on the development of children and youth with mental retardation is an area in need of research. Questions regarding the nature and impact of peer relationships and whether they can be used systematically in training and education programs to enhance development need to be asked and researched. It may be that careful inclusion of friendship and other peer relationships in special education programs may help to compensate for some of the role restrictions discussed in this chapter. Thus, while complementary roles provide a rich variety of social learning experiences for most people, they may provide only a restricted experience for those with retardation. The child with MR will have complementary role interactions, but those experiences will be within the restricted range defined by the deviant status of MR (i.e., few complementary roles with which to interact and limited variation of those complementary role enactments). Further, because of the limited array of persons filling complementary roles, the parents or other primary caregivers will assume even more importance and impact as complementary role enactors.

We note that serious problems in the socialization of persons with MR frequently become most evident in their transition from special school adolescents to young adults who try to succeed in the marketplace, in special work settings, and in independent or semi-group living situations. Social difficulties and severe role restrictions generally continue far beyond the transition period and into the adult working and living situations. We propose that the study of social role phenomena and role modification training for those with mental retardation is important for understanding and correcting the role-restriction phenomena and for improving the socialization and achievement for persons with MR.

X. Chapter Summary

This chapter has discussed social role dimensions in the context of the social position of mental retardation. The model holds that persons with mental retardation are labeled as members of an MR social position and are socialized into an MR social role that is characterized by a restricted role repertoire, noncomplex and little-varied role enactments, and a generalized submissive-dependent character. The latter is in contrast to nearly all complementary roles, and those are characterized by dominance-superiority over the person with mental retardation.

It follows that persons with MR have relatively few complementary roles with which to interact, and as a result, they suffer severely restricted access to social resources. Restricted role resource access is here tentatively identified as the major point of impact and influence of all of the social role restrictions placed on the retarded person. Those restrictions become operational as social mechanisms that go into effect when the person is labeled as a member of the deviant social position mental retardation. When operating, these social mechanisms are geared to the maintenance of the MR role. They interfere with the person's general social, intellectual, and occupational development, and they constrain the learning of important tacit knowledge and thus truncate the person's development of practical intelligence.

We have also hypothesized that role strain is generated by persons' recognition of the limitations imposed differentially upon them and their inability to overcome those limitations. We hypothesize that as a result, persons with mild mental retardation experiences pervasive, poorly understood, low-intensity feelings of dissatisfaction, leaving them in a constant condition of generalized, low-level dissatisfaction and frustration.

Persons with MR, then, already constrained by intellectual deficits, are further burdened by lifelong social mechanisms that make their optimum development difficult indeed. These people are thus doubly handicapped, and their lives lack the variety, richness, and satisfaction associated with less restricted role development. It is understandable that, with their double handicap, they maintain marginal social lives, develop minimal practical intelligence, and demonstrate little motivation for conventional success.

The model presented here has attempted to identify those restrictive social mechanisms so they can be studied and modified toward the goal of personal enhancement of those with mental retardation. The mechanism that seems most central in carrying the restrictions to the person is that of limiting role resource access. We assume that the MR role is modifiable and that specific training and education of the person and their most significant complementary role enactors can help improve the functioning of persons with retardation.

KEY TERMS

Know these important terms. Check the chapter and the Glossary for their meanings.
They are listed in the approximate order of their appearance in the chapter.

Interference hypothesis	Implicit norms	Role violation
Active socialization hypothesis	Expectancies	Role conflict
Primary negative effects	Demands (social)	Role vacuum
Secondary negative effects	Direct modeling	Role strain
Social agent	Symbolic modeling	Role sectors
Social role	Position entry	Role resource access
Social role development	Position maintenance	Personal identity
Mental retardation social role	Position exit	Self-esteem
Socially devalued role	Positional status	Social role metacognition
Social role resource access	Positional set	MR social position
Restricted role resource access	Deviance	Deviant identity
Personal competence	Role imposition	MR social role enactments
Adaptive intelligence	Role improvisation	Mental age
Social position	Complementary roles	Dependent-submissive character
Social norms	Role multiplicity	Practical intelligence
Person	Role set status	Tacit knowledge
Position setting	Role complexity	Zone of proximal development
Explicit norms	Role variation	

SUGGESTED READING

Biddle, B. J. (1986). *Role theory: Expectancies, identities, and behaviors.* New York: Academic Press.

Edgerton, R. B. (1967). *The cloak of competence: Stigma in the lives of the mentally retarded.* Berkeley: University of California Press.

Scheff, T. J. (1966). *Being mentally ill: A sociological theory.* Chicago: Aldine.

Stryker, S., & Statham, A. (1985). Symbolic interaction and role theory. In G. Lindzey & E. Aronson (Eds.), *The handbook of social psychology* (3rd ed., Vol.1, pp. 311–378). New York: Random House.

S T U D Y   Q U E S T I O N S

10-1. Explain, as if to a student, the active socialization hypothesis and the interference hypothesis as they apply to mental retardation.

10-2. Define social role and social position.

10-3. Consider your own current life. Write down all of the social positions you have occupied in the past few months. Can you determine your own positional set and position set status?

10-4. Given the social positions you identified in 10-3, what are the social roles that you enact? For each of your social roles, identify the associated complementary roles.

10-5. For each complementary role, identify the social resources controlled by that complementary role enactor. Identify how you access those resources. Identify those that are most important to you.

10-6. Now put yourself in the place of a person with moderate MR and a restricted role repertoire. How different is that person's life from yours?

10-7. Define and explain the importance of the concept zone of proximal development.

In the 1940s, Leo Kanner (1943) described a childhood disorder now known as *infantile autism* or *autistic disorder.* The term **autism** means absorption in self-centered activity and extreme withdrawal or divorce from external reality. Similar observations had been made in the midnineteenth and early twentieth century and by Hans Asperger (1944) (as reviewed by Frith, 1991). It was Kanner's description of a clinical sample of eleven children that sparked so much professional interest. Kanner described young children with numerous severe impairments including six common characteristics:

1. profoundly impaired social interactions including **aloofness** and **aloneness** (i.e., lack of affective contact with others)
2. an obsessive **preservation of sameness** in behavior that is markedly rigid, repetitive, lacking the usual play behavior of most children, and overall, lacking in creative or imaginative dimensions
3. **impaired language** and social communication, including language that is absent (*mutism*), deficient, or deviant and, if present at all, is characteristically not aimed at communication. Two frequent verbal behaviors are echolalia (insistent repetition of words that may continue well beyond the normal age of about 3 years) and **pronoun reversal,** in which the I and you forms are not used correctly. For example, Gerry, one of the children in our program, when requesting something (e.g., a cookie), would insist loudly, "Gerry, do you want a cookie!"
4. a strong fascination for objects that are often handled with considerable fine motor coordination
5. exceptional memory feats may be performed by some of these children, such as repeating verbatim whole television commercials or song lyrics
6. autism is evident early in life and is typically diagnosed by 2.5 to 5 years

The first three characteristics were identified as the primary autistic characteristics and eventually became known as the essential **autistic triad** (Wing, 1989). Whatever other characteristics individual children might display, the autistic triad constitutes the necessary factors that must be present in some degree for the diagnosis of autistic disorder. Despite the shared characteristics within this diagnostic classification, person with autism can be very different from each other. The most evocative statement we have seen regarding the variability among persons with autism is the following:

> If one collected all of the individuals who are diagnosed as having autism in one room, probably the most striking fact would not be their similarity, but how vastly different they are among themselves. [There are] three-year-old children and senior citizens, people with profound mental handicap and university graduates, adults who barely have a word of expressive vocabulary (and almost undetectable receptive language) and adults who read encyclopedias for recreation and speak with pedantic exactitude. Some individuals with autism are self-destructive, while others are over-conscious about their physical well-being. There are individuals with autism who memorize road maps and train schedules, and others who couldn't make sense of either. (Baron-Cohen, Tager-Flusberg, & Cohen, 1993, p. 5)

I. Three Cases

Following are three brief case descriptions. The first two case are drawn from our early work (Graziano, 1974). The third is a recent case.

Frankie.   The parents described Frankie, their firstborn, as a "very good baby" who slept well, made few demands, and lay quietly even when not asleep, often for hours at a time. Eventually, his parents wondered if he was "too quiet" and unresponsive. Holding and hugging him, his mother began to note a consistent lack of positive response, and when she picked him up, he stiffened and vigorously arched way from her. Try as she might, she could not get him to hug and cuddle, and she knew by his 6th month that he was pulling away from her every attempt at affection. She could not even stimulate eye contact, which he consistently avoided not only as an infant but throughout his life.

After their next two children were born, Frankie's "strangeness" became more evident. Over the next 4 years, he moved through, within, but never as an interacting part of the family. His younger siblings soon caught up with and surpassed him. His childhood was without the joys of normal play with toys or with other children. Aloof, alone, and silent, he sat for hours apparently staring at a revolving fan or perhaps at an empty corner. Sometimes he knotted rope over and over and made a low humming sound. Whereas other children his age had developed language and speech, Frankie remained with neither. His parents also noted bizarre, repetitive motions of head and hands and his insistence on certain routines. He required, for example, always the same chair, a particular pair of pajamas, and absolutely no substitutes for 7-Up, the only liquid he would drink. Even minor changes in any of these would throw him into loud, raging tantrums.

By the time he was 5, he was still an aloof, nonverbal little boy who played neither with normal toys nor with other children. He could not tolerate even minor changes in routine, was still not toilet trained, had no communicative language, and in general, seemed never to have experienced normal childhood. He had been hospitalized once and examined at several clinics and special schools by pediatricians, neurologists, psychiatrists, psychologists, and speech pathologists. Frankie had been thought to be deaf, mute, aphasic, to have cerebral palsy, and mental retardation. He was eventually diagnosed as having autistic disorder, with severe mental retardation.

Cathy.   By 6 years of age, Cathy had been examined frequently. Following are quotes from one of the reports. Cathy exhibits "grossly disordered behavior . . . hyperactivity, lack of judgement, temper tantrums, failure to be toilet trained, inability to understand directions, refusal to chew solid food . . . solitary play with household objects such as a spoons, toothpaste tubes and cosmetics." She was described as having no communicative language, being in a "world of her own most of the time . . . waving and staring at a soup ladle for long periods while making a sound such as 'ee' and moving her body back and forth." Her typical day was described as "usually spent in running, jumping, or climbing aimlessly. She loves to hear records and could spend hours doing this. She shows no interest in (normal toys) and other children refuse to play with her."

At age 6, Cathy had no communicative language. She still did not respond to verbal stimuli and had a limited vocabulary that was used rarely and inappropriately, consisting of endlessly repeated fragments from television commercials. Her limited language development at the age of 6 suggested a very poor prognosis for Cathy. She refused to eat solids but had progressed to a limited range of strained baby foods. Cathy was not yet toilet trained and she frequently wet and soiled herself. She used no eating utensils, had no social skills, and played with none of the usual childhood toys. Cathy was not aware of normal dangers and was apt to walk in front of moving cars and get herself into other dangerous situations. She sometimes wandered through her neighborhood, entered any house and rummaged through boxes, cabinets, and drawers, frequently taking and losing things.

Generally highly active, Cathy engaged in apparently nondirected physical activity. She ran, jumped, climbed, screamed, and engaged in violent headshaking and constant toe walking (the calves of her legs became very muscular). The physical activity intensified whenever there was even mild frustration: It consisted of severe tantrums, screaming, kicking people, throwing herself on the floor, knocking over or throwing and smashing objects, and in general, violently disrupting her surroundings for as long as 3 hours at a time. These tantrums occurred several times daily, in church, stores, and other public places, as well as at home.

One of her frequent activities consisted of lining several dolls along a windowsill, holding a small doll by the legs, against her mouth, and for an hour or more, wildly spinning and jumping in front of the dolls. This may have been in imitation of the rock 'n' roll performers she saw on television.

In the mornings, when her mother attempted to arouse, bathe, and dress her, Cathy invariably resisted, fought, and screamed. The rest of her day was spent in aloof isolation, solitary and rigidly stereotyped behavior, battles over feeding, and invariably, one or more severe tantrums. She made no positive contact with any family member. She usually was put to bed at night with no problems.

At age 6, Cathy was taken to kindergarten in a public school where she lasted only a few minutes of the first day, erupting into a major tearing tantrum. Within several months, she began in our program (discussed in Graziano, 1974) where she remained until age 12. In those 6 years, Cathy made spectacular progress. She developed not only a good vocabulary but also communicative language and, eventually, could hold brief conversations. She learned excellent emotional control and no longer erupted in wild tantrums. Cathy became far more socially interactive at home as well as in our program. She achieved well academically in our school, learning to read and to write very nearly at her appropriate grade level. Although not formally tested, Cathy's intellectual level was judged to be higher than average.

We cannot claim that Cathy's marvelous improvement in our program was due to the program itself. Unfortunately, we did not have adequate experimental validation of our procedures but only "before and after" measures and behavioral observations. As discussed later in this chapter, children with autism who are high functioning (high-functioning autism, or HFA) often make excellent progress as they grow older, as did Cathy. However, despite that progress, she remained a youngster with marked social deficits, and this is commonly observed in HFA.

When our program ended, Cathy was enrolled in a local private special education school where her good academic achievement continued. However, her clumsy, insistent attempts to interact with other children and her continued general high activity level were met by unceasing rejection and torment by the other children. Deemed to be "too disruptive," Cathy was expelled by the school and no longer had any program involvement (in the late 1960s there was no state mandate for educating autistic children).

Gino. Gino is a 25-year-old man with autism. He works steadily in his father's automobile service station, serving customers by pumping gas, checking oil and water, repairing tires, and under his father's direction, making some minor repairs on cars. He takes telephone messages for his father and drives the truck to dealers to pick up parts ordered by his father. Gino greets customers, presents bills, and makes change for purchases. He is responsive to customers, although conversations do not go beyond a few sentences. At times, he behaves in ways that appear peculiar to many customers—walking on his toes, standing and rocking in place, and endlessly wiping and washing his hands.

As long as he is employed by his father, Gino will probably continue doing well, but what will happen to him after his father sells his business and retires?

II. Pervasive Developmental Disabilities and Autistic Spectrum Disorders

Many developmental disorders occur in infancy, childhood, or adolescence (the developmental years). Some are specific disorders, such as sleeping, eating, language, or phobic disorders. In such cases, the problems are centered in one area of difficulty, and the child may function normally in all others. Some, however, such as autism, Asperger's syndrome, and Rett's syndrome are **pervasive developmental disorders (PDD),** and they involve severe impairments in more than one area of development. These children may be severely impaired intellectually, in language, social interaction, emotional development, and so on. The pervasive developmental disorders typically appear early in life, are severe and permanent, and most cases also include mental retardation. Before the recognition of PDD, most such cases were included under the label of childhood psychoses.

The etiologies of PDD are not yet fully known but are thought to be mostly prenatal and to involve some combinations of CNS pathologies, chromosomal anomalies, genetic defects, and congenital infections. In PDD, there are severe developmental delays in several functional areas. Pervasive disorders are also marked by "developmental deviations or distortions" (Nelson, D. L., 1984) that are deviant at any developmental time. Children with autism, for example, exhibit deviant behavior such as repetitive, stereotyped mannerisms and lack of imaginative play, distorted language, markedly poor social relationships, and much of their functioning seems bizarre as well as delayed or slow. These children seem not so much to travel a slower developmental path as they appear to travel a *different* developmental path.

As shown in Box 11.1 and discussed in the following paragraphs, autistic disorder is one of several that are grouped under the PDD concept in the ***Diagnostic and Statistical Manual*** (*DSM-IV*, American Psychiatric Association, 1994). There is still a question as to whether these are truly different conditions or are varying degrees of the same condition, autistic disorder.

BOX **11.1**

Pervasive Developmental Disorders

Autistic Disorder
Rett's Syndrome
Childhood Disintegrative Disorder
Asperger's Syndrome
Pervasive Developmental Disorder (not Specified)

Based on *DSM-IV,* 1994

III. Autistic Disorder

Etiology

Because of many findings from different research disciplines, most researchers believe that the etiology of autism lies in multiple biological factors with a heavy genetic contribution resulting in neurological problems in the brain. That is, we are reasonably confident that autism is biologically determined. However, despite such belief and confidence, we need to keep in mind that the identification of the precise etiology and biological pathways to autism is not yet known.

Consider that autism appears early in life. This suggests prenatal biological origins and casts doubt on the etiological importance of parental and emotional-developmental factors. In addition, the prevalence of autism and the defining characteristics are the same wherever it has been studied, despite strong social class, national, and cultural differences. For example, children with autism in Japan display the same triad of autistic characteristics as those in the United States, Canada, England, and Europe, as do autistic children whose families are poor or rich. These observations make it unlikely that psychological, social, or cultural factors determine the condition.

Genetic and chromosomal hereditary factors are suggested by the findings in twin studies. In monozygotic (identical) twins, the concordance rate for autism is 65 to 90 percent, and 5 to 10 percent among same-sex dizygotic twins (Bailey, Luther, Bolton, LeCouteur, & Rutter, 1995). Among nontwin siblings, the rate of autism is 2 to 3 percent (Smalley, Asarnow, & Spence, 1988). While this does not seem high by absolute standards, it is a twenty to fifty times greater risk than in the general population (Happe & Frith, 1996). Bolton et al. (1994) reported that while most siblings of autistic children develop normally, 10 to 15 percent of the siblings have a variety of cognitive impairments (e.g., language or reading difficulties or mental handicaps). This suggests that some common genetic factors may cause a range of cognitive difficulties that are more pronounced in some siblings (e.g., autism) and less severe in others (e.g., reading difficulties). Links between autistic parents and autistic children are not readily studied since so few autistic persons become parents.

In one study noted in the Harvard Mental Health Letter (1997), a state survey in Utah in the 1980s found eleven families with autistic fathers, and more than half of their children were autistic.

A recessive gene metabolic disorder (phenylketonuria, or PKU) and a chromosome anomaly (fragile X syndrome) are present in some cases of autism. When they are found in autism, the inference is usually made that these conditions play some part in the etiology of autism. PKU is increasingly rare, largely because of early detection and dietary treatment (as discussed in Chapter 4) and is thus not a major contributor to autism. Fragile X, however (see Chapter 5), is seen by some researchers (e.g., W. T. Brown et al., 1986; Hagerman, 1996) as possibly the single most common biomedical cause of autism. Because it is an X-linked disorder, fragile X affects more boys than girls and is more disabling in males. Boys with fragile X are usually moderately to severely retarded, show speech delays and language deficiencies, and often have hyperactivity and emotional problems. The suggestion that the chromosomal anomaly that causes fragile X syndrome might also contribute to some cases of autism is another hint that autism may be genetically determined.

No "autistic genes" have been identified, but as reviewed by Rapin (1997), evidence suggests the interaction of one or more genes and possibly other nongenetic factors. In their review, Happe and Frith (1996) note that some evidence suggests that transmission may be through autosomal recessive and X-linked recessive genes, and some researchers believe multiple genes operating together may be responsible. Although many hints abound, at this point it is too early to assert definitely that genetic or chromosomal factors operate (Gillberg, 1998b). In time, research will determine the degree of genetic/chromosomal contributions to autism.

Whatever the transmission mechanisms may be, autism seems to have some (as yet unknown) neurobiological bases. Piven et al. (1995) noted that researchers have found "neuroimmunological, neurochemical, and neurophysiological abnormalities" in persons with autism. Piven et al. (1995) used magnetic resonance imaging (MRI) and found larger than normal brain size in twenty-two males with autism. The larger size was due both to a greater amount of brain tissue and to larger lateral ventricles (brain cavities). Other researchers have reported greater brain circumference and weight in persons with autism (Bailey et al., 1995; Bailey et al., 1993). These results have led to hypotheses of abnormal prenatal brain development (Bauman & Kemper, 1994). It is speculated that perhaps there is an interruption of the normal neural paring-down process in which damaged and miswired neurons are presumably deleted, resulting in larger, heavier brains. Reviewing this work, Piven et al. (1995) suggested that a promising line of research to help understand the pathological brain development may be investigation of the genes and proteins that are involved in these neural paring-down processes in prenatal brain development. In this interpretation, the larger brain size gives further hints that genetic factors may be involved. That is, some specific genes would, presumably, signal at the correct developmental time for the production of proteins necessary to initiate and carry out the paring process. If those genes contain some defect, then that signaling and the subsequent processes may be interrupted.

Autism is often associated with other medical disorders. For example, it is estimated that epilepsy occurs in 35 to 45 percent of cases of autism (Happe & Frith, 1996). In about half of these cases, seizures begin in puberty (Volkmar & Nelson, 1990), and the seizure frequency peaks in adolescence (Rapin, 1997). Even high-functioning persons with autism have a high rate of epilepsy (Happe & Frith, 1996). Thus, epilepsy or the conditions leading to epilepsy may also be etiological factors in some cases of autism.

It has also been suggested that prenatal and perinatal events can contribute to autism. During those periods, damaging events can occur (e.g., maternal infections such as rubella, herpes, encephalitis; maternal bleeding during mid- to late pregnancy; medications and drugs taken during pregnancy; Rh incompatibility; see Chapter 7). These reduce the optimum conditions in pregnancy and birth, and such "reduced optimality" in the prenatal and perinatal periods may be associated with autism (Steffenberg & Gillberg, 1989).

Although a precise picture has not yet emerged, the accumulating research data support a biological model of autism (i.e., autism as a biologically determined behavioral disorder; Gillberg, 1988). Further, because of the association of so many conditions with the autistic syndrome, it is increasingly thought that autism is not a single disease entity at all. Rather, as argued by Gillberg (1988) autism is best viewed as an "administrative" or "umbrella" term that includes several biological conditions that share common behavioral characteristics (i.e., the autistic triad).

Characteristics of Autism

Many specific behavioral characteristics make up the functional picture of autism. Three were initially described by Kanner (1943) and remain as the major defining autistic characteristics. These are (a) isolation or "aloneness," (b) language/speech disabilities, and (c) repetitive, rigid, and stereotyped functioning (including lack of "imaginative" activity). The severity of these major characteristics is not uniform across children but varies in their relative intensities and frequencies from one child to another. The other characteristics to be described are commonly found among the group as a whole but are not necessarily demonstrated in each case. The following descriptions are drawn from our own work since 1960 (e.g., Graziano, 1974) with children and families with autism.

A generalized description of a child with severe autistic disorder shows an infant whose parents began to notice "strange" or "different" behavior even in the first few months of life. Rather than "cuddling" or molding to the parent, the child would not respond or would shrink away from physical contact, the little body going limp or perhaps stiffening in apparent protest. He seems remarkably oblivious to others, and as the child grows, it becomes increasingly clear that he or she is grossly impaired in social interaction and communication. The child is markedly aloof and unresponsive and does not develop the normal attachment patterns to parents or to others. Language and speech development are impaired. The child may be mute but more likely has some language that is limited and distorted, perhaps echoing words someone else has said or endlessly repeating meaningless sounds that seem to be words but have no meaning. It is not possible to have a conversation with the child.

The child ignores other children and seems to have little imagination. He or she engages in solitary play, with a stereotyped, rigid quality, such as staring for hours at a revolving fan or turning around in circles. He or she insists on particular, unvarying orders of things and sequences of events, such as wearing the same pair of pajamas each night or following exactly the same routine at mealtimes. If the order or routine should be changed, the child will become agitated, throw tantrums, and even become physically aggressive.

Frequently, the child will engage in bizarre, repetitious behavior for long periods of time, perhaps even hours. These include arm flapping, bobbing back and forth from foot to foot in a rigid, repetitious "dance," finger flicking, toe walking, spinning, and long periods of body rocking. Some autistic children become self-injurious, banging their heads against walls or with their fists, biting their hands or arms, and picking at their scalps until bloody sores form. These children may be hyperactive, seemingly in frenzied activity with no apparent purpose. Oversensitivity to light, sounds, and smells is common.

As noted earlier, most persons with autism are in the retarded range of intelligence. They do not typically show substantial improvement with age and require lifelong care. Some autistic children improve as they grow older, and this seems to be directly related to their cognitive level and language ability. For those in the approximately 20 percent with average or higher levels of intelligence, improvements do seem to occur, but they are not necessarily due to education, treatment, or training (Howlin, 1998). The intensity of outbursts and general agitation seems to decrease in some, and although severe social deficits persist, some may become more responsive to other persons. Systematic training programs with painstakingly detailed and repeated learning trials may direct and spur the higher-functioning autistic child's personal, social, and academic functioning. The basic autistic syndrome, however (the three major autistic characteristics), will remain a severe lifelong disorder.

Major characteristics of children with autistic disorder are briefly discussed in the following paragraphs. These include the original descriptions by Kanner (1943) and observations made since then.

Severe Social Isolation.   The most notable feature is the impairment in social interaction. Unable to relate to others, these children typically reject close physical and psychological contact and appear to remain alone and aloof. Infants and young children often violently struggle to get away and to remain away from others. This also takes the form of no response even to intense stimuli such as loudly shouting the child's name. In some cases, the unresponsiveness is so severe that the child is thought to be profoundly deaf, whereas in actuality the child's sensory abilities in hearing are not at all impaired. As they grow older, their isolation generally continues but, in many cases, moderates. Some older children and adolescents, primarily those at higher cognitive levels, do begin to show increased interest in social contact, but lacking good social skills, they become intensively aversive or annoying in their attempts to socialize and are rebuffed by others.

It is generally thought that children with autism cannot be affectionate and do not develop any attachment with parents. However, many of these children do show affection for and attachment to their mothers (Dissanayake, Crossley, & Stella, 1996), but "on their own terms and without the [normal] joy and reciprocity" (Rapin, 1997, p. 97). Their attachment patterns tend to be disorganized, but the children do show preference for being near their mothers in attachment-testing situations (Buitelaar, 1995).

Atypical Language.   For nearly 50 percent of children with autism (i.e., those with IQ of 50 or less), substantial usable language does not develop. When language does develop, it is typically limited and distorted. Conversational ability is rare, and language is typically not used for communication. Mutism is frequent; pronoun reversals and other language problems are evident. A common development is a seemingly endless repetition of simple sounds and echolalia (repeating without understanding what another has said). Speech patterns are typically stilted, monotonous, rigid, repetitious, and rarely show spontaneity or humor. In about 20 percent (those with average or higher IQ), substantial improvement may occur in language and social behavior.

Preservation of Sameness.   Autistic children display an intense insistence on maintaining the environment without change and often react with rage and violent tantrums if routines are upset. A child may insist on wearing the same shirt every day, always use the same cup for drinking, and maintain exactly the same order of books or other small objects lined up on the floor or a shelf.

Repetitive and Stereotyped Behavior.   This includes often bizarre-appearing behavior such as hand flapping, head waving, facial grimacing, finger flicking, head and body rocking, dipping, and swaying. Exaggerated movements, posturing, and toe walking may be evident. Stereotyped "play" with small objects such as lining up kitchen utensils on the floor always in the same order is typical. The child may engage in such rigid, repetitious behavior for long periods, even for hours at a stretch. Apparent intense fascination with moving, spinning objects such as fans or lights may occur. Strong attachment to objects such as a piece of string, foil from a candy wrapper, or a piece of a toy is common.

Lack of Imaginative Play, Creativity, and Humor.   The typical stereotyped, repetitive, and rigid behavior leaves little room for normal child playfulness and creativity. Autistic children do not ordinarily engage in games and jokes, do not play with toys in an appropriate manner (a toy truck, a teddy bear, and spoon are all used in the same rigid manner), and spontaneous play and humor are absent. They will sometimes engage in physical "tumble" games with adults but not in games that are rule-driven and require taking turns. One exception to the lack of appropriate use of toys is the facility shown by some autistic children to assemble blocks and picture puzzles. Typically, these children are not creative or imaginative, although in some cases, as in savants, impressive art may be produced.

Early Onset.   The disabilities are typically evident in infancy, within the first 30 months. This early onset suggests prenatal biological causation. Typically, in autistic disorders, there is no time during which development appears to be normal. Thus, the characteristics of the autistic disorder are not regressions from a more normal level but rather are delayed, distorted developments from a very early age. (As we will see, there is a quite different pattern in some of the other autistic spectrum disorders.)

Severe Tantrum Behavior.   Particularly if frustrated, such as if the child's rigid arrangement of objects or familiar routines are changed, severe, apparently raging tantrums may occur and can last for long periods, even hours at a time.

Isolated Ability Areas.   Many autistic children show unusual abilities in isolated areas, often leading parents to think the child is highly intelligent. These abilities may include rote memory feats such as correctly reciting lyrics from television commercials or deftly assembling jigsaw puzzles. At extreme levels, this is called "savant functioning." For example, one young autistic man whom we know has limited and distorted verbal and social interaction but can correctly identify the name, year, and model of virtually any car or truck. He works steadily in a laundry and keeps his co-workers apprised (and impressed) on the identification of each vehicle that pulls into the parking lot. Baron-Cohen and Bolton (1993) discuss several cases of autistic children with remarkable abilities in drawing, music, and rote memory and arithmetical calculations.

Mental Retardation.   Approximately 75 to 80 percent of persons with autism have significantly subaverage cognitive abilities, with IQs less than 70 (Wing & Attwood, 1987), most commonly in the moderate range of 35 to 50 (American Psychiatric Association, 1994). Most of the remaining 25 percent are in the low-average to average IQ range, and a small proportion have exceptionally high intelligence. In the latter cases of high-functioning autism (HFA), it appears that the level of expressive language (i.e., vocabulary) is greater than that for receptive language (language comprehension).

Associated Characteristics.   In addition to the features that are so closely associated with autism, these children may also show additional individual patterns of problem behaviors. These may include aggressiveness, hyperactivity, self-injurious behavior, severe temper tantrums, short attention span, and oversensitivity to lights, sounds, or to being touched. Rigid and strange food preferences and fears may be present. Distorted emotional expressions may occur, such as excessive crying or giggling or no emotional reactions at all.

IV. Other Autistic Spectrum Disorders

The following descriptions are based on those in the *DSM–IV* (American Psychiatric Association, 1994) and include Rett's syndrome, childhood disintegrative disorder, and Asperger's Syndrome.

Rett's Syndrome

This is an autisticlike pervasive developmental disorder for which we have no definitive incidence or prevalence estimates. Although apparently quite rare in the population, it may be one of the most common causes of severe retardation in females. Rett's has so far been diagnosed only in females (American Psychiatric Association, 1994), which suggests a possible X chromosome mutation as an etiological factor. In recent research (Amir et al., 1999), it was suggested that a defect in a gene (MECP2) on the X chromosome causes disruption of a process known as "gene silencing," which results in genetic messages being sent out incompletely or at incorrect times and sequences. If this occurs in males (with their single X chromosome), there would be no compensating healthy allele. As a result, the male conceptions with this defect do not survive.

The outstanding feature of Rett's syndrome is that, unlike autistic disorder, the child has a period of apparently normal development and functioning followed by a clear pattern of deterioration. Prenatal and perinatal development are normal as is postnatal development through approximately the first 5 months. From 5 months to about 30 months, there is a noticeable slowing of development, including a deceleration in head-circumference growth rate and loss of some of the child's previously developed or developing motor and speech skills. Stereotyped hand movements (resembling hand washing or wringing) begin to appear. Over the next few years, the child loses interest in social interactions and develops a variety of motor coordination problems, specifically in trunk or gait movements. Expressive and receptive language are seriously impaired, and severe to profound mental retardation becomes evident.

Childhood Disintegrative Disorder

This is a rare disorder, far less prevalent than autistic disorder. Its major feature is the child's severe regression in several functional areas after at least 2 years of normal development. The child begins to lose developed skills in two or more functional areas such as language skills, social interaction, play, and general adaptive behavior. As the disorder progresses, the child increasingly exhibits the deficits that are characteristic of autistic disorder such as deficient social interaction, aloofness, language and communication deficits, and repetitive, stereotyped behaviors. Severe mental retardation is associated with this disorder. By the age of 5 or 6, the child appears much like those with autistic disorder. Carefully gathering historical information from the parents will reveal the characteristic regression following the 2 or more years of apparently normal development.

As with other pervasive PDDs, etiology is not yet known, but prenatal, possibly chromosomal or genetic, defects may be involved. This disorder is similar to Rett's except that it has a longer period of normal development, and both sexes are affected whereas Rett's has so far been seen only in females. Like Rett's and autistic disorder, this is a severe, pervasive, lifelong disability (Volkmar & Cohen, 1989).

Asperger's Syndrome (AS)

This syndrome was described by Hans Asperger, a Viennese pediatrician, in a German-language journal in 1944 (as discussed by Wing, 1981) and has since been described in detail (e.g., Frith, 1991; Gillberg, 1998a; Wing, 1981). The person with Asperger's syndrome has several features much like those with autistic disorder, but other features are lacking or are present to a relatively minor degree. The person with AS (a) is seriously impaired in social interactions and (b) shows rigid, repetitive behavior, much like the autistic child. However, language development is not delayed. Language usage, although sometimes oddly insistent and perseverative, is not markedly distorted or bizarre, as it is in autism, and the person is able to communicate effectively. Further, cognitive development appears normal, and intellectual functioning is above average for most persons with Asperger's syndrome. Indeed, high-function cognitive abilities seem to be characteristic of AS and are used diagnostically to help differentiate it from other forms of autism (Gillberg, 1998a). In particular, these children seem to thrive on word usage—often repetitive, obsessively insistent, but often at quite high levels. They show obsessive interest in things and are often involved in reciting their interests to others, as if lecturing to them. Their obsessive involvement may be with things such as clocks or radios or a fascination with long train, bus, or airline schedules. Noting their obsessive word use, Asperger is reported to have called these children "little professors" (O'Neill, 1999).

The child with AS develops normal self-help skills and most adaptive behaviors (except in the social interaction area). This child will have many normal abilities and interests and may want to interact at times with other children and engage them in his or her own markedly stereotyped interests. As infants and preschoolers, they often appear to parents to be normal, very bright children, whose oddities are often attributed to their high intelligence. However, because of the social skills deficits and the obviously "odd" behavior and content of their interests and activities, these children are not easily accepted by other children. As a result, Asperger's syndrome is generally not diagnosed until the child is in school and the social interactive problems become clearly observable. Autism, in contrast, is now generally diagnosed in early childhood, long before school.

This child is in school with other children, is very bright and often able to meet and even exceed academic demands, and wants to have friends and to interact with other children. But the child's behavior is odd, insistent, and often irritating for others. Unfortunately, other children often ridicule and reject this child, and teachers, unless they have been specifically prepared, tend to attribute this child's disruptions to some deliberate, troublemaking intent. Adolescence is particularly difficult for these youngsters, as they continue to be highly aware of themselves and others, motivated to develop close friendships, but still feel the harsh social rejections. Throughout their lives, despite their high intelligence, these children, youth, and adults cannot perceive the myriad subtle social cues that even young children have mastered.

Adults with AS may seem rigid, odd, and intense in their insistent interests in such things as train schedules. They may lack empathy for others but do not behave in the obviously bizarre or disturbed ways as the person with autistic disorder. Because of their high IQ and good language ability, many persons with AS are able to succeed in school and achieve occupational success and independence. Recall that the best indicators of future adjustment in autism are IQ and language development, both of which are characteristically high in AS. Because of these abilities, some persons with AS are able to recognize their limitations and problems and to discuss them with others. This degree of self-awareness and evaluation is not common in other forms of autism.

It should be noted that although this person is much closer to "normal" behavior than one with autistic disorder, a diagnosis of AS is made only after it has been determined that significant impairments exist in at least two or three functional areas. Not as evidently bizarre-behaving as the person with autism, people with AS are still developmentally disabled and, depending on the individual, in need of some degree of support services.

Little data yet exist on the prevalence of Asperger's syndrome, but it does appear to be much more common than autistic disorder. One of the few population studies (referenced by Gillberg, 1998a) suggests a prevalence of 36 to 70 per 10,000 children ages 7 to 16 years, compared with perhaps 20 per 10,000 with autistic disorder. As Gillberg (1998a) notes, this would mean that AS is the largest subgroup included in the spectrum of autistic disorders. Further, because person's with AS have high IQ, we may have to revise the currently held view that 70 to 75 percent of persons with autism also have mental retardation. Gillberg suggests that figure would drop to about 15 percent, a major change in the description of this group. Further epidemiological studies will have to clarify this issue. There also appears to be a stronger genetic link in AS than in other forms of autism.

Nonspecific Pervasive Developmental Disorder

Some children have severe and pervasive impairments, showing some features of the autistic characteristics but perhaps not showing others. They may not meet all of the criteria for autistic disorder, for Rett's, Asperger's, or disintegrative disorder, but autisticlike characteristics are present. For diagnostic purposes, this category is used to label those cases that do not quite fit into the other groups.

V. Diagnosis of Autism

Autistic spectrum disorders are diagnosed clinically by observing the person's functioning, obtaining a developmental history, and determining the presence of the major autistic characteristics. There are no physical examinations or genetic, chemical, or psychological tests that will positively determine the diagnosis. Although biological etiologies are strongly suspected, autism is nevertheless diagnosed *behaviorally*. Given the standard definition of autism, a diagnosis requires that all of the major characteristics (the triad of autistic disorders) be present in each case. Thus, to diagnose autism there must be evidence of impairments in social communication and social interaction, and presence of stereotyped, repetitive behavior with impaired imaginative activity.

As noted by Wing (1989), the diagnosis would be relatively easy if made when children are between 2.5 and 5 years old, presented the same level of severity, and had only the autistic disorder configuration. Indeed, most cases are diagnosed by about age 5. At that age, the developmental delays have become evident, patterns of development and regression such as in Rett's and Asperger's syndromes have already occurred, the major autistic characteristics are already emerging, and the parents can report recent developmental events without the confusion of looking back over many years. Prior to about 30 months, a definitive diagnosis is difficult because language is just developing in most children and language problems have not yet become so evident.

Compounding the diagnostic task is the great variability among persons with autism. It can be associated with any level of intelligence, widely different degrees of severity, and may be accompanied by any number of other medical conditions, such as epilepsy and mental retardation. There may also be significant changes in language and behavior as persons age. If the diagnosis is attempted in adulthood, then it may be difficult to distinguish autism from schizophrenia or to determine which of the several autistic spectrum of disorders is involved. The diagnostician is thus faced with such variability that exactly the same clinical picture is never seen twice.

In each case, the differential diagnostic task is to determine if the condition is one of mental retardation, schizophrenia (a concern with adults), or autistic spectrum disorder. If the first two are ruled out, then it must be determined which of the spectrum of disorders is present. One major complicating problem is that so much overlap exists among these conditions that differential diagnoses, especially with adults, can be difficult to make.

The diagnosis is best made, then, when the child is about 2.5 to 5 years of age. Clear indications of the autistic triad of characteristics must be observed, and their relative presence and strength need to be determined. The child's developmental history needs to be obtained from the parents. Attention needs to be paid to the possibility of patterns of seemingly normal development followed by regression. Psychological testing is usually difficult or impossible with these children, but some estimate of intellectual level must be made. Likewise, an assessment of language development needs to be carried out carefully. With this information, the diagnosis of autistic disorder and the differentiation from other autistic spectrum disorders, such as Rett's and Asperger's, and from mental retardation can be made.

Medical and neurological examinations should also be carried out. Although those findings will not bear directly on the diagnosis of autism, they can reveal associated problems that can then be treated. Periodic reevaluations need to be carried out to track changes as the person matures and help to refine education and treatment programs.

VI. Population Estimates of Autism

Autistic disorder is evident in infancy or childhood, is lifelong, and affects primarily boys, with a ratio of nearly 3 to 1 (Burd, Fisher, & Kerbeshian, 1987). It is found throughout the world (Morgan, 1996) and in every ethnic and socioeconomic group. Early population estimates of autism were low, about 2 to 4 per 10,000 (Wing & Gould, 1979), and autism was thought to be a rare childhood disorder. However, most current estimates place the prevalence in the United States as being up to 20 per 10,000 children, which yields perhaps 116,000 children with autism out of the population of about 58 million children ages 1 to 15 years (Rapin, 1997). The prevalence of autism among adults is not currently known, but if the same rate (0.002) holds for the entire U.S. population of 275 million, then there are some 550,000 autistic persons of all ages in the United States. Some researchers have suggested that the overall prevalence is actually so high as to make autism one of the most common developmental disabilities. The basis for this change in suspected prevalence is the recognition that the major autistic characteristics (impaired social interaction, limited communication and imagination, stereotyped and rigid behavior patterns) can occur to varying degrees in large numbers of persons of any age. These persons include many with mental retardation, with psychiatric or severe emotional disorders, and those included in the list of pervasive disorders shown in Box 11.1. All of those conditions taken together constitute a spectrum of autistic disorders (Wing, 1996). The earlier prevalence estimates of 2 to 4 per 10,000 were based on the cases that would now fall into the autistic disorder category alone (i.e., the "classic autistic syndrome") (Howlin, 1998). However, as reviewed by Howlin (1998) and by Fombonne (1997), if persons across the total autistic spectrum are included, then the estimate is much greater, perhaps even as high as 91 per 10,000 (Howlin, 1998). The latter suggests a prevalence of some 2.5 million autistic persons (of all ages) in the United States, including 500,000 children, putting autism not far below mental retardation in prevalence (see Table 1.3). However, as noted, the most common estimate is up to 20 per 10,000 children. These estimates generate a wide prevalence range from 550,000 to 2,500,000 persons with autism in the United States, including some 116,000 to 500,000 children. Better records and much more demographic research is needed to develop definitive figures. However, if there is any validity in the higher estimates, then much more service is needed than is now available. To offer more and better service, we need research to discover etiologies and lifelong courses and to develop effective educational and training procedures for children, for their parents, and for adults with autism. We need many more effective programs to be developed around the country, and we must carefully train professionals and paraprofessionals to carry out those programs.

Autism commands a great deal of professional attention, probably because it is a complex, dramatic, puzzling, and resistive phenomenon. Our own literature search, for example, found more than 500 publications on autism from 1996 to 1998. Despite such activity, few professionals have had extensive experience treating or educating autistic children or counseling their parents. Also, there are still few reliably systematic, experimentally validated programs for these children. Although we can find a great variety of suggested approaches, there is general agreement that the most effective procedures entail long-term, systematic, detailed, and perhaps intensive educational programs that include cognitive-behavioral, teaching-training procedures.

VII. The Final Common Pathway Model

Several descriptive models of autism have been proposed. They include the early psychogenic models, biological/neurological, behavioral, and cognitive models. The psychogenic models of etiology have been long discarded as having no validity in the face of modern science (Steffenberg & Gillberg, 1989). The term *autism* is an umbrella term that covers a number of biologically caused conditions that share common functional characteristics (i.e., the autistic triad). Early in the study of autism, there was a tendency to conceptualize it as either psychological or biological in nature, with either cognition or behavior as the critical issue for intervention. As a result, one-dimensional biological, behavioral, or cognitive interventions were developed. Today, our models describe autism as being so complex that interventions must include all dimensions.

Modern researchers view autism as a spectrum of many biologically caused disorders that share common functional characteristics. This view is summarized in the **final common pathway model** (Baron-Cohen & Bolton, 1993). In this model, there are multiple biological etiologies that can operate in various combinations and to different degrees of severity. The most probable etiologies are thought to be genetic defects and chromosomal anomalies, but other biological risk factors may be involved, such as maternal infections in pregnancy and other "reduced pregnancy optimality" factors. The final common pathway model holds that the etiological factors result in damage to those areas of the brain that control the development of language and communication, social behavior, play, and creativity. The brain damage sets up the final common pathway, which in turn underlies the range of cognitive and behavioral deficits that characterize autism and mental retardation.

We must emphasize that this model is tentative and best used as a guide for research. For example, it assumes brain damage as a necessary condition of autism and predicts its existence in every case. However, in most of the cases studied, no brain damage or other neurological anomaly has been found. Clearly, more research in all three of the dimensions noted earlier is needed.

Biological factors are identified as the necessary and sufficient etiologies in autism. However, psychosocial variables are important additional factors in enhancing or further degrading the person's functioning. That is, once the biological etiologies—and thus, the presence of autism—exist, then the person's learning environment and experience come into play. Training and education in communication, social functioning, emotional control and expression, and overall behavior can have significant influences on the person's functioning. Recall that in Chapter 1 we defined etiology as including all direct and indirect causes of disease or pathology. Thus, the lack or distortion of such learning experience may be seen as additional risk factors and becomes part of the overall etiological picture. This theoretical model is useful as a general guide for research but is still without most of the needed detail. As suggested by the model, research in autism needs to investigate the biological etiology and the cognitive and the behavioral development and functioning of persons with autism. All three domains are critical for eventual understanding of and effective programs for persons with autism.

The limitations of the model point out several observations about autism that attest to how much we seem to know and how much we still do not understand. For example, it is now generally agreed that autism clearly has biological etiologies with prominent genetic components, but the exact determination of those biological causes has not yet been made. Autism is believed to be a complex disorder or set of disorders with multiple causality, with many, most likely prenatal, routes to autism, but we have not yet mapped those routes. We have considerable confidence in its essentially biological nature, but autism is now recognized and diagnosed by its behavioral characteristics. There are some promising leads to understanding some of the biology of autism, but as yet there are no clear medical/biological markers, diagnostic or treatment factors of any consequence. Finally, nearly all of our current major services, including treatment, training, and education, are psychological in nature (i.e., educational, cognitive, behavioral, social). Thus, on the one hand, we have strong confidence in its essentially biological nature and, on the other hand, a clear set of behavioral characteristics and diagnostic criteria. Hence, two large and rich realms of research in autism exist: (a) the psychosocial research realm and (b) the biological realm. The former involves studying the functional aspects of autism (i.e., psychosocial, cognitive/emotional, education, treatment, and training). The latter involves studying etiologies, discovering biological pathways to autism, developing future medical therapies, and discovering and mapping out potential primary prevention routes. If there is ever to be full understanding of autism, it will involve the separate research advances within many disciplines and the eventual understanding of their interactions.

This research picture mirrors the whole developmental disabilities field: the separate and interactive actions of both biological and psychosocial factors. It is certainly true in the field of autism that more questions than answers now abound and that basic and applied research in both domains, biological and psychosocial, is critical. We no longer think in terms of a single etiology or some critical one-factor "key" to autism. Rather it is seen as a complex developmental disability with many contributing events, developmental pathways, and phenotypic expressions. "Understanding" autism means understanding different parts of its many functional and/or structural elements and their interactions. The study of autism can be approached through any number of disciplines that, singly and in combinations, can make significant contributions. There is no expectation at present of "cures" for autism and no procedures to halt or reverse its many forms. As will be discussed, there is a good technology of specific training/teaching procedures that can be applied systematically to carefully assessed individuals. Such procedures include a large body of cognitive-behavioral approaches, good educational technology, and highly specialized technologies such as those of speech and language specialists and physical therapists. Autism cannot now be cured, but many persons with autism can be taught improved functioning in many areas, thereby removing or muting some of their handicaps and helping them to achieve a more substantial life quality.

VIII. Autism and Theory of Mind

A recent line of research that is potentially important in understanding the autistic child's characteristic cognitive deficits is the **theory of mind** hypothesis (see Baron-Cohen et al., 1993, for a thorough discussion of theory of mind concepts applied to autism). This cognitive model is from the field of child development. It asserts that as children mature normally they develop an appreciation and understanding not only of the physical world but also of the mental world of ideas. Part of this development is the recognition of one's own and other people's mental states and the growing ability to make inferences about other people's thinking, feelings, and attitudes. This ability, referred to as "mind-reading" (Baron-Cohen, 1993), is thought to develop to sophisticated levels in normal children and adults and to be used automatically in social relationships. People are thought to infer other persons' thoughts, desires, knowledge, and intentions, and they do so as a natural part of all social situations. According to this model, adults and older children infer the thinking of others and also understand and describe others in mentalistic terms. That is, people explain and understand the behavior of others in terms of inferences about the other person's attitudes, desires, knowledge, intentions, emotions, and so on. Further, in social situations, we base our own behavior on our mind-reading of others, taking into consideration our inferences about the expectations of other persons. This "everyday mentalism" (Wellman, 1993) is said to pervade all of our social relationships and to constitute a major functional dimension of our interactions. Notice that these hypothesized mentalistic skills for inferring the expectations of others fit nicely with the social role model discussed in Chapter 10. That is, the functional limitations that are occasioned by complementary role deficits are fed not only by the limited support coming from complementary role enactors, but also by the retarded or autistic person's impaired ability to engage in the active "reading" of the other person's social expectancies.

The theory of mind concepts led to research on the form and development of this hypothesized ability. Is it a valid phenomenon, and if so, when and how does it develop in children, how is it used, and how important is it? Considerable research on theory of mind in normal child development was generated by the work of Premack and Woodruff (1978) and Wimmer and Perner (1983). In a review of the field, Wellman (1993) noted that children as young as 3 to 5 years have already developed a fair degree of this ability to think about their own and others' mental states. This ability to do so rests upon their already developed recognition that "minds" and thoughts do exist in their otherwise very concrete world. This development, according to Wellman (1993), begins very early in life, just as an infant's language and social development have early beginnings.

The first study to apply the ideas to autism was reported by Baron-Cohen, Leslie, and Frith (1985). From a series of studies, Baron-Cohen and colleagues have proposed that autistic children have a developmental deficit in this theory of mind. Baron-Cohen (1993) noted that persons with autism fail to develop an understanding that other people have mental lives and their mental activity affects their overt behavior. These deficits in autistic children begin early in life and have a long course of interference with subsequent cognitive and social development. Peterson and Siegal (1999) found that autistic children, compared with hearing-impaired and normal children, are significantly less developed in theory of mind. They suggest that autistic children may have specific neurological damage that makes it particularly difficult to develop an understanding of the mental states of others.

If such theory of mind deficits do, indeed, exist in the autistic child, then this cognitive model may provide a good basis for our eventual understanding of at least two of the autistic characteristics: the social and the language deficits. According to this model, the autistic child lives in a world devoid of the mental sphere of other people. The child would be unable to understand other's intentions, needs, implied meanings, feelings, and so on. He or she would not be able to anticipate what others might do based on their reading of others' intentions. He or she could not "read" facial expressions, connect them with others' feelings and thoughts, and then anticipate the others' behavior. Nor would this child be able to engage in the "joint-attention" activities (Curcio, 1978) that emerge in preverbal young children. These are important behaviors with which children learn to understand and to use gestures in social interaction, to obtain and direct attention, and to engage in shared attention with others during some activities, such as play. The handicapping effects in social give-and-take would be enormous. Likewise, how would this child ever have the concepts and the language to express ideas such as "I know how you feel," "I understand your needs," and so on? How could this child anticipate how others might "read" his or her thoughts? How will this child understand his or her own thoughts? Metacognition—the development of skills in "thinking about thinking" (as was discussed in Chapters 3 and 9)—would be seriously impaired in this child. Lacking the appreciation of others' thoughts and feelings, this child could have no conception of how his or her own behavior might make another person feel or affect what others think about and how they evaluate the child.

In an excellent summary, Baron-Cohen and Howlin (1993) discuss briefly the types of errors made by autistic persons because of their theory of mind deficits. Such errors are commonly seen clinically in persons with autism, and they include (from Baron-Cohen & Howlin, 1993, p. 467):

Insensitivity to other people's *feelings*
Inability to take into account what other people *know*
Inability to read the *intentions* of other people
Inability to read a listener's *level of interest* in one's speech
Inability to anticipate what other persons may *think of one's actions*
Inability to understand common *misunderstandings* among people
Inability to deceive or to *understand deceptions*
Inability to *understand motives* that lie behind people's actions

And we will add impaired ability to *think about thinking* (i.e., in metacognition) and impaired ability to consider one's own feelings as related to one's behavior.

In essence, this model asserts that while autistic children are "aloof," do not interact emotionally with others, and have great difficulties in communication, their deficits may not be due to any general active rejection of other people, as was earlier believed. Rather, these characteristics may (largely) be the result of the child—lacking the development of a theory of mind—being *unable to recognize and share in the mental experiences of others or even to recognize and share one's own mental experiences.* The model helps to explain the odd combination of strengths and weaknesses of high-functioning autistic (HFA) persons. In some cases, they are able to master fairly high levels of technical information and skills and can learn large vocabularies and even correct syntax (the systematic, organizational "flow") of their language. However, because they cannot share in the mental life of others, their social interactions are distorted.

As can be seen, such "errors" commonly occurring in persons with autism would constitute major impediments to normal human interaction and certainly would affect their communication and social behavior. A potentially important line of research currently under way is the development of methods to teach the missing mentalistic skills to persons with autism. Future research will determine the effectiveness of these approaches.

As was discussed in Chapter 9, impairments in metacognition are characteristic of mental retardation. In that group, cognitive impairments in general occur, including impaired metacognitive skills. Persons with mental retardation, then, should also have theory of mind impairments. Thus, we can ask: To what degree are the theory of mind deficits attributed to autism actually metacognition deficits, and to what degree are these deficits part of the overall cognitive limitations of MR? Since autism commonly includes MR (i.e., 70 to 75 percent of persons with autism are also MR), this theory of mind deficit may be an expression of general mental retardation rather than a unique feature of autism. One fact that argues against that interpretation is that persons with high-functioning autism are not mentally retarded but still demonstrate the limitations associated with theory of mind deficits. Metacognition and theory of mind skills do appear to be related, and perhaps they are different levels of the same processes. Ideally, future research will clarify these issues.

IX. Education, Training, and Treatment

As we have noted several times, autism is a lifelong developmental disability. It has biological etiologies and is expressed functionally as severe deficits in cognitive, social, and emotional behavior. By definition, all persons with autism share the triad of autistic characteristics. However, the group is markedly heterogeneous, with cognitive and overall functioning levels ranging between individuals from severe mental retardation to high academic achievement and good personal functioning.

A great deal has been written about the education, training, and treatment of persons with autism. We will briefly summarize some of the major ideas that apply to programming. This discussion assumes the availability of ideal resources, an assumption that unfortunately can seldom be met.

Treatment and Cure

Because autism is a permanent disability, it cannot be "cured" by any known procedure. As Gillberg (1988) noted from his clinical experience, many parents have been gulled into believing that their children would be cured by following particular regimens such as psychoanalytic treatment, holding therapy, long-term immersion in residential treatment, behavior modification, and others. (Other claims of cure are summarized in Howlin's, 1998, excellent review for practitioners.) Cure is not a concept that can be applied to autism. Those who claim such cures should be viewed with skepticism.

However, the concepts of treatment and cure are appropriately applied to any accompanying medical condition such as a microbial infection. Persons with autism become ill just as anyone else does, and appropriate treatment toward cure of the pathology needs to be provided.

Teaching Is the Essential Task

While treatment for an overall cure is not possible, persons with autism are capable of learning. We cannot treat and cure, but we can *teach and educate.* Thus, as we noted many years ago (Graziano, 1971), the essential remedial task is *teaching.* The fact that such great variability among persons exists suggests that our teaching approaches need to be highly individualized and tailored to each specific person. Professional efforts will best be aimed at the development and validation of specialized teaching procedures that will be applied in highly customized form to individual students. As discussed by S. L. Harris (1998), the most widely used and successful teaching methods are those known as intensive behavioral intervention (IBI). *We believe that behavior modification carried out in systematic, highly individualized, daily programming is the best overall approach now available to persons with autism.*

Persons with Autism Are Individuals

Despite their general sharing of the autistic triad, autism comprises a very heterogeneous group. This means that whatever approaches we may believe are most useful, the education, training, and treatment must all be based on a careful, highly individualized assessment of each person. What will work for one, or even for most, may not work at all for many. Therefore, a major principle in working with autistic children, youth, or adults is not to think of each person as a member of a homogeneous group of autistic persons but as *an individual.* Before planning any approaches, we must spend time with the individual persons interacting as much as possible, observing carefully, and trying to engage them in verbal, motor, or social activity to whatever degree is possible. We must try to learn each person's usual, consistent behavior, preferences, fears, modes of communication, and to appreciate each person's total functioning as an individual human being.

Likewise, we need to learn the person's history—medical, developmental, social, and so on. It is important to interact with the family because these are the people who have the most experience with this person, the longest observational period, and the most knowledge to date. Particularly if this is a child or youth or an adult living with his or her family, we need to see them all at home and learn to appreciate what the family life is like and what resources and obstacles are present. Do not rush into your favorite programming. Instead, take some time and let them tell you, in all the observable ways possible, what each person is like before you begin to plan programs.

Autism Is a Highly Complex Condition

Many professional resources are needed to achieve maximum understanding and to develop the best approaches. This is not a condition that can be "treated" by a single therapist in an office, and it is not a condition for which a single approach is sufficient. Multidimensional approaches must be brought to bear, and this requires the skills of many professions, multidisciplinary cooperation, and a professional setting such as a school or clinic where these many factors can be brought together. No single professional person has all of these skills. However, it is important to have at least one professional who becomes thoroughly familiar with the student and is responsible for the *overall management* of each case.

Thorough Diagnostic Study Is Needed

One must assess as many dimensions as possible to establish functional baselines for program planning. These include evaluation of cognitive levels, language development, social and emotional development, academic achievement, sensory capabilities (vision, hearing), standard physical status measurements (height, weight, muscular development, etc.), and fine and gross motor coordination to assess developmental delays and distortions. Medical and dental health and neurological and nutritional status need to be assessed as well. The person's daily functioning needs to be assessed such as typical daily behavior, areas of frustration, social skills, play behavior, sleep patterns, eating preferences, emotional expression and control, general likes and dislikes, and so on. This is where the case manager would arrange for consulting professionals such as psychologist, physician, social worker, speech therapist and perhaps speech pathologist, special education teacher, and perhaps physical and vocational therapists. Specialists in speech and language training and in behavior modification need to be consulted. Each professional would prepare a separate evaluation, and the case manager, in consultation with each, would try to integrate the findings and begin designing a program for that particular person.

In reality, it is often not possible to carry out all of those evaluations. For example, formal psychological testing to obtain measures of cognitive functioning might simply not be possible with a particular person. In that event, we need to make estimates of intelligence based on our daily observations of the person and detailed reports from parents.

Multidimensional Programming Is Needed

Any program for the autistic person must address several of the autistic dimensions and not limit the focus to only one. There will be need for work on language development and social interaction skills. But other dimensions are important, too, such as emotional control, academic development, job training and placement for adult clients, and so on. A program would best not try to initiate all dimensions at once but begin with one or two and then, as progress is made on those, phase in additional program dimensions. The decisions as to which dimensions to include, with which to begin, the sequence of other dimensions to phase in, and so on need to be made by considering all of the highly individualized diagnostic information in each specific case.

The Involvement of Parents and Family in Any Treatment or Other Services Is Essential

Involvement of the person's family in programming is essential, although complex. S. L. Harris, Glasberg, and Delmolino (1998), for example, discuss the major issues that beset the family with an autistic teenager. This family faces not only the usual upheavals of an adolescent but also must understand and deal with the special demands made by autism. Those demands change as the autistic teenager develops, and the family needs to anticipate issues that are looming ahead. There are special stresses placed on parents and the nonautistic children by the developmental demands of the autistic youngster—sexuality being just one of those issues. Specific attention and programming must be aimed at issues such as living arrangements for the young adult, continuing education when appropriate, job placement, and so on.

One of the major values of family involvement lies in the generalization process. Whatever is taught to the person within the structure of a teaching/training program will have value to the degree that the new skills can be generalized to the real world. By having the parents and other family members maintain program approaches and help the person to practice new skills at home, that generalization will be enhanced. Family members can be taught to carry out home practice in social skill development, emotional control, reduction of fears, phobias, compulsive behavior, and so on. Several descriptions, ranging over many years, of home programs are available in the literature (e.g., Graziano, 1974; S. L. Harris et al., 1998; Howlin, 1989; Ozonoff & Cathcart, 1998).

Enlisting the parents' active participation in home-based programs carries some difficulties with it (Howlin, 1998). Some of those potential issues are:

> We need to be careful to train parents well in specific techniques and to have adequate monitoring of their work. If this is not done carefully, parents' approaches may gradually "decay" into less useful, perhaps even harmful, practices. Further, such monitoring should be alert to the problems that arise when some particular approach or goal is no longer working, or has become inappropriate, and it is time to change or to discard it. We should point out that monitoring to prevent decay and other problems is also essential to professional staff within the program itself.

> We need to avoid placing overbearing time and effort responsibilities on the parents, thereby unwittingly making their already burdensome tasks even more difficult.

> Problems can arise if the parents have unstated goals that conflict with those of the program. Likewise, some program goals and approaches may not be easily integrated into a given family, causing strains and conflicts.

Generally, the procedures taught to parents to be carried out at home should incorporate much of the effective coping strategies that already exist in the family (i.e., use the family resources that are already there).

Improving the Communication Abilities of Staff and Family Members

An important point made by Howlin (1998) bears repeating here. While the professional staff and parents work to improve the behavior and communication skills of their students with autism, it is also important to improve their own (a) communications and (b) understanding of what the student may be trying to communicate. When communicating with persons with autism, our language should be clear, direct, and unambiguous. The use of quips, puns, metaphors, and colloquialisms may not be easily understood by the students and may create distress and uncooperative responses. Others who interact with the person with autism should learn what phrasings are best understood and to use them consistently.

Likewise, we must become sensitive to the student's particular ways of communicating and his or her characteristic responses to our communications. Some of the bizarre, negative behavior may be ineffective expressions of needs, distress, and so on. It is not always easy or even possible to do so successfully, but we should be prepared to ask: Is there some meaning that impels this particular behavior? Is this behavior a communicative sign of some need of the child? We assume that, like our own behavior, much of the child's behavior will be habit driven and will have no "meaning" or motivation beyond its overt occurrence. However, much of it may be motivated, and it is important in such instances for staff to try and understand those motivational factors.

Frequent, Detailed Evaluation of Progress Is Needed

As noted earlier, it is essential to maintain evaluative monitoring of any programming, at home or in a professional program setting. Procedures may lose their effectiveness or become problematic; new problems may arise; the person may grow and develop with age and training and may have new needs that are not met by current procedures.

Objective, Valid, Experimental-Based Procedures Are Needed to Evaluate the Effectiveness of Education/ Training Approaches

This is a critical need in our field. As discussed in Box 11.2 on facilitated communication, autism is so complex, puzzling, and resistive to change that we are too often tempted to accept very simple solutions based on little valid data. The impact of such false leads on parents, clients, and the field in general can be destructive, and we must try to avoid such errors. Procedures applied in a program must be evaluated objectively by persons with proper training in experimental methodology. Few programs have experimentally sophisticated persons on staff; indeed, many programs harbor the belief that scientific approaches are not even needed, as argued, for example, by Allen and Allen (1996). Clearly, we are absolutely opposed to such antiscience notions and recommend that if the expertise is lacking in the program staff, then it is imperative to bring in consultations with scientists to evaluate the procedures.

Behavior Modification and Behavior Therapy

Behavior modification is a general term for psychological learning theory approaches in education and mental health. Since the 1960s, researchers and practitioners have been applying behavior modification procedures to children with autism. These behavioral approaches constitute a large array of appropriate tools that have been highly successful in many cases. Researchers have applied intensive behavioral interventions (IBI) to children with autism (e.g., S. L. Harris, 1998; Lovaas, 1996; many others) and have reported significant improvement in functioning. No other set of approaches has been so thoroughly researched and validated by so many investigators as have these behavior modification procedures. It appears to us that any program for autistic persons, particularly children, *must* include behavior modification as an important (but not the only) dimension. To do that, we need professionals with expertise in learning theory and behavior modification to help plan, carry out, and evaluate programming and to train professionals and paraprofessionals.

Behavior therapy, a more specific term, refers to behavior modification concepts and procedures that are applied as therapy for pathological conditions. "Treatment" does not apply to the condition of autism but is appropriately applied to specific pathological conditions that may occur in autism as well as in any other person. For example, behavior therapy such as relaxation (see Graziano, 1974; Graziano & Kean, 1968, for the first account of relaxation training for autistic children) and graded desensitization are appropriate to reduce fears, phobias, and severe tantrums or outbursts of autistic children, and to help teach better emotional control. These do not "cure" the autism, but they may help individuals to function significantly better and should be available to use where appropriate.

Developmentally Graded Programming

It is essential for programming to be developmentally graded, changing to meet the emerging needs and abilities of the maturing child. Thus, continued monitoring and fine-tuning of the program is needed as the child matures. The younger child needs training in basic language development, emotional control, and social interaction, and the input of language and early education specialists is critical. Programming for the younger child should include basic information and training for the parents about the nature of autism, ways of interacting with their children, the nature of the program, and their potential involvement in it. A parent support group can be very helpful.

As the children reach school age, evaluations are needed of each child's readiness and potential for academic work. To whatever degree their particular abilities allow, the appropriate teaching needs to be provided. We believe that the settings and subject matter of academic programming should mimic that for nonautistic children to maximize its "real-world" generalization. Only a small proportion of autistic children—perhaps the upper IQ 20 to 30 percent—will be able to progress very far academically. However, each student should be given the opportunity to learn to whatever degree each is capable.

Graded social experiences and teaching about their expanding world would accompany the academic programming, mimicking the progress of nonautistic children. In this schoollike atmosphere, the teaching task is critical and should not be left to amateurs. Thus, special education teachers are needed to carry this out.

New needs will arise as the children grow into youth and adulthood, and the programming must be modified. Behavior appropriate to increasing age needs to be taught; planning for possible job training and placement and/or additional or higher-level education needs to be carried out. As higher-functioning persons with autism grow older, their transition to work and/or higher education needs to be carefully programmed. Temple Grandin (1992b), who has autism, has provided "tips" from her own experience. These include programming for gradual transitions, continued association with a mentor (in our terms, reciprocal interaction with a complementary role enactor of "mentor and friend"), and specifically dealing with anxieties and fears. Potential needs for lifelong programming and support must be assessed as well as potential for independent adult functioning. At all times, we need to be guided by the idiosyncratic nature of the individual.

Special Education and Mainstreaming

In its broadest sense, teaching and education are the most essential components of programs for persons with autism. **Special education** is not a separate topic, but virtually everything we have discussed so far in programming falls under the special education rubric. By definition, special education refers to all specially designed instruction for persons with disabilities. These include academic instruction, physical education, speech and language development, vocational education, and any other specially designed instruction or service to meet the needs of the student. Thus, special education teachers, social workers, psychologists, and speech therapists become interactive components in all special education programs.

Autistic persons present particular problems for the special education teacher. For example, all of the students have communication problems, and this alone makes the task a formidable one. In addition, autistic children are typically preoccupied with ritualistic and stereotyped activity, and the teacher cannot depend on their sustained attention to planned lessons. Allowing the children to drift off into such preoccupations interferes with the teaching tasks. However, breaking into that preoccupation may stimulate disruptive outbursts, which must then be dealt with. The program needs to be highly structured, defined, and predictable—one in which the autistic student moves from one familiar activity to the next familiar *and predictable* activity in the program's daily sequence. In this way, the autistic preoccupations and outbursts can be reduced and the teaching tasks maintained.

Repeated, careful, individualized educational assessment will determine the kind of training and/or education that is required in each case. Whether the student should be maintained in a special education program or partly or wholly mainstreamed in regular classes needs to be determined. In our view, the younger child with autism will benefit most from special class settings where the needed specialized resources exist. As gains are made, small mainstreaming steps into regular settings can be carefully planned, initiated, and evaluated.

Additional Therapies and Special Training Are Needed

In developing communication skills training, the expertise of language development specialists and speech therapists is essential. Some of the children who do not develop spoken language might benefit from alternative communication procedures, such as signing, sign language, and the use of keyboards. Occupational and physical therapy may be helpful in addressing specific deficits. In doing so, the parents need instruction for appropriate home monitoring and practice with their children.

Art and music therapy or instruction may also be valuable adjuncts for some persons with autism. Close student–professional interactions in these artistic areas may be particularly effective in role enhancement (see Chapter 10 for a discussion of social roles). Artistic activity can be inherently rewarding for the student, particularly if the student proves to be among the small group who have some innate ability. Given the inherently rewarding nature of the activity, the complementary roles of art/music teacher/therapist and student can be rehearsed with a minimum of friction and frustration. Again, as in other therapies, involvement of professionals in art and/or music instruction or therapy is needed. A great deal can be communicated among the participants, and the student may be able to learn the enactment of a "successful student" role. According to our role model (discussed in Chapter 9), this kind of role-enactment success may contribute positively to the student's social role development, self-identity, and positive self-evaluation. At this point, we have no objective experimental data on which to base these suggested effects. We hope such research will be carried out.

Highly Structured Programs Are Needed

To paraphrase the review by Rapin (1997), there is general agreement that the most effective programming for remediation in autism is early and intensive teaching that deals with deficits in communication and behavior, is individualized and intensive, and is carried out in highly structured teaching environments, with a high teacher-to-student ratio. The high structure is important largely because it enhances predictability. Generally, for persons with autism, life is smoothed considerably when they are able to predict what is coming next in their daily program. We see this is as being part of the need for clarity in communication that we noted earlier. When the language, the instructions, and the sequence of activities are clearly presented, the person with autism appears better able to function.

X. Prognosis and the Older Person with Autism

Autism is a lifelong condition. We have seen that there is great variability among autistic persons whose cognitive levels and functional adjustment range from severe and profound retardation to significant academic and personal success. Some 75 percent of persons with autism are within the MR range (at least according to our current information and concepts). A small proportion function at above average and superior intellectual levels. Whatever the cognitive level or lifelong adjustment may be, the triad of autistic characteristics remains, to varying degrees of severity, in virtually all cases.

Children who are diagnosed as autistic will remain autistic. The older person with autism continues the autistic functioning that was displayed as a child, but generally with less of the earlier bizarre intensities (Howlin, 1996). Improvement with age is closely related to the person's cognitive ability and language development. Those with severe to profound cognitive deficits will show little improvement and will require lifelong care. The approximately 20 to 30 percent with average and higher intelligence typically improve to some degree, and the few who are high functioning may achieve complete independence, including high academic achievement. For the majority, an estimated 75 percent, autism remains a lifelong, severe disability, requiring residential care in sheltered settings (Baron-Cohen & Bolton, 1993). In general, the degree and quality of language development in the children by about age 5 or 6 are good predictors of adult functioning.

In puberty and adolescence, people with autism experience the same physical changes as do other young persons, and sexual feelings and interests become new issues for them. We have little information on particular problems of autistic persons around sexual issues. It is assumed that because of their disabilities, they are more prone to inappropriate sexual behavior such as public masturbation and becoming victims of sexual exploitation than are other youngsters. Programs for these youth should therefore include teaching appropriate sexual behavior and prudent awareness of possible exploitation.

Some higher-functioning autistic adults have been able to function in group homes and even to maintain paid employment. A few with exceptionally high cognitive and language abilities (those with AS) have completed college and even graduate studies, earning advanced degrees and functioning as professional persons. However, even in the best of adjustments, the higher-functioning person still retains some of the social problems, a restricted range of interests, and some noticeably stereotyped, rigid behavior. Some who have achieved at high levels have written about their experiences growing up as a person with autism (e.g., Grandin, 1992a, b; 1995a, b; Grandin & Scariano, 1986; McDonnell, 1993).

Cohen (1998) discusses anecdotal case reports of apparently recovered autistic persons. Some achieved high academic success, and some married and raised children. "Recovery" is not equated with "cure," as there are residuals of autistic characteristics, even in the most successful cases. What causes improvement in each case is not clear, and different people attribute the changes to different types of therapy. This suggests that there is so much variability among persons with autism that any given approach may be useful for some, and perhaps even for many, but not necessarily useful for all. This reinforces the admonition to view each person as an individual. Thus, in addition to using generalized approaches that may be effective for many people, we must tailor specific approaches to each person's needs. Services should proceed, then, on a "best fit" of person, needs, and approaches.

XI. Some Comments on History

This chapter will end with some comments drawn from my clinical experiences with autistic children and their families. Beginning in 1961, when there were few guidelines, we developed treatment, training, and educational approaches to autistic children (Graziano, 1963, 1967, 1969, 1974; Graziano & Kean, 1968). The following discussion has been shaped by our observations during those early years. Others might have different views of that time.

In 1943, Kanner described autistic children as persisting in socially aloof, stereotyped, repetitive, and often bizarre behavior, including sometimes violent, uncontrollable outbursts. He suggested these children had been born with an innate inability to form normal biologically based emotional contact with other people. This deficit was inborn,

Kanner (1943) speculated, much like other children who are born with innate handicaps. Kanner also described the parents as being overly formal and intellectual, cold and aloof. "Autistic disturbance of affective content" was Kanner's label for the disorder, and the term, *infantile autism* became commonly used.

Since Kanner's description, many clinicians and researchers have added information about autism, and the more we learned, the more puzzling it became. Clinicians began applying the label too broadly, to almost any puzzling, serious, childhood condition, and autism soon became a grab-bag label for conditions we did not understand. "Autistic" children included some with severe intellectual disabilities and some with exceptionally high intelligence; some had no language, others had limited distorted language, and some had high-level, albeit still distorted, language. Some of the children were physically well-formed, with beautiful countenances and well-coordinated movements, but others had distorted features and clumsy, stilted, and even bizarre grimaces, gestures, and peculiar trunk movements and gait. Many children showed autistic features very early (with hindsight, virtually from birth), thus suggesting prenatal etiologies. Others, however, did not exhibit autistic functioning until after 3 or more years of what appeared to be normal development, leading some to speculate about psychological causes in early infancy. Autism was variously thought to be a type of schizophrenia or other psychosis, a form of mental retardation, possibly a neurological impairment and/or brain damage. It was thought to be genetically transmitted or, conversely, psychologically determined (i.e., a psychogenic disorder). Some thought there were whole, complete, even intellectually superior children "locked inside" impervious psychological "shells," just waiting to get out. Others saw only children with severe cognitive disabilities.

For many years, even into the 1970s, there were virtually no public school and few private school programs for autistic children and little confidence that these children could be educated even if programs were made available. Parents had virtually no support groups and very few professionals or programs to turn to for information, child education, and treatment. They were emotionally buffeted by conflicting professional and nonprofessional claims, frustrated by indifferent public officials, and left alone with all of the responsibility but little guidance. Parents complained that if one had never tried to raise an autistic child, then one could not fully appreciate the problems—and they were right!

Parents under such intense strain were easy prey to their own despairing need for answers and the often blind-alley enthusiasms of well-meaning professionals. They avidly sought and often tried to adopt subjective biographical reports by other parents who claimed to have found one or another "key" to autism and to have "brought out" and "cured" their own child. Misdirection was common but unintentional. It was born of frustration, of the conflicting pictures presented by the children, of insufficient knowledge, of strong needs to believe that progress can be made, and too often, of professionals' rigid adherence to old "certainties" that had not yet been recognized as being inappropriate for these children. An early example discussed by Graziano (1967, 1969, 1974) was the now discarded belief that long-term psychoanalytic therapy for the child and parent (primarily the mother) was the treatment of choice. These professionals applied concepts that were familiar to them, but like everyone else in those early years, they operated from an unfortunate combination of little knowledge about these children and adherence to familiar but inappropriate treatment concepts that had seemed useful in the past for other problems.

Several erroneous ideas became commonly accepted in the years from the 1950s through the 1980s, as parents and professionals cast about for answers. These ideas had significant and, too often, negative effects on some parents. They constitute a set of solidly persistent false beliefs about the nature of autism, its etiology, and its treatment. Following are a few of the main erroneous ideas that we encountered at the time.

There was general agreement that, at least on a descriptive level, autism involves an emotional/developmental disorder in which the child's "self" or ego fails to develop properly, making the child incapable of relating warmly to other people and disturbing virtually all of the child's emotional growth. As a general descriptive statement, this may still have some value. The problem was in the inferences about the etiology of such ego deficiency, the central importance it was thought to have, and the treatment implications of those inferences. For example, this developmental failure of the child was attributed to the parents' failures, particularly the mother's. These parents were thought to be cold, aloof, rejecting people who were focused on the precision and objectivity of the material world and had little patience or skill in warm, supportive parenting. As a result, they were thought never to have developed in themselves or in the child the normal warm, emotional relationships that were thought to be necessary for healthy child development. Autism, with its characteristic lack of warm relationships, was thought to be the result. This idea arose from Kanner's (1943) early descriptions of some of the parents whom he saw as having a mechanical style of human interaction and little or no emotional warmth. In a later article, Kanner (1954) emphasized the parents' behavior as a critical factor in helping to create the child's psychopathology. The idea was further reinforced by the concept of the "frigid mother" or "schizophrenogenic mother" proposed by Despert (1951) and supported by others to help explain the etiology of schizophrenia and autism. Kanner gave power to this idea when he commented on the destructive effects of the "emotional refrigeration" to which the autistic children were subjected by their parents. The now discarded idea of the etiological power of the "cold, rejecting parent" profile became an accepted stereotype that persisted in the clinical field for many years despite Kanner's (1971) later attempts to temper the notion and to emphasize a biological model of causation.

This psychogenic etiological model was the basis for a coherent explanation, and if valid, it meant that autism is of psychogenic origin, and the treatment of choice is psychotherapy for the parents (i.e., mother) and the child. Bruno Bettelheim (1967), a noted psychoanalyst of the time, was so enamored of the "schizophrenogenic mother" concept that he went so far as to prescribe separation of the child and parent while the long psychoanalytic-based therapy was conducted, often for years. The psychogenic model was an early attempt to understand autism, but it proved not to be a productive treatment direction.

An alternative model, holding that biological deficits make up the etiology, was proposed by many (e.g., Rimland, 1964; Rutter, 1977; Wing, 1976) and has become the generally accepted current view (Rapin, 1997). The treatment implications of a biological model and the understanding of the parental role are, of course, very different from those of the psychogenic models. Most obviously, there is no "blaming" the parent.

Unfortunately, the early psychogenic model may have had some arguably destructive effects on the parents because of the explicit (and erroneous) identification of the mother's poor parenting as the major etiological factor in autism. No matter how subtly or sensitively that explanation was presented to parents, the message conveyed was clearly one of blame.

The resulting guilt and distress could then, of course, be "worked through" in the long hours of therapy prescribed for the parent. As we worked with the families in our own program beginning in 1961, one of our first goals was to dispel the implied blame that the parents had assumed from their earlier treatment experiences.

Three major metaphors were commonly employed by parents and clinicians in these early attempts to explain autism: the fortress metaphor, the picture puzzle metaphor, and the lock and key metaphor. In the fortress metaphor, mentioned earlier, the autistic child is viewed as an "intact" child who is somehow trapped within a surrounding wall of silence (the wall being the fortress). Many parents were convinced that "inside that wall" there existed an intact, functioning brain and personality. The task was somehow to "get through" to the child and to "bring out" the "real" child, to help the child "break through" the wall to express his or her "true" self. It was inferred that the child had already developed a personal identity and many cognitive and language skills but was, for unknown reasons, incapable of expressing them.

The other common metaphors employed the imagery of a picture puzzle with a piece missing. Parents and many professionals were convinced that "the puzzle of autism" would be solved by finding "the missing piece." The missing piece, of course, was the "key" (here we have the "lock and key" metaphor as discussed by Graziano, 1975b). Once the missing piece is found, and the key put into place and activated, then all else would "click together" and the child would function as a whole person. The belief in a "key" to autism is truly a romantic philosophical notion, grossly simplistic in its application to human beings. Despite a lack of supporting evidence, it persisted. Parents and many professionals were receptive to simplistic single-factor remedies (e.g., megavitamin doses, teaching language as *the* key element, establishing adaptive behaviors and even "curing" autism through systematic operant conditioning, etc.).

One of the implications of these ideas, at least for the psychodynamic adherents, was that training, education, or treatment need not be so heavily focused on teaching cognitive and behavioral skills, because the child presumably already possessed those skills but could not use or communicate them. Rather, the emphasis would best be placed on methods to find the "inner child" to enable the child's full expression of the hidden skills.

This set of ideas became a part of the general, unsystematic surround of information and misinformation, and it allowed parents and many professionals to maintain erroneous conceptions of the nature of autism. The variability among persons with autism is so great that at least one case could always be found to provide some apparent support for almost any hypothesis. Thus, as long as validation of ideas was based on naive single-case descriptions, all of the metaphors seemed to have some validity. Parents were led to believe that perhaps their children can be "cured" of autism. They also believed that the key to unlock the mystery might be near at hand and that professionals and parents should emphasize over all else "understanding the real inner child" and be less concerned with teaching new cognitive and personal skills. For many parents, these beliefs held out false hopes and led to greater disappointment than was necessary. In some cases, they served to delay or even to prevent more productive lines of inquiry and treatment. It is easy now to criticize these early ideas and their implications, but it should be realized that such beliefs arose largely from the frustrating nature of the condition and the desperate needs of the parents. Autism is a puzzling phenomenon with great variability, inconsistencies, and apparent contradictions, powerfully resistant to change, and it generates strong needs for answers. The vulnerability of parents and professionals to the allure of simple answers is understandable. We may be tempted to believe that such naiveté is restricted to that earlier time because of our lack of experience then. However, consider that 30 years later, in the mid 1990s—a generation later—a procedure called facilitated communication (FC) with autistic persons was widely and enthusiastically embraced by thousands of well-intentioned professionals and desperate parents (see Box 11.2). This phenomenon illustrates the same factors—powerful needs for simple, immediate answers to frustrating, puzzling questions, and lack of scientific sophistication, all leading to gullibility, even in trained professionals. However, compared with the earlier gullibility, this recent example of FC is inexcusable. As discussed in Box 11.2, one major factor leading to the gullibility is professionals' ignorance about experimental methodology and the nature of evidence. It appears that modern professionals in any science-based discipline should certainly know this!

The dangers of oversimplifying issues, particularly issues about treatment of autism and suggestions of actual cures, are still with us, and oversimplification still temptingly misleads many parents and professionals, as illustrated by the facilitated communication events. Howlin (1997) has identified a number of current therapies that have attracted attention but have not yet been fully validated. These include "holding" therapy, music therapy, scotopic sensitivity training (use of special eyeglasses), "auditory integration," several drug and vitamin therapies, and even "dolphin" therapy. As Howlin points out, some autistic children show improvements with age, some quite substantially, and such improvement might be mistaken as the results of particular treatment. However, although some treatments may prove to be useful for some limited goals, the best predictors for improvement in autism are the young child's cognitive and language development levels. High-functioning persons with autism, for example, can show considerable improvement with age (Piven, Harper, Palmer, & Arndt, 1996), but this is not necessarily dependent on treatment. Such observed improvements may lead to erroneous conclusions about the effectiveness of various treatments.

Most researchers now agree that highly specific, detailed teaching of the children and parents based on behavior modification principles can be effective in improving specific areas of functioning, such as social skills, emotional control, and academic achievement. But it is also true that there are now no "cures" for autism and no overall therapies that will bring about a generalized significant improvement or cure for autistic children in general.

XII. Chapter Summary

This chapter has discussed two groups of severe disabilities: pervasive developmental disabilities and autistic spectrum disorders. They involve disabilities in more than one functional area, are lifelong, and are severe. There are no known "cures" for these disorders, but a great deal can be accomplished through special education to help each person function as best as possible.

Autistic disorder is characterized by three major diagnostic characteristics: severe social isolation (aloneness, aloofness), atypical language development, and stereotyped, repetitive behavior with impaired imaginative play (preservation of sameness). Several

B O X **11.2**

Facilitated Communication: Gullibility and the Lack of Scientific Training

In the 1990s, scores of previously mute or otherwise noncommunicative autistic children and adults in the United States suddenly began to type messages on keyboards. For the first time, it seemed, autistic persons had been provided with technology in the form of electronic or mechanical keyboards that enabled them to communicate with other persons. The procedure, called *facilitated communication* (FC), originated in Australia in the 1960s and 1970s. In 1989, it was brought to the United States by Douglas Biklen (Biklen, 1990) of Syracuse University and was quickly introduced to professionals in speech therapy and special education. FC involved a professional (the facilitator) who assisted the autistic or other developmentally disabled student. This consisted of physical support, such as holding the student's hand, arm, or sleeve, and encouragement and emotional support while the student presumably typed messages on the keyboard. The facilitator tried to help the student to remain focused on the task without influencing the student's actual typing. If the student gained communicating skills, the facilitator was to fade gradually out of the process (Biklen, 1992).

An outpouring of personal messages, poetry, stories, observations, and essays were produced via FC in clear, grammatically correct, and even creative language. Success had apparently been achieved in breaking through the autistic wall of silence, revealing the "real person" who had been locked inside! The concept of autism was being radically changed as professionals now took seriously the idea that the children did not lack language but had been incapable of expressing their thoughts through the standard means of speech. Many professionals enthusiastically adopted FC and eagerly sought communication with their previously uncommunicative autistic and other students. Imagine the rapture of a parent who sees her autistic teenager, after years of silence, type "I love you, Mom!"

Through FC, some autistic children seemingly began to achieve at unexpectedly high academic levels, mastering literature, creative writing, and mathematics. They appeared to revel in their new freedom to express, finally, their own thoughts and feelings that had for all of their lives been "bottled up"! Some autistic children, on the strength of their work with FC, were moved into regular classrooms where, accompanied by their facilitators, they presumably learned normal academic material.

What helped to make this development so startling and exciting is that virtually all of the students who were suddenly communicating so smoothly and at such high levels were invariably those who had never before managed any communication remotely similar. They were nearly all persons who were at the lower levels of cognitive abilities.

More than 2000 professionals sought training in FC, became members of a newly formed professional organization, attended conferences, presented papers, and attended presentations by professionals and autistic persons. A major "breakthrough" was proclaimed, and the field of developmental disabilities was on the verge of major reconceptualizations of the nature of autism and, possibly, mental retardation.

The FC technology revived a discarded model of autism—that is, the autistic person is cognitively intact, with internal language, ideas, feelings, and cognitive abilities that, for unknown reasons, he or she cannot express to others. FC seemed to validate the idea that "getting through" to that "real person" who is "trapped inside" is the major goal of education and treatment programs. FC, if valid, was arguably the single most important development to have occurred in the entire study of autism since Kanner's early descriptions.

Those clinicians, unfortunately, had little scientific training and were convinced by the dramatic FC demonstrations. Scientists, however, were skeptical. In time, controlled research was

(continued)

BOX **11.2**   **Continued**

carried out, and FC was shown to be an artifact—a phenomenon that people so intensively wanted to believe that it beguiled and duped them into a failure to apply even the most basic scientific skepticism. In introductory research methods courses, students are taught that every experimental hypothesis about a phenomenon is but one of many alternative hypotheses. They learn that it is not sufficient only to demonstrate support for one hypothesis, perhaps one's favorite, out of all of those hypotheses, no matter how compelling the demonstrations may be. What is necessary before accepting any hypothesis as valid is to provide evidence to support the hypothesis *and to rule out alternative hypotheses* as explanations of the phenomenon. Experimental research is the process of systematically ruling out alternative hypotheses by using carefully controlled experimental methodology and arriving at valid conclusions. That, as discussed by Graziano and Raulin (2000), is the essence of an experimental research methodology that is aimed at establishing causal relationships, such as the relationship of FC to outcomes such as improved communication.

Those who so avidly embraced FC and its implications about the nature of autism had failed to rule out the alternative hypotheses. What they saw and believed is that the autistic person was producing the typed messages (that is one hypothesis). The major alternative hypothesis, of course, is that the *facilitator* produced the messages. It had been observed that in the dramatic cases of students' messages, the facilitators had not faded out of the procedures as Biklin (1992) had originally instructed. Instead, they had remained very much actively involved as facilitators. Since the facilitated messages were the products of two very closely interacting persons, the question had to be asked: Who was communicating, the student or the facilitator? A series of experiments designed to rule out one or the other hypothesis was carried out (as reviewed by Jacobson, Mulick, & Schwartz, 1995). The experiments were well-controlled *single-blind* and *double-blind* procedures that used variations of the following protocol: The facilitator and student were individually shown a series of simple pictures (a dog, a boat, a person, etc.). The student was then asked to identify the picture by typing on the keyboard with the facilitator's help. When both facilitator and student were shown the same picture, the identification was invariably correct. When only the student was shown the picture, the identification was invariably wrong. When the facilitator was shown one picture and the student a different picture, invariably the typed message identified the one seen by the facilitator. The experimental evidence was very clear. It was the second hypothesis that was supported. That is, *the facilitators and not the autistic students were producing the messages!* There had been no breakthrough; only illusion, only artifact.

Several professional organizations, including the American Psychological Association, the Academy of Child and Adolescent Psychiatry, the American Association of Mental Retardation, and the American Academy of Pediatrics developed policy statements urging the discontinuation of FC except as a research tool (American Psychiatric Association, 1994). To their credit, most of the facilitators quickly discontinued the procedure after they saw the experimental evidence. However, despite the evidence against FC, some professionals continue to maintain their allegiance to it.

How do we explain the professionals' failure? The eagerness to have some positive findings to support an optimistic model of autism was certainly a blinding factor, as it had been many years before. But here was an added problem—the failure to exercise even the most rudimentary principles of scientific research. These events certainly fault some professions for their failure to teach their members even the most basic rudiments of scientific procedure and the nature of evidence. As a result, countless professional hours were misdirected, and so many students were engaged in pointless activities instead of more productive learning. Perhaps most sadly, many parents were mislead into false hopes about their children's abilities and their future intellectual and social development.

Ideally, the lesson has been learned that it is critical for practitioners in any science-based discipline to learn and understand the nature of scientific evidence, to assess the effectiveness of their therapies, and to avoid similar occurrences in the future. Unfortunately, questionable claims are still being made for treatments for autism. One such claim is for "dolphin therapy" in which distraught and desperate parents travel to Florida or California where they are charged for immersing their children in tanks with dolphins. To date, there is no scientifically valid experimentation to support the claims.

Caution is needed, however, not to dismiss the entire procedure as having no potential value. The use of assistive technology such as keyboards by persons with developmental disabilities may have value in many cases. The specific technique, FC, may have some potential use as a teaching tool for some autistic persons and others with developmental disabilities, probably a small minority of the total group. For example, FC could be tested as a graduated teaching method for selected students. The facilitator's initially heavy supportive involvement would be gradually faded out (as Biklen originally advised) to see if the student can eventually become truly independent in keyboard use (i.e., with no facilitator involved at all). The systematic fading of heavy prompts in teaching special students is a well-tried teaching procedure. Any student who cannot eventually function independently on the keyboard must always leave the question: Who is communicating?

Further, research needs to demonstrate and validate that with some students FC leads to gains not only in specific keyboard use but also in objectively measurable language use and social functioning. Finally, criteria need to be developed for identifying the particular students who might profit from training in the use of FC. If all of those are demonstrated in well-designed, controlled studies, then a useful place for FC will have been established. What must not be done is to continue its unexamined and indiscriminate use and to allow its continuation by persons who are not equipped to evaluate it. We also need to be careful not to perpetuate the "autism-as-fortress" myth that we discussed earlier.

For an excellent review of facilitated communication, see Jacobson, J. W., Mulick, J. A., & Schwartz, A. A. (1995). A history of facilitated communication: Science, pseudo-science, and anti-science. *American Psychologist, 50*(9), 750–765.

---

additional characteristics may also be present in some cases, such as severe tantrum behavior and hyperactivity. Most children with autism are also mentally retarded. About 20 to 30 percent have average intelligence and some have very high IQs. One of the facts of autism is that it is a heterogeneous group of persons with a great deal of individual variation in intelligence, language, and social behavior. Other autistic spectrum disorders are Rett's syndrome, Asperger's syndrome, and childhood disintegrative disorder.

At this time, there is general agreement that autism's etiologies are biological in nature, causing brain disturbances in those areas that control language and social learning. Older psychogenic concepts have been virtually discarded.

KEY TERMS

Know these important terms. Check the chapter and the Glossary for their meanings. They are listed here in their approximate order of appearance in the chapter.

Autism	Aloneness	Impaired language
Aloofness	Preservation of sameness	Pronoun reversal

Mutism

Autistic triad

Pervasive developmental
 disorders

Autistic spectrum disorders

*Diagnostic and Statistical
 Manual (DSM-IV)*

Severe social isolation

Atypical language

Rett's syndrome

Childhood disintegrative disorder

Asperger's syndrome

Nonspecific pervasive
 developmental disorder

Final common pathway model

Theory of mind

Facilitated communication

SUGGESTED READING

Baron-Cohen, S., Tager-Flusberg, H., & Cohen, D. J. (1993). *Understanding other minds: Perspectives from autism.* Oxford: Oxford University Press.

Gillberg, C. (1998). Asperger syndrome and high functioning autism. *British Journal of Psychiatry, 172,* 200–209.

Grandin, T. (1995). *Thinking in pictures: And other reports from my life with autism.* New York: Doubleday.

Howlin, P. (1996). *Autism in adulthood: The way ahead.* London: Routledge.

Jacobson, J. W., Mulick, J. A., & Schwartz, A. A. (1995). A history of facilitated communication: Science, pseudo-science, and anti-science. *American Psychologist, 50*(9), 750–763.

STUDY QUESTIONS

11-1. Describe in detail the autistic triad.

11-2. What is meant by the term, *autistic spectrum disorder?*

11-3. What are some fairly common shared characteristics (in addition to the autistic triad) found in children with autism?

11-4. Explain the theory of mind hypothesis and how it applies to autism.

11-5. Explain why Rett's syndrome is found only in females.

11-6. Describe the final common pathway model as it applies to autism.

11-7. What was the appeal of facilitated communication procedure for persons with autism? What is the problem with this procedure? How might better scientific training for those professionals have helped to prevent the problems?

11-8. Describe the nature of the atypical language in children with autism.

11-9. Several studies indicate that some persons with autism have larger/heavier brains than is normal. Explain how this may have occurred in some cases.

CHAPTER

12 Seizure Disorders

I. Seizures and Epilepsy

Epilepsy is a general term that covers a variety of events involving seizure activity. A single seizure that occurs on only one occasion and is due to unusual conditions such as a head injury or high fever does not constitute epilepsy. For epilepsy to be diagnosed, the seizures must be recurrent, and the person must have had *more than one seizure on more than one occasion.* It is the repetitiveness, the chronic nature of the seizures, and the tendency to have seizures that characterize the condition of epilepsy.

Seizure refers to sudden disruption or marked change in the electrical activity of the brain and the subsequent uncontrolled effects on the body. Normally, millions of electrical charges move among brain cells and to all other areas of the body. In epilepsy, this normal condition is briefly interrupted by sudden, intense bursts of electrical energy that can temporarily disrupt motor control, consciousness, sensations, and memory. These excessive neural discharges may begin in a localized point in the brain and spread to other parts of the central nervous system where they interrupt normal brain and other central nervous system (CNS) functioning.

Prior to a seizure, a person may experience an **aura,** feelings of anxiety, unease, or discomforting sensations such as flickering lights or visual "sunbursts." Seizures range from major **convulsions** accompanied by losing consciousness and falling down to brief, invisible seizures in which the person might only blink an eye or "stare" for a moment. Following a seizure, the person may feel confusion, memory lapse, fatigue, alarm, irritation, fright, and/or anger, particularly after severe seizures. Loss of consciousness occurs in many, but not all, seizures.

Seizures can occur frequently or with long periods between occurrences. In some cases, where the cause of epilepsy is specific and known (e.g., brain damage due to a head injury or sudden exposure to a toxin), surgical or medical treatment can remove the cause and end the epilepsy. In most cases, however, cures are not possible and lifelong medication is used to control the seizures and to keep the person above the **seizure threshold,** a concept that is usefully descriptive but imprecise. It refers to each person's combination of hereditary, physiological, psychological, and environmental factors that appears to make the person more or less prone to seizures. Box 12.1 describes the types of seizures.

People sometimes misinterpret and label ordinary sensory experiences or temporary episodes of dizziness or forgetfulness as "seizures" (Gumnit, 1997). In **psychogenic seizures,** the seizures are genuine, but no abnormal brain activity is found with electroencephalogram (EEG) examinations. These have most of the appearances of **neurogenic seizures** (induced by abnormal brain activity). The inferred causes of psychogenic seizures are psychological in nature, possibly involving high stress on the person. Some persons experience both neurogenic and psychogenic seizures (Gates & Hemmes, 1990; Williams, Walczak, Berten, Nordi, & Bergtraum, 1993). In those cases, medication to control neurogenic seizures and psychological counseling to identify the precipitating stress and relieve the seizures are necessary.

Seizures can occur in anyone, given the right precipitating conditions in susceptible persons (O'Donohoe, 1994). Those include high fevers in infants and young children, head trauma such as in automobile crashes and child abuse, a sudden drop in blood sugar, loss of oxygen, extreme exertion, lack of sleep, high doses of drugs or sudden drug withdrawal, and failure to take seizure control medication as prescribed. Most people do not have seizures because they do not encounter such severe conditions and their seizure thresholds are high, which is the normal condition. Some, however, have abnormally low seizure thresholds. They are prone to multiple seizures that occur on more than one occasion. They have epilepsy.

Epilepsy is not a single condition. Rather, the term refers to a variety of conditions and etiological factors. Therefore, a more descriptive term is *the epilepsies.*

BOX **12.1**

Types of Seizures

Seizures are categorized as *partial seizures,* which occur in one specified area of the brain, and *generalized seizures,* which occur throughout the brain. A special condition, *status epilepticus,* is also recognized.

A. Partial Seizures

1. **Simple partial seizures** (formerly called Jacksonian, focal, or auras): There is no loss of consciousness. The person is aware of the seizure but is unable to control the movements. These typically involve the arms and or legs, starting at the periphery (hands, feet), and "marching" up the limb. Depending on which part of the brain is affected, there can be accompanying strong emotion such as fear, excitement, or anger and sometimes smells, tastes, or dizziness will be experienced.

2. **Complex partial seizures** (also called psychomotor or temporal lobe seizures): The person loses awareness during the seizure. Repetitive behavior may occur, such as picking at clothing, hand rubbing, or walking about apparently in a "daze." The seizure is fairly brief, perhaps 1 or 2 minutes. Recovery may take longer and the person may feel confusion, irritability, and anger. More common in adults and adolescents than in children, it accounts for nearly two-thirds of all cases of known epilepsy.

3. **Generalized partial seizures:** Partial seizures sometimes develop into a second phase of generalized tonic-clonic seizures in which the person loses consciousness, falls down, and has convulsions (see below).

B. Generalized Seizures

1. **Generalized tonic-clonic seizures** (formerly called grand mal seizures): The entire brain and body are affected, and immediate loss of consciousness occurs. There is often no warning of the coming seizure. The person becomes rigid (tonic phase), falls down, and the body alternately stiffens and relaxes (clonic phase) and has violent convulsions lasting perhaps 1 or 2 minutes. Physical injury can occur when the person falls. During recovery, there is confusion, fatigue, often headache and muscle soreness, and there is no awareness or memory of the seizure.

2. **Absence seizures** (formerly called petit mal seizures): Usually occurring in children from about 4 to 12 years of age, absence seizures are brief, sometimes lasting only a few seconds. The child is unaware of what is happening, seems to be "in a fog," staring, "daydreaming," and not paying attention. Sometimes there is rapid eye blinking, mouthing motions, or arm waving.

3. **Atonic seizures:** There is a sudden loss of muscle tone so severe that the person falls down. Injury may occur when the person falls. No tonic-clonic movements are involved (unless caused by head injury in the fall).

C. Status Epilecticus

This is a serious emergency situation usually occurring in young children. It involves seizures that continue for at least 15 to 30 minutes or more or recur at short intervals. Immediate emergency treatment is necessary.

II. Etiology of Seizures and the Epilepsies

Symptomatic and Idiopathic Epilepsy

Seizures can be caused by a number of factors operating alone or together (see Box 12.2). Many are unusual and traumatic events that can occur to anyone (e.g., high fevers, head injuries). In several studies carried out in different countries, about one-third of the cases were **symptomatic** (the etiologies are known), about two-thirds were **idiopathic** (the etiologies are unknown), and a very small proportion was not classifiable (Hauser & Hesdorffer, 1990).

Anyone can have a seizure under the right conditions, but not everyone has epilepsy. An important question not yet completely answered is: What causes some persons to have abnormally low seizure thresholds and thus to experience repeated seizures? In symptomatic epilepsy, the presumed cause is known, such as a head injury that leaves permanent

BOX **12.2**

Causes of Seizures

Head Trauma: Seizures can be stimulated by severe head blows as in automobile crashes, falls from playground equipment and bicycles, falling down stairs, intended head injuries such as in child abuse, unintended blows to the head in sports such as by baseballs, bats, golf clubs, hockey pucks, and so on.

Strokes, brain tumors, and Alzheimer's disease: In older persons, these conditions are related to later seizures and epilepsy.

Misuse of medications and other drugs: Seizures may be triggered by taking too high a dose of medications. For example, overdose of medication prescribed in treatment of asthma or overuse of amphetamines may trigger a seizure. Also, the sudden withdrawal of drugs that had been taken for a long period, including barbiturates, anticonvulsant medication, or alcohol, can trigger a seizure.

Infections and high fever: Meningitis and other illnesses with high fever can result in seizures. Those triggered by high fevers are known as febrile seizures and are most common in young children. As the children grow older, febrile seizures decrease markedly. Although febrile seizures are associated with later nonfebrile epilepsy, febrile seizures are fairly common in children and, in most cases, do not lead to epilepsy.

Environmental triggers: In some cases, a seizure can be triggered by environmental stimuli that are innocuous for most people. These include flickering and fluorescent lights, patterns of lights and movement on television and computer screens, extreme heat, and problems and conflicts that cause personal stress.

Toxins: Lead poisoning is of particular threat to children (see Chapter 6) and can trigger seizures, as can exposure to insecticides and other chemicals. Children have been known to have seizures while playing on a lawn recently sprayed with insecticides.

Emotions and Fatigue: Extreme excitement or fear, being overtired, and lacking sufficient sleep can all trigger seizures in some persons.

brain damage, and the epilepsy can be accounted for. In the majority of cases (idiopathic epilepsy), "cause" cannot be specified, but many risk factors have been identified, at least tentatively (see Box 12.3).

Prenatal and Perinatal Risk Factors

There is general agreement that both prenatal and perinatal risk factors exist. Two factors that are most predictive of later epilepsy are (a) a fetus that is small for gestational age and (b) the occurrence of neonatal seizures. Other factors have been implicated, but the supporting data are not conclusive. These include low birth weight, toxemia, **eclampsia** (maternal seizures during pregnancy), maternal hemorrhage during pregnancy, and a variety of birth complications, particularly those increasing the risks of anoxia.

Recall from our discussion of teratogens in Chapter 6 that some substances taken by the pregnant woman are associated with fetal growth retardation and with reduction of oxygen to the fetus. Tobacco is a substance that has both effects. Anoxia and fetal growth retardation are associated with epilepsy. Thus, there may be a connection between smoking in pregnancy and subsequent childhood epilepsy. This suggestion is speculative, but the pathways seem to be there, at least theoretically.

Association with Other Disabilities

Cerebral palsy (CP), mental retardation (MR), and multiple sclerosis (MS) are risk factors for epilepsy. It is generally thought that none of these conditions is a direct cause of epilepsy. However, all (CP and MS in particular) are suggestive of brain damage, which may be the effective risk factor that elevates the probability of epilepsy in children who have CP, MR, or MS (Hauser & Hesdorffer, 1990). In the case of MS, it has been suggested that the lesions that destroy myelin on the axons may be the "irritative triggers" for seizures (Kinnunin & Wilkstrom, 1986).

Seizures due to high fevers (febrile seizures) occur in about 3 percent of young children, with a peak occurrence between 9 and 20 months. They rarely occur under 6 months of age or over 5 years (O'Donohoe, 1994). **Febrile seizures** are associated with risks of later nonfebrile seizures and of epilepsy, although the degree of risk is uncertain (O'Donohoe, 1994). Children with CP and those with MR have an increased risk for febrile seizures. Therefore, both CP and MR are risk factors for epilepsy because of their association with febrile seizures and with brain damage. High fevers also accompany CNS infections such as **encephalitis** or **meningitis,** and both are associated with a high rate of seizures and epilepsy. The effects are greatest in encephalitis, although they are significant in both.

Phenylketonuria (PKU) is a disability due to hormonal disorder controlled by a recessive autosomal gene (see Chapter 4). Children with PKU or other inheritable diseases such as tuberous sclerosis and neurofibromatosis may have elevated risks of seizures (Gumnit, 1997). This is suggestive of a genetic link to some epilepsies, as will be discussed.

In older persons, seizures and epilepsy are associated with Alzheimer's disease. As in CP, MR, and MS, the apparent effective factor is brain damage, which may be due to old age or indirectly to collateral changes that occur in aging. In Alzheimer's disease, brain damage presumably elevates the risk of seizures and epilepsy. **Strokes** (occlusive cardiovascular disease) and brain tumors are also associated with seizures and epilepsy in older persons.

Genetic Risk Factors

The evidence indicates a significant genetic component in the etiologies of some epilepsies (O'Donohoe, 1994), and there is probably some genetic contribution to each person's seizure threshold (Freeman, 1995). As reviewed by Hauser and Hesdorffer (1990), studies of twins, of nontwin siblings, of offspring of parents with epilepsy, and of clusters of epilepsy in families all indicate a genetic component in some epilepsy. Among the strongest evidence are twin studies. Monozygotic twins share the same genetic makeup, while dizygotic twins share about 50 percent of their genetic makeups. Twins are the same age and, when reared together, have similar family environments. By comparing monozygotic and dizygotic twins, and assuming the environmental factors are held fairly constant, researchers have tried to estimate the contribution of genetics to epilepsy. With all types of epilepsy, the disorder is far more prevalent in monozygotic twins than in dizygotic twins, and both have higher rates than nontwin siblings or the general population of nonrelated persons.

Having a parent with epilepsy increases the epilepsy risk for children. Children whose mothers have epilepsy have a risk that is about twice as great as for children whose afflicted parent is the father (Ottman, Annegers, & Hauser, 1988). When one parent has epilepsy, the incidence in the children is about 4 percent; when both parents have epilepsy, the rate for their children rises to 10 percent (O'Donohoe, 1994). Genetic counseling is recommended for parents with epilepsy or who have at least one child with epilepsy. In addition, children with heritable diseases such as PKU have an increased risk of epilepsy. There are more than 100 single-gene disorders that are associated with the epilepsies, but these account for only about 2 percent of cases (O'Donohoe, 1994).

The epilepsies appear to result from complex interactions of genetic and environmental factors, but the details are not yet known. In most cases, neither genetic nor environmental factors alone can account for epilepsy. It appears, however, that a genetic risk factor is part of the etiological picture. Much more research is needed.

Head Trauma

Head trauma, particularly where penetration occurs, is clearly associated with the epilepsies. In adolescents and adults, head trauma occurs primarily in automobile crashes but also in work injuries and in physical attacks, including gunshot wounds. Children are particularly vulnerable to head injury in crashes, in playground and sports injuries, and in physical abuse. In the latter, infants and young children who are violently shaken by irate caregivers (**shaken baby syndrome**) may suffer permanent brain damage and have increased risks of disorders such as cerebral palsy and epilepsy.

Alcohol and Other Drugs

Definitive studies are not yet available, but some data suggest that alcohol and heroin are associated with seizures and epilepsy in adults. They might involve a sudden overdose or abrupt cessation of the drug. The latter would generate drug withdrawal distress.

BOX **12.3**

Risk Factors in Epilepsy

Prenatal and perinatal risk factors: A number of these factors have been identified, and the most clearly associated are a fetus that is small for gestational age and the occurrence of neonatal seizure.

Association with other disabilities: Conditions such as cerebral palsy, multiple sclerosis, and mental retardation, presumably because of the brain damage associated with them (particularly CP and MS), are predictive of later epilepsy. Febrile seizure in infancy and childhood is also a risk factor for epilepsy, as are inherited conditions such as phenylketonuria. In older persons, strokes and Alzheimer's disease are also associated with later seizures and epilepsy.

Genetic factors: Genetic factors operate in epilepsy, although the extent of their influence is not yet known. Family influence is seen in studies of identical and fraternal twins, siblings, and children of parents who have epilepsy.

Head trauma: Persons of all ages are susceptible to head trauma, which is associated with epilepsy. In children, head trauma occurs in automobile crashes, in playground and sports injuries, and in child abuse. For adolescents, a major cause of head trauma is automobile crashes. Adults suffer head trauma in work-related injuries and automobile crashes. Gunshot wounds in the head affect primarily adolescents and adults.

Abuse of alcohol and other drugs: The research is not yet definitive, but alcohol and drug use may be associated with some epilepsy. Presumably, this would affect primarily adults and adolescents.

III. Incidence and Prevalence of Epilepsy

The annual incidence of epilepsy for all ages ranges from 30.9 to 56.8 per 100,000, and its prevalence is estimated at 642 per 100,000 (Hauser & Hesdorffer, 1990). These estimates, applied to the U.S. population of 275 million, yield an estimated annual incidence of up to 156,200 new cases and a prevalence of 1,765,500 cases. The Epilepsy Foundation of America (1998) estimates the annual incidence to be about 125,000. Others put the prevalence at about 2 percent of the population for a total of 5.5 million cases. Shorvon (1990) estimated that 1 in 20 persons will have a seizure at some time in life, and 1 in 200 will have epilepsy. For all ages, 50 percent began under 25 years (Epilepsy Foundation of America, 1998).

The epilepsies are most frequent in children under 1 year of age, continue at a high rate up to age 4, decrease through childhood, adolescence, and adulthood, and sharply increase in persons over 50 (O'Donohoe, 1994). Half of all cases begin before the age of 25 (Epilepsy Foundation of America, 1998). Its incidence among children under 14 years is between 45.6 and 83.1 per 100,000. Its prevalence in children under age 14 is estimated to be more than 500,000 (based on Hauser & Hesdorffer, 1990). Compared with Caucasians, African and Hispanic Americans have a higher incidence and prevalence, and the differences may be due more to socioeconomic factors than to ethnicity. Epilepsy is more prevalent among males than females by a ratio of up to 3.3:1 (Hauser & Hesdorffer, 1990).

IV. Major Effects of Epilepsy on the Person

Physical Effects

Appearance. Unlike developmental disabilities such as FAS, severe MR, Prader-Willi syndrome, and cerebral palsy, there are no visible characteristic features of most persons with epilepsy until a seizure occurs. When the seizures are massive, as in generalized tonic-clonic seizures, the person might be injured during a fall or during recovery if he or she is disoriented. In severe cases, children with epilepsy must wear protective headgear and sometimes guards for face protection to avoid injury in falls during seizures.

Mortality. The mortality rate is greater for most types of epilepsy than in the general population. However, persons with absence seizures or idiopathic complex partial epilepsy do not have elevated mortality. The excess in the death rate tends to occur within 10 years of first diagnosis and affects males more than females (Hauser & Hesdorffer, 1990). Studies (e.g., Henriksen, Juul-Jensen, & Lund, 1970) indicate that persons with infrequent seizures do not have a higher mortality rate than the general population, but frequent seizures are associated with a higher rate. Unfortunately, "frequency" is not well defined in the literature. It has been suggested that death may be due to the conditions that cause epilepsy (e.g., neurological damage, severe infectious disease, etc.) rather than to the seizures (Hauser & Hesdorffer, 1990). The risks of death from accidental trauma such as head injuries and drowning are elevated in persons with epilepsy.

   Suicide is more prevalent in persons with epilepsy (Satischandra, Chandra, & Schoenberg, 1988; Stagno, 1993). The incidents seem linked to depression, and the most frequent method of suicide is overdose of seizure control medication. That medication may increase the risk of suicide. That is, common seizure control medications are barbiturates, and barbiturates can induce depression. Thus, suicide might be a response to drug induced depression. Although a greater risk of suicide has been measured in epilepsy, the causal pathways are not yet fully understood, and much more research is needed.

Injury. There are risks of injuries during and following seizures, but injuries can be minimized by careful planning. Injuries and even death can occur when the surrounding conditions pose risks for the person. It is important to know if there is any predictability in seizure occurrence: Do they occur under particular external conditions (e.g., heat, noise, etc.)? Is the person's condition a factor (e.g., stress, fatigue, lack of medication, etc.)? For example, a person who has frequent seizures must be careful when bathing because of the risk—albeit small—of drowning. Care needs to be taken to use only a small amount of water in the tub. The bathroom door should not be locked, and there should be other people nearby in case of an emergency. Persons may be injured in falls during seizures or while disoriented following a seizure. Such disorientation can cause a person to trip and fall over obstacles or even wander into dangerous situations such as heavy vehicle traffic. Children who are prone to frequent seizures should wear helmets when riding bicycles or playing sports (actually, that is a good idea for all children).

Effects on Pregnancy and Reproduction

Pregnancy, delivery, and neonatal problems are greater for women with epilepsy than for those without epilepsy. Epilepsy, particularly in men, is associated with decreased fertility as measured by live births. However, much of this increased risk may be due to factors other than the epilepsy itself. For example, conceiving and having fewer children than the general population might be due to a reduced desire by persons with epilepsy to have children rather than directly to the epilepsy (Hauser & Hesdorffer, 1990). In addition, the complications of pregnancy and birth and greater rate of birth defects may be due more to the medications given to control epilepsy during pregnancy than to the epilepsy itself.

During pregnancy, the seizure rate changes for about half of the women. Most of the changes involve more frequent seizures, and a smaller proportion shows a decrease in seizures (Hauser & Hesdorffer, 1990). Many of the seizure control drugs administered during pregnancy may have teratogenic effects resulting in minor and, in some cases, major birth defects. They may include cleft palate, neural tube defects, foot and finger anomalies, and digestive track anomalies. Researchers generally agree that teratogenesis is a problem in using antiepileptic drugs during pregnancy, that no antiepileptic drug is completely safe in pregnancy, and that great care must be taken in supervising these pregnancies. However, the details of the relationships and what other factors may be involved are not yet clear. There are potentially confounding factors, such as genetics and the mother's physical condition, that may contribute to the birth defects (Hauser & Hesdorffer, 1990), and these variables need to be controlled in future research. Despite the still equivocal nature of the research, mothers with epilepsy have two or three times the normal rate of congenital malformations in their newborns (i.e., 4 to 8 percent of births). We need to emphasize, however, that 90 percent of the pregnant women with epilepsy have normal, healthy children (Gumnit, 1997).

Psychological and Social Effects

Epilepsy, particularly when it is generalized tonic-clonic epilepsy, can have major effects on the person's social functioning and psychological well-being. The person's life may be strongly influenced by how well he or she is able to understand, accept, and control the condition. In children and adolescents, major problems of self-evaluation and fears of peer rejection can arise. For young adults, questions of friendships, romance, careers, marriage, and parenthood must be faced. It seems that the social and psychological reactions to the physical condition may be as potent in the person's life as the physical condition itself.

The question of intelligence in epilepsy is a complicated one. Most of the early studies showed that children with epilepsy had lower than normal intelligence levels. One of the problems in testing children with epilepsy is the great variability from one time to another in each child's performances on IQ tests, which is much more variable than in nonepileptic children. Thus, a single administration of a test to a child with epilepsy cannot be considered reliable in establishing that child's intellectual level. Further, there are intellectual differences between various types of epilepsy. For example **infantile spasms** are commonly associated with developmental delay and mental retardation, while absence seizures are not. In many cases of infantile spasms, developmental delay had been present before the spasms began. One inference (O'Donohoe, 1994) is that the same factors that lead to infantile spasms (and to other organic-associated epilepsy) also lead to developmental delay. Rutter, Graham, and Yule (1970) found that 28 percent of their sample of children with epilepsy also had organic brain disorder such as cerebral palsy, and the tested intellectual levels were lower than normal. However, in 72 percent of their sample, the epilepsy was not associated with organic brain disorder. That large proportion showed a normal range of intelligence, with an average IQ of 102. *The general conclusion is that most children with epilepsy have the same range of intelligence as any other sample from the general population, while the smaller proportion of epileptic children with organic disorders accounts for the lower IQ found in earlier studies.*

Despite the findings that general intelligence is not usually compromised by epilepsy, it is clear that, as a group, children with epilepsy do less well in school than do other children (Seidenberg, Beck, & Geisser, 1986). A large proportion is seen by their teachers to be inattentive, absent-minded, lethargic, and to have learning disorders and behavioral difficulties (Holdsworth and Whitmore, 1974). Academic problems are greatest in arithmetic and also occur in spelling and reading comprehension (Seidenberg et al., 1986). There are probably many reasons for these academic deficiencies. Research suggests that antiepileptic medication may cause drowsiness and inattention and, particularly when used in conjunction with other medications, may be a major factor (e.g. Brent et al., 1990). Social and psychological factors might also operate, such as an overdependence on parents (Hartlage & Green, 1972) and low expectations and negative attitudes of teachers (Holdsworth & Whitmore, 1974). In addition, there may be subtle, not yet understood organic effects of epilepsy on cognition.

Some research indicates a higher risk of psychological problems (e.g., depression, anxiety disorders, aggression) in persons with epilepsy. However, most of those studies were conducted with patients being treated for mental health problems and thus were not representative of all persons with epilepsy (Dodrill & Batzel, 1986; Trostle, Hauser, & Sharbrough, 1989). As concluded by Hermann (1991), the estimates of high risk for psychiatric disorders in epilepsy may be much inflated because of the confounded nature of the research. At this time, it has not been established that epilepsy is highly correlated with psychopathology. However, Hermann also points out that epilepsy ranges from mild to severe levels, and it would not be surprising to find that persons at the most severe end of this continuum have heightened risks of psychopathology. Continued research is needed. At the least, persons with epilepsy do have fears and anxieties about their condition.

The negative psychological and social factors in epilepsy may be effects of the medication and/or the person's psychological reactions to the complex condition rather than directly caused by the epilepsy. For example, a child with epilepsy might not achieve as well as other children academically, not because of cognitive deficit, but because of social and anxiety reactions to seizures. It is here, *with the person in the social context,* that the greatest impairments occur. The disruptive impact of epilepsy is largely social and psychological in nature, affecting how others view and behave toward that person and how he or she resolves the emotions and negative self-definitions that can be created.

When a person is diagnosed with epilepsy, the entire family is affected. If it is a child or adolescent, then not only that young person but also parents, siblings, other relatives, and friends must develop some understanding and acceptance of the condition. The general public does not understand epilepsy and harbors many misconceptions (see Box 12.4). For many persons, epilepsy has an aura of finality, dark mystery, and family catastrophe. When parents learn of their child's diagnosis, all of the questions, confusion, misinformation, and fear create powerful feelings of family devastation and even grief for their child (Livingston, 1972). In time, given good professional services and the psychological support of others, parents can gain knowledge, correct misconceptions, and begin to understand the reality of their child's condition. They can learn that epilepsy can be controlled in nearly all cases, that serious physical or other long-term disruptions need not occur, and that one can learn to manage and to live with the condition. This can reassure the parents and help them to cope with the child's condition and teach the child how to do so also.

How the parents accommodate to the condition will affect the child's ability to "live well with epilepsy" (Gumnit, 1997). If the parents become frightened and panicked at each seizure, then the child and the siblings will also respond with emotion and confusion. Through modeling and direct teaching, the parents need to help the child understand and learn how to manage the condition with effective, lifelong self-care skills. Parents' must also teach the siblings to respond effectively, without panic, to help the child when needed.

For the growing child, epilepsy becomes an important, perhaps central, factor in life as one's self-definitions, role development, and social interactions are all impacted by epilepsy. The child grows and learns more about his or her condition and becomes increasingly aware of the reactions of others, particularly the negative and distressed reactions when the seizures are witnessed. Budding friendships can be interrupted, and peer rejection can become a growing burden on the child. The child's sense of adequacy and self-esteem may be undermined, and it is not uncommon to find the children beginning to shun their peers and to become increasingly isolated.

The Epilepsy Social Role

It is important for the child to avoid developing a primary and generalized sick role (see Chapter 10). This **epilepsy social role** would be defined by negative norms developed from other persons' biases, misunderstandings, and lack of knowledge of epilepsy. These expectancy norms would be communicated as social demands for the proper "epileptic role" enactment. For our discussion, let us list some of the behavioral norms that describe a very negative epilepsy role that could conceivably develop. These norms mirror common misconceptions about epilepsy (see Boxes 12.4 and 12.5).

Box 12.5 presents an admittedly overstated epilepsy role enactment. It is probably rare for a person with epilepsy to develop such a thoroughgoing negative role and to generalize its enactment across most situations. However, to a degree that varies among individuals, aspects of this role may in fact be developed, internalized, and enacted by the growing child. To whatever degree this occurs, that person will have created self-imposed limitations on the potential richness of his or her life. If such a role were to be enacted in a widely generalized manner, it would constitute that person's dominant role enactment. Thus, by enacting this role in a generalized manner, he or she would be a person with epilepsy even

BOX **12.4**

Misconceptions about Epilepsy

Epilepsy is a mental illness: No. It is distinct from conditions such as psychiatric disorders and mental retardation.

Persons with epilepsy have lower intelligence: No. In most types of epilepsy, there is no difference in intelligence.

Persons with epilepsy cannot be employed: No. Employment prejudice does exist, but persons with epilepsy work as well as others and have no more work absences, accidents, or injuries than other people.

Persons with epilepsy have distinct facial features and look different from others: No. There are no identifying facial or other body features. In terms of appearance, persons with epilepsy are indistinguishable from the general population.

Epilepsy is hereditary in nature: There may be some genetic components, and the presence of epilepsy is a risk factor in having children. Medical and genetic counseling are recommended to prospective parents if one has epilepsy. However, epilepsy is not primarily a hereditary condition.

---

if seizure free most of the time. This person's life would be characterized by restricted role multiplicity, which leads to reduced interactions with complementary roles and to markedly restricted role resource access (see Chapter 9). It seems reasonable to assume that this role is most powerful in cases in which the epilepsy is at the most severe levels.

Although we have overstated the case, negative social roles can develop in children with epilepsy. However, if they are significantly moderated, those attitudinal and behavioral norms can actually be useful. For example, instead of a prohibition against driving, a more positively stated and useful norm could be: "I may drive an automobile as long as I know and respect the limiting conditions that apply specifically to me." Guiding children to moderate the prohibitive norms and to reduce the role's potential negative effects is a major task and responsibility of the parents and other caregivers. But not many parents, given their own distress at the diagnosis for their children, may be clearly aware of the potential stultification of this role development or have the required knowledge and skills to moderate the role (see Box 12.6).

Santilli (1993) has discussed the importance for persons with epilepsy to learn about their condition. They need to understand what epilepsy is and to recognize and avoid conditions that may trigger or otherwise increase the probability of seizures. They need to understand the importance of continuing to take medication, even when no seizures have occurred in a long time. They need to learn to recognize the possible side effects of medication, such as drowsiness, depression, and anxiety and bring them to their physician's attention. They must develop good personal problem-solving skills because, according to Santilli, failure to solve personal problems as they arise may lead to further problems and to increased stress, thus complicating the condition. Persons can learn to live well with epilepsy (Gumnit, 1997). To do so, they must have knowledge and understanding of epi-

---

B O X 12.5

Behavioral Norms That Might Be Included in a Generalized Epileptic Role

These are some of the negative self-limiting norms that a young person with epilepsy might be taught to internalize.

Do not try to be popular or become too friendly with anyone or you will be hurt when they eventually reject you.

Do not be too visible socially (e.g., do not stand out in class) because that will increase your embarrassment when you have seizures.

Do not engage in physical activity, especially organized sports.

Do not try to keep up with your friends and all of their activities.

Do not think you can drive an automobile.

Do not become too fond of persons of the opposite sex because persons with epilepsy should not marry or, if they do, should not have children.

Do not be too ambitious; people with epilepsy cannot become professionals such as doctors or lawyers. Be satisfied with whatever good job comes your way and "don't rock the boat."

Never go too far away from home, where your parents can't take care of you.

B O X 12.6

Norms That Could Be Included in a Moderated Epilepsy Social Role

A more positive and better-serving role would include the central idea, "I am a person with epilepsy. I accept that fact and therefore I must *learn* all I can to: *understand* this condition; *understand* the special problems it imposes on me; *recognize* the potential triggering events that operate for me; *become* an active participant with doctors and others in the control of the condition; *live* my life to the fullest extent, within the limitations that apply specifically to me; *recognize* that I am fully capable of achieving any academic, career, and personal goals within my abilities—just as I would if I did not have epilepsy."

---

lepsy and develop an active role within their own "treatment team" of professionals such as doctors, nurses, and pharmacists. As noted, the parents of children with epilepsy have the responsibility of teaching their children the skills necessary to maintain control over the condition and to live satisfying and successful lives.

Social Biases against Persons with Epilepsy

Persons with epilepsy are not readily identifiable except when they are experiencing a seizure. There are no physical anomalies such as facial or other deformities and no generalized language, mood, or psychological problems. Indeed, persons with epilepsy appear to be quite normal in all respects until a seizure occurs. When that happens in public, others understandably become frightened, upset, and are surprised at the suddenness and degree of change in the behavior of the person they had seen, but no longer see, as a perfectly "normal" person. People become edgy around a person who is prone to seizures, and relationships are often disrupted, hard to establish, or at least made uneasy. The suddenness and unpredictability of seizures mean that the person who enacts a normal social role might unexpectedly, at any time, be thrown into a clearly deviant role of a person with serious disability. This in turn demands a sudden switch in complementary role enactors. The person who was, a moment ago, a friend, must now assume the role of helper with much more responsibility. But most of us do not know the behavioral norms of that helper role, and as a result, we feel frustration, inadequacy, and distress in our own inability to switch roles rapidly and help the afflicted person. Such unpredictable and rapid role switches may cause a good deal of role strain (see Chapters 9 and 10) for all concerned, and make it difficult to develop and to maintain friendships. Box 12.7 lists important responses of helpers when seizures occur.

This role strain, caused perhaps by fear and poor information, may have been the basis for prejudice against persons with epilepsy. Historically, this prejudice has even been codified, institutionalized, and then played out by individuals in everyday interactions and also by society collectively through its laws and its agencies. For example, as late as 1982, it was illegal in the state of Missouri for a person with epilepsy to marry. In 1986, it was still legal in South Carolina to order the *forced sterilization* of any woman with epilepsy (Yerby, 1994). Happily, these extremely prejudicial restrictions have been lifted.

Other social biases occur in employment of persons with epilepsy, and that has only recently improved substantially. It has been estimated that employment prejudice still results in 20 to 30 percent underemployment of persons with epilepsy (Gumnit, 1994), a percentage far beyond that of the general population. (Such codified and institutionalized prejudice is also evident today in the restrictive actions taken against persons who are gay by numerous municipalities, by agencies such as the Boy Scouts, and most interesting, even by some Christian church denominations.) Although there is general agreement that employment prejudice against persons with epilepsy does exist, its importance has been questioned. For example, Hauser and Hesdorffer (1990) have argued that the research is equivocal because of the presence of so many confounding factors, and employment prejudice may be more perceived than real. In either event, persons with epilepsy are, or believe they are, discriminated against by employers.

Nearly all states restrict driver's licenses for people with epilepsy for fear they might lose consciousness while driving and cause accidents. This is a prudent position, and persons with epilepsy must be careful when deciding whether to drive and while driving. However, it appears that persons with well-controlled epilepsy have no more driving mishaps than do nonafflicted persons (Gumnit, 1997). Certainly, persons who are afflicted with alcoholism are responsible for many more driving fatalities and injuries, but they are generally not restricted by states until they are caught, after the fact, driving while intoxicated.

B O X **12.7**

Important Responses of the "Helper" When Seizures Occur

The person with epilepsy should wear a medivac alert bracelet or necklace that, if a seizure occurs, will inform others of the person's condition. When coming to the aid of a person having a seizure, one should:

1. Remain calm.
2. Remove the person's eyeglasses and loosen tight clothing.
3. Clear the immediate area of sharp or otherwise dangerous objects.
4. Not try to force anything into the person's mouth.
5. Not try to restrain the tongue—it is physically impossible for the person to "swallow the tongue."
6. Not try to restrain the person—you cannot stop the seizures and your restraint might injure the person or yourself.

After the seizure, the person will wake up and will be confused and disoriented.

1. Turn the person to one side to allow saliva to drain from the mouth.
2. Arrange for someone to remain near until the person is completely awake.
3. Do not offer the person food or drink.
4. Call 911 or the local police if:
   The person does not begin breathing within 1 minute after the seizure. Call for help and begin mouth-to-mouth resuscitation.
   The person is injured.
   The person continues to have seizures.
   The person requests an ambulance.
   The person becomes aggressive toward you and you need help.

These points have been gleaned from a number of sources, such as Gumnit's book, *Living Well with Epilepsy* (1997), New York: Demos Vermonde, pages 88–89, which has been written as a guide for the person with epilepsy (paraphrased by permission).

V. Epilepsy in Adolescence

Epilepsy is the most commonly occurring neurological disorder in adolescence (O'Donohoe, 1994). It is a condition with many etiologies and many developmental paths. Adolescence, a time of rapid changes— physically, psychologically, and socially—imposes special conditions that affect seizure activity. The myriad of changes, including altered lifestyles as the adolescent becomes more distanced from family control and more involved with peers, may trigger seizures. Lifestyle changes in adolescence include stress from longer days and less sleep, increased physical activity in athletics, emotional surges, increased sexual activity, bouts of social anxieties, dependence–independence struggles, traumatic injuries such as in automobile crashes, use of alcohol and other drugs, and so on.

Conversely, in many cases, adolescence is associated with reduction of seizure activity. For example, in most cases, the febrile seizures of infancy tend to disappear as the child grows. Some 50 percent of the absence seizures of childhood are arrested or significantly improved by adolescence, as are some other types of epilepsy (O'Donohoe, 1994). Others, such as primary tonic-clonic seizures (**grand mal**), seem to become more severe with adolescence. It has been speculated that grand mal episodes may be triggered by the adolescent's increased activity and resulting fatigue, lack of sleep, and use of alcohol or other drugs. A particular adolescent may have always had a lower seizure threshold but had never before been "challenged" and now, subject to facing the challenging environmental stimuli, experiences seizures. In other cases, absence seizures (**petit mal**) may have occurred earlier but had gone unnoticed. Adolescents have special problems with epilepsy that seem related to the seriousness of the condition and the fear of peer rejection, and as discussed earlier, a negative social role may develop, with its personally restrictive effects.

Further complicating the adolescent's coping with epilepsy are the growing relationships with the opposite sex, increased involvement in athletics, obtaining a driver's license, thinking about career choices, going away to college, and generally, trying to develop greater independence from the protective family.

In most cases, the seizures can be controlled in adolescents with medication and careful medical monitoring. However, a major problem when seizure control medications fail in adolescence appears to be the youth's failure to take the medication regularly, as prescribed (O'Donohoe, 1994). Adolescents' refusal to cooperate is also evident in the difficulty in getting them to wear identifying bracelets or necklaces. We can see why wearing such an obvious declaration of disability is not easily accepted by the adolescent.

As O'Donohoe (1994) sums up, an adolescent with epilepsy requires regular medical care and monitoring, support, encouragement, clear information about the condition, and good education or vocational training. Most important, in the framework of our social role model, the persons who enact significant complementary roles—the parents, siblings, peers, teachers, prospective employers—need to develop enlightened attitudes, expectancies, and demands about epilepsy and apply them in supportive ways to the young person.

VI. Treatment and Prevention of Epilepsy

Epilepsy is a condition that affects the entire person, biologically, psychologically, and socially. Therefore, the management of epilepsy needs to be comprehensive. The seizures, so prominent a part in the person's experience of epilepsy, do not constitute a disease. Rather, they are the expressions or symptoms of complex underlying conditions. To the person, of course, the seizures are the most evident, disruptive, and distressing aspects of the condition and often create further problems. The underlying conditions might include cerebral palsy, mental retardation, traumatic brain injury, Prader-Willi syndrome, other neurological problems, and so on. In response to the epilepsy, some children will have cognitive difficulties, academic, social, and/or behavioral problems. Few will have epilepsy alone with no additional issues that preceded or that have been created by the epilepsy. Thus, there is a range of issues to be faced by the person who has epilepsy.

Drug Therapy

The core of management of epilepsy is the control of seizures. If the seizures can be eliminated or significantly reduced with medication, then much of the person's psychological as well as physical distress can be alleviated. The major treatments are with antiepileptic medications, and their goal is to maintain the person at a physiological level that is above his or her seizure threshold. To achieve this, one needs close contact with and monitoring by physicians, as medications often need to be changed and dosages adjusted.

There are many difficulties in maintaining effective drug treatment, including the possibility of negative side effects. For example, anticonvulsant medication used in pregnancy creates problems for the mother and the fetus. When more than one drug is simultaneously applied (**polytherapy**), additional problems can be created. The toxicity of drugs increases as the dose levels and as the number of drugs used increases, serious problems of drug interactions can arise, and the presence of more than one drug makes it difficult to evaluate each drug's effectiveness and side effects (Bourgeois, 1988).

Another difficulty that commonly occurs in treating any long-term disorder is the failure to comply with the medication regimen. Some persons, on being seizure free for a long period, think that the medication is no longer necessary, and they stop taking it. Some, adolescents in particular, are prone to reject authoritative advice. Children must depend on adults (who are not always dependable) to see that the medication is properly taken. Despite these and other problems in maintaining an effective drug regimen, some 80 to 85 percent of persons with epilepsy do achieve good control over their seizures (Livingston, 1972).

Surgery

About 15 to 20 percent of persons with epilepsy do not respond well to drug therapy, and a small proportion of those persons is appropriate for surgery. The criteria for deciding who should be considered for surgery are the severity of the seizures, the lack of response to drug treatment, and the judgment that there is little chance of any spontaneous recovery in the future (O'Donohoe, 1994). For that small proportion, surgery may be indicated if the seizures have a specific focus in the brain. Most are temporal lobe seizures, and most of the surgery thus involves temporal lobe surgery. Some have their locus in other parts of the brain (frontal or parietal lobe), and the surgery is appropriately carried out in those areas. Surgical procedures have apparently achieved high success rates for full or partial remission of seizures, especially the temporal lobe surgery, with up to 70 percent of the persons becoming seizure free and up to 90 percent of persons showing improvement (Gumnit, 1997). The appropriateness and success of surgery vary with the type of epilepsy.

Surgery is appropriate for only a small minority of persons with epilepsy and, of course, is not risk free. There is some risk of death and of further damage or complications, including brain cavity hemorrhage and neural deterioration. A potential problem of temporal lobe surgery is interference with language and memory. The fears and potential psychological trauma of surgery for a child are additional problems. Consideration of surgery should be approached very carefully and in only the most intractable cases.

Psychological Treatment

There is a general and continuing need to counsel and educate children and youth with epilepsy to help them learn how best to cope with the condition. A small minority of children with epilepsy might be best taught in special school situations. There, teachers would be trained to understand and accept the child's epilepsy, to respond to their seizures without panic and with appropriate action, and to help provide the psychological support and guidance that these children need so much. Besag (1987) noted that the reasons for referral of children to special school placement include particularly severe epilepsy, the presence of other medical problems, cognitive deficits (mental retardation), behavioral and psychiatric problems, and dysfunctional families. However, *nearly all children with epilepsy alone can be taught adequately in the normal school situation* if teachers and administrators have the necessary attitudes, information, and skills regarding children with epilepsy.

In addition to the everyday natural environment support and guidance at home and school, specific psychological treatment may also be helpful. In cases of psychogenic seizures, psychological treatment, including family therapy, and behavior modification are recommended. Persons with epilepsy typically experience some degree of distress over their seizures. For some, the anxiety causes more severe psychological problems, and psychological treatment is then indicated in addition to the medical control of seizures.

Mostofsky (1993) notes that some part of seizure behavior is learned. As reviewed by Goldstein (1990) and Mostofsky (1993), such learned behavior can be significant, and psychological treatments, particularly behavior modification therapies, can be important adjuncts to the basic drug therapies.

As in all behavior modification or behavior therapy, it is necessary to carry out a detailed **functional analysis** of the person's behavior in relation to the immediate environment. This analysis focuses on each specific person and his or her own particular behavior. It specifies the behavior to be studied (in this instance, seizures and related pre- and postseizure behavior), thoughts, and emotions such as anxiety and depression. Once the behaviors have been specified (targeted), the functional analysis asks the central questions: For this particular person, under what specific conditions do the targeted behaviors occur? What are the personal, subjective, and environmental conditions that appear to lead up to, precipitate, and maintain the targeted behaviors, including seizures?

Behavioral treatment programs that derive from the analysis must be highly individualized for each specific person. For a particular person, it may be found, for example, that psychological stress is induced under certain predictable conditions, and the stress then increases the probability of seizures. The functional analysis might reveal that stimuli such as particular emotions, thoughts, sounds, smells, lights, and even temperature extremes increase the probability of a seizure. It can also show that, following a seizure, the person behaves in maladaptive ways, thus worsening his or her social relationships. Once the most important stimulus–response (S–R) relationships are identified through the functional analysis, then a large variety of behavior modification approaches can be applied to modify the S–R relationships and thus reduce some aspects of the seizures and/or reduce their negative impact. Behavioral approaches can modify the S–R relationships by eliminating maladaptive behaviors, creating and strengthening new adaptive behaviors, and by creating cognitive-behavioral self-control skills. The behavior that is studied and modified includes overt actions and the person's thoughts and emotions that are associated with the seizures.

There are three groups of behavioral approaches to epilepsy. **Operant conditioning** approaches use contingent rewards, usually in academic or social settings, to strengthen or weaken existing targeted behavior and to create new behavior. In **cognitive-behavioral self-control training,** the person learns to recognize cues for maladaptive behavior and to apply learned cognitive (thought) and other strategies to control that behavior. In **classical conditioning** approaches, specific S–R bonds are strengthened or weakened as suggested by the findings of the functional analysis. A mix of approaches can be applied, all based on the original functional analysis. Once a behavioral program is begun, there must be careful long-term monitoring of results and appropriate adjustments to the treatment program.

A comprehensive approach to long-term management combines seizure control through medication; general support, guidance, and education for the child and the family; and counseling for the minor psychological problems and for major decisions such as those involving education and career choices. For some persons, more specific psychological treatment is indicated, and behavior modification offers an array of therapeutic procedures for long-term management programs (Mostofsky, 1993). Medical control of seizures is the major and necessary central component of treatment. However, we suggest that general concern for the child's social role development and avoiding or moderating the potential "epilepsy role" is also of great importance in each case. There has not been much research on this concept, and ideally, interest and research in it will develop.

The Ketogenic Diet

About 20 percent of children with epilepsy do not respond well to drug treatment because the medication might not control the seizures and/or might have serious negative side effects. A dietary treatment, the **ketogenic diet,** has been developed for persons with hard-to-control seizures that occur several times a week. To date, it has been used almost exclusively with children and rarely with adolescents or adults.

The diet is very high in fat and low in protein and carbohydrate. It is a rigidly prescribed regimen, and the intake of calories and liquid is carefully controlled. Food must be accurately measured, such as on a gram scale, to achieve and maintain the prescribed balance of fat, protein, and carbohydrate. The four major food groups of this diet are shown in Box 12.8.

The ratio of fats to carbohydrate and protein is 3 or 5 to 1. With its high fat content (butter, oil, margarine, mayonnaise, heavy cream), the diet is not particularly palatable for most adults. Like the dietary restrictions in cases of PKU (see Chapter 3), the demands on the person to comply are heavy and often troublesome. The ketogenic diet demands special and detailed preparation of the food and very careful monitoring.

Freeman, Kelly, and Freeman (1996) have applied the diet for many years at Johns Hopkins Medical Center, and they report improvement in seizures in nearly 75 percent of the children, including 20 percent who reach complete cessation of seizures. After 2 years on this rigid diet, many of the children can return to a more normal diet, and they reportedly

---

BOX **12.8**

The Four Basic Food Groups of the Ketogenic Diet

Meat, fish, poultry, eggs, or cheese (for protein)

Fruits or vegetables (for carbohydrate)

Butter, oil, margarine, or mayonnaise (for fat)

Heavy whipping cream (for protein/carbohydrate/fat)

From: Freeman, J. M., Kelly, M. T., & Freeman, J. B. (1996). *The epilepsy diet treatment: An introduction to the ketogenic diet.* New York: Demos Vermande, page 35.

---

maintain their seizure control. These results are remarkable when we consider that the children treated are those who were the most difficult to treat with medication.

The mechanisms that make the diet effective are not yet known. In essence, it is an empirically supported approach that currently has no coherent explanatory theory. Despite the theoretical lack, it is thought that its effectiveness may be based on three factors associated with dietary fasting: (a) ketosis, (b) acidosis, and (c) restriction of water intake.

According to Freeman et al. (1996), it has long been known that seizure activity decreases during dietary fasting. However, abstinence from food cannot be maintained for more than a few days. The ketogenic diet essentially mimics the effects of fasting, while making it possible to maintain the diet for long periods without nutritional harm.

Ketones, acidic organic compounds found in blood and urine, result from the body's incomplete burning of fats. The accumulation of ketones has mildly sedating and appetite-suppressing effects. High levels of their presence in blood and urine and the sedative effects constitute a condition of *ketosis.*

Acidosis is the accumulation of higher than normal levels of acid in the blood and other tissues (i.e., an abnormal reduction of alkalinity). The accumulation of ketones contributes to acidosis. Acidosis is known to raise the threshold for seizures. It is believed that the interactions of ketosis, acidosis, and liquid restriction affect metabolism in as yet unknown ways and result in raising the seizure threshold.

Prevention of Epilepsy

There have been no remarkable campaigns for the prevention of epilepsy. Consistent with the three levels of prevention that will be discussed in Chapter 16 (primary, secondary, and tertiary prevention), prevention can be conceptualized as follows (M. H. Thomas, 1973):

    An etiological focus to prevent the onset of seizures

    Monitoring and treatment to prevent the recurrence of seizures

    Monitoring, education, and treatment to prevent the negative consequences of epilepsy

At the primary level of prevention, research would focus on discovering and modifying genetic contributions to epilepsy and on correcting conditions that are risk factors for epilepsy. The latter would include attempts to reduce brain damage during birth and in childhood and adolescence, to improve the nutrition of pregnant women and of infants and children, and to reduce the incidence of infectious diseases, particularly those such as meningitis which involve the central nervous system.

At the secondary and tertiary levels, close monitoring of children with epilepsy by health and education professionals is needed. Appropriate educational supports and medical and psychological treatments need to be available. General public education about epilepsy is also important not only to provide information but also to try and offset the generally held negative attitudes toward and fears about persons with epilepsy.

What has been described is not a systematic epilepsy-prevention program, but they are general points to focus such programs were they to be initiated. Most of these points address issues of general good health. Thus, whatever government, health, educational, and social agencies can do to enhance the general health of pregnant women, infants, children, and adolescents will be useful in preventing many problems, including epilepsy. Perhaps at some future time, specific epilepsy-prevention programs will be planned and set into motion.

VII. Prognosis in Epilepsy

Overall, there is a generally positive prognosis for persons with epilepsy. In his extensive review, Donohoe (1994) comments on how unfortunate it is that this positive outlook is not more generally discussed, particularly by pediatricians when they counsel parents of children with epilepsy. As disruptive and dire as the condition might appear, studies show complete control of seizures in 60 percent of cases over a 35-year period and significant reduction in frequency and/or severity in another 25 percent of cases (Livingston, 1972). The remaining 15 percent were not responsive to the treatments then available. We assume, although we have not found recent data on this, that the resistant 15 percent have been decreased over the three decades since Livingston's review. The resistant cases appear to be those in which seizures began early (prior to age 2), where other neurological or mental disabilities prevailed since birth, where there were difficulties controlling the seizures early in the case, and where the seizures were predominantly of the complex partial seizure type.

This is not to suggest that the psychological effects of epilepsy are light. Rather, we want to emphasize that seizures can be effectively controlled in the majority of cases, 85 percent or perhaps more. These persons can lead quite normal lives provided they understand their conditions and take active, positive roles in their own control of the seizures.

VIII. Chapter Summary

The epilepsies are chronic conditions of repeated seizures. Anyone can have seizures under conditions that exceed each person's seizure threshold. Some persons have lower thresholds than most, and they are prone to epilepsy. The concept of seizure threshold is not a precise term. It is descriptive and refers to the person's particular combination of genetic, physical, psychological, and environmental characteristics that account for the seizure threshold, making that person more or less prone to seizures.

Seizures can be symptomatic (the etiologies are known) or idiopathic (the etiologies are not identified). They may be frequent or rare and can range from absence seizures (petit mal) to generalized tonic-clonic seizures (grand mal) in which the person loses consciousness, falls down, and has clearly visible seizures. Injury from falls or other accidents can occur during and following a seizure.

In most cases (up to about 85 percent) seizures can be well controlled by medication, and the prognosis for a healthy and successful life within the ability limits of the person is quite positive. In all cases, personal issues of self-definition and academic and career planning can be impacted and must be worked with. In many cases, ancillary psychological treatment is indicated, and the most promising approaches are behavior therapy and cognitive-behavior modification. It is generally accepted that comprehensive treatment programs are indicated.

Surgery may be indicated for a small proportion of the 15 to 20 percent of persons with epilepsy who do not improve with drugs. Surgery has resulted in good success rates, depending largely on the type of epilepsy, but it has risks and must be approached with great caution.

The ketogenic diet has been effectively used with children whose seizures are not controlled by medication. Clinical data indicate that up to 70 to 75 percent of these children show improvement, including about 20 percent who have a complete cessation of seizures.

The social and psychological stresses of epilepsy create challenges and personal difficulties. We have suggested that among the most important issues may be the potential development of a negative and self-stultifying "epilepsy social role." The parents of a child with epilepsy have a heavy responsibility to support their children, to provide good medical treatment for seizure control, and to help the children develop healthy views of their conditions and to learn to moderate the negative social role. This parental responsibility includes understanding all they can about epilepsy, knowing how to use their medications to control seizures, and operating on the belief that persons with epilepsy can accomplish any reasonable personal, academic, or career goals they may set for themselves.

K E Y   T E R M S

Know these important terms. Check the chapter and the Glossary for their meanings.
They are listed here in the approximate order of their appearance in the chapter.

Epilepsy	Generalized partial	Seizure threshold
Seizure	Generalized tonic-clonic	Symptomatic epilepsy
Convulsions	Absence	Idiopathic epilepsy
Aura	Atonic	Eclampsia
Types of seizures	Status epilepticus	Febrile seizures
Simple partial	Psychogenic seizures	Encephalitis
Complex partial	Neurogenic seizures	Meningitis

Stroke
Shaken baby syndrome
Infantile spasms
Epilepsy social role
Role strain
Grand mal seizures
Petit mal seizures

Ketosis
Ketones
Acidosis
Polytherapy
Behavior modification
Behavior therapy
Functional analysis

Operant conditioning
Cognitive-behavioral self-control
  training
Classical conditioning
Ketogenic diet

SUGGESTED READING

Gumnit, R. J. (1997). *Living well with epilepsy* (2nd ed.). New York: Demos Vermonde. This is an excellent book filled with practical information for persons who have epilepsy or who have family members with epilepsy.

O'Donohoe, N. V. (1994). *Epilepsies of childhood* (3rd ed.). Cambridge, England: Butterworth/Heineman.

STUDY QUESTIONS

12-1. Compare the concepts of neurogenic and psychogenic seizures.

12-2. Explain the nature of the ketogenic diet and the bases on which it is thought to work.

12-3. Explain: Anyone can have seizures but not everyone has epilepsy.

12-4. What are the prenatal and neonatal risk factors for eventual epilepsy?

12-5. What are the major postnatal risk factors for epilepsy?

12-6. What should you do to aid a person who is having a seizure?

12-7. What are some of the problems in seizure management that are associated particularly with adolescents?

13 Cerebral Palsy

There are several disorders of childhood that are grouped under the label the **cerebral palsies,** which are a heterogeneous collection of conditions that involve motor control problems. Brain damage that occurs prior to or during birth or in the child's first 4 years (Copeland & Kimmel, 1989) causes serious problems in the child's ability to control body movements. Although it is a chronic, lifelong condition, cerebral palsy is a **nonprogressive disorder;** that is, the neurological or brain damage occurs just once (Pellegrino & Dormans, 1998) and does not worsen over time such as it does in muscular dystrophy, cystic fibrosis, Parkinson's, or Tay-Sachs disease. The brain damage is not progressive, but the person's overall functioning can worsen significantly if appropriate treatment or programming is not maintained or if additional severe illness or injury occur. As will be discussed later, these problems can also interact with aging to create a deterioration of function over time.

The cerebral palsies involve movement disorder, and the severity varies from one person to another. Some children display only minor difficulties in fine motor control such as in drawing or writing. Others are unable to walk or control gross body motions. Some have uncontrolled writhing hand motions, and some have severely impaired speech. Many are ambulatory and pursue quite normal lives, although with difficulty. Others use wheelchairs for mobility and are dependent on caregivers. Persons with cerebral palsy can be diagnostically described on several dimensions, including the severity of the impairment (mild, moderate, severe), the particular muscle groups that are involved, and the specific functional problems that result. In addition, there are differences in age, gender, socioeconomic class, and in some, the presence of other illness or disability. With such variability, we can see that two persons, even if they have the same type of cerebral palsy, can present very different clinical pictures and require very different treatment/training programs. As we have emphasized throughout this book, each person is an individual despite common diagnostic labels, and it is essential to develop detailed person-specific programs.

The most severe cases of cerebral palsy are completely dependent on others for their care and on *assistive technology devices* such as wheelchairs and letter boards. In most cases, the disability is apparent, and the person is easily identifiable as a person with disabilities.

The prevalence of cerebral palsies in the United States is approximately 500,000 persons of all ages. Its incidence is about 1 per 1000 newborns, or about 4000 new cases each year (Turk, Overeynder, & Janicki, 1995). Some believe its prevalence may have increased slightly since about 1970 because more preterm babies are surviving, and they have increased risks for disorders including cerebral palsy (NINDS, 1999). Pharaoh, Platt, and Cook (1996) suggest there is a changing epidemiological pattern of cerebral palsy. They found that the rate of cerebral palsy among normal-weight births in England remained the same, but it increased considerably for low-birth-weight babies (LBW). In the 1980s, LBW accounted for more than 50 percent of all new cases, and this has changed the relative contributions of LBW and normal-weight babies.

I. Diagnosing Cerebral Palsy

Cerebral palsy (CP) is typically diagnosed in the first 2 years of life and almost always by about age 4. Early diagnosis, however, can be problematic because many of the early diagnosed children will no longer meet the CP criteria by the time they reach age 7 (Dormans & Pellegrino, 1998). However, many of those children who seem to "outgrow" the early signs appear to have other neurodevelopmental problems. Thus, the early signs of CP are also suggestive of later non-CP neurological problems.

The CP diagnosis is based on the three major aspects of its definition. Cerebral palsy:

1. is a syndrome of *motor* impairment, with *posture* and *movement* disorder
2. results from brain abnormalities early in life (prenatal, perinatal, or in the first few postnatal years)
3. is a nonprogressive disorder

Early events such as premature birth, problems during birth that might interrupt oxygen flow to the baby, the use of instruments in birth such as forceps that might cause brain damage, and the presence of jaundice at birth are risk factors for later cerebral palsy. They are not highly predictive of cerebral palsy, but their presence should alert pediatricians and parents to maintain close monitoring of the baby's progress. Typically, parents note that their child seems not to be progressing normally—there may be developmental delays, observed muscular weakness and/or rigidity, and so on. As the baby grows older, these and other motor problems become more apparent. When brought to professional attention, the diagnosis of cerebral palsy is eventually made. It is important first to rule out the possibility that the condition may be a progressive (degenerative neurological) disorder. When that has been ruled out, the examinations focus on identifying the type and degree of motor disabilities.

After the diagnosis is made, continued observation, monitoring, and examination must be carried out to determine the type and extent of the motor disabilities. The cerebral palsy diagnosis is made on the basis of motor dysfunction and nonprogressive brain damage. However, these children often have sensory and cognitive deficits as well as major motor deficits (Burstein, Wright-Dreschel, & Wood, 1998). Therefore, it is important to examine for other disorders (e.g., seizures, mental retardation, hearing loss, etc.). Those are not part of the CP definition but are important factors in the child's development and function, and they have significant implications for treatment, education, and management.

As the child grows, the motor disabilities become more apparent, and patterns of developmental delays and motor disabilities appear. Evaluation focuses on what parts of the body are affected and how severely. How much are the normal developmental motor skills interfered with such as reflexes, reaching and grasping, rolling, sitting, creeping, crawling, walking, and so on? Are there motor problems with feeding (sucking, chewing, swallowing, etc.)? Is the motor development necessary for vocalizing, language, and communication skills interfered with?

For each child, a developmental and functional profile needs to be developed. This profile will indicate the type of cerebral palsy (areas of the body that are involved and the degree and type of impairment) and will identify the related functional limitations. Those include the types and degree of the child's handicaps in meeting normal age-appropriate demands such as walking, communicating, and self-care. That information needs to be kept up to date and is important in the management plans for treatment and education.

II. Types of Movement Disorders

The conditions that make up the cerebral palsies are categorized in five groups of movement disorders.

Spastic Cerebral Palsy

Spastic cerebral palsy affects about 70 to 80 percent of persons with cerebral palsy. It is a condition in which muscles are stiff and permanently contracted in a state of continual high muscle tone (**hypertonicity**) so the person has poor control over the use of limbs. Walking, reaching, even sitting may be affected. The spasticity may be of various degrees of severity and can affect different limbs in different people. In some persons, it is a persistent tremor in one area of the body. In others, when both legs are affected with spasticity, a characteristic walk called the **scissors gait** occurs. The legs are stiff, and they turn in drastically at the knees, sometimes crossing each other, resulting in the scissors gait.

Athetoid Cerebral Palsy

About 10 to 20 percent of all persons with cerebral palsy are affected by this type, which is also called **dyskinetic cerebral palsy.** There are continuous, uncontrolled, slow, writhing movements of the legs, feet, hands, arms, and in some, of facial muscles including the tongue. There may be uncontrolled facial grimacing and drooling and a condition called **dysarthria** (severe speech difficulties) as the person cannot easily control the muscles needed for speech. Hearing impairment is also common in this group (Turk et al., 1995). Most persons with **athetoid cerebral palsy** are ambulatory, although they move with difficulty. In this group, as in all cerebral palsies, self-care is a problem. The person does not have the flexibility and control for all of the small acts of personal self-care that most persons take for granted. For example, brushing one's teeth, putting on a pair of socks, or using bathroom facilities is not easily accomplished if one's arms or fingers are severely spastic.

Ataxic Cerebral Palsy

Ataxic cerebral palsy is rare, affecting about 5 to 10 percent of persons with cerebral palsy. Balance, depth perception, and fine motor coordination are affected. There is unsteadiness and difficulty in walking, and the person characteristically places the feet wide apart and proceeds unsteadily. Sudden, rapid, or fine movements are problematic, so the person will have difficulty in sudden changes of direction or in trying to write, button, or tie a lace. **Intention tremors** may occur in which a voluntary movement, such as reaching for an object, can stimulate trembling that worsens as the person continues trying to reach.

Hypotonic Cerebral Palsy

Hypotonia refers to weak, flaccid, "floppy" muscle tone and is rare in cerebral palsy. When present in infants, it may be a precursor to later more common spastic and athetoid forms (Turk et al., 1995). In hypotonia, the muscles are weak and the person has great difficulty moving against any resistance, including gravity, making control over limbs and locomotion very difficult.

Mixed Types of Cerebral Palsy

Frequently, there is a mix of the types, most commonly with both spasticity and athetoid characteristics. Although more than one type is present, typically one will predominate. Cerebral palsy is identified diagnostically by the type of movement disorder (spastic, athetoid, etc.) and the particular muscle groups affected. For example, **hemiplegia** (half-paralysis) is a condition in which one whole side of the body is involved. Box 13.1 summarizes the descriptive terms used for the muscle groups that are involved.

BOX 13.1

**Terms Used to Describe the Muscle Groups
Involved in Cerebral Palsy**

> **Monoplegia:** One limb (arm or leg) is affected. This is rare in cerebral palsy.
>
> **Hemiplegia:** One side of the body, including one arm and one leg, is involved.
>
> **Triplegia:** Three limbs are affected. This usually includes both legs and one arm.
>
> **Paraplegia:** The legs only are affected. This is a rare condition in cerebral palsy.
>
> **Diplegia:** Both arms and both legs are affected.
>
> **Quadriplegia:** The entire body—both arms, both legs, and the trunk—is affected.

III. Etiologies of Cerebral Palsy

Cerebral palsy has many forms and the etiologies are varied. Most cerebral palsy is congenital, although (a) the condition may not be detected for many months after birth and (b) in most cases the particular causes are not known (NINDS, 1999). It is thought that 75 to 90 percent of cerebral palsies begin prior to or during delivery (**congenital cerebral palsy**) and 10 to 25 percent after birth, usually during infancy (**acquired cerebral palsy**) (Noetzel & Miller, 1998). In the following sections, some of the known causes and risk factors are discussed.

Prenatal Events

Events that can cause brain damage in the developing fetus or during birth can be causes of congenital cerebral palsy. As discussed in Chapter 6, a number of events such as maternal infections, illness, drugs, and toxic substances can have teratogenic effects and compromise the nervous system of the developing child. Infections during pregnancy that can cause damage to the motor centers of the fetal brain and are associated with later cerebral palsy are rubella, cytomegalovirus (viral infections), and toxoplasmosis (NINDS, 1999).

Rh incompatibility (see Chapter 6) can destroy blood cells in a short time and result in the buildup of bile pigments in the blood. These are normally found in small amounts in the bloodstream, but in this condition, they increase to toxic levels. The abnormal buildup of these yellow pigments can result in **jaundice.** When severe and untreated, jaundice in the infant can damage brain cells and, thus, possibly cause cerebral palsy. Jaundice in infants can be caused by other conditions, too, with the same potential for brain cell damage.

Additional maternal factors that are associated with an elevated risk of cerebral palsy include maternal hyperthyroidism, epilepsy, or mental retardation; maternal vaginal bleeding in the 6th to 9th month of pregnancy; and severe **proteinuria** (excess protein in the mother's urine). Premature birth and low birth weight are other major risk factors in cerebral palsy (Bhushan, Paneth, & Kieley, 1993; Hack, Klein, & Taylor, 1995) in a third or more of the cases (Scherzer & Tscharnuter, 1990). Children born too soon and/or too small are less developed than full-term or normal-weight babies (see Chapter 7). They are more prone to cerebral hemorrhages and breathing difficulties and therefore to anoxia and potential brain damage. They also tend to have feeding problems that will affect their general health.

Problems during Delivery

Oxygen deprivation in body tissues (**hypoxia**), if severe and prolonged so as to cause permanent tissue damage (**anoxia,**) can be a general cause of brain damage and of eventual cerebral palsy. Long delays in labor and delivery, precipitous birth, and breech presentations (see Chapter 7) can interfere with the normal oxygen supply and cause damage to brain cells. Severe squeezing of the still-malleable skull in rapid or precipitous birth may cause many small hemorrhages, and the use of instruments (e.g., forceps) during delivery may depress the skull and damage the brain. Such hemorrhaging and brain damage can result in later cerebral palsy in the infant.

In some cases, **asphyxia,** tissue damage from oxygen deficiency that is due to the interruption or lack of breathing, such as in **newborn respiratory distress,** may occur. If it is severe and prolonged, asphyxia may result in brain damage that is a type of **encephalopathy.** A high proportion of babies with encephalopathy die, and many others may develop cerebral palsy, seizure disorders, and mental retardation.

Asphyxia can result if the umbilical cord is wrapped around the baby's neck, and if prolonged, the lack of oxygen can affect brain cells. Preterm birth and low birth weight (see Chapter 7) are implicated in brain damage leading to cerebral palsy. When the newborn is underdeveloped, such as in those conditions, the baby is at risk for asphyxia because there may not be sufficient development of lung function for normal breathing to occur.

When asphyxia occurs during birth, it is usually of brief duration because of the rapid and effective responses of the obstetrical team. Few of the babies who experience asphyxia during birth develop encephalopathy, cerebral palsy, or other neurological disorders (NINDS, 1999). Only up to 13 percent of congenital cerebral palsy results from asphyxia and other birth complications. Most or all of the rest are due to prenatal causes.

Postnatal Events

About 10 to 26 percent of children with cerebral palsy acquire the disorder early in infancy or childhood (Noetzel & Miller, 1998) from brain injury or illness. Among the causes are brain infections such as viral encephalitis and bacterial meningitis. The infection and perhaps the accompanying fever can cause brain damage, leading to cerebral palsy and seizure disorders. Other illnesses such as stroke can occur to children, although stroke is most often associated with old age. In strokes, abnormal blood cells or clogged or broken blood vessels can cause bleeding in the brain and subsequent damage to brain cells. Some children suffer stroke even prior to birth. Prenatal or postnatal strokes can result in cerebral palsy.

Unintentional head injuries such as in automobile crashes and playground falls are also postnatal causes. **Intentional injuries** to children (i.e., child abuse) result in the investigation of more than 3 million children a year and leave an estimated 18,000 children per year with "serious disabilities" (NCCAN, 1995) such as mental retardation and/or permanent sensorimotor disabilities (Baledarian, 1991a). Many of those children, according to Diamond and Jaudes (1983), develop cerebral palsy. One form of abuse, the violent shaking of a baby, can cause serious brain damage. As the head and neck are whipped around, the brain is repeatedly slammed violently against the inside of the baby's skull, causing brain damage (**shaken baby syndrome**). Damage from the physical battering of the brain, plus the additional damage from hemorrhages that can occur, can result in cerebral palsy. Older children, too, are put at similar risk when they are violently shaken by irate caregivers, including teachers. Recently, the shaken baby syndrome has received so much public attention that there is no longer any valid defense of ignorance about the consequences, and such horrendously vicious behavior toward children cannot be tolerated.

Additional risk factors for brain damage and cerebral palsy include signs of nervous system malformations. Microcephaly, for example, suggests that the baby's brain has not developed sufficiently. Other factors include neonatal seizures and multiple births. The latter increase the chances that one or more of the babies will not have developed fully.

Prevention

Usually, the causes of CP are not known, and therefore, primary prevention programs to reduce CP are not common. However, it is prudent to provide good prenatal care and nutrition and to maintain well-trained and alert obstetrical teams. For example, when jaundice is diagnosed at birth, **phototherapy** can be immediately applied. This involves the use of special blue-toned lights. These result in the breakdown of the bile pigments, preventing their accumulation and thus reducing their potential for causing damage to brain cells. Sensitivity to the known risk factors is critical. Reduction of child abuse and the increased general use of automobile child restraints and child bicycle helmets will help. Vaccinations against rubella, the timely treatment for Rh-negative mothers, and reducing drug addiction in pregnancy (alcohol, nicotine, and illicit drugs) are important in preventing or reducing the occurrence of brain damage and cerebral palsy.

IV. Associated Disorders

Any disorder involving brain impairment can increase major risks of other problems, particularly cognitive and neurological problems. There is an association of the severity of cerebral palsy and intellectual deficit, and children with spastic quadriplegia have a higher rate of mental impairment than do children with other forms of cerebral palsy. However, some persons with cerebral palsy have no additional disorders except for the secondary problems, such as eating problems and poor nutrition that stem from disabled motor control. For example, while about two-thirds of persons with cerebral palsy have some degree of mental retardation (Lipkin, 1991), one-third has normal intelligence (NINDS, 1999). Among that one-third, however, specific learning disabilities are common (see Chapter 14).

A common problem among children with cerebral palsy is growth retardation or **failure to thrive syndrome.** Despite adequate care and feeding, some babies do not gain weight or develop at the normal rate. As the months go by, the parents see that the baby is not as active as expected and is not reaching the normal developmental milestones at the expected ages (i.e., developmental delay). Often, they will note the presence of *hypotonia,* or decreased muscle tone, in which the muscles are flaccid and "floppy," or **hypertonia,** in which the muscles are rigid and inflexible. These early signs lead parents to consult their doctors, and the diagnosis of cerebral palsy is usually made by the child's 4th year.

Seizures (see Chapter 12) occur in about half of the children with cerebral palsy, and about one-third develop epilepsy, most of which begins in the first 2 years of life (Aksu, 1990). Seizures may be of any type, from tonic-clonic seizures to partial simple seizures. In the most severe instances, the child will have both cerebral palsy and epilepsy (repeated seizures over time). Tonic-clonic seizures involve the loss of consciousness, twitching, convulsions, and bladder-control loss. They are followed by disorientation, fatigue, and emotional reactions such as anger, fear, and confusion. Clearly, the presence of seizures constitutes a major complication for many persons with cerebral palsy.

Sensory problems in persons with cerebral palsy are common. About 25 percent of cases have visual problems, and more than 50 percent have hearing and speech abnormalities (Scherzer & Tscharnuter, 1990). **Strabismus** is a visual problem in which the eyes are not aligned in their movements. In children, this can lead to poor eyesight in one eye as the brain adapts by ignoring the discrepant signals from that eye. In time, strabismus in children may impede the development of visual-motor coordination. Surgery to correct the differences between the controlling muscles of the eyes can correct strabismus.

The functional aspects of cerebral palsy involve problems in motor control in any motor function, not just the limbs. For example, poor bladder and bowel control is common (G. Miller & Clark, 1998). This **incontinence,** plus the person's other difficulties in motor control, causes many to depend on others for everyday care, including personal hygiene. Oral hygiene can be a problem. If it is insufficient, halitosis, gum infections and degeneration, and tooth decay can result, adding to the already complex care needed by the child. Excessive drooling can result from poor muscle control of the throat and mouth. In children, this excessive, uncontrolled drooling can have physical effects, such as continually irritated skin around the mouth, constituting uncomfortable, malodorous, and even painful conditions. There is also a social cost. The child who continuously drools and who may also be incontinent is not going to be easily accepted by other children, thus forcing more rejection and social isolation.

Poor nutrition is also common, despite the availability of sufficient food. The infant with cerebral palsy may have problems with motor control in eating, drinking, chewing, and swallowing. This increases the risk of poor nutrition, which in turn increases risks of growth retardation and vulnerability to infections. The demands of time and effort in the preparation and presentation of food several times daily can become onerous for caregivers. As seen in the list of possible problems that affect eating (Box 13.2), the difficulties in eating can arise from any single or combination of oral-related problems and can become very complex. G. Miller and Clark (1998) suggest that a professional "feeding team" (see Box 13.2) needs to include professionals who can understand and deal with the details of the various systems that may be involved.

Another serious problem, **contracture,** is a condition of shortened muscles and tendons, in which muscles become rigidly fixed in abnormal positions. It is a common lifelong complication in persons with cerebral palsy, and therapy is required to prevent or reduce it.

BOX **13.2**

**Associated Problems That Affect Eating and a List
of Professionals Needed for Management**

The following factors can contribute to the person's eating difficulties.
The child may:

be unable to maintain an upright seated posture

be unable to turn and hold steady the neck and head to receive food

have uncontrolled tongue thrusting, making feeding difficult

have an insufficient or prolonged or exaggerated bite reflex

have an abnormal gag reflex, increased or decreased

have abnormal drooling

have surplus or insufficient saliva

have problems in controlling muscles for chewing and swallowing

have an inadequate attention span or level of consciousness for feeding

Professionals comprising the "feeding team" would include:

a dietitian, gastroenterologist, nurse, psychologist, occupational therapist, speech pathologist,
speech therapist

The information in this box is based on the discussion by Lifschitz, C. H., Browning, K. K., Linge, I., McMeans,
A. R., & Turk, C. L. (1998). Feeding the child with cerebral palsy. In G. Miller & G. D. Clark (Eds.). *The cerebral
palsies: Causes, consequences, and management* (pp. 309–319). Boston: Butterworth-Heinemann.

In normal development, children are physically active. They run, jump, walk, throw balls,
roll around and wrestle on the floor, grasp objects, talk, sing and shout, chew and swallow,
and so on. Growing children use their limbs, trunk, and facial muscles in a myriad of ways
and in seemingly constant motion. Through their varied activity, children stretch all of their
muscles and tendons, and this normal stretching helps those tissues to grow at the same rate
as the bones are growing. In cerebral palsy, however, there is a significant curtailment of
this normal activity and, thus, of the normal stretching processes. As a result, muscle growth
does not keep pace with the continually lengthening bones. This contracture is an imbal-
ance in growth and can interfere not only with later motor development but can disrupt
some already learned motor skills such as grasping, reaching, and balance. Physical therapy
and the use of various braces can prevent or reduce contracture.

　　Because the functional impairments in cerebral palsy can be so severe, the child is
prevented from full exploration of the environment. This reduces the sensory, motor, per-

ceptual, and cognitive/intellectual stimulation and learning experiences that are so necessary for child development. Thus, many children with cerebral palsy may appear to have severe cognitive limitations and to have failed to develop any understanding of spoken language. Such deficits may be present, but if so, they are not due to brain damage. Rather, they may be the results of lack of experience, and much can be accomplished through special therapies and education.

Cerebral palsies are conditions of serious motor impairments with often severe associated disorders. The motor deficits have their origins in brain damage that may be localized in a single area or in more than one area. Because of the functional restrictions caused by the brain damage, the child may also suffer secondary cognitive deficits due to lack of proper stimulation and learning experiences, as well as additional physical problems. Clearly, cerebral palsies are serious multiple handicapping conditions.

V. Management of Cerebral Palsy

Comprehensive Programming

There is no cure for cerebral palsy, so all treatment must focus on the best management that is possible for each individual. As we have emphasized throughout this text, each person is a unique individual, and all planning for management programs must focus in great detail on the specific characteristics—the deficits, needs, and strengths of each individual. Medical, physical, educational, psychological, and social factors appropriate for each individual need to be studied and integrated into any person's unique management program. The programming is focused on preventing physical and functional deterioration and promoting the fullest possible participation in normal and modified life activities. This means that any management plan for a person with cerebral palsy must be a comprehensive multidimensional plan with multidisciplinary professional involvement. It is not sufficient to focus on only one or two prominent aspects such as locomotion. Rather, the psychological and social aspects must also be addressed. Cerebral palsies can be so encompassing that persons can be easily dismissed as having few or no personal assets, and others may lose sight of the person who is so often obscured by the disabilities. Some glimpses of the persons behind the veil of disabilities are available, however. Grandin (1995a, b) has written several papers and books about her experiences growing up with autism; M. Smith (1995) has written about his life with cerebral palsy, and Fries (1997) has edited a volume of nonfiction, fiction, and poetry written by and about persons with disabilities. These sources can give us some indications of the private thoughts and responses of persons with disabilities. They can also show us often graphic and startling pictures of ourselves as seen by these writers and are recommended reading for anyone working in this field.

The discussion of social roles in Chapters 9, 10, and 12 should be recalled here, and we can readily think of a dismissive, constraining **cerebral palsy social role,** a negative, deviance role. The expectancies and demands of complementary role enactors are particularly important in cases of severe motor disability because that person will be so completely dependent on caregivers. If the complementary role enactors have low or negative expectations, they will not provide the myriad role resources necessary for the person's best functioning. Although this is a nonprogressive disorder, the failure to provide necessary resources—education, therapy, training, companionship, support, assistive technology, and so on—can result in functional deterioration. That is, failing to gain skills, the person becomes increasingly incapacitated, thus actually or at least apparently deteriorating.

Once cerebral palsy has been diagnosed in an infant, an individualized, comprehensive treatment program needs to be started. This program will involve the interaction of several professions (see Box 13.3) to deal with the different dimensions of disability. It must also be guided by the unfolding developmental needs of the child. Thus, the program must be repeatedly monitored and adjusted as the child grows older.

BOX 13.3

Professions Involved in a Management Program for Persons with Cerebral Palsy

A physician, such as a pediatrician, a pediatric neurologist, or a pediatric psychiatrist, trained to help developmentally disabled children; this physician, often the leader of the team, works to synthesize the professional advice of all team members into a comprehensive treatment plan, implements treatments, and follows the patient's progress over a number of years

An orthopedist, a surgeon who specializes in treating the bones, muscles, tendons, and other parts of the body's skeletal system; an orthopedist might be called on to predict, diagnose, or treat muscle problems associated with cerebral palsy

A physical therapist, who designs and implements special exercise programs to improve movement and strength

An occupational therapist, who can help patients learn skills for day-to-day living, school, and work

A speech and language pathologist, who specializes in diagnosing and treating communication problems

A social worker, who can help patients and their families locate community assistance and education programs

A psychologist, who helps patients and their families cope with the special stresses and demands of cerebral palsy; in some cases, psychologists also oversee therapy to modify unhelpful or destructive behaviors or habits

An educator, who may play an especially important role when mental impairment or learning disabilities present a challenge to education

Reprinted, with permission, from: National Institute for Neurological Disabilities and Stroke (1999). *Cerebral Palsy—Hope through research*. National Institutes of Health. Bethesda, MD: 20892. Publication No. 93-159.

Parent and Family Involvement

As with any developmental disability, the involvement of the child's family is of major importance. The family needs to learn all about the condition, their child's strengths and limitations, the needed resources, and how best to access them. The love, support, and guidance of the parents and other family members are critical for the child's best development. Along with the varied professionals needed to work with the child, the family members are the significant persons who enact the child's complementary social roles, and they control the child's access to many important resources.

Perhaps the most important starting point once the diagnosis has been made is to counsel, educate, and psychologically support the parents. Counseling should help them to accept the reality of their child's condition and teach them how best to help the child. It can stimulate and support their active involvement in the program and their continued acquisition of skills to cope with the child's changing needs as he or she grows. Psychologists and social workers are typically the professionals who carry out parent counseling. Parents need to be put in contact with local and national agencies that have information about and services for children with disabilities. Education in the form of classes, reading material, and videos needs to be made available. Parent support groups can help in sustaining motivation, learning how other parents deal with the many issues that arise, and providing all important support at those times when the task becomes overwhelming. Such support groups are important for all of the parents, but particularly for single parents or those who are relatively isolated. Such education and counseling are, of course, a continuing process.

Parenting is a demanding task in general, but it is even more demanding when the child has a serious disability. The anxiety and stress can be overwhelming. Depression, marital discord, and breakups are common results of the continuous demands of dealing with a child with a disability (F. Miller & Bachrach, 1995). It is important for parents to recognize that their own good health—physical and psychological—is necessary if they are going to be effective caregivers for their child with a disability. Parent counseling and support groups are important; arranging for periodic breaks away from the demands can be of major help in reducing stress. Many agencies will take a child for a weekend or longer respite for the parents. These and other resources are available, and parents need to know about them and take advantage of their services.

Caring for children with cerebral palsy can put considerable physical stress on the caregivers. An obvious example is the handling, moving, and lifting of a child or adult with cerebral palsy that is necessary many times each day. The caregiver not only faces the sheer physical burden but must also learn how to manipulate and lift so as to avoid injury to the child and to oneself. Serious back problems for the parent can result from poor lifting techniques, and those problems can interfere with good care of the child. Everyday infant basic care involves carrying, lifting, bathing, dressing, and feeding. All are complicated by the muscular problems of the child, and the parent needs to learn not only how to avoid injury to the child but how best to handle and position the child in order to foster good muscle use and development.

Parents must also learn to use many mechanical and electronic devices such as braces, special boards for standing and sitting, seats for the home and automobile, wheelchairs, special exercise and therapy equipment, and many other assistive devices. In addition, with the child's limitations and the presence and use of special equipment, parents often need to modify their homes—for example, building special access ramps, modifying the heights of tables and the widths of doors, repositioning light switches, and so on. Box 13.4 lists a number of useful home modifications. Many manuals for care are available and can be used by parents and professionals (e.g., Levitt, 1995; F. Miller & Bachrach, 1995), and training and assistance are often available at local agencies.

As important as it is, parental involvement may be an increasingly difficult component to include in programming because it depends on the availability of parents who can share the responsibility and the required time and effort for all of the specialized care of the child. The traditional nuclear family of two married parents and one or more children is no longer the norm, and today it accounts for a scant 26 percent of families in the United States. If this holds true for families in which there are children with disabilities, then there may be a growing problem of the lack of family resources, specifically of the available number of responsible adults to care for a child with disabilities. It is not clear how this may be affecting programming for children with disabilities, but it does suggest that greater responsibility is being pushed onto single parents, relatives, and public and private agencies.

Environmental Stimulation

As discussed earlier, normal child development involves a great deal of age-appropriate environmental stimulation. Parents construct the immediate stimulating environments for children and provide the objects, sounds, sights, and spaces for the child to explore. Of particular importance are the many repeated social interactions of the caregiver and child—talking and singing to the child and the physical stimulation in picking up, rocking, and playing with the baby. The growing child becomes increasingly active and mobile and in exploring the environment becomes an active seeker of stimulation through exploration.

All children need stimulating and varied environments. The child with cerebral palsy, however, can be grossly limited in responding to the caregiver's stimulation and limited in the ability to explore the environment and obtain stimulation. For those reasons, it is important for parents and other caregivers to assume major responsibility for providing the necessary objects and events that will supply that stimulation for the child who is physically unable to explore actively. **Infant stimulation therapy** can be provided for these children. The therapist provides age-graded, increasingly complex visual, auditory, and motor stimulation and trains parents and others to maintain the program at home. It includes limb and trunk movements, placing the child in various sleeping, standing, and sitting positions, play therapy, and sensory stimulation (F. Miller & Bachrach, 1995).

Attention and Motivational Issues

Successful therapy is much more than the application of movement exercise or other procedures to a passive child. It requires the child's active involvement, attention, and concentration. However, severe disabilities may create apathy, hyperactivity, and attention deficits in the child (Levitt, 1995). In cerebral palsy, these may be due to brain damage, the side effects of drugs, exhaustion, discomfort or pain, or emotional stress on the child. The child may then, understandably, lack motivation, be uncooperative, inattentive, difficult to handle, and

B O X **13.4**

Some Home Modifications That Can Be Useful
for Persons with Physical Disabillities

Rearrange:

> *furniture* to remove obstructions and allow room for wheelchair turning
>
> *kitchen cabinets and refrigerator,* placing needed items on low shelves
>
> *bathroom accessories* for easy reach

Remove:

> plush wall-to-wall *carpeting;* apply nonslip finish to wood floors

Widen:

> *doorways*

Replace:

> *doorknobs* with lever handles
>
> *entrance steps* with ramps
>
> *bathtubs* with wheel-in showers

Install:

> *hinged arm support* for toileting
>
> *a high-rise toilet*
>
> *single-mix faucets* with antiscald device
>
> an adjustable-height, open-front *sink and counter* in kitchen and bath
>
> an intercom system
>
> an *angled mirror* above stove burners to allow view of pot contents from wheelchair
>
> a *fire extinguisher* at an accessible level

Adjust:

> *height* of light switches and electric plugs to be within reach

Buy:

> *portable telephones* and program them so the child can have access to other people
>
> *home automation system* to allow child to control TV, intercom, and thermostat from a central device
>
> *a lounge chair* with electric-powered positioning and lifting

Use:

> *adaptive devices* such as bath chairs, lifts, hospital bed, etc.

Increase accessibility:

> with a properly trained *service dog*

Adapted by permission: Miller, F., & Bachrach, S. J. (1995). *Cerebral Palsy: A complete guide for caregiving.* Baltimore, MD: Johns Hopkins University Press, p. 283.

unresponsive to therapy attempts. The parent or therapist needs to minimize these distracting responses and increase the child's motivation and attention. In general, the adult needs to have a good understanding of the child's state of fatigue, his or her mood, and the particular objects and activities that are pleasurable and reinforcing. It is also important to try and discern some of the child's own goals or desires, rather than impose all of the therapy or training goals on the child. By being sensitive to these and other child factors, the adult can increase the child's attention, motivation, involvement, and achievement by:

> choosing the best time of day for the procedures
> avoiding periods when the child is fatigued or stressed
> breaking down the tasks into small steps to avoid fatigue and attention loss
> using effective, idiosyncratic positive reinforcement
> matching tasks carefully to the child's developmental level
> knowing what other impairments may be present so as to anticipate their effects
> keeping the length of session well within the child's current attention span
> avoiding distractions during the sessions

Therapy

Physical Therapy, Occupational Therapy, and Language and Speech Therapy.   Several different types of therapy are applied to address various issues. Therapy is provided by specialists in each area—that is, physical therapists (PT), occupational therapists (OT), and language and speech pathologists and therapists (LSP). Because these specialists are focused largely, but not completely, on the child's physical (primarily motor) disabilities, there is some overlap in their functions, and a good deal of communication normally occurs among them. All of these specialists might at various times in the child's treatment become involved in helping with the same area of problems, such as eating behavior. Although these professionals might work simultaneously with the same child, it is more typical that they will come into the case at different times, depending on the development and needs of the child. Each of these professionals conducts detailed diagnostic evaluations of the child (focusing on each particular domain of expertise), assesses developmental delays, plans therapy programs, advises and counsels parents, communicates with other professionals involved with the child, and plans, conducts, and evaluates therapy procedures. The general shared goal of these professionals is to optimize the child's functioning. Although overlapping, the three professions differ in their specific focus, as briefly described here.

In addition to the shared functions that have been noted, the occupational therapist focuses on the assessment, development, and function of fine motor control, sensory and perceptual development and impairment, and functioning such as self-care, school, and work (Lowes & Greis, 1998). The occupational therapist works, for example, on fine motor control of hands and fingers for movements needed in everyday self-care, such as dressing and eating, and in school activities, such as drawing and writing. In treatment, a range of assistive technology is employed as well as exercises. As the child grows older, occupational therapy focuses on skills needed for subsequent phases of life, such as work.

The **language and speech pathologist** or therapist carries out the tasks common to the three professions. In addition, this specialist is concerned primarily with evaluation and treatment of motor function involved in activities such as feeding and speech and with language development. Depending on the child's motor involvement, the language and speech therapist will focus on enhancing verbal communication or some form of **augmentative communication.** This can involve sign language training, use of low-tech equipment such as letter boards and pointers, and electronic devices involving computer-assisted nonverbal communication.

Physical therapy can start early in the child's life (infant stimulation therapy is an example) and continue into adulthood. Focused primarily on gross motor development and function, the physical therapist assesses and attempts to improve muscle tone, patterns of movement and movement disorders, balance, posture, sitting, range of motion such as in limbs, and the ability to move from place to place. Standardized assessments of physical developmental status and motor delays are made. Among these diagnostic evaluations is **gait analysis,** a complex and specialized laboratory study of the details of the person's locomotion (F. Miller, 1998). Gait analysis is carried out by physicians and by physical therapists. The procedure is carried out in a specialized laboratory and entails the use of special cameras, computers, force-plates to determine the weight placed on each foot, electrodes to record muscle activity, and direct observation. This detailed analysis helps to determine the treatment program most appropriate for the child and to evaluate the effects of treatment and the child's progress over time.

The focus and procedures of physical therapy change to meet new needs as the child is introduced to settings outside the home, such as school. Focus is then placed on new physical skills needed in those settings, including the child's ability to communicate and to assume more self-care responsibilities. Skills in moving around a classroom, such as maneuvering a wheelchair, and those needed to use learning materials are worked on.

Physical therapy focuses on three broad goals: to prevent atrophy of muscles due to lack of use, to prevent contracture, and generally, to improve the child's motor development. The successes in physical therapy are important foundations for a wide array of skills in which other therapists may be involved, ranging from large muscle control to speaking and even to chewing and swallowing. To achieve these broad goals, the physical therapist must assess the specific condition of the child, develop and apply specific treatments, monitor their effects and the child's development, and modify the therapy to meet the child's changing needs. The treatments include specific physical exercises, whirlpools, and a range of assistive technology to promote gross motor functioning and the use of assistive devices.

Medical Therapy. Drugs are used to control associated disorders such as epilepsy in children with cerebral palsy. Many of these children also have epilepsy, and in severe cases, more than one drug (polytherapy) may be used. Many of the problems in using seizure control medication (see Chapter 12) are compounded when the person also has the serious limitations of cerebral palsy. Other drugs may be used for short-term control of spasticity but have limited long-term value. One study (K. B. Nelson & Grether, 1995) found a significantly lower incidence of cerebral palsy among low-birth-weight babies whose mothers had been given magnesium sulfate. Magnesium is commonly found in green vegetables, beans, meat, and even chocolate. Magnesium sulfate is an inexpensive natural chemical used commonly to prevent preterm labor and high blood pressure in pregnancy. If this initial suggestion holds up in subsequent research, then the chemical might eventually be used to reduce the rate of cerebral palsy that now occurs in low-birth-weight babies.

Surgery is used in some cases to lengthen problematic muscles and tendons. Because of the complexities involved in coordinated movements, surgery is a difficult undertaking. In preparation for surgery to improve locomotion, gait analysis (see above) is carried out. Using those data, the surgeons identify which muscles and tendons are problematic, and they monitor the results of surgery. One of the complications of this surgery is that when muscles are lengthened, they are actually made weaker. As a result, long recuperation and therapy to strengthen the muscles are required. The stress on a child can be heavy.

Diet and Nutrition. As noted in Chapter 12, in some cases of epilepsy, medication fails to control seizures. This is also true in cases with both cerebral palsy and epilepsy. In these cases, the ketogenic diet (Chapter 12) may help to control seizures. The foods are carefully chosen and measured, and the diet needs to be systematically monitored. Cerebral palsy often involves motor problems of facial muscles, thus interfering with normal ingestion, biting, and swallowing. In such cases, the usual demands of maintaining the ketogenic diet are compounded by the additional limitations of cerebral palsy.

Other Therapies. Many other therapies are important in the overall management procedures, and they are used according to the needs of the particular person and family. For example, individual and family counseling may be useful for helping parents and siblings adjust to the demands made on them. Behavior modification can be used to reward and strengthen the child's own movement attempts. It can be used as an integral part of all of the educational programming that may be carried out.

VI. Assistive Technology

In our technological world, so much of which is computer driven, we have a growing frontier of products, knowledge, and procedures to apply to the task of helping persons with disabilities to function more successfully. In its broadest sense, *assistive technology* refers not only to the devices—mechanical, electronic, optical, and so on—but also to knowledge and to the services and professional skills that are applied to the assistive task.

Assistive technology and services may be relatively simple, such as spoons with built-up handles for easier grasping and tables with adjusting height levels. They may also be high tech and complex, such as the use of specialized computers and programs integrated with voice synthesizers and light pointers to allow the person to communicate despite severe motor disabilities. Whatever the technological level, the critical issue is that the technology be devised, adapted, and applied to individuals specifically to meet the particular needs of that individual. It follows that development of assistive technology for any individual is a continuous process, requiring monitoring and repeated adjustments, particularly for children as they grow, change, and face new developmental challenges.

As discussed by Burstein et al. (1998), assistive technology focuses on specific skill areas. For children, these are communication, mobility, environmental mastery, learning, and recreation. A particular child might benefit from assistive technology in all of those areas; another child might need help in only one or a few. For example, a child with severe deficits in productive language can learn to communicate through a variety of devices, including picture or symbol boards, electronic alphabet boards, electric typewriters and computers, and even voice synthesizers. The child needs to have control over some response—a simple sound, a finger point, a slight head nod, an eye blink, a puff of air, a foot or toe push, and so on. With that and the assistive devices, the child can answer questions, can agree with statements, can point to symbols to produce complex communications and/or spell words, can type messages, and even, with a breath puff or a minor toe press, can activate an electronic voice synthesizer.

Chapter 3 discussed the importance of children's games and active play for physical, cognitive, emotional, and social development. But for children with cerebral palsy, with their severe motor impairments, much or all of this play is not possible. They cannot run and jump and make silly sounds. Nor can many of these children manipulate the myriad of toys that are so common. Many cannot operate CD players, radios, or televisions, move pieces across a board, or simply play with dolls and trucks and things. Many toys and other stimulating objects such as mobiles and light and sound boxes can be adapted for use by the child with cerebral palsy. For example, large handles and knobs can be adapted to toys to make them more easily used. Imagination and creativity are needed by a caregiver to make these modifications and then to engage the child in their use.

VII. Cerebral Palsy and Aging

Recall the brief discussion in Chapter 3 of aging and disabilities. Aging is a lifelong, continuous process that begins at conception, proceeds through complex developmental sequences, and ends with death. The normal processes of aging are fairly predictable. However, for persons with disabilities, there may be special events and processes that occur, making aging a significantly different set of processes for them. Turk et al. (1995) point out that all persons with disabilities undergo the natural changes in aging. However, they also face two additional important factors: the changes brought about by the nature of each specific disability and the new issues created by the interactive effects of their conditions with the normal aging process. As discussed by Turk et al. (1995), persons with cerebral palsy have additional aging problems, including:

> In general, muscle and skeletal problems that began at an earlier age may worsen in persons with cerebral palsy, resulting in more pain, discomfort, and greater limits to mobility.
>
> Spasticity appears to increase with age and is accompanied by more fatigue and pain.
>
> Muscle flexibility, strength, and endurance may decline sharply with age, decreasing mobility and increasing the risk of falls and attendant injuries such as fractures; this decrement may also cause greater problems in daily self-care, such as eating and hygiene, necessitating more help in these areas.
>
> There may be long-term negative effects of vigorous therapies that had been applied earlier in life, and these effects may begin to appear as the person grows older; in addition, the suspension of therapy as one grows older may have negative effects on functioning.

Dental problems can become severe after many years of poor oral hygiene due to poor muscle control of hands and arms; gum disease becomes more likely and serious as the person ages; pain and general oral discomfort can also occur, and declining nutrition can result as serious oral health problems interfere with proper eating.

Osteoporosis may be a particular problem in cerebral palsy, increasing with age and resulting in greater susceptibility to serious fractures in falls.

General reduced mobility and increased discomfort, pain, and fatigue may occur; the energy expenditure demands to achieve even minor mobility may be very taxing for anyone with cerebral palsy and may become even more onerous as the person ages and experiences physical decline.

Communication, which may have always been difficult for many persons with cerebral palsy, may pose even greater problems with aging. The person may find it extremely difficult to communicate to health-care providers any new sensations, problems, pains, malfunctions, fears, and so on that may be occurring with age; as a result, adequate treatment might not be forthcoming.

In general, as we get older and move into the final years, maintaining previous social roles, interacting with persons in complementary roles, and accessing the social resources provided by those roles become increasingly difficult. Aging in those latter years involves a diminution of role multiplicity, complexity, and status, and the elder person cannot derive as much personal identity and self-esteem as were once possible. That is, a "role vacuum" (Cavan, 1962) may be created. For some persons with cerebral palsy, who may have already had limited role enactment, these further reductions with aging may create a particularly bleak life quality. In this group, aging may pose significantly different and more severe problems due to the interaction of the natural changes in aging with specific changes and problems resulting from the condition itself. As our population of persons with developmental disabilities continues to increase and to age, more attention needs to be directed to these issues.

Turk et al. (1995) make the point that these and other potential problems of the aging person with cerebral palsy demand that care providers in all professions become sensitive to these issues in their clients and develop adequate procedures to deal successfully with them. Attention must be paid not only to the physical needs and changing health of the aging person but also to the psychological and social aspects. It is important, for example, to help the person maintain friendships and **social networks** as he or she grows older, thus maintaining the possibility of continued role interactions and of retaining at least some of the benefits a person can derive from those interactions.

VIII. Chapter Summary

The cerebral palsies are a group of nonprogressive motor disabilities that result from brain damage occurring early in life. Etiologies are mostly of prenatal origin. Although the organic damage does not worsen, the person's functioning can deteriorate over time due to many factors such as poor health or lack of training. Cases of cerebral palsies vary in their severity and type of involvement. Major types are spastic, athetoid, ataxic, hypotonic, and mixed types.

Usually diagnosed by about age 4, the cerebral palsies cannot be cured. Lifetime comprehensive management of the condition is needed. Management includes parent and family counseling, medical care, education, and training and involves a number of professional areas. The management goals for the child with cerebral palsy are to provide assistance, education, and specialized therapies in order to acquire, maintain, and improve the skills needed to have the highest possible level of functioning. Because the cerebral palsies are disorders of movement and posture, the core therapies used are various forms of physical therapy. Assistive technology refers to the knowledge, services, procedures, and devices (mechanical, optical, electronic, etc.) that are developed and made available to help the person function better despite the presence of disabilities. The chapter concluded with a discussion of aging in cerebral palsy.

KEY TERMS

Know these important terms. Check the chapter and the Glossary for their meanings. They are listed in the approximate order of their appearance in the chapter.

Cerebral palsies	Paraplegia	Phototherapy
Nonprogressive disorder	Diplegia	Failure to thrive syndrome
Assistive technology	Quadriplegia	Hypertonia
Spastic cerebral palsy	Jaundice	Strabismus
Hypertonicity	Congenital cerebral palsy	Incontinence
Scissors gait	Acquired cerebral palsy	Contracture
Athetoid cerebral palsy	Proteinuria	Cerebral palsy social role
Dyskinetic cerebral palsy	Oxygen deprivation	Parent support groups
Dysarthria	Anoxia	Infant stimulation therapy
Ataxic cerebral palsy	Hypoxia	Physical therapy
Intention tremors	Asphyxia	Occupational therapy
Hypotonic cerebral palsy	Newborn respiratory distress	Language and speech pathologist
Hypotonia	Encephalopathy	Augmentative communication
Monoplegia	Shaken baby syndrome	Gait analysis
Hemiplegia	Intentional injuries	Social networks
Triplegia	Unintentional injuries	

SUGGESTED READING

Dormans, J., & Pellegrino, L. (1998). *Caring for children with cerebral palsy: A team approach.* Baltimore, MD: Paul H. Brookes.

Miller, F., & Bachrach, J. T. (1995). *Cerebral palsy: A complete guide for care giving.* Baltimore, MD: Johns Hopkins University Press.

Smith, M. (1995). *Growing up with cerebral palsy.* Waco, TX: WRS Publishers.

STUDY QUESTIONS

13-1. What are some important assistive devices for use by persons with cerebral palsy?

13-2. Explain: Cerebral palsy is a nonprogressive disorder.

13-3. What important information needs to be obtained early in the child's life for a functional profile?

13-4. What are major risk factors for cerebral palsy during delivery and at any postnatal time?

13-5. Identify and define each of these types of CP: spastic, athetoid, ataxic, hypotonic, mixed types.

13-6. What are some of the major causes of asphyxia in the etiology of CP?

13-7. Issues arise for everyone as we age. What are some of the important issues that arise in aging specifically for the person with CP?

CHAPTER

14 Learning Disabilities

Learning disabilities (LD) is a complex and puzzling phenomenon. It lacks a clear de-limiting definition that is necessary if a useful explanatory theory is ever to be developed (Torgesen, 1994). As Kavale and Forness (1995) noted, the question "what is LD?" still does not have a satisfactory answer. Nevertheless, more grammar and middle school children are diagnosed with LD than with any other developmental disability, it is the largest group of children being served in the field of special education, and an extensive research and applied literature is developing.

Some (e.g., Finlan, 1993) argue that LD is not a true disability but may derive from misunderstanding the nature of normal variability in human skills, resulting in a popular and convenient category that is of doubtful validity. That is, there are natural variations among persons in the many different skills necessary for reading and other academic tasks, and these skills have a statistically normal distribution among the population. Thus, some portion of the population will fall at the lower levels of language, math, or reading skills, others at the highest levels, and most will fall in between. To label persons at the lower end of the distribution as having a disability may be a distortion. Most professionals, however, assume that LD is a true phenomenon of **specific learning disorders** that are not yet well understood. This chapter presents the major concepts in the field, keeping in mind the field's still unfinished nature.

Learning disabilities is an umbrella term that refers to a large and heterogeneous group of persons with impaired learning skills that interfere with normal functioning. The impairments are specific in each person and occur in one or more areas of language development (spoken, written, reading), mathematical processes, and/or other intellectual tasks such as memory, reasoning, and problem solving. In addition, many children with LD have **secondary problems** with attention and motivation, and they may be highly distractible, impulsive, overactive, disruptive, and socially impaired. These secondary problems are not considered part of the core condition of LD, and they do not occur in some cases.

Specific learning disabilities vary among children, but what is shared and is so frustrating for children and parents is the apparent contradiction that these severe difficulties in learning and behavior occur in children of normal intelligence. As a result, these apparently bright youngsters do not achieve as well as expected in school, and there are no obvious reasons why. How can a child be bright in so many obvious ways and still have such difficulty with reading or math? The children are often considered unmotivated, lazy, undisciplined, or otherwise willfully oppositional. As we will discuss, this discrepancy between the child's apparent overall ability and poor academic achievement is a cornerstone of diagnosis and education in LD, but it also poses problems.

It is generally thought that LD has multiple and interactive etiologies—genetic factors, central nervous system (CNS) dysfunction, poor learning environments—although etiology is not yet well understood. There is no known "cure" for LD. (Note that cure is not an appropriate expectation for those who adopt the position that LD is actually an artifact of a normal distribution of skills.) In any event, education and training are best aimed at compensatory skills—that is, finding ways of "teaching around" each child's actual or assumed specific disabilities. Children of high intelligence with LD can develop their own compensating strategies (these children and adults are sometimes referred to as "compensated LD"), and they may be successful enough in the early schoolyears that their disabilities are not noticed until much later, perhaps in high school. By then, their years of struggle may have taken a personal toll, and of course, their LD condition continues. Children do not spontaneously or naturally outgrow LD. When they become adults, they generally continue to have the same or similar functional problems in personal and work-related spheres.

I. Prevalence of Learning Disabilities

It has been estimated (Lyon, 1996) that half of the 5.3 million children in special education programs in the United States have learning disabilities, accounting for 5 percent to 6 percent of all schoolchildren aged 6 to 18 (Lewitt & Baker, 1996; U.S. Department of Education, 1995). While prevalence estimates of emotional disorders, speech and language disabilities, and mental retardation have not changed much since 1977, the estimate for specific learning disabilities grew from less than 2 percent of the school population in 1976 to more than 6 percent, or about 2.5 million, in 1994 (U.S. Department of Education, 1995). Applying the 6 percent estimate to the current U.S. population of about 90 million children and youth (ages 0 to 17) yields an estimated 5.4 million children and youth with one form or another of LD in the year 2000. The approximate ratio of adults to children and youth is 2:1. Thus, we estimate 10.8 million adults with LD in the United States, for a total of some 16.2 million persons of all ages. Compare this with the approximately 8 million persons with mental retardation, and it is clear that LD may be one of our most prevalent developmental disabilities (Gerber & Reiff, 1994). It should be added, however, that some researchers (e.g., Kavale & Forness, 1995) believe the LD prevalence estimates to be far too large and on the order of twice as high as they believe to be a reasonable estimate.

Many attempts have been made to determine the LD prevalence among adults, but the results vary widely depending on the particular group being studied. For example, Vogel, Leonard, Scales, Hayeslip, and Hermanson (1998) reported that, on average, 2.6 percent of college and university student bodies had documented LD ranging from 0.5 percent in the most highly selective colleges to 10 percent in open admission colleges. The highest rate (30 percent) was reported for persons who are in poverty and are underemployed (Giovengo, Moore, & Young, 1998).

Traditionally, LD has been identified primarily in males, with a male–female ratio of 4:1 (Shaywitz, Shaywitz, Fletcher, and Ecsobar, 1990). This disparity may reflect a true male–female difference, or it might be an artifact. Boys are, or are perceived to be, more active and disruptive than girls and tend to be more readily noticed and labeled. Girls with learning disabilities may be more passive and thus less obtrusive and noticeable. Recently, there has been a change of perception, and we now see no sex differences in prevalence. More research is needed on this issue of gender and LD.

Although there is general agreement that LD encompasses a large group of persons, the prevalence estimates are unreliable because we still do not have clear definitions of LD, of the specific conditions subsumed by the label LD, or of the criteria for diagnosis and treatment. The field suffers from a lack of consensus on the nature of LD. This lack of information and agreement appears due to a number of factors. The most apparent factors are the heterogeneity of the group—indeed, it may not even be a single group—and the complexity of the disabilities, making it difficult to focus and to refine definitions and criteria. Another factor is the involvement of so many different professions (e.g., audiology, education, medicine, occupational therapy, psychology, speech and language pathology and therapy, etc.), each of which has its own focus on which issues are most important. This results in different working definitions of LD depending on one's professional discipline. A third factor may be the overlap in functioning of children with LD and those with some emotional/behavioral problems, attention disorders, hyperactivity, or mild mental retardation. Children in these groups behave in similar ways, and it is often difficult to distinguish one from the other. A final reason may be that the field is still primarily one of application, in which observations are made and concepts and criteria are developed primarily in the pursuit of applied education. According to Kavale and Forness (1995), the field is so focused on the practicalities of providing educational services that it has been content with practical definitions that have some everyday utility but has not been invested in the research needed for deeper and fuller *understanding* of the phenomenon. This suggests that specific immediate needs of specific children, arising in specific schools, take the attention of the practitioners. Therefore, those educators and psychologists might not develop a larger view of the entire group or have the bases for developing standardized criteria. There is need for objective scientific study of the whole field to break away from narrow discipline-oriented ideas, to standardize concepts, measures, and approaches, and to develop standardized definitions for diagnoses. Progress is being made, but there is still a long way to go. With improved standardization, we will eventually be able to make more informed estimates of incidence and prevalence and be more successful in diagnosis, education, therapy, and training. Out of this heterogeneity, some general assumptions emerge that seem important for both research and practice (see Box 14.1).

BOX 14.1

Some Assumptions about the Nature of Learning Disabilities

1. *LD appears primarily in terms of academic learning:* That is, it is tied closely to the school context. It is in school, in relation to academic tasks, that the problems are seen first and at their most severe levels.
2. *The discrepancy criterion is important:* The child with LD is not simply functioning at a level that is lower than average but is functioning at a lower level than is expected given *that particular child's* apparent abilities.
3. *A child's LD seen in school is lifelong:* LD children eventually leave school, but their learning difficulties persist and affect their functioning in many aspects of adult life, from personal to occupational functioning.
4. *LD is not a single disorder:* Rather it appears in different forms, combinations, and severity in different children.
5. *LD most commonly occurs as some type of language defects,* accounting for 80 to 85 percent of LD cases.
6. *The specific areas of functional difficulty are:* language, arithmetic, and motor function.
7. *LD reflects true disabilities* that reside within the child and/or arise in child–environment interactions.
8. *Those intrinsic disabilities are cognitive problems* arising from brain function or malfunction which derive from genetic factors or from damage due to disease or trauma injury.
9. *What emerges as LD in school is the product of developmental processes and/or impairments that had been in effect long prior to entering school.* Those processes and/or impairments constitute the major (but not sole) etiological factors for LD. At this time, they are inferred constructs and are not yet demonstrably known.
10. *LD is multiply determined.* No single etiological factor accounts for the disabilities demonstrated by a particular child or by the group as a whole.
11. *LD can be predicted early in development.* If LD in each case is based in specific deficits and if those deficits are developmental products, as assumed above, then it is at least theoretically possible to determine and to trace out developmental sequences that lead to the demonstrated LD. If so, then early diagnosis and the development of specific remedial programming for specific deficits are theoretically possible.
12. *Dual exceptionality* (a child with LD and giftedness) presents special difficulties.

II. Learning Disabilities Criteria

Inclusion and Exclusion Criteria

The term *LD* includes a variety of disabilities that can be grouped into several categories of specific disabilities. It is generally agreed that children with LD have some combinations of problems in the academic performance areas listed in Box 14.2. Although there is general agreement that different specific disabilities exist, there is insufficient agreement on which specific disabilities should be included and on the definitions of each. Further, there is a continuing need to develop valid and reliable procedures for identifying and measuring specific disabilities.

Box 14.3 presents two definitions of LD (proposed in federal guidelines and by the National Joint Commission on Learning Disabilities, (N.J.C.L.D., 1988). These definitions recognize that LD (a) is not a single disorder but is a heterogeneous category, (b) occurs within the individual (is intrinsic), (c) is related to central nervous system defects, and (d) is not the same as disabilities caused by pervasive disorders such as mental deficiency.

The definitions suggest at least a two-step diagnostic approach. First, they propose **inclusion criteria** to identify areas of disabilities (spoken or written language and mathematical calculations). If significant difficulties in these areas are identified, then the next part of the definitions comes into play, the **exclusion criteria,** to determine that the disabilities are *not* due to visual, hearing, or motor impairment, mental retardation, emotional disturbance, environmental, cultural, or economic disadvantage. By ruling out these conditions, these definitions suggest that etiological factors in LD are either unknown (in the majority of cases) or are some type of known CNS dysfunction. In most instances, inferences are made that some CNS dysfunction or damage is involved, but it is rarely identified. Although widely accepted, the exclusion criteria pose some difficulty in application because, on a functional level, children with mild mental retardation, LD, attention deficit, or some types of emotional problems behave so much alike as to be nearly indistinguishable.

B O X 14.2

Academic Problem Areas for Children with LD

1. receptive language
2. expressive language
3. basic reading skills
4. reading comprehension
5. written expression
6. mathematical calculation
7. mathematical reasoning

Based on Lyon, G. R. (1996). Learning disabilities. In *Special Education for Students with Learning Disabilities,* 6(1), Los Altos, CA: Center for the Future of Children (pp. 54–76). The David and Lucille Packard Foundation.

BOX 14.3

Definitions of Learning Disabilities

1. From: Public Law 94-142, as amended by Public Law 101-76 (Individuals with Disabilities Education Act—IDEA)

"Specific learning disability" means a disorder in one or more basic psychological processes involved in understanding or in using language, spoken or written, that may manifest itself in an imperfect ability to listen, speak, read, write, spell, or do mathematical calculations. The term includes such conditions as perceptual disabilities, brain injury, minimal brain dysfunction, dyslexia, and developmental aphasia. The term does not apply to children who have learning problems that are primarily the result of visual, hearing, or motor disabilities, or mental retardation, or emotional disturbance, or of environmental, cultural, or economic disadvantage.

2. From: National Joint Commission on Learning Disabilities (N.J.C.L.D., 1994)

"Learning disabilities" is a general term that refers to a heterogeneous group of disorders manifested by significant difficulties in the acquisition and use of listening, speaking, reading, writing, reasoning, or mathematical abilities. These disorders are intrinsic to the individual, presumed to be due to central nervous system dysfunction, and may occur across the life span.

Problems in self-regulatory behavior, social perception, and social interaction may exist with learning disabilities but do not by themselves constitute a learning disability.

Although learning disabilities may occur concomitantly within other handicapping conditions (for example, sensory impairment, mental retardation, serious emotional disturbance) or with extrinsic influences (such as cultural differences, insufficient or inappropriate instruction), they are not the result of those conditions or influences.

Discrepancy Criterion

Related to the exclusion criterion is the **discrepancy criterion.** By ruling out (excluding) mental retardation, LD is defined as a condition of specific disabilities that exist in a person with normal *general* intelligence. Diagnostically, the LD child is one who functions with significant problems in some area(s) of learning despite normal general intelligence. There is a discrepancy between the child's low level of performance in a specific area and the higher level that is expected, given that child's general intelligence (e.g., a child with average IQ who is reading far below grade level). However, the questions of how much of a discrepancy is required for a diagnosis of LD and how the discrepancy is to be measured do not have any consistent or standardized answers. Various formulas have been proposed for calculating the discrepancy, such as comparing intelligence and achievement test scores from standardized tests that have the same mean and standard deviation. The calculation takes into account the measured reliability of the tests, thus reducing statistical error associated with the tests (Schuerholz et al., 1995).

However, neither practitioners nor researchers have adopted standard criteria or mathematical formulas to measure and evaluate the discrepancy. Therefore, studies may be difficult to compare. It is often not clear if the children sampled in different studies are truly equivalent or if they represent different populations. Likewise, in the applied educational setting, there is so much variability in how school psychologists define and measure the concept of LD that a child might be diagnosed and labeled LD in one school district but not in a neighboring district (Lyon, 1996). What diagnostic label or services a child receives, if any at all, are affected by where that child lives (Lewitt & Baker, 1996).

Perhaps the greatest problem is that the IQ–achievement discrepancy cannot be assessed until the child has been in school for some time and learning problems have become evident. Therefore, most children with LD are not diagnosed until the third grade or later (Foorman, Francis, & Shaywitz, 1996), sometimes even as late as adolescence. The problem is that remedial steps are therefore delayed. If a learning disability affects language or other cognitive development from the earliest years, a child might experience much of his or her formative years under the handicap of LD before anything is done about it.

The condition becomes more problematic the longer remedial action is delayed (Lyon, 1996). If the child experiences many years of LD without being provided with some help, it is reasonable to assume that intellectual and other academic skills will be compromised. In addition, the commonly associated problems of poor self-esteem, loss of motivation for learning, and behavioral problems may develop. In effect, reliance on the discrepancy criteria forces a delay in diagnosis and in remedial action and may thus serve to worsen the child's condition.

What is needed is the development of concepts and procedures that will allow *early identification* of specific learning disabilities. However, that may be difficult to achieve. Consider that some 80 percent of LD involves learning how to read (Lerner, 1989), and for most children, reading does not begin until the schoolyears. Unless some early developmental predictors of later academic performance can be identified, then the diagnosis of LD will not occur until after children have been in school for several years.

Academic Underachievement

Academic **underachievement** is clearly a defining factor in LD, but the two are not synonymous. A child might underachieve for many reasons including LD, ill health, poor motivation, inadequate study and preparation, poor home and family setting, the interference of social and other distracting factors, and so on. LD is one set of specific factors that lead to underachievement. For most children, LD involves problems in language development; for others, it involves problems in mathematics. The focus of study and understanding of LD is not on the fact of underachievement but, as discussed by Kavale and Forness (1995), on the *nature of the specific disabilities* that have brought about that underachievement. Research needs to focus on identifying and understanding these specific defects. That understanding would make it possible in individual cases to identify specific deficits and to develop and apply specific teaching procedures that are focused on those targeted defects. With such clarification, early preschool diagnoses may then also be possible.

Variability in Learning Disabilities

Relatively poor skills in specific areas of language and math are quite common in persons with normal or better general intelligence (Lokerson, 1999). Consider, for example, successful mathematicians who cannot spell well or the educated minister who cannot balance a checkbook. However, these persons are not considered to have learning disabilities unless the difficulties reach a level of severity that interferes significantly with some aspects of normal functioning. It is the child who fails in school or the adult who cannot hold a job because of specific learning difficulties who is considered to have LD. There is a continuum of specific learning difficulties ranging from common mild problems through severe disrupting difficulties. It is at the severe end of this continuum that the term LD is applied.

Among persons diagnosed with LD, there is a confusing variability in their characteristics. The disabilities range in severity among persons, the specific disabilities can occur in many different areas of functioning, and the details of each set of problems can vary significantly from one person to another. One person might have problems in only one area of learning, while another might have several problem areas. Further variability is created by differences in personality and environment. Different people react differently to the disabilities, and their total functioning thus varies from one person to another. People diagnosed with LD can be very different from each other in the number, type, and severity of disorder and may be greatly dissimilar in their educational profiles and general levels of achievement and success. Their common LD label, does not mean they are all the same; they are a very heterogeneous group. Often, the only similarity is the common label.

III. Specific Learning Disabilities

Several classification systems have been proposed to organize and describe the varied deficits in LD. Our organization of this material is based on the *International Classification of Diseases (ICD-10)* (World Health Organization 1993, 1996) and the *Diagnostic and Statistical Manual (DSM-IV)* (American Psychiatric Association, 1994). Both classification systems organize LD into at least three major categories of "specific developmental disabilities": **speech and language disorders, scholastic (academic) skills disorders,** and **motor function disorders.** Each system includes categories for **mixed, other,** and even a somewhat confusing **unspecified disorders** category. These learning disabilities (listed in Box 14.4) are distinguished from "pervasive disorders," such as autism, and from disorders that are clearly due to mental retardation or to organic factors.

Developmental Speech and Language Disorders

A child's speech and language problems may be the earliest indicators of LD and thus may provide bases for early diagnoses of LD. Speech and language disorders include problems in producing clear speech sounds (**developmental articulation disorders**), understanding the speech sounds of others (**developmental receptive language disorders**), and communicating clearly with others (**developmental expressive language disorders**).

Articulation Disorders.   Speech articulation refers to the quality of speech sounds. Articulation problems include the clarity, precision, accuracy, crispness, and so forth of the child's speech sounds. Individual variation in the rate at which children master speech

---

B O X **14.4**

Types of LD

Specific Disorders of Psychological Development

Specific Developmental Disorders of Speech and Language

    Speech articulation disorder

    Expressive language disorder

    Receptive language disorder

    Acquired aphasia with epilepsy

    Other developmental disorders of speech and language

    Developmental disorders of speech and language, unspecified

Specific Developmental Disorders of Scholastic Skills

    Reading disorder

    Spelling disorder

    Arithmetic skills disorder

    Mixed disorders

    Other academic skills disorders (n.b. in the *ICD-10,* this category includes *Expressive writing disorder*)

    Developmental academic skills disorders, unspecified

Specific Developmental Disorders of Motor Function

Mixed Specific Developmental Disorders

Other Disorders of Psychological Development

Unspecified Disorders of Psychological Development

Note: those in italics are the most commonly included and diagnosed as LD, and the others may be included depending on specific local usage. These categories are similar to those presented in *DSM-IV* (American Psychiatric Association, 1994).

Based on *International Classification of Disease,* World Health Organization *ICD-10* (WHO, 1996).

---

sounds needs to be considered when trying to determine if there is a developmental delay in articulation. Young children normally have common articulation errors such as omitting some sounds or mispronouncing some combinations (e.g., "thmile" rather than smile, "wun" rather than run, "aminal," "pasghetti," or "ephelants"). These approximations are no longer considered cute if they persist into schoolyears. By about age 8, most children have developed adequate articulation and can be easily understood by others. Mastery of virtually all speech sounds is expected by about age 11.

Specific articulation disorders are diagnosed when the child's articulation is significantly delayed, and the problems are not attributable to mental retardation, sensory problems, or neurological damage. However, the diagnosis is not reliably made until after about
age 8. In many cases, timely speech therapy can reduce or correct the problems.

Expressive Language Disorders.   As outlined in Chapter 3, the first true words emerge
by about 18 months, and a vocabulary spurt begins by about age 2. The 2- to 3-year-old
rapidly produces an increasing number of single words and holophrases. The average
3-year-old has about a 900-word vocabulary and actively engages in conversations with
children and adults. By about school age, vocabulary has grown to some 8,000 to 14,000
words, and complex sentences, correct tense, and language comprehension continue their
rapid development. Serious problems in expressive language development should alert
parents to possible developmental delays and to possible future LD. The child might use
incorrect words or seem not to have the words to name things, cannot easily create answers
to simple questions, and persists in using simple one- or two-word phrases long after other
children have mastered word strings and sentences. Some of the children do not speak very
much, a lack that is apparent to persons outside the family. These children communicate
with gestures and a limited number of two- or three-word combinations. The parents easily
learn to understand the children's nonverbal communications that are so difficult for others
to understand. The children's language use is far below their age levels. When these problems are (a) true developmental delays and not age-appropriate language approximations
and (b) not attributable to other causes (e.g., mental retardation, pervasive disorders, deafness, etc.), then a **specific developmental expressive language disorder** can be diagnosed. This involves problems in adequately expressing oneself in speech. Although these
children seem to understand well what is said to them and their speech is clear, with no
serious articulation delays, they do not easily create words, strings of words, and sentences
that are expected for their age. Expressive language problems in preschoolers may be predictive of later problems in school.

Receptive Language Disorders.   While expressive (or productive) language is developing in normal children, there is a corresponding normal development of receptive language
(see Chapter 3), and these receptive language skills are normally greater than one's productive language skills. Problems with receptive language mean difficulties understanding
what others say. This includes a 1-year-old who typically fails to respond to familiar names
or the 2-year-old who cannot follow simple directions or understand questions or commands. As the child grows older, the lack of understanding becomes even greater because
appropriate language levels are more complex for older children. Sentence structure, complex issues such as negatives and comparatives, and more subtle aspects such as tone of
voice leave the child puzzled and/or unresponsive. In an adult, this may be a worker who
cannot follow directions correctly. Often, a hearing loss is suspected, but in most cases,
the child's hearing is normal. In some cases, there is a hearing deficit, but it is not severe
enough to account for the language difficulties (WHO, 1996). In some cases, too, the
parents or teachers believe the child is being negative and willfully disobedient. The resulting criticisms and/or punishments do not help the child. At times, the receptive language-
impaired child may appear almost autistic in his or her language errors or lack of response

to language. But these children are not autistic: They do engage in creative make-believe play, develop social interests and relationships, show emotional ties with parents, can communicate nonverbally, and maintain interaction with others.

Among all language problems, receptive language disabilities have the greatest rate of associated social and behavioral problems (WHO, 1996). This may be so because spoken language is so important in the intellectual, personal, and social development of children. In most cases, the child with receptive language disabilities also suffers from serious delays in expressive language (WHO, 1996).

Developmental Academic Skills Disorders

This category includes significant learning difficulties in basic academic areas (reading, spelling, writing, and arithmetic), and they are not usually diagnosed until third grade or later. As with specific language and speech disabilities, the etiologies of academic skill disorders are not known. There is a general assumption that, like all specific learning disabilities, they stem from specific cognitive limitations, which in turn are due to genetic and/or other organic factors such as CNS damage. Those assumed factors are thought to operate early in development and in interaction with environmental factors such as quality of home life, educational opportunity, guidance, and support. Because details of the inferred cognitive and organic factors are not known, this is still a very general and tentative model.

In diagnosing developmental academic skill disorders, we must be sure that the child is substantially below the expected performance age level. Further, the delay is not due to conditions of general cognitive level (as in mental retardation) or due to other conditions, including brain trauma or pervasive developmental disorders. The child is clearly underachieving and doing so in specific functional areas, such as reading, spelling, writing, and arithmetic (WHO, 1996).

Reading Disorders.   Learning to read is a complicated process, but most children master reading skills. Consider that in order to read and comprehend a written passage, a child must carry out many cognitive tasks (see Box 14.5). Some must be done in rapid sequence or even simultaneously. The cognitive tasks must also be successfully coordinated with controlled motor tasks such as proper and sustained eye movement. Further, the child needs to have good attention skills, be motivated, and find pleasure and reinforcement in the tasks.

As children learn to read, they master these and other tasks in a gradual accumulation of the skills. Impairments in any of those areas will create problems in learning to read and may constitute a reading disability. The term **dyslexia** refers to reading disabilities, although it has lost its precision because it is often used generally for all language disabilities. It seems more useful to refer to the specific disabilities by name (e.g., expressive language, specific reading, etc.) rather than use the term dyslexia.

Although estimates vary widely, some believe that up to 20 percent of schoolchildren have serious reading difficulties (e.g., Shaywitz, 1996), and for some 8 to 10 percent of the school population, those difficulties are severe enough to constitute "reading disability," making this probably the most prevalent learning disability.

BOX **14.5**

Some of the Tasks That a Child Needs to Master in Learning How to Read

The child must:

Understand that printed letters represent spoken sounds
Recognize specific letters and their associated sounds
Recognize the sounds that make up words (phonemes)
Know the meanings of the words
Have sufficient metacognitive skills for approaching the reading task
Understand the grammar in the passage
Be able to build new ideas and images from what is read
Have a memory store of information and be able to sort through it quickly
Be able to compare the new ideas that are read with those stored in memory
Be able to store new images and ideas in memory
Be able to focus and maintain one's attention on the printed material
Be able to control eye movements across and down the page

Most children with reading disabilities have average intelligence. Some children with severe reading disabilities nevertheless have high intelligence, excellent comprehension, language production, and reasoning ability, but they have inordinate trouble reading the printed word. Developmental reading disabilities are not due to low intelligence, visual or hearing problems, psychological disorder, or inadequate schooling.

Preschoolers with reading disabilities often show difficulties learning the alphabet, recognizing and correctly naming letters, knowing the sounds represented by letters, being able to make up rhymes and invented words, or generally playing with words and word sounds. Some early warnings of possible later LD are listed in Box 14.6. Later, problems with oral reading become apparent in school (see Box 14.7). As the reading tasks become more complex in later grades, the child or youth with LD will have increasing problems and more difficulty in academic achievement.

Spelling Disorders. Some children have inordinate difficulty trying to master spelling skills, oral and written, although other academic skills and general intelligence levels are adequate. In this diagnosis, it is important to distinguish children who have motor-control-based handwriting problems that might appear to be a spelling disorder. As in the other academic disabilities, we assume there is a specific cognitive deficit resulting in the spelling disorder, although the inferred deficit is seldom clearly identified. Standardized spelling tests can identify these children.

Expressive Writing Disorders. In the *ICD-10,* expressive writing disorder is included in the "other developmental disorders" category and is not well described or defined.

BOX 14.6

Some Common Signs of Early Difficulties
That May Predict Later LD

Preschool
Babies who do not respond well to visual or auditory stimuli
Delayed motor development such as sitting and walking
Babies with little vocalizing such as cooing, babbling, and playing with vocal sounds
Delays in speaking and vocabulary growth (e.g., no real words by about age 2)
Problems with pronunciation
Difficulty rhyming or otherwise "playing with" words
Difficulty learning colors, days of the week, numbers, and the alphabet
Is very restless; has trouble with siblings and peers
Has trouble following simple directions; "does not listen"

The 3- or 4-Year-Old
who speaks very little, especially to nonfamily members
whose speech is not easily understood by nonfamily members
with persistent problems trying to think of and produce common words
who uses incorrect words
who speaks spontaneously but cannot follow or engage in a conversation
who dislikes having stories read to him or her

BOX 14.7

Common Difficulties in Oral Reading Shown by Children
with Developmental Reading Disabilities

    (a) omissions, substitutions, distortions, or additions of words or parts of words;
    (b) slow reading rate;
    (c) false starts, long hesitations or 'loss of place' in text, and inaccurate phrasing;
    (d) reversals of words in sentences or of letters within words; there may also be deficits in reading comprehension as shown by, for example:
    (e) an inability to recall facts read;
    (f) inability to draw conclusions or inferences from material read; inability to use general knowledge as background information . . .

Reprinted with permission from: World Health Organization (1996). *Multiaxial classification of child and adolescent psychiatric disorders (ICD-10).* pp. 189–190.

Expressive writing is a complicated process. Children may have difficulties with basics such as word sounds, vocabulary, syntax, grammar, and so on. Their production of meaningful, smoothly flowing written language is thus compromised.

Arithmetic Disorders (Mathematical Disabilities).   These involve significant difficulties in one or more aspects of mathematics such as basic arithmetic calculation in subtraction, addition, multiplication, and/or division and possibly in more advanced areas such as geometry and algebra. Most of the research and the diagnostic and remedial services for children with LD are primarily for those with reading disabilities. They are seldom for mathematical disabilities despite the estimates that some 6 percent of all schoolchildren have significant math disabilities (Badian, 1984).

As with reading, accurate mathematical calculation requires combinations of many basic skills, and cognitive deficits may exist in any of them. In *ICD-10* (WHO, 1996, p. 192), these problems include **conceptual deficits** in understanding as well as **procedural deficits,** and they may involve the child's failure in areas such as those listed in Box 14.8.

Most of the research in mathematical disability has been carried out in the most basic areas of arithmetic, and little is yet known about disabilities in more advanced areas such as geometry and algebra. Even in elementary calculations, however, children need to master the skills that have been listed and these basic skills can be categorized as skills in **number concepts, counting,** and **basic arithmetic.**

Consider the tasks of understanding number concepts. Children need to know the correct word for each number as well as the standard sequence (one, two, three, etc.). They also need to know the Arabic numerals, their sequences, and which numerals are named by which number words (1, 2, 3, etc. and one = 1, two = 2, etc.). The concepts of number sequence and larger and smaller values must be learned. Children need to understand some of the characteristics of our standard number system. These include the concept of ordinality (numbers progress in sequence from smaller to greater values and, in reverse, from greater to smaller values) and the idea that numbers can be "decomposed" or broken down into

---

B O X **14.8**

Conceptual and Procedural Deficits in Math Disabilities

The child fails to:

> understand concepts that underlie particular arithmetic operations
> understand mathematical terms and symbols
> understand which of the numbers are relevant for the specific problem
> recognize numerical symbols
> carry out standard calculations
> align numbers properly (and failures in spatial organization of calculations)
> insert decimal points or symbols properly during calculations
> learn multiplication tables

smaller units (e.g., 53 = 30 + 20 + 3, and any other combinations that total 53). They need to understand the base-ten structure of the number system (that numbers progress in sequence 1–10 and then repeat that sequence 11–20 and so on). It is a difficult concept for most children to understand but is essential for later more complex calculations.

In addition to mastering number concepts, children need to develop skills in counting. A rote recitation of one, two, three, and so on. is not difficult for most children to master. The ability to recite the sequence and to count to 100 does not necessarily indicate good math ability. Many other rules of counting need to be learned and used to perform mathematical calculations (see Box 14.9). Deficits in any one of these skills can result in later problems for the child in arithmetic.

Basic arithmetic skills involve the integration and use of number concepts and counting skills. How well do children put it all together? One factor is memory, and there appear to be at least two types of memory problems involved in math disabilities. Children with math disabilities compared with children without the disabilities seem to have greater difficulty remembering number facts—that is, (a) storing facts in memory and (b) accessing them when needed. When these facts, such as multiplication tables and simple sums (e.g., 2 + 3 = 5), are not readily available, the child then has difficulties with math.

The other memory problem is that while some children with math disabilities are able to store and retrieve number facts, they have difficulty in keeping out other facts that are actually irrelevant for the particular problem. For example, the child might recall the fact 3 + 2 = 5 but also retrieve the fact that 6 immediately follows 5 in a counting sequence. Then, in selecting an answer to 3 + 2 = ?, 6 may be as likely to be given as 5. The difficulty inhibiting irrelevant facts clearly interferes with the child's ability to solve math problems. Deficits in memory functions thus appear basic in math disabilities.

B O X **14.9**

Some Counting Rules That Children Must Understand
to Perform Mathematical Calculations

One-to-one correspondence: When counting objects, each object is counted only once and only one word tag (label) (e.g., four, seven, etc.) is assigned to each object.

Stable order: The ordinality must be preserved. It is stable over different sets of objects (i.e., the sequence four, five, six proceeds in the same low–high order no matter what objects are counted).

Cardinality: Children must understand that in a correct sequence of counting, the total number of objects is indicated by the final number or word tag. Some children may be able to count five pennies, for example, but might not understand that five is the answer to the question: How many pennies are there?

Abstraction: Counting can be applied to any set of objects, and the counting rules remain the same.

Order irrelevance: When counting rules are applied to any set of objects, the objects can be arranged in any order—front to back, up and down, and so on—and the counting is accurate as long as the order is preserved and each object is counted once and only once.

Developmental Motor Function Disorders

Fine and gross motor coordination problems not due to other conditions such as general or specifically diagnosed neurological disorder or mental retardation are included in this category. There may be effects on fine coordination required in printing and other academic tasks and in games and the use of toys. Some coordination tasks, such as learning to tie shoelaces, may be delayed, and the child may be seen as generally clumsy. There are often associated language problems (WHO, 1996) and, later, academic difficulties.

Mixed, Other, and Unspecified Disorders

The *ICD-10* (WHO, 1996) category "mixed disorders" is intended to include children with more than one disorder, such as both language and motor disabilities, where one does not clearly predominate. The *ICD-10* categories "other" and "unspecified" are poorly defined catch-all categories that are necessary to have a place for observed LD conditions that do not quite fit the other categories. These disorders presumably include few children.

IV. Phonological Awareness and Central Processing Deficits

Phonological Awareness

Since the 1970s, a growing interest has developed in the of concept of **phonological awareness** in language disabilities. In spoken language, a **phoneme** is the smallest unit of meaningful speech sounds, and spoken words are combinations of phonemes. A word as simple as cat is composed of three phonemes: /"kuh"/ /"ahh"/and /"tuh"/. Combinations of forty-four phonemes make up all of the words in the English language. In normal speech, we blend these sounds to produce words that are smooth, unbroken sound units. For example, one seldom asks, "Did you feed the kuh ahh tuh?"

Infants are surrounded by speech sounds and soon begin to imitate them. In acquiring language, children play with sounds, as they play with everything else in their worlds. Children make up new words, silly words, rhyming words, and they have fun with funny-sounding word combinations. They sing and chant and even call each other names ("You're a doodoo-head!" "Oh yeah? Well you're a doodoo-boodoo-head!"). The production of speech sounds, words, and sentences becomes an integral part of play; indeed, it becomes an inseparable component of their socialization experience.

Children learn, among many things, the essential phonemes. They do not label the sounds as phonemes, and most people will never even learn what phonemes are. But the children are learning a range of phonemic skills: They learn to hear and recognize the sounds, to understand the meanings of a growing number of sound combinations (i.e., words), and to reproduce them and use them in their own speech. These skills remain largely unlabeled and preconscious. Hearing, recognizing, understanding, and producing these sounds—becoming skilled at their manipulation—are critically important basic skills. It is largely on this phonemic foundation that, according to the adherents of the phonological awareness model, fluent, meaningful speech, reading, language comprehension, and composition are developed.

Acquiring spoken language skills occurs for most children as part of normal growing up—a part of everyday experience. A major assumption is that parts of the human brain are prewired for normal language acquisition. An innate structure and capacity for the development of spoken language are presumed to exist, and language unfolds naturally as the child grows (e.g., Chomsky, 1965) and continues to experience his or her expanding environment. We assume that language development is the result of genetic X environmental interaction and that little extra effort beyond normal growing-up is required of children to achieve spoken language.

However, reading, writing, and math calculations require special effort and concentration. They are not normally learned in everyday infant and preschool activities, although such everyday activities to enhance language development can be created for the preschooler (Lundberg, Frost, & Peterson, 1988). Instruction, practice, and guidance such as occurs in school are needed to master these skills. A written text is a set of symbols that represents spoken language. Reading is a complex *decoding process* in which the child transforms those written symbols into sounds, words, and sentences. In order to read, the child needs to know that various combinations of the twenty-six letters of the written alphabet represent the forty-four phonemes used in the spoken English language. Children must be able to recognize the printed symbols, to know what sounds the symbols represent, what words are created by which combinations of those sounds and symbols, and the meanings of the resulting words, phrases, and sentences. The new reader is faced with the task of recoding the printed letters (i.e., the **graphemes**) into the phonemes that correspond to those letters. Most children adequately master the complicated decoding skills, but some have great difficulty doing so. For those children who do not learn to read adequately (i.e., to decode the symbols) in spite of their normal intelligence, the general term *dyslexia* is applied.

The phonological model posits that language is processed in the brain in a hierarchical set of processing components (Shaywitz, 1996). It is assumed that these inferred components are each concerned with a particular aspect of language function (i.e., phonology, semantics, grammar, and pragmatics) (see Box 14.10). It is further assumed that they are arranged hierarchically, with the most basic aspect being the phonological processing component. It is at this basic processing level that the specific sounds that constitute language are processed. At higher levels in this processing hierarchy are components for processing **semantics** (the meanings of words and sentences), **grammar** (the structure of language), and **pragmatics** (the use of connected sentences to communicate with others). Box 14.10 defines each of these processing components.

For those higher-order functions to occur in spoken or written form, the words must first be disassembled or parsed into their basic phonemic units in the phonological processing component of the brain. That is, the basic sounds and the resulting words must be first clearly identified if upper-level processing is to occur. If this basic phonological processing activity is impaired, then all of the upper-level processing will be affected. How can a child know the meaning and proper usage of a word that he or she was not even able to identify? According to this model, a child might possess the higher-order processing skills for meaning and comprehension, but those skills cannot be adequately used because the basic elements—the specific words—have not been clearly identified.

Phonological awareness is the child's ability to manipulate phonemes—that is, to recognize, recall, think about, manipulate, and understand the basic word sounds (Torgesen, 1998). With that growing ability, the child is increasingly able to access the language functions farther up in the hierarchy and to gain meaning from a written text. There are individual differences among children in phonemic awareness, and most children gradually develop these skills to an adequate degree. Some children, however, do not. According to the **phonological deficit model,** weakness in phonological processing interferes with the decoding process and prevents the child's adequate word identification. That lack in turn prevents access to the higher functions and interferes with comprehension of the text and other language functions. The phonological deficit is thought by many to be the most common reason for early reading and other language problems (e.g., Liberman, Shankweiler, & Liberman, 1989).

Phonological awareness is well into development prior to school age. It should be possible to assess it in preschoolers, to provide special training for children with deficits, and to enrich the phonemic development of children in general. Tests of phonological awareness and letter recognition have been developed (Torgesen, 1998; Yopp, 1988). The results of early prevention attempts are mixed. Some large-scale prevention studies (Foorman et al., 1996; Torgesen, Wagner, & Rashotle, 1997) indicate that most children at risk for reading difficulties can be helped to reach average reading skills if special instruction is given early, in kindergarten or early first grade. However, a sizable proportion of children with reading disabilities do not profit from these programs (Torgesen, 1998).

Reading skills are of critical importance in education and, indeed, in much of modern life. The early diagnosis and prevention of reading problems and the general enrichment of early prereading experiences are potentially significant for the future of a literate, well-informed society. It is not surprising that so much interest has been generated in these problems and that basic and applied research in language development is a dynamic and expanding area of inquiry.

Central Processing Deficits

It is assumed that the etiologies of LD include some as yet unspecified CNS disturbances. These in turn are thought to create difficulties in central processing functions that are expressed as various specific learning disabilities. Central processing is the perception (the two terms are here used interchangeably) of sensory stimulation—that is, the sense that one makes of auditory, visual, proprioceptive, and other sensory stimuli. The sense organs such as the eye and the outer and inner ear receive and transmit sensory stimuli to the brain. At the brain level, central processes (perception) then "make sense" of those stimuli so that we understand what sights, sounds, and so on they represent. Of particular concern in LD are **auditory and visual central processing defects.** The child with one of these defects may have normal sensory acuity (normal vision and hearing) but is unable to make clear sense of the signals that reach the brain. That is, he or she may see and hear adequately, but cannot easily translate the sensory signals into meaningful messages.

Children learn about the world through all of the senses. They see, hear, touch, taste, smell, and detect sensory stimuli arising from their own bodies. As children approach and enter school, vision and hearing will become the primary senses through which informa-

B O X **14.10**

The Inferred Hierarchical Structures That Process Language in the Phonological Processing Model

Pragmatics: Refers to the many rules for actual language usage in real settings (i.e., how the meaning of words relates to the actual context in which the words occur). Children learn not only effective use of words and sentences but must also develop an appreciation of the settings in which the language occurs and the appropriateness of the language for each setting. Children speak differently to each other than to their teachers and when in church or on the playground. Language becomes more formal when writing, less formal in conversation, and so on. Pragmatics, then, involves rules for the use of language in social interaction for appropriate and effective communication.

Grammar: Includes morphology and syntax and refers to the rules for the structure of language. **Syntax** refers to the rules for combining words into meaningful sentences. The sequence of words in a sentence can be altered and still convey the same meaning, but the various forms of the sentence must follow syntactic rules to make sense. Rules also indicate, for example, how to express negation ("I will not go to the store" rather than "I will go to the store, not.") and interrogation ("Do you want a cookie?" rather than "A cookie want you do?"). **Morphology** refers to the rules for proper use of morphemes, which are the smallest units of meaning in a language. These include suffixes and prefixes and the root words that form the bases of other words. How words are modified to form different tenses, plural and singular forms, and so on are guided by the morphological rules of the language.

Semantics: Refers to the meanings of words and phrases. Children's vocabularies grow and the children learn not only the sound and form of words and phrases, but also to comprehend their meanings. Semantic rules help to determine which words to use and how words are sequenced in phrases and sentences to produce the meanings that are intended.

Phonology: Refers to the processing of the distinctive basic elements of sounds that make up a language. The phoneme is the smallest meaningful unit of sound in a language. Children must learn to recognize and reproduce these basic sounds, as well as all of the rules for combining the phonemes to produce the 900 words that the average child knows by about age 3 and up to some 14,000 known by about school age. Phonological rules guide the ways that sounds of words change as we alter their morphology (e.g., turning "goose" into "geese"). A major inference of the phonological processing model in LD is that if children have deficits in this basic level of phonological processing, they will also have difficulties in the higher-order processing (semantics, grammar, pragmatics), possibly resulting in dyslexia.

tion is transmitted. Increasingly, the child will be directed to process visual and auditory information in order to achieve in school. The major deficits that result from auditory and visual central processing disorders are summarized in Box 14.11.

As can be seen from Box 14.7, the child with auditory or visual central processing problems, despite normal vision and hearing acuity, will be hard pressed to develop phonemic awareness skills, learn to read, write, understand teachers' verbal instructions, pay

B O X **14.11**

Major Deficiencies Resulting from Auditory and Visual Central Processing Disorders

Deficiencies Found in Auditory Central Processing Disorders (Based on: the American Speech-Language-Hearing Association, 1996).
A child might have one or more of the following problems in:

> locating direction of sound stimuli (left, right, etc.);
> discriminating among specific sounds;
> recognizing patterns of sounds in auditory stimuli;
> recognizing the timing (temporal aspects) among sound stimuli;
> maintaining performance when competing signals are present;
> maintaining performance when the signals degrade (become less clear or intense).

Deficiencies Found in Visual Central Processing Disorders (from National Center for Learning Disabilities, 1999).
A child might have one or more of the following problems in:

> perceiving accurately the spatial relationships among objects
>
> visual discrimination: the ability to discriminate common objects from each other and symbols based on their characteristics such as shape, color, position, and size
>
> visual closure: the ability to recognize objects that are only partially presented (i.e., being able to complete or have "closure" when presented with an incomplete figure)
>
> object recognition: being able to recognize visually common objects. A child might have difficulty recognizing a familiar object visually (also called visual agnosia) but be able to do so through another sense, such as touch.
>
> whole–part relationships: the ability to recognize the parts of a configuration and the whole. For example, recognizing a word (the "whole") and the letters that make up the word (the "parts"). Some children can do one but have difficulty with the other, thus interfering with learning to read.
>
> integrating visual perceptions with other developmental areas: visual perceptions often guide motor actions, and the two need to be integrated to produce smooth functioning. Some children have difficulty with this integration, thus producing a marked clumsiness and difficulties in, for example, trying to learn to print or write.

---

attention, take notes, and so on. Losing the thread of what is being presented orally, this child will begin to appear inattentive, distractible, forgetful, uninterested, and unmotivated in class and may even be thought of as hearing or visually impaired.

The diagnoses of these conditions require auditory, visual, and speech assessments. Audiologists and optometrists or ophthalmologists assess sensory functioning to rule out auditory and/or visual impairments. Speech and language therapists then assess linguistic skills and try to identify specific language weaknesses. Special education teachers and educational psychologists evaluate academic and cognitive functioning to identify the child's strengths and problem areas. With that type of information, special education teachers can plan individually oriented teaching procedures.

V. Primary and Secondary Characteristics

Attention and Hyperactivity Problems

The **primary characteristics** of persons with LD are specific deficits and functional problems in the development and use of language and arithmetic skills. It is assumed these primary characteristics are the cognitive problems in learning, and they in turn are due to genetic and biological processes and conditions inherent in the person. There are also **secondary characteristics** that are found in many but not in all cases. LD is defined by the primary characteristics, not by the secondary characteristics. Although secondary, these characteristics might nevertheless be extremely disruptive, interfering with the child's progress in school and perhaps even leading to early withdrawal from school. Secondary does not mean they are of little consequence. When trying to develop diagnostic criteria, it is necessary to clarify which factors are primary and which are secondary.

Common secondary issues include problems in attention and overactivity. Children with LD often cannot remain attentive to a task for long periods, become restless, easily distracted, forget details, and fail to carry through on instructions. These are frequent features of LD cases and are considered to be the results of specific learning deficits rather than causes of LD. However, if present, attention and overactivity problems can certainly further complicate learning problems.

These associated characteristics should not be confused with primary **attention deficit disorder (ADD)** and **attention deficit hyperactivity disorder (ADHD)** (*DSM-IV*, American Psychiatric Association, 1994), although there are similarities. ADHD is not considered a learning disability per se and is diagnosed separately from LD. The criteria for the *DSM-IV* ADHD diagnosis are summarized in Box 14-12. Many of those characteristics can also be seen in LD children, although not in the number and intensity that are required for a diagnosis of ADHD. (ADHD is treated very briefly because, as explained earlier, we have made the decision not to include it as a developmental disability.) An estimated 3 to 10 percent of elementary school students have ADHD symptoms (Stoudemire, 1998). For these children, treatment with a combination of medication and behavior modification can improve attention and reduce hyperactivity. The medication, methylphenidate (the generic form of Ritalin), is a stimulant, and it has the paradoxical effect of helping to calm the child. With that accomplished, the child is presumably more able to profit from regular or, in some cases, special education. Unfortunately, for years, there has been a tendency to overprescribe stimulants to control children's behavior. Zito et al. (2000) found a significant increase in prescriptions for *preschoolers,* even though there is considerable doubt that such young children can meet the definitional requirements for ADHD. Another reason for caution is that we do not know very much about the effects of such mood and behavior control drugs on the developing brain. To administer these drugs to young children might threaten that brain development.

BOX **14.12**

A Summary of the Criteria for the Diagnosis of ADHD

To meet the criteria for the ADHD diagnosis, eight of the following must have been present for at least 6 months, must be excessive for age and intelligence, and the attention deficit patterns must have begun prior to age 7.

1. Often fidgets and squirms
2. Difficulty remaining seated
3. Easily distracted
4. Difficulty waiting to take turns
5. Often blurts out answers before the question has been completed
6. Difficulties following instructions; often fails to complete tasks
7. Difficulties sustaining attention on tasks
8. Often shifts from one activity to another
9. Difficulty playing/working quietly
10. Often talks excessively
11. Interrupts or intrudes upon others
12. Often seems not to listen
13. Often loses necessary things (toys, books, assignments, pencils, etc.)
14. Often behaves in physically dangerous ways, seemingly without thought

(Based on *DSM-IV,* American Psychiatric Association, 1994)

Anxiety, Panic, Phobias

Children and adults with LD are susceptible to all of the psychological problems that beset other people. Indeed, because of their learning difficulties and the associated social problems, they may be even more prone than most to problems of poor self-esteem, anxiety, panic, fears, and phobias. The LD condition does not preclude those other issues from arising. When they do occur, usually as secondary factors to the LD, there is no reason why direct therapeutic help cannot be given for those specific secondary problems. For children, there are many effective, behaviorally oriented treatments for anxiety problems, and they can be applied to children with LD as well as to other children. One of the limitations in our perceptions of children with DD, LD, MR, or even children who suffer from physical abuse is that serious anxiety problems are seen as "symptoms" of the primary condition. Therefore, it is mistakenly thought that these symptoms are not likely to be improved without improving the primary condition. Unfortunately, as discussed in Chapter 1, too many professionals fail to understand that while those problems are not independent of the disabilities, they can and should be treated separately (Graziano & Mills, 1992). Even though such direct treatment does not reduce the primary disability, it can help to improve the child's quality of life by ameliorating those secondary issues.

Intellectually Gifted Children with LD

It may seem a contradiction, but some children with LD are intellectually gifted. Consider the major defining factor: persons with normal or higher intellectual ability who have severe, specific learning difficulties. By definition, all children with specific LD are at or above the mean in the IQ distribution. This suggests that theoretically about 5 percent are 2 standard deviations above the mean of the IQ distribution. At least one study (Baum, 1985) found one-third of their sample of students with LD had superior intellectual ability!

A "gifted" child is one with outstanding ability in any of five areas: general intelligence, high aptitude in specific academic areas, productive thinking, leadership abilities, and visual and performing arts (Marland, 1972, as modified by later legislation; see Brody & Mills, 1997). A child with LD has significant disabilities in one or more specific areas of learning. When the LD and gifted factors are combined in one person, the child then has special needs in two areas—that is, needs stemming from specific learning disabilities *and* from high intellectual or other abilities (Fox, Brody, & Tobin, 1983). Children of such marked **dual exceptionality** present particularly difficult problems and are not well served by our schools (Cline & Schwartz, 1999). This is a heterogeneous group, with at least three major subgroups (Brody & Mills, 1997; summarized in Box 14.13). To complicate the issues further, each factor alone (LD and Gifted) presents serious definitional problems (Vaughn, 1989) that are compounded when the two are combined. Consider the issues of identification and diagnoses. This group of children includes all types of LD and all types of giftedness. The possible combinations of patterns are so great that no single set of test scores could possibly suffice as definitional and diagnostic indicators.

BOX **14.13**

Three Major Subgroups of Children with LD and Giftedness (Dual Exceptionalities)

Some students are recognized as gifted but have academic problems due to LD. Their learning disabilities are not identified, and no special programming is provided to help them. Unfortunately, these students are labeled "underachievers," seen as having self-concept problems, poor motivation, or even more pejoratively, as being lazy and indifferent.

In another group, the learning disabilities are recognized but not the child's outstanding abilities and potential. They are not referred for "gifted" programs and continue to be significantly underestimated, probably to the child's serious decrement.

In what Brody and Mills (1997) suggest may be the largest group, the dual exceptionalities mask each other, and neither their LD nor their particular giftedness is recognized. These students appear to function at least passably in regular classes. As academic work increases in difficulty in upper grades, their disabilities may become apparent, but their high potential is never recognized, the students continue to be underestimated, and little or no help is provided.

Based on Brody, L. E., & Mills, C. J. (1997). Gifted children with learning disabilities: A review of the issues. *Journal of Learning Disabilities, 30*(3), 282–286.

Likewise, because of the heterogeneity, no single remedial approach will meet all needs. Rather, individually designed approaches are needed. There appears to be a general consensus that the emphasis ought to be placed on strengthening the students' particular assets rather than trying to remediate the disabilities, and there are a variety of strategies that should be used (Brody & Mills, 1997). The programs could include full-time or part-time special classes for gifted students with LD and/or the provision of resource rooms. In either case, these students would gain support and stimulation from the other students, as well as from the materials and faculty. Keeping these students in general education classes is another option. However, meeting the varied needs of widely diverse students in the same classroom, as in mainstreaming, can be a difficult endeavor.

VI. Assistive Technology for Learning Disabilities

For all children with specific LD, many forms of **assistive technology** are available. These are designed to aid the person to function despite the disability rather than to correct or cure the problem, much as a person uses a cane to help in walking. A child's *individualized educational plan* (IEP) will include the particular technology to help the child work around the disability. The person's learning difficulties are not limited to school but occur in all set-tings—home, school, work, and even recreation (e.g., keeping score in a bowling match). Hence, some technologies are "portable," thus helping the person to be more successful and independent in many settings.

Assistive technologies can be low-tech devices. For example, some LD children have problems writing or adding numbers in straight horizontal lines or, in reading, cannot keep adjacent lines of text from intruding into the field of vision. For these and similar problems, simple straight edges, enhanced lines on the paper, highlight markers, cardboard cutout windows, and large text can serve as guides or masking devices. Graph paper, vertically lined paper, and color-coded or shaded columns and rows can help the child to keep straight the vertical and horizontal lines of arithmetic calculations. These guides can be gradually faded out as the child's skills improve.

Assistive technologies can also be high-tech ranging from audiotape-recorded lec-tures to sophisticated interactive computer programs. For example, for students with a va-riety of reading problems, computer software can include a spelling and grammar checker, dictionary, and thesaurus and can present textual material that allows the reader to alter the font size and the number of lines or even words on a single page (i.e., screen). Text and graphics can be altered in color, background material, and size so as to improve the salience of the material. New computers can have speech capability to reduce or supplement the visual components of reading or scanning. With a computer, speech capability, a color scan-ner, and a color printer, a knowledgeable and creative special education teacher can produce effective, highly individualized, custom-designed material for LD students.

Other high-tech devices include books on tape, hand-held and talking calculators, CD recorders and players, large screen displays, and keyboards with oversized characters. With the development of laptop and notebook computers, much of the technology is made portable, and the student need not be limited to working only at a desk or in school. The potential is vast for new and creative ideas in developing useful procedures to improve the person's functioning and independence. The technology exists to help every LD student. The major impediments are those due to administrative inertia.

VII. The Personal Toll of LD

Druck (1994), who grew up with a learning disability, discusses the pervasive feelings of sadness and the self-label "stupid" that he experienced. Repeated failures in school, all of them very public and obvious to peers, teachers, and parents, made him feel humiliated, stupid, and incompetent. Those feelings were reinforced by the advice given by teachers and counselors that he was "limited" and should have only low-level expectations for his future. He eventually earned his doctorate. Druck never forgot how the schools missed seeing his strengths and how he was made to feel stupid and inadequate. He succeeded because, despite his LD, he was a bright, capable, and hardworking person. The first 30 years of his life were largely devoted to the laborious tasks of creating complex, roundabout strategies to hide his limitations and to compensate for what he then believed was his basic stupidity. As an adult, he eventually came to know that he was not stupid after all.

That firsthand account illustrates the personal toll of LD. Children may develop what Druck calls "learned stupidity" and feelings of inadequacy. They suspect they are just as smart as other students (Bear & Minke, 1996), although they perceive that they do not achieve as well in academic areas (Cooley & Ayers, 1988). The discrepancy leads to their puzzlement: "I know I'm as smart as they are. Why can't I understand? Why can't I learn like others? Why me?" Many of the students try to compensate for their limitations by studying or working longer, harder hours by constantly creating novel alternative ways to learn. Many are successful at this, but the cost in energy and time can be high. Others eventually weary of the struggle and give in to their "stupidity."

Social skills may also suffer. LD often involves language and communication limitations. The person with LD may also have difficulties perceiving and understanding subtle nonverbal cues that are part of every social interaction. Reading the intent and moods of others may be difficult (see the discussion of "reading other's minds" in Chapter 11, section VIII.). Poor understanding of such nuances can lead to misunderstandings and impatience and can cause social and employment problems. As a result, some may seem socially inept, fail to behave appropriately in many small ways, and not recognize what others are trying to communicate.

Life for the families of children with LD is often stressful. If the LD is accompanied by attention and hyperactivity problems, then life can be a daily round of sibling bickering with the LD child seemingly always in the center and the parents feeling exhausted. Even without the ADHD component, parents of LD children often find themselves pressed for extra attention, striving to help the child learn academics and understand social rules, and repeatedly intervening to settle conflicts.

For the child with LD, struggling to keep pace academically with peers means extra hours and harder work, and it can be exhausting. The already tired child comes home from school and is expected by teachers and parents to work even more on homework, which takes this child an inordinately long time and is often accompanied by resistance, postponements, struggles, and demands on the parents. They, too, become fatigued.

Perhaps the greatest cost—for the person and for society—is when the LD child's strengths are not recognized and nourished. Many children can become worn down by the emphasis on their limitations and the lack of support for their abilities. Then not only the child but also society loses.

VIII. Learning Disabilities in Adulthood

Every year, many thousands of youngsters with LD move from school into the adult population. One of the persistent myths about LD is that it will be "outgrown" by adulthood. But that optimistic expectation is not borne out (Gerber & Reiff, 1994). LD is a lifelong condition. It may be less obvious in adults because the persons are not challenged daily and publicly as in school. But adults face many challenges that demand the very skills that are so uncertain in the person with LD. The most common problems revolve around language-based deficits such as in reading and spelling (Blalock, 1982). It has been estimated that 30 million Americans are functionally illiterate, and half is due to LD (Anderson, 1994). Everyday events such as shopping require the person to read labels, make simple calculations of comparative prices, determine relative nutritional values, and keep within a budget. Going to a supermarket can be overwhelming for some. Reading airline, bus, and train schedules, contracts, utility bills, instructions for operating appliances, instructions for the safe use of medications, and so on are beyond many. It is difficult or even impossible for many persons with LD to understand a note from their child's teacher, income tax report forms, or write a check, especially spelling out the amount. Many adults with LD have problems with "directionality"—they cannot read maps, understand or remember directions to places, often confuse right- and left-hand turns, and have inordinate difficulty reading street names and road signs quickly enough while driving. Many report "organizational problems" in keeping order in their lives, knowing where everyday objects are stored, such as in a kitchen, keeping a schedule, and so on. Seeking employment is difficult if one cannot easily read newspapers, advertisements, or fill out employment applications (this is one of the most common problems).

Life is marked by transitional periods such as moving from school to work, college, or the military; from one job to another; from a single to married state; entering parenthood, middle age, and old age. Each transition requires shifting to new roles and discarding and/or modifying old roles. Transition means change, often generates anxiety, and demands that we react with good solutions to a myriad of new demands. Succeeding in these common transitions may be particularly difficult for persons with LD (Gerber et al., 1990).

Even those with LD who have been successful report many continuing problems as they struggle to compensate for their limitations (Druck, 1994). One of the common issues described is that of the inordinate amount of time required to complete many ordinary work and leisure tasks that others can accomplish quickly and seemingly with ease. Another is the residual anger that many adults still feel over their treatment as youngsters by insensitive adults, including teachers, counselors, and relatives (Reiff & Gerber, 1994). When they were in school, they were made to "feel stupid," as only their academic weaknesses were recognized while their strengths were not. One person with LD who eventually earned a

PhD recalls a common experience: the guidance counselor explaining to his parents that their son could always be a "janitor or something" (Druck, 1994). Strong feelings of being stupid, of being the marginal person in a group, stress and anxiety, low self-esteem, helplessness, anger, and grief over lost opportunities appear frequent among those LD adults who seek counseling and psychotherapy (Barton & Fuhrman, 1994).

Attending to the issues of LD children in school is difficult and only partially successful. How do we deal with the issues over their next 60 or so years? Although there has been a marked increase in the literature on issues of adults with LD (Patton & Polloway, 1992), a great deal more research is still needed. An excellent book by Gerber and Reiff (1994) is recommended for its discussions of major issues of adults with LD.

It is the children with LD who may have the greatest burdens because in school they are challenged daily to read, write, or do arithmetic. In addition, the constant challenges posed and their struggles and failures are so very public. They fail repeatedly in front of their friends and other peers, and they are constantly subjected to the evaluating and judgmental scrutiny of their teachers and parents. School can become a feared battleground for these children.

For many, the struggles continue throughout life, leaving them puzzled, deeply frustrated, and less successful and fulfilled than they might have been. However, LD is a heterogeneous population, and the escape from school and moving into adulthood are often liberating events. As suggested by Reiff and Gerber (1994), many adults with LD, freed from the demands and scrutiny of childhood and school, succeed in creating their own structure. They learn to direct their lives toward their own strengths and interests—in essence, gaining control—and successfully adapting to the demands of adulthood.

We need to be reminded that many persons, apparently with LD, have been enormously successful and important despite negative and dismissive judgments by teachers and others. We need only recall Einstein, Edison, Woodrow Wilson, or many others (see Jordan, 1996, for vignettes) to realize that even though some children have trouble reading or remembering facts, they may nevertheless have other powerful talents that enable them to conceptualize in ways far above more "intact" people.

IX. Chapter Summary

Learning disabilities (LD) is an umbrella term that refers to a large and heterogeneous group of persons, an estimated 16 million children and adults in the United States. This makes LD one of the most prevalent disabilities. LD has multiple and interactive etiologies—genetic factors, CNS dysfunction, poor learning environments—but its etiology is not yet well understood. It has been estimated that 5 to 6 percent of all schoolchildren and 50 percent of those in special education have learning disabilities. Two important diagnostic criteria are academic underachievement and the exclusion of other intellectual deficits such as mental retardation.

LD is a lifelong disability that sets up many handicaps. Although it cannot be "cured" or reversed, persons with LD can, through careful educational programming, still learn and achieve academic, personal, and occupational success.

KEY TERMS

Know these important terms. Check the chapter and the Glossary for their meanings.
They are listed here in their approximate order of appearance in the chapter.

Specific learning disorder
Learning disabilities (LD)
Secondary problems
Inclusion criteria
Exclusion criteria
Discrepancy criteria
Underachievement
Dyslexia
Dyscalcula
Speech and language disorders
Scholastic skills disorders
Motor function disorders
Unspecified disorders
Developmental articulation
   disorders
Developmental receptive
   language disorders

Developmental expressive
   language disorders
Specific reading disorders
Specific spelling disorders
Specific expressive writing
   disorders
Phonological awareness
Phonemes
Graphemes
Semantics
Grammar
Morphology
Syntax
Pragmatics
Phonological deficit model
Auditory central processing
   defects

Visual central processing defects
Specific arithmetic disorder
Developmental motor function
   disorder
Mixed (learning) disorder
Other (learning) disorder
Unspecified (learning) disorder
Primary characteristics of LD
Secondary characteristics of LD
Attention deficit disorder
Attention deficit hyperactivity
   disorder
Dual exceptionality
Individual educational plan
Assistive technology

SUGGESTED READING

Brody, L. E., & Mills, C. J. (1997). Gifted children with learning disabilities: A review of the issues. *Journal of Learning Disabilities, 30*(3), 282–296.

Gerber, P. J., & Reiff, H. B. (Eds.). (1994). *Learning disabilities in adulthood: Persisting problems and evolving issues.* Boston: Andover Medical Publishers.

Jordan, D. R. (1996). *Overcoming dyslexia in children, adolescents, and adults* (2nd ed.) Austin, TX: Pro-Ed.

Vaughn, S., & Bos, C. (1994). (Eds.). *Research issues in learning disabilities: Theory, methodology, assessment, and ethics.* New York: Springer-Verlag.

ONLINE LIST OF ORGANIZATIONS

An updated list of organizations providing LD services and/or information for professionals and parents is available online: http//www.ldonline.org/ccldinfo/5.html

STUDY QUESTIONS

14-1. Think this through: What are some of the secondary problems that can occur and complicate the life of a child in grammar school who has a primary LD?

14-2. What is meant by inclusion criteria, exclusion criteria, and discrepancy criteria in the diagnosis of LD?

14-3. Describe each of the following types of LD: developmental speech and language disorder; articulation disorder; expressive language disorder; receptive language disorder; developmental academic skills disorder.

14-4. What are some important early signs of possible LD development in the future for a child?

14-5. What is the concept of phonological awareness and why is it important in, for example, the development of reading and other academic skills?

14-6. What is meant by central processing deficits and what is their importance in LD?

14-7. Distinguish between primary and secondary characteristics of LD.

14-8. What are some useful assistive devices for children with LD?

CHAPTER

15 Services for Persons with Developmental Disabilities

I. The Twentieth-Century Revolution

Restated Romanticism, Empirical Science, and Technology

Services for persons with disabilities have been discussed, where appropriate, in earlier chapters. This chapter presents a brief discussion of the contemporary model of service. The intent is to provide the model's rationale and, in broad terms rather than in specific procedures, its major characteristics.

Chapter 1 presented a brief account of the history of social responses to disabilities. We noted that at any time in history treatment was mixed, ranging from exemplary care for some to brutality for others, and that mix still exists today. Included in that historical mix have been infanticide, abandonment of children, murder, abuse, rejection, ridicule, and institutionalized isolation, the latter being primarily for the protection of society from the demands and depredations of those "afflicted" persons. There has, however, been significant improvement in much of the world. Brutality continues to be part of the picture, but there has been a shift and long, slow progress toward more humanitarian approaches. In the mid- to late nineteenth and early twentieth centuries, the revolutionary (but not new) ideas of training and educating persons with disabilities gained support in Europe and the United States. In the last half of the twentieth century, largely through the pressures applied by civil rights reformers, advocacy groups such as those formed by parents and persons with disabilities, and protesters in general, public policy began to change dramatically, and services were improved and expanded.

It has been fairly recent, in about the last four decades of the twentieth century, that the growing weight of changing public opinion gained enough force to create a new model of the status of persons with disabilities and the services provided for them. This model is one of equal humanity, with a core idea that disability is a reality but that reality does not define the person. *Person-first language*—"a child with autism"—rather than "an autistic child," becomes a clear signal and a reminder of the importance of primary focus on the person rather than on the disability. The model directs services to bring about not just inclusion in society, but the fullest active participation in culture and society within limits of each person's abilities and desires. Like the humanitarian reform models of the late eighteenth and early nineteenth centuries (e.g., *moral treatment*), this is a concept derived from the romantic philosophy of the time. That philosophy believed in the dignity and worth of all persons and in a natural human potential for individuals to grow and to evolve to higher levels of function and integration when artificial social barriers are removed. The present restatement of romanticism is buttressed by the added strength of modern empirical science and technology. This newly integrated model recognizes the essential human equality of persons with or without disabilities and extends in concept, if not always in reality, all of the human rights, the social acceptance, inclusion, and respect that is generally extended to other people. What is new about the current model is the combination of romantic humanitarianism with modern empirical science—an alliance that would have earlier been quite thoroughly conflicting because the nineteenth-century romantic ideas grew largely as protest against the eighteenth-century emergence of objective science! But as has happened often in history, two initially conflicting world-views may eventually come together in alliance for common cause. The romantic, humanitarian philosophy is now informed by objective science and uses that knowledge and technology to assist people in their striving for optimum personal development.

We should note that many of the changes in service delivery over the past four decades have involved the resumption by parents of responsibilities and rights involving the care of their children with disabilities. This development follows a long history in which, as Newman (1991) pointed out, parents had gradually relinquished those rights and responsibilities to social agencies. A significant part of the revolution we are discussing has been the overturning of that historical trend and the resumption of parental control.

We have asserted that one of the major central, organizing, and revolutionary ideas in this sea change in attitudes and behavior has been the rediscovery in the 1950s and 1960s of the power of iatrogenic circumstances in molding the overall functioning of human beings. Like the Romans of A.D. 300 and the nineteenth-century humanitarian reformers, we have again been struck by the realization that how we treat people and what expectations we communicate to them are, indeed, powerful influences. This model of extended humanity and new sensitivity to social/environmental factors and its alliance with empirical science help define our public attitudes, policy decisions, and professional services. This realization seems to be at the center of virtually all of the powerful and important protest movements of the twentieth century—civil rights, deinstitutionalization, and environmental protection—and has been particularly visible and important in the demands for improved lives for persons with disabilities.

Normalization, Advocacy, and Consumer Empowerment

Many ideas and events have swirled together over the past several decades to help form our current views and approaches. Three ideas have been of particular importance: normalization, advocacy, and consumer empowerment.

Normalization.   This became an influential idea in the 1970s and 1980s. It asserted the principle that persons with disabilities need to have available to them all of the usual, ordinary facilities, resources, and patterns of everyday life such as are found in mainstream society (Nirje, 1969). According to this principle, the personal and service goals for socialization for persons with disabilities and the social supports or means of achieving those goals (Wolfensberger, 1972) should be located within and derived from *normal social settings* rather than from specialized segregated settings. Adoption of this principle constituted a major shift of emphasis away from segregation-based settings such as special isolated schools, residential institutions, and special workshops. Persons with disabilities were now seen as best served when placed, as much as possible, in normal everyday settings and given opportunities to play, learn, and work among other persons who were without disabilities.

The concept had an enormous impact on how service agencies were operated, and they modified their mission statements and resulting activities toward increased commitment to normalization. Public policy was affected as new laws incorporated the principle. It gave major impetus to the development of community residences for persons with disabilities, inclusion in regular classes in school, and more training and employment opportunities in normal job settings. Over a period of some 30 years, the influence of the normalization principle brought increased numbers of persons with disabilities into daily contact with many other people, increased their social experiences, and radically changed the field.

In terms of our social role model, we can see that this movement reshaped the very social position and social role of persons with disabilities. The position and role norms for behavior were now different than they had been. Persons in this new role were expected to function with more independence, more freedom to move in society, to have more interactions with more persons in complementary roles, and therefore to gain by the increased opportunities to utilize the social resources that are controlled by other persons. Thus, normalization opened up new opportunities but also imposed new demands on the persons with disabilities and on the service providers who now had to help them adapt to the new demands and opportunities. Wolfensberger (1983, 1984, 1992) recognized that normalization was also altering the social status (i.e., value) of persons with disabilities. By redefining the role and bringing these persons into everyday society, one result could be an increased value of the role. Wolfensberger discussed this new valuation as **social role valorization.**

Advocacy and Consumer Empowerment.   Advocacy has long been part of social movements to improve the condition of specific groups of people, and it has been no less so in this field. To be an advocate is to "take up the cause" and to work toward achieving the goals of the cause. In the disabilities field, parents have been critically important advocates for their children, as have others such as professionals in human services, education, law, medicine, psychology, public service, and many others.

As normalization continued to develop in the field, it became apparent that in addition to significant gains, new problems were emerging (Wolfe, Kregel, & Wehman, 1996). Persons with disabilities, increasingly interacting in the "normal" social world, were beginning to experience new difficulties in their normalized worlds, such as facing job discrimination, social rebuffs, opposition to neighborhood residences, and so on. In addition, it seemed to many that what was "normal" and therefore desirable for the person with disabilities was increasingly being defined by service providers, sometimes in opposition to the client's own wants. Thus, service providers appeared to be gaining a great deal of power over their clients in the new normalized worlds, and agencies began to be seen as contemporary reflections of the paternalistic, controlling agencies of previous decades. Normalization notwithstanding, it was feared that a new kind of authoritarian control by providers and a new form of passive dependence of clients were being fostered.

Advocacy then began to take on a new character of advocacy for the civil rights of persons with disabilities and for consumer empowerment. In essence, this was a new coalition: (a) governmental policy and law were needed to guarantee the civil rights of persons with disabilities to function in society without discrimination and (b) the clients themselves needed to develop more control over their own lives to practice consumer empowerment. Consumer empowerment is self-advocacy—taking up the cause, speaking out for oneself and for the group, and working actively to bring about changes to improve each person's opportunities to develop their own lives without prejudice and unwarranted social obstacles.

We do not want to suggest that the civil rights guarantees and consumer empowerment movements have replaced all previous ideas and approaches. Rather, we now have a considerable mix of options for persons with disabilities, their families, and the professionals who provide services. There are still residential institutions and service agencies with clients and professional service providers. We still operate by the normalization principle, although we might not call it that. We have the Americans with Disabilities Act of 1990 to protect civil rights. We encourage self-advocacy and consumer empowerment but also know that these alone are not sufficient because, in addition to the self-assertive actions of persons with disabilities, society must also accept responsibilities, make resources available, and even intervene in individual cases and assume direct control when required. The major responsibility of society with regard to persons with disabilities has become that of guaranteeing the rights of individuals, making resources available, and providing direct help in each case to the degree necessary for each individual.

Each person with disabilities, then, to the degree each is capable, can help to create and control his or her own life, utilizing whatever portions of the available resources may be needed at various times in life. For some persons, a heavy dependence on service providers may be needed; for others, a greater degree of autonomy is possible. There is no longer a "one rule for all" approach. This means, of course, that the social agencies need to continue redefining their own social positions and the roles of their individual agents. They need to incorporate the new norms of accommodating and assisting individuals as they function to develop their own lives. They need to train future staff in the new model.

In the new model, the relative roles of the service agencies and the individuals have changed. Greater directive control is now with the individual, while the agency becomes the general repository of resources to be used by the person. The specific mix of individual control and agency resources will vary from one case to another. As a result, the experiences and overall development of persons with disabilities who are born today will be very different from those born just 20 or so years ago. Our expectations for them are more positive, our services are more sensitive and responsive, our procedures are better, and more resources are available. A person's chances for full participation, independent living, and personal development are greater now than ever before. Recognition of biological issues and needs for medical services and the availability of those services are greater now. Our recognition that this is a *person* who has a disability is sharper now. And our attention to a full range of human needs in biological, cognitive, personal/emotional, educational, social, economic, and self-development areas is greater than ever before. The science and technology that underlie our understanding of and services to persons are more developed than ever before. The elderly person with disabilities in the year 2070 will have had a significantly different development and overall quality of life than his or her counterpart today.

This is not to say that all is well, that we have all the answers, all the research, all of the programs in place, or the assurance that those will continue. There is still a vast amount to learn and much research to be done. There are still deep prejudices and discriminations, too many social and political obstacles, and too many places where services are not available or do not measure up to the quality needed. We are still heavily dependent on a peaceful world and healthy economic times to provide the resources needed for expanded research, training, and services. And there are still new revolutions to come, such as, perhaps, in the *prevention* of disabilities, which will alter our approaches once again (see Chapter 16).

Our current conceptions of the relative roles of society, service agencies and agents, and individuals with disabilities are driven by many factors such as science and technology, romantic-humanitarian philosophy, activism, empowerment, social protests, advocacy, professional development, and governmental policy. The latter, as expressed in legislation since 1960, reflects the significant attitudinal, philosophical, and technological changes and prescribes our current model of services to preschool and school-age children, youth and adults with disabilities, and their families. Some of the important legislation is listed in Box 15.1. A revolution has occurred and we are now working from a new and still developing humanitarian-scientific model that informs and guides our services to persons with disabilities.

The service model described here tries to conceptualize optimum services. The model will need modification through continued research and experience in practice. This

BOX **15.1**

Some of the Important Legislation
for Persons with Disabilities

1964. The Civil Rights Act prohibits discrimination based on race, religion, ethnicity, national origin, and creed. In later amendments, gender was added. This legislation was an important precedent for later legislation aimed specifically at persons with disabilities.

1968 & 1970. Architectural barriers to access in all federal buildings are prohibited, and the 1970 *Mass Transit Act* required wheelchair lifts on mass transit vehicles. Political moves delayed the implementation for some 20 years.

1972. President Nixon vetoes the *Rehabilitation Act* that had aimed to encourage independent living for persons with disabilities. Disability activists protested across the country, and Congress overrode Nixon's veto in 1973.

1975. PL 94-142, *The Education of All Handicapped Children Act,* states that all children with disabilities are eligible for a free and appropriate public education in the least restrictive environment. The act mandates that a detailed written contract (the individual education plan, or IEP), based on the unique characteristics and needs of each particular child, be produced and implemented for each child.

1986. PL 99-457 expands services provided to children 3 to 5 years of age with disabilities. This later becomes part of PL 94-142.

1990. PL 101-476, *The Individuals with Disabilities Education Act* (IDEA) reauthorized PL 94-142. It maintains the main provisions and alters some of the terminology (e.g., "handicaps" to "disabilities"). Most important, it expands the ages covered from the original 5 to 18 years of age to include children from birth and youth up to age 21. The new focus on the younger ages puts more emphasis on services for the child in the family context, including a detailed individual family services plan (IFSP), much like the IEP. It also emphasized the need for carefully planned transitions from home to school and from school to young adulthood, work, and more independent living.

1990. *The Americans with Disabilities Act* was the culmination of civil rights and self-advocacy movements. The law provides civil rights protection for persons with disabilities. It guarantees equal opportunities in five broad areas: Employment (Title I); Public Services (Title II); Public Accommodations (Title III); Telecommunications (Title IV); Miscellaneous (Title V). For example, under Title I, public or private employers may not discriminate against those with disabilities in employment practices (i.e., recruitment, hiring, advancement, firing, etc.). Under Title II, public services that are available to all citizens, such as transportation or social programs, cannot be denied to persons with disabilities. Under Title III, all new construction must be accessible to persons with disabilities, and in existing facilities, all barriers to use must be removed where feasible.

discussion is thus a working draft subject to additions, refinements, and corrections. Some of this material was discussed in various sections of earlier chapters in the contexts of specific disabilities. The following is an attempt at an integrated overview of services for persons with disabilities. Box 15.2 summarizes some of the important assumptions of this model.

BOX **15.2**

Summary of the Major Assumptions of the Current Model of Services

Current approaches to persons with developmental disabilities (indeed, all disabilities) are predicated on a model that coalesced in the last decades of the twentieth century and is still developing. The basic assumptions of this model are:

1. the shared humanity of *all* persons and the inviolability of their civil rights
2. that iatrogenesis is a powerful phenomenon, and alertness to the potential iatrogenic effects of any service and/or social action is necessary
3. an alliance of (a) early nineteenth-century romantic philosophy that assumes all persons' dignity, shared humanity, and natural tendency, when barriers are removed, to grow and develop toward one's fullest potential and (b) modern empirical science and technology that assume all phenomena can be understood through systematic empirical study and that knowledge gained through science can be used as the bases for practical applications to the solution of human problems
4. acceptance of the validity of the developmental hypothesis—that is, human development proceeds along known, predictable dimensions of growth that occurs according to a shared timetable of gradually emerging forms and functions
5. acceptance of the concept that such development continues throughout the entire life span from conception to death
6. belief that persons with developmental disabilities proceed along the same dimensions of lifelong development as do all other persons (i.e., all share the same developmental tasks), but their progress is interfered with by the specific nature and extent of their impairments and by social/personal issues and barriers related to those impairments
7. the importance of *lifelong* normalizing experiences for persons with developmental disabilities, including as normal as possible home and family life, accessible and effective health care, social interaction and development with peers, appropriate levels of schooling, occupational training and placement, independent living, gainful employment, and personal achievement within the limits of individual ability and desires
8. the need for civil and legal empowerment of individuals with disabilities to control their own lives
9. the need for service-delivery systems composed of many professional disciplines that will individually and interactively aim their services at helping persons with disabilities to achieve their fullest possible personal development and participation in society
10. the need for local, state, national, and worldwide advocacy for individuals, for specific groups of persons, and for all persons with disabilities
11. the need for (a) public awareness and education about the nature of developmental disabilities, (b) enlightened public policy that is informed by personal experiences, by modern science, and by humanitarian philosophy, and (c) increased research in and large-scale social application of methods for the *prevention* of developmental disabilities

II. Dimensions of Service

Early Diagnostic Evaluation and Timely Intervention

This model has developed in interaction with the growth of technology. For example, the development of prenatal testing and neonatal diagnoses (see Chapter 2) makes timely medical treatment and other services possible, as in the cases of children born with spina bifida, PKU, Prader-Willi, or Down syndrome. For children with spina bifida, for example, corrective surgery, sometimes even in utero, can significantly improve the condition. Children with PKU can be placed on the low-phenylalanine diet within just weeks after birth to prevent brain damage. Parents of children with Prader-Willi or Down syndrome can be prepared, counseled, and trained in effective care for their children beginning in infancy. Early detection makes it possible for immediate treatment, for timely preparation of parents for the special demands they will face, and for quick initiation of a range of special services, all aimed at giving this child the best opportunities for optimum development.

It is important that services and effective childrearing start as early as possible in the life of the child. This emphasis on early diagnosis and service is obvious in children whose disabilities are due to prenatal or neonatal factors. It is just as important in those instances of developmental disabilities stemming from injury or disease at later times during childhood and youth.

The Need for Continued Health Care

Children with developmental disabilities, just like all other children, need general health monitoring and care, but sometimes health problems are masked by major disabilities, and thus ignored or perhaps exacerbated by the impairment. Based on earlier work (Doherty & Baird, 1987), Jackson (2000) has proposed a useful "level of intervention" model for medical services to children with chronic conditions. Level I care, the most basic, involves routine health care for children who do not have chronic conditions such as developmental disabilities. The remaining five levels describe health care for children with chronic conditions. The model recognizes that these children need general, routine care but also will require specialized, sometimes emergency, care because of the nature of the disabilities. The skills needed by the various health providers vary from one level to another depending on the nature of the care needed.

The model includes not only direct care of the children but also family services such as case management, family education, and referral services. Included in this model is a level at which health-care providers and others assume responsibility for advocating for the children with chronic conditions. This requires knowledge and skills not only concerning childhood disabilities but also about legislative processes, community services and agency networking, and skills in working with legislators. Jackson's comprehensive model is focused on children, but its basic ideas also apply to the person as he or she grows older and is appropriate for the entire life span.

The Developmental Emphasis and Family Support

The developmental hypothesis, which is a product of the early to midtwentieth century, is of major importance. It is assumed that persons proceed through normal, predictable developmental sequences from conception throughout his or her *entire life span,* and the person's developmental rate and form will be affected by many biological and social factors, including the nature of specific impairments. Impairments may cause delays in some areas and preclude development in others. However, a basic assumption of the model is that every person has the potential for some level of development along the normal sequences. A general goal for service providers is to help ensure as normal a developmental sequence and attainment of developmental skills as is possible in each case. It is assumed that to achieve optimum development, the infant will need all of the affection, attention, and care that is found in most normal family interactions. This becomes the central principle for much of the special services: *maintaining the child in a home/family environment that is assisted to operate in a positive, developmentally supportive manner* (see Birenbaum, 1971; Darling, 1991; Voysey, 1975). As the child grows into youth, young adulthood, middle and old age, the person's needs for services change, but the central idea remains (i.e., to help maintain the maturing person in planned, supportive, and well-equipped environments in order to enhance optimum developmental success). Clearly, this is a focus on *lifelong development.*

Carrying out the central idea of normalizing each child's development requires family support services. Few families are trained or equipped for the special demands created by a child's severe impairments. Thus, family evaluation, training, counseling, and monitoring from the beginning become important parts of the services. The focus is on helping the family guide and assist the child through normalized experiences. Parent–child interaction that supports the achievement of sequenced developmental tasks is encouraged. These include keeping the child at home rather than institutionalized, enhancing parent–child attachment formation, early stimulation, play with peers, normalized school experiences, broadening social interactions as the child grows into adolescence, helping the young adult in transition to more independent living and working, and dealing with illness, aging, and death. The concept embraces the full life span, but parental and family support services are most usually focused on about the first third of the person's life, when family ties and lingering dependence on parents are greatest. Later, the emphasis shifts to the person's adult status, including his or her peer group, employment, and "new family" such as those created in group-home settings.

As early as possible, a family evaluation is carried out by a team of professionals and paraprofessional assistants, followed by periodic monitoring to assess the child's and family's progress and changing needs. We should note that "family" today is not limited to the two-parent plus siblings and often one or more grandparents that may have existed at some earlier time. The diversity in families today is great. A family may be headed by two biological parents or some combination of male–female, biological, and/or stepparents and/or foster parents. There may be a single adult, consanguineously related to the children or not, as the responsible caregiver. Unmarried couples, heterosexual or homosexual, are heading more families than before. Divorce and other family breakups seem now to be the rule rather than the exception. Such variability may have significant implications for family stability and cohesiveness, for individual member's acceptance of responsibility, and perhaps even for funding eligibility. The family evaluators need to be aware of these factors and their possible implications in each case.

There are several models on which family evaluations can be based such as family systems theory (Minuchin, 1974), in which the family is seen as operating as an integrated model, and social ecological models (Bronfenbrenner, 1979), which view the family as it exists within a larger social/ecological context. Whatever the theoretical model, the evaluators recognize the heavy demands made on parents by a child with disabilities, and they try to evaluate the parents' and family's strengths and resources for dealing with those demands. Service providers then try to help the family cope successfully with those issues. The following list summarizes the major issues faced by parents of children with disabilities. These are the issues that evaluators and service providers need to understand and work with.

1. There is initial shock and then combinations of total despair, depression, fear, deep guilt, and anger when parents first learn their child has a severe disability. Intense negative feelings can eventually center on the child and cause problems in forming parent–child attachment or in generally expressing affection and providing good care. Family cohesion may be threatened. A period very much like mourning for the lost "perfect" baby is common. Parents' contacts with and dependence on professionals are heavy at this time of initial adjustment.

2. As the parents and family are helped to accept the reality of the child's condition, they need to be educated about the child's impairments and their implications for development. Family service providers can help by giving information, correcting misinformation, showing where and how to obtain information (from libraries, clinics, Web sites, etc.), referring parents to appropriate local agencies, and introducing the family to education and support groups that can provide emotional support as well as information. Detailed information on how the disability will affect the child's development in specific areas such as motor, language, cognitive, and social development is important so the parents will know what to expect and how best to proceed.

3. As the parents become immersed in the care of the infant (or older child if the disability occurred later, e.g., in an automobile collision), they will be faced with a long succession of challenges involving everyday care. For example, how can parents successfully feed the infant with Prader-Willi syndrome and how are they to control the eventual voracious eating, marked obesity, and aggressive behavior? How is a child with severe myelomenigocele to be handled physically, as in bathing, using diapers, and so on? How is a child with severe cerebral palsy to be bathed, moved, and dressed without injury? What is expected of how relatives, friends, and other children will behave toward the child with disabilities? How does one deal with stares and questions about the child in public places? Parents will need information, training, and even emotional counseling regarding everyday practical child care issues depending on the nature of the child's disabilities.

4. Parental respite is needed not only from the constant weight of responsibility but also from the sheer fatigue of hard work for long hours. Trying to diaper and keep clean a resistant, developmentally delayed 4-year-old is far more demanding than with a smaller, lighter, less mobile 1-year-old. The physical exertion involved in lifting older children with severe physical problems can result in physical stress and injury for the parent. Behavioral problems such as negative resistance, aggression, and conflicts with siblings can wear down any parent. Service providers can help by providing access to home aid personnel or to **respite settings** where for a few days children can be cared for, just long enough for the family to have a brief break from the constant demands. Access to support groups and counseling needs to be provided in many cases, such as when the demands and the parents' reactions reach crisis levels.

5. In time, the child grows older, and the parents are faced with taking the child into more public settings—a period described by Seligman (1991) as when the family "goes public." Issues of the reactions of others and of the child's own behavior in public create new parental anxieties. Decisions about preschool or day care need to be made, and concerns over how the child can have peer contact and the nature of those contacts will arise. Parents eventually will need to determine what type of school placement will most likely be best for the child (e.g., a mainstreamed or a special class setting). As the child is introduced to more public settings, the parents and other children in the family may have to deal with new problems of siblings who may experience stress as more of their peers learn that they have a brother or sister with disabilities.

6. Parents need to recognize and accommodate to an altered parental role. They will soon realize that their parental role regarding this child is considerably different from the roles of other parents and from their own role enactments with reference to other children in the family. In our role theory terms (recall our discussion in Chapter 10), the social position of parent remains largely the same, and most of the role enactments that are guided by the positional norms for parent, are the same as for other parents. That is, the normative rules for parent behavior include the general responsibilities for child care. However, in addition to enacting that normal role, the parents of a child with severe disabilities will have to behave differently with reference to that particular child than he or she behaves toward the other children in the family. In role terms, they need to develop a **specialized role sector** and be able to enact differentially the norms of the general role and of the specialized role sector. But how are they to develop a specialized role sector when they have had little or no socialization in such role enactments? They will do so through experience, learning by trial and error, by discussions with other parents of special children, by reading, and by direct teaching and training provided by professionals. This means, of course, that the professionals working with the family need to understand the nature of this specialized role sector, know what the normative demands are and be able to teach it to parents, and to monitor and evaluate the parents' progress in this role development. It also means that the parents must realize their need to develop the altered role. The demands on the parents will often be taxing. They will need to be motivated, to sustain hard work, to study, and to learn. These specialized demands will fall on them and not on other parents. One of the implications of the need for differential role enactments, often simultaneously, is the possibility of role conflict. The parent may often be put in the situation where treatment of two children, one with disability and one without, must be different, sometimes seemingly unfair and favoring the child with the disability. There may be intrarole conflicts, too, as the parent may devote far more time and attention to the children with the disabilities, while relatively neglecting the other children. All such conflicts arising from specialized role sector demands will take their toll on parents, and ideally, the professionals will be able to help the parents in their resolution of these conflicts.

The specialized norms demand that the parent must be, for many more years, the major teacher, trainer, companion, and source of affection and support for their son or daughter. In addition, as part of their new role, they must become the child's major advocate in relation to schools, agencies, government, and in general, all of society. Their advocacy for their own child will help ensure the availability of needed resources. Moving successfully into this public and often political domain requires even more effort and learning within of the specialized role sector, and the service providers need to help guide and counsel the parents in this development.

7. In similar fashion, the parents will later face new issues arising in adolescence. These include issues of sexual behavior and relative independence. The usual turmoil of most adolescents is here compounded by the nature of the disabilities and by the restrictions and frustrations they impose.

8. Transition to young adulthood brings new issues. Is employment training appropriate? If so, what type is best and where is it available? How will the young person adapt to these changed circumstances? Decisions need to be made as to whether and/or when the young person will move out of the family into a peer-oriented setting such as a group home.

9. At some point, as all parents must, they need to face the prospect of relinquishing control in the event the young adult successfully moves into a semi-independent living and work setting. The parents' specialized role of intense involvement will be reduced, although not eliminated, in their lifetime. This relinquishing of control that they had developed with so much effort for so many years requires parental adjustment. In some cases of severe disability, independent living facilities are not available in the community, and the parents then must maintain the more active role well into their own old age. This leaves parents with a distressing question: Who will care for our son/daughter when we die or are otherwise no longer able to maintain the active parental role?

Throughout these long 20 or more years of the intensely active parental role, professional service providers serve as important supports by bringing information, guidance, and counseling to the parents and family. It is a critical professional role, and when available to families, it greatly enhances the developmental environment for the person, thus improving the person's attainment of the best possible quality of life. The amount of professional involvement and the specific professional disciplines involved will vary with the nature of the child's disabilities and the characteristics of the family. Ideally, societies will find the resources to expand and maintain such important parent–family support services.

Specialized Services

The degree to which specialized services are required depends on the specific conditions of each child. The child's needs and strengths and the services provided are understood within the context of the family's characteristics and procedures aimed at normalizing the child's development. It is within the reality of the family that an **individualized family service plan (IFSP),** which is a detailed written document, is developed. The IFSP is required by law in all cases where federal monies are used to support the early intervention services, and the law clearly directs that the plan be "family centered" (Dunst, Johanson, Trivette, & Hamby, 1990). As summarized by Sandall (1993), the IFSP is a detailed written document, a contract, that is developed by a multidisciplinary team of professionals *and the child's parents,* describing the specific individualized services for that particular child and family. The IFSP includes the following:

1. A clear statement of the child's physical, cognitive, communication, social, emotional, and adaptive development is basic. This is developed through evaluations using observation and specific tests where possible. The evaluation of the child includes assessment of sensory development, such as vision and hearing, and an evaluation of overall health status. There typically are professionals from various disciplines carrying out different parts of this evaluation and producing reports.
2. Assessment of the family is critical. This includes the family structure, resources available to the family, and its priorities and concerns.
3. Specification of the expected outcomes for the child and family includes the goals, the procedures for attaining them, the procedures and expected time line for monitoring and evaluating progress, and modifying procedures when needed.
4. A clear statement of the specific services to be delivered, predicated on the evaluation and the method(s) to be used for service delivery, must be developed.
5. A specification and description of the characteristics of the child-family natural environment in which services are to be performed are needed.
6. Specifications of the date for service initiation and the probable duration of services are needed.
7. There is an identification, by name, of the professional who is to be the service coordinator. This coordinator is to be in the profession that is most closely associated with the needs of the child and carries the major responsibility for implementing and coordinating the plan.
8. The IFSP must also indicate the procedures that will be used to ensure continuation of services and transition into the services provided by public school districts.

The specific services provided depend on the particular condition and needs of the child and the needs and resources of the family. Clearly, the task of providing many services needing different professional areas of expertise and involving many service providers can be complex, demanding, and requires close coordination. There may be many different professionals entering the home for several years, and the possibility of conflicting styles, goals, and advice to and interaction with parents is a real concern of the coordinator.

Transition to School

Vessey and Jackson (2000) note that school experience is particularly important for children with disabilities because it is an important setting for social, emotional, and cognitive development. School provides settings for socialization that may be otherwise not accessible to these children; it can provide interest and enjoyment, and the inclusion of these children provides opportunities for children without disabilities to broaden their own social perspectives.

According to law (PL94-142), all children with disabilities must be provided with educational experiences in the least restrictive setting. In accordance with the aim of normalization, the educational setting for each child must be as normal as is possible, given the child's needs. A school setting is more or less "restrictive" depending on the degree to which it departs from a normal school setting. Children with severe disabilities may be placed in school settings that are far removed from usual school settings and are therefore highly restrictive, such as in-home teaching or state special residential schools. The least restrictive setting is the normal classroom in a normal school. Between those is a range of settings from most to least restrictive, as shown in Figure 15.1. An important goal is to place each child in the *least restrictive setting* (i.e., most normal) that is possible for the particular child. Children are placed in the least restrictive setting according to the children's strengths and needs.

In a procedure similar to the development of the IFSP, the school is responsible for developing an **individualized education plan (IEP)** for each child who has been referred for special education. The Individuals with Disabilities Education Act (IDEA) and its amendments specify that the IEP must be a written document developed by an interdisciplinary team that is composed of:

the child's parents
at least one regular and one special education teacher
a qualified representative of the school district
a person qualified to interpret evaluation results
other qualified persons who may be selected at the parents' or schools' discretion
the child in question may be included, if appropriate

The IEP specifies an assessment plan and, based on assessment results, makes recommendations for school placement. If parents agree to it, the child is enrolled as

**FIGURE 15.1   Examples of School Placement Along a Dimension
of Most- to Least-Restrictive Settings.**

Most-Restrictive Settings

Home teaching, hospitals, and residential institutions
Special public or private day schools in the community
Special classes in regular schools, public or private
Special classes in regular schools with some involvement in regular classes
Regular class placement with special services provided outside of class
Regular class placement with special services provided in the classroom

Least-Restrictive Settings

Adapted with permission from Vessey, J., & Jackson, P. (2000). School and the child with a chronic condition. In P. L. Jackson & J. A. Vessey (Eds.). *Primary care of the child with a chronic condition*. St. Louis, MO: Mosby.

recommended, and an annual review of progress is required. The child's placement may be modified based on the annual review.

Although the specific form of the IEP varies from one school district to another, all must include certain information such as: (IEP Checklist, 1998):

> *Current level of performance.* The most basic information is an evaluation of the child's current level of performance. Included in this evaluation is recognition of the parents' concerns, the child's needs and strengths, and a description of how the disability is most likely to affect the child's participation in school.

> *Yearly goals.* The IEP must delineate specific goals that can be accomplished within the academic year, what specific behavioral supports will be needed, and exactly how progress is to be measured. It must also indicate how parents are to be kept informed of progress.

> *Related services.* The IEP specifies what special services are needed to help the child attain the goals, when and where the services will be initiated, their frequency, location, and expected ending dates.

> *Placement.* The child must be placed in the least restrictive setting. Explanations must be given if the child is not participating in all of the general school activities.

> *Instruction.* The IEP specifies the special education tasks, the place (school), the schedule, and the personnel who will carry them out (e.g., special education teacher, general education teacher, parents, aides, etc.). It also details the nature of the class setting such as class size, special seating arrangements, and assistive devices needed.

> *Transition plans.* Transition from school to young adulthood is an important period of preparation and adaptation. The IEP must attend in detail to transition issues and procedures. Before the youth reaches age 14, there must be a careful consideration and a statement of what training or other preparation will most likely be needed to prepare for the transition. By age 14, there needs to be a specification of what classes will be needed for that transition. By age 16, the IEP must specify the transition-related needs of the youth, the specific services, and the agencies that are to be included. Before age 18, the IEP must identify what rights the youth will have on transition and afterward.

Transition to Adulthood

As reviewed by Sawin, Cox, and Metzger (2000), youth with disabilities do not generally fare well in their transition to adulthood. Compared to those without disabilities, they have higher rates of school dropout, unemployment, poverty, behavioral problems such as depression and attempted suicide, physical and psychological abuse by others, and dependence on others (e.g., parents) for their living arrangements. Spurred by the Americans with Disabilities Act (1990), by the general influence of the civil rights movement, cultural and attitudinal changes, and technology that has resulted in greater longevity, the emphasis on normalizing life experiences for persons with disabilities has been extended throughout the entire life span. The new model holds that *all persons* have the right to live freely in the community, to a free public education, to access to public transportation and places (e.g., stores, etc.), health care, employment, and protection from discrimination. Given the reality of transition problems as noted, the growing numbers of older persons with disabilities, and the new emphasis on empowerment and life-span normalization, service providers now have a major task of planning for adolescent-to-adult transition for persons with disabilities. The task does not end there, as service providers now also have a greater task in continuing the services throughout the increasing life spans of ever-greater numbers of adults.

As we noted in the previous section, the IEP requires planning for transition to adulthood. Thus, most of that preparation is carried out in the school context and with the parents' involvement. Transition from adolescence to adulthood is a process that takes many years to accomplish. It requires not only adaptation to new social and physical factors external to the person but also cognitive and emotional changes within the person. Among the adolescent's many developments are a personal identity, finding one's place in a peer group, a positive sense of one's worth, developing skills in using social resources, learning how to be useful to others, and developing the anticipation of a positive personal future (Carnegie Council, 1995). Natural changes in and knowledge about sexuality and appropriate sexual behavior and expectations are important developments in adolescence for a full adult life. The major transitions from adolescence to young adulthood involve psychological, social, and physical movement from home and school into new settings. These may involve postsecondary education, moving away from the family, vocational training, transition to work, personal and sexual relationships, and generally, greater autonomy and personal control.

Adolescents with disabilities, like everyone else, need to progress through these transitions, but they have the added burdens of their impairments that affect the degree and success of some of the transitions. The service providers need to work closely with the parents and family of the adolescent. They need to understand the adolescent's level of cognitive abilities and any impairment that might affect successful transition to the relative independence of adulthood. In addition to helping with the psychological and social transitions, service providers need to plan for continuation of the person's general health care and for specialized health care for the person's specific disabilities.

Adulthood and Aging

It is in the adult years, some 70 percent of the normal life span, that people make their most significant contributions to others and to society. The reality of life for most seems to be our lives as adults, from about 20 to 75 years of age. As we noted in Chapter 1, the longevity of persons with disabilities has increased markedly, and that population is attaining a life span that is very similar to that of persons without disabilities (Herr & Weber, 1999a). One estimate has the life span of persons with developmental disabilities reaching 70 to 74 years (Straus & Eyman, 1996). The field of developmental disabilities, however, still focuses primarily on the first one-third of life. Only recently has there been general acknowledgment that the adulthood and aging of this population demand even more research, understanding, services, and public policy action. The new model of service that we have been discussing includes recognition of the life-span reality of disabilities and the needs of adults. There has been a noted increase in interest in this area, as indicated by compilations such as those of Herr and Weber (1999b) and Janicki and Dalton (1999), but our social policy and service resources have not yet been developed sufficiently to serve this population. We suggested in an earlier chapter that the prevention of developmental disabilities is one of the important areas of potential development in this field, and as we discussed in Chapter 3, another critical area is that of providing services for the aging population.

As persons with developmental disabilities move into adulthood, it is to be hoped that the earlier IEP- and IFSP-based services through schools and homes had adequately provided helpful transitions from childhood and youth to adulthood. The issues and tasks facing these young adults once they leave the protective environment of school are essentially the same as those for all people. They involve becoming independent from parents and developing one's own control over life. Finding personal relationships, good living arrangements, marriage and family, preparing for and obtaining employment, developing a sense of personal worth as an adult, maintaining healthy lifestyles, and knowing how to obtain proper medical care are some of the normal tasks of adulthood. For persons with disabilities, all of these are complicated issues, many are extremely difficult, and some are precluded by impairment. From a service point of view, each person will need specific supports to succeed in those tasks.

Transitions continue to make demands throughout life as we age, and persons with disabilities continue to need assistance in making those transitions. However, there is no policy-mandated detailed planning for adults such as the IEP and IFSP that drive services for children and youth. Specific protections of civil rights are available, such as those guaranteed by the Americans with Disabilities Act, but these are not the same intensity of individualized planning and mandated services as those applied earlier in life.

The service model for children and youth that we have been discussing is influencing the services provided for adults with disabilities. No longer are the major adult services those of segregation and seeking appropriate institutional placement. Rather, the emerging model of services for adults—in keeping with the precedents set for children and youth—is one of individualized support services that aim to enhance full community participation. Heller (1999) identifies several major factors that make up this emerging model for adults. In all of their work with clients, service providers now focus on a commitment to maintain *person-centered* planning and programming to help individuals to:

> maximize use of family and community resources
> develop and maintain human relationships such as friendships
> create individualized life plans
> foster and maintain self-choice and personal life control
> maintain a focus on high quality of life for each person

The support service programs that proceed from this model are applied to the major areas of life for adults with disabilities. Some of the major areas of service are described in the following paragraphs.

Residential Services.   Residential services in the community are critical, particularly because so many large residential institutions have been closed over the past three decades. Most adults with disabilities, an estimated 60 percent (Fujiura, 1998), live at home with parents or other family members. Indeed, even when institutionalization was at its highest levels in the United States, an estimated 90 percent of persons with mental retardation lived at home (Willer & Intagliata, 1984). The family was, and still is, the major social resource for persons with disabilities. Assisting families to maintain the person at home is important because this is where the majority of persons with disabilities actually live, it keeps the individual in real-world community settings, and ideally, it increases the potential for full integration into community life. The continuing demands on the family, particularly on aging parents, however, can be daunting. Important services, then, aim at helping the family maintain the person at home. Specifically, these services can help to create individualized plans for living and help the families carry out the individualized plans. Often, counseling and advice for the parents on how to deal with personal issues of adjustment and on planning for future care when they are no longer able to do so are needed. Service providers can help to place the person in day care, in occupations, and in social and recreation settings. Transportation can be provided, as well as financial assistance to the families. These services are thus aimed at helping to make the in-home placement as successful as possible in achieving the goals of the individualized plan and in carrying out the general goal of community inclusion and personal development.

Because of the need to foster independence and autonomy, and because clients are living longer and their parents become older or die, there is a growing demand for out-of-home community residential facilities. However, supply has not kept up with the demand, and around the country, there are tens of thousands of adults on waiting lists (Prouty & Lakin, 1998). Development and maintenance of adult group homes in residential communities have become a major area of service. Agencies now devote considerable effort to building or purchasing and remodeling houses to serve as residences for six or so adults and training staff to supervise the settings, depending on the degree of need of the intended residents. These small residences have proved to be successful alternatives to earlier institutional models, as they allow greater inclusion in local communities. Unfortunately, there is often community opposition to establishing these adult residences.

Health-Care Services.   Whether they live with their families or in group residences, adults with disabilities have normal health-care issues, as well as those health concerns directly related to their disabilities. An area of service is that which helps to monitor health and health behavior and provides access to regular medical examinations and to clinics or other facilities for specialized health services.

Age-related decline in physical health is to be expected, and health-care providers may not be trained sufficiently to meet the ordinary health needs of persons with disabilities. For example, persons with cognitive disabilities may not be as aware of health problems or may not be able to identify and describe problems clearly. Maintaining a home regimen of prescribed medication is difficult for most people and may be even more difficult for persons with disabilities, particularly with cognitive disabilities. Failures in treatment compliance may become even greater as the individual ages. Service providers need to be aware of these problems and to provide appropriate degrees of support depending on the needs of the person.

Occupational Services.   As reviewed by Heller (1999), after ending their school years, usually at about age 21, most adults with disabilities do not have regular or sufficient involvement in daily activities outside of their homes, such as occupations, sheltered work-shops, or day programs. Given the importance of work in our society in sustaining us not only economically but also psychologically, and with research data showing that persons with disabilities desire to work (e.g., Heller, Sterns, Sutton, & Factor, 1996), placement in work roles seems a major step in any programs for normalization and empowerment. But success in finding and maintaining an occupational role is made extremely difficult by the nature of disabilities and by the attitudes of employers. Persons with severe physical or cognitive handicaps cannot fulfill many occupational requirements. However, the range of jobs, the variety in duties, hours, and so on in our economy are very large. The variety is so great that it would seem possible to match the needs of individuals with the demands of jobs and find appropriate placement for the *majority* of persons with disabilities. Many constraints operate against individuals, such as transportation, local availability of jobs, and the severity and type of disability. The task of training persons in job skills, of matching individuals with specific appropriate work, overcoming problems such as transportation, monitoring and helping them to sustain good work performance, and assisting employers in finding, hiring, and maintaining persons with disabilities are all possible. Indeed, in many instances, these have been carried out successfully. However, it is a complex and difficult set of tasks and costly to carry out on a large scale. The investment in training a sufficient number of service providers to carry out these tasks would be very large.

Although the costs are great, the benefits, too, would appear large. For adults in our society, there may be few areas of activity more positive than that of successfully maintaining a useful and satisfying occupation. In our role theory model, one derives not just new skills, knowledge and personal satisfaction from a successful occupational position and role, but one's very self-evaluation, self-definition, and social status would derive largely from it. The social resources accessed by enacting an occupational role also include a wage and comradeship with other workers.

It appears to us that successful occupational placement and maintenance would be one of the major positive services that society can provide for persons with disabilities. A large-scale national effort to carry this out would be a powerful gain in the development of normalization and empowerment for people with disabilities. A society as rich as ours can certainly afford to invest its resources here.

Affiliation and Recreation.   Quality of life concerns for persons with disabilities must also address the human need for affiliation and for recreational activity. Friendships and acquaintances can emerge from well-run group living situations and in school and work settings. But as noted earlier, most adults with disabilities are not heavily involved in out-of-home school, work, or social settings. Many are prevented from seeking outside friend-ships by the nature of their disabilities, by transportation problems, and by the paucity of appropriate recreational settings. Healthy within-family affiliation is vastly important, but so is contact and affiliation outside of the home. Service providers will contribute much to the person's life quality by providing or arranging for outside-of-home daily programs, special activities, trips, attendance at public events (e.g., concerts, movies), and so on and by making these resources available to all persons with disabilities. As noted, the limita-tions appear to be insufficient funding for providing large-scale services, and not the lack of potential activities. Many agencies provide these services, but it is doubtful that the services are available to any significant proportion of this population.

Aging. The aging of persons with disabilities is a growing specialized area of concern, as noted earlier and in Chapter 1 (it may be a good idea to reread the brief section, VII. Growth beyond the "Developmental" Years, in Chapter 3). As most people age beyond their work years, they usually experience a diminution of vigor, strength, stamina, and sensory sharpness. Sometimes the decline is marked with physical illness, cognitive loss, and serious dementia, such as Alzheimer's disease. However, as we also know, many aging persons can still remain vigorous, highly active, socially involved, and creative. Retired persons in their 70s, 80s, and some even older still play tennis, write books, maintain businesses, give lectures, paint pictures, play music, create beautiful gardens, produce gourmet meals, travel the world, enjoy family affiliations with children and grandchildren, maintain close friendships, and remain in control of their own lives. To do so, they must make intelligent accommodations with their changing physical and cognitive conditions; they must monitor and control their nutrition, health, activity level, and social involvement. (There is a good deal of "luck," too, in not falling victim to serious illness that can hasten decline.) Knowing what accommodations to make in order to enjoy one's later years is part of the necessary skill of the successfully aging person.

That picture of the successfully aging person is the "ideal" model we hold for persons with disabilities for whom aging will be a parallel experience, but with the addition of its own particular issues. These people will experience all of the usual aging events and declines, plus those specifically related to their disabilities, and the interactions of one set of factors with the other, as discussed by Turk, Overeynder, and Janicki (1995). Service providers need to understand the processes involved in normal aging as well as those occurring in persons with disabilities. As with all aging people, decline in older persons with disabilities is inevitable, but to a significant degree, the quality of life in those years can be under one's personal control. This means understanding and effectively dealing with the challenges and issues that occur during these years. Persons with disabilities will experience the loss of specific persons—parents, perhaps siblings, other relatives, and close friends. They will feel their physical decline and will undergo cognitive decline as well. They suffer losses in health and stamina. This aging person may become increasingly vulnerable to physical, psychological, and even economic abuse from family or caregivers, and is not well prepared or skilled in the face of such abuse. The service provider has the task of helping the person deal with these and other specific issues of aging, while remaining focused on the general goal of maintaining a good quality of life. These and other problems attendant on a disability make their task of personal control more difficult than it is for most people. The task for service providers is to assist persons with disabilities in developing and exercising control and dealing with those issues. Each person is different from each other, and the type and the degree (or intensity) of supports needed for what Herr and Weber (1999b) call a "good old age" must be assessed in each case by the service provider(s) in close collaboration with the person.

Consistent with the new model of service, the overall goal is to assist and enhance the person's own personal control over life during these years. The overall emphasis is on as much decision making as is possible by the person and a consistent sensitivity to maintaining one's civil rights and exercise of self-advocacy. More specific goals include:

maintaining a safe and stable living environment that is supportive of the person's own needs and preferences

supporting emotional and physical health by providing counseling, problem-solving assistance, and when needed, psychological treatment/training

maintaining good physical health by monitoring and training the person to monitor for nutrition, physical exercise, and common ailments

helping the person to obtain medical treatment when needed

maintaining special therapeutic/maintenance services that derive from specific impairments

helping the person to maintain personal interactions with families, friends (both close friends and more distant acquaintances), and generally, to maintain satisfying social contacts with others

helping the person to maintain personal development activities that will stimulate interest and cognitive, physical, and social skills

helping the person deal with personal loss

As a final idea, consider the role-vacuum concept in old age put forth by Cavan (1962). As discussed in Chapter 9, each person develops many different roles during a lifetime and sequentially enacts several roles in any given day. By the time we reach middle age, most people have had experiences in roles such as child, son or daughter, father or mother, student, professional (e.g., doctor, professor, minister), worker, tradespeople, craftspeople (e.g., carpenter, painter), parishioner, and so on. In adulthood, we derive much of our self-identity, self-value, and social status from our particular role set. Enacting these roles well gives us a sense of worth and accomplishment, and the multiplicity of roles is a source of richness and variety in our lives. As we age and move into retirement, we make our transitions out of the active enactment of many of those roles. One by one, the roles and positions from which we derived so much drop out of our lives. As the roles are lost, so too are most of the complementary roles that had been important in our lives. For many aging persons, the only new role attained is that of senior citizen, an uncertain, ill-defined role at best, and one that has little status and thus little power to convey worth and dignity to the individual. It is this progressive loss of roles and complementary roles and the attendant loss of status, meaning, and richness for older persons that Cavan referred to. In the most extreme cases, the person has been stripped of virtually all roles, and with that loss has gone much of one's own identity and sense of worth.

Chapter 10 argued that persons with developmental disabilities tend to develop and enact fewer roles than do most people, and the roles they do have are generally of lower social status. In many cases, their disability defines their social position and thus their appropriate roles. As they age, they lose roles just as everyone else does, and whatever meaning in life had been provided by their role enactment is also lost. Because their roles are more tenuous than most (i.e., fewer roles in number, less complex, and of lower status), the impact of the role-loss process may be particularly hard for those with disabilities because very little is left. It appears to us that a major task of the service provider is to help the person develop and maintain alternative positive roles from which they can derive value, pleasure, and enrichment.

III. Chapter Summary

This chapter has discussed a current model of service delivery, presenting general principles rather than detailed discussions of service techniques. We have noted a revolution in service models occurring in the latter half of the twentieth century. Significant ideas and events that formed that revolution include iatrogrenesis, acceptance of developmental models of human growth, and humanitarian, educational, and civil rights reform movements. Emerging models have been largely formed around a coalition of (a) nineteenth-century romantic philosophy with its emphasis on human dignity and the natural tendency of persons to grow and develop toward ideal optimality when artificial social barriers are removed and (b) twentieth-century empirical science and technology. As that coalition formed, it was translated into actions that significantly reshaped societies' responses to persons with disabilities. Since the 1960s and 1970s, there has been a significant turn in thought and action from a segregation approach to that of inclusion, normalization, advocacy, self-advocacy, and consumer empowerment, all organized with a view of services to persons throughout the entire life span.

The new service models focus on ideals of helping persons to attain the best possible life quality with dignity and respect in natural environments in which the individual can exercise maximum personal control within his or her abilities, needs, and desires. Normalization, self-advocacy, consumer empowerment, civil rights, and personal choice and control are major goals of service that are applied throughout the entire life span, in addition to the more traditional provision of medical, educational, physical, psychological, social, and other forms of assistance.

KEY TERMS

Know these important terms. Check the chapter and the Glossary for their meanings.
They are listed here in the approximate order of their appearance in the chapter.

Respite settings	Individualized education plan	Consumer empowerment
Specialized role sector	(IEP)	Social role valorization
Individualized family service	Normalization	
plan (IFSP)	Advocacy	

SUGGESTED READING

Bockoven, J. S. (1963). *Moral treatment in American psychiatry.* New York: Springer.

Brown, W., Thurman, S. K., & Pearl, L. (Eds.). (1993). *Family-centered early intervention with infants and toddlers: Innovative cross-disciplinary approaches.* Baltimore, MD: Paul H. Brookes.

Darling, R. B. (1979). *Families against society: A study of reaction to children with birth defects.* Beverly Hills, CA: Sage.

Edgerton, R. B., & Gaston, M. A. (1991). *I've seen it all: Lives of older persons with mental retardation in the community.* Baltimore, MD: Paul H. Brookes.

Jackson, P. L. (2000). The primary care provider and children with chronic conditions. In P. L. Jackson & J. A. Vessey (Eds.), *Primary care of the child with a chronic condition* (3rd ed., pp. 3–19). St. Louis, MO: Mosby.

Jackson, P. L., & Vessey, J. A. (Eds.). (2000). *Primary care of the child with a chronic condition* (3rd ed.). St. Louis, MO: Mosby.

Janicki, M. P., & Dalton, A. J. (1999). (Eds.). *Dementia, aging, and intellectual disabilities: A handbook.* Philadelphia, PA: Brunner/Mazel.

Safford, P. L., & Safford, E. J. (1996). *A history of childhood and disability.* New York: Teacher's College Press.

Seligman, M. (Ed.). (1991). *The family with a handicapped child* (2nd ed.). Boston: Allyn & Bacon.

Voysey, M. (1975). *A constant burden: The reconstitution of family life.* London: Routledge and Kegan Paul.

Disabilities Rights Advocacy Group. This is a national organization dedicated to the social, occupational, and political empowerment of persons with disabilities. www.draginc.com/history.htm

STUDY QUESTIONS

15-1. What major philosophical position makes up a substantial part of the service "revolution"? What ideas from that philosophy are most important for service delivery today, and how do they affect services?

15-2. What does consumer empowerment mean? How is this idea translated into services for persons with disabilities?

15-3. How have the civil rights movements of the 1960s and 1970s affected services for persons with disabilities?

15-4. What is the concept of normalization? What are the perceived advantages and disadvantages of the normalization movement?

15-5. What is an IFSP? An IEP? Why are they important?

15-6. What are some of the major problems that face all persons as they grow into old age?

15-7. What specific problems face persons with disabilities as they grow into old age?

15-8. Why is it so important for service providers to focus on transitions and to do so throughout the entire life span?

16 Deviance, Responsible Social Agents, and Prevention in Developmental Disabilities

More than 13 million persons in the United States across all ages and socioeconomic levels have some form of developmental disabilities. They constitute about 5 percent of the total population, and as our population grows, so too will the number of persons with developmental disabilities (see Table 1.3). As noted in Chapter 1, new causes and even new types of disabilities will emerge. These will present new challenges to persons with disabilities, to the professionals, and to society in general. In response, our society seems to have become more sensitive and successful in helping people make the best of their disabilities. Our efforts typically involve diagnoses of existing disabilities and the procedures that aim to prevent the worsening of each condition, to avoid, decrease, or correct the physical, social, and personal problems that can be created by the disabilities, and to help people attain success-ful and satisfying lives. Those procedures are ameliorative after the fact attempts to limit the negative impact of conditions that already exist in individuals.

When applied to developmental disabilities, ameliorative approaches *do not reduce the incidence or prevalence of developmental disability in the population.* The lives of persons with developmental disabilities can be significantly improved through treatment, training, and education, but the disabilities are permanent, and no amount of amelioration removes them.

The ameliorative model is part of a total approach to disabilities. **Prevention** is another, and both are necessary components of society's response to developmental dis-abilities. Prevention has developed primarily within a public health model (Levine & Perkins, 1987). A prevention approach to developmental disabilities would (a) focus pri-marily on groups of persons who are at risk for future occurrences of the disabilities and (b) aim to reduce the incidence and prevalence of the disabilities in these groups. A co-herent, systematic, and long-term prevention approach to developmental disabilities is needed, but creating one is a complex and difficult task. Recall from Chapters 10 and 11 the concepts of social role theory: social positions, roles, norms, expectancies, and devi-ance. In this chapter, these concepts will be applied to the prevention of developmental disabilities to help us understand some of the difficulties. We begin by presenting the concept of a particular social position, the **responsible social agent,** with its attendant roles and norms.

I. A Traditional Social Position:
The Responsible Social Agent

Throughout history, people have experienced natural events, gained knowledge, and passed it on to successive generations. They observed regularities in natural cycles, such as sea-sonal changes, daytime and nighttime sky patterns, tidal flows, food availability, birth, life, and death, and human behavior. By noting such regularities, people realized that irregulari-ties (deviations) also occurred. In addition, the repeated observations of what *had* occurred led to predictions and expectations of what *should* and/or *will* occur. Predictable sequences in the human life span must have been recognized early, such as that people are born, grow from infancy into robust adulthood, function in daily activities with others, repro-duce, and then gradually weaken and die. Some people move through this sequence to its end, whereas others survive only part of the process. Some follow the predictable patterns, whereas others deviate. (It is little wonder that predictable cycles of seasonal change are a near universal metaphor for birth, life, and death and that religions across time and cultures have incorporated that metaphor into their beliefs and ceremonies.)

The recognition of life-span regularities forms a conceptual model, a time-line frame-work for organizing knowledge about human life cycles. It brackets, as with parentheses, the beginning and end of each life. Within those opening and closing parentheses, the human condition can be observed and anticipated. In time, new and more sophisticated ob-servations and inferences were added to that framework to produce elaborated conceptual models of normal and deviant human development and functioning.

Although early people lacked the finesse of modern statistical thinking, they had developed elementary concepts of what is normal human functioning and what are deviations from expected function. Those expectations became traditional wisdom. With such conceptual models, even at an elementary level, people could assess any person's condition and functioning and evaluate them against the expectations contained in the model.

Early society recognized physical, cognitive, and behavioral deviations, observing that some persons were born with deformities and some behaved in distorted, bizarre, destructive, and/or incompetent ways. Such deviations can have powerful effects on others in society and thus cannot be ignored. We hypothesize that in the course of their natural evolution, all societies, even nonliterate societies, developed conceptual and social systems for recognizing, understanding, explaining, and dealing with those human deviations (Graziano, 1971). That is, all societies construct specialized social positions in response to the recognition of human deviance, and these positions and roles emerged with considerable similarity in virtually every society. We have named this hypothetical social position the *responsible social agent* (Graziano, 1969), the norms for which define the agents' powers and duties to society.

II. The Responsible Social Agent and Deviance

The identity of responsible social agents who deal with deviance has varied throughout history. In nonliterate societies, it could have been the shaman, witch doctor, king, priest, or reigning elder. Later, magistrates and sheriffs became the identified social agents. More recently, physicians, psychologists, psychiatrists, nurses, social workers, special educators, speech therapists, physical therapists, and other professional groups have been accorded that social position. As societies grew larger and more complex, individuals were no longer adequate as the responsible social agents, and it became necessary to form larger social units to carry out the responsibilities. In the United States, every state has some office of mental health, mental retardation, developmental disabilities, child welfare, health and welfare, juvenile justice, and so on. Coalesced at the top are several federal agencies. Indeed, there are so many agents that it is often confusing as to exactly where responsibility lies.

The complexity of our social agents for health in general is necessary because of the size and complexity of society. Such complexity creates problems of coordination among so many different persons and agencies, and there tends to be confusion in the assumption of responsibility for specific areas. For example, who is responsible for reducing the incidence of neural tube-related birth defects? Obstetricians, the medical professions in general, the federal Food and Drug Administration? To take another example from developmental disabilities, who is responsible for preventing traumatic brain injury (TBI) in youth due to gunshots, automobile crashes, and other violence? The police, hospitals, federal agencies, schools, religious agencies, automobile manufacturers? For some tasks, the responsible social agent is clearly identified; for instance, the medical profession is clearly responsible for the treatment (but not the prevention) of TBI. No other social agent has the resources to carry out those complex treatment tasks.

For other tasks, however, the assignment of responsibility is not so apparent. The growth of state and federal agencies reflects a hierarchical structure in which responsibility can easily be lost and pursued up or down the hierarchy until it is so diffuse that it disappears. For example, we might demand that the local police and various local health agencies assume responsibility for TBI prevention in youth. But their resources are largely controlled by local and state legislatures. The legislatures in turn will point out that these are health issues that are the proper domain of the state health departments. They will maintain that resources are controlled by state legislatures and federal health agencies. Those bodies then refer us to the U.S. Congress as the body that controls financial resources and sets policies for action. Congress, of course, will claim that it is dependent on the "will of the people" in whom the responsibility lies. Thus, we are all responsible, and therefore, we are none of us responsible, and as a result, progress is slow and even halted at times. Who, then, is or are the responsible social agents for dealing with developmental disabilities? An effective prevention enterprise will be a complex undertaking and will involve numerous social agents, each dealing with some aspects of the prevention enterprise. If the prevention of developmental disabilities is ever to assume a coherent, long-term character, then we need to identify clearly the identity of the responsible social agents. A case in point is the recent Supreme Court decision regarding the regulation of tobacco as a drug (see Box 16.1).

Society determines the identity of the social agents (police for criminal behavior, physicians for health, teachers for education, clergy for religion, etc.). Society also defines appropriate functions (i.e., *services to benefit society*) to be carried out by each responsible social agent. With reference to health and behavioral deviance (e.g., physical illness, developmental disabilities, mental disorder, criminality, etc.), we hypothesize there are four critical functions that are demanded by society of the responsible social agent. That is, four major *norms of this position* specify the behavior of persons who occupy the position. The responsible social agent must:

1. create an explanatory model of the phenomena (in this case, developmental disabilities)
2. identify the deviating individuals and/or groups
3. create and carry out specific actions to deal with the imputed or observed deviations
4. maintain a primary responsibility to society, *for the benefit of society*

Creating Explanatory Models

In defense of its own well-being, a society needs to recognize and understand deviance, such as ill health, disabilities, and criminality. It is the task of the social agent to create and present to society conceptual models of the deviance phenomenon. These models need to explain the phenomenon, identify its origins, chart its course of development, and predict likely outcomes and the potential impact on society. The explanatory model must be understood by and acceptable to the society. Thus, it must present a clearly articulated model which, to be readily understood, must derive from knowledge and beliefs *that already exist in the society and are readily familiar to the people.*

The social agent, like everyone else, is immersed in the society, and the explanatory model that is developed is of necessity drawn from the culture's already existing belief systems and values. The models are metaphors, drawing on familiar concepts, and they make puzzling phenomena understandable to the society. Two thousand and more years ago, the

B O X **16.1**

Identifying the Responsible Social Agent in the Tobacco-Control Controversy: The U.S. Supreme Court's Role

As discussed in Chapter 6, tobacco use is a major factor in the etiologies of some developmental disabilities and other serious diseases, such as cancer, emphysema, and heart disease. Supreme Court Justice Stephen Breyer (Breyer, 2000) noted that annually tobacco use causes "more than 400,000 people (to) die," killing "more people in this country every year than…AIDS, car accidents, alcohol, homicides, illegal drugs, suicides, and fires, combined." It seems appropriate that a substance as dangerous as tobacco ought to be regulated by the agency that was created specifically to regulate such substances, the federal Food and Drug Administration. In terms of our discussion, it seems appropriate that the FDA would be the recognized responsible social agent for regulating this hazardous substance and helping to protect the nation's health.

As the responsible social agent for regulating tobacco, the FDA could institute long-term prevention programs to reduce smoking initiation by young people and reduce the myriad negative effects of tobacco use. Powerful resources controlled by the FDA would be made available to reduce cigarette use, and for the first time, a concerted, organized, and well-funded national prevention policy on tobacco could be initiated. The potential public health benefits for this nation, and the value as a precedent for action by other countries would, presumably, be immense.

It was that very issue—is the FDA the responsible social agent for regulating tobacco?—that was decided by the Supreme Court in March 2000 (*Food and Drug Administration v. Brown and Williamson Tobacco Corp.*, No. 98-1152). The court ruled, in a 4–3 split decision, that the FDA does *not* have that jurisdiction and, therefore, cannot now be the responsible social agent. By one vote, the potential for significant improvement in public health was negated. According to the Supreme Court's ruling, the responsible social agent is the Congress of the United States—only the Congress can properly act to regulate tobacco. But how long will it be before Congress acts on this, if ever? According to critics, the greatest problem here is the lobbying influence of the tobacco industry over Congress. In the last two election cycles, the industry spent $30 million to lobby Congress (Martin, 2000), a vast amount of money that is rarely matched in politics. Public health issues are not necessarily decided by science or humanity (Graziano, 1969); clearly, one of the greatest obstacles to disease and disabilities prevention programs is the power and self-interest that is wielded in our politics. Such is reality.

metaphor was an animistic one—the person had fallen ill or became insane or behaved in bizarre ways because some malicious spirit had invaded the body. The afflicted person was seen as a largely passive victim. Later, religious metaphors were used and illness was explained as the punishment or trials meted by a deity or mischief caused by evil forces, such as the devil. In both models, the person was thought to be controlled or possessed by external sentient and self-directing forces that he or she could not control. In twelfth-century Europe, a variation of the religious/animistic models became prominent, and it included the notion of individual responsibility. That is, the person was thought to have willingly made a pact with evil (the devil), and the person's subsequent bizarre or otherwise deviant behavior was the combined result of his or her own action and the power of superior, albeit evil, creatures. The deviant person, then, was not a completely passive victim but bore some personal responsibility for the deviance. The great witchcraft campaigns that scoured Europe and England for some 300 years utilized that metaphor.

Since the midnineteenth century, industrialized societies have turned to a more naturalistic and scientific metaphor that has pushed the religious/animistic metaphor to a secondary, but by no means abandoned, position. The modern scientific metaphor views deviance as the result of organic or learning disorders caused by physical or psychological trauma, genetic and chromosomal defects, brain damage, or germ, parasitic, physical, or chemical toxic invasion of the body. Some forms of deviance such as delinquency and criminal behavior are attributed largely to deficient or distorted developmental processes influenced by powerful social environments.

Identifying Deviant Individuals and Groups

The responsible social agent is also charged with the task of alerting society—that is, to identify groups and individuals that deviate from expectations. This is, in essence, an investigative process. With regard to health, many modern professions are charged with this duty and given the social power to carry out investigations such as public health studies of toxic environments or the sophisticated diagnostic procedures used in medicine, mental health, and education. In the United States, this investigative task falls to a variety of agencies: the schools, medical and other health agencies, and the police (as in identification of delinquent youth). In modern society and with reference to developmental disabilities, identification has evolved into sophisticated concepts and procedures for diagnosis. For example, psychologists in schools are the agents to carry out this function for diagnosing intellectual deficiency; for birth defects, it is physicians who make the diagnoses. From the identifications originally carried out by shamans, witch doctors, and priests, there has evolved a sophisticated and highly professional group of procedures and agents. These investigative/diagnostic functions derive from norms that help define the positions and roles of responsible social agents.

Applying Corrective Procedures

The social agent is also charged with developing and applying corrective procedures to deal with the deviance. In the health fields, there are many areas, four of which are particularly important for our discussion: therapeutics, prevention, research, and training.

A current major approach in modern medicine is characterized by diagnosing an already existing disorder and applying treatment to alleviate the disorder and return the person to a prior condition of health.

Another major area is prevention, and this stands in contrast, but not in opposition, to traditional therapeutics. The prevention concept is arguably a more sophisticated development than that of therapeutics because it includes and goes beyond the application of remedies to already existing conditions. The core of prevention requires knowledge that will allow predictions of what has not yet occurred, as well as the observation of what has already occurred. For prevention, we must be able to predict where and when in healthy populations such disorders are likely to occur, to understand what actions can be taken to reduce the probability of the disorder's occurrence, and to apply preventive measures. The use of inoculations to prevent disease in children, reduction of lead content of gasoline to prevent lead toxicity, and public campaigns to reduce alcohol and tobacco use are classic examples of prevention approaches. The modern public health field is largely one of prevention.

For therapeutic and prevention functions to be carried out, two other functions are necessary: appropriate *education and training* of the social agents and *research* to understand the causes, courses of development, treatment, and prevention of the disorders. In modern societies, both training and research have developed into huge social enterprises.

There is some tension between proponents of prevention and those of therapeutics. Both, of course, are essential and they are complementary, but our contemporary commitment of resources by professions, government agencies, and elected officials appears generally not to favor prevention. For example, training in the health professions appears to emphasize therapeutics over prevention. We can also see this preference in the public's demands for cures for various disorders, while it pays less attention to the many prevention approaches that are immediately available. Society demands cures for cancer, brain deterioration, and so forth but powerfully resists the prevention-aimed reduction of toxic environments, changing risk behavior in drug use and sexual practices, improving diets, lowering highway speed limits, reducing poverty, or restricting the availability of guns.

Maintaining the Agents' Primary Responsibility to Society, for the Benefit of Society

Society creates these positions *for its own protection,* and the functions of the social agents have traditionally been carried out *primarily in the interests of society.* Historically, the interests of the identified individuals have gradually emerged, and they remain secondary. This powerful norm of primary responsibility to society is most obvious where the deviance is criminal in nature. Here the social agents (police, courts, etc.) are clearly responsible to society in general for the protection of society against those individuals, and any therapeutics for those deviant individuals are, at best, only recent and secondary concerns. This norm is less obvious in the health fields but is still powerful. One need only review the history of the treatment of persons we now recognize as having had mental illness or intellectual disability. The humanitarian reform movement of the nineteenth century was largely an attempt to shift the social agents' responsibilities to include concern for the individual. For most of the twentieth century, individuals were routinely locked away into mental hospitals, training schools, and other institutions for the protection (and convenience) of society. Our current concern with AIDS, for example, seems primarily a concern for the society that might become infected, with less concern for the persons who are already infected. A recent case in point (in April 2000) is a presidential statement that labels AIDS as a threat to the security of the United States. The statement attracted attention to the AIDS issues and stimulated controversy, both supportive and critical. The president may very well be correct, and we do not argue that point. However, the statement reflects the agents' ascendant norm of responsibility to protect society. Had the president stated that AIDS is a "threat to the security of individuals," little attention would have been paid, despite the obvious validity of that statement.

Individuals are still too often given secondary value, while the "system" is given priority; people still "get lost in the system." There is still the norm that demands we must deal with a particular (deviant) group to protect the rest of us. This traditional norm is being challenged and may be changing, at least at some levels of operation of the responsible social agent. Responsibility to individuals may be more apparent at the direct care level, as it ought to be. In addition, however, norm conflicts and role strain may be more likely there. An example is an event in the city of Buffalo early in 2000. A private agency provided shelter for abused women and their children in safe locations that are not known to the abusers. Most of these women and children were traumatized and needed this safe respite. As part of their program, the agency provided a school for the children to minimize disruption of their academic learning and to maintain interactions with other children. By all observations, it was a good program, and the children were well served. However, when the state education department learned of this clandestine school, they forced it to close, saying the children would have to attend proper public school in their own neighborhoods. The agency argued that sending these traumatized children all over the city to public settings would leave the children and, through them, their mothers vulnerable to the abusers. What the children needed, they argued, was at least some time period of safety, of the security of the private setting, and to be with other children who understood what they each had experienced. The program was closed, and the children were shipped out to public schools. To whom is the social agent responsible? In this instance, the norm conflict was settled in favor of the responsibility to the larger system (i.e., the prerogatives of the state educational system rather than to the individuals in need).

At higher organizational levels in the system, concern shifts and the agents' responsibility to society becomes paramount. This seems reasonable because the concerns for the larger society need to be maintained at some level in the system. Even at those higher levels, there can be norm conflicts and role strains (the incident just described can be seen in those terms). For example, when higher administrative action is taken for the specific benefit of a particular individual, the agents' norms are in conflict. Perhaps the individual's case is compelling; perhaps some special interest and untoward influence is at work. In either case, norm conflict and role strain have occurred.

As professionals in the field of developmental disabilities, or in the health field in general, we need to assess and clarify continuously where our responsibilities lie—primarily with individuals or primarily with society. A balanced system would include both, with each emphasis operating at different levels in the total system of the social agent. At each level, this issue must be clarified. As noted, it seems a matter of clarifying roles and norms. The responsible social agent concept is summarized in Box 16.2.

These are important issues still in need of clarification. For many current social problems (e.g., violence, poverty), there is not only a good deal of public concern and discussion but also confusion and conflicting actions. Much of the confusion, we suggest, is because these issues of identifying the responsible social agents and clarifying to whom responsibility is to be accorded have not been properly thought through and clarified. Perhaps in a democracy, this is difficult to do, but difficult or not, it is essential if progress is to be made.

As with other social issues, the successful prevention of developmental disabilities is complicated and diluted by conflicting interests, directions, and uncertain responsibilities. If we are to have coherent, successful, and long-term prevention efforts, then we need to

BOX **16.2**

Summary of the Responsible Social Agent Concept

Throughout human history, virtually all societies:

1. recognized the existence of physical defects and the bizarre and otherwise disturbing behavior of some people
2. developed ideas of regularities and deviance in human conditions and behavior
3. recognized that some of the deviations were threatening or disturbing to social order or, perhaps, that some were of positive value
4. identified specific persons or groups as the responsible social agents with regard to the deviancies
5. prepared the responsible social agents through apprenticeships, training, and education
6. invested the social agents with some degree of social power greater than that for most individuals
7. charged the social agents to perform four major duties, as follows:
    a. to develop conceptual models that describe each type of deviance and to provide coherent explanations of its origins and predictable course and its possible effects on society
    b. to develop effective procedures to identify persons who are deviant as described by the explanatory conceptual models
    c. to develop specific procedures of deviance control
    d. to carry out those deviance control procedures for the benefit of society

identify and clarify in detail the nature of this social position (the responsible social agents for these prevention tasks).

1. We need to identify clearly which individuals and agencies are to be the responsible social agents for these tasks.
2. We need the identified agents then to carry through on the four critical norms of their roles (create theoretical models, identify the populations at risk, create and apply the prevention procedures, and clarify to whom their responsibilities lie).
3. Finally, our legislators must provide the resources for those social agents to carry out their tasks. Here the realm of politics is clearly entered, but if legislators can be presented with systematic models, definitions, and procedures, the probability of significant support may be improved.

III. Levels of Prevention

Three levels of prevention—primary, secondary, and tertiary—have been defined (Caplan, 1964). We will use these distinctions in our discussion of developmental disabilities, although Caplan's original distinctions applied to the field of mental health rather than to developmental disabilities.

Tertiary Prevention

This level of prevention has an ameliorative focus. Tertiary applications prevent and/or reduce some of the handicapping effects of already existing disabilities. For example, a person with cerebral palsy who cannot speak or use his or her hands might be provided with a computerized pointing device that is held between the teeth. With this device, the person can point to pictures and words on a screen, ask and answer questions, write text, and engage in conversations. The disability is not corrected, but the person's quality of life will have been vastly improved. What are prevented are many of the negative personal and social effects that derive from the condition.

All of the developmental disabilities can be approached with tertiary prevention procedures. Indeed, our service programs for individuals with developmental disabilities are tertiary prevention programs. They are aimed at improving individuals' life quality by reducing or preventing handicaps that result from the disabilities. Training persons with mental retardation in personal care is an example. Providing wheelchairs or walkers for those with ambulatory problems and training them in their use is another example. Educating persons with severe visual and auditory problems, providing occupational training for those with mental retardation, and so on are tertiary prevention approaches.

That this tertiary approach now characterizes most of the field of disability services is seen in the nature of virtually all of the service providing agencies. They are geared to creating and maintaining tertiary prevention services and bringing individuals who have been diagnosed with the disabilities into that service system. The goals of the direct care, clinical, and educational work with individuals are virtually all aimed at reducing the impact of disability by providing training, education, counseling, assistive devices, and social support. The tertiary nature of our focus is also incorporated in the character of the education and training of workers in the field. Training is geared heavily toward teaching skills for tertiary services. Whether in special education, speech therapy, occupational and physical therapy, counseling and psychology, or social services, the aim is to equip the professional with skills and/or devices that will help ameliorate for their clients the impact of the conditions.

Our culture is invested heavily in a tertiary approach to developmental disabilities. Our social resources—funding, personnel, training institutions, and service agencies—are focused on the tertiary approach, and less is devoted to other levels of prevention. This is not a suggestion to reduce tertiary approaches in this field. If anything, we need even more than we have now. However, much more attention needs to be paid to other levels of prevention.

Secondary Prevention

Secondary prevention, while important in medicine and mental health, is not appropriately applied to developmental disabilities. As defined by Levine and Perkins (1987), secondary prevention aims at reducing the *prevalence* of a disorder by early diagnosis and treatment, thus reducing its duration. In medicine, when therapeutic approaches are successfully applied to an already existing disorder, the condition can be corrected (i.e., the condition that did exist no longer exists). Its duration has been made shorter. The person who had been ill is no longer so and is removed from the "count" of persons with that particular disorder. Thus, the prevalence of the disorder in the population is reduced. In medical practice, the early detection of disease followed by appropriate therapeutic treatment that reduces the duration of the disease is a standard and highly successful secondary prevention approach. However, because developmental disabilities are, by definition, *permanent in nature,* we cannot, with present knowledge, shorten their duration. We can and do apply tertiary prevention measures to reduce the impact of the disability and to prevent associated problems from developing, but we cannot shorten the duration of the disability itself.

Note that secondary prevention in medicine can reduce the prevalence of a disorder but does not reduce its *incidence.* That is, the duration of already existing cases can be reduced, but the emergence of new cases is not usually affected by secondary prevention. It can be argued that communicable diseases may be exceptions. When new cases of a communicable disease are largely due to contact with persons who already have the disease, then by treating and curing the existing cases we can, theoretically at least, reduce the incidence of new cases. But this does not apply to developmental disabilities because we cannot, now, "cure" persons of mental retardation, autism, cerebral palsy, phenylketonuria, and other developmental disabilities. Once a person is diagnosed with one of those disabilities, assuming the diagnosis is accurate, no treatment will remove him or her from that category.

Primary Prevention

Primary prevention strategies focus on reducing the *incidence* of a disorder (Levine & Perkins, 1987), to avoid the disability before it starts (Hollowell & Adams, 1997). Eradicating mosquito populations to reduce malaria is an example from the early twentieth century. Contemporary campaigns to reduce smoking and alcohol use by pregnant women, measles and polio vaccinations, fluoridation of water to prevent tooth decay, and nutritional campaigns such as including foliates in the diets of pregnant women to prevent neural tube defects are all examples of primary prevention. Vaccinations against smallpox, diphtheria, polio, and measles have virtually eliminated these diseases from the United States. (Measles still results in some 1 million deaths annually worldwide.) It is in primary prevention strategies that the public health model is most clearly seen. Primary prevention is aimed at identified target populations, such as pregnant women and children that are presently healthy but are potentially susceptible to an identified illness or disability. It has been estimated, for example, that half of all mental retardation can be prevented through the use of large-scale primary prevention methods (Guthrie & Edwards, 1990). Another example of primary prevention is the reduction of teenagers' use of "gateway drugs" (i.e. tobacco, alcohol, and nicotine; U.S. Department of Health and Human Services, 1991). This gateway concept holds that adolescents experiment with these drugs, which serve as an introduction to the larger world of other even more dangerous drugs. Education programs in schools aimed at avoiding or delaying that experimentation may have primary prevention value in reducing risks of future illness, of addiction, and later, of drug use during pregnancy.

IV. Obstacles to Prevention

A coherent national policy for the prevention of developmental disabilities requires legislative and political actions as well as professional activity. Most of the prevention activity is being carried out at state and local levels, but ultimately, national and worldwide policy will be required for a coordinated and sustained effort. We now have sufficient understanding of the etiologies of developmental disabilities and many prevention procedures to form a coherent and successful national program. Our limitations are not scientific or technological, but are political, personal, and social. Crocker (1990) suggests there are psychological obstacles to the large-scale adoption of prevention strategies. He doubts that we have a sufficient national consensus and commitment to prevention to overcome the political and social inertia. One of the major obstacles is a strong, seemingly paradoxical emotional and moral objection by persons with disabilities and parents of children with disabilities. They argue that, in promoting prevention, there is a strong implicit acceptance that persons with disabilities are of less value. It is heard when a parent of a child with, for example, Down syndrome, argues that if primary prevention had been in effect, this loving child "would never have been born."

It is difficult to answer these genuine emotional arguments other than to maintain that preventing developmental disabilities is a humane and ethical position. In pursuing this, we need to pay close attention to the ethical limits of what our technologies allow us to do, and ethical guides need to be developed and followed.

It is important to point out that the major ethical objections have been aimed at some of the primary prevention methods and not at secondary or tertiary prevention. Specifically, the critics point to procedures such as abortion that result in blocking the birth of a child, thus denying life to that human being. Even in situations where the outcome is clear, such as a fetus with anencephaly (see Chapter 5), parental decisions are emotionally wrenching. If born, that baby will have no chance at human functioning, but will exist, briefly and without awareness, only at the mercy of sustaining machines. Should this pregnancy be aborted? Should a Down syndrome fetus be terminated? These are difficult decisions, and the parents must make them.

Fortunately, most primary prevention aims at the *prevention of pathology* and not at the prevention of life. Programs for maternal inoculation against diseases that have teratogenic effects, to improve nutrition before and during pregnancy, to reduce maternal tobacco, drug, and alcohol use, or to reduce lead and other serious environmental pollutants are primary prevention strategies to which we see no ethical objections. This describes nearly all of the primary prevention strategies.

Further, tertiary prevention procedures aim to ameliorate existing disabilities and to improve life quality, and thus, they are not the targets of concern. (As noted, secondary prevention does not apply to developmental disabilities.) In sum, the psychological barriers to accepting a prevention mode are most pointedly aimed at only a small portion of *primary* prevention, which in turn is only part of the full array of prevention strategies.

There have been other objections. One of the most frequently voiced, particularly in legislative debates, is that prevention costs a great deal of money. In response, a number of estimates have been made of the costs savings that would result from prevention programs. For example, as summarized by Guthrie and Edwards (1990), huge financial savings can be achieved through prevention by the resulting reduction of social costs of care for persons with severe disabilities. In one study, for example (Browder, 1977), a rubella (German measles) vaccine was successfully used to prevent the disorder and its resulting disabilities. Given the number of children involved and the expected rate of severe disabilities had the vaccine not been used, the estimated costs of not using the vaccine (i.e., costs of medical and social care and special education) were thirty times the costs of using the vaccine as prevention. Arguably, a society as rich as ours should not be concerned with a cost-savings analysis of health issues, but unfortunately, this issue is repeatedly raised. It certainly appears that prevention is very cost effective as well as focused on its more important human values.

In addition to psychological and financial barriers, several other issues have impeded a national policy of prevention of developmental disabilities. Boggs (1980) discusses a number of probable obstacles. Among them are the competition for funds by so many different social concerns, ethical problems in making decisions for persons who often cannot make decisions themselves (e.g., infants and persons with severe cognitive disabilities), and lack of clear collaboration between national and state agencies. Of the barriers discussed by Boggs, we believe that one of the most basic and serious is the lack of awareness and understanding by the national constituency. That is, most people may think that preventing developmental disabilities is an issue limited to those persons who have disabilities. Further, individuals who already have disabilities cannot personally be helped by primary prevention programs. This means that their involvement in primary prevention must be altruistically based; thus, there may be sufficient motivation only among a few to support primary prevention. Persons who do not have or who are not closely associated with developmental disabilities might not perceive the value of prevention for their own future children and descendants or for society in general. This lack of personal motivation may be a major impediment. Of course, it need not be. Perhaps large-scale education campaigns to inform the public of the human costs of developmental disabilities and what can be done through prevention can reduce this obstacle. To these issues we will add our earlier suggestion that two additional major impediments need to be addressed: We need to identify clearly the responsible social agents for prevention and must clarify their positional norms.

It has been argued that some prevention is a modern form of eugenics in which, historically, the limits of humane behavior have been overreached, as was done by the Germans under Hitler in the 1930s and 1940s. They point to one modern view of eugenics (e.g., Kuhse & Singer, 1985; Singer, 1979) that advocates euthanasia for severely disabled neonates. These authors present a carefully reasoned philosophical position. They maintain that parents have the moral right to end the life of their severely disabled child to "end the child's suffering" and to enhance the family's life quality. This position has doubtful primary prevention value because the disabilities to be ended have already occurred, and the incidence will not decrease. The prevalence of disabilities would, of course, decrease but at what price? It has no secondary or tertiary prevention value since it does not improve the person's quality of life. This position, in our personal view, is the ultimate expression of the social agent's norm of *service to society, for the benefit of society*. The position completely devalues the individual, eliminating that person for the convenience of the rest of society. In our view, it is not a position to be taken seriously.

Barriers to prevention also exist on a more individual level. As will be discussed later in this chapter, parents are among those with responsibility for providing prevention services to children. It is clearly a normative mandate of the social position of parent to protect children from injury and harm and to guide and support their healthy development. There is, however, considerable variation among parents in their motivation and ability to enact these norms. Some children, then, suffer injury and even disabilities because of parental abuse, neglect, indifference, and/or ignorance. It might not be possible for large-scale programs to reach into every maladaptive parent–child relationship and to secure a good environment for all children.

V. Partial Solutions in Our Less Than Ideal World

Even before conception, important issues need to be considered and decisions made by the prospective parents. In some idealized, best of all possible worlds, the couple would be mature, stable, healthy, and have adequate economic and social resources. They would have knowledge about child development and realistic concepts of the nature of children at different ages, would already possess the start of good childrearing skills, and would have made conscious, informed decisions to have this child. In that ideal world, too, the environment would not be polluted with teratogenic toxins, local, state, and federal governments would be enlightened about health policy, and all health agencies would have clear understanding of their roles and norms. Health education for the general public and social and medical services to promote healthy pregnancies and babies would be generously funded and easily available to everyone. There would be no famines and starving children, no epidemics and dying children, no abuse and terrorized children, and no child labor and exploited children. And of course, the world would be at peace.

That idealized world stands far distant from our real world, and we despair that it might never be reached. However, by conceptualizing an ideal, we can at least construct guiding models that tell us where to focus our efforts to encourage healthier pregnancies and children. (An ambitious federal attempt to create such a preventive model is the project "Healthy Children, 2000," and it is described in Box 16.3.) Such models tell us that environmental pollution and poverty must be reduced; that programs to reduce teenage and out-of-wedlock pregnancies need to be strengthened, multiplied, and maintained; that large-scale health-promoting educational, medical, and social programs are essential. They point out the importance of maintaining high levels of research, and they remind us of the need for continued efforts to reach those prevention goals despite the obstacles erected by politicians, industry, and other special interests.

An important point too often overlooked in prevention discussions is that all of our prevention efforts are, of necessity, only *partial solutions*. Indeed, there are no complete solutions, no 100 percent solutions; there are only partial solutions. The overall issue of developmental disabilities is a large and complex aggregate of factors consisting of many complex problems. There is no single solution because there is no single problem. Thus, all we have are many smaller solutions to many problems; we have *only* partial solutions (Graziano & Mills, 1992).

That point is important to recognize because so much resistance and active opposition to prevention efforts seem based on the criticism that any particular effort will not "solve the problem" because there are other, presumably more important, issues involved that are not addressed by a given strategy. This argument is heard against gun control, slower highway speed limits, improved child automobile restraints, reducing lead in paint and gasoline, and eliminating other environmental toxins. The argument is made in opposition to needle-exchange programs to reduce the spread of AIDS, to legislation to reduce public alcohol use by pregnant women and to create tobacco smoke-free public areas, and so on. In each issue for which prevention legislation is suggested, many arguments are raised by a variety of special interest groups. Among those, one invariably finds the argument that, for example, mandating the licensing of guns will not reduce gun violence because the "criminal" or the teenager will always find ways to get guns or will simply use other weapons. Prohibiting television advertisements for alcoholic products or reducing media presentations of violence, it is argued, will not reduce teenage alcohol use or violence because youngsters will be stimulated by other social factors, such as their peers and individual psychopathology, anyway.

Those objections implicitly and correctly recognize the reality that the proposed prevention programs are but partial solutions to many-faceted problems. The error they make, however, is to equate "partial solution" with "no value" and then, having labeled it so, to dismiss it. What is ignored is that partial solutions, while they leave much to be done, do provide some degree of relief from and improvement of some portion of a problem. It seems reasonable to expect that multiple partial solutions will each contribute to some degree of improvement. Thus, partial solutions—whether 10 percent of the problem or 20 percent or more or less—are of value. In the aggregate, constructing the combination of several partial solutions to a complex problem may bring us very close to solving the whole of that problem.

VI. Prevention of Developmental Disabilities in a Time-Line Perspective

In the following sections, discussion of prevention of developmental disabilities is organized along a human time-line framework. Prevention concepts and procedures are grouped as those used *prior to conception, during pregnancy, during perinatal* and *neonatal periods, in infancy, childhood, and youth* (this discussion is based on the organization used by Pueschel & Mulick, 1990, in their excellent volume).

Prevention Goals Prior to Conception

Out-of-Wedlock and Teen Pregnancy. In my opinion, marriage—not just cohabitation, but marriage—may be one of the best factors in protecting the health of children. Out-of-wedlock pregnancy and the young age of the mother (17 years and under) are major risk factors for birth defects, premature births, low birth weight, developmental disabilities, and infant mortality. As reviewed by Evrard and Scola (1997) 80 percent of these teenage mothers are high school dropouts and thus have inadequate education and poor employment and economic prospects. Further, pregnancies and divorce occur in 60 percent of teenage marriages within 5 years, leaving most of the children to be raised—for at least some part of their lives—by single mothers. Children born to teenage unmarried mothers are at high risk

---

BOX **16.3**

Healthy Children, 2000

The U.S. Department of Health and Human Services (D.H.H.S., 1990) report *Healthy People 2000* specified 300 health objectives to have been met by the year 2000. D.H.H.S believed that we already have the social resources (scientific research and knowledge, professional skills, individual commitment, community support, and political will) for significantly expanded efforts toward major ideals of health promotion and disease prevention. The ideals included preventing disabilities and premature death, preserving life-supporting physical environments, cultivating family and community supports, and enhancing individuals' inherent abilities and maximum levels of functioning. The report's overall purpose was to commit the nation to strive for three broad goals:

> Increase the span of healthy life for Americans
> Reduce health disparities among Americans
> Achieve access to preventive services for all Americans

Here was a challenge to citizens, state and local governments, and private agencies to translate those broad national goals into specific local action.

The report included a section, "Healthy Children, 2000," with 170 health promotion and disease prevention objectives for mothers, infants, children, and adolescents. Prevention at all levels is a major component of the report.

The report covered twenty-two priority areas (listed below), each one of which specified many objectives for mothers, children, and youth. For example, the priority area *unintentional injuries* includes twenty-two objectives for improving health and/or reducing risks. These objectives include: reducing child and youth deaths from motor vehicles, falls, fire, and poisoning; reducing head and spinal cord injuries; increasing education for safety; increasing use of protective clothing in sports (e.g., helmets, pads); and increasing the availability of emergency trauma services. The priority area *alcohol and other drugs* includes fourteen risk-reduction objectives such as increasing the age of the first use of the "gateway drugs" alcohol, tobacco, and marijuana; reducing annual alcohol consumption to no more than 2 gallons of ethanol per person (age 14 and over) from the base of 2.54 gallons; and increasing the proportion of high school seniors who perceive the health risks of alcohol, tobacco, and marijuana.

Those 277 health status and risk-reduction objectives are specific enough to be used as focused program goals by state, local, and private agencies. This is truly a landmark document that organizes vast amounts of information and sets out a coherent model for all levels of prevention that can realistically be created. At this writing, we have reached the year 2000 but do not yet know exactly what degree of success has been achieved in seeking those objectives. The document still stands as an excellent guide and source of specific program goals for our continuing efforts to prevent developmental disabilities. We recommend strongly that anyone interested in the prevention of disabilities study this document.

The twenty-two priority areas are:

1. Physical Activity and Fitness
2. Nutrition
3. Tobacco
4. Alcohol and Other Drugs
5. Family Planning

6. Mental Health and Mental Disorders
7. Violent and Abusive Behavior
8. Educational and Community Based Programs
9. Unintentional Injuries
10. Occupational Safety and Health
11. Environmental Health
12. Food and Drug Safety
13. Oral Health
14. Maternal and Infant Health
15. Heart Disease and Stroke
16. Cancer
17. Diabetes and Chronic Disabling Conditions
18. HIV Infection
19. Sexually Transmitted Diseases
20. Immunization and Infectious Diseases
21. Clinical Preventive Services
22. Surveillance and Data Systems

for poverty. They are likely to be raised in a home that is run by a single parent who is immature, who has poor childrearing skills, insufficient education and knowledge, poor economic prospects, and who may be socially isolated, with limited family or social support. This child faces a higher probability of fetal and childhood disorders, poor medical care, serious injuries, and generally, poor parental supervision. This child will also be at risk for limited parental support for academics and for poor academic achievement. As Evrard and Scola (1997) noted, a child with poor academic skills because of faulty and nonsupportive parenting may be just as handicapped as one with a learning disability. *Thus, nationwide efforts to reduce out-of-wedlock pregnancy and to delay pregnancy until the midtwenties* (Tarjan, 1982, cited by Crocker, 1990) *are two prevention goals worthy of very serious public investment and effort.* An important role for governmental and private local, state, and federal agencies is to carry out large-scale public education programs aimed at reducing teenage marriages and pregnancies.

Several social agents can be involved in these prevention efforts, including schools and religious groups. For example, sex education programs in schools may be useful to help preteens and adolescents avoid pregnancy. Religious groups could do much more to educate parents and to counsel youngsters to postpone sexual activity and pregnancy until they are older. Unfortunately, in our opinion, too many religious organizations devote efforts to criticizing and blocking sex education programs, while doing little or nothing themselves to reduce early, unplanned, and irresponsible pregnancy.

Public Awareness of Early Pregnancy Risks and Prevention Strategies. Many risks to fetal and mothers' health can occur early in pregnancy, and many can be avoided or at least reduced by taking action prior to conception. These issues need to be addressed on an individual basis with each woman who is or is planning to become pregnant and the current or potential father in their preconception and early pregnancy examinations and counseling, as discussed later. But there is also an important role for large-scale educational programs aimed at the general public to inform and remind people of the early pregnancy risks and of available prevention procedures. For example, neural tube defects, fetal alcohol effects, radiation, and many chemical toxin effects can all occur very early, even within the first few weeks of pregnancy and often without the parents' awareness (see Chapters 6 and 7). Public education programs can contribute to the solution of these problems by alerting the public to those issues and informing the public about preconception and early pregnancy nutrition needs, the dangers of alcohol, tobacco, and other drug use, and the threats of many environmental toxins. Such public education programs must, of course, be continual because each new generation of potential parents needs to hear and understand the messages. The more such information is made available to the public, we believe, the more individuals will behave knowledgeably and responsibly and perhaps help to reduce the incidence of developmental disabilities.

Preconception Physical Examinations and Counseling.   Anything that can be done to improve the physical and psychological health of future parents prior to pregnancy will have primary prevention value. In a time when close extended and multigeneration families seem to have decreased, potential parents need to obtain their preconception and pregnancy information from other sources. In the best of all possible worlds, women planning on pregnancy would have physical examinations and prepregnancy screening to determine if family or individual high-risk conditions exist. Treatment and counseling for maternal conditions such as diabetes may be needed, and genetic counseling may be appropriate if inheritable genetic and chromosomal disorders are found to have occurred in the families. A health and personal habits history needs to be taken prior to conception to help prepare for the pregnancy.

It is important to maximize good nutrition prior to conception so the woman will be in good nutritional standing when she becomes pregnant. Ensuring adequate intake of foliates, for example, to reduce neural tube defects and avoiding potential teratogens such as ethanol (alcohol) are important even before pregnancy occurs. It is never too early to provide information and counseling on the importance of avoiding tobacco and drug use prior to and during pregnancy.

Admittedly, we do not live in the best of all possible worlds, and many millions of prospective parents do not have access to any systematic preconception health examinations and counseling. A systematic national prevention policy would include the large-scale establishment of clinics or centers for such preconception examinations for individuals that would be available to all women as well as to all prospective fathers. It seems reasonable to believe that making these services available to all people at nominal or no individual costs is a wise and valuable investment in the future strength of our country.

In addition to the focus on individual parents, large-scale dissemination of preconception information needs to be increased through public information programs on television and radio, in videotapes, pamphlets, magazines, and books, in preparenting classes, and so on. The social agents would include educational, social, and health agencies as well as local, state, and federal offices.

Prevention Goals during Pregnancy

Public Education.   Prevention during pregnancy is the continuation and extension of prevention principles applied prior to conception, and the basic issues are the same. That is, efforts need to be made to ensure the good physical and psychological health of the mother during pregnancy, to anticipate any problems that may arise as pregnancy progresses, and to ensure the continued health, responsibility, help, and support of the father or spouse. As in preconception prevention, there is a major role here for general public education about health risks to mother and fetus during pregnancy. The issues raised in examinations of individual pregnant women are the same issues that need to be presented to the general public. The importance of thorough and continuing public education cannot be overstressed. State and local health and education agencies are probably the social agents most appropriate for this important public education task, and while they have accomplished much, a good deal more needs to be done. These efforts, it seems to us, need to be maintained as a *permanent* and well-funded part of our social commitment to our own healthy futures.

Individual Examination and Counseling.   In our idealized, best of all possible worlds, the pregnant woman and her spouse will have easy access to good prenatal care and counseling. Von Oeyen (1990) writes about the need for optimal prenatal health care. He describes its organization around procedures of pregnancy risk assessment that is based on three other areas of assessment for each pregnant woman: the pregnancy duration and projected date of delivery; the mother's nutrition and weight status throughout pregnancy; prenatal screening for potential problems. Each of these areas of assessment is carried out with the primary prevention goals of blocking the occurrence of pathology and secondary and tertiary goals of early diagnosis and treatment to curtail the duration of pathology and/or reduce its negative effects on individual functioning. Risk assessment is an overriding and continuing activity throughout the whole of pregnancy, and ideally, it should begin during the preconception examinations.

Risk assessment in pregnancy involves obtaining a personal and medical history and a physical prenatal examination. The personal and medical history should identify potential psychological problems and physical/medical conditions that might adversely affect the pregnancy. For example, maternal depression, high anxiety and/or hypertension, drug use such as alcohol, tobacco, cocaine, and medications prior to pregnancy all need to be evaluated if found. Maternal physical problems identified in the medical history include menstrual problems such as excessive bleeding, disorders such as diabetes, PKU, recent viral infections, and exposure to possible teratogens such as in the workplace. Both parents' family histories of congenital disorders, genetic disorders, alcoholism, mental retardation, autism, and so forth and other family history that suggests pregnancy or child developmental problems need to be examined.

Physical examinations such as the pelvic examination can diagnose possible physical anomalies and/or infections that can affect the fetus, particularly during birth. Laboratory tests are conducted to rule out or identify blood type, presence of sexually transmitted disease (e.g. syphilis, gonorrhea), hepatitis B, and rubella immunity. Several prenatal screening procedures (see Chapter 2) that are useful at different times during pregnancy are available (e.g., amniocentesis, ultrasonagraphy, chorionic villus sampling, fetoscopy, alpha-fetoprotein assay, etc.).

With all of the information obtained from the history taking, the physical examination, and laboratory tests, a pregnancy risk assessment is carried out and a problem list of actual or potential problems is created to be used throughout the pregnancy (von Oeyen, 1990). Throughout the duration of pregnancy, the health status of the mother and fetus are repeatedly assessed. Psychological status (e.g., mood, anxiety), weight gain or loss, and the occurrence of new or previously undiagnosed medical problems are carried out. As can be seen, early diagnosis and prevention, particularly secondary and tertiary prevention, are an overall major goal of preconception and prenatal assessments.

Perinatal and Neonatal Prevention Goals

During these periods, the focus is on good perinatal medical care to prevent problems such as hypoxia, birth delays, and tissue damage due to excessive pressure during birth. Neonatal screening (see Chapter 2) evaluates the child's condition shortly after birth (e.g., Apgar and Brazelton screening procedures), and neonatal intensive care is provided if needed. A number of screening tests for metabolic disorders are performed, including the phenylalanine assay developed by Guthrie and Susi (1963) for early PKU detection before significant brain damage and mental retardation occur (see Chapter 3). Blood and urine testing can be done (and in some states, is routinely used) by taking samples from newborns and/or by providing parents with a filter paper kit to take urine samples. These are then mailed to a regional or local testing site where the various tests are performed. Such testing can be prohibitively expensive in some areas of the country, and therefore, regional testing sites, serving large areas, can be efficient ways to use resources (Levy, 1990). Newborn screening can provide early diagnosis of many treatable conditions, making tertiary prevention of disabilities possible.

Young children such as low-birth-weight children who had required neonatal intensive care constitute a high-risk population for neurological disturbances. For all children, and for this group particularly, screening in infancy and childhood for neurological problems is necessary. There is considerable value of such screening for early diagnosis and for tertiary prevention. As outlined by Vohr (1990), screening in the 1st year can identify a number of problems such as:

> motor deficits (e.g., cerebral palsy)
> seizure disorders
> hearing and visual disorders
> head growth abnormalities
> congenital malformations
> some mental retardation
> some syndromes, such as autism

Prevention Goals for Childhood and Adolescence

Good nutrition, physical safety, availability of health and medical services, emotional support and guidance by adults, physical exercise, appropriate education, and freedom from abuse are some of the major factors in a healthy life for children and youth. Prevention of developmental disabilities for older children and for youth involves these and other factors. Constant informed monitoring by adults, presumably the parents, is required. Parents and children are in complementary social role relationships, and among the most important norms that define the parental social position are those of responsibility for providing children with a healthy and supportive environment. This means, of course, that parents need easy access to resources such as appropriate knowledge of what constitutes risks for disabilities and what actions will reduce those risks. They need access to health care, education for the children, and so on. In cases where the parents are unable or unwilling to carry out those responsibilities, then the state, through social service and family court systems, needs to intervene on the children's behalf.

Growing children need to be protected from infections and physical traumas that can cause disabilities. Inoculation programs for protection against potentially serious diseases such as diphtheria, measles, mumps, and rubella can prevent disabilities from occurring. Measles and mumps, for example, thought by most parents to be benign childhood disorders, can in some cases result in blindness, deafness, and other disabilities. Children need to be protected from environmental hazards, such as poisoning from toxic materials and lead in paint, water, and the atmosphere (see Chapter 7). Brain damage can occur from the physical trauma of intentional or unintentional injuries as discussed in Chapter 8. For adolescents, automobile mishaps are a major cause of death and injury, and for all children, falls in playgrounds, from bicycles, and physical trauma in sports events are serious risks. Reducing adolescent alcohol use, improving drivers' training, automobile seat restraints and vehicle design and construction, modifying the design and construction of playground equipment, and greater use of sports protective gear are all prevention methods. Keeping children safe from the many common risk factors requires the efforts of parents, educators, health personnel, policymakers, and of course, of the children and youth themselves.

VII. A Final Note

This textbook ends with a chapter on prevention of developmental disabilities. Throughout the text, we have tried to present a time-line-based discussion of etiology, impairment, disability, and handicap with the goal of informing students about many developmental disabilities. The introduction to etiology that constitutes nearly the first half of this text was deemed important for that understanding. We believe it is necessary information for all of us who work at all levels of prevention in developmental disabilities, including tertiary prevention, where the vast majority of our efforts are now focused. By ending the text on prevention, we hope to underscore its importance and to reinforce the point that much of our future thrust in this field will do well to more fully emphasize prevention. In closing, we must repeat an idea stated several times throughout this work: Groups, populations, and diagnostic categories of developmental disabilities are, after all, made up of individuals. Each individual, whatever the type or depth of his or her particular disability, is a complex human being who deserves all of the respect, consideration, personal attention, and friendship that we would want for ourselves. In our reciprocal, complementary roles as professionals, paraprofessionals, relatives, friends, neighbors, employers, or acquaintances, we need to remember that our own identity and stature are enhanced by how well we help to enhance the lives of others.

KEY TERMS

Know these important terms. Check them in the text and the Glossary for their meanings.
They are listed here in the approximate order of their appearance in the chapter.

Prevention   Secondary prevention   Responsible social agent
Primary prevention   Tertiary prevention   Eugenics

SUGGESTED READING

Levine, M., & Perkins, D. (1987). *Principles of community psychology: Perspectives and applications.* New York: Oxford University Press.

Pueschel, S. M., & Malik, J. A. (Eds.). (1990). *Prevention of developmental disabilities.* Baltimore, MD: Paul H. Brookes.

STUDY QUESTIONS

16-1. Explain this statement: Ameliorative approaches do not reduce the incidence and prevalence of developmental disabilities.

16-2. Distinguish and explain primary, secondary, and tertiary prevention.

16-3. What is the concept of the responsible social agent? Describe the social role. What is its importance in a society's response to deviance?

16-4. The term *unintentional injury* is replacing *accident.* Why is this important?

16-5. If you were the person responsible for creating a developmental disabilities prevention program in your community, what are the major obstacles you would face? How would you approach them?

16-6. In developing that prevention program, what would be your major goals?

GLOSSARY

Abortion: The spontaneous or induced expulsion of a fetus (usually a nonviable fetus) (Ch. 2, 7).

Absence seizures (petit mal): Brief (a few seconds) of momentary lapses, staring, occurring primarily in children; person is not aware of the seizure and it is often not recognized by others (Ch. 12).

Abstract thinking: Thought that transcends representations of immediate concrete reality; conceptions of what "might be," "the future," etc. (Ch. 3, 9).

Academic intelligence: Types of intelligence necessary for scholastic success (Ch. 9, 10).

Achievement tests: Tests to measure acquired information, such as in academics (Ch. 14).

Acidosis: Accumulation of higher than normal levels of acid in the blood and other tissues; high levels of ketones contribute to acidosis; important in the ketogenic diet (Ch. 12).

Acquired cerebral palsy: Cerebral palsy that occurs after birth (Ch. 13).

Acquired immune deficiency syndrome (Aids): The final stage of immune system deterioration due to HIV infection (Ch. 6).

Active socialization hypothesis: The concept that society forces persons with disabilities into a negative social role and reinforces the person's handicaps (Ch. 3, 10).

Adaptive behavior: Overt functioning aimed at successfully meeting life tasks (Ch. 9).

Adaptive intelligence: Intellectual skills needed to function successfully in most everyday affairs (Ch. 10).

Adenine: A base chemical in RNA and DNA; in double-stranded DNA such as in human cells, it pairs with thymine (Ch. 2).

Advocacy: To take up a cause; to plead the case for another or for oneself (Ch. 15).

AIDS: *See* Acquired immune deficiency syndrome (Ch. 6, 7).

Allele: Alternate forms of a single gene locus. The genetic information found at a given locus on a chromosome (Ch. 2).

Aloneness: In autistic children, a characteristic preference for maintaining one's isolation (Ch. 11).

Aloofness: Lack of response to others; a major characteristic of autistic children (Ch. 11).

Alphafetopotein (AFP) assay: A blood test (assay) in pregnacy to determine fetal Down syndrome, neural tube, or other CNS defects (Ch. 2).

Alpha particle: A positively charged nuclear particle ejected at high speed in some radioactivity events (Ch. 4).

Alveoli: Air sacs in the lungs (Ch. 8).

Alzheimer's disease: A group of disorders characterized by severe memory and skill loss in older persons. Some variations are due to a dominant gene disorder (Ch. 3).

Amino acids: The material from which proteins are synthesized under genetic direction. There are twenty different amino acids from which all proteins are made (Ch. 2).

Amniocentesis: A procedure used to examine fetal development by withdrawing amniotic fluid and fetal cells using a long needle inserted into the abdomen of the pregnant woman. The sample is evaluated for chromosomal defects and other biochemical characteristics (Ch. 2).

Amnion: The closed membrane containing amniotic fluid and the growing fetus; the "fetal sac" (Ch. 2).

Amniotic fluid: The liquid within the amnion in which the fetus is suspended and protected from most physical shocks or pressure (Ch. 2).

Amphetamines: Drugs used to stimulate the cerebral cortex. Often used in treatment of hyperactivity (Ch. 6, 7, 14).

Amputations, congenital: An abrupt noncompletion of a body part during prenatal development, giving almost the appearance of amputation (Ch. 1).

Anaclitic depression: Withdrawal, sadness, depression in young children due to serious social and sensory neglect and/or separation from caregivers (Ch. 3).

Anemia: A deficiency of red blood cells and corresponding reduction in oxygen transport (Ch. 6, 7).

Anencephaly: A severe fetal condition in which most of the brain fails to develop. The failure begins in the embryonic period, weeks 3 to 8, when the cephalic end of the neural tube fails to close properly (Ch. 3, 5).

Aneuploidy: Having a chromosome number that is not an exact multiple of the usual haploid number. Includes nullisomy, monosomy, trisomy, and tetrasomy (Ch. 2, 3, 5).

Anomalies: Irregularities or deviations from the common rules such as in cases of genetic and chromosomal conditions, birth defects, etc. (Ch. 2).

Anoxia: Hypoxia (oxygen deficiency) of such severity as to result in permanent damage (Ch. 13).

Antibody: A protein molecule that attaches to foreign substances, such as disease organisms; fights infections (Ch. 6, 7).

Antigen: A chemical substance, usually protein or carbohydrate, that stimulates production of antibodies (Ch. 3).

Anxious-insecure attachment: A tenuous emotional connection of infant and caregiver characterized by uncertainty and anxiety (Ch. 3).

Apgar test: Developed by Virginia Apgar, a short series of quick visual observations are made at 1 minute and at 5 minutes after birth for a quick assessment of the newborn's condition and to help determine if immediate emergency care is required (Ch. 2).

Aphasia: Language disorders in children not caused by mental retardation (Ch. 13).

Apraxia: Impairment in carrying out purposeful movements in a person who does not have significant motor problems (Ch. 13).

Articulation: In speech, refers to the production of speech sounds from vocal tract movements (lips, jaw, tongue). The age-appropriateness, quality, precision, accuracy, etc. of speech sounds are assessed (Ch. 14).

Articulation disorder: Incorrect speech production (Ch. 14).

Asperger's syndrome: A type of autism characterized by high-level cognitive and language ability and some autistic characteristics (Ch. 11).

Asphyxia: Lack of oxygen due to poor oxygen supply or to breathing difficulties (Ch. 13).

Assistive technology: Any procedures or mechanical or electronic devices that are designed to assist a person with disabilities to function better (Ch. 13, 14).

Ataxia: Lack of balance (Ch. 13).

Ataxic cerebral palsy: A type of cerebral palsy characterized by ataxia (Ch. 13).

Athetoid cerebral palsy: A type of cerebral palsy characterized by athetoid movements (Ch. 13).

Athetoid movement: Involuntary movements associated with cerebral palsy, seen as discordant, jerky movements especially of the wrist and fingers (also Athetosis. Ch. 13).

Atonic seizures: Sudden loss of muscle tone so severe the person may fall down; injury can result in falls (Ch. 12).

Attachment: A strong bond that develops between a child and caregiver. Disruptions in the attachment process are thought to have potentially harmful effects on development (Ch. 3).

Attention deficit disorder (ADD): A disability in children characterized by poor attentional skills, impulsive and poorly controlled behavior, and sometimes accompanied by hyperactivity (e.g., ADHD—attention deficit hyperactivity disorder) (Ch. 1, 14).

Attention deficit hyperactivity disorder (ADHD): *See* Attention deficit disorder (Ch. 14).

Attention span: Period of time during which person is able to maintain focus on a task (Ch. 9).

Atypical language: Characteristic language distortions of groups such as autism (Ch. 11).

Audiologist: A professional trained in diagnosing and treating hearing problems (Ch. 1).

Auditory central processing deficits: Disabilities that prevent adequate perception of sound (Ch.14).

Auditory impairments: Hearing losses from various structural or functional disorders (Ch. 1).

Augmentative communication: The use of various procedures and apparatus to enable or assist persons with speech and language disabilities to communicate (Ch. 13).

Autism: A severe, complex syndrome involving the child's cognitive functioning, language and social skills development, emotional life, and motor performance. Autistic children are characterized by severe aloofness, stereotyped behavior, language distortions, and sometimes violent behavior (Ch. 11).

Autistic spectrum disorders: A group of disorders that have severe autistic impairments in more than one area of function (Ch. 11).

Autistic triad: Three major characteristics necessary for diagnosis of autism: impaired social interactions, preservation of sameness, impaired language (Ch. 11).

Autonomic nervous system: That portion of the nervous system that controls involuntary action such as the physiological changes in emotion (Ch. 4).

Autosome: In humans, one of the twenty-two chromosomes other than the sex chromosomes (Ch. 2).

Aura: A strange feeling experienced by a person, predictive of a seizure about to occur; term also used formerly for simple partial seizures (Ch. 12).

Babbling: Repetitive consonant–vowel patterns such as "bababa" and "mamama" that begin at about 3 months and continue to about 12 months when single words begin to appear (Ch. 3).

Bacteria: Single-celled spherical, spiral, or rod-shaped microorganisms that can have pathogenic effects on plant and animal bodies (Ch. 2).

Base pairs: Nitrogen-based molecules (nucleotides) (adenine and thymine [A-T] and guanine and cytocine [G-T]) that bind together the molecular strands of phoshate and sugar of the DNA molecule (Ch. 2, 4, 5).

Behavior modification: Concepts and procedures to study and alter behavior based on psychological learning theory concepts (Ch. 11, 12).

Behavior therapy: Behavior modification concepts and procedures used to improve functioning of persons with psychopathology (Ch. 11).

Behavioral teratology: Study of substances and events that cause damage in the prenatal CNS, affecting future cognitive, emotional, and behavioral functioning (Ch. 6, 7).

Beta particle: An electron or positron released from an atom nucleus during radioactive decay (Ch. 8).

Birth defect: A general term for disabilities that are discernible at birth; also called congenital malformations and congenital anomalies (Ch. 4).

Blastocyst: The hollow sphere of inner cells (endodermal) and outer cells (ectodermal) that forms from the human zygote in 2 to 4 days following conception (Ch. 2).

Bonding: An immediate attachment of mother and child that forms quickly when there is close physical contact at and following birth. While a positive event, its long-term effects are unclear (Ch. 3).

Brazelton Neonatal Behavioral Assessment scale (NBSA): A behavioral rating scale applied to newborns and infants; it rates twenty-six items of behavior to assess the baby's well-being (Ch. 2).

Breech presentation or birth position: At birth, the baby is positioned buttocks-first rather than head-first, usually requiring attempts to turn it around for its birth (Ch. 2).

Cannabinoids: Chemical molecules of cannabis (marijuana) (Ch. 6, 7).

Carrier: An individual whose genotype includes a recessive gene (Ch. 2).

Causal agents: Any factors, such as a pathogen, with a direct, causal relationship with pathology, as distinguished from correlates (correlated), contributory, or risk factors (Ch. 1).

Cell differentiation: *See* Differentiation (Ch. 2).

Central nervous system (CNS): The brain and spinal cord (Ch. 4).

Cephalo-caudal development: A normal, general developmental sequence that proceeds directionally from head to foot (Ch. 2).

Cerebellum: The upper-back part of the brain that controls muscle coordination and equilibrium (Ch. 3).

Cerebral: Relating to the two hemispheres of the brain (Ch. 3).

Cerebral cortex: The outer layer of the brain in which higher cognitive processes are controlled (Ch. 3).

Cerebral palsy: A nonprogressive developmental disability caused by damage to the central nervous system before, during, or soon after birth and manifest by speech disturbances, muscular incoordination, and in more than half of the cases, mental retardation (Ch. 13).

Cerebral palsy social role: A deviance social role enacted by persons with cerebral palsy (Ch. 13).

Cerebrum: The major front and upper-back portions of the brain, where voluntary muscle control is located (Ch. 3).

Cervix: The neck or lower part of the uterus leading into the vaginal canal (Ch. 2).

Cesarean section: A surgical procedure used when the normal process of the baby moving through the birth canal is not possible or advised. It entails cutting through the abdomen and the uterus and lifting out the neonate (Ch. 2).

Chelation therapy: Treatment procedures using chemical compounds to bind with metal toxins, such as lead, and to neutralize, slow their absorption, or remove them from the bloodstream (Ch. 8).

Childhood disintegrative disorder: Rare childhood disorder with severe regression in several functional areas after at least 2 years of normal development (Ch. 11).

Chlamydia: Caused by the parasite *Chlamydia trachomatis,* this infection occurs in the cervix, urethra, or anus. It is the most common sexually transmitted disease, affecting more than 3 million persons annually (Ch. 6, 7).

Chorea: A movement disorder primarily involving fingers and toes (Ch. 13).

Chorion: A membrane layer covering the placenta and uterus (Ch. 2).

Chorionic villus sampling: An invasive prenatal examination of the fetus by means of taking and examining a biopsy from the chorion (Ch. 2).

Chromosome: DNA molecules in the cell nucleus that carry genetic material (Ch. 2).

Chromosome anomalies: Distortions in the number or structure of chromosomes, often resulting in fetal death or developmental disabilities (Ch. 2).

Classical conditioning: Psychological learning model that focuses on stimulus–response (S–R) association to account for increased or decreased strength of some classes of behavior; also called respondent or Pavlovian conditioning (Ch. 12).

Cognition: Higher-order mental processes such as thinking and problem solving (Ch. 2).

Cognitive behavioral self-control training: Integration of behavior modification and cognitive function concepts, used to teach persons to self-monitor, analyze, modify, and maintain their own behavior (Ch. 10).

Comorbidity: When a person has more than one clearly diagnosable disorder (Ch. 1, 9).

Complex partial seizures (psychomotor or temporal lobe seizure): A brief seizure of 1 or 2 minutes in which person is unaware of his or her repetitive behavior or walking about in a "daze"; confusion is typical during recovery, is usually in adults, and accounts for about two-thirds of epilepsy (Ch. 12).

Conception: The process in which a haploid sperm cell unites with a haploid ovum, creating a diploid zygote (Ch. 2).

Conceptus: The developing organism after conception (Ch. 2).

Concrete thinking: Thought characteristic of young children; focused on "real" or immediate things and events, as opposed to abstract thoughts (Ch. 3, 9).

Concussion: Jarring of organs (e.g., the brain) due to physical force. May cause loss of consciousness and temporary or permanent brain damage (Ch. 8).

Congenital: A condition present at birth (Ch. 4).

Congenital anomalies: Disorders and defects present at birth (i.e., "born with") (Ch. 4).

Congenital cerebral palsy: Cerebral palsy present at birth (Ch. 13).

Congenital factors: Structures and conditions present at birth but not caused by heredity (Ch. 4).

Congenital toxoplasmosis: Toxoplasmosis present at birth (Ch. 6, 7).

Constitution: All of the person's behavioral and biological characteristics that exist at birth (Ch. 2).

Consumer empowerment: In developmental disabilities, a movement of the 1990s of persons with disabilities to assume greater power in managing their own lives (Ch. 15).

Contracture: A permanent shortening of a muscle or tendon causing deformity (Ch. 13).

Convulsions: Uncontrolled seizure activity usually with loss of consciousness involving the whole body or large portions (Ch. 12).

Correlate: A factor that is related to a condition but does not directly cause it (Ch. 6, 7).

Correlational research: Research in which the degree and direction of relationship among variables is tested. Unlike experimental research, variables are not manipulated to determine causality (Ch. 6, 7).

Craniofacial anomalies: Distortions of the head and face, as in fetal alcohol syndrome (Ch. 1).

Cretinism (or hypothyroidism): Severe physical stunting and mental retardation due to thyroid deficiency which may have genetic or environmental etiologies (Ch. 3).

Cri du chat syndrome (cat's cry syndrome): Caused by a deletion on chromosome 5, it includes severe mental retardation, microcephaly, maldeveloped vocal chords (hence the name), and death in early infancy (Ch. 3, 5).

Critical period: A time of particularly rapid or important development of an organ in which disruptions result in especially severe damage (Ch. 6, 7).

Crossing over: Exchange of genetic material across portions of chromosomes, leading to recombinants (Ch. 2).

Cultural-familial retardation: A subset of mild mental retardation accounting for more than 70 percent of all MR, in which there are no known organic etiologies. Risk factors are inherited intelligence levels (familial) and social/environmental (cultural) (Ch. 9).

Cystic fibrosis: A recessive-gene defect, located on chromosome 7, in which lungs become filled with mucus and infected, causing death before adulthood (Ch. 3).

Cytomegalovirus (CMV): A herpes virus that is usually fatal to an embryo. It is the most common fetal viral infection, and nearly 20 percent of infected fetuses will have congenital defects (Ch. 6, 7).

Cytoplasm: The protoplasm within a cell but outside of the nucleus (Ch. 2).

Cytosine: A base chemical in RNA and DNA; in double-strand DNA such as in human cells, cytosine pairs with guanine (Ch. 2).

Cytotoxin: Any substance that has toxic effects on cells (Ch. 6, 7).

Deductive thinking (or inferences): Higher-order thought processes that proceed from general ideas to more specific ideas such as hypotheses or predictions about events (Ch. 3).

Deficit vs. difference model: Alternative models to explain the cognitive limitations of persons with mild mental retardation. The deficit model attributes low functioning to inherited intellectual limitations; the difference model attributes them to normal intelligence variation and to disadvantaged personal/social conditions (Ch. 9).

Deletions: A mutation in which there is a loss of part of the chromosomal material and its information (Ch. 4, 5).

Demands (normative): Role-based social expectations that have been communicated, thereby taking on the power of social "demands" (Ch. 10).

Dementia: A severe, degenerating impairment in thinking and problem solving, usually associated with aging and Alzheimer's disease (Ch. 5).

Deoxyribonucleic acid (DNA): The basic chemical carrier of the genetic code; DNA molecules make up genes and chromosomes (Ch. 2).

Detoxification: Process of removing a toxin or its effects (Ch. 4).

Developmental articulation disorder: A specific learning disability involving problems with speaking clearly (Ch. 14).

Developmental delay: A failure to acquire an ability at the time expected according to child developmental norms (Ch. 1).

Developmental disability: A severe, permanent, physical or psychological impairment originating before age 22 and causing severe functional disruptions (handicaps) in the person's life (Ch. 1).

Developmental expressive language disorder: A specific learning disability involving cognitive-based problems in communicating through speech. Not to be confused with physical speech disorders (Ch. 14).

Developmental motor function disorder: A specific learning disorder involving fine motor problems that interfere with academic achievement (Ch. 14).

Developmental psychopathology: The study and treatment of severe psychological impairments in children (Ch. 1).

Developmental receptive language disorder: A specific learning disability involving problems in understanding language (Ch. 14).

Developmental tasks: Behaviors and ideas that are presumed necessary to master at various points in development (Ch. 3).

Developmental vs. difference controversy: Conflicting theoretical models concerning the nature of mild mental retardation. *See* Deficit vs. difference models (Ch. 9).

Deviance positions: Low-status, negatively valued social positions that depart significantly from the accepted array of social positions (Ch. 10).

Deviant identity: Defining oneself with the norms of one's position of deviance (Ch. 10).

Dexedrine: Commercial trade name for one of several stimulant drugs used to treat hyperactivity in children (Ch. 14).

Diabetes mellitus: A metabolic disorder in which insulin is not properly secreted or utilized, causing an excess of sugar in the blood and urine and excessive thirst (Ch. 6, 7).

Diagnostic and Statistical Manual (DSM-IV): A nomenclature for all psychiatric conditions, published by the American Psychiatric Association, and used commonly throughout the mental health field (Ch. 11).

Diagnostic overshadowing: A response tendency by professionals in which a person is nearly totally defined by a diagnosis, such as "mental retardation," with the result that the person's other positive characteristics are obscured (Ch. 1).

Diathesis: An innate or constitutional predisposition to a disease or disorder (Ch. 1, 2).

Diethylstilbestrol: A synthetic estrogen hormone given to pregnant women in the 1940s through 1960s to prevent miscarriages but found to be teratogenic and carcinogenic for the offspring (Ch. 6, 7).

Differentiation: In fetal development, the formation of different types of cells, tissues, and organs, directed by gene functioning. In general, it is the development of a more specialized level of structure or function (Ch. 2).

Diffuse axonal injury: Severe damage to axons throughout the brain caused by violent movements of the head, (e.g.,as in automobile crashes). Immediate loss of consciousness, probable permanent brain damage, and functional disability vary in seriousness with the severity of the force (Ch. 8).

Dilation stage: The first of three phases in the human birth process is the dilation/effacement phase. Dilation is the enlargement of the cervical opening to about 10 centimeters in diameter (Ch. 2).

Diplegia: In cerebral palsy, where both legs are involved. A paralysis of corresponding parts on both sides of the body, such as both legs. *See* Spastic diplegia (Ch. 13).

Diploid: The condition of a cell when it has the full complement of chromosomes (forty-six in humans) (Ch. 2).

Direct modeling: Live teaching by demonstrating behavior to a person (Ch. 10).

Disability: An impairment of such severity that the impaired function or state of health is significantly disrupted or made ineffective. Literally, when a function is disabled, it is "put out of commission" (Ch. 1).

Discrepancy criteria (in learning disabilities): Academic achievement that is significantly lower than expected based on the person's intellectual level. This is a major diagnostic criterion for learning disabilities (Ch. 14).

Disease: An illness, sickness, malady (Ch. 1).

Disorder: The basic disruption or disturbance that can constitute a disability. In this text, disorder is used synonymously with "impairment" (Ch. 1).

Dizygotic twins: Twins resulting from the union of two different ova and sperm at about the same time. Genetically, these twins are as different as any siblings, sharing about half of their genes (Ch. 2).

DNA: Deoxyribonucleic acid (Ch. 2).

Dominant gene: The gene that takes precedence over a recessive gene in genetic expression (Ch. 4).

Dose-effect relationship: The concept that the size of the effects of a toxin or other pathogen is related to the amount or strength of the pathogen (Ch. 6, 7).

Double-blind procedure: A control procedure for experimentation in which neither the participants nor the researchers who interact with the participants are aware of the hypotheses or the nature of the experimental conditions. *See* Single-blind procedure (Ch. 11).

Double helix: Double spiral; descriptive of DNA molecule (Ch.2).

Down syndrome: A developmental disability caused by a genetic defect (i.e., presence of an extra chromosome in chromosome pair 21). Associated with characteristic facial features and mental retardation. Also called trisomy 21 (Ch. 4).

Dual diagnosis: The determination that a person with a developmental disability such as cerebral palsy or mental retardation also has a psychiatric/behavioral/emotional disorder (Ch. 1).

Dual exceptionality: The cooccurrence of a specific learning disability and giftedness. Special needs in two areas cause serious problems, and this person is poorly served in school (Ch. 12).

Duchenne's muscular dystrophy: A severe form of muscular dystrophy involving only boys and manifest by progressive muscle weakening, being wheelchair confined by about age 12, and death by about age 18 (Ch. 5).

Duplications: The doubling of a chromosome segment (Ch. 4, 5).

Dysarthria: Speaking difficulties caused by poor control of facial muscles needed for speech (Ch. 13).

Dyscalcula: A specific learning disability involving problems in arithmetic (Ch. 14).

Dysgraphia: Problems producing legible handwriting at age-appropriate quality and speed (Ch. 14).

Dyskinesis: Abnormal involuntary movements often following voluntary movement by persons with cerebral palsy (Ch. 13).

Dyskinetic cerebral palsy: Cerebral palsy characterized by dyskinesis (Ch. 13).

Dyslexia: A group of disorders that involves problems in expressive or receptive oral or written language (reading, spelling, writing, speaking, listening) (Ch. 14).

Echolalia: Repeating the speech of others. It is commonly found in autism (Ch. 11).

Eclampsia: Maternal seizures during pregnancy or birth (Ch. 12).

Ectoderm: The outer layer of cells in the blastocyst which develops into the skin, central nervous system, nails, and parts of the teeth and eyes (Ch. 2).

Educational therapist: A professional trained to assess children's educational achievement and behavior; develops and implements appropriate remedial programs (Ch. 14).

EEG: *See* Electroencephalograph (Ch. 2).

Effacement (in birth): The first of three phases in the human birth process is the dilation/effacement phase. Effacement is the shortening of the cervical canal from its normal 2 centimeters opening to about 10 centimeters in diameter (Ch. 2).

Electroencephalograph (EEG): An electronic device that measures brain activity by sensing small electrical changes on the head (Ch. 2).

Embryo: The developing organism in the uterus; in humans, from approximately 2 weeks postconception to 8 weeks (Ch. 2).

Embryonic period: Approximately gestation weeks 3 through 8 in which cell differentiation and development of supporting systems occur (Ch. 2).

Encephalitis: Infection and inflammation of the brain (Ch. 13).

Encephalopathy: *See* Encephalitis (Ch. 13).

Encoding: Process of language expression; selecting, sequencing and producing in speech the appropriate words for ideas (Ch. 14).

Endoderm: The inner layer of cells of the blastocyst from which the embryo develops (Ch. 2).

Endogenous: Events originating within a specified system; contrasted with exogenous (Ch. 3, 4).

Endometrium: The lining of the uterine wall in which the blastocyst becomes embedded at about 7 to 14 days after conception and which provides nutrients for development (Ch. 2).

Enzymes: Complex proteins produced by cells and which are basic to specific chemical reactions in the body (Ch. 4).

Epidemiology: Study of the incidence and prevalence of disease or other disorders in a population (Ch. 5).

Epilepsy: Various disorders marked by disturbed electrical rhythms of the central nervous system, manifest by convulsive attacks (seizures) and clouding of consciousness. *See* Idiopathic epilepsy, Psychogenic seizures, Symptomatic epilepsy (Ch. 12).

Epilepsy social role: An hypothesized "sick role" that can develop in persons with epilepsy and result in unecessarily restricted lives; develops from others' negative concepts about and ignorance and fear of epilepsy (Ch. 12).

Epinephrine: An adrenal hormone (Ch. 6, 7).

Erythroblastosis: The condition in which antibodies formed by the mother's Rh- blood attack the Rh+ blood of the fetus, causing fetal death or serious disabilities (Ch. 5, 6, 7).

Ethanol: Alcohol (Ch. 6, 7).

Etiology: The study of all of the factors, causal and correlated, which result in a pathological condition (Ch. 1).

Exclusion criteria: Ruling out conditions to help diagnose one particular condition. For example, ruling out mental retardation to diagnose learning disability (Ch. 14).

Exogenous: Events originating externally to a system (Ch. 3, 4).

Expectations (or expectancies): Social norms, when communicated, comprise the expectations of society (Ch. 3, 10).

Experimental research: Research in which careful controls are used to test the hypothesis that a causal relation exists between the independent and dependent variables (Ch. 6, 7).

Explicit norms: Norms that are codified and/or recorded (Ch. 10).

Expressive language: Communication through writing, speaking, and/or gestures (Ch. 3, 14).

Expulsion: The second phase of the birth process; the amnionic membrane ruptures, amnionic fluid is discharged, and the neonate is pushed through the birth canal (Ch. 2).

Extremely low birth weight (ELBW): Birth weight that is below 2.2 pounds (1000 grams), usually due to premature birth (Ch. 8).

Facilitated communication: A now discredited procedure in which professionals sought to provide supports for autistic and other persons with severe communication problems to communicate with others (Ch. 11).

Failure to thrive: Poor rate of growth and development in young children (Ch. 7, 13).

Fallopian tubes: Two tubes, each leading from one ovary to the uterus, through which the sperm and ovum move (Ch. 2).

Febrile seizures: Seizures caused by high fevers such as occur in infections (e.g., encephalitis, meningitis). These are most common in young children (Ch. 12).

Fetal alcohol effects (FAE): A cluster of pathological characteristics similar to fetal alcohol syndrome but at a lower level of severity and caused by maternal alcohol use during pregnancy (Ch. 5).

Fetal alcohol syndrome (FAS): A cluster of characteristics in birth defects caused by maternal alcohol use during pregnancy (Ch. 5).

Fetal period: From about the 8th week to the end of pregnancy (Ch. 2).

Fetoscopy: An invasive procedure for prenatal examination of the fetus by means of an optical scanner inserted into the uterus through an abdominal incision (Ch. 2).

Fetus: A developing organism in the uterus. In humans, approximately 8 weeks post-conception to birth (Ch. 2).

Final common pathway model: A theoretical model of autism's etiology in which it is thought that a spectrum of biological causes results in damage to those areas of the brain that control language, communication, social behavior, play, and creativity (Ch. 11).

Fragile X syndrome: A sex-linked (twenty-third pair) chromosomal anomaly in which the lower arm of the chromosome has a constricted or pinched form and is subject to breakage. It is associated with mental deficiency in a third of the females who carry it and in more than half of the males (Ch. 4).

Functional analysis: In behavior modification, a detailed study of behavior and its antecedents and reinforcing contingencies; essential basis for behavior and cognitive-behavior modification in education and mental health (Ch. 12).

Functional disorder: A malfunction of the behavior of an organism, as contrasted with the structural aspects (Ch. 1).

Functional endpoints: Negative impact of teratogens on behavior (Ch. 6).

Functional severity: The degree to which a disability interferes with the normal functioning of an organ, an organ system, or of overt behavior (Ch 1).

Gait analysis: A highly detailed, specialized study of a person's movements to determine the specific muscular problems in locomotion (Ch. 13).

Gametes: The mature sex cells (ovum and sperm), each carrying half of the total chromosome complement (i.e., haploid), that can combine to form the zygote (Ch. 2).

Gamma rays: Photons or other radiation particles emitted spontaneously by a radioactive substance (Ch. 8).

Gene: The portions of the chromosome that carry genetic material and direct development (i.e., segments of DNA that are responsible for production of particular proteins) (Ch. 2).

Gene map: A representation of the location and order of genes on a chromosome (Ch. 2).

Generalized partial seizures: When a partial seizure develops a second phase of generalized tonic-clonic seizure (Ch. 12).

Generalized tonic-clonic seizures (grand mal): Severe, sudden involvement of the entire brain and body, with immediate loss of consciousness and physical control; body alternately stiffens and relaxes (tonic-clonic movement); injury can occur in falls; no awareness or memory of the seizure (Ch. 12).

Genetic code: The sequence of DNA chemical bases (Ch. 2).

Genetic counseling: A procedure to assess the probabilities of conceiving children with genetic defects. Detailed family history and physical examinations are used (Ch. 2).

Genetic defect: Disabilities based on mutations in the smallest units of heredity, the base pairs in specific genes; can be autosomal or X-linked, dominant or recessive (Ch. 4).

Genetic determination: The principle that phenotypic characteristics are directly determined all or in part by the inherited genetic information (Ch 2).

Genome: All of the genetic information contained in a haploid cell (Ch. 2)

Genotype: The total genetic makeup of an organism. *See* Phenotype (Ch. 2).

Germ cells: The sex cells of an organism, contrasted with the somatic (body) cells (Ch. 2).

Germinal period: In humans, approximately the first 7 to 14 days from conception to implantation in the endometrium and during which cell division occurs rapidly, multiplying to about 150 cells (Ch. 2).

Gestation: The period of development of young in the uterus from conception to birth. In humans, about 38 to 42 weeks (Ch. 2).

Gestational diabetes: Diabetes mellitus of the mother during pregnancy; it has negative consequences for the fetus, particularly macrosomia (Ch. 6, 7).

Global intelligence: Overall general intelligence as distinguished from specific areas of intelligence (Ch. 9).

Gonads: The reproductive organs; ovaries in females, testes in males (Ch. 2).

Gonorrhea: A highly contagious sexually transmitted bacterial infection that usually lodges in the penis, vagina, throat, and anus and can spread to the eyes; it can cause sterility, blood infection, arthritis, and heart problems (Ch. 5).

Grammar: The rules for the structure of a language. Grammar includes syntax and morphology (Ch. 14).

Grand mal seizures: Severe epileptic seizures, with loss of consciousness and memory for the event. *See* Petit mal seizures (Ch. 12).

Graphemes: Written symbols that represent phonemes (Ch. 14).

Guanine: A base chemical in RNA and DNA; in double strand DNA, such as in human cells, guanine pairs with cytosine (Ch. 2).

Handicap: The effects of a disability on a person's functioning. A handicap exists when a disability is so serious or disruptive that it makes it uncommonly difficult for the person to pursue normal life activities (Ch. 1).

Haploid: A cell with a single copy of each chromosome (Ch. 2).

Head trauma: Physical injury to the head, nearly always causing brain injury (Ch. 2).

Heart defects, congenital: A variety of heart anomalies that are present at birth (Ch. 1).

Hemiplegia: Paralysis of a lateral half of the body, or portion of it, usually one arm and one leg on the same side, caused by damage to the motor centers of the brain (Ch. 13).

Hemophilia: A sex-linked genetic disorder in which the material necessary for normal blood clotting is missing. Hemophiliacs bleed profusely if injured (Ch. 3).

Herpes simplex virus (HSV): The most common sexually transmitted disease. It is passed to a child by an infected mother usually through contact with lesions during birth, but can infect the fetus early in pregnancy; infected children have high rates of spontaneous abortions, blindness, deafness, brain damage, mental retardation, and death (Ch. 5).

Heterozygous: In humans (diploid organisms), having two different alleles at a given gene locus; contrast with homozygous (Ch. 2).

Holophrase: In language development, at about 18 months, when children use single words to convey complete thoughts (Ch. 3).

Homologous chromosomes: Members of a pair of chromosomes that have the same overall genetic composition and sequence. One homologous chromosome is from each parent (Ch. 2).

Homozygous: In humans (diploid organisms), having the same allele in each chromosome, producing genotypically identical gametes. These may be homozygous dominant or homozygous recessive; contrast with heterozygous (Ch. 2).

Human Immunodeficiency Virus (HIV): A viral disease factor carried in the blood and other fluids of the infected person that overwhelms the body's immune system and leads to AIDS (Ch. 4).

Huntington's chorea: A dominant gene defect that does not manifest phenotypically until adulthood. It causes progressive neurological, physical, intellectual, and personality deterioration and death (Ch. 3).

Hydrocephalus (hydrocephaly): An abnormally large amount of cerebrospinal fluid in the brain cavity, causing head enlargement, brain atrophy, and mental retardation (Ch. 3, 5).

Hyperactivity: A high level of overt motor activity by a child that is particularly distressful to parents and teachers. It is often associated with inappropriate social behavior, attentional, and academic problems (Ch. 4).

Hyperthyroidism: A hormonal condition in which excess thyroid hormone (thyroxin) is produced, causing rapid heart rate, high blood pressure, and increased metabolism (Ch. 5).

Hypertonia (also hypertonicity): Increased muscle tone (Ch. 13).

Hypoglycemia: Low blood sugar (Ch. 6, 7).

Hypothetical-deductive reasoning: An advanced form of thinking and problem solving in which predictions are generated and tested and their implications thought out (Ch. 3).

Hypothyroidism: A hormonal condition in which insufficient thyroid hormone (thyroxin) is produced by the thyroid gland; in pregnancy, it increases the risk of cretinism (Ch. 5).

Hypotonia: Decreased muscle tone (Ch. 13).

Hypotonic cerebral palsy: Cerebral palsy manifested by hypotonia (Ch. 13).

Hypoxia: An oxygen deficiency (Ch. 2).

Iatrogenic: The inadvertent creation of disorder caused by a treatment (Ch.1).

Identity: A person's own enduring self-description (Ch. 10).

Idiopathic epilepsy: Epilepsy where the causes are not known (Ch. 12).

Impairment: Any lessening or weakening in some ability or state of health which leaves the person at less than an optimal level of performance or health for his or her age. Impairments can occur in any physical or psychological area (Ch. 1).

Implicit norms: Prescriptions for behavior that are not codified or recorded (Ch. 10).

Impulsivity: A tendency to act hastily, quickly, without reflection (Ch. 5).

Incidence: The number of new cases in a population of a disease or pathology, usually expressed as the ratio of new cases per 1000 population in a given time period (Ch. 1).

Incidental learning: Additional learning that occurs while a person is focused on some specific learning task. This is limited in persons with mental retardation (Ch. 9).

Inclusion criteria: Specifying what factors are part of a diagnosis (Ch. 14).

Incontinence: Problems controlling urination and/or defecation (Ch. 7).

Individualized educational plan (IEP): A detailed written document prepared by a multidisciplinary team and the child's parents that specifies the details of special education services and transition to adult life (Ch. 15).

Individualized family services plan (IFSP): A detailed written document prepared by a multidisciplinary team and the child's parents that identifies and describes the services to be provided for the child and family (Ch. 15).

Inductive thinking: Thinking process in theory building that proceeds from more specific observations or ideas to more general ideas (Ch. 3).

Infant mortality: Death at an early age, in infancy (Ch. 8).

Infant stimulation therapy: Used for infants with cerebral palsy to provide the sensorimotor stimulation that the child cannot obtain on his or her own because of the severe motor disabilities (Ch. 13).

Infantile spasms: Frequent seizures in infancy; associated with developmental delay and mental retardation (Ch. 12).

Influenza: A group of acute, highly contagious viral diseases (Ch. 6, 7).

Innate factors: Structures or tendencies due to heredity (Ch. 4).

Intention tremors: In cerebral palsy, trembling of limbs, such as when reaching for something, that increases as the person gets closer to the desired goal (Ch. 13).

Intentional injuries: Injuries to a child caused deliberately by another person (i.e., not accidental) (Ch. 8).

Interdependence: Shared responsibility that supports all persons in a relationship (Ch. 9).

Interference hypothesis: The model that normal child development is skewed toward disabilities by the intrusions and disruptions of factors such as impairments (Ch. 3).

Internalizing disorder: Psychological disorders characterized by anxiety (e.g., fears, phobias, depression, anxiety disorders) (Ch. 1).

International Classification of Disease (ICD-10, 1996): The World Health Organization system of disease classification and nomenclature (Ch. 14).

Inversion: A chromosomal mutation in which a chromosome segment is separated and then reattached but at 180° from its original position (Ch. 3, 5).

In vitro: An event occurring outside of a living body in a controlled laboratory, clinic, or other "artificial" setting (Ch. 4).

In vivo: Occurring within the living body of an organism (Ch. 4).

Ionizing radiation: Radiation that causes atoms to become charged (creating an ion) and thereby altering the nature of the substance. Ionizing radiation can alter the structure of chromosomes, resulting in mutations (Ch. 6, 7).

Jaundice: A disorder of the blood involving accumulation of bile pigments in the bloodstream (Ch. 13).

Juvenile paresis: A gradual motor and cognitive deterioration in children, often caused by maternal syphilis and ending in an early death (Ch. 5).

Karyotype: A photomicrograph of all of an individual's chromosomes, arranged in pairs and ordered by size and type (Ch. 2)

Ketogenic diet: A high-fat, low-protein, low-carbohydrate, rigidly prescribed diet used successfully to control seizures in epilepsy, based on ketones, ketosis, and acidosis (Ch. 13).

Ketones: Acidic organic compounds that, in accumulation, have mild sedative and appetite suppressing effects; believed to be the basis for success of the ketogenic diet in epilepsy treatment (Ch. 13).

Ketosis: A condition of high concentration of ketones in body fluids, important in the ketogenic diet for control of seizures in epilepsy (Ch. 13).

Klinefelter's syndrome: A sex-linked genetic trisomic disorder with two X and one Y chromosome (47, XXY) (Ch. 3).

Kohl: Powdered lead used as a cosmetic, usually around the eyes of women in some cultures such as India, and a source of lead poisoning (Ch. 9).

Kwashiorkor: Malnutrition in which a child's body bloats from water accumulation, hair drops out, skin sores erupt. Cognitive and other disabilities result if the child survives physically (Ch. 9).

Language and speech pathologist: A professional trained in diagnosing and treating speech and language disabilities (Ch. 14).

Lead encephalopathy: Inflammation of the brain due to lead poisoning; a severe toxic level (Ch. 8).

Lead toxicity (lead poisoning): A toxic condition caused by lead that is ingested or otherwise taken into the body (Ch. 5).

Learning disabilities: A marked difficulty in learning basic academic skill(s), with no apparent deficits in intelligence. Involves problems in thinking, listening, talking, reading, writing, spelling, arithmetic, and/or fine motor coordination (Ch. 1, 14).

Least restrictive environment: The concept that handicapped persons have the right to live in conditions that are as normal as possible, such as with nonhandicapped students, workers, and neighbors (Ch. 9).

Lesch-Nyhan syndrome: A severe neurological disorder caused by a metabolic defect that is genetically transmitted. Symptoms appear at about 6 months of age, and the children seldom live beyond adolescence (Ch. 4).

Lightening: About 10 to 14 days before delivery, the fetus settles lower in the pelvic inlet, reducing pressure on maternal organs and resulting in a "lighter" feeling (Ch. 2).

Limited cognitive abilities: Less than normal general and/or specific intelligence (Ch. 9).

Linked genes: Two genes lying close together (Ch. 2).

Locus (pl.: loci): The specific location of a gene on a chromosome (Ch. 2).

Low birth weight (LBW): A newborn, full-term or preterm, whose weight is significantly below the norm (i.e., below 3500 grams or 7.5 pounds) (Ch. 8).

Macrocephaly: An unusually large head with fluid accumulation, ordinarily with severe mental retardation (Ch. 6, 7).

Macrosomia: An unusually large fetus and neonate. May be caused by mother's diabetic condition in pregnancy; can cause serious problems during birth (Ch. 6, 7).

Macular degeneration: Progressive damage to the maculae, a specific area in the central region of the human retina (Ch. 4).

Magnetic resonance imaging (MRI): A body-imaging process that employs radio waves, magnetic fields, and computer analyses (Ch. 2).

Mainstreaming: Placing persons with disabilities in normal settings to enhance their development (e.g., placing children with disabilities in regular classrooms) (Ch. 9).

Malnutrition: A condition of undernutrition due to insufficient calories, protein, and/or vitamins and minerals (Ch. 6, 7).

Marasmus: Extreme condition of malnutrition in which the child's growth literally stops, the body deteriorates, and the child dies (Ch. 8).

Maternal phenylketonuria (MPKU): Developmental disabilities, including severe intellectual disabilities, can occur from the teratogenic effects of a mother's PKU condition, even if the child is heterozygous for the PKU allele. *See* Phenylketonuria (Ch. 4).

Maturation: An organism's normal growth and development that are relatively independent of environmental influences (Ch. 3).

Meiosis: The maturation process in the sex cells that results in the haploid state—that is, gametes with half of the total number of chromosomes (twenty-three in humans) (Ch. 2).

Memory skills: Cognitive abilities relating to memory (e.g., rehearsal, organization, and storage strategies) developed largely during middle childhood (Ch. 3).

Meninges (pl. of meninx): Any of the three membranes that envelop the brain and spinal cord (Ch. 14).

Meningitis: A disease, usually of bacterial origin but also can be viral, involving inflammation of the meninges (brain covering), with high fever, often convulsions, and frequently resulting in brain damage (Ch. 7, 12).

Meningocele: A neural tube defect in which the meninges protrude through the spinal cord, forming a skin-covered cystic "sack" filled with cerebral spinal fluid. Neural disorders are common, and hydrocephaly often accompanies this condition (Ch. 5).

Mental age: The performance level of person that equals the level attained by a normative group of the same age (Ch. 9).

Mental retardation: A permanent disability consisting of (a) significant subaverage intellectual function and (b) significant impairments in social functioning (Ch. 10).

Mental retardation social position: A construction of society that identifies the characteristics of persons with mental retardation and specifies their expected behavior (Ch. 10).

Mental retardation social role: An enactment of a mental retardation social position (Ch. 10).

Mesoderm: The middle layer of cells in the blastocyst that develops into the bones, muscles, circulatory, excretory, and reproductive systems (Ch. 2).

Metabolic disorders: A large group of disorders due to single gene defects, resulting in abnormal enzymes or proteins and thus in metabolism disorders (Ch. 4, 5).

Metacognition: Thinking about thinking. In child development, it is the acquisition of rules and skills for how to learn (Ch. 3).

Microcephaly: An unusually small skull, brain case, and brain, accompanied by mental retardation (Ch. 3).

Microenvironment: A subset of family environment; daily, detailed, mother-child interaction; its quality may be critical in optimal child development (Ch. 9).

Mild mental retardation: The largest category of mental retardation, encompassing about 70 percent of all MR and defined by 50 to 70 IQ (Ch. 9).

Minimal brain dysfunction (MBD): An inferred or hypothetical condition that cannot be directly measured, based on the hypothesis that in children of average or higher intelligence, some cognitive and behavioral problems are caused by brain malfunctioning that is not easily or directly detectable (Ch. 8, 14).

Miscarriage: Expulsion of a human fetus after week 12 of gestation and before it is viable (Ch. 2).

Mitosis: The maturation process in somatic cells that results in the reproduction of new cells, each carrying the full complement of chromosomes (twenty-three pairs in humans) (Ch. 2).

Mixed learning disorder: The presence in a person of more than one learning disorder in which one disorder does not dominate or take precedence over the other(s) (Ch. 14).

Model: An organized and tentative set of facts and constructs used to describe some aspects of the real universe. Models are used analogically (i.e., "as if" they are correct). They are neither "correct" nor "incorrect"; rather they are important because they are useful (Ch. 2).

Moderate mental retardation: A category of mental retardation, encompassing about 10 percent of all MR and defined by 35 to 49 IQ (Ch. 9).

Monoplegia: Paralysis involving a single limb (Ch. 13).

Monosomy: A chromosomal anomaly (aneuploidy) in which there is a loss of one chromosome from a pair (Ch. 4, 5).

Monozygotic twins: Twins produced from the division of a single zygote. Unlike dizogotic twins, their genetic characteristics will be identical (Ch. 2).

Morphemes: The smallest units of meaning in a language (Ch. 14).

Morphology: In a language, the rules for proper use of morphemes (Ch. 14).

Mosaicism: Two types of cells in the same individual, one having forty-seven chromosomes and others having forty-six. For example, a type of Down syndrome in which only some of the cells are characterized by trisomy 21, with the result that these persons do not have the full degree of impairment as in full Down syndrome (Ch. 3, 5).

Motor function disorder: *See* Developmental motor function disorder (Ch. 14).

Multifactorial traits: Characteristic of the offspring produced by the interactions of several genetic and environmental factors (Ch. 3).

Multifactorial transmission: Hereditary passing of characteristics through operation of more than one gene and/or gene–environment interaction (Ch. 4).

Multiple sclerosis: A disease with patches of hardened tissue in the brain and/or spinal cord resulting in partial or complete paralysis and muscle tremor (Ch. 1)

Muscular dystrophy: A sex-linked chromosomal anomaly affecting males primarily, characterized by progressive wasting away of muscles and death before adulthood (Ch. 3, 5).

Mutagen: Any agent that significantly increases the rate of mutations (Ch. 4).

Mutation: A sudden change in a gene's molecular structure occurring spontaneously or through the influence of some factors early in pregnancy. If the organism survives, the mutation will be passed on to the next generation (Ch. 3).

Mutism: An unwillingness or inability to speak, associated with autism (Ch. 11).

Myelin: A sheath of fatty substance that insulates neurons and facilitates neural transmission (Ch. 3).

Myelination: Process of developing the myelin sheath that covers axons (Ch. 3).

Myelomeningocele: A spinal cord defect in which the cord protrudes through an opening in the vertebra. Neurological deficits and hydrocephaly are virtually always involved, and internal shunts are needed to reduce fluid buildup (Ch. 3).

Neonatal: The newborn baby, usually from birth to end of 1st month (Ch. 2).

Neonate: A newborn child, up to about 1 month of age (Ch. 2).

Neural differentation: Rapid development of supporting and connecting neural networks. Neural size and myelination increase (Ch. 3).

Neural proliferation: Rapid development of new neurons; occurs primarily before birth (Ch. 2, 3).

Neural tube: A long fold that develops about 3 weeks postconception and from which the central nervous system develops (Ch. 2).

Neural tube defects: Improper closure at the cephalic or caudal ends of the neural tube, resulting in serious disabilities such as anencephaly and spina bifida (Ch. 6, 7).

Neurofibromatosis: A genetically based (autosomal dominant) disease in which neurons develop lesions and tumors (Ch. 2).

Neurogenic seizures: Seizures induced by abnormal brain activity (Ch. 12).

Neuropsychological assesment: Using various psychological and neurological tests to evaluate central nervous system functioning indirectly (Ch. 12).

Neurotransmitter: A chemical substance, such as norepinephrine, that transmits nerve impulses across synapses (Ch. 6, 7).

Newborn respiratory distress: Serious breathing difficulties in a newborn (Ch. 13).

Nondisjunction: An error during meiosis in which homologous chromosomes fail to separate, often resulting in a trisomic condition (Ch. 4, 5).

Nonprogressive disorder: A disorder in which the basic impairments do not typically become more severe with time (e.g., cerebral palsy). The person's functioning, however, can still deteriorate (Ch. 13).

Nonspecific pervasive developmental disorder: A category of severe and pervasive disorders with some autistic features (Ch. 11).

Normal curve: A statistical construct describing a common range of events (e.g., IQ scores) in which most scores occur around the middle or mean of the distribution and the rest are distributed equally above and below the mean score (Ch. 9).

Normalization principle: A guiding principle that services must aim to provide as normal as possible life experiences for persons with disabilities (Ch. 8, 15).

Norm violation: Breaking behavioral rules associated with social positions (Ch. 10).

Norms (social): The explicit or implicit rules for behavior that define a social position and its accompanying social roles (Ch. 3, 10).

Nucleoplasm: The protoplasm within the cell nucleus (Ch. 2).

Nucleotides: Nitrogen-based molecules of adenine, thymine, guanine, and cytosine which bind together in repeating pairs (A-T; G-C) in the DNA molecule (Ch. 2).

Nucleus: A membrane-bound structure within the cell that contains nucleoplasm and structures such as genes and chromosomes (Ch. 2).

Nullisomy: A chromosomal anomaly (aneuploidy) in which there is a loss of one pair of chromosomes (Ch. 4, 5).

Occupational therapy: A professional discipline to assess and treat impaired motor or sensory function (Ch. 13).

Oocyte: The egg cell (Ch. 5).

Oogenesis: The development, through meiosis, of the female germ cell (ovum) (Ch. 2).

Operant conditioning: A psychological learning model that focuses on responses and their immediate antecedent and reinforcing conditions to account for some types of learning; extremely important in behavior modification; also called Skinnerian learning; similar to instrumental conditioning concepts (Ch. 12).

Organogenesis: Prenatal period when organ systems are at their highest rate of development (Ch. 6, 7).

Other learning disorder: A catchall category of learning disorders that do not fit into major categories (Ch. 14).

Overnutrition: Intake of nutrients, particularly calories, significantly above the amount required for good health; usually involves obesity (Ch. 8).

Ovum (pl. ova): Female reproductive cells that are present in the ovaries from birth (Ch. 2).

Oxygen deprivation: A lack of oxygen to the bloodstream and/or tissues. *See* Anoxia (Ch. 13).

Palsy: Paralysis or difficulties in voluntary muscle control (Ch. 13).

Paraplegia (or paraparesis): A type of cerebral palsy in which both legs are affected by spasticity but the arms are not affected or only mildly affected by spasticity (Ch. 13).

Parasite: An organism that lives in or on and draws its sustenance from another, often causing disease for the host (Ch. 6, 7, 8).

Parent support groups: Groups of people, normally parents of children with disabilities, who find help and support in the experiences of each other (Ch. 13).

Paresis (or plegia): Paralysis, as in juvenile paresis and in cerebral palsy (Ch. 5, 12).

Passive smoking: Breathing the smoke from cigarettes, cigars, and pipes of others. It has been identified as a risk factor in SIDS (Ch. 7).

Pathogen: A specific disease-causing agent, such as a virus or bacterium (Ch. 1).

Pathology: Literally, the study of disease and its causes. Used generally also to refer to conditions of disease and their causes. Pathology may be physical or psychological in nature (Ch. 1).

Perception: The higher-order processes of interpreting sensory stimuli based on experience (Ch. 3).

Perinatal: The time period at and around a child's birth; from about the 28th prenatal week to the end of the first postnatal month (about 14 to 16 weeks) (Ch. 2).

Personal competence: A person's general set of skills for successful everyday functioning (Ch. 10).

Personal identity: An individual's enduring self-description (Ch. 10).

Pervasive developmental disorder: A group of childhood disorders in which there are problems in more than one area of function; as distinguished from specific developmental disorders (Ch. 11).

Petit mal seizures: Minor or small epileptic seizures, with brief clouding but no loss of consciousness or memory as in grand mal (Ch. 12).

Phenotype: The observable behavioral and biological characteristics of a person that result from interaction of genes within the individual and of genotype and the environment (Ch. 2).

Phenylalanine: A protein found in many foods such as milk products; incomplete metabolism of phenylalanine is a basic factor in phenylketonuria (PKU) (Ch. 4).

Phenylketonuria (PKU): A genetic disorder in which the child is unable to metabolize certain proteins, resulting in a buildup of phenylpyruvic acid, damage to the central nervous system, and mental retardation (Ch. 3).

Phonemes: The basic sounds that make up a language. English has forty-four phonemes (Ch. 14).

Phonological awareness: Children's growing skills in manipulating phonemes (Ch. 14).

Phonological deficit model: Theoretical model of hierarchical language problems based on poor phonological skills (Ch. 14).

Phonology: Processing the distinctive basic elements of sounds (phonemes) (Ch. 14).

Phototherapy: Use of blue-toned lights to neutralize yellow bile pigment in babies with jaundice (Ch. 13).

Physical therapy: A professional discipline in which persons with disabilities are helped to function better, with focus on physical factors (Ch. 13).

Pica: Seen mostly in children with severe disorders, it is the habitual eating of nonfood material such as dirt and hair (Ch. 8).

Placenta: An organ composed largely of blood vessels that is attached to the uterine wall and, through the umbilical cord, to the fetus, through which oxygen, nutrients, and fetal waste matter are transported (Ch. 2).

Placental phase (in birth): In a normal human birth, the final 10 to 20 minutes immediately after emergence of the baby in which the placenta, the remainder of the amniotic fluid, and umbilical cord are expelled (Ch. 2).

Play years: From about age 2 to 6 years, children engage in great deal of play, and it is vital in their healthy development (Ch. 3).

Plegia (or paresis): Paralysis, as in juvenile paresis or in cerebral palsy (Ch. 5, 12)

Plumbism: Lead poisoning (Ch. 8).

Polygenic determinism: The concept that any particular phenotypical characteristics are brought about not by single gene action but by the interaction of several genes (Ch. 3).

Polygenic traits: Phenotypical characteristics of the offspring produced by interaction of many genes (Ch 3).

Polyploidy: Chromosomal condition in which cells have more than the usual number of sets of chromosomes (Ch 4).

Polytherapy: Use of more than one factor or substance in treatment of a single disorder (e.g., prescribing two medications to control seizures); polytherapy creates potential problems of negative treatment interaction effects (Ch. 12).

Position entry: The factors involved in one's assuming (entering) a social position (Ch. 10).

Position exit: The factors involved in leaving a social position (Ch. 10).

Position maintenance: The factors involved in preserving one's social position(s) (Ch. 10).

Position set: All of the social positions held by an individual (Ch. 10).

Positional status: The value placed by society on a social position (Ch. 10).

Postnatal: The 6 months following a child's birth (Ch. 2).

Postpartum depression: A usually temporary condition of overwhelming sadness, crying, and despondence, in about half of the mothers in the week following birth due to sharp hormonal fluctuations (Ch. 2).

Practical intelligence: A form of intelligence for everyday functioning; different from academic intelligence (Ch. 10).

Prader-Willi syndrome: Caused by a deletion on chromosome 15, the baby has a poor sucking reflex, becomes a compulsive eater by about age 5 and grossly obese, has behavioral problems, mental retardation, and generally poor social and sexual development (Ch. 3, 5).

Pragmatics: The rules for the practical use of language in real settings (Ch. 14).

Precipitous birth: Abnormally rapid birth, less than about 10 minutes; associated with anoxia and physical trauma to neonate (Ch. 8).

Premature birth (or preterm birth): Any birth occurring 3 or more weeks before the due date (Ch. 8).

Prenatal: The entire time period from conception to a child's birth or other ending of pregnancy (Ch 2).

Preservation of sameness: A major characteristic of children with autism to maintain behavior and other conditions and strongly resist change (Ch. 11).

Preterm birth: Birth that occurs early, preventing full development of the fetus; it is a major factor in infant mortality (Ch. 8).

Prevalence: The number of cases in a population of a disease or pathology, usually expressed as a ratio of cases per 10,000 or 100,000 population at a given time (Ch. 1).

Primary characteristics: The major necessary identifiable factors that define a given diagnostic entity (Ch. 14).

Primary negative effects: The direct disruptive effects of some factor such as a teratogen (Ch. 10).

Primary prevention: Interventions aimed at reducing the occurrence of disorders. For example, reducing lead in the environment will reduce the occurrence of new cases of lead poisoning (Ch. 9).

Principle of critical periods: Teratogens have their most severe effects during the time of the highest rate of development of tissues and organs (Ch. 6, 7).

Principle of genetic determination: The effects of a teratogen vary between species and between individuals within a species (Ch. 6, 7).

Principle of target access: Teratogens vary in terms of their specific routes to the fetus (Ch. 6, 7).

Productive (or expressive) language: The language that is expressed by a person to communicate with others; contrast with receptive language (Ch. 3, 14).

Profound mental retardation: A category of mental retardation; together with the category severe MR, it encompasses 10 percent of all MR. It is defined by an IQ of about 34 and below and has a high incidence of genetic, chromosomal, and other biological etiologies (Ch. 9).

Prognosis: The prediction of the outcome of a disease or disorder (Ch. 1).

Pronoun reversal: Distorted speech in which persons refer to themselves as "you," "he," or "she" and to others as "I" or "me." Frequent in children with autism (Ch. 11).

Proteinuria: The presence of protein in the urine (Ch. 13).

Protoplasm: The complex of organic and inorganic substances that constitutes the living cell within the cell membrane (Ch. 2).

Protozoa: Acellular or unicellular animals, some of which are serious human parasites (Ch. 6, 7, 8).

Proximodistal development: A normal developmental sequence in which development proceeds from the center of the body to the extremities (Ch. 2).

Psychoactive drugs: Chemical substances such as tranquilizers, ethanol, and stimulants that affect psychological functioning (behavior, thinking, emotions) (Ch. 6, 7, 8).

Psychogenic seizures: Seizurelike behavior with no measurable brain discharge such as occurs in "true" seizures. The etiology is thought to be psychological stress (Ch. 12).

Psychomotor retardation: A slowing down of large- and small-muscle movement (speech, level of energy, body movement, etc.) often associated with mental retardation, brain damage, and depression (Ch. 1, 10).

Psychopathology: Disorders that are psychological in nature, such as anxiety disorders and phobias. It is assumed they are reversible rather than permanent (Ch. 1).

Psychosocial dwarfism (Kaspar-Hauser syndrome): Severe physical and psychological growth retardation caused by prolonged stress due to severe child abuse (Ch. 8).

Psychosocial factors: Events of a psychological and/or social nature; as distinguished from biological events (Ch. 2).

Pulmonary surfactant: A substance that develops in the fetal lungs late in pregnancy and helps keep alveoli open for the neonate to breathe properly (Ch. 8).

Quadriplegia (or quadriparesis): A type of cerebral palsy in which all four limbs and trunk are affected by spasms (Ch. 13).

Quickening: The sudden increase in fetal movements felt by the mother beginning in about the 16th gestational week (Ch 2).

Reaction range: The concept that the genotype sets upper limits for development (e.g., intelligence) and the phenotype develops within those limits (Ch. 2).

Receptive language: The ability to understand language that is spoken by others; contrast with productive or expressive language (Ch. 3).

Recessive gene: A gene that carries control of some characteristic or function and is held relatively inoperative in the presence of a dominant gene in the other allele (Ch. 4).

Relative rates of cognitive development: Children with mental retardation are thought to develop at significantly slower rates than normal children; because all children continue to develop, those with MR never "catch-up," and the difference increases with age (Ch. 9).

Reliability (of a test):   The ability of a test to provide substantially the same results over time and conditions. An unreliable test is useless (Ch. 9).

Respite setting: A place that provides responsible temporary care of persons with disabilities to give relief to parents and children from their daily intense interactions, demands, and conflicts (Ch. 15).

Rett's syndrome: A rare autisticlike, pervasive developmental disorder with progressive neurological deterioration; thus far diagnosed only in females (Ch. 11).

Rh incompatibility: A condition in which an Rh– mother conceives an Rh+ fetus, and the mother's antibodies attack the fetal blood cells, causing fetal death (Ch. 5).

Rheumatic disease: Any of several diseases characterized by inflammation and pain in joints (Ch. 1).

Ribosomes: Complex cellular structures in the cytoplasm that are involved in protein synthesis (Ch 2).

Risk factor: Any event that increases the probability of occurrence of a pathology (Ch. 2).

RNA: Riboneucleic acid, or "messenger RNA," carries particular messages from the nucleus to the ribosomes to synthesize proteins (Ch. 2).

Role complexity: Social roles vary in the number of role sectors and the breadth and difficulty of role enactments (Ch. 10).

Role conflict: When the norms within a role or between roles are in opposition (Ch. 10).

Role imposition: The degree to which a position and role are structured by society so they preexist any individual; as distinct from role improvisation (Ch. 10).

Role improvisation: The degree to which a social position and/or role are created by the person; as distinct from role imposition (Ch. 10).

Role multiplicity: More than one role is typically held/ enacted by any person (Ch. 10).

Role resource access: A major concept in the role model of developmental disabilities presented in this text. By virtue of adopting a position and enacting its role(s), the person gains access to the resources that are controlled by complementary roles (Ch. 10).

Role sectors: Reliable variations in enactments of a particular role by a person (Ch. 10).

Role set: All of the roles typically held/enacted by any person (Ch. 10).

Role set status: The combined social "value" of all of the roles held/enacted by a person (Ch. 10).

Role strain: Discrepancies within and/or between the norms of a person's social role(s) creating role-enactment difficulties (Ch. 10, 11, 12).

Role vacuum: The concept that becoming elderly involes the loss of social role enactments that had derived from the family, school, occupations, and leisure. In extreme cases—such as institutionalization of the elderly—the person may be left with only one meager role—nursing home resident thus existing in a social role vacuum (Ch. 10).

Role variation: A social role can be enacted differently by a person from one time to another, contributing to variability and "richness" in life (Ch. 10).

Rubella: A type of measles (German measles) that is usually benign but, if occurring to the mother in pregnancy, can cause fetal blindness, deafness, and CNS damage (Ch. 6, 7).

Scholastic skills disabilities: In the *DSI-10,* a category of specific learning disabilities (Ch. 14).

Scissors gait: In motor disorder conditions, such as cerebral palsy, muscle and tendon shortening can result in a crossing of the legs and the characteristic "scissors gait" (Ch. 13).

Scoliosis: An abnormal curvature of the spine (Ch. 13).

Secondary characteristics: Factors that frequently accompany some defined diagnostic condition but are not necessarily present (Ch. 14).

Secondary negative effects: The indirect disruptive effects of some factor (Ch. 10).

Secondary prevention: Efforts aimed at reducing the severity and/or duration of already existing cases of illness in the population (Ch. 9).

Secure attachment: A healthy emotional connection of baby and caregiver, established by about 18 months of age (Ch. 3).

Seizure: A sudden, uncontrolled discharge of electrical activity in the CNS, as in epilepsy; may be accompanied by convulsions, loss or clouding of consciousness (Ch. 12).

Seizure threshold: A theoretical concept concerning the amount of stimulation that is minimally necessary to trigger seizure activity. Individuals have different seizure thresholds (Ch. 12).

Seizure, types of: Seizures are categorized as partial seizures and generalized seizures, with subtypes in each category (Ch. 12).

Selective attention: Focus on some event or stimulus and disregard of other associated events (Ch. 3).

Self-awareness: Knowledge about oneself (Ch. 3).

Self-esteem: One's own evaluation of oneself, derived partly from one's role set status (Ch. 10).

Self-injurious behavior (SIB): Injury repeatedly inflicted on oneself, seemingly without control, such as head banging, severe scratching, digging, etc.; seen often in children with autism (Ch. 5, 11).

Self-regulation: The ability to monitor oneself and control impulses, needs, etc. (Ch. 3).

Self-stimulatory behavior: Behavior engaged in by a person that serves to stimulate the person; seen often in children with autism, it includes behaviors such as repeated, intense hand flapping, arm waving, and rapid, stereotyped, and loud sounds (Ch. 11).

Semantics: The meanings of words and phrases (Ch. 14).

Sensation: The immediate experience that results from stimulation of a sense organ (Ch. 3).

Sensitive populations: Particular subgroups of organisms that are specifically affected by a given event or substance, such as environmental toxins (Ch. 8).

Separation anxiety: Severe upset in children when separated from their caregiver, usually the mother (Ch. 3).

Severe mental retardation: A category of mental retardation that, together with the category profound MR, includes about 10 percent of all MR and is defined by IQs up to about 34 (Ch. 10).

Severe social isolation: A characteristic of children with autism: the children reject human contact and clearly prefer to remain alone. The severity varies among children (Ch. 11).

Sex chromosomes: The X and Y chromosomes that control sexual characteristics (Ch. 4).

Shaken baby syndrome: Brain damage in a baby caused by being violently shaken, usually by irate parents (Ch. 13).

Sickle cell anemia: A recessive-gene disorder in which red blood cells are damaged and their oxygen-carrying capacity is reduced (Ch. 3).

SIDS (Sudden infant death syndrome): Death occurs suddenly during sleep, in healthy babies up to 6 months of age. Risk factors include parents' cigarette smoking, poverty, young maternal age, and sleeping position, placing the infant face-down (Ch. 6,7).

Simple partial seizure (Jacksonian or "aura"): No loss of consciousness, person is aware of the seizure but cannot control arm and leg movements; often with strong emotions (Ch. 12).

Single-blind procedure: A control procedure in experimentation in which the participants are not aware of the hypotheses or the research conditions; not as powerful a control as double-blind procedures (Ch. 11).

6-hour retardation: When the definition and diagnosis of mental retardation are highly dependent on school conditions (Ch. 9).

Social agents: Persons who carry out particular role-related functions that serve to maintain social structure and functions (Ch. 9).

Social cognition: The thinking processes that organize and understand social experience (Ch. 3).

Social communication: Interactive understandings based on verbal and nonverbal exchanges among persons in social situations; a common area of difficulty in many developmental disabilities (Ch. 9).

Socialization: The developmental process of learning the rules and behaviors necessary for interpersonal functioning (Ch. 3).

Social networks: The web of relationships a person has with other people (Ch. 13).

Social norms: *See* Norms.

Social position: A construction of society that identifies a class of persons and identifies their positional behavior (e.g., parent, doctor, etc.) (Ch. 10).

Social referencing: Learning to self-regulate one's behavior based on observing and interacting with other people (Ch. 3).

Social role development: Lifelong process of socialization in which social roles are learned (Ch. 10).

Social role metacognition: Intellectual skills in how to learn and enact social roles (Ch. 10).

Social roles: The enactment of social positions (Ch. 3).

Social role valorization: The hypothesis that in the process of normalization persons with disabilities will acquire enhanced social value (i.e., status) (Ch. 15).

Socially devalued role: Any role, such as mental retardation or other developmental disability, that has a low social status (Ch. 10).

Socioeconomic status (SES): An index consisting of measures of a person's levels of income, education, and occupational status (Ch. 2).

Somatic cells: Most of the cells in the human body are somatic (body) cells, as contrasted with germ (sex) cells (Ch. 2).

Somatogenesis: Biological or psychological events that originate within the body; usually refers to disorders (Ch. 2).

Sonogram: A prenatal ultrasound screening procedure to determine the size and skeletal structure of the fetus (Ch 2).

Spastic cerebral palsy: *See* Spastic diplegia (Ch. 13).

Spastic diplegia: A type of cerebral palsy in which both arms and both legs are affected (Ch. 13).

Special education: A professional field focusing on specially designed educational instruction for persons with disabilities (Ch. 11).

Specific arithmetic skills disorder: In the *ICD-10,* one of the specific developmental disorders of scholastic skills (Ch. 14).

Specific expressive writing disorder: In the *ICD-10,* one of the specific developmental disorders of scholastic skills (Ch. 14).

Specific learning disorders: Cognitive problems with learning that are not due to general or pervasive conditions such as mental retardation or autism (Ch. 14).

Specific reading disorder: In the *ICD-10,* one of the specific developmental disorders of scholastic skills (Ch. 14).

Specific spelling disorder: In the *ICD-10,* one of the specific developmental disorders of scholastic skills (Ch. 14).

Speech and language disabilities: A general term for all language problems; includes specific speech and language disabilities as defined in *ICD-10* (Ch. 14).

Sperm: The male reproductive cells; sperm production begins at puberty in the testicles (Ch 2).

Spermatogenesis: The creation in the testes of mature sperm cells through meiosis (Ch 2).

Spina bifida: A developmental disability characterized by incomplete closure of the neural tube at the caudal end, resulting in protrusion of some portion of the spinal cord and causing paralysis of lower limbs, often accompanied by mental retardation (Ch. 3).

Spinal meningitis: Inflammation of the membranes that enclose the spinal cord (Ch. 5).

Spirochetes: Spiral shaped bacteria, such as those causing syphilis (Ch. 6, 7).

Stage theories of development: Models of human development that postulate a progression of qualitatively different steps or stages that occur in fixed sequence (Ch. 2).

Status epilecticus: A serious emergency condition usually in children in which seizures continue for at least 15 to 30 minutes or recur at short intervals; immediate emergency treatment is necessary (Ch. 12).

STD: Sexually transmitted disease (Ch. 6,7).

Stimulus over selectivity: A tendency to focus attention on a minor or nonessential part of a complex stimulus, and thus fail to perceive the whole; common in autism and MR (Ch. 9).

Strabismus: A disorder in which eyes are not properly aligned. Can often be surgically corrected (Ch. 13).

Stroke: Occlusive cardiovascular disease; blockage causes increased pressure and weak area of blood vessel breaks; brain damage can result (Ch. 14).

Submissive-dependent character: Characteristic functioning of persons with MR, presumably developed through MR role socialization (Ch. 10).

Super male syndrome (47, XYY):   An anomaly of the sex chromosomes caused by nondisjunction in which the male has two X chromosomes (Ch. 3).

Surfactant: A substance in the lungs of newborns that enables easier breathing by keeping alveoli open. A lack of surfactant resulted in many deaths, particularly in preterm births. It can now be synthesized and given to those newborns who lack it (Ch. 2).

Surma: Powdered lead used as a cosmetic. *See* Kohl (Ch. 8).

Symbiotic support groups: Often informal organizations of persons with common issues (e.g., disabilities) who help each other (Ch. 9).

Symbolic modeling: Demonstrating, as through video, behavior that is to be imitated (Ch. 10).

Symptomatic epilepsy: Epilepsy in which the causes are known (Ch. 12).

Syndrome: A group of fairly distinctive characteristics that occur together in a disorder (Ch. 2, 3).

Synergistic effects: The interaction of two or more variables, such as medications, to form a new factor or condition (Ch. 8).

Syntax: Rules in a language for combining words into meaningful sentences (Ch. 14).

Syphilis: A sexually transmitted disease which, in pregnancy, increases risks of fetal death and, in children who survive, increases risks of blindness and deafness, seizures, mental retardation, and juvenile paresis (Ch. 5).

Tacit knowledge: The kind of knowledge, intelligence, and skills needed for success in real-world pursuits, as distinguished from academic knowledge (Ch. 10).

Target access: The teratogenic principle that there are two main routes for teratogens to reach the fetus: (a) move directly and unchanged through maternal tissue to the fetus and (b) move across the placenta where they can be modified by maternal tissues (Ch. 5).

Tay-Sachs disease: A severe recessive-gene disorder associated with chromosome 15, marked by physical and mental degeneration and leading to death by 4 to 6 years of age (Ch. 3).

Temperament: Innate, generalized, and stable behavioral style of the child's intensity or activity level, mood, adaptability, and distractibility (Ch. 2, 3).

Teratogen: Any toxic substance that crosses the placenta during gestation and causes disability in the developing embryo or fetus. *See* Behavioral teratogens (Ch 5).

Teratogenic endpoints: The effects of teratogens: (a) embryo and fetal death, (b) growth retardation and birth defects, (c) functional (i.e., cognitive-behavioral) disorders (Ch 5).

Teratology: The study of birth defects (Ch 5).

Tertiary prevention: Efforts aimed at reducing the severity and/or duration of disorders that are secondary to, or associated with, primary disorders (Ch. 9).

Tetrasomy: A chromosomal anomaly in which there is an extra pair of chromosomes resulting in four rather than two chromosomes. *See* Aneuploidy (Ch. 5).

Thalidomide: A drug prescribed in the 1960s and 1970s to control morning sickness in pregnancy, thalidomide was later found to be a powerful teratogen (Ch 5).

Theory building: Hypothetical-deductive thinking that allows use of explanatory and predictive models; develops in many, but not in all, adolescents (Ch. 3).

Theory of mind: Idea that people normally develop skills in making correct inferences about the thoughts of others; considered to be limited in autism (Ch. 11).

Thymine: A base chemical found in DNA but not in RNA; in double-stranded DNA, as in human cells, thymine pairs with adenine (Ch. 2).

Tourette's disorder: Severe, uncontrolled motor and vocal tics with explosive vocalizations that are often obscene.

Toxoplasmosis: A blood and tissue infection caused by a parasitic protozoan that lives its full life cycle in the cat (Ch. 6, 7).

Transfer of learning: Applying skills or information learned in one situation to another situation (Ch. 9).

Translocations (or transpositions): Chromosomal mutations in which there is a change in the position of parts of a chromosome (Ch. 4, 5).

Trauma: A physical or psychological injury that constitutes serious damage in an organism (Ch. 8).

Traumatic brain injury: Severe physical damage to the brain (Ch. 8).

Triplegia: A type of cerebral palsy (Ch. 13).

Triple X syndrome (47, XXX): A polyploidal chromosome anomaly in which three X chromosomes occur instead of the normal number (two for females, one for males). Triple X occurs only in females; they appear to be normal in all other physical respects and have somewhat lower than normal intelligence but are typically not mentally retarded (Ch. 3).

Trisomy: A chromosomal anomaly (aneuploidy) in which there is an extra chromosome in what is usually a pair of chromosomes (Ch. 4, 5).

Trisomy-21 (Down syndrome): A chromosomal disorder caused by an extra chromosome on the twenty-first chromosome pair (Ch. 4).

Tuberous sclerosis: An autosomal dominant-gene disorder manifest by severe mental retardation and multiple tumors (Ch. 3).

Turner's syndrome: A chromosomal anomaly of the sex chromosomes (45, X0) of females caused by nondisjunction during meiosis, in which the second X chromosome is missing. Physical anomalies include webbed neck, short stature, lack of secondary sexual characteristics, sterility, learning and behavioral problems (Ch. 3).

Ultrasonagraphy: A diagnostic procedure using reflections of ultrasonic waves (above human limits of about 20,000 cycles per second) to represent the developing fetus and detect many abnormalities (Ch 2).

Umbilical cord: A flexible tube connecting the placenta and the fetus through which nutrients and waste material pass (Ch. 2).

Underachievement: A level of academic work that is significantly lower than what is expected given the person's general ability level (Ch. 14).

Undernutrition: *See* Malnutrition (Ch. 6, 7).

Unintentional injuries: Injuries to children caused without deliberate action (i.e., "accidents" as in automobiles, etc.) (Ch. 8).

Unspecified learning disorder: A category of learning disabilities that is not included in other categories (Ch. 14).

Uterus: Organ that contains the amniotic fluid, placenta, and developing fetus (Ch. 2).

Validity (of a test):   The ability of a test to measure what it is supposed to measure. An invalid test (e.g., reading tea leaves to understand personality) is, at best, useless (Ch. 9).

Varicella: Chicken pox (Ch. 5).

Very low birth weight (VLBW):   Significantly below average birth weight; below 3.75 pounds, or 1500 grams (Ch. 8).

Virus: Complex molecules or simple noncellular organisms that function only within other organisms and are the source of many animal diseases (Ch. 5).

Visual central processing deficits: Disabilities that prevent clear perception of visual messages (Ch. 14).

Visual impairments: Any difficulties in vision (Ch. 1).

Vocabulary spurt: In language development, around age 18 months, when children engage in a rapid development of new words (Ch. 3).

Wasserman reaction: A serum test for diagnosing syphilis (Ch. 5).

X-linked recessive-gene disorders: Recessive gene disorders that occur from mutations on the X chromosome (Ch. 4).

Zone of proximal development: The theoretical range formed by genetic limits and environmental supports within which a child's intelligence can develop (Ch. 10).

Zone of uncertainty: The variability in an IQ score, usually 5 points above and below the obtained score (Ch. 9).

Zygote: A single cell formed by the union of two gametes (ovum and sperm); the fertilized egg. In humans, the cell is termed a zygote from conception to about 2 weeks (Ch. 2).

REFERENCES

A.A.M.R. (American Association on Mental Retardation). (1992). *Mental retardation: Definition, classification, and systems of supports* (9th ed.). Washington, DC: American Association on Mental Retardation.

Aase, J. M. (1994). Clinical recognition of FAS: Difficulties of detection and diagnosis. *Alcohol Health and Research World, 18*(1), 5–9.

Abel, E. L. (1980). Smoking during pregnancy: A review of effects on growth and development of offspring. *Human Biology, 52,* 593–625.

Abel, E. L. (1989). *Behavioral teratogenesis and behavioral mutagenesis: A primer in abnormal development.* New York: Plenum Press.

Abel, E. L. (1990). *Fetal alcohol syndrome.* New York: Plenum Press.

Abel, E. L. (1992). Paternal exposure to alcohol. In T. B. Sonderegger (Ed.), *Perinatal substance abuse: Research findings and clinical implications* (pp. 132–160). Baltimore, MD: Johns Hopkins University Press.

Abel, E. L., & Sokol, R. J. (1987). Incidence of fetal alcohol syndrome and economic impact of FAS-related anomalies. *Drug & Alcohol Dependence, 19,* 51–70.

Adams R. J. (1989). Newborns' discrimination among mid- and long-wavelength stimuli, *Journal of Experimental Child Psychology, 47*(1), 130–141.

Adler, T. (1994). The return of thalidomide. *Science News, 146*(26 & 27), 424–425.

Ainsworth, M. (1973). The development of infant–mother attachment. In B. M. Caldwell & H. N. Ricciutti (Eds.), *Review of child development research* (Vol. III). Chicago: University of Chicago Press.

Ainsworth, M. (1993). Attachment as related to mother–infant interaction. In C. Rovee-Collier & L. Lipsitt (Eds.), *Advances in infancy research* (Vol. 8). Norwood, NJ: Ablex.

Aksu, F. (1990). Nature and prognosis of seizures in patients with cerebral palsy. *Developmental Medicine and Child Neurology, 32,* 661–668.

Alexander, G. R., & Korenbrot, C. C. (1995). The role of prenatal care in preventing low birth weight. *The Future of Children, 5*(1), 103–120.

Alexander, R. C., & Hanson, J. W. (1988). Overview. In L. R. Greenswag & R. C. Alexander (Eds.)., *Management of Prader-Willi syndrome.* New York: Springer-Verlag.

Alford, J. D., & Locke, B. J. (1984). Clinical responses to psychopathology of mentally retarded persons. *American Journal of Mental Deficiency, 89,* 195–197.

Allen, B., & Allen, S. (1996, September). Can the scientific method be applied to human interaction? *American Psychologist, 51,* 986.

Aloia, G. F., & MacMillan, D. L. (1983). Influence of the EMR label on initial expectations of regular classroom teachers. *American Journal of Mental Deficiency, 88,* 255–262.

Altman, L. K. (2000, July 9). In effort to save lives, South Africa creates an anti-AIDS campaign that minces no words. *The New York Times,* p. 8.

American Association on Mental Retardation. (1992). *Mental retardation: Definition, classification, and systems of support.* Washington, DC: Author.

American Psychiatric Association. (1994). *Diagnostic and statistical manual* (4th ed.). Washington, DC: Author.

American Speech-Language-Hearing Association. (1996). Task force on central auditory processing consensus development. *American Journal of Audiology, 5*(2), 41–54.

Anastasi, A. (1988). *Psychological testing* (6th ed.). New York: Macmillan.

Anderson, C. W. (1994). Adult literacy and learning disabilities. In P. J. Gerber & H. B. Reiff (Eds.), *Learning disabilities in adulthood: Persisting problems and evolving issues.* Boston: Andover Medical Publishers.

Andiman, W. A., & Horstmann, D. M. (1984). Congenital and perinatal viral infections. In M. B. Bracken (Ed.), *Perinatal epidemiology.* New York: Oxford University Press.

Andrich, D., & Styles, I. (1994). Psychometric evidence of intellectual growth spurts in early adolescence. *Journal of Early Adolescence, 14,* 328–344.

Angell, N. F., & Lavery, J. P. (1982). The relationship of blood lead levels to obstetric outcome. *American Journal of Obstetrics and Gynecology, 142,* 40–46.

Annan, K. (1997, December 3). Secretary general's message on International Day of Disabled Persons cites discrimination against "world's largest minority." *United Nations Press Release.* New York: United Nations.

Annas, G. J., & Elias, S. (1999). Thalidomide and the *Titanic*: Reconstructing the technology tragedies of the twentieth century. *American Journal of Public Health, 89*(1), 98–101.

Apgar, V. A. (1953). Proposal for a new method of evaluation of the newborn infant. *Anesthesia and Analgesia, Current Researches, 22,* 260.

Apgar, V. A., & Beck, I. (1974). *Is my baby all right?* New York: Pocket Books.

Apgar, V. A., & James, L. S. (1962). Further observations on the newborn scoring system. *American Journal of Diseases of Children, 104,* 418–428.

Aries, P. (1962). *Centuries of childhood: A social history of family life.* New York: Knopf.

Asch, A. (1984). The experience of disability: A challenge for psychology. *American Psychologist, 39*(5), 529–536.

Ash, P., Vennart, J., & Carter, C. O. (1977). The incidence of hereditary disease in man. *Lancet, 1,* 849–851.

Asperger, H. (1944). Die autistichen psychopathen im kindesalter. *Archiv fur Psychiatrie und Nervenkrankheiten, 117,* 76–136.

Astley, S. J., & Little, R. E. (1990). Maternal marijuana use during lactation and infant development at one year. *Toxicology and Teratology, 12,* 161–168.

Avery, M. E., & Taeusch, H. W. (1984). Maternal conditions and exogenous influences that affect the fetus/newborn. In M. E. Avery & H. W. Taeusch (Eds.), *Schaffer's diseases of the newborn* (5th ed.). Philadelphia, PA: Saunders.

Badian, N. A. (1984). Reading disability in an epidemiological context: Incidence and environmental correlates. *Journal of Learning Disabilities, 17,* 129–136.

Baer, A. S. (1977). *The genetic perspective.* Philadelphia, PA: W. B. Saunders.

Bailey, A., LeCouteur, A., Gottesman, I., Bolton, P., Simonoff, E., Yuzda, E., & Rutter, M. (1995). Autism as a strongly genetic disorder: Evidence from a British twin study. *Psychological Medicine, 25,* 63–78.

Bailey, A., Luther, P., Bolton, P., LeCouteur, A., & Rutter, M. (1993). Autism & megalencephaly. *Lancet, 34,* 1225–1226.

Baledarian, N. J. (1991a). *Abuse causes disabilities. Disability and the family.* Culver City, CA: Spectrum Institute.

Baledarian, N. J. (1991b). Sexual abuse of people with developmental disabilities. *Sexuality and Disability, 9*(4), 323–335.

Barlow, D. H., & Durand, V. M. (1995). *Abnormal psychology: An integrative approach.* Boston: Brooks/Cole.

Barnes, D. M. (1989). Fragile X syndrome and its puzzling genetics. *Science. 243,* 171–172.

Baroff, G. S. (1991). *Developmental disabilities: Psychosocial aspects.* Austin, TX: Pro-Ed.

Baron-Cohen, S. (1993). From attention-goal psychology to belief-desire psychology: The development of a theory of mind and its dysfunction. In S. Baron-Cohen, H. Tager-Flusberg, & D. J. Cohen (Eds.), *Understanding other minds: Perspective from autism.* Oxford: Oxford University Press.

Baron-Cohen, S., & Bolton, P., (1993). *Autism. The facts.* New York: Oxford University Press.

Baron-Cohen, S., & Howlin, P. (1993) The theory of mind deficit in autism: Some questions for teaching and diagnosis. In S. Baron-Cohen, H. Tager-Flusberg, & D. J. Cohen (Eds.), *Understanding other minds: Perspectives from autism* (pp. 466–480). Oxford: Oxford University Press.

Baron-Cohen, S., Leslie, A. M., & Frith, U. (1985). Does the autistic child have a "theory of mind"? *Cognition, 21,* 37–46.

Baron-Cohen, S., Tager-Flusberg, H., & Cohen, D. J. (1993). *Understanding other minds: Perspectives from autism.* Oxford: Oxford University Press.

Barrett, M. D. (1985). Issues in the study of children's single-word speech. In M. D. Barrett (Ed.), *Children's single-word speech.* Chichester, England: Wiley.

Bartecchi, C. E., MacKenzie, T. D., & Schrier, R. W. (1995). The global tobacco epidemic. *Scientific American, 272*(5), 44–51.

Barton, R. S., & Fuhrman, B. S. (1994). Counseling and psychotherapy for adults with learning disabilities. In P. J. Gerber & H. B. Reiff (Eds.), *Learning disabilities in adulthood: Persisting problems and evolving issues.* Boston: Andover Medical Publishers.

Batshaw, M. L., & Perret, Y. M. (1997). *Children with disabilities: A medical primer* (4th. ed.). Baltimore, MD: Paul H. Brookes.

Bauer, S. (1995). Autism and the pervasive developmental disorders: Part 2. *Pediatric Review, 16*(5), 168–176.

Baum, S. (1985). *Learning disabled students with superior cognitive abilities: A validation study of descriptive behaviors.* Unpublished doctoral dissertation, University of Connecticut.

Bauman, M. L., & Kemper, T. L. (1994). Neuroanatomic observations of the brain in autism. In M. L. Bauman & T. L. Kemper (Eds.). *The neurobiology of autism.* Baltimore, MD: Johns Hopkins University Press.

Beal, S. M., & Finch, C. F. (1991). An overview of retrospective case control slides investigating the relationship between prone sleep positions and SIDS. *Journal of Paediatrics and Child Health, 27,* 334–339.

Bear, G. G., & Minke, K. M. (1996). Positive bias in maintenance of self-worth among children with LD. *Learning Disability Quarterly, 19,* 23–32.

Becker, H. S. (1963). *Outsiders: Studies in the sociology of deviance.* New York: Free Press.

Beckwith, L., & Rodning, C. (1991). Intellectual functioning in children born pre-term: Recent research. In L. Okagaki & R. J. Sternberg (Eds.), *Directors of development: Influences on the development of children's thinking.* Hillsdale, NJ: Erlbaum.

Bee, H. (1992). *The developing child* (6th ed.). New York: HarperCollins.

Begley, S., & Carey, J., (1982, January 11). How human life begins. *Newsweek 159*, 38–43.

Behrman, R. E. (Ed.). (1992). *Nelson textbook of pediatrics* (14th ed.). Philadelphia, PA: Saunders.

Bellenir, K. (1996). *Genetic disorders sourcebook.* Detroit, MI: Omnigraphics.

Bellenir, K. (Ed.). (1999). *Diabetes sourcebook.* Detroit, MI: Omnigraphics.

Berger, K. S., & Thompson, R. A. (1995). *The developing person: Through childhood and adolescence.* New York: Worth Publishers.

Besag, F. M. C. (1987). The role of the special school for children with epilepsy. In J. Oxley & G. Stores (Eds.), *Epilepsy and education* (pp. 65–71). London: Education in Practice for the Medical Tribune Group.

Bettelheim, B. (1967). *The empty fortress: Infantile autism and the birth of the self.* New York: Free Press.

Bhushan, V., Paneth, N., & Kiely, J. L. (1993). Impact of improved survival of very low birth weight infants on recent secular trends in the prevalence of cerebral palsy. *Pediatrics, 91,* 1094–1100.

Bickel, H., & Hickmans, G. J. (1953). Influence of phenylalanine intake on phenylketonuria. *Lancet, 2,* 812–813.

Biddle, B. J. (1979). *Role theory: Expectations, identities, and behaviors.* New York: Academic Press.

Biddle, B. J. (1986). Recent developments in role theory. *Annual Review of Sociology, 12,* 67–92.

Biklen, D. (1990). Communication unbound: Autism and praxis. *Harvard Educational Review, 60,* 291–314.

Biklen, D. (1992). Autism orthodoxy versus free speech: A reply to Cummins and Prior. *Harvard Educational Review, 62,* 242–256.

Birenbaum, A. (1971). The mentally retarded child in the home and the family cycle. *Journal of Health and Social Behavior, 12,* 55–65.

Bjorklund, D. F., & Bjorklund, B. R. (1992). *Looking at children: An introduction to child development.* Pacific Grove, CA: Brooks/Cole.

Blake, J. (1990). *Risky times.* New York: Workman Publishing.

Blalock, J. (1982). Persistent problems and concerns of young adults with learning disabilities. In W. Cruickshank & A. Silver (Eds.), *Bridges to tomorrow* (Vol. 2, pp. 3–56). Syracuse, NY: Syracuse University Press.

Blau, Z. S. (1973). *Old age in changing society.* New York: New Viewpoints.

Blumer, H. (1980). Social behaviorism and symbolic interactionism. *American Sociological Review,* 409–419.

Boggs, E. M. (1980). Toward a national policy for prevention of developmental disabilities. In M. D. McCormack (Ed.), *Prevention of mental retardation and other developmental disabilities* (pp. 641–654). New York: Marcel Dekker.

Bologna, L., & Castellino, N. (1995). Unusual sources of non-occupational plumbism. In N. Castellino, P. Castellino, & A. M. Alimandi (Eds.), *Inorganic lead exposure: Metabolism and intoxication* (pp. 487–497). Boca Raton, FL: Lewis Publishers.

Bolton, P., Macdonald, H., Pickles, A., Rios, P., Goode, S., & Crowson, M. (1994). A case-control family history study of autism. *Journal of Child Psychology and Psychiatry, 35,* 877–900.

Boswell, J. (1988). *The kindness of strangers: The abandonment of children in Western Europe from late antiquity to the Renaissance.* New York: Pantheon Books.

Bourgeois, B. F. D. (1988). Problems of combination drug therapy in children. *Epilepsia, 29* (Suppl. 3), S20–S24.

Brazelton, T. B. (1973). *Neonatal behavioral assessment scale.* Philadelphia, PA: Lippincott.

Brazelton, T. B. (1989). Observations of the neonate. In C. Rovee-Collier & L. P. Lipsitt (Eds.), *Advances in infancy research* (Vol. 6). Norwood, NJ: Ablex.

Brazelton, T. B., Nugent, J. K., & Lester, B. M. (1987). Neonatal behavioral assessment scale. In J. D. Osofsky (Ed.), *Handbook of infant development* (2nd ed.). New York: Wiley.

Brent, D. A., Crumrine, P. K., Varma, R. (1990). Phenobarbitol treatment and major depressive disorder in children with epilepsy: A naturalistic follow-up. *Pediatrics, 85,* 1086–1091.

Brent, R. L. (1977). Radiation and other physical agents. In J. G. Wilson & F. C. Fraser (Eds.), *Handbook of teratology: General principles and etiology* (pp. 153–223). New York: Plenum Press.

Breyer, J. (2000). *Food and Drug Administration v. Brown & Williamson Tobacco Corp.* U.S. Supreme Court (No. 98-1152).

Brody, L. E., & Mills, C. J. (1997). Gifted children with learning disabilities: A review of the issues. *Journal of Learning Disabilities, 30*(3), 282–286.

Bronfenbrenner, U. (1979). *The ecology of human development.* Cambridge, MA: Harvard University Press.

Bronfenbrenner, U., & Ceci, S. J. (1994). Nature-nurture reconceptualized in developmental perspective: A bio-ecological model. *Psychological Review, 101,* 568–586.

Browder, J. A. (1977). *Immunizations and what can be done to improve their use.* Proceedings of an International Summit on Prevention of Mental Retardation from Biomedical Causes. Racine, WI.

Brown, B. (1999). Optimizing expression of the common human genome for child development. *Current Directions in Psychological Science, 8*(2), 37–41.

Brown, B., & Rosenbaum, L. (1985). Stress and competence. In J. H. Humphrey (Ed.), *Stress in childhood* (pp. 127–154). New York: AMS Press.

Brown, R. (1965). *Social psychology.* New York: Free Press.

Brown, W. T., Jenkins, E. C., Gross, A. C., Chan, C. B., Krawczun, M. S., Duncan, C. J., Sklower, S. L., & Fisch, G. S. (1987). Further evidence for genetic heterogeneity in the fragile-X syndrome. *Human Genetics, 75,* 311–321.

Brown, W. T., Jenkins, E. C., Krawczun, M. S., Wisniewski, K., Rudelli, R., Cohen, I. L., Fisch, G., Wolf-Schein, E., Miezejeski, C., & Dobkin, C. (1986). The fragile X syndrome. In H. M. Wisniewski & D. A. Snider (Eds.), *Mental retardation: Research, education, and technology transfer. Annals of the New York Academy of Sciences, 477,* 129–150.

Brown, W., Thurman, S. K., & Pearl, L. F. (1993). *Family-centered early intervention with infants and toddlers: Innovative cross-disciplinary approaches.* Baltimore, MD: Paul H. Brookes.

Bryson, S. E. (1996). Brief report: Epidemiology of autism. *Journal of Autism and Developmental Disorders, 26*(2), 165–167.

Buitelaar, J. K. (1995). Attachment and social withdrawal in autism: Hypotheses and findings. *Behaviour, 132*(5–6), 319–350.

Bukatko, D., & Daehler, M. W. (1992). *Child development: A topical approach.* Boston: Houghton Mifflin.

Bulterys, M. (1990). High incidence of infant death syndrome among northern Indians and Alaska natives compared with southwestern Indians: Possible role of smoking. *Journal of Community Health, 15*(3), 185–194.

Burd, I., Fisher, W., & Kerbeshian, J. (1987). A prevalence study of pervasive developmental disorders in North Dakota. *Journal of the American Academy of Child and Adolescent Psychiatry, 26,* 700–703.

Burd, L., & Martsolf, J. T. (1989). Fetal alcohol syndrome: Diagnosis and syndromal variability. *Physiology and Behavior, 46,* 39–43.

Bureau of the Census. (1993). *Statistical abstract of the United States* (113th ed.). Washington, DC: Department of Commerce.

Burrow, G. (1965). Neonatal goiter after maternal propylthiouracil therapy. *Journal of Clinical Endocrinology, 25,* 403–408.

Burstein, J. R., Wright-Dreschel, M. L., & Wood, A. (1998). Assistive technology. In J. P. Dormans & L. Pellegrino (Eds.), *Caring for children with cerebral palsy: A team approach* (pp. 371–389). Baltimore, MD: Paul H. Brookes.

Butler, S. (1950). *The way of all flesh.* New York: Random House. (Original work published 1867)

Butterworth, G. (1997, May). Starting point. *Natural History, 106*(4), 14.

Camras, L. A., & Sachs, V. B. (1991). Social referencing and caretaker expressive behavior in a day care setting. *Infant Behavior and Development, 14,* 27–36.

Caplan, G. (1964). *Principles of preventive psychiatry.* New York: Basic Books.

Carey, S. (1977). The child as a word learner. In M. Halle, J. Bresnan, & G. A. Miller (Eds.), *Linguistic theory and psychological reality.* Cambridge, MA: MIT Press.

Carlson, B. M. (1994). *Human embryology and developmental biology.* St. Louis, MO: Mosby

Carnegie Council. (1995). *Great transitions: Preparing adolescents for a new century.* New York: The Carnegie Council on Adolescent Development.

Caron, A. J., Caron, R. F., & MacLean, D. J. (1988). Infant discrimination of naturalistic emotional expressions: The role of face and voice. *Child Development, 59,* 604–616.

Carpenter, S. (1999). Cocaine use boosts heart attack risks. *Science News, 155*(23), 356.

Carroll, B. A. (2000). Sickle cell disease. In P. L. Jackson & J. A. Vessey (Eds.), *Primary care of the child with chronic disease* (pp. 808–836). St. Louis, MO: Mosby.

Carson, R. (1962). *Silent spring.* Boston: Houghton Mifflin.

Castellino, N., Castellino, P., & Sannolo, N. (Eds.). (1995). *Inorganic lead exposure: Metabolism and intoxication.* Boca Raton, FL: Lewis Publishers.

Castellino, P., & Alimandi, A. M. (1995). Lead exposure during fetal life and childhood. In N. Castellino, P. Castellino, & N. Sannolo (Eds.), *Inorganic lead exposure: Metabolism and intoxication* (pp. 467–485). Boca Raton, FL: Lewis Publishers.

Cataldo, C. Z. (1984). Infant toddler education. *Young Children, 39*(2), 25–32.

Cavan, R. S. (1962). Self and roles in adjustment during old age. In A. M. Ross (Ed.), *Human behavior and social processes.* Boston: Houghton Mifflin.

Centers for Disease Control. (1991, December 13). Injury mortality atlas of the United States, 1979–1987. *Morbidity and Mortality Weekly Report, 40*(49), 846–848.

CF Foundation (1997). *National patient registry data.* Bethesda, MD: Author.

Chalmers, B. (1983). Psychosocial factors and obstetric complications. *Psychological Medicine, 13*(2), 333–339.

Chalmers, B. (1984a). A conceptualization of psycho-social obstetric research. *Journal of Psychosomatic Obstetrics and Gynecology, 3*(1), 17–26.

Chalmers, B. (1984b). Behavioral associations of pregnancy complications. *Journal of Psychosomatic Obstetrics and Gynecology, 3*(1), 27–35.

Chasnoff, I. J. (1992). Cocaine, pregnancy, and the growing child. *Current Problems in Pediatrics, 302*–321.

Chasnoff, I. J., Hatcher, R., & Burns, W. J. (1980). Early growth patterns of methadone-addicted infants. *American Journal of Diseases of Children, 134,* 1049–1051.

Chavez, G. F., Mulinare, J., & Cordero, J. F. (1989). Maternal cocaine use during early pregnancy as a risk factor for congenital urogenital anomalies. *Journal of the American Medical Association, 262,* 795–798.

Cherry, S. H. (1987). *Planning ahead for pregnancy.* New York: Viking Press.

Children's Defense Fund. (1988, April). Piecing together the teen pregnancy puzzle. *CDF Reports, 9,* 1, 5–6.

Chomitz, V. R., Cheung, L. W. Y., & Lieberman, E. (1995). The role of lifestyle in preventing low birth weight. *The Future of Children, 5*(1), 121–138.

Chomsky, N. (1965). *Aspects of the theory of syntax.* Cambridge, MA: MIT Press.

Christensen, D. (1999, February 6). AIDS virus jumped from chimps. *Science News, 155*(6), 84.

Chrousos, G. P., & Gold, P. W. (1992). The concepts of stress and stress system disorders: Overview of physical and behavioral homeostasis. *Journal of the American Medical Association, 267,* 1244–1252.

Cicchetti, D., & Beeghly, M. (1990). *Children with Down syndrome: A developmental perspective.* New York: Cambridge University Press.

Cicchetti, D., & Carlson, V. (Eds.). (1989). *Child maltreatment: Theory and research on the causes and consequences of child abuse and neglect.* Cambridge: Cambridge University Press.

Cicero, T. J. (1994). Effects of paternal exposure to alcohol on offspring development. *Alcohol Health and Research World, 18*(1), 37–41.

Claverie, J-M. (2001). What if there are only 30,000 human genes? *Science.* Feb. 16, 2001, *291*(5507), 1255–1257.

Cline, S., & Schwartz, D. (1999). *Diverse populations of gifted children.* Upper Saddle River, NJ: Merrill.

Cockcroft, D. L. (1991). Vitamin deficiency and neural tube defects: Human and animal studies. *Human Reproduction, 6,* 148.

Cohen, D. J., & Volkmar, F. R. (Eds.). (1997). *Autism and pervasive developmental disorders: A handbook.* New York: Wiley.

Cohen, S. (1998). *Targeting autism.* Berkeley: University of California Press.

Coker, S. B. (1989). *Developmental delay and mental retardation.* New York: PMA Publishing.

Cole, R. (1996, January 24). Down syndrome patient gets heart-lung transplant. *Buffalo News,* p. A-3.

Coles, C. (1994). Critical periods for prenatal alcohol exposure: Evidence from animal and human studies. *Alcohol, Health and Research World, 18*(1), 22–29.

Collins, N. L., Dunkel-Schetter, C., Lobel, M., & Scrimshaw, S. C. M. (1993). Social support in pregnancy: Psychosocial correlates of birth outcomes and postpartum depression. *Journal of Personality and Social Psychology, 65*(6), 1243–1258.

Committee on Genetics (1994). American Academy of Pediatrics: Prenatal genetic diagnosis for pediatricians. *Pediatrics, 93,* 1010–1014.

Committee on Genetics (1996). Newborn screening fact sheet. *Pediatrics, 98,* 473–501.

Condon, W., & Sander, L. (1974). Synchrony demonstrated between movements of the neonate and adult speech. *Child Development, 45,* 456–462.

Connor, E. M., Sperling, R. S., Gelber, R., Kiselev, P., Scott, G., O'Sullivan, M. J., Van Dyke, R., Bey, M., Shearer, W., & Jacobsen, R. L. (1994). Reduction of maternal-infant transmission of human immunodeficiency virus type 1 with treatment. Pediatric AIDS clinical trial group protocol 076 study group. *New England Journal of Medicine, 331,* 1173–1180.

Connor, J. M., & Ferguson-Smith, M. A. (1987). *Essential medical genetics* (2nd ed.). Oxford: Blackwell Scientific Publications.

Cooley, E. J., & Ayers, R. R. (1988). Self-concept and success–failure attributions of nonhandicapped students and students with learning disabilities. *Journal of Learning Disabilities, 21*(3), 174–178.

Copeland, M. E., & Kimmel, J. R. (1989). *Evaluation and management of infants and young children with developmental disabilities.* Baltimore, MD: Paul H. Brookes.

Craft, L. T., & Wolraich, M. L. (1997). Conditions. In H. M. Wallace, R. F. Biehl, J. C. MacQueen, & J. A. Blackman (Eds.), *Mosby's resource guide to children with disabilities and chronic illness* (pp. 441–465). New York: Mosby.

Cragan, J. D., Roberts, H. E., Edmonds, L. D., Khoury, M. J., Kirby, R. S., Shaw, G. M., Velie, E. M., Merz, R. D., Forrester, M. B., Williamson, R. A., Krishnamurti, D. S., Stevenson, R. E., & Dean, J. H. (1995). Surveillance for anencephaly and spina bifida and the impact of prenatal diagnosis—United States, *Morbidity and Mortality Weekly Report, 44*(4), 1–13.

Creasy, R. K., & Resnik, R. (1989). *Maternal-fetal medicine: Principles and practice* (2nd ed.). Philadelphia, PA: Saunders.

Crocker, A. C. (1986). Prevention of mental retardation: 1985. *Annals of the New York Academy of Science, 477,* 329–338.

Crocker, A. C. (1990). Societal commitment toward prevention of developmental disabilities. In S. M. Pueschel & J. A. Mulick (Eds.). *Prevention of developmental disabilities* (pp. 337–343). Baltimore, MD: Paul H. Brookes.

Crossette, B. (2000, February 24). U.N. food agency says famine threatens 8 million in Ethiopia. *The New York Times,* p. A11.

Crow, T. J., & Done, D. J. (1992). Prenatal exposure to influenza does not cause schizophrenia. *British Journal of Psychiatry, 161,* 390–393.

Cuckle, H. S. (1995). Screening for neural tube defects. *Ciba Foundation Symposium, 181,* 253–269.

Curcio, F. (1978). Sensorimotor functioning and communication in mute autistic children. *Journal of Autism and Childhood Schizophrenia, 8,* 283–292.

Dagna-Bricarelli, F., Pierluigi, M., Grasso, M., Strigini, P., & Perroni, L. (1990). Origin of extra chromosome 21 in 343 families: Cytogenics and molecular approaches. *American Journal of Medical Genetics—Supplement, 7,* 129–132.

Dalterio, S. L., & Fried, P. A. (1992). The effects of marijuana use on offspring. In T. B. Sonderegger (Ed.), *Perinatal substance abuse: Research findings and clinical implications* (pp. 161–183). Baltimore, MD: Johns Hopkins University Press.

Darling, R. B. (1991). Initial and continuing adaptation to the birth of a disabled child. In M. Seligman (Ed.), *The family with a handicapped child* (2nd ed., pp. 55–90). Boston: Allyn & Bacon.

Dasa, U., Takei, N., Sham, P. C., & Murray, R. M. (1995). No association between prenatal exposure to influenza and autism. *Acta Psychiatrica Scandinavica, 92*(2), 145–149.

Davies, P. (1988). Alzheimer's disease and related disorders: An overview. In M. K. Aronson & R. N. Butler (Eds.), *Understanding Alzheimer's disease.* New York: Charles Scribner's Sons.

Davison, A. N., & Dobbing, J. (1966). Myelination as a vulnerable period in brain development. *British Medical Bulletin, 22,* 40–44.

Day, N. L., & Richardson, G. A. (1994). Comparative teratogenicity of alcohol and other drugs. *Alcohol Health and Research World, 18*(1), 42–46.

Despert, L. (1951). Some considerations relating to the genesis of autistic behavior in children. *American Journal of Orthopsychiatry, 21,* 335–350.

Detterman, D. K. (1986). Human intelligence is a complex system of separate processes. In R. J. Sternberg & D. K. Detterman (Eds.), *What is intelligence?* Norwood, NJ: Ablex.

Detterman, D. K. (Ed.). (1994). *Current trends in human intelligence: Vol. 4. Theories of intelligence.* Norwood, NJ: Ablex.

De Vries, B. B. A., van den Ouweland, A. M. W., & Mohkamsing, S. (1997). Screening and diagnosis for the fragile X syndrome among the mentally retarded: An epidemiological and psychological survey. *American Journal of Human Genetics, 61,* 660–667.

Dexter, L. A. (1960). Research on problems of subnormality. *American Journal of Mental Deficiency, 64,* 835–838.

Dexter, L. A. (1964). *The tyranny of schooling.* New York: Basic Books.

D.H.H.S. (1990). *Healthy people, 2000* (Department of Health and Human Services, U.S. Public Health Service, Publication No. HRSA-M-CH 91-12). Washington, DC: U.S. Printing Office.

D.H.H.S. (1991). *Ageing America: Trends and projections* (Department of Health and Human Services Publications No. FCoA 91-28001). Washington, DC: Department of Health and Human Services.

Diamond, J. (1989, February). Blood, genes, and malaria. *Natural History,* pp. 8–18.

Diamond, L. J., & Jaudes, P. K. (1983, April). Child abuse in cerebral palsied populations. *Developmental Medicine and Child Neurology,* pp. 169–174.

DiPietro, J. A., Hodgson, D., Costigan, K. A., & Johnson, T. R. B. (1996). Fetal antecedent of infant temperament. *Child Development, 67,* 2568–2583.

Dissanayake, C., Crossley, S., & Stella, A. (1996). Proximity and sociable behaviors in autism: Evidence for attachment. *Journal of Child Psychology & Psychiatry & Allied Disciplines, 37*(2), 149–156.

Dobbing, J. (1987). *Early nutrition and later achievement.* London: Academic Press.

Dobson, J. C., Williamson, M. L., & Koch, R. (1977). Intellectual assessment of 111 four-year-old children with phenylketonuria. *Pediatrics, 60*(6), 822–827.

Dodrill, C. B., & Batzel, L. W. (1986). Interictal behavioral features of patients with epilepsy. *Epilepsia, 27*(2), 64–76.

Doherty, W., & Baird, M. A. (1987). *Family-centered medical care: A clinical casework.* New York: Guilford Press.

Dormans, J. P., & Pellegrino, L. (Eds.). (1998). *Caring for children with cerebral palsy: A team approach.* Baltimore, MD: Paul H. Brookes.

Dow-Edwards, D., Chasnoff, I. J., & Griffith, D. R. (1992). Cocaine use during pregnancy. In T. B. Sonderegger (Ed.), *Perinatal substance abuse: Research findings and clinical implications.* (pp. 184–206). Baltimore, MD: Johns Hopkins University Press.

Down, J. L. H. (1866). Observations on an ethnic classification of idiots. *Journal of Mental Science, 13,* 121–123.

Drew, C. J., Hardiman, M. L., & Logan, D. R. (1996). *Mental retardation: A life-cycle approach.* Englewood Cliffs, New Jersey, Merrill.

Driscoll, C. D., Streissguth, A. P., & Riley, E. P. (1990). Prenatal alcohol exposure: Comparability of effects with humans and animal models. *Nuerotoxicology and Teratology, 12,* 231–237.

Drotan, D., Eckerle, D., Satola, J., Pallotta, J., & Wyatt, B. (1990). Maternal interactional behavior with nonorganic failure-to-thrive infants: A case comparison study. *Child Abuse and Neglect, 14,* 41–51.

Druck, K. (1994). Personal perspectives on learning differences: Coming out of the shadow. In P. J. Gerber & H. B. Reiff (Eds.), *Learning disabilities in adulthood: Persisting problems and evolving issues.* Boston: Andover Medical Publishers.

Dryfoos, J. (1994). *Full service schools: A revolution in health and social services for children, youth, and families.* San Francisco: Jossey-Bass.

Dufour, M. C., Williams, G. D., Campbell, K. E., & Aitken, S. S. (1994). Knowledge of FAS and the risks of heavy drinking during pregnancy, 1985 and 1990. *Alcohol Health and Research World, 18*(1), 82–85.

Dunn, J., & Munn, P. (1985). Becoming a family member: Family conflict and the development of social understanding in the second year. *Child Development, 56,* 480–492.

Dunn, J., & Shatz, M. (1989). Becoming a conversationalist despite (or because of) having an older sibling. *Child Development, 60,* 399–410.

Dunst, C. L., Trivette, C. M., Hamby, D. M., & Pollack, B. (1990). Family systems correlates of the behavior of young children with handicaps. *Journal of Early Intervention, 14*(3), 204–218.

Dwyer, J. (1983). Impact of maternal nutrition on infant health. *Medical Times, 111, 30–38.*

Eaton, L., & Menolascino, F. J. (1982). Psychiatric disorders in the mentally retarded: Types, problems, and challenges. *American Journal of Psychiatry, 139,* 1297–1303.

Edgerton, R. B. (1967). *The cloak of competence: Stigma in the lives of the mentally retarded.* Berkeley: University of California Press.

Edgerton, R. B. (1988). Perspectives on the prevention of mild mental retardation. In F. J. Menolascino & J. A. Stark (Eds.), *Prevention and curative intervention in mental retardation* (pp. 325–342). Baltimore. MD: Paul H. Brookes.

Eimas, P. D., Sigueland, E. R., Jusczyk, P., & Vigorito, J. (1971). Speech perception in infants. *Science, 171,* 303–309.

Eisinger, J. (1996). Sweet poison. *Natural History, 105*(7), 48–53.

Elwood, J. M., & Elwood, J. H. (1980). *Epidemiology of anencephalus and spina bifida.* Oxford: Oxford University Press.

Environmental Protection Agency. (1986). *Air quality criteria for lead* (Vols. 1–4). Washington, DC: Author.

Epilepsy Foundation of America. (1998). *Epilepsy facts and figures* [On-line]. Available: http://www.efa.org

Epstein, C. J. (1995). Down syndrome (Trisomy 21). In C. R. Scriver, A. L. Beaudet, W. S. Sly, & D. Valle (Eds.). *The metabolic and molecular bases of inherited intelligence,* Vol. I (7th. ed.) pp. 749–794. New York: McGraw-Hill.

Epstein, L. H., & Wing, R. R. (1987). Behavioral treatment of childhood obesity. *Psychological Bulletin, 101,* 331–342.

Ericson, J. E., Smith, D. R., & Flegal, A. R. (1991). Skeletal concentrations of lead, cadmium, zinc, and silver in ancient North American Pacos Indians. *Environment and Health Perspectives, 93,* 217–223.

Esquirol, J. E. (1838). *Des Maladies mentales: Considerees sous les hygieniques, et medico-legaux, 1772–1840.* Paris: Bailliere.

European Collaborative Study. (1991). Children born to women with HIV-1 infection: Natural history and risk of transmission. *Lancet, 337,* 253–260.

Evans, D. P. (1983). *The lives of mentally retarded people.* Boulder, CO: Westview Press.

Evrard, J. R., & Scola, P. S. (1997). Preparation for parenthood. In S. M. Pueschel & J. A. Mulick (Eds.), *Prevention of developmental disabilities* (pp. 27–36). Baltimore, MD: Paul H. Brookes.

Ewer, D. (1992). *Maternal infant bondings: A scientific fiction.* New Haven, CT: Yale University Press.

Fabri, G., & Castellino, N. (1995). Chelating agents and lead. In N. Castellino, P. Castellino, & N. Sannolo (Eds.), *Inorganic lead exposure: Metabolism and intoxication* (pp. 257–286). Boca Raton, FL: Lewis Publishers.

Fahrner, R., & Manio, E. (2000). HIV infection and AIDS. In P. L. Jackson & J. A. Vessey (Eds.), *Primary care of the child with a chronic condition.* St. Louis, MO: Mosby.

Fantuzzo, J., DePaola, L., Lambert, L., Martino, E., Anderson, E., & Sutton, S. (1991). Effects of interparental violence on the psychological adjustment and competencies of young children. *Journal of Consulting and Clinical Psychology, 59,* 258–265.

Farley, J. A., & Dunleavy, M. J. (2000). Myelodysplasia. In P. L. Jackson & J. A. Vessey (Eds.), *Primary care of the child with a chronic condition* (pp. 658–675). St. Louis, MO: Mosby.

Farley, J. A., & McEwan, M. (2000). Epilepsy. In P. L. Jackson & J. A. Vessey (Eds.), *Primary care of the child with a chronic condition* (pp. 475–494). St. Louis, MO: Mosby.

Feinman, S., (1985). Emotional expressions, social referencing, and preparedness for learning in infancy—Mother knows best, but sometimes I know better. In G. Ziven (Ed.), *The development of expressive behavior.* Orlando, FL: Academic Press.

Feldman, H. A. (1982). Epidemiology of toxoplasma infections. *Epidemiological Review, 4,* 204–213.

Felt, J. P. (1971). Children at work. In T. R. Frazier (Ed.), *The underside of American history.* New York: Harcourt Brace Jovanovich.

Fenster, L., Schaefer, C., Mathur, A., Hiatt, R. A., Pieper, C., Hubbard, A. E., Von Behren, J., & Swan, S. H. (1995). Psychological stress in the workplace and spontaneous abortion. *American Journal of Epidemiology, 142*(11), 1176–1183.

Finlan, T. (1993). *Learning disability: The imaginary disease.* Westport, CT: Bergin & Garvey.

Fishler, K., Azen, C. G., Friedman, E. G., & Koch, R. (1987). Psycho-educational findings among children treated for phenylketonuria. *American Journal of Mental Deficiency, 92*(1), 65–73.

Fishler, K., Azen, C. G., Friedman, E. G., & Koch, R. (1989). School achievement in treated PKU children. *Journal of Mental Deficiency Research, 33,* 493–498.

Flavell, J. H., Miller, P. H., & Miller, S. A. (1993). *Cognitive development* (3rd ed.). Englewood Cliffs, NJ: Prentice Hall.

Folling, A. (1934). Ueber ausscheidung von phenylbrenz traubensaure in dens als staffwechselanomalie in verbindung mit imbezilitaet [Excretion of urinary phenylpyruvic acid as metabolic anomaly in connection with imbecility]. *Physiological Chemistry, 227,* 169–176.

Fombonne, E. (1997). Epidemiological studies of autism. In F. Volkmar (Ed.), *Autism and developmental disorders.* New York: Cambridge University Press.

Foorman, B. R., Francis, D. J., & Shaywitz, S. F. (1996). The case for early reading intervention. In B. Blachman (Ed.), *Cognitive and linguistic foundations of reading acquisition: implications for intervention.* Mahwah, NJ: Erlbaum.

Forness, S. R., & Kavale. (1993). The Balkanization of special education: Proliferation of categories and sub categories for "new" disorders. In J. Marr, G. Sugai, & G. Tindal (Eds.), *The Oregon conference mono-*

graph (pp. ix–xv). Eugene: University of Oregon Press.

Foucault, M. (1965). *Madness and civilization.* New York: Random House.

Fox, L. H., Brody, L., & Tobin, D. (1983). *Learning disabled/gifted children: Identification and programming.* Austin, TX: Pro-Ed.

France, D. (1999, September 7). AIDS outbreak feared for U.S. tribes. *The New York Times.*

Francis, P. A., Self, P. A., & Horowitz, F. D. (1987). The behavioral assessment of the neonate: An overview. In J. R. Osofsky (Ed.), *Handbook of infant development* (2nd ed., pp. 723–779). New York: Wiley.

Freeman, J. M. (1995). A clinician's look at the developmental neurobiology of epilepsy. In P. A. Schwartzkroin, S. L. Moshe, J. L. Noebels, & J. W. Swann (Eds.), *Brain development and epilepsy.* New York: Oxford University Press.

Freeman, J. B., Kelly M. T., & Freeman, J. B. (1996). The epilepsy diet treatment: An introduction to the ketogenic diet. New York: Demos Vermande.

Freij, B. J., South, M. A., & Sever, J. L. (1988). Maternal rubella and the congenital rubella syndrome. *Clinics in Perinatology, 15,* 247–258.

Fried, P. A. (1982). Marijuana use by pregnant women and effects on offspring: An update. *Neurobehavioral Toxology and Teratology, 4,* 451–454.

Fried, P. A. (1986). Marijuana and human pregnancy. In I. J. Chasnoff (Ed.), *Drug use in pregnancy: Mother and child.* Lancaster, England: MTP Press.

Fried, P. A., Watkinson, B., & Dillon, R. (1987). Neonatal neurological status in a low-risk population after prenatal exposure to cigarettes, marijuana, and alcohol. *Developmental and Behavioral Pediatrics, 8,* 318–326.

Fries, K. (1997). *Staring back: The disability experience from the inside out.* New York: Plume.

Frith, U. (Ed.). (1991). *Autism and Asperger syndrome.* New York: Cambridge University Press.

Fryers, T. (1984). *The epidemiology of severe intellectual impairment: The dynamics of prevalence.* London: Academic Press.

Fuhrmann, W., & Vogel, F. (1983). *Genetic counseling* (3rd ed.). New York: Springer-Verlag.

Fujiura, G. (1998). Demography of family households. *American Journal on Mental Retardation, 103,* 225–235.

Gajria, M., & Hughes, C. A. (1988). Introduction to mental retardation. In P. J. Schloss, C. A. Hughes, & M. A. Smith (Eds.), *Mental retardation: Community transition.* Boston: Little, Brown.

Galler, J. R., Tonkiss, J., & Maldonado-Irizarry, C. S. (1994). Prenatal protein malnutrition and home orientation in the rat. *Physiology & Behavior, 55*(6), 993–996.

Garber, H. L. (1988). *The Milwaukee project: Preventing mental retardation in children at risk.* Washington, DC: American Association on Mental Retardation.

Garrison, W. T., & McQuiston, S. (1988). *Chronic illness during childhood and adolescence.* London: Sage.

Gates, J. R., & Hemmes, R. (1990). Role and implementation of long-term monitoring for epilepsy. *Seminars in Neurology, 10,* 357–365.

Geary, D. C. (1999). Mathematical disabilities: What we know and don't know [LD On-line]. Available: http://www.ldonline.org/ld_indepth/math_skills/geary_math_dis.html

Gelfand, D., Jenson, W. R., & Drew, C. J. (1988). *Understanding child behavior disorders* (2nd ed.). Fort Worth, TX: Holt, Rinehart & Winston.

Gerber, P. J., Ginsberg, R. J., & Reiff, H. B. (1992). Identifying alterable patterns in employment success for highly successful adults with learning disabilities. *Journal of Learning Disabilities, 25,* 475–487.

Gerber, P. J., & Reiff, H. B. (1994). Perspectives on adults with learning disabilities. In P. H. Gerber & H. B. Reiff (Eds.), *Learning disabilities in adulthood: Persistent problems and evolving issues.* Boston: Andover Medical Publishers.

Gibbs, R. S., & Sweet, R. L. (1989). Maternal and fetal infections—Clinical disorders. In R. K. Creasy & R. Resnick (Eds.), *Maternal fetal medicine: Principles and practice* (2nd ed.). Philadelphia, PA: Saunders.

Gibson, G. T., Baghurst, P. A., & Colley, D. P. (1983). Maternal alcohol, tobacco, and cannabis consumption and the outcome of pregnancy. *Australia and New Zealand Obstetrics and Gynecology 3,* 16–19.

Gillberg, C. (1984). Infantile autism and other childhood psychoses in a Swedish urban region. Epidemiological aspects. *Journal of Child Psychology and Psychiatry, 25,* 35–43.

Gillberg, C. (1988). The neurobiology of infantile autism. *Journal of Child Psychology and Psychiatry, 129,* 245–256.

Gillberg, C. (Ed.) (1989). *Diagnosis and treatment of autism.* New York: Plenum Press.

Gillberg, C. (1998a). Asperger syndrome and high-functioning autism. *British Journal of Psychiatry, 172,* 200–209.

Gillberg, C. (1998b). Neuropsychiatric disorders. *Current Opinions in Neurology, 11,* 109–114.

Giovengo, M., Moore, E., & Young, G. (1998). Screening and assessment results of the learning disabilities initiative: Identification of individuals with learning disabilities in the job opportunities and basic skills program. In S. A. Vogel & S. Reder (Eds.), *Learning disabilities, literacy, and adult education* (pp. 179–194). Baltimore, MD: Paul H. Brookes.

Glenn, M. C. (1984). *Campaigns against corporal punishment: Prisoners, sailors, women, and children in antebellum America.* Albany: State University of New York Press.

Goldsmith, H. H., Buss, K. A., & Lemery, K. S. (1997). Toddler and childhood temperament: Expanded content, stronger genetic evidence, new evidence for the importance of environment. *Developmental Psychology, 33,* 89–105.

Goldson, E., & Hagerman, R. J. (1992). The fragile-X syndrome. *Developmental Medicine and Child Neurology, 34,* 822–832.

Goldstein, L. H. (1990). Behavioral and cognitive-behavioral treatments for epilepsy: A progress review. *British Journal of Clinical Psychology, 29,* 257–269.

Gonzalez, N. M., & Campbell, M. (1994). Cocaine babies: Does prenatal exposure to cocaine affect development? *Journal of the American Academy of Child and Adolescent Psychiatry, 33,* 16–19.

Goode, E. (2000, February 23). Sharp rise found in psychiatric drugs with the very young. *The New York Times,* p. A-1.

Gortmaker, S., & Sappenfield, W. (1984). Chronic childhood disorders: Prevalence and impact. *Pediatric Clinics of North America, 31,* 3–18.

Gottesman, I. I. (1974). Developmental genetics and ontogenetic psychology: Overdue détente and propositions from a matchmaker. In A. D. Pick (Ed.), *Minnesota Symposia on Child Psychology* (Vol. 8, p. 60). Minneapolis: University of Minnesota Press.

Grandin, T. (1992a). An inside view of autism. In E. Schopler & G. B. Mesibov (Eds.), *High functioning individuals with autism* (pp. 105–125). New York: Plenum Press.

Grandin, T. (1992b). Needs of high functioning teen-agers and adults with autism: Tips from a recovered autistic. *Focus on Autistic Behavior, 5*(1), 16.

Grandin, T. (1995a). *How people with autism think.* New York: Plenum Press.

Grandin, T. (1995b). *Thinking in pictures: And other reports from my life with autism.* New York: Doubleday.

Grandin, T., & Scariano, M. (1986). *Emergence: Labeled autistic.* Novato, CA: Arena Press.

Graziano, A. M. (1963). *A description of a behavioral day-care and treatment program.* Report to the Connecticut State Department of Mental Health, Division of Children's Services, Hartford, CT.

Graziano, A. M. (1967). *Programmed psychotherapy: Treating autistic children.* Paper presented at the meeting of the Eastern Psychological Association, Boston, MA.

Graziano, A. M. (1969). Clinical intervention and the mental health power structure. *American Psychologist, 24,* 10–18.

Graziano, A. M. (1971). (Ed.). *Behavior therapy with children* (Vol. I) Chicago: Aldine-Atherton.

Graziano, A. M. (1974). *Child without tomorrow.* New York: Pergamon Press.

Graziano, A. M. (Ed.) (1975a). *Behavior therapy with children* (Vol. II). New York: Aldine.

Graziano, A. M. (1975b). Modification of psychotic behavior. In A. M. Graziano (Ed.), *Behavior therapy with children* (Vol. II, pp. 153–159). New York: Aldine.

Graziano, A. M. (1987, May). *Role modification: Application of social role theory to mental retardation.* Paper presented at meeting of the Association of Behavior Analysis, Nashville, TN.

Graziano, A. M. (1992). Why we should study sub-abusive violence against children. *The Child, Youth, and Family Services Quarterly, 15,* 4, 8–9.

Graziano, A. M., & Kean, J. E. (1968). Programmed relaxation and reciprocal inhibition with psychotic children. *Behaviour Research and Therapy, 6,* 433–437.

Graziano, A. M., Kunce, L., Lindquist, C. M., & Munjal, K. (1991). Physical punishment in childhood and current attitudes: A comparison of college students in the U.S. and India. *Journal of Interpersonal Violence, 7,* 147–155.

Graziano, A. M., & Mills, J. (1992). Treatment for abused children: When is a partial solution acceptable? *Child Abuse and Neglect, 16,* 217–228.

Graziano, A. M., & Raulin, M. (2000). *Research methods: A process of inquiry* (4th ed.). New York: Allyn & Bacon.

Greenhouse, S. (2000, August 6). Farm work by children tests labor laws. *The New York Times,* p. Y-10.

Greenland, S., Staisch, K., Brown, N., & Gross, S. (1982). The effects of marijuana use during pregnancy. *American Journal of Obstetrics and Gynecology 143,* 408–413.

Greenswag, L. R., & Alexander, R. C. (Eds.). (1988). *Management of Prader-Willi syndrome.* New York: Springer-Verlag.

Greven, P. (1977). *The Protestant temperament: Patterns of child rearing, religious experience, and the self in early America.* New York: Knopf.

Griesbach, L. S., & Polloway, E. A. (1990). *Fetal alcohol syndrome: Research review and implications* (Report No. EC232650). Lynchburg, VA: Lynchburg College. (ERIC Document Reproduction Service No. ED326035)

Grossman, H. J. (Ed.). (1983). *Classification in mental retardation.* Washington, DC: American Association on Mental Deficiency.

Grossman, H. J., & Tarjan, G. (Eds.). (1987). *AMA handbook on mental retardation.* Chicago: American Medical Association.

Grossman, K., Thane K., & Grossman, K. E. (1981). Maternal tactual of the newborn after various postpartum conditions of mother-infant contact. *Developmental Psychology, 17,* 158–169.

Gumnit, R. J. (1994). Epilepsy: Presentation to United States House of Representatives Appropriations Committee. *Departments of Labor, Health and Human Services,* Appropriation for 1995 (Part 7). Hearing. Washington, DC: U. S. Government Printing Office.

Gumnit, R. J. (1997). *Living well with epilepsy* (2nd ed.). New York: Demos.

Guthrie, R. (1961). Blood screening for phenylketonuria. *Journal of the American Medical Association, 178*(8), 863.

Guthrie, R. (1986). Lead exposure in children: The need for professional and public education. In H. M. Wisnewski & D. A. Snider (Eds.), *Mental retardation: Research, education, and technology transfer.* New York: New York Academy of Sciences.

Guthrie, R., & Edwards, J. (1990). Prevention of mental retardation and developmental disabilities. In S. M. Pueschel & J. A. Mulick (Eds.), *Prevention of developmental disabilities* (pp. 11–23). Baltimore, MD: Paul H. Brookes.

Guthrie, R., & Susi, A. (1963). A simple phenylalanine method for detecting phenylketonuria in large populations of newborn infants. *Pediatrics, 32,* 338–343.

Guttmacher, A. F., & Kaiser, I. H. (1986). *Pregnancy, birth, and family planning.* New York: New American Library.

Hack, M., Klein, N. K., & Taylor, H. G. (1995). Long-term developmental outcomes of low birth weight infants. *The Future of Chidlren, 5*(1), 176–196.

Haddow, J. E. (1998). Antenatal screening for Down's syndrome: Where are we and where next? *Lancet, 352,* 336–337.

Hagberg, B., Hagberg, G., Lewerth, A., & Lindberg, U. (1981). Mild mental retardation in Swedish school children: II. Etiologic and pathogenetic aspects. *Acta Paediatrica Scandinavica, 70,* 445–452.

Hagerman, R. J. (1996). Biomedical advances in developmental psychology: The case of the fragile-X syndrome. *Developmental Psychology, 32*(3), 416–424.

Hagerman, R. J. (2000). Fragile-X syndrome. In P. L. Jackson & J. A. Vessey (Eds.), *Primary care of the child with a chronic condition* (3rd ed., pp. 495–513). St. Louis, MO: Mosby.

Haglund, B., & Cnattingius, S. (1990). Cigarette smoking as a risk factor for sudden infant death syndrome: A population-based study. *American Journal of Public Health, 80*(1), 29–32.

Hall, B. D., & Smith, D. W. (1972). Prader-Willi syndrome: A resume of 32 cases. *Journal of Pediatrics, 81,* 286–293.

Hankin, J. R. (1994). FAS prevention strategies: Passive and active measures. *Alcohol Health and Research World, 18*(1), 62–66.

Happe, F., & Frith, U. (1995). *Theory of mind in autism.* New York: Plenum Press.

Happe, F., & Frith, U. (1996). The neuropsychology of autism. *Brain, 119,* 1377–1400.

Harmon, J. P., Hiett, A. K., Palmer, C. G., & Golichowski, A. M. (1995). Prenatal ultrasound detection of isolated neural tube defects: Is cytogenetic evaluation warranted? *Obstetrics and Gynecology, 86*(4), 595–599.

Harris, J. C. (1995). *Developmental neuropsychiatry: Assessment, diagnosis, and treatment of developmental disorders* (Vol. II.) Oxford: Oxford University Press.

Harris, S. L. (1994). *Siblings of children with autism.* Bethesda, MD: Woodbine House.

Harris, S. L. (1995). Educational strategies in autism. In E. Schopler & G. B. Mesibov (Eds.), *Learning and cognition in autism: Current issues in autism.* New York: Plenum Press.

Harris, S. L. (1998). Behavioral and educational approaches to the pervasive developmental disorders. In F. R. Volkmar (Ed.), *Autism and pervasive developmental disorders* (pp. 195–208). New York: Cambridge University Press.

Harris, S. L., Glasberg, B., & Delmolino, L. (1998). Families and the developmentally disabled adolescent. In V. B. Van Hasselt & M. Hersen (Eds.), *Handbook of psychological treatment protocols for children and adolescents* (pp. 519–548). Mahwah, NJ: Erlbaum.

Hartladge, L. C., & Green, J. B. (1972). The relation of parental attitudes to academic and social achievement in epileptic children. *Epilepsia, 13,* 21–26.

Harvard M. H. Letter. (1997, March). Autism. *Harvard Mental Health Letter, 13*(9), 1–4.

Haskins, R. (1986). Social and cultural factors in risk assessment and psychosocial development. In D. C. Farran & J. D. McKinney (Eds.), *Risks in intellectual and psychosocial development* (pp. 29–60). New York: Academic Press.

Hauser, W. A., & Hesdorffer, D. C. (1990). *Epilepsy: Frequency, causes and consequences.* New York: Demos.

Havighurst, R. J. (1972). *Developmental tasks and education.* New York: David MacKay.

Havighurst, R. J. (1980). More thoughts on developmental tasks. *Personnel & Guidance Journal, 58,* 330–335.

Hawley, T. L., & Disney, E. R. (1992). Crack's children: The consequences of maternal cocaine abuse. *Social*

Policy Report: Society for Research in Child Development. 6(4), 1–23.

Hayes, C. D. (Ed.). (1987). *Risking the future: Adolescent sexuality, pregnancy, and childbearing* (Vol. 1). Washington, DC: National Academy Press.

Hecht, C. A., & Hook, E. B. (1996). Rates of Down syndrome at live birth at one-year maternal age intervals in studies with apparent close to complete ascertainment in populations of European origin: A proposed revised rate schedule for use in genetic and prenatal screening. *American Journal of Medical Genetics, 62,* 376–385.

Heller, T. (1999). Emerging models. In S. S. Herr & G. Weber (Eds.), *Aging, rights, and quality of life: Prospects for older people with developmental disabilities* (pp. 149–165). Baltimore MD: Paul H. Brookes.

Heller, T., Sterns, H., Sutton, E., & Factor, A. R. (1996). Impact of person-centered, later-life planning training program for older adults with mental retardation. *Journal of Rehabilitation, 62,* 77–83.

Henley, E. D., & Altman, J. (1978). The young adult. In D. W. Smith, E. L. Bierman, & N. M. Robinson (Eds.). *The biologic ages of man from conception through old age* (pp. 187–208). Philadelphia, PA: Saunders.

Henriksen, B., Juul-Jensen, P., & Lund, M. (1970). The mortality of epileptics. In R. D. C. Brackenridge (Ed.), *Proceedings of the 10th International Congress of Life Assurance Medicine.* London: Putnam.

Hermann, B. P. (1991). The relevance of social factors to adjustment in epilepsy. In O. Devinsky & W. H. Theodore (Eds.), *Epilepsy and behavior* (pp. 23–36). New York: Wiley-Liss.

Herr S. S., & Weber, G. (1999a). Aging and developmental disabilities. In S. S. Herr & G. Weber (Eds.), *Aging, rights, and quality of life: Prospects for older people with developmental disabilities* (pp. 1–16). Baltimore, MD: Paul H. Brookes.

Herr, S. S., & Weber, G. (Eds.) (1999b). *Aging, rights, and quality of Life: Prospects for older people with developmental disabilities.* Baltimore, MD: Paul H. Brookes.

Hetherington, E. M., Parke, R. D. & Locke, V. O. (1999). *Child psychology: A contemporary viewpoint,* (5th edition). New York: McGraw Hill.

Hingson, R., Alpert, J. J., Day, N., Dooling, E., Kayne, H., Morlock, S., Oppenheimer, E., & Zuckerman, B. (1982). Effects of maternal drinking and marijuana use on fetal growth and development. *Pediatrics, 70,* 539–546.

Hinman, A. R. (1990). Immunoprophylaxis of developmental disabilities. In S. M. Pueschel & J. A. Mulick (Eds.), *Prevention of developmental disabilities* (pp. 287–302). Baltimore, MD: Paul H. Brookes.

Hobbs, N., Perrin, J., & Ireys, H. T. (1985). *Chronically ill children and their families.* San Francisco: Jossey-Bass.

Hofman, K. J. (1991). Phenylketonuria in U.S. Blacks: Molecular analysis of the phenylalanine hydroxylase gene. *American Journal of Human Genetics, 48,* 791–798.

Holdsworth, L., & Whitmore, K. (1974). A study of children with epilepsy attending ordinary schools: II. Information and attitudes held by their teachers. *Developmental Medicine and Child Neurology, 16,* 759–765.

Hollowell, J. G., & Adams, M. J. (1997). Evolving concepts in the prevention of developmental disabilities. In H. M. Wallace, R. F. Biehl, J. C. MacQueen, & J. A. Blackman (Eds.), *Mosby's resource guide to children with disabilities and chronic illness* (pp. 203–212). Baltimore, MD: Mosby.

Holmes, L. B. (1992). Teratogens. In R. E. Behrman (Ed.), *Nelson textbook of pediatrics* (14th ed.). Philadelphia, PA: Saunders.

Hormuth, R. P. (1963). A proposed program to combat mental retardation. *Children, 10,* 29–31.

Householder, J., Hatcher, R., Burns, W., & Chasnoff, I. (1982). Infants born to narcotic-addicted mothers. *Psychological Bulletin, 92,* 453–468.

Howes, C., & Hamilton, C. E. (1992). Children's relationships with caregivers: Mothers and child-care teachers. *Child Development, 63,* 859–866.

Howlin, P. (1989). Help for the family. In C. Gillberg (Ed.), *Diagnosis and treatment of autism* (pp. 185–202). New York: Plenum Press.

Howlin, P. (1996). *Autism in adulthood: The way ahead.* London: Routledge.

Howlin, P. (1997). Prognosis in autism: Do specialist treatments affect outcome? *European Child and Adolescent Psychiatry, 6,* 55–72.

Howlin, P. (1998). Practitioner review: Psychological and educational treatments for autism. *Journal of Child Psychology and Psychiatry, 39*(3), 307–322.

Howlin, P., & Yates, P. (1989). Treating autistic children at home: A London-based programme. In C. Gillberg (Ed.), *Diagnosis and treatment of autism.* New York: Plenum Press.

Hughes, D., & Simpson, L. (1995). The role of social change in preventing low birth weight. *Future of Children, 5*(1), 87–102.

Hunt, J. McV. (1961). *Intelligence and experience.* New York: Ronald Press.

Hunt, J. McV. (1964). The psychological basis for using preschool enrichment as an antidote for cultural deprivation. *Merrill-Palmer Quarterly, 10,* 209–248.

IEP Checklist. (1998). *Parents educational advisory training center, 20*(2), 16–17.

Iivanainen, M., & Lahdevirta, J. (1988). Infectious diseases as causes of mental retardation and other concomitant neurological sequelae. *Australia and New Zealand Journal of Developmental Disabilities, 14*(3 & 4), 201–210.

Institute of Medicine. (1990). Subcommittee on nutritional status and weight gain during pregnancy. *Nutrition during pregnancy.* Washington, DC.: National Academy Press.

Institute of Medicine. (1996). *Fetal alcohol syndrome: Diagnosis, epidemiology, prevention, and treatment.* Washington, DC: National Academy Press.

Ireys, H. T., & Katz, S. (1997). The demography of disability and chronic illness among children. In H. M. Wallace, R. F. Biehl, J. C. MacQueen, & J. A. Blackman (Eds.), *Mosby's resource guide to children with disabilities and chronic illness* (pp. 3–13). Baltimore: Mosby.

Istvan, J. (1986). Stress, anxiety, and birth outcomes: A critical review of the evidence. *Psychological Bulletin, 100,* 331–334.

Jackman, M. (1983). Enabling the disabled. *Perspectives: The Civil Rights Quarterly, 15,* 23–36.

Jackson, M. (1933). *Human anatomy.* New York: McGraw-Hill.

Jackson, P. L. (2000). The primary care provider and children with chronic conditions. In P. L. Jackson & J. A. Vessey (Eds.), *Primary care of the child with a chronic condition.* St. Louis, MO: Mosby.

Jackson P. L., & Vessey, J. A. (Eds.) (2000). *Primary care of the child with a chronic condition.* St. Louis: Mosby.

Jacobs, P. A., & Hassold, T. J. (1995). The origins of numerical chromosome abnormalities. *Advances in Genetics, 33,* 101–133.

Jacobson, J. W., Mulick, J. A., & Schwartz, A. A. (1995). A history of facilitated communication: Science, pseudo-science, and anti-science. *American Psychologist, 50*(9), 750–765.

Janicki, M. P. (1993). *Building the future: Planning and community development in aging and developmental disabilities.* Albany: New York State Office of Mental Retardation and Developmental Disabilities.

Janicki, M. P. (1994a). A vision for the future: Aging and developmental disabilities working together. In D. Vasiliou (Ed.), *Conference proceedings of the National Conference on Aging and Disabilities: A vision for the future* (pp. 7–40). Minot: University of North Dakota Press.

Janicki, M. P. (1994b). Policies and supports for older persons with mental retardation. In M. M. Seltzer, J. W. Krauss, & M. P. Janicki (Eds.), *Life course perspectives on adulthood and old age* (pp. 143–165).

Washington, DC: American Association on Mental Retardation.

Janicki, M. P. (1999). Public policy and service design. In S. S. Herr & G. W. Weber (Eds.), *Aging, rights, and quality of life: Prospects for older persons with developmental disabilities* (pp. 289–310). Baltimore, MD: Paul H. Brookes.

Janicki, M. P., & Dalton, A. J. (Eds.). (1999). *Dementia, aging, and intellectual disabilities: A handbook.* Philadelphia, PA: Brunner/Mazel.

Janicki, M. P., & Jacobson, J. W. (1986). Generational trends in sensory, physical, and behavioral abilities among older mentally retarded persons. *American Journal of Mental Deficiency, 90,* 490–500.

Jarvik, M. E. (1973). Further observation on nicotine as the reinforcing agent in smoking. In W. L. Dunn, Jr. (Ed.), *Smoking behavior: motives and incentives* (pp. 33-51). Washington, DC: Winston.

Jones, K. L., & Smith, D. W. (1975). The fetal alcohol syndrome. *Teratology, 12,* 1–10.

Jones, K. L., Smith, D. W., Ulleland, C. N., & Streissguth, A. P. (1973). Pattern of malformation in offspring of chronic alcoholic mothers. *Lancet, 1,* 1267–1271.

Joos, S. K., Pollitt, E., Mueller, W. H., & Albright, D. L. (1983). The Bacon Chow study: Maternal nutritional supplementation and infant behavioral development. *Child Development, 54,* 669–676.

Jordan, D. R. (1996). *Overcoming dyslexia in children, adolescents, and adults.* Austin, TX: Pro-Ed.

Kahn, J. (2000, July 19). U.S. offers Africa $1 billion a year for fighting AIDS. *The New York Times,* p. 1.

Kalil, R. E. (1989, December). Synapse formation in the developing brain. *Scientific American, 261,* 76–85.

Kampen, D., & Grafman, J. (1986). Neuropsychological evaluation of penetrating injury. In M. D. Lezak (Ed.), *Assessment of the behavioral consequences of head trauma* (pp. 49–60). New York: Alan R. Liss.

Kanner, L. (1943). Autistic disturbances of affective content. *Nervous Child, 2,* 217–250.

Kanner, L. (1954). To what extent is early infantile autism determined by constitutional inadequacies? Reprinted in L. Kanner (1973). *Childhood psychosis: Initial studies and new insights* (pp. 69–76). Washington, DC: Winston.

Kanner, L. (1971). Follow-up study of eleven autistic children originally reported in 1943. *Journal of Autism and Childhood Schizophrenia, 1,* 112–145.

Kanner, L. (1973). *Childhood psychosis: Initial studies and new insights.* New York: Wiley.

Karp, R. J. (Ed.) (1993). *Malnourished children in the United States: Caught in the cycle of poverty.* New York: Springer.

Katz, K. S. (1978). Inherited disorders: Down syndrome and phenylketonuria. In P. R. Magrab (Ed.), *Psy-chological management of pediatric problems: Vol. 1. Early life conditions and chronic diseases* (pp. 89–128). Baltimore, MD: University Park Press.

Katz, V. L., Jenkins, T., Haley, L., & Bowes, W. A. (1991). Catecholamine levels in pregnant physicians and nurses: A pilot study of stress and pregnancy. *Obstetrics & Gynecology, 77,* 338–342.

Kauffmann, J. M. (1977). *Characteristics of behavior disorders of children and youth* (1st ed.) Columbus, OH: Merrill.

Kauffmann, J. M. (1989). *Characteristics of behavior disorders of children and youth* (4th ed.). Columbus, OH: Merrill.

Kavale, K. A., & Forness, S. R. (1995). *The nature of learning disabilities: Critical elements of diagnosis and classification.* Mahwah, NJ: Erlbaum.

Kaye, K. (1982). *The mental and social life of babies.* Chicago: University of Chicago Press.

Kaye, K., & Fogel, A. (1980). The temporal structure of face-to-face communication between mothers and infants. *Developmental Psychology, 16*(5), 454–464.

Keith, L. G., MacGregor, S., Friedell, S., Rosner, M., Chasnoff, I. J., & Sciarra, J., (1989). Substance abuse in pregnant women: Recent experience at the Perinatal Center for Chemical Dependence of Northwestern Memorial Hospital. *Obstetrics and Gynecology, 73,* 715–720.

Keren, B., & Rommens, J. M. (1990). Identification of the cystic fibrosis gene: Genetic analysis. *Science, 245*(4922), 1073.

Keuhne, E. A., & Reilly, M. W. (2000). Prenatal cocaine exposure. In P. L. Jackson & J. A. Vessey (Eds.), *Primary care of the child with a chronic condition* (pp. 758–776). St. Louis, MO: Mosby.

Khalfa, J. (Ed.). (1994). *What is intelligence?* Cambridge: Cambridge University Press.

Kinnunin, E., & Wilkstrom, J. (1986). Prevalence and prognosis of epilepsy in patients with multiple sclerosis. *Epilepsia, 27,* 729–733.

Klonoff-Cohen, H. S., Edelstein, S. L., Lefkowitz, E. S., Srinivasan, I. P., Kaegi, D., Chang, J. C., & Wiley, K. J. (1995). The effects of passive smoking and tobacco exposure through mother's milk on sudden infant death syndrome. *Journal of the American Medical Association, 273*(10), 795–798.

Klopfer, P. (1971). Mother love: What turns it on? *American Scientist, 49,* 404–407.

Knobloch, H., & Pasamanick, B. (Eds.). (1974). *Gesell and Amatruda's developmental diagnosis* (3rd ed.). Hagerstown, MD: Harper & Row.

Kolata, G. (1985). Down syndrome-Alzheimer's linked. *Science, 230,* 1152–1153.

Koop, C. E. (1986). *Surgeon General's report on acquired immune deficiency syndrome.* Washington, DC: U.S. Department of Health and Human Services

Kopp, C. B. (1983). Risk factors in development. In J. J. Compos & M. Haith (Eds.), *Handbook of child psychology* (Vol. 2). New York: Wiley.

Kopp, C. B., & Kaler, S. R. (1989). Risk in infancy: Origins and implications. *American Psychologist, 44,* 224–230.

Kopp, C. B., & Parmelee, A. H. (1979). Prenatal and perinatal influences on behavior. In J. D. Osofsky (Ed.), *Handbook of infant development.* New York: Wiley.

Korones, S. B. (1986). *High-risk newborn infants: the basis for intensive nursing care* (4th ed.). St. Louis, MO: Mosby.

Kotelchuck, M., Schwartz, J. B., Anderka, M. T., & Finison, K. S. (1984). WIC participation and pregnancy outcomes: Massachusetts statewide evaluation project. *American Journal of Public Health, 74*(10), 1086–1148.

Kowles, R. V. (1985). *Genetics, society, and decisions.* Columbus, OH: Merrill.

Kramer, M. S. (1987). Determinants of low birth weight: Methodological assessment and meta-analysis. *Bulletin of the World Health Organization. 65,* 663–737.

Krasnegor, N. A. (1987). Introduction. In N. A. Krasnegor, E. M. Blass, M. A. Hofer, & W. P. Smotherman (Eds.), *Perinatal development: A psychobiological perspective* (pp. 1–8). Orlando, FL: Academic Press.

Kuhn, M. H. (1964). Major trends in symbolic interaction theory in the past twenty five years. *Sociology Quarterly, 5,* 61–84.

Kuhse, H., & Singer, P. (1985). *Should the baby live?: The problem of handicapped infants.* New York: Oxford University Press.

Kurent, J. E., & Sever, J. L. (1977). Infectious diseases. In J. G. Wilson & F. C. Fraser (Eds.), *Handbook of teratology: I. General principles and etiology* (pp. 225–259). New York: Plenum Press.

Kurtz, L. A., Dowrick, P. W., Levy, S. E., & Batshaw, M. L. (Eds.) (1996). *Handbook of developmental disabilities: Resources for interdisciplinary care.* Gaithersburg, MD: Aspen.

Lagerstrom, M., Bremme, K., Eneroth, P., & Janson, C-G. (1991). School marks and I.Q.-test scores for low birth weight children at the age of 13. *European Journal of Obstetrics, Gynecology, and Reproductive Biology, 40,* 129–136.

Langerstrom, M., Bremme, K., Eneroth, P., & Janson, C-G. (1994). Long-term development for girls and boys at age 16–18 as related to birth weight and gestational age. *International Journal of Psychophysiology, 17,* 175–180.

Lamb, M. E., & Bornstein, M. H. (1987). *Development in infancy: An introduction* (2nd ed.). New York: Random House.

Largo, R. H., & Schinzel, A. (1985). Developmental and behavioural disturbances in 13 boys with fragile-X syndrome. *European Journal of Pediatrics, 143,* 269–275.

Larson, J. E., Morrow, S. L., Happel, L., Sharp, J. F., & Cohen, J. C. (1997). Reversal of cystic fibrosis phenotype in mice by gene therapy in utero. *Lancet, 349*(9052), 619–620.

Larsson, G., Bohlin, A., & Tunnell, R. (1985). Prospective study of children exposed to variable amounts of alcohol in utero. *Archives of the Diseases of Children, 60,* 315–321.

Lashley, F. R. (1998). *Clinical genetics in nursing practice* (2nd ed.). New York: Springer.

Lee, K., & Corpuz, M. (1988). Teenage pregnancy: Trend and impact on rates of low birth weight and fetal, maternal, and neonatal mortality in the United States. *Clinics in Perinatology, 15,* 929–942.

Lefkowitz, B. (1997). *Our guys: The Glenn Ridge rape and the secret life of the perfect suburb.* Berkeley: University of California Press.

Legit, E. M., & Baker, L. S. (1995). Unintentional injuries. *The Future of Children, 5*(1), 214–222.

Lemert, E. M. (1967). *Human deviance, social problems, and social control.* Englewood Cliffs, NJ: Prentice Hall.

Lemoine, P., Harousseau, H., Borteyru, J. P., & Menuet, J. C. (1968). Les enfants de parents alcooliques. Anomalies observees. A propos de 127 cas. Paris. *Ouest Medical, 21,* 476–482.

Lenke, R. R., & Levy, H. L. (1980). Maternal phenylketonuria and hyperphenylalaninemia: An international survey of the outcome of untreated and treated pregnancies. *New England Journal of Medicine, 303,* 1202–1208.

Lenke, R. R., & Levy, H. L. (1982). Maternal phenylketonuria—results of dietary therapy. *American Journal of Obstetrics and Gynecology, 142,* 548–553.

Lennox, W. G (1960). *Epilepsy and related disorders* (Vols. 1 & 2). London: Churchill.

Lerner, J. W. (1989). *Educational interventions in learning disabilities. A report to Congress.* Bethesda, MD: National Institutes of Health.

Lester, B. M., & Dreher, M. (1989). Effects of marijuana use during pregnancy on newborn cry. *Child Development, 60,* 765–771.

Lester, B. M., Lagasse, L., & Brunner, S. (1997). Data base of studies on prenatal cocaine exposure and child outcome. *Journal of Drug Issues, 27,* 487–499.

Levin, R. (1986). *Reducing lead in drinking water: A benefit analysis* (EPA 230/09-86-019). Washington, DC: U.S. Environmental Protection Agency.

Levine, A. G. (1982). *The Love Canal: Science, politics, and people.* Lexington, MA: Heath.

Levine, M., & Perkns, D. (1987). *Principles of community psychology: Perspectives and applications.* New York: Oxford University Press.

Levitan, G. W., & Reiss, S. (1983). Generality of diagnostic overshadowing across disciplines. *Applied Research in Mental Retardation, 4,* 59–64.

Levitt, S. (1995). *Treatment of cerebral palsy and motor delay* (3rd ed.). London: Blackwell Science.

Levy, H. L. (1990). Neonatal screening for metabolic disorders. In S. M. Pueschel & J. A. Mulick (Eds.), *Prevention of developmental disabilities* (pp. 217–225). Baltimore, MD: Paul H. Brookes.

Lewin, B., Siliciano, P., & Klotz, M. (1997). *Genes VI.* Oxford: Oxford University Press.

Lewis, M., & Miller, S. M. (Eds.). (1990). *Handbook of developmental psychopathology.* New York: Plenum Press.

Lewitt, E. M., & Baker, L. S. (1996). Child indicators: Children in special education. *The Future of Children, 6*(1), 139–152.

Liberman, I. Y., Shankweiler, D., & Liberman, A. M. (1989). The alphabetic principle and learning to read. In D. Shankweiler & I. Y. Liberman (Eds.), *Phonology and reading disability: Solving the reading puzzle* (pp. 1–33). Ann Arbor: University of Michigan Press.

Lifschitz, C. H., Browning, K. K., Linge, I., McMeans, A. R., & Turk, C. L. (1998). Feeding the child with cerebral palsy. In G. Miller & G. D. Clark (Eds.), *The cerebral palsies: Causes, consequences, and management* (pp. 309–319). Boston: Butterworth-Heinemann.

Light, W. H. (1988). *Alcoholism and women: Genetics and fetal development.* Springfield, IL: Charles C Thomas.

Limb, C. J., & Holmes, L. B. (1994). Anencephaly: Changes in prenatal detection and birth status, 1972 through 1990. *American Journal of Obstetrics and Gynecology, 170*(5), 1333–1338.

Lindzey, G., & Byrne, D. (1968). Measurement of social choice and interpersonal attractiveness. In G. Lindzey & E. Aronson (Eds.), *The handbook of social psychology* (2nd ed., Vol. 2). Reading, MA: Addison-Wesley.

Linton, R. (1936). *The study of man.* New York: Appleton-Century.

Lipkin, P. H. (1991). Epidemiology of the developmental disabilities. In A. J. Capute & P. J. Accardo (Eds.),

Developmental disabilities in infancy and childhood (pp. 43–47). Baltimore, MD: Paul H. Brookes.

Little, R. E., Graham, J. M., & Samson, H. H. (1982). Fetal alcohol effects in humans and animals. In B. Stimmel (Ed.), *The effects of maternal alcohol and drug abuse on the newborn* (pp. 103–125). New York: Haworth.

Littman, G., & Parmelee, A. H. (1978). Medical correlates of infant development. *Pediatrics, 61,* 470–474.

Livingston, S. (1972). *Comprehensive management of epilepsy in infancy, childhood, and adolescence.* Springfield, IL: Charles C. Thomas.

Lokerson, J. (1999). *Learning disabilities.* Reston, VA: ERIC. (ERIC Clearinghouse on Handicapped and Gifted Children, ERIC Digest No. E516).

Lovaas, O. I. (1996). The UCLA young autism model of service delivery. In C. Maurice (Ed.), *Behavioral intervention for young children with autism* (pp. 241–250). Austin, TX: Pro-Ed.

Lovett, S. B., & Flavell, J. H. (1990). Understanding and remembering: Children's knowledge about the differential effects of strategy and task variables on comprehension and memorization. *Child Development, 61,* 1842–1858.

Lowes, L. P., & Greis, S. M. (1998). Role of occupational therapy, physical therapy, and speech and language therapy in the lives of children with cerebral palsy. In G. Miller & G. D. Clark (Eds.), *The cerebral palsies: Causes, consequences and management* (pp. 333–346). Boston: Butterworth-Heinemann.

Lowrey, G. H. (1986). *Growth and development of children* (8th ed.). Chicago: Yearbook Medical Publishers.

Lozoff, B. (1989). Nutrition and behavior. *American Psychologist, 44,* 231–236.

Lundberg, I., Frost, J., & Peterson, O. (1988). Effects of an extensive program for stimulating phonological awareness in pre-school children. *Reading Research Quarterly, 23,* 263–284.

Lyon, G. R. (1996). Learning disabilities. *Special education for students with disabilities. 6*(1), 54–76.

Maaskant, M. A. (1993). *Mental handicap and aging.* Dwingeloo, the Netherlands: KAVANAH.

MacKenzie, T. D., Bartecchi, C. E., & Schrier, R. W. (1994). Human costs of tobacco use. *New England Journal of Medicine, 330*(14), 975–980.

MacLeod, C. L., & Lee, R. V. (1988). Parasitic infections. In G. N. Burrow & T. F. Ferris (Eds.), *Medical complications during pregnancy* (3rd ed.). Philadelphia, PA: Saunders.

Macmillan, D. L., Siperstein, G. N., & Gresham, F. M. (1996). A challenge to the viability of mild mental retardation as a diagnostic category. *Exceptional Children, 62*(4), 356–371.

Main, M., & George, C. (1985). Responses of abused and disadvantaged toddlers to distress in age-mates: A study in the day-care setting. *Developmental Psychology, 21,* 407–412.

Malamud, C. (1964). Neuropathology. In H. A. Stevens & R. Heber (Eds.). *Mental retardation* (pp. 429–452). Chicago: University of Chicago Press.

Malatesta, C. Z., Culver, C., Tesman, J. R., & Shepard, B. (1989). The development of emotional expression during the first two years of life. *Monographs of the Society for Research in Child Development, 54* (1-2, Serial No. 219).

Malina, R. M. (1990). Physical growth and performance during the transitional years (9–16). In R. Montemayer, G. R. Adame, & T. P. Gullotta (Eds.), *From childhood to adolescence: A transitional period?* Newbury Park, CA: Sage.

March of Dimes. (1993). *March of Dimes statbook: Statistics for healthier mothers and babies.* White Plains, NY: March of Dimes Birth Defects Foundation.

Marland, S. P. (1972). *Education of the gifted and talented.* Report to the subcommittee on Education, Committee on Labor and Public Welfare, U.S. Senate. Washington, DC: U.S. Government Printing Office.

Marlowe, M. (1995). The violation of childhood: Toxic metals and developmental disabilities. *Journal of Orthomolecular Medicine, 10*(2), 79–86.

Martin, J. (2000). *The poisoning of America: Latest tobacco ruling reveals government denial* [On-line]. Available: www://ABC News.Com.

Masci, O., & Bongarzone, R. (1995). Toxicity of lead. In N. Castellino, P. Castellino, & N. Sannolo (Eds.), *Inorganic lead exposure: Metabolism and intoxication* (pp. 203–214). Boca Raton, FL: Lewis Publishers.

Maugh, T. H. (1999, July 26). Study ties crib deaths to smoke. *The New York Times.*

Mayo, L. W. (1963, February). Report of the president's panel on mental retardation. *Health, Education, and Welfare Indicators,* pp. 5–14.

McAbe, E. R. B., & McAbe, L. (1986). Issues in the dietary management of phenylketonuria: Breastfeeding and trace-metal nutriture. In H. M. Wisniewski & D. A. Snider (Eds.), *Mental retardation: Research, education, and technology transfer.* New York: American Academy of Sciences.

McAnarney, E. R. (1987). Young maternal age and adverse neonatal outcome. *American Journal of Diseases of Children, 141,* 1053–1059.

McAnarney, E. R., & Stevens-Simon, C. (1990). Maternal psychological stress/depression and low birth weight. *American Journal of Diseases of Children, 144,* 789–792.

McCarver, R. B., & Craig, E. M. (1974). Placement of the retarded in the community: Prognosis and outcome. *International Review of Research in Mental Retardation, 7,* 145–207.

McCauley, E., Ito, J., & Kay, T. (1986). Psychosocial functioning in girls with Turner syndrome and short stature. *Journal of the American Academy of Child Psychiatry, 25,* 105–112.

McCauley, E., Kay, T., Ito, J., & Treeler, R. (1987). The Turner syndrome: Cognitive defects, affective discrimination and behavior problems. *Child Development, 58,* 464–473.

McClearn, G. E., Plomin, R., Gora-Maslak, G., & Crabbe, J. C. (1991). The gene chase in behavioral sciencce. *Psychological Science, 2,* 222–229.

McDonnell, J. (1993). *News from the border: A mother's memoirs of her autistic son.* New York: Ticknor & Fields.

McGue, M. (1993). From proteins to cognitions: The behavioral genetics of alcoholism. In R. Plomin and G. E. McClearn, (Eds.), *Nature, nurture, and psychology.* Washington, DC: American Psychological Association.

McKusick, V. (1988). *Mendelian inheritance in man* (8th ed.). Baltimore, MD: Johns Hopkins University Press.

McKusick, V. & Amberger, J. S. (1995). Genetic map of the human genome: The autosomes and X, Y, and mitochondrial chromosomes. In C. R. Scriver, A. L. Beaudet, W. S. Sly, & D. Valle (Eds.). *The metabolic and molecular bases of inherited disease.* Vol 1, New York: McGraw-Hill.

McLaren, J. & Bryson, S. E. (1987). Review of recent epidemiological studies of mental retardation: Prevalence, associated disorders, and etiology. *American Journal of Mental Retardation, 92,* 243–254.

McMullen, A. H. (2000). Cystic fibrosis. In P. L. Jackson & J. A. Vessey (Eds.). *Primary care of the child with a chronic condition* (pp. 401–425). St. Louis, MO: Mosby.

McNeil, J. M. (1993). *Americans with disabilities, 1991–1992.* Current Population Reports, Series p70, No. 33). Washington, DC: U.S. Department of Commerce, Economics, and Statistics Administration, Bureau of the Census.

Mead, G. H. (1934). In C. W. Morris (Ed.), *Mind, self, and society.* Chicago: University of Chicago Press.

Mednick, S. A., Machon, R. A., Huttenen, M. O., & Bonett, D. (1988). Adult schizophrenia following prenatal exposure to an influenza epidemic. *Archives of General Psychiatry, 45,* 189–192.

Meier, J. H. (1975). Screening, assessment and intervention for young children at developmental risk. In B. Z. Friedlander, G. M. Sterritt, & G. E. Kirk (Eds.), *Exceptional infant: Assessment and intervention* (Vol. 3). New York: Brunner/Mazel.

Menaghan, E. G. (1989). Role changes and psychological well-being: Variations in effects by gender and role repertoire. *Social Forces, 67,* 693–714.

Menninger, K. A. (1926). Influenza and schizophrenia: An analysis of post-influenzal "dementia praecox" as of 1918 and five years later. *American Journal of Psychiatry, 5,* 469–529.

Menninger, K. A. (1928). The schizophrenic syndrome as the product of acute infectious disease. *Archives of Neurology and Psychiatry, 20,* 464–481.

Menolascino, F. J. (1990). The nature and type of mental illness in the mentally retarded. In M. Lewis & S. M. Miller (Eds.), *Handbook of developmental psychology* (pp. 397–408). New York: Plenum Press.

Menolascino, F. J., & Stark, J. A. (Eds.). (1984). *Handbook of mental illness in the mentally retarded.* New York: Plenum Press.

Mercer, J. R., (1970). Sociological perspectives on mild mental retardation. In H. C. Haywood (Ed.), *Sociocultural aspects of mental retardation* (pp. 378–391). New York: Appleton-Century-Crofts.

Mercer, J. R. (1973). *Labeling the mentally retarded.* Berkeley: University of California Press.

Meyer, M. B., & Tonascia, J. A. (1977). Maternal smoking, pregnancy complications, and perinatal mortality. *American Journal of Obstetrics and Gynecology, 128,* 494–502.

Michaelis, E. K., & Michaelis, M. L. (1994). Cellular and molecular bases of alcohol's teratogenic effects. *Alcohol Health and Research World, 18*(1), 17–20.

Miller, E., Hare, J. W., Cloherty, J. P., Dunn, P. J., Gleason, R. E., Soeldner, J. S., & Kitzmiller, J. L. (1981). Elevated maternal hemoglobin A, C in early pregnancy and major congenital anomalies in infants of diabetic mothers. *New England Journal of Medicine, 304,* 1331.

Miller, F. (1998). Gait analysis in cerebral palsy. In J. P. Dormans & L. Pellegrino (Eds.), *Caring for children with cerebral palsy: A team approach* (pp. 169–192). Baltimore, MD: Paul Brookes.

Miller, F., & Bachrach, S. J. (1995). *Cerebral palsy: A complete guide for caregiving.* Baltimore, MD: Johns Hopkins University Press.

Miller, G., & Clark, G. D. (1998). *The cerebral palsies: Causes, consequences, and management.* Boston: Butterworth-Heineman.

Miller, W. A. (1990). Prenatal genetic diagnosis. In S. M. Pueschel & J. A. Mulick (Eds.), *Prevention of developmental disabilities* (pp. 123–141). Baltimore, MD: Paul H. Brookes.

Minuchin, S. (1974). *Families and family therapy.* Cambridge, MA: Harvard University Press.

Money, J. (1992). *The Kaspar-Hauser syndrome of "psychosocial dwarfism": Deficient statural, intellectual, and social growth induced by child abuse.* Buffalo, NY: Prometheus Books.

Money, J., Annecillo, C., & Hutchison, J. W. (1985) Forensic and family psychiatry in abuse dwarfism: Munchausen's Syndrome by proxy, atonement, and addiction to abuse. *Journal of Sex and Marital Therapy, 11*(1), 30–40.

Moore, K. L. (1977). *The developing human: Clinically oriented embryology* (2nd ed.). Philadelphia, PA: Saunders.

Moore, K. L. (1988). *The developing human: Clinically oriented embryology* (4th ed.). Philadelphia, PA: Saunders.

Moore, K. L. (1989). *Before we are born.* Philadelphia, PA: Saunders.

Moore, K. L., & Persaud, T. V. N. (1993). *The developing human: Clinically oriented embryology* (5th ed.). Philadelphia, PA: Saunders.

Moore, K. L., & Persaud, T. V. N. (1998). *The developing human: Clinically oriented embryology* (6th ed.). Philadelphia, PA: Saunders.

Morgan, H. (1996). *Adults with autism: A guide to theory and practice.* Cambridge: Cambridge University Press.

Mostofsky, D. I. (1993). Behavior modification and therapy in the management of epileptic disorders. In D. I. Mostofsky & Y. Loyning (Eds.), *The neurobehavioral treatment of epilepsy* (pp. 67–82). Hillsdale, NJ: Erlbaum.

Muccigrosso, L. (1991). Sexual abuse prevention strategies and programs for persons with developmental disabilities. *Sexuality and Disability, 9*(3), 261–271.

Murray, A., Youings, S., & Dennis, N. (1996). Population screening at the FRAXA and FRAXE loci: Molecular analyses of boys with learning difficulties and their mothers. *Human Molecular Genetics, 5,* 727–735.

Mussen, P. H., Conger, J. J., Kagan, J., & Huston, A. C. (1990). *Child development and personality* (7th ed.). New York: HarperCollins.

Myers, R. E. (1975). Maternal psychological stress and fetal asphyxia: A study in the monkey. *American Journal of Obstetrics and Gynecology, 122,* 47–59.

Nathaniels P. W. (1995). The role of basic science in preventing low birth weight. *The Future of Children, 5*(1), 57–70.

National Academy of Science. (1999). *Marijuana and medicine: Assessing the science base.* Washington, DC: Institute of Medicine, National Academy Press.

National Association for Perinatal Addiction Research and Education. (1988, October). Innocent addicts: High rate of prenatal drug abuse found. *ADAMHA News.*

National Center on Addiction and Substance Abuse at Columbia University. (1996). *Illicit drug use during pregnancy, substance abuse and the American woman* [On-line]. Available: http://.casacolumbia.org/pubs/jun96/womc25.htmmml.

National Center for Health Statistics. (1984). Advanced report on final natality statistics, 1982. *Monthly Vital Statistics Report, 33*(6). Hyattsville, MD: Public Health Service.

National Center for Health Statistics (1989). Final data from the National Center for Health Statistics. *Monthly Vital Statistics Report, 40*(8, Suppl. 2). Hyattsville, MD: Public Health Service.

National Center for Health Statistics (1996). Life expectancy at birth: United States. *Monthly Vital Statistics Report, 45*(3). Hyattsville, MD: Public Health Service.

National Center for Learning Disabilities (1999). *Visual and auditory processing disorders.* New York: Author.

National Committee for Injury Prevention and Control. (1989). *Injury prevention: Meeting the challenge.* New York: Oxford University Press.

National Plan to Combat Mental Retardation (1962, October). Washington, DC: U.S. Government Printing Office.

National Research Council. (1972). *Lead: Air-born lead in perspective.* Washington, DC: National Academy Press.

National Research Council, Committee on Mapping and Sequencing the Human Genome. (1988). *Mapping and sequencing the human genome.* Washington, DC: National Academy Press.

National Research Council, Committee on Measuring Lead in Critical Populations. (1993). *Measuring lead exposure in infants, children, and other sensitive populations.* Washington, DC: National Academy Press.

NCCAN. (1995). National Center on Child Abuse and Neglect. *Child maltreatment 1993: Reports from the states to the National Center on Child Abuse and Neglect.* Washington, DC: Department of Health and Human Services.

Needleman, H., Rabinowitz, M., Leviton, A., Linn, S., & Schoenbaum, S. (1984). The relationship between prenatal exposure to lead and congenital anomalies. *Journal of the American Medical Association, 251,* 2956–2959.

Neerhof, M. G., MacGregor, S. N., Retsky, S. S., & Sullivan, T. P. (1989). Cocaine abuse during pregnancy: Peripartum prevalence and perinatal outcome. *American Journal of Obstetrics and Gynecology, 161,* 633–638.

Nehring, B., & Vessey, J. A. (2000). Down syndrome. In P. L. Jackson & J. A. Vessey (Eds.). *Primary care of the child with a chronic condition* (pp. 445–474). St. Louis, MO: Mosby.

Nelson, D. L. (1984). *Children with autism and other pervasive disorders of development and behavior: Therapy through activities.* Thorofare, NJ: Slack Publishing.

Nelson, K. B., & Grether, J. K. (1995). Can magnesium sulfate reduce the risk of cerebral palsy in very low birthweight infants? *Pediatrics, 95*(2), 263.

Newacheck, P. W., & Taylor, W. R. (1992). Childhood chronic illness: Prevalence, severity, and impact. *American Journal of Public Health, 82,* 364–371.

Newton, R. W., & Hunt, L. P. (1984). Psychosocial stress in pregnancy and its relation to low birth weight. *British Medical Journal, 288,* 1191–1194.

Newman, J. (1991). Handicapped persons and their families: Historical, legislative, and philosophical perspectives. In M. Seligman (Ed.), *The family with a handicapped child* (2nd ed.). Boston: Allyn & Bacon.

New York Times (2000, April, 30). That whining sound of money and lives, section 4, p. 2.

Niccols, G. A. (1994). Fetal alcohol syndrome: Implications for psychologists. *Clinical Psychology Review, 14*(2), 91–111.

N.I.C.H.H.D. (1993, January). *The mental retardation and developmental disabilities branch report to Council.* Washington, DC: National Institute of Child Health and Human Development.

Nichols, R. C. (1981). Origins, nature, and determinants of intellectual development. In M. J. Begab, H. C. Haywood, & H. L. Garber (Eds.), *Psychological influences on retarded performances. Vol. I: Issues and theories in development* (pp. 127–154). Baltimore, MD: University Park Press.

NINDS (1999). *Cerebral palsy: Hope through research.* National Institute of Neurological Disorders and Stroke. U.S. Department of Health and Human Services. Available: http://www.ninds.nih.gov/patients/disorder/cp/cphtr.HTM.

Nirje, B. (1969). The normalization principle and its human management implications. In R. B. Kugel & W. W. Wolfensberger (Eds.), *Changing patterns in residential services for the mentally retarded* (pp. 179–188). Washington, DC: U.S. Government Printing Office.

N.J.C.L.D (1994). *Learning disabilities, Issues and definitions. Collective perspectives on issues affecting learning disabilities.* Austin, TX: Pro-Ed.

Noetzel, M. J., & Miller, G. (1998). Traumatic brain injury as a cause of cerebral palsy. In G. Miller & G. D. Clark (Eds.), *The cerebral palsies: Causes, consequences, and management.* Boston: Butterworth-Heinemann.

Noller, K. L. (1990). In utero DES exposure. In E. J. Quilligan & F. P. Zuspan (Eds.) *Current therapy in obstetrics and gynecology* (Vol. 3). Philadelphia, PA: Saunders.

Norbeck, J. S., & Tilden, V. P. (1983). Life stress, social support, and emotional disequilibrium in complications of pregnancy: A prospective multivariate study. *Journal of Health and Social Behavior, 24*(1), 30–46.

Northam, E. (1997). Psychosocial impact of chronic illness in children. *Journal of Paediatric Child Health, 33,* 369–372.

N.P.H.S. (National Pregnancy and Health Survey). (1992). *Drug use among women delivering live births.* Bethesda, MD: (H.H.S. National Institute on Drug Abuse, NIH Publication # 96-3819).

O'Callaghan, E., Sham, P., Takei, N., Glover, G., & Murray, R. M. (1991). Schizophrenia after prenatal exposure to the 1957 A-2 influenza epidemic. *Lancet, 337,* 1248–1250.

O'Donohoe, N. (1994). *Epilepsies of childhood* (3rd ed.). Oxford: Butterworth-Heinemann.

Olds, S. B., London, M. L., & Ladewig, P. A. (1988). *Maternal-newborn nursing.* Menlo Park, CA: Addison-Wesley.

Olegard, R., Sabel, K. G., Aronsson, M., Sandin, B., Johansson, P. R., Carlson, C., Kyllerman, M., Iversen, K., & Hrbek, A. (1979). Effects on the child of alcohol abuse during pregnancy. *Acta Paediatrica Scandinavica Supplement, 275,* 112–121.

Oller, D. K., & Eiler, R. (1988). The role of audition in infant babbling. *Child Development, 59,* 441–449.

Olshan, A. F., Baird, P. A., & Teschke, K. (1989). Paternal occupational exposures and the risk of Down syndrome. *American Journal of Human Genetics, 44,* 646–651.

Olsho, L. (1982). Auditory frequency discrimination in infancy. *Developmental Psychology, 18*(5), 721–726.

O'Neill, J. (1999, April 6). A syndrome with a mix of skills and deficits. *The New York Times,* pp. D1, D4.

Orden, S. R., & Bradburn, N. (1969). Working wives and marriage happiness. *American Journal of Sociology, 74,* 392–407.

O'Shea, J. S. (1990). Preventing accidents in children. In S. M. Pueschel & J. A. Mulick (Eds.), *Prevention of developmental disabilities* (pp. 303–318). Baltimore, MD: Paul H. Brookes.

Osofsky, J. D., Osofsky, H. J., & Diamond, M. O. (1988). The transition to parenthood: Special tasks and risk factors for adolescent parents. In G. Y. Michaels & W. A. Goldberg (Eds.), *The transition to parenthood: Current theory and research* (pp. 209–234). New York: Cambridge University Press.

Ottman, R., Annegers, J. F., & Hauser, W. A. (1988). Higher risk of seizures in offspring of mothers than fathers with epilepsy. *American Journal of Human Genetics, 43,* 257–264.

Ozonoff, S., & Cathcart, K. (1998). Effectiveness of a home program intervention for young children with autism. *Journal of Autism and Developmental Disorders, 28*(1), 25–32.

Paneth, N. S. (1995). The problem of low birth weight. *The Future of Children, 5*(1), 19–34.

Parker, S. M., & Barrett, D. E. (1992). Maternal type A behavior during pregnancy, neonatal crying and infant temperament: Do type A women have type A babies? *Pediatrics, 89,* 474–479.

Parmelee, A. H., Kopp, C. B., & Sigman, M. (1974). Selection of developmental assessment techniques for infants at risk. *Merrill Palmer Quarterly, 22,* 177–201.

Parmelee, A. H., & Sigman, M. (1983). Perinatal brain development and behavior. In M. Haith & J. Compos (Eds.), *Biology and infancy.* New York: Wiley.

Parsons, J. A., May, J. G., & Menolascino, F. J. (1984). The nature and incidence of mental illness in mentally retarded individuals. In F. J. Menolascino & J. A. Stark (Eds.), *Handbook of mental illness in the mentally retarded* (pp. 3–44). New York: Plenum Press.

Parsons, T. (1965). *Social structure and personality.* London: Free Press.

Patlak, M. (1992). Controlling epilepsy: Science replaces superstition. *F.D.A. Consumer, 26*(4), 28–31.

Patterson, D. (1987). The causes of Down syndrome. *Scientific American, 257,* 52–61.

Patton, J. R., & Polloway, E. A. (1992). Learning disabilities: The challenges of adulthood. *Journal of Learning Disabilities, 25,* 410–416.

Pellegrino, L., & Dormans, J. P. (1998). Making the diagnosis of cerebral palsy. In J. P. Dormans & L. Pellegrino (Eds.), *Caring for children with cerebral palsy: A team approach* (pp. 31–54). Baltimore, MD: Paul H. Brookes.

Perez-Reyes, M., & Wall, M. E. (1982). Presence of delta-9-tetrahydrocannabinol in human milk. *New England Journal of Medicine, 307,* 819–820.

Perrin, James M. (1997). Systems of care for children and adolescents with chronic illness. In H. M. Wallace, R. F. Biehl, J. C. MacQueen, & J. A. Blackman (Eds.), *Mosby's resource guide to children with disabilities and chronic illness* (pp. 156–161). New York: Mosby.

Peterson, C. C., & Siegal, M. (1999). Representing inner worlds: Theory of mind in autistic, deaf, and normal hearing children. *Psychological Science, 10*(2), 126–129.

Pharaoh, P. D., Platt, M. J., & Cooke, T. (1996). The changing epidemiology of cerebral palsy. *Archives of the Disabled Child, 75,* 169–173.

Phelps, L. (2000). Long term developmental outcomes of prenatal cocaine exposure. In press, *Journal of Psychoeducational Assessment,* March, 2000.

Phelps, L., & Grabowski, J. (1992). Fetal alcohol syndrome: Diagnostic features and psychoeducational risk factors. *School Psychology Quarterly, 7*(2), 112–128.

Phelps, L., Wallace, N. V., & Bontrager, A. (1997). Risk factors in early child development: Is prenatal cocaine/polydrug exposure a key variable? *Psychology in the Schools, 34*(3), 245–252.

Phillipson, R. (1988). The fetal alcohol syndrome: Recent international statistics. *Australia and New Zealand Journal of Developmental Disabilities, 14*(3), 211–217.

Pianta, R., Egeland, B., & Erickson, M. F. (1989). The antecedents of maltreatment: Results of the mother-child interaction research project. In D. Cicchetti & V. Carlson (Eds.), *Child maltreatment: Theory and research on the causes and consequences of child abuse and neglect* (pp. 203–253). New York: Cambridge University Press.

Pierce, B. A. (1990). *Family genetic sourcebook.* New York: Wiley.

Pipp, S., Fischer, K. W., & Jennings, S. (1987). Acquisition of self and other knowledge in infancy. *Developmental Psychology, 23,* 86–96.

Piven, J., Arndt, S., Bailey, J., Havercamp, S., Andreasen, N. C., & Palmer, P. (1995). An MRI study of brain size in autism. *American Journal of Psychiatry, 152*(8), 1145–1149.

Piven, J., Harper, J., Palmer, P., & Arndt, S. (1996). Course of behavioral change in autism: A retrospective study of high-IQ adolescents and adults. *Journal of the American Academy of Child and Adolescent Psychiatry, 35*(4), 523–529.

Plomin, R. (1990). *Nature and nurture.* Belmont, CA: Wadsworth.

Plomin, R. (1994). *Genes and experience: The interplay between nature and nurture.* Thousand Oaks, CA: Wadsworth.

Plomin, R., DeFries, J. C., & McClearn, G. E. (1990). *Behavior genetics: A primer* (2nd ed.). New York: Freeman.

Polani, P. E. (1966). Chromosome anomalies and abortions. *Developmental Medicine and Child Neurology, 8,* 67–70.

Pollitt, E., Gorman, K., Engle, P., Martorell, R., & Rivera, J. (1993). Early supplementary feeding and cognition: Effects over two decades. *Monographs of the Society for Research in Child Development, 58* (6, Serial No. 235).

Potocnik, U., & Widhalm, K. (1994). Long-term follow-up of children with classical phenylketonuria after diet discontinuation: A review. *Journal of the American College of Nutrition, 13*(3), 232–236.

Powers, C. (1980). *Role imposition or role improvisation: Some theoretical principles.* Paper presented at the meeting of the Pacific Sociological Association.

Powell, T. H., Aiken, J. M., & Smylie, M. A. (1982). Treatment of involuntary euthanasia for severely handicapped newborns: Issues of philosophy and public policy. *Journal of the Association for Persons with Severe Handicaps, 6,* 3–10.

Prader, A., Labhart, A., & Willi, H. (1956). Ein syndrom von Adipositas, Klein-wuchs, Kriptorchismus, und Oligophrenie nach myatonieartigem Zustand im Neugeborenalter. *Schweizerische Medizinische Wochenschrift, 86,* 1260–1261.

Pratt, O. E. (1984). Introduction: What do we know of the mechanisms of alcohol damage in utero? In *Ciba Foundation Symposium 105: Mechanisms of alcohol damage in utero* (pp. 1–7). London: Pitman.

Prechtl, H. F. R. (1977). *The neurological examination of the full-term newborn infant* (2nd ed.). London: Heineman.

Premack, D., & Woodruff, G. (1978). Does the chimpanzee have a theory of mind? *The Behavioral and Brain Sciences, 4,* 515–526.

Prouty, R., & Lakin, K. C. (Eds.). (1998). *Residential services for persons with developmental disabilities: Status and trends through 1997.* Minneapolis: University of Minnesota, Institute on Community Integration.

Provence, S. (1995). Forward. In Sperry, V. W., Fragile success: *Nine autistic children, childhood to adulthood.* North Haven, CT: Archon Books.

Pruett, K. D. (1987). *The nurturing father.* New York: Warner.

Pueschel, S. M., & Mulick, J. A. (1990). (Eds.). *Prevention of developmental disabilities.* Baltimore, MD: Paul H. Brookes.

Raloff, J. (1994). The great nicotine debate. *Science News, 145,* 314–317.

Rapin, I. (1997). Current concepts in autism. *New England Journal of Medicine, 337*(2), 97–104.

Rapin, I., & Katzman, R. (1998). Neurobiology of autism. *Annuals of Neurology, 43,* 7–14.

Ramey, C. T., & Finkelstein, N. W. (1981). Psychosocial mental retardation: A biological and social coalescence. In M. Begab, H. Haywood, & H. Garber (Eds.), *Psychosocial influence in retarded performance: Vol. I. Issues and theories in development* (pp. 65–92). Baltimore, MD: University Park Press.

Reeder, S. J., & Martin, L. L. (1987). *Maternity nursing: Family, newborn, and women's health care* (16th ed.). Philadelphia, PA: Lippincott.

Reiff, H. B., & Gerber, P. J. (1994). Social/emotional and daily living issues for adults with learning disabilities. In P. J. Gerber & H. B. Reiff (Eds.), *Learning disabilities in adulthood: Persisting problems and evolving issues* (pp. 72–81). Boston: Andover Medical Publishers.

Reiff, H. B., Gerber, P. J., & Ginsberg, R. (1993). Definitions of learning disabilities from adults with learning disabilities. The insider's perspective. *Learning Disability Quarterly, 16,* 114–125.

Reisman, J. E. (1987). Touch, motion, and proprioception. In P. Salapatek & L. Cohen (Eds.), *Handbook of infant perception: Vol. 1. From sensation to perception.* Orlando, FL: Harcourt Brace Jovanovich.

Reiss, S., Levitan, G. W., & Szyszko, J. (1982). Emotional disturbance and mental retardation: Diagnostic overshadowing. *American Journal of Mental Deficiency, 86,* 567–574.

Reiss, S., & Szyszko, J. (1983). Diagnostic overshadowing and professional experience with mentally retarded persons. *American Journal of Mental Deficiency, 87,* 396–402.

Reschly, D. J. (1987). *Adaptive behavior.* Tallahassee: Florida Department of Education.

Reschly, D. (1988). Minority mild mental retardation: Legal issues, research findings, and reform trends. In M. C. Wang, M. C. Reynolds, & H. J. Walberg (Eds.), *Handbook of special education: Research and practice* (Vol. 2, pp. 23–41). Oxford: Pergamon Press.

Rett, A. (1996). Uber ein eigenartiges hirnatrophisches syndrom bei hyperammonamie im kindersalter. *Wienar Medizinische Wochenschrift 116*: 723–738.

Revkin, A. C. (2000, July 11). Milestone report on mercury emissions. *The New York Times,* p. A12.

Ricci, J. M., Fojaco, R. M., & O'Sullivan, M. J. (1989). Congenital syphilis: The University of Miami/Jackson Memorial Medical Centre Experience, 1986–1988. *Obstetrics and Gynecology, 74*(5), 687–693.

Ricciutti, H. N. (1991). Malnutrition and cognitive development: Research policy linkages and current research directions. In L. Okagaki & R. K. Sternberg (Eds.), *Directors of development.* Hillside, NJ: Erlbaum.

Rimland, B. (1964). *Infantile autism.* New York: Appleton-Century-Crofts.

Robbins, W. J., Brody, S., Hogan, A. G., Jackson, C. M., & Green, C. W. (1928). *Growth.* New Haven, CT: Yale University Press.

Robinson, N. M., & Robinson, H. B. (1976). *The mentally retarded child: A psychological approach* (2nd ed.). New York: McGraw-Hill.

Rosenblatt, J. S. (1982). Birth interaction and attachment. Johnson & Johnson Roundtable. (Referenced in Berger, & Thompson (1995). *The developing person through childhood and adolescence* (4th ed.) New York, N.Y.: Worth.

Rosenblith, J. F., & Sims-Knight, J. E. (1985). *In the beginning: Development in the first two years of life.* Monterey, CA: Brooks/Cole.

Rosenstein, D., & Oster, H. (1988). Differential facial response to four basic tastes in newborns. *Child Development, 59,* 1555–1568.

Rosenthal, E. (1990, February 4). When a pregnant woman drinks. *New York Times Magazine,* pp. 30–32.

Rosett, H. L., & Weiner, L. (1984). *Alcohol and the fetus: A clinical perspective.* New York: Oxford University Press.

Roth, M., Wischik, C. M., Evans, N., & Mountjoy, C. (1985). Convergence and cohesion of recent neurobiological findings in relation to Alzheimer's disease and their bearing on its aetiological basis. In M. Bergener, M. Ermini, & H. B. Stahelin (Eds.), *Thresholds in aging.* London: Academic Press.

Rowitz, L. (1981). A sociological perspective on labeling in mental retardation. *Mental Retardation, 19,* 47–51.

Rowitz, L. (1991). Social and environmental factors and developmental handicaps in children. In J. L. Matson & J. A. Mulick (Eds.), *Handbook of mental retardation* (Vol. 121, 2nd ed., pp. 158–165). New York: Pergamon Press.

Rubin, R. (1984). *Maternal identity and the maternal experience.* New York: Springer.

Rudolph, A. (1987). *Pediatrics.* (18th ed.). Norwalk, CT: Appleton-Lange.

Russell, M. (1982). The epidemiology of alcohol-related birth defects. In E. L. Abel (Ed.), *Fetal alcohol syndrome. Volume II: Human studies.* Boca Raton, FL: CRC Press.

Russell, M. (1991). Clinical implications of recent research on the fetal alcohol syndrome. *Bulletin of the New York Academy of Medicine, 67*(3), 207–222.

Russell, M. (1994). New assessment tools for drinking in pregnancy: T-ACE, TWEAK, and others. *Alcohol Health Research World, 18,* 55–61.

Russell, M., Martier, S. S., Sokol, R. J., Mudar, P., Jacobson, S., & Jacobson, J. (1996). Detecting risk drinking during pregnancy: A comparison of four screening questionnaires. In Press, *American Journal of Public Health.*

Russell, P. J. (1994). *Fundamentals of genetics.* New York: HarperCollins.

Rutter, M. (1977). Infantile autism and other child psychoses. In M. Rutter & L. Hersov (Eds.), *Child psychiatry: Modern approaches.* Oxford: Blackwell.

Rutter, M., Graham, P., & Yule, W. (1970). *A neuropsychiatric study in childhood.* Philadelphia, PA: Lippincott.

Safford, P. L., & Safford, E. J. (1996). *A history of childhood and disability*. New York: Teacher's College Press.

Samuels, M., & Samuels, N. (1986). *The well pregnancy book*. New York: Summit Books.

Sandall, S. R. (1993). Curricula for early intervention. In W. Brown, S. K. Thurman, & L. F. Pearl (Eds.), *Family-centered early intervention with infants and toddlers: Innovative, cross-disciplinary approaches.* Baltimore, MD: Paul H. Brookes.

Sannolo, N., Carelli, C., DeLorenzo, G., & Castellino, N. (1995). Sources, properties, and fate of airborne lead. In N. Castellino, P. Castellino, & N. Sannulo (Eds.), *Inorganic lead exposure: Metabolism and intoxication* (pp. 53–82). Boca Raton, FL: Lewis Publishers.

Santilli, N. (1993). Psychosocial aspects of epilepsy: Education and counseling for patients and families. In E. Wylie (Ed.), *The treatment of epilepsy: Principles and practice* (pp. 1163–1167). Philadelphia, PA: Lea & Febiger.

Satischandra, P., Chandra, V., & Schoenberg, B. S. (1988). Case-control study of associated conditions at the time of death in patients with epilepsy. *Neuroepidemiology, 7,* 109–114.

Sawin, K. J., Cox, A. W., & Metzger, S. G. (2000). Transitions to adulthood. In P. L. Jackson & J. A. Vessey (Eds.), *Primary care of the child with a chronic condition* (pp. 140–162). St. Louis, MO: Mosby

Scarr, S. (1993). Biological and cultural diversity: The legacy of Darwin for development. *Child Development, 64,* 1333–1353.

Scarr, S., & Kidd, K. K. (1983). Developmental behavior genetics. In M. M. Haith & J. J. Compos (Eds.), *Handbook of child psychology: Infancy and developmental psychobiology* (Vol. 2, pp. 345–434). New York: Wiley.

Scheff, T. J. (1966). *Being mentally ill: A sociological theory.* Chicago: Aldine.

Scherzer, A. L., & Tscharnuter, I. (1990). *Early diagnosis and therapy in cerebral palsy: A primer on infant developmental problems* (2nd ed.). New York: Marcel Dekker.

Schiavi, R. C., Thelgaard, A., Owen, D., & White, D. (1984). Sex chromosome anomalies, hormones, and aggressivity. *Archives of General Psychiatry, 41,* 93–99.

Schloss, P. J., Hughes, C. A., & Smith, M. A. (1988). *Mental retardation: Community transition.* Boston: Little, Brown.

Schroeder, B. A. (1992). *Human growth and development.* New York: West.

Schuerholz, L. J., Harris, E. L., Baumgardner, T. L., Reiss, A. L., Freund, L. S., Church, R. P., Mohr, J., & Denckla, M. B. (1995). An analysis of two discrepancy-based models and a processing-deficit approach in identifying learning disabilities. *Journal of Learning Disabilities, 281*(1), 18–19.

Schurz, B. J., & Scrimshaw, N. S. (Eds.). (1990). *Activity, energy expenditure and energy requirements of infants and children.* Lausanne, Switzerland: Nestle Foundation.

Schwartz, J., Angle, C., & Pitcher, H. (1986). Relationship between childhood blood-lead levels and stature. *Pediatrics, 77,* 281–288.

Scriver, C. R., Beaudet, A. L., Sly, W. S., & Valle, D. (1995). *The metabolic and molecular bases of inherited disease* (Vol. 1). New York: McGraw-Hill.

Seabrook, C. (1987, February). Children: Third wave of AIDS victims. *Atlanta Journal.*

Seidenberg, M., Beck, M., & Geisser, M. (1986). Academic achievement of children with epilepsy. *Epilepsia, 27,* 753–759.

Seligman, M. (Ed.). (1991). *The family with a handicapped child* (2nd ed.). Boston: Allyn & Bacon.

Seltzer, M. M., (1992). Aging in persons with developmental disabilities. In J. E. Birren, R. B. Sloane, & G. D. Cohen (Eds.), *Handbook on aging and mental health* (2nd ed., pp. 583–599). San Diego, CA: Academic Press.

Seltzer, M. M., & Seltzer, G. B. (1985). The elderly mentally retarded: A group in need of service. In G. Getzel & J. Mellor (Eds.), *Gerontological social work practice in the community* (pp. 99–119). New York: Haworth Press.

Serdulla, M., Williamson, D. F., Kendrick, J. S., Anda, R. F., & Byers, T. (1991). Trends in alcohol consumption by pregnant women: 1985–1988. *Journal of the American Medical Association, 265*(7), 876–879.

Shahar, S. (1990). *Childhood in the Middle Ages.* London: Routledge.

Shaywitz, S. E. (1996, November). Dyslexia. *Scientific American.*

Shaywitz, S. E., Shaywitz, B. A., Fletcher, J. M., & Escobar, M. D. (1990). Prevalence of reading disability in boys and girls: Results of the Connecticut longitudinal study. *Journal of the American Medical Association, 264,* 998–1002.

Sheehan, M. (2000). Autism. In P. L. Jackson & J. A. Vessey (Eds.), *Primary care of the child with a chronic condition.* St. Louis, MO: Mosby.

Shepard, T. H. (1986). Human teratogens: How can we sort them out? In H. M. Wisniewski & D. A. Snider (Eds.), *Mental retardation: Research, education, and technology transfer, Annals of the New York Academy of Sciences, 477,* 105–115.

Sherman, S. (1996). Epidemiology. In R. J. Hagerman & A. Cronister (Eds.), *Fragile X syndrome: Diagnosis, treatment, and research* (2nd ed.). Baltimore, MD: Johns Hopkins University Press.

Shiono, P. H., & Behrman, R. E. (1995). Low birth weight: Analysis and recommendations. *The Future of Children, 5*(1), 4–18.

Short, R. H., & Hess, G. C. (1995). Fetal alcohol syndrome: Characteristics and remedial implications. *Developmental Disabilities Bulletin, 23*(1), 13–29.

Shorvon, S. D. (1990). Epidemiology, classification, natural history and genetics of epilepsy. *Lancet, 336,* 93–96.

Sieber, S. D. (1974). Toward a theory of role accumulation. *American Sociological Review, 39,* 567–578.

Sigman, M. (1995). Nutrition and child development: Food for thought. *Current Directions in Psychological Science, 4*(2), 52–55.

Siller, J. A., Chipman, A., Ferguson, L., & Vann, D. H. (1967). *Studies in reaction to disability. Vol. II: Attitudes of the non-disabled toward the physically disabled.* New York: New York University School of Education.

Singer, P. (1979). *Practical ethics.* Cambridge: Cambridge University Press.

Slotkin, T. A., Lappi, S. E., McCook, E. C., Lorber, B. A., & Seidler, F. J. (1995). Loss of neonatal hypoxia tolerance after prenatal nicotine exposure: Implications for sudden infant death syndrome. *Brain Research Bulletin, 38*(1), 69–75.

Smalley, S. L., Asarnow, R. F., & Spence, M. A. (1988). Autism and genetics: A decade of research. *Archives of General Psychiatry, 45,* 953–961.

Smilkstein, G., Helsper-Lucas, A., Ashworth, C., Montano, D., & Pagel, M. (1984). Prediction of pregnancy complications: An application of the biopsychosocial model. *Social Science and Medicine, 18*(4), 315–321.

Smith, I., Beasley, M. G. & Ades, A. E. (1990). Intelligence and quality of dietary treatment in phenylketonuria. *Archives of Diseases of Children, 65,* 472–478.

Smith, I., Beasley, M. G., Wolff, O. H., & Ades, A. E. (1988). Report from the MRC/DHSS phenylketonuria register. *Journal of Pediatrics, 3,* 403–408.

Smith, M. (1995). *Growing up with cerebral palsy.* Waco, TX: WRS Publishers.

Snodgrass, S. R. (1994). Cocaine babies: A result of multiple teratogenic influences. *Journal of Child Neurology, 9*(3) 227–233.

Snow, J. H. & Hooper, S. R. (1994). *Pediatric traumatic brain injury.* London: Sage.

Sobsey, D., & Mansell, S. (1990). The prevention of sexual abuse of people with developmental disabilities. *Developmental Disabilities Bulletin, 18*(2), 51–66.

Sokol, R. J. & Abel, E. L. (1988). Alcohol-related birth defects: Outlining current research opportunities. *Neurotoxicology and Teratology, 10,* 183–186.

Sokol, R. J., & Clarren, S. J. (1989). Guidelines for the use of terminology describing the impact of prenatal alcohol on the offspring. *Alcoholism: Clinical and Experimental Research, 13,* 597–598.

Sokol, R. J., Martier, S., & Ernhart, C. (1985). Identification of alcohol abuse in the prenatal clinic. In N. C. Chang & H. M. Chao (Eds.), *Early identification of alcohol abuse.* (NIAA Research Monograph 17, DHHS Publication No. ADM 85-1258). Washington, DC: U.S. Department of Health and Human Services.

Sonderegger, T. B. (Ed.). (1992). *Perinatal substance abuse: Research findings and clinical implications.* Baltimore, MD: Johns Hopkins University Press.

Sperry, V. W. (1995). *Fragile success: Nine autistic children: Childhood to adulthood.* North Haven, CT: Archon Books.

Spiker, D., Lotspeich, L., & Kraemer, H. C. (1994). Genetics of autism: Characteristics of affected and unaffected children from 37 multiplex families. *American Journal of Medical Genetics. 54,* 27–35.

Spitz, H. H. (1994). Fragile-X syndrome is not the second leading cause of mental retardation. *Mental Retardation, 32*(2), 156.

Spreitzer, E., Snyder, E. & Larson, D. (1979). Multiple roles and psychological well-being. *Sociological Focus, 12,* 141–148.

Sroufe, L. A., Fox, N. E., & Pancake, Van R. (1983). Attachment and dependency in developmental perspective. *Child Development, 54,* 1615–1627.

Stagno, S. (1993). Psychiatric aspects of epilepsy. In E. Wylie, (Ed.), *The treatment of epilepsy: Principles and practice* (pp. 1178–1183). Philadelphia, PA: Lea & Febiger.

Steffenberg, S., & Gillberg, C. (1989). The etiology of autism. In C. Gillberg (Ed.), *Diagnosis and treatment of autism.* New York: Plenum Press.

Stein, A. (1983). Pregnancy in gravidas over age 35 years. *Journal of Nurse-Midwifery, 28,* 17–20.

Stein, Z. (1984). Epidemiologic considerations in assessing adverse reproductive outcomes following genotoxic exposure. In F. J. DeSerres & R. Pero (Eds.), *Individual susceptibility to genotoxic agents in the human population* (pp. 459–480). New York: Plenum Press.

Sternberg, C. R., & Compos, J. J. (1990). The development of anger expressions in infancy. In N. L. Stein, B. Leventhal, & T. Trabasso (Eds.), *Psychological and biological approaches to emotion.* Hillsdale, NJ: Erlbaum.

Sternberg, R. J. (1982). *Intelligence applied.* New York: Harcourt.

Sternberg, R. J. (1985). *Beyond I.Q.: A triarchic theory of human intelligence.* Cambridge: Cambridge University Press.

Sternberg, R. J., & Detterman, D. K. (1986). (Eds.). *What is intelligence? Contemporary viewpoints on its nature and definition.* Norwood, NJ: Ablex.

Sternberg, R. J., & Slater, W. (1982). Conceptions of intelligence. In R. J. Sternberg (Ed.), *Handbook of human intelligence.* Cambridge: Cambridge University Press.

Sternberg, R. J., & Wagner, R. K. (Eds.). (1986). *Practical intelligence: Nature and origins of competence in the everyday world.* Cambridge: Cambridge University Press.

Sternberg, S. (1996). Risky sex breeds neglected epidemic. *Science News, 150,* 22, 343.

Stoudemire, A. (1998). *Clinical psychiatry.* Philadelphia, PA: Lippincott-Raven.

Stratton, K., Howe, C., & Battaglia, F. (1996). *Fetal alcohol syndrome: Diagnosis, epidemiology, prevention, and treatment.* Washington, DC: National Academy Press.

Straus, D., & Eyman, R. K., (1996). Mortality of people with mental retardation in California with and without Down syndrome, 1986–1991. *American Journal on Mental Retardation, 100,* 643–653.

Streissguth, A. P. (1994). A long-term perspective on fetal alcohol syndrome. *Alcohol Health and Research World, 18*(1), 74–81.

Straus, R. (2000). Adult functional outcome of those born small for gestational age: Twenty-six year follow-up of the 1970 British birth cohort. *Journal of the American Medical Association,* Feb. 2, 2000, *283*(5) 625–632.

Streissguth, A. P., Aase, J. M., Clarren, S. K., Randels, S. P., La Due, R. A., & Smith, D. F. (1991). Fetal alcohol syndrome in adolescents and adults. *Journal of the American Medical Association, 265,* 1961–1967.

Streissguth, A. P., Clarren, S. K., & Jones, K. L. (1985). Natural history of the fetal alcohol syndrome. A 10-year follow-up of 11 patients. *Lancet, 2,* 85–91.

Streissguth, A. P., Herman, C. S., & Smith, D. W. (1978). Intelligence, behavior, and dysmorphogenesis in the fetal alcohol syndrome: A report on 20 patients. *Journal of Pediatrics, 92,* 363–367.

Streissguth, A. P., & LaDue, R. A. (1985). Psychological and behavioral effects in children prenatally exposed to alcohol. *Alcohol Health and Research World, 10,* 6–12.

Streissguth, A. P., & LaDue, R. A. (1987). Fetal alcohol syndrome and fetal alcohol effects: Teratogenic causes of mental retardation and developmental disabilities. In S. R. Schroeder (Ed.), *Toxic substances and mental retardation: Neurobehavioral toxicology and teratology* (pp. 1–32). Washington, DC: American Association on Mental Deficiency.

Streissguth, A. P., Randels, S. P., & Smith, D. F. (1991). A test-retest study of intelligence in patients with fetal alcohol syndrome: Implications for care. *Journal of the American Academy of Child and Adolescent Psychiatry, 30,* 584–587.

Streissguth, A. P., Sampson, P. D., Barr, H. M., Claren, S. K., & Martin, D.C. (1986). Studying alcohol teratogenesis from the perspective of the fetal alcohol syndrome: Methodological and statistical issues. In H. M. Wisniewski & D. A. Snider (Eds.), *Mental retardation: Research, education, and technology transfer.* The New York Academy of Sciences, *477,* 63–86.

Stryker, S., & Statham, A. (1985). Symbolic interaction and role theory. In G. Lindzey & E. Aronson, *The handbook of social psychology* (Vol. 1, 3rd ed., pp. 311–378). New York: Random House.

Suomi, S. (1982). Biological foundations and developmental psychobiology. In C. B. Kopp & J. B. Krakow (Eds.), *The child: Development in a social context.* Reading, MA: Addison-Wesley.

Super, C. M., Herrera, M. G., & Mora, J. O. (1990). Long-term effects of food supplementation and psychosocial intervention on the physical growth of Colombian infants at risk of malnutrition. *Child Development, 61,* 29–49.

Sutherland, G. R. (1977). Marker X chromosomes and mental retardation. *New England Journal of Medicine, 299,* 1472.

Tager-Flusberg, H., & Baron-Cohen, S. (1993). An introduction to the debate. In S. Baron-Cohen, H. Tager-Flusberg, & D. J. Cohen (Eds.), *Understanding other minds: Perspectives from autism.* Oxford: Oxford University Press.

Takei, N., Murray, G., O'Callaghan, E., Sham, P., Glover, G., & Murray, R. M. (1995). Prenatal exposure to influenza epidemics and risk of mental retardation. *European Archives of Psychiatry and Clinical Neuroscience, 245*(4–5), 255–259.

Tanner, J. M. (1978). *Foetus into man: Physical growth from conception to maturity.* Cambridge, MA: Harvard University Press.

Taylor, H. G., Barry, C. T., & Schatschneider, C. W. (1993). School-age consequences of haemophilus influenzas, type b meningitis. [Special issue: The neuropsychological basis of disorders affecting children and adolescents]. *Journal of Clinical Child Psychology, 22*(2), 196–206.

Taylor, R. (1989). Cracking cocaine's legacy in babies of drug abusers. *Journal of NIH Research, 1,* 29–31.

Tellegen, A., Lykken D. T., Bouchard, T. J., Wilcox, K. J., Segal, N. L., & Rich, S. (1988). Personality similarity in twins reared apart and together. *Journal of Personality and Social Psychology, 54,* 1031–1039.

Thomas, A., & Chess, S. (1977). *Temperament and development.* New York: Brunner-Mazel.

Thomas, A., Chess, S., & Birch, H. C. (1963). *Behavioral individuality in early childhood.* New York: New York University Press.

Thomas, E. J., & Biddle, B. J. (1966). Basic concepts for classifying the phenomena of role. In B. J. Biddle & E. J. Thomas (Eds.), *Role theory: Concepts and research* (pp. 23–46). New York: Wiley.

Thomas, M. H. (1973). The ultimate challenge of epilepsy prevention. In M. J. Parsonage (Ed.), *Prevention of epilepsy and its consequences* (pp. 5–9). London: International Bureau for Epilepsy.

Thompson, M. W., McInnes, R. R., & Willard, H. F. (1991). *Thompson and Thompson: Genetics in medicine* (5th ed.). Philadelphia, PA: Saunders.

Thompson, R. A. (1991). Attachment theory and research. In M. Lewis (Ed.), *Child and adolescent psychiatry: A comprehensive textbook.* Baltimore, MD: Williams and Wilkins.

Thompson, R. A., & Limber, S. P. (1990). "Social anxiety" in infancy: Stranger and separation anxiety. In H. Leitenberg (Ed.), *Handbook of social anxiety.* New York: Plenum Press.

Thompson, R. I., & O'Quinn, A. N. (1979). *Developmental disabilities: Etiologies, manifestations, diagnoses, and treatments.* New York: Oxford University Press.

Todd, L. P., & Curti, M. (1966). *The rise of the American nation.* New York: Harcourt Brace & World.

Tonkiss, J., Galler, J. R., Formica, R. N., Shukitt-Hale, B., & Timm, R. R. (1990). Fetal protein malnutrition impairs acquisition of a DRL task in adult rats. *Physiology & Behavior, 48,* 73–77.

Torgesen, J. K. (1998, Spring/Summer). Catch them before they fall: Identification and assessment to prevent reading failure in young children. *American Educator.*

Torgesen, J. K. (1994). Learning disabilities theory: Issues and advances. In S. Vaughn & C. S. Bos (Eds.), *Research issues in learning disabilities.* New York: Springer-Verlag.

Torgesen, J. K., Wagner, R. K., & Rashotte, C. A. (1997). The prevention and remediation of severe reading disabilities: Keeping the end in mind. *Scientific Studies of Reading, 1,* 217–234.

Travis, J. (1997). Cystic fibrosis controversy. *Science News, 151,* 292.

Trostle, J. A., Hauser, W. A., & Sharbrough, F. W. (1989). Psychological and social adjustment to epilepsy in Rochester, Minnesota. *Neurology, 39,* 633–637.

Turk, M. A., Overeynder, J. C., & Janicki, M. P. (1995). *Uncertain future: Aging and cerebral palsy—clinical concerns.* Albany: New York State Developmental Disabilities Planning Council.

Turner, G., Till, R., & Daniel, A. (1978). Marker X chromosomes, mental retardation, and macroorchidism. *New England Journal of Medicine, 299,* 1472.

Turner, G., Webb, T., & Wake, S. (1996). Prevalence of the fragile-X syndrome. *American Journal of Medical Genetics, 64,* 196–197.

Turner, J. S., & Helms, D. B. (1991). *Life-span development.* (4th ed.). Chicago: Holt, Rinehart and Winston.

Turner, R. H. (1956). Role-taking, role standpoint and reference group behavior. *American Journal of Sociology, 61,* 316–328.

Turner, R. H. (1978). The role and the person. *American Journal of Sociology, 84,* 1–23.

Ulfelder, H. (1986). DES-transplacental teratogen and possible carcinogen. In J. L. Sever & R. L. Brent (Eds.), *Teratogen update: Environmentally induced birth defect risks.* New York: Alan R. Liss.

UNICEF (2000, July 12). Young people found uninformed on AIDS. *The New York Times,* p. A-11.

U.S. Advisory Board on Child Abuse and Neglect. (1995). *A nation's shame: Fatal child abuse and neglect in the United States.* Washington, DC: Department of Health and Human Services, Administration for Children and Families.

U.S. Department of Agriculture. (1992). *World tobacco situation.* (Document FT-8-92). Washington, DC: Department of Agriculture, Foreign Agricultural Service.

U.S. Department of Commerce. (1995). *The statistical abstracts of the United States.* Washington, DC: United States Printing Office.

U.S. Department of Education. (1993). *Implementation of the Individuals with Disabilities Education Act: Fifteenth annual report to Congress.* Washington, DC: U.S. Department of Education.

U.S. Department of Education. (1995). *Seventeenth annual report to Congress on the implementation of the Individuals with Disabilities Education Act.* Washington, DC:

U.S. Department of Health and Human Services (1991). *Healthy people 2000: National health promotion and disease prevention objectives* (DHHS Pub. No. PHS 91-50213). Washington, DC: U.S. Government Printing Office.

US: DHHS. (1998). *Child maltreatment 1966. Reports from the states to the national child abuse and neglect data system.* Washington, DC: U.S. Government Printing Office.

U.S. Public Health Service. (1979). *Smoking and health* (A report of the Surgeon General, U.S. Department of Health, Education, and Welfare Publication No. PHS 79-50066). Washington, DC: U.S. Public Health Service, Office on Smoking and Health.

U.S. Senate Special Committee on Aging. (1991). *Aging America: Trends and predictions 133.* Washington, DC: U.S. Government Printing Office.

Valleroy, L. A. (1990). Pediatric AIDS and HIV-1 infection in the United States: Recommendations for research, policy, and programs. *Society for Research in Child Development Social Policy Report, 4*(3), 1–12.

Valleroy, L. A., Harris, J. R., & Way, P. O. (1990). The impact of HIV infection on child survival in the developing world. *AIDS, 4,* 667–672.

VanHasselt, V. B., Lutzker, J. R., & Hersen, M. (1990). Overview. In M. Hersen & V. B. VanHasselt (Eds.), *Psychological aspects of developmental and physical disabilities: A casebook* (pp. 11–54). Newbury Park, CA: Sage.

Vaughn, S. (1989). Gifted learning disabilities: Is it such a bright idea? *Learning Disabilities Focus, 4*(2), 123–126.

Venter, J. C. et al. (2001). The sequence of the human genome. *Science.* Feb. 16, 2001, 291 (5507), 1153.

Verbrugge, L. (1983). Multiple roles and physical health of women and men. *Journal of Health and Social Behavior,* 24, 16–30.

Vessey, J. A., & Jackson, P. L. (2000). School and the child with a chronic condition. In P. L. Jackson & J. A. Vessey (Eds.), *Primary care of the child with a chronic condition.* St. Louis, MO: Mosby.

Vogel, S. A., Leonard, F., Scales, W., Hayeslip, P. & Hermanson, J. (1998). The national LD data bank: An overview. *Journal of Learning Disabilities, 31*(3), 234–247.

Vohr, B. R. (1990). In S. M. Pueschel & J. A. Mulick (Eds.), *Prevention of developmental disabilities* (pp. 227–240). Baltimore, MD: Paul H. Brookes.

Volkmar, F. (1996). *The disintegrative disorders: Childhood disintegrative disorders and Rett's disorder.* Washington, DC: American Psychiatric Press.

Volkmar, F. R., & Cohen, D. J. (1989). Disintegrative disorder or "late onset" autism. *Journal of Child Psychology and Psychiatry, 30,* 717–724.

Volkmar, F. R., & Nelson, D. S. (1990). Seizure disorders in autism. *Journal of the American Academy of Child and Adolescent Psychiatry, 29,* 127–129.

von Oeyen, P. T. (1990). Optimal prenatal care. In S. M. Pueschel & J. A. Mulick (Eds.), *Prevention of developmental disabilities* (pp. 55–76). Baltimore, MD: Paul H. Brookes.

Voorhees, C. V., & Mollnow, E. (1987). Behavioral teratogenesis: Long-term influences on behavior from early exposure to environmental agents. In J. D. Osofsky (Ed.), *Handbook of infant development* (2nd ed., pp. 913–971). New York: Wiley.

Voysey, M. (1975). *A constant burden: The reconstitution of family life.* London: Routledge & Kegan Paul.

Vygotsky, L. S. (1978). *Mind in society: The development of higher psychological processes.* Cambridge, MA: Harvard University Press.

Wade, N. (2001). Reports on human genome challenge long-held beliefs. *The New York Times.* Mon. Feb. 12, 2001, p. A-1.

Wagner R. K., & Sternberg, R. J. (1985). Practical intelligence in real-world pursuits: The role of tacit knowledge. *Journal of Personality and Social Psychology, 49*(2), 436–458.

Wallace, H. M., Biehl, R. F., MacQueen, J. C., & Blackman, J. A. (1997). *Mosby's resource guide to children with disabilities and chronic illness.* New York: Mosby.

Washington Research Project. (1974). *Children out of school in America.* Washington, DC: Children's Defense Fund.

Watson, J. D., & Crick, F. H. C. (1953). Genetical implications of the structure of deoxyribonucleic acid. *Nature, 171,* 964–969.

Webb, T. P., Bundey, S. E., Thake, A. I., & Todd, J. (1986). Population incidence and segregation ratios in the Martin-Bell syndrome. *American Journal of Medical Genetics, 23,* 573–580.

Wechsler, D. (1991). *Wechsler Intelligence Scale for Children-III.* San Antonio, TX: Psychological Corp.

Weir, M. (1982). Mental retardation. In E. Zigler & D. Balla (Eds.), *Mental retardation: The developmental-difference controversy* (pp. 203–205). Hillsdale, NJ: Erlbaum.

Weiss, P. A. M., & Coustan, D. R. (Eds.). (1988). *Gestational diabetes.* Wien, NY: Springer-Verlag.

Weisz, J. R. (1982). Learned helplessness and the retarded child. In E. Zigler & D. Balla (Eds.), *Mental retardation: The developmental-difference controversy* (pp. 27–40). Hillside, NJ: Erlbaum.

Wellman, H. M. (1993). Early understanding of mind: The normal case. In S. Baron-Cohen, H. Tager-Flusberg, & D. J. Cohen (Eds.), *Understanding other minds: Perspectives from autism.* New York: Oxford University Press.

Welsh, M. J., & Smith, A. E. (1995, December). Cystic fibrosis. *Scientific American.*

Wenar, C. (1990). *Developmental psychopathology from infancy through adolescence.* New York: McGraw-Hill.

Wendel, G. D. (1988). Gestational and congenital syphilis. *Clinics in Perinatology, 15,* 287–303.

White, L. R., & Sever, J. Y. (1967). Etiological agents: I. Infectious agents. In A. Rubin (Ed.), *Handbook of congenital malformations.* Philadelphia, PA: Saunders.

White, M., & Gribbin, J. R. (1992). *Stephen Hawking: A life in science.* London: Penguin Books.

WHO. (1996). *Multiaxial classification of child and adolescent psychiatric disorders.* Cambridge: Cambridge University Press.

Wicks-Nelson, R., & Israel, A. C. (1991). *Behavior disorders of childhood* (2nd ed.). Englewood Cliffs, NJ: Prentice Hall.

Widerstrom, A. H., Mowder, B. A., & Sandall, S. R. (1991). *At-risk and handicapped newborns and infants: Development, assessment, and intervention.* Englewood Cliffs, NJ: Prentice Hall.

Widmayer, S., & Field, T. (1980). Effects of Brazelton demonstrations on early patterns of preterm infants and their teenage mothers. *Infant Behavior and Development, 3,* 79–89.

Willer, B., & Intagliata, J. (1984). *Promises and realities for mentally retarded citizens.* Baltimore, MD: University Park Press.

Williams, D. T., Walczak, T., Berten, W., Nordi, D., & Bergtraum, M. (1993). Psychogenic seizures. In D. I. Mostofsky & Y. Loyning (Eds.), *The neurobehavioral treatment of epilepsy* (pp. 83–106). Hillsdale, NJ: Erlbaum.

Williamson, H. A., LeFevre, M., & Hector, M. (1989). Association between life stress and serious perinatal complications. *Journal of Family Practice, 29,* 489–496.

Wilson, G. S. (1992). Heroin use during pregnancy: Clinical studies of long-term effects. In T. B. Sonderegger (Ed.), *Perinatal substance abuse: Research findings and clinical implications* (pp. 224–238). Baltimore, MD: Johns Hopkins University Press.

Wilson, J. G. (1977). Current status of teratology. In J. G. Wilson & F. C. Fraser (Eds.), *Handbook of teratology: Vol. 1. General principles and etiology* (pp. 47–74). New York: Plenum Press.

Wimmer H., & Perner, J. (1983). Beliefs about beliefs: Representation and constraining function of wrong beliefs in young children's understanding of deception. *Cognition, 13,* 103–128.

Windle, C. (1962). Prognosis of mental subnormals. *American Journal of Mental Deficiency, 66* (Monograph Supplement).

Wing, L. (1976). *Early childhood autism* (2nd ed.). New York: Pergamon Press.

Wing, L. (1981). Asperger's syndrome: A clinical account. *Psychological Medicine, 11,* 115–130.

Wing, L. (1989). The diagnosis of autism. In C. Gillberg (Ed.), *Diagnosis and treatment of autism* (pp. 5–22). New York: Plenum Press.

Wing, L. (1996). Autistic spectrum disorders. *British Medical Journal, 312,* 327–328.

Wing, L., & Attwood, A. (1987). Syndromes of autism and atypical development. In D. J. Cohen, A. Donnellan, & R. Paul (Eds.), *Handbook of autism and pervasive developmental disorders* (pp. 3–19). Silver Springs, MD: Winston.

Wing, L., & Gould, J. (1979). Severe impairments of social interactions and associated abnormalities in children: Epidemiology and classification. *Journal of Autism and Developmental Disorders, 9,* 11–29.

Winick, M. (1976). *Malnutrition and brain development.* New York: Oxford University Press.

Winick, M. (1981, January). Food and the fetus. *Natural History, 88,* 38–44.

Winick, M., & Rosso, P. (1969). The effect of severe early malnutrition on cellular growth of human brain. *Pediatric Research, 3*(2), 181–184.

Wolfe, P., Kregel, J., & Wehman, P. (1996). Service delivery. In P. J. McLaughlin & P. Wehman (Eds.), *Mental retardation and developmental disabilities.* Austin, TX: Pro-Ed.

Wolfensberger, W. (1972). *The principle of normalization in human services.* Toronto: National Association for the Mentally Retarded.

Wolfensberger, W. (1983). Social role valorization: A proposed new term for the principle of normalization. *Mental Retardation, 21,* 234–239.

Wolfensberger, W. (1984). A reconceptualization of normalization as social role valorization. *Canadian Journal on Mental Retardation, 34*(2), 22–26.

Wolfensberger, W. (1992). *A brief introduction to social role valorization as a higher order concept for structuring human services.* Syracuse, NY: Syracuse University Press.

Wolraich, M. (Ed.). (1996). *Disorders of development and learning: A practical guide to assessment and management.* St. Louis, MO: Mosby.

World Health Organization, Expert Committee on Maternal and Child Health. (1950). *Public health aspect of low birth weight* (WHO Technical Report Series No. 27). Geneva, Switzerland: Author.

World Health Organization. (1980). *International classification of impairments, disabilities, and handicaps.* Geneva, Switzerland: Author.

World Health Organization. (1993). *The ICD-10 classification of mental and behavioural disorders. Diagnostic criteria for research.* Geneva, Switzerland: Author.

World Health Organization. (1996). *Multiaxial classification of child and adolescent psychiatric disorders.* Cambridge: Cambridge University Press.

Xu, K., Ming, Shi Z., Veek, L. L., Hughes, M R., Rosenwaks, Z. (1999). First unaffected pregnancy using preimplantation genetic diagnosis for sickle-cell anemia. *Journal of the American Medical Association,* May 12, 1999, *281*(18), 1701–1706.

Yen, I. H., Khoury, M. J., Erickson, J. D., James, L. M., Waters, G. D., & Berry, R. J. (1992). The changing epidemiology of neural tube defects: United States,

1969–1989. *American Journal of Diseases of Children, 146*(7), 857–861.

Yerby, M. S. (1994). Pregnancy, teratogenics, and epilepsy. *Neurologic Clinics, 12*(4), 749–771.

Yopp, H. K. (1988). The validity and reliability of phonemic awareness tests. *Reading Research Quarterly, 23,* 159–177.

Yule, K. S. (2000). Phenylketonuria. In P. L. Jackson & J. A. Vessey (Eds.), *Primary care of the child with a chronic condition* (pp. 706–731). St. Louis, MO: Mosby.

Zelazo, P. R. (1979). Infant reactivity to perceptual-cognitive events: Application for infant assessment. In R. B. Kearsley & I. E. Sigel (Eds.), *Infants at risk: Assessment of cognitive functioning.* Hillsdale, NJ: Erlbaum.

Zellweger, H. (1984). The Prader-Willi syndrome. *Journal of the American Medical Association, 25*(4), 18–35.

Zigler, E., & Balla, D. (Eds.). (1982). *Mental retardation: The developmental-difference controversy.* Hillsdale, NJ: Erlbaum.

Zigler, E., & Harter, S. (1969). The socialization of the mentally retarded. In D. A. Goslin (Ed.), *Handbook of socialization theory and research* Chicago: Rand McNally.

Zigler, E., & Hodapp, R. M. (1986). *Understanding mental retardation.* New York: Cambridge University Press.

Zigler, E., & Hodapp, R. M. (1991). Behavioral functioning in individuals with mental retardation. *Annual Review of Psychology, 42,* 29–50.

Zito, J. M., Safer, D. J., Dos Reis, S., Gardner, J. F., Boles, M., & Lynch, F. (2000). Trends in the prescribing of psychotropic medications to pre-school children. *Journal of the American Medical Association,* Feb. 23, 2000. *283*(8) 1025–1030.

Zuckerman, B., Frank, D. A., Hingson, R., Amaro, H., Levenson, S. M., Kayn, H., Parker, S., Vinci, R., Aboagye, K., Fried, L. E., Cabral, H., Timperi, R., & Bauchner, H. (1989). Effects of maternal marijuana and cocaine use on fetal growth. *New England Journal of Medicine, 320*(12), 762–768.

AUTHOR INDEX

SUBJECT INDEX

475

SUBJECT INDEX

489

valorization, 375, 433
zone of proximal development, 257–258
Social role sensitivity, 9
Social role valorization, 375, 433
Social skills, in autism, 264, 271
Socioeconomic status
defined, 433
developmental disabilities and, 41
and mental retardation, 211–212, 221–223
Somatic cells, 42, 433
Somatogenesis, 433
Spastic cerebral palsy, 324–325, 434
Special education, 288, 434
Specialized role sector, 382
Specialized services, 383–384
Specific learning disorders, 434
Speech disorders, 350–353, 358–360
articulation disorders, 350–352, 418
defined, 434
incidence in U.S., 35
Speech pathologist, 336–337, 426
Spelling disorders, 354
Sperm, 47, 49, 434
Spermatogenesis, 47
Spina bifida, 124–125
defined, 58, 434
fetal development, 54
prenatal detection, 57, 58, 379
Spinal cord, fetal development, 54
Spontaneous abortion, 41
Stage theories of development, 434
State law, developmental disabilities, 24–25
Status epilepticus, 301, 434
Status validation, 240–241, 245–246
STDs. See Sexually transmitted diseases
Stereotyped behavior
in autism, 270, 272
in Rett's syndrome, 274
Stimulus overselectivity, 205, 434
Strabismus, 329, 434

Stress
during pregnancy, 168–169
effect on children, 186–187
Stroke
cerebral palsy and, 327
defined, 434
seizures and, 304
Substance abuse
preventing, 405
teratogenicity of, 156–157, 214
Sudden infant death syndrome (SIDS), 153–154, 433
Suicide, in epileptics, 306
Super male syndrome, 121, 434
Surfactant, 55, 178, 431, 434
Surgery, for epilepsy, 315–316, 320
Surma, 191, 434
Symbiotic support groups, 223, 434
Symptomatic epilepsy, 302, 434
Synergistic effects, 194, 434
Syntax, 361, 434
Syphilis, 139, 434

Tacit knowledge, 256–257, 434
Tantrums, in autism, 272
Target access, 133, 431, 434
Tay-Sachs disease, 45, 100–101, 435
TBI. See Traumatic brain injury
Teen pregnancy, 409, 411
Temperament
defined, 76, 435
inheritability of, 48–49
Temporal lobe seizures, 301, 420
Teratogens, 53, 129–159, 161–173
autism and, 270
critical periods, 134, 135, 420, 431
defined, 435
delayed effects, 134, 135
drugs as, 142–159
endpoints of, 132, 134, 145, 435
environmental toxins, 161–164
genetic determination, 133–134, 424, 431
infectious diseases as, 136–141
lead as, 162–163

mental retardation and, 213
public education, 412
radiation as, 162
target access, 133, 431, 434
Teratology, 132, 133–136, 435
Tertiary prevention, 404, 406, 435
Tetrasomy, 109, 112, 435
Thalassemia, genetics of, 45
Thalidomide, teratogenic effects of, 132, 133–134, 142, 435
Theory building, 75, 205, 435
Theory of mind, 233, 280–282, 435
Thymine, in DNA, 43, 435
Thyroid gland, cretinism, 104–105
Thyroxin, 104–105, 164
Tobacco use
birth weight and, 153, 178
responsible social agent, 399
teratogenicity of, 152–155
Tonic-clonic seizures, 301, 307, 314, 424
Tonic phase, 301
Tourette's disorder, 435
Toxoplasmosis, 138, 420, 435
Transfer of learning, 205–206, 435
Translocation (chromosomal structure), 108, 109, 112, 113, 115, 127, 435
Traumatic brain injury (TBI), 187–190, 397, 435
Trimesters of pregnancy, 50–51
Triplegia, 326, 435
Triple X syndrome, 121, 435
Trisomy, 109, 112
causes of, 113–114
defined, 435
Down syndrome (trisomy 21), 85, 92, 112, 114–118, 170, 422, 429, 435
super male syndrome, 121, 434
trisomy 13, 112
trisomy 18, 112
Tuberous sclerosis, 45, 435
Turner's syndrome, 113, 120, 435
Twin studies, 268, 304
"Two-group" model, mental retardation, 213
Tyrosine, in PKU, 97